Ethical, Legal, and Professional Issues in Counseling

Theodore P. Remley, Jr.

University of New Orleans

Barbara Herlihy

University of New Orleans

Merrill
Prentice Hall

Upper Saddle River, New Jersey
Columbus, Ohio

Library of Congress Cataloging-in-Publication Data
Remley, Theodore Phant,
 Ethical, legal, and professional issues in counseling / Theodore P. Remley, Jr., Barbara Herlihy.
  p. cm.
 Includes bibliographical references and index.
 ISBN 0-13-573718-4
   1. Counseling—Moral and ethical aspects—United States. 2. Counselors—Professional
ethics—United States. 3. Counseling—Law and legislation—United States. 4.
Counselors—Legal status, laws, etc.—United States. I. Herlihy, Barbara. II. Title.

BF637.C6R45 2001
174′.915—dc21

00-055018

Vice President and Publisher: Jeffery W. Johnston
Executive Editor: Kevin M. Davis
Editorial Assistant: Christina M. Kalisch
Development Editor: Heather Doyle Fraser
Production Editor: Linda Hillis Bayma
Production Coordination: Clarinda Publication Services
Design Coordinator: Diane C. Lorenzo
Cover Designer: Jason Moore
Cover art: © SuperStock
Production Manager: Laura Messerly
Director of Marketing: Kevin Flanagan
Marketing Manager: Amy June
Marketing Services Manager: Krista Groshong

This book was set in Times Roman by The Clarinda Company. It was printed and bound by R.R. Donnelley & Sons Company. The cover was printed by The Lehigh Press, Inc.

Merrill
Prentice Hall

10 9 8 7 6 5 4 3 2 1
ISBN: 0-13-573718-4

*To Dr. Patrick M. Flanagan,
this counselor's counselor
and a true role model.*
                    —Ted Remley

*To my colleagues—far too numerous to mention—
who have questioned my assumptions,
challenged my thinking, asked me the tough questions,
and in so many other ways helped me learn and grow
as a scholar and teacher of ethics.*
                    —Barbara Herlihy

Preface

We think you will find it useful to know something about us, the coauthors of this text, and how we came to write this book. Currently, we are both professors in the counseling graduate program at the University of New Orleans. Ted Remley is an attorney with several years of legal experience and also has been a school and community college counselor. Barbara Herlihy has worked as a school counselor and a Licensed Professional Counselor in private practice, and is presently a counselor educator with a special interest in counselor ethics.

Although we have only recently become colleagues at the same institution, we have worked together for many years. We have coauthored articles and presented a number of workshops on law and ethics in counseling. It was through these workshops that the idea for this book was born. The counselors who attended our workshops had much in common, although they practiced in a variety of settings with diverse clientele. They shared a deep and abiding commitment to the welfare of their clients, a desire to stay current with the ethical standards of their profession, and a need to feel competent in dealing with legal issues that arose in their work. At the same time, they sometimes felt overwhelmed by the complex and conflicting demands of situations they encountered. They frequently had difficulty distinguishing between legal and ethical issues. As we worked with these counselors, we found that we very rarely disagreed with each other, but we did bring differing perspectives. Barbara's ethics orientation led her to focus on client welfare and to emphasize protecting the client. Ted, with his legal orientation, helped us to consider another dimension, that of protecting the counselor. We believe *both* perspectives are important.

Since both of us regularly teach graduate courses in professional orientation and ethics, we found ourselves discussing the need for a textbook written specifically for *counselors* that would address ethical, legal, and professional issues. Thus, out of our backgrounds and shared interests was conceived a textbook that is unique in that it approaches each professional issue in counseling from both an ethical perspective and a legal viewpoint. We believe you will find this integrated approach particularly helpful as you grapple with the complexities inherent in the work of the counselor.

We also believe that the best learning is active rather than passive and personalized rather than abstract. We hope that you will actively discuss and even argue the issues that are raised throughout the book and that you will work to develop your own personal stance on these issues. Typical situations and dilemmas that counseling practitioners encounter are presented in each chapter and are depicted in the accompanying videotaped vignettes. We ask you to imagine that you are the counselor in each vignette and attend to what you would think, how you would feel, and what you might do in the situation. In these vignettes, as in real life, there is rarely a single right answer to the counselor's dilemma, so we hope that the vignettes will spark lively discussion.

ACKNOWLEDGMENTS

The comments of the following reviewers were invaluable: L. DiAnne Borders, University of North Carolina—Greensboro; David Capuzzi, Portland State University; Ellen Fabian, University of Maryland; Thomas Froehle, University of Indiana; Samuel Gladding, Wake Forest University; Lowe S. MacLean, University of Missouri—St. Louis; Marty Sapp, University of Wisconsin—Milwaukee; Simeon Schlossburg, Western Maryland College; Holly Stadler, Auburn University; Gerald Tolchin, Southern Connecticut State University; and Susan Walden, University of Houston—Clear Lake.

DISCOVER THE COMPANION WEBSITE
ACCOMPANYING THIS BOOK

The Prentice Hall Companion Website: A Virtual Learning Environment

Technology is a constantly growing and changing aspect of our field that is creating a need for content and resources. To address this emerging need, Prentice Hall has developed an online learning environment for students and professors alike—Companion Websites—to support our textbooks.

In creating a Companion Website, our goal is to build on and enhance what the textbook already offers. For this reason, the content for each user-friendly website is organized by topic and provides the professor and student with a variety of meaningful resources. Common features of a Companion Website include:

For the Professor—

Every Companion Website integrates Syllabus Manager™, an online syllabus creation and management utility.

- Syllabus Manager™ provides you, the instructor, with an easy, step-by-step process to create and revise syllabi, with direct links into Companion Website and other online content without having to learn HTML.
- Students may logon to your syllabus during any study session. All they need to know is the web address for the Companion Website, and the password you've assigned to your syllabus.
- After you have created a syllabus using Syllabus Manager™, students may enter the syllabus for their course section from any point in the Companion Website.
- Clicking on a date, the student is shown the list of activities for the assignment. The activities for each assignment are linked directly to actual content, saving time for students.
- Adding assignments consists of clicking on the desired due date, then filling in the details of the assignment—name of the assignment, instructions, and whether or not it is a one-time or repeating assignment.
- In addition, links to other activities can be created easily. If the activity is online, a URL can be entered in the space provided, and it will be linked automatically in the final syllabus.
- Your completed syllabus is hosted on our servers, allowing convenient updates from any computer on the Internet. Changes you make to your syllabus are immediately available to your students at their next logon.

For the Student—

- **Topic Overviews**—outline key concepts in topic areas
- **Electronic Bluebook**—send homework or essays directly to your instructor's email with this paperless form
- **Message Board**—serves as a virtual bulletin board to post—or respond to—questions or comments to/from a national audience
- **Chat**—real-time chat with anyone who is using the text anywhere in the country—ideal for discussion and study groups, class projects, etc.
- **Web Destinations**—links to www sites that relate to each topic area
- **Professional Organizations**—links to organizations that relate to topic areas
- **Additional Resources**—access to topic-specific content that enhances material found in the text

To take advantage of these and other resources, please visit the *Ethical, Legal, and Professional Issues in Counseling* Companion Website at

www.prenhall.com/remley

Brief Contents

Contents

CHAPTER 3   DIVERSITY, CLIENT WELFARE, AND INFORMED CONSENT   47

CHAPTER 4   CONFIDENTIALITY AND PRIVILEGED COMMUNICATION   79

CHAPTER 5   RECORDS, TECHNOLOGY, AND SUBPOENAS   109

CHAPTER 6   COMPETENCE AND MALPRACTICE   135

CHAPTER 10   EVALUATION, TESTING, AND DIAGNOSIS   206

CHAPTER 11   PROFESSIONAL RELATIONSHIPS, PRIVATE PRACTICE, AND HEALTH CARE   220

Introduction

PROFESSIONAL ORIENTATION

This book is intended primarily for prospective counselors. We hope that as you read and discuss the material, you will acquire a thoughtful understanding of ethical, legal, and professional issues in counseling. These issues, collectively, make up the "professional orientation" content area of your graduate studies. The Council for Accreditation of Counseling and Related Educational Programs (CACREP), an organization that sets standards for counselor preparation and accredits training programs that meet these standards, defines professional orientation as "studies that provide an understanding of all aspects of professional functioning including history, roles, organizational structures, ethics, standards, and credentialing" (Council for Accreditation of Counseling and Related Educational Programs [CACREP] 1994, p. 52).

The National Board for Certified Counselors (NBCC), a voluntary organization that credentials counselors, also requires the counselors it certifies to complete course work in this area. If you plan to become licensed as a professional counselor, you should be aware that state counselor licensure boards mandate that licensees demonstrate knowledge of professional orientation issues, which include ethical and legal issues.

Beyond external requirements, an important part of your professional development as a counselor is to acquire a firm grounding in the area of professional orientation. This content area includes three main components:

- Developing a *professional identity* as a counselor. This includes understanding the history and development of counseling and related professions, knowing the professional roles and functions of counselors and how these are similar to and different from other professions, learning about and becoming involved in professional organizations, gaining awareness of counselor preparation standards and credentialing, and knowing how to advocate for your clients and your profession.
- Learning about *ethics*. This involves becoming familiar with ethical standards for counselors, understanding the ethical issues that counselors encounter, developing ethical reasoning and decision-making skills, and being able to apply your knowledge and skills in your day-to-day professional activities.
- Learning about the *law* as it applies to counseling. This includes being able to distinguish among legal, ethical, and clinical issues; acquiring a basic knowledge of

legal issues in counseling and laws that affect the practice of counseling; and knowing what to do when you are faced with a legal problem.

It is essential that you develop a strong professional identity as a counselor during this time in our history when we are a relatively new profession. Counselors today are constantly being asked questions such as, "What kind of counselor are you?" or "Is being a counselor like being a psychologist?" These are legitimate questions, and you must be prepared to clearly explain who you are as a member of a professional group, what you believe, how you are similar to other mental health professionals, and, more importantly, how you are different. You must also be prepared to practice in ways that are ethically and legally sound and that promote the welfare of your clients. Information throughout this book will provide you with an understanding of your chosen profession of counseling and will prepare you to practice in an ethical and a legal manner.

We hope that seasoned practitioners, as well as counselors in training, will read this book and find it useful. Professional, ethical, and legal standards are constantly changing, and it is important to keep up to date. Too, as Corey, Corey, and Callanan (1993) have pointed out, issues that students and beginning practitioners encounter resurface and take on new meanings at different stages of one's professional development.

Morality, Ethics, Law, and Professionalism

The terms *ethical* and *moral* are sometimes used interchangeably, and they do have overlapping meanings. Both ethics and morality involve judgments about what is good and bad or right and wrong, and both pertain to the study of human conduct, relationships, and values. In this book, however, we will define these two terms differently. *Moral* actions are determined within a broad context of a culture or society. Thus, it is important to remember that what you view as moral behavior is based on the values you espouse, which have been influenced in turn by your upbringing, the culture in which you live, and quite possibly your religious beliefs. Conduct that you evaluate as moral might be judged as immoral by another person or by people in another society. Although some moral principles, such as "do no harm to others," are almost universally shared among civilized groups of people, how these moral principles are interpreted and acted upon will vary from individual to individual. Thus, when we refer to moral conduct, we ask you to think in terms of your *personal* belief system and how this affects your interactions with others in all aspects of your life.

Ethics is a discipline within philosophy that is concerned with human conduct and moral decision making. Mental health professionals have defined ethics as standards of conduct or actions in relation to others (Levy, 1972) and as "moral principles adopted by an individual or group to provide rules for right conduct" (Corey, et al., 1993, p. 3). Certainly, you have developed your own individual ethical stance that guides you in the ways you treat others, expect them to treat you, and make decisions about what behaviors are good or right for you. In this book, however, we will think of ethics as it relates to the profession of counseling; that is, ethics refers to conduct judged as good or right for counselors as a professional group. When your fellow professionals have come to sufficient consensus about right behaviors, these behaviors have been codified and have become the ethical standards to which you are expected to adhere in your professional life. Therefore, think about ethics as referring to your *professional* behavior and interactions.

Law is different from morality or ethics, even though law, like morality, is created by a society and, like ethics, it is codified. Laws are the agreed-upon rules of a society that set forth the basic principles for living together as a group. Laws can be general or specific regarding both what is required and what is allowed of individuals who form a governmental entity. Criminal laws hold individuals accountable for violating principles of coexistence and are enforced by the government. Civil laws allow members of society to enforce rules of living with each other.

Our view is that there are few conflicts between law and ethics in professional counseling. Keep in mind, though, that there are important differences. Laws dictate *minimum* standards of behavior that society will tolerate, while ethics represent the *ideal* standards expected by the profession. Laws are created by elected officials, enforced by police, and interpreted by judges. Ethics are created by members of the counseling profession and are interpreted and enforced by ethics committees and licensure boards.

Where does the notion of *professionalism* fit into the picture? Many factors, including the newness of the counseling profession, the interpersonal nature and complexity of the counseling process, and the wide variety of types of counselors and their work settings, make it essential for counselors to conduct themselves in a professional manner. It is not easy to define what it means to be "professional," and we discuss this in more detail in Chapter 2. At this point, we will note only that professionalism has some relationship to legal and ethical behavior, but it is possible to be unprofessional and still not behave unethically or illegally.

The relationship among ethics, law, and professionalism is complex. Clifford Stromberg (1988), an attorney, offered an elaborate diagram composed of interlocking circles to illustrate the relationships among professionalism, law (specifically malpractice), licensure, and ethics. We have drawn a more simplified picture (see Fig. 1-1) that may help you see how these concepts can be both overlapping and distinct from each other.

A Model for Professional Practice

One source of very real frustration for prospective and beginning counselors is that there are so few absolute, right answers to ethical or legal questions. Throughout your career you will encounter dilemmas for which there are no "cookbook" solutions or universally acceptable answers (Bersoff, 1996). We visualize professional practice as entailing a rather precarious balance that requires constant vigilance. We also see counseling practice as being built from within the self but balanced by outside forces, as shown in Figure 1-2.

In this model of professional practice, the internal building blocks are inside the triangle. The most fundamental element, at the base, is *intentionality*. Being an effective practitioner has to start with good intentions, or wanting to do the right thing. The overwhelming majority of counselors in training and practitioners have the best intentions; they want to be helpful to those they serve.

The second building block contains the *moral principles of the helping professions.* Moral principles are a set of shared beliefs or agreed-upon assumptions that guide the ethical reasoning of helping professionals (including physicians, nurses and other medical specialists, teachers, and mental health professionals). Basic moral principles include autonomy (respecting freedom of choice), nonmaleficence (doing no harm), beneficence (being helpful), justice (fairness), fidelity (being faithful), and veracity (being honest). We will discuss these in more detail later.

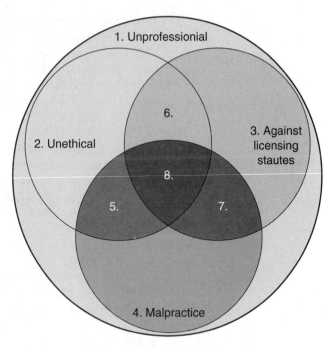

Figure 1-1   Relationship among professionalism, ethics, malpractice, and licensure. (Adapted from Stromberg, 1988.)

1   Behavior that might be considered unprofessional; practices that are not admirable but are not in violation of an established code of conduct—such as consistently running late for appointments with clients.

2   Behavior that is unethical without being against the law as defined either by licensing boards or in a malpractice suit—such as taking on so many clients that you are not performing to your best capacity.

3   Behavior that violates a licensing law but does not violate the code of ethics or constitute malpractice—such as failing to display your license in your office when the licensing law requires you to do so.

4   Behavior that may constitute legal malpractice but is not unethical or against your licensing statute. For example, an otherwise competent counselor could make a poor decision in working with a suicidal client and be sued and found guilty by a jury of negligence and malpractice.

5,6,7   Usually rare instances in which conduct is a combination of two of these three: unethical, against licensure statute, and malpractice.

8   Misconduct that violates all standards—is unethical, against your licensing law, and likely to result in a malpractice suit—such as entering into a sexual relationship with a current client.

The third element is *knowledge* of ethical, legal, and professional standards. You will find that there are a wealth of resources available to you as you work to gain, maintain, and

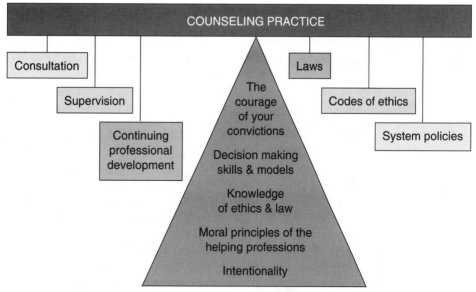

Figure 1-2　Professional Practice—Built from within and balanced from outside the self

expand your knowledge base. Textbooks such as this one, casebooks, professional journals, codes of ethics, workshops and seminars, professional conferences, and your colleagues are all excellent resources that can help to increase your knowledge.

Knowing the rules is not sufficient, however. It is necessary to have *skills* for applying your knowledge and reasoning through the questions and dilemmas that will arise in your practice. It also helps to have a *model* that will serve as a road map to guide your ethical decision making and bring some consistency to the process.

The final internal element is *the courage of your convictions.* This element can challenge even the most conscientious counselors who have the best intentions. We illustrate by sharing a story told at a conference several years ago by Dr. Deena Davis (1996), a law professor. A young actor was called to testify before the House Un-American Activities Committee during the McCarthy hearings in the 1950s and was asked to name colleagues in the movie industry who were members of the Communist Party. (McCarthy was a federal legislator who used his position in Congress to hold highly public hearings to expose Communists in the United States at a time when citizens were fearful of being attacked and overpowered by Communist governments, particularly the Soviet Union.) The actor wanted to do the right thing, and he knew what he ought to do, which was to refuse to cooperate in this witch hunt. But he also realized that refusal would likely lead to his being blacklisted and would end the career in which he had struggled so hard to succeed. Desperate to find a compromise that would "do no harm," he decided to give names, but only of people who were already dead. When he did this, the Committee continued to badger him, so he agreed to give more names, but only of people who had already been named by someone else. The actor ultimately gave out names he had intended to withhold.

The story goes on, but the point is clear. This actor apparently lacked the moral courage to act on his convictions when the personal price was very high. It is easy to see where he first set foot on an ethical slippery slope. The slippery slope phenomenon is a term used by moral philosophers to describe what happens when one begins to compromise one's principles—it becomes easier and easier to slide down the slope, diminishing one's sense of moral selfhood along the way. As a counselor, you will face ethical quandaries. It can take courage to do what you believe is right, especially when there is a high cost to yourself, when your personal needs are involved, when you know that others may not agree with or approve of your actions, or when (as is the case in ethical dilemmas) there is no single, clear, right answer to the problem.

The diagram of the model also includes external forces that can support counselors in their efforts to maintain sound, professional practice. External sources of guidance and support include consulting with colleagues, seeking supervision, and increasing your knowledge and skills through continuing education activities. Your code of ethics is certainly a major source of guidance. Some laws support counselors in fulfilling ethical obligations; for example, privileged communication statutes can help you to uphold your clients' confidentiality when called to testify or produce records in court. The system (school, agency, or institution) in which you are employed may also have policies on which you can rely when confronted with a challenge or request to compromise your ethics.

PROFESSIONAL ETHICS

Concern about ethics acknowledges the awesome responsibilities inherent in the practice of counseling. A counselor's work can make a difference in whether an abused child's life situation is recognized and addressed, whether a battered spouse finds the self-affirming courage to move to a safe environment, or whether a suicidal client finds the hope needed to choose life. Other clients come with less dramatic, more mundane problems, yet counseling can play a vital role in their struggle to lead more meaningful and effective lives (Pope & Vasquez, 1991). Ethical counselors take these responsibilities seriously.

Foundations of Ethics: Principles and Virtues

A number of thoughtful mental health professionals have struggled with questions of ethical ideals, concepts, principles, and values, and how to link these to ethical decisions in professional practice (Beauchamp & Childress, 1994; Jordan & Meara, 1990; Kitchener, 1984; Meara, Schmidt, & Day, 1996). Two perspectives that we find helpful are *principle ethics* and *virtue ethics*. Even though these two approaches are quite different from one another, they are complementary. When integrated into a holistic framework for ethical decision making, they can serve as a bridge from philosophy to practice.

Principle ethics have their foundation in moral principles, which are agreed-upon assumptions or beliefs about ideals that are shared by members of the helping professions. They are prima facie obligations that are always considered in ethical decision making (Meara, et al., 1996). Although moral philosophers do not agree about the nature or number of moral principles, the following six have been suggested in the professional literature in counseling.

- *Autonomy* means to foster self-determination. According to this principle, counselors respect the rights of clients to choose their own directions, act in accordance with their beliefs, and control their own lives. Counselors work to decrease client dependency and foster independent decision making.

- *Nonmaleficence* means to do no harm. This principle, long established in the medical profession, obligates counselors to avoid actions that risk hurting clients, even inadvertently.
- *Beneficence* is the flip side of the coin of nonmaleficence. It could be argued that the obligation of ordinary citizens in our society ends with doing no harm to others, while professionals have a higher obligation to provide a service that benefits society. Thus, counselors actively do good or are helpful, and work to promote the mental health and wellness of their clients.
- *Justice* refers to the counselor's commitment to fairness in professional relationships. Counselors' actions and decisions must be fair to all concerned. Justice demands equality, which has implications for nondiscrimination and equitable treatment of all clients.
- *Fidelity* refers to fulfilling a responsibility of trust in the counseling relationship. Counselors strive to be faithful to the promises they make, such as keeping clients' disclosures confidential.
- *Veracity* means truthfulness, and addresses the counselor's obligation to deal honestly with clients.

In theory, all of these principles have equal value and each should be considered along with all the others when weighing an ethical decision. In reality, however, these principles can compete with one another, and counselors may need to sacrifice one in order to uphold another. For example, a counselor who is counseling a suicidal client may decide to intervene by notifying family members against the client's wishes or by seeking involuntary hospitalization (thus sacrificing client autonomy) in order to uphold the obligations to prevent harm and do good.

Virtue ethics start from a very different premise than principle ethics. The basic assumption of this viewpoint is that professional ethics involves more than just moral actions; it also involves traits of character or virtue. Virtue ethics focus on the actor rather than the action. Principle ethics ask the question, "What should I do?" while virtue ethics ask "Who should I be?" Patterns of virtuous behavior are evident throughout the career of a professional, rather than being found in any particular action or decision. Thus, this perspective asks you to look at who you are, rather than what you do. Some characteristics of virtuous agents that have been suggested as appropriate for mental health professionals (Meara, et al., 1996) are discussed below. We hope that you will read about these characteristics with an eye to whether you see them as representing the ideals you hold for yourself, and that you will assess their relevance for you as an aspiring counselor.

- *Integrity.* Virtuous agents are motivated to do what is right because they believe it is right, not because they feel obligated or fear the consequences. They have stable moral values and are faithful to these values in their actions.
- *Discernment.* Discerning counselors are able to perceive the ethically relevant aspects of a situation, know what principles apply, and take decisive action. Discernment involves a tolerance for ambiguity, the ability to maintain perspective, and an understanding of the links between current behaviors and future consequences.

- *Acceptance of emotion.* Without discounting the value of logic and systematic deliberation about ethical issues, virtuous agents also recognize the role of emotion in ethical decisions. Rather than assume that emotion hinders reason, they believe that emotion informs reason. For instance, compassion is an important virtue for health care professionals.
- *Self awareness.* Virtuous agents know their own assumptions, convictions, and biases and how these may affect their relationships and interactions with others.
- *Interdependence with the community.* Virtuous agents realize that values cannot be espoused without awareness of context. They are connected with their communities.

Both perspectives—a focus on principles and a focus on virtues—can contribute to your understanding of the basis for professional ethics. Principle ethics help you systematically evaluate what you should do when trying to resolve an ethical dilemma. Virtue ethics can help you examine your ideals and define the kind of person you aspire to be as a helping professional. Thinking about principles and virtues requires you to look inward in order to identify internal resources that can assist you in ethical decision making. There are external resources as well, and primary among these is your professional code of ethics.

Codes of Ethics

Promulgating a code of ethics is one way that a group of practitioners can establish their professional status. Codes of ethics serve a number of other important purposes as well. Most fundamentally, they exist to protect and promote the welfare of clients.

Some counselors practice *mandatory ethics;* that is, they function at a level of ethical reasoning that merely keeps them in compliance with minimal standards. By complying with these basic "musts" and "must nots," they meet the letter but not the spirit of the ethical standards. According to Pope and Vasquez (1991), counselors who set their sights at this level are vulnerable to denial and other means of distorting, discounting, or dismissing ethical questions they encounter. Some of the self-statements that these counselors use to justify their actions include the following:

"It can't be unethical if I don't see it as an ethical issue."

"It isn't unethical if I don't know an ethical standard that prohibits it."

"It can't be unethical if I know other practitioners who do it."

"It isn't an ethical problem so long as no client has ever complained about it."

"It's not unethical as long as no one finds out about it."

Other counselors practice *aspirational ethics,* a term that describes the highest standards of conduct to which counselors can aspire. They understand the spirit behind the code and the moral principles on which it rests. They not only look outward to established standards, but also look inward and ask themselves whether what they are doing is best for their clients. Corey et al., (1993) have emphasized that clients' needs are best met when counselors monitor their own ethics and challenge their own thinking and behavior.

While we certainly would encourage you to practice aspirational, rather than mandatory, ethics, we must caution you against becoming overly judgmental of the practices and ethical decisions of your peers. You may some day be a member of an ethics committee or state licensure board. In those roles, you would be required to review the actions (or failures to act) of counselors to determine whether they were ethical. In addition, you could be called upon at some point in your career to accuse a peer of ethical conduct according to the procedures set forth in Section H.2 of the American Counseling Association (ACA) Code of Ethics (1995). Unless you are an ethics committee or licensure board member or are in a rare situation in which you should report a peer's suspected unethical conduct, you should be very reluctant to label another counselor's actions as unethical, illegal, or unprofessional.

When you see a colleague making difficult ethical decisions, your role should be to assist that person. When you hear of actions taken by a peer that may seem unusual, keep in mind that you may be hearing only part of the story and do not judge that person's actions precipitously or harshly. Remember that you will be placed in difficult ethical situations many times during your career, and you will want understanding and support from your peers, rather than their inappropriate and sanctimonious judging. A counselor's reputation and career can be irreparably harmed by rumors or by unfounded or inappropriate allegations of unethical conduct. This caution against judging too quickly must be balanced, however, with your obligation to address practices of your peers that you view as unethical.

Herlihy and Corey (1996); Mappes, Robb, and Engels (1985); and Van Hoose and Kottler (1985) have suggested that codes of ethics have the following purposes:

- Educate members of the profession about what constitutes sound, ethical conduct.
- Provide a means to ensure accountability by enforcing the standards.
- Serve as a catalyst for improving practice.
- Protect the profession from government, allowing the profession to regulate itself and function more autonomously.
- Help control internal disagreement, thus promoting stability within the profession.
- Protect practitioners—if professionals behave according to established guidelines, their behavior is more likely to be judged in compliance with accepted standards in a malpractice suit or licensing board complaint.

A code of ethics that would address every possible situation that a counselor might encounter would probably fill an entire library. You cannot expect your code of ethics to provide an answer to every question you might have. Codes are a crucial resource, but they are not a substitute for an active, deliberative, and creative approach to fulfilling your ethical responsibilities (Pope & Vasquez, 1991). You will need to attend to both the letter and the spirit of the code, and work to understand the intentions that underlie each standard. As Herlihy and Corey (1996) have noted, there is a very real difference between merely following the ethics code and living out a commitment to practice with the highest ideals.

Your primary professional association, the American Counseling Association (ACA) has established a code of ethics to guide you in your practice. This code is presented in Appendix A. We encourage you to review it when you complete this chapter to become familiar with how the code relates to issues discussed throughout the book. Figure 1-3 presents a brief overview of the eight sections of the code and their general provisions:

The current *ACA Code of Ethics and Standards of Practice,* adopted in 1995, is the fifth version of the ethics code established by ACA and its predecessor organizations. Development of the first code was initiated in 1953 by Donald Super, then president of the newly

Section A: The Counseling Relationship addresses important issues in forming, maintaining, and ending the counseling relationship. This section includes guidelines to help counselors keep client welfare foremost and respect client rights. It contains standards that emphasize the importance of respecting diversity and being aware of one's own personal needs and how these can influence the counseling relationship. It provides guidance on how to handle troublesome issues such as dual relationships, fees, and termination. Guidelines for working with multiple clients and the use of computer technology are also included in this section.

Section B: Confidentiality addresses the client's right to privacy of information shared during counseling sessions and of records. Exceptions and limitations to confidentiality are specified, and special considerations in working with minors, families, and groups are addressed. Guidelines are offered for maintaining confidentiality when consulting or conducting research.

Section C: Professional Responsibility contains standards related to competence. It emphasizes the importance of advertising services and credentials in an accurate manner. It also addresses the counselor's responsibilities to the public.

Section D: Relationships with Other Professionals offers guidelines for employer/employee and consultative relationships. This section highlights the importance of respecting and establishing good working relationships with professionals in related mental health professions.

Section E: Evaluation, Assessment, and Interpretation includes standards on competence to select, use, and interpret tests. Client rights in testing, test security, and proper testing conditions are addressed. This section also includes standards related to diagnosis of mental disorders.

Section F: Teaching, Training, and Supervision presents guidelines for counselor educators and trainers, counselor preparation programs, and students and supervisees. Guidance is provided on issues such as relationship boundaries, evaluation, and endorsement of students to enter the profession.

Section G: Research and Publication describes research responsibilities, informed consent practices, and the reporting of research results. A range of issues are covered from protection of human subjects to ethical procedures in seeking publication.

Section H: Resolving Ethical Issues addresses the responsibility of counselors to know their ethical standards and explains procedures for resolving and reporting suspected ethical violations.

Figure 1-3   ACA Code of Ethics and Standards of Practice: A Synopsis

formed American Personnel and Guidance Association (APGA). It was adopted in 1961. It was revised in 1974 and has been revised every seven years since that time. The current document, the result of a lengthy revision process that began in 1991, was adopted after the membership gave input and suggestions regarding two earlier proposed versions. In 1995, for the first time, the ethical standards of the association were presented in two separate documents. In the *Casebook* that accompanies these standards, Herlihy and Corey (1996, p. 7) explained the rationale for creating not only an ethics code but also practice standards:

> The Standards of Practice were developed in response to the needs of nonmembers of ACA to understand our minimal expectations for ethical behavior and to enforce these expectations in legal arenas. Increasingly, courts of law and state licensure boards are demanding that the counseling profession define its minimal standards to which all counselors may be held accountable. The Standards of Practice are relatively brief and specify minimal behaviors required of professional counselors (mandatory ethics) that can be understood and evaluated by individuals outside the counseling profession. The Code of Ethics is lengthier, gives more detailed guidance regarding the standards of practice, and includes statements describing the best practice that represents the ideals of the profession (aspirational ethics).

As you learn about ethical standards that you will be expected to uphold, keep in mind that codes of ethics are living documents that change over time. They are periodically revised as the profession's knowledge base grows and as consensus emerges about controversial ethical issues. You will need to stay aware of these issues and ongoing developments throughout your professional career.

It is also important to keep in mind that historically, counseling has not been a unified profession. Codes of ethics have proliferated as various specialty groups within counseling, certification bodies, and state licensure boards have developed their own ethical standards. When you are established in your own professional practice, it is likely that you will hold multiple affiliations and will be bound to know and adhere to multiple codes. For instance, you might be a member of ACA and several of its divisions that have published specialty guidelines, be a National Certified Counselor (NCC), and be licensed as a counselor in your state. Holding each of these credentials will require you to abide by its particular code of ethics. The existence of multiple codes of ethics creates difficulties in enforcement, confusion for consumers of counseling services, and confusion for counseling professionals themselves (Herlihy & Remley, 1995). Until a single, universally accepted code of ethics for the counseling profession is established, you will need to thread your way carefully through this maze.

Ethical Decision Making

As you undoubtedly realize at this point, ethical decisions are rarely easy to arrive at, and dilemmas can be complex. Several writers (Blocher, 1987; Corey et al., 1993; Forester-Miller & Davis, 1995; Jordan & Meara, 1990; Kitchener, 1984; Rave & Larsen, 1995; Stadler, 1986; Van Hoose & Paradise, 1979) have offered models for ethical decision making, all of which help bring order and clarity to the reasoning process. Rather than elaborate on any one particular model, we will instead describe steps that many of them seem to have in common, incorporating lessons that can be learned from principle and virtue ethics. We have kept in mind the caution offered by feminist writers (Hill, Glaser, & Harden, 1995; Meara et al., 1996; Rave & Larsen, 1995) that most ethical decision making models represent the information processing style of white males. Traditional models have tended to be linear, logical, rational, dispassionate, abstract, and paternalistic. Ethical decision making that is also holistic, intuitive, emotional, compassionate, personal and contextual, and mutual may be more inclusive of other processing styles and more culturally appropriate.

The general goal in presenting steps in the decision making process is to assist you in becoming an "Ideal Problem Solver" (Bransford & Stein, 1993) who can (1) identify problems and opportunities, (2) define goals, (3) explore possible strategies, (4) anticipate outcomes, (5) act, and (6) look back and learn.

Identify and define the problem. Before deciding what action to take when faced with an ethical problem, it is prudent to take time to reflect and gather information. Although you may feel some sense of urgency, there really is no such thing as an ethical emergency. Take time to consider what you know (or what you can find out) about the situation, applicable ethical guidelines, and any laws that might be relevant. Review the professional literature and your code of ethics. If a legal issue is involved, consult with an attorney. Try to examine the problem from several perspectives and avoid searching for simplistic solutions.

Consider the moral principles. Reflect on how the moral principles apply to the problem. Identify ways that they compete with each other, and rank them in order of their priority in this situation.

Tune in to your feelings. Virtue ethicists believe that emotion informs judgment. Consider what emotions you are experiencing as you contemplate the situation and your possible actions. To what extent are you being influenced, for instance, by emotions such as fear, self-doubt, or an overwhelming sense of responsibility? Your emotions can help guide you in your decision making.

Involve your client in the decision making process. This is not a separate step in ethical decision making; rather, it should occur throughout the process. Walden (1997) reminded counselors that the client is an integral part of the ethical community of the counseling relationship. Including clients in the process both empowers them and is culturally appropriate practice. We can think of very few situations that would preclude making the client an active partner in decisions affecting that client. Counselors should avoid making decisions *for* the client when those decisions can be made *with* the client.

Identify desired outcomes. Even after thoughtful consideration, a single desired outcome rarely emerges in an ethical dilemma. There may be a number of outcomes you would hope to see achieved in a situation; some may seem essential and others may be desirable but not altogether necessary. Two helpful strategies are brainstorming to generate new options and consulting with colleagues who may see possibilities that have not occurred to you.

Consider possible actions that you could take to achieve the desired outcomes. It may even be useful to list desired outcomes on one side of a page, and on the other side generate possible actions that would facilitate the achievement of each of those outcomes. Ponder the implications and consequences of each option for the client, for others who will be affected, and for yourself.

Choose and act on your choice. Once you have selected an action or series of actions, check to see whether your selected options are congruent with your ranking of the moral principles. Pay attention to how you feel about your choice. This final step involves strengthening your ego or gathering the moral courage to allow you to carry out your decision.

Even after the most careful deliberation, conscientious counselors cannot help but ask the question, "How can I know whether I've done the right thing?" Van Hoose and Paradise

(1979) suggested that decisions are probably ethically responsible if the counselors (1) maintained personal and professional honesty, coupled with (2) the client's best interests, (3) without malice or personal gain, and (4) can justify their actions as the best judgment regarding what should be done based on the current state of the profession.

You can also apply four self-tests after you have resolved an ethical dilemma. First is the test of *justice,* in which you ask whether you would treat others the same in this situation. Second is the test of *universality,* which means that you would be willing to recommend the course of action you followed to other counselors who find themselves in a similar situation. Third is the test of *publicity:* you would be willing to have your actions come to light and be known by others. These three tests were suggested by Stadler (1986). Finally, you can check for *moral traces,* which are lingering feelings of doubt, discomfort, or uncertainty that counselors may experience after they have resolved an ethical dilemma, particularly when expediency, politics, or self-interest have influenced the decision. Moral traces are unpleasant but serve an important function. They act as a warning sign that you may have set foot on an ethical slippery slope, which was discussed earlier in this chapter.

In summary, being an ethical professional involves a combination of knowledge, problem solving skills and strategies, understanding of philosophical principles, and a virtuous character that leads one to respond with maturity, judgment, and wisdom (Bersoff, 1996). It is a task that requires a lifelong commitment and is never really finished.

LEGAL ISSUES

The discussion of professional ethics that preceded this section emphasized the serious responsibility you have to clients, the difference you can make in their lives, and the duty you have to practice in an ethical manner. Understanding the legal system and your role in it, the legal rights of your clients, and your legal responsibilities to clients is also essential to practicing counseling in a professional manner. Legal issues within counseling are somewhat frightening because the law is an area that is complex, often vague, threatening, antithetical to the nature of counselors, and difficult to fully grasp. The process of decision making around legal issues will be presented to you in this chapter. In addition, throughout this text, you will be given information about the legal dimensions that surround your functions as a professional counselor.

Origins of Law

There are a number of sources of law in the United States. The basic source is the U.S. Constitution. The fifty states, the District of Columbia, and the U.S. possessions also have constitutions. Laws created by the federal, state, district, and possession governments cannot violate either federal or state constitutional principles. The United States has adopted the English common law. It includes a set of societal principles that were not written into documents, but have been accepted over time as obvious within our society. An example of common law that is very important to counselors is the law of torts. Tort law relates to the principle that individuals will be held accountable for any harm they cause to other members of society. Malpractice is an area of tort law that holds professionals accountable for any harm they might cause to the public. The public relies upon the professionals to provide services in a manner that benefits and does not harm them.

A primary source of law is statutes that are passed by federal and state legislatures. These statutes may modify the common law, but may not violate constitutional principles. Governmental regulations, both federal and state, are procedures adopted by agencies to carry out laws created by statutes. Regulations may implement statutes, but may not exceed the authority of the statute. Finally, federal and state courts interpret the law. While some accuse judges of creating law, courts are limited to interpreting constitutions, common law principles, statutes, and regulations.

Almost all areas of counselor practice are affected by law. Most counselors are keenly aware of the law of malpractice and the fact that they might be sued by a client. You will probably come to share this awareness. You also must be aware of laws related to confidentiality, records, parental rights, and licensing statutes, among others. In addition, you must be able to identify legal problems as they arise, and you must adhere to legal requirements when you are involved in any way with a legal proceeding. Legal issues are an important part of the day-to-day professional practice of counselors in all settings.

Recognizing Legal Issues

Many of the ethical and professional judgment questions you will encounter as a counseling practitioner will have legal implications as well. Many counselors find it difficult to determine when they have a legal problem or to know what to do once a legal problem has been identified. This section of the chapter will discuss how to recognize legal issues, how to get legal advice, and steps to take to ensure proper and professional practice.

The following are examples of legal issues that counselors face in their practices:

- The secretary tells you that there is a deputy sheriff in the reception area asking for you. When you introduce yourself, the deputy hands you a subpoena that orders you to produce your case notes and any other documents related to one of your current clients.
- One of your clients asks you to come to a child custody hearing that will determine whether she will get permanent custody of her children.
- One of your clients has been arrested for drug possession. You receive a subpoena in the mail that orders you to appear at her criminal trial.
- A new client tells you that his lawyer sent him to see you. He is suing his employer for having fired him and wants you to verify that he has emotional stress that is job related.
- A client tells you that her former husband's lawyer called and told her she had to let her former husband have their children for the summer. She wants to know if the lawyer is right.
- A former client has sent you a letter demanding her money back. She thinks the ten sessions she had with you were a waste of money since you did not help her. She has sent a copy of the letter to her lawyer.
- A client you are seeing appears suicidal and refuses to go voluntarily to the local hospital for a psychiatric evaluation.
- You receive a notice from your state licensure board that a formal complaint has been filed against you and that a hearing will be held on the matter.
- In your office mail, there is a formal legal complaint that has been filed with the local court. One of your clients murdered his girlfriend nine months ago.

The complaint alleges that you were responsible for the girl's death and asks for one million dollars in damages.

A simple test to determine whether there is a legal issue involved is to review the situation to see if any of the following apply: (1) legal proceedings of some type have been initiated, (2) lawyers are on the scene in some capacity, or (3) you are vulnerable to having a complaint filed against you for misconduct. If you are providing professional counseling services and any of these three components exist, then you definitely are dealing with a legal issue. Sometimes, all you need to do with a legal situation is clarify the nature of a counselor's role with your client and refer the client to attorneys for legal advice. When you are dealing with a legal issue and you are unsure which course of action you should take, often you will need to consult a lawyer.

Obtaining Legal Advice

Most counselors are employed by organizations or entities that provide counseling services, such as community mental health agencies, schools, businesses, hospitals, outpatient treatment programs, colleges, and others. These entities all have administrators and organizational structures that require the regular services of attorneys. It is the employees' responsibility to request legal advice when dealing with an issue that has legal implications beyond their ability to resolve. It is the obligation of employers to provide employees with the legal advice they need to perform their job appropriately.

Counselors seldom have direct access to lawyers, primarily because the cost is prohibitive. Also, administrators seek the advice of lawyers but they must maintain their authority in making administrative decisions. When a counselor identifies a legal issue in the work setting and defines the legal questions to ask, the counselor should pose the questions to the immediate supervisor and ask for assistance. If the counselor thinks an attorney needs to have special information regarding the situation in order to render sound advice, the individual should request a personal consultation with the attorney, although such consultations are not normally allowed. The supervisor will then either answer the counselor's questions based on previous experience with similar issues or seek legal advice through proper administrative channels within the organization.

In some circumstances, it is possible for counselors to give their legal problems to administrators within their agency. Many legal issues that arise are administrative in nature and should be handled by administrators rather than counselors. Examples of legal issues that counselors might easily turn over to administrators include the following:

- A noncustodial parent demands from a school counselor that he be allowed to see his child's academic records.
- The police arrive at a counselor's door and want to see the counseling file for a current client.
- A health insurance company representative calls a counselor and wants to know why the counselor's agency has so many claims signed by the same psychiatrist.
- A client becomes irate because a counselor terminates the counseling relationship after five sessions because that is the agency's policy.
- A lawyer for a former client calls a counselor and threatens to sue if the counselor does not immediately give the lawyer the information being sought.

- A secretary who reports to an administrator appears to be revealing confidential information about clients to friends.
- A client tells you that a counselor colleague in your agency has made sexual advances during a counseling session.

If legal problems cannot be handed over to an administrator, then counselors themselves must take responsibility for resolving situations in an appropriate manner. Once counselors have disclosed their legal questions to their immediate supervisors and have received a response either from the supervisor or an attorney advising them as to the proper course of action, counselors must follow that advice. It is essential for counselors to follow legal advice given to them, even if they do not agree with it. Only then will counselors be indemnified by their employers and supported if problems arise later. By seeking and following legal advice when legal questions arise, counselors are protecting themselves from being held individually responsible in the event their actions are challenged.

Counselors in independent private practice do not have the luxury of seeking legal advice without charge within their work environment, and they are not protected from responsibility since they do not have employers. Private practitioners must establish relationships with attorneys for legal advice just as they must retain accountants to handle their financial and business affairs. The cost of legal advice for a counselor in private practice is a necessary expense related to establishing and maintaining a business. However, finding a lawyer who understands the nature of mental health practices and is prepared to represent counselors effectively is not always an easy task (Remley, 1991). Counselors who are planning to open private practices are advised to identify an attorney while they are establishing their business so they will have a working relationship in place when problems arise. The best attorney probably would be a local one who is already representing one or more successful mental health practitioners—counselors, social workers, or psychologists. Such an attorney would already have been educated regarding the special issues surrounding mental health practices. If an attorney who is experienced in representing mental health professionals is not available, then a lawyer who represents other types of professionals, such as accountants, other lawyers, or physicians, would be a good alternative.

Some counselors have jobs in which they testify in court on a routine basis or provide services to clients who frequently are involved in litigation. These counselors learn their roles over time and do not need to consult attorneys for advice each time they encounter a legal situation. For most counselors, however, it is infrequent that they deal with legal proceedings, have clients who are represented by lawyers, or think they are in danger of being sued. When such situations arise for the majority of counselors, it is essential for them to obtain legal advice.

Exercising Professional Judgment

Throughout the work day, counselors often have to exercise their professional judgment in areas that are difficult. They are held accountable for making professional decisions that are sound and reasonable, given the information they have available when they make such judgments. If a client believes that he or she was harmed because of a professional decision made by a counselor, then the client might sue a counselor for malpractice. As a result, when a counselor exercises professional judgment, there is always a risk of being accused of wrongdoing afterwards.

A few of the areas in which counselors make judgments that are particularly vulnerable to later legal challenges include the following:

- Determining whether a client is suicidal or a danger to others.
- Deciding what to do to prevent harm after determining that a client is a danger to self or others.
- Rendering a clinical diagnosis that could have negative implications for a client at a later time.
- Terminating a counseling relationship over the client's objections.
- Deciding whether to enter into a counseling relationship with a client who has a problem that you have not treated before or have not been specifically trained to treat.
- Reacting appropriately to a client who has expressed an interest in having a sexual relationship with you.
- Using a paradoxical intervention with a client.

When counselors face issues that require them to exercise their clinical judgment, particularly where there are no clear right or wrong responses, it is essential to consult with colleagues to the extent possible. In some situations consultation might be impossible, such as when emergencies arise. When time does allow, however, consulting about clients provides a substantial protection to counselors whose clinical decisions are later challenged. The legal standard of care for counselors is that counselors must practice in a manner consistent with the way in which a reasonable, similarly educated counselor would practice in the same set of circumstances. By consulting with others, counselors can prove later that they indeed met the standard of care by doing what other, presumably reasonable, counselors advised or agreed upon. If experts are available for consultation, it is wise to talk with them as well. Experts might include former university professors, counselors who are known for their expertise in a particular area, or counselors with extensive clinical experience.

It is impossible for counselors to know for certain whether they are making decisions that will protect their clients or others from harm. Because of this uncertainty, it is essential that counselors maintain a current personal professional liability insurance policy at all times. Professional liability insurance policies are discussed in detail in Chapter 6.

SUMMARY AND KEY POINTS

This introductory chapter has familiarized you with some key concepts that form the foundation for studying ethical, legal, and professional issues in counseling. The professional orientation content area of graduate training involves the study of professional identity, ethics, and law. Morality, ethics, law, and professionalism are all interrelated terms but they have different meanings. As used in this book, the term *morality* refers to personal beliefs and how these beliefs affect your conduct, while *ethics* refers to professional values and behaviors. Laws are agreed-upon rules that set forth principles that allow people to live together in a society. Laws dictate minimal standards of behavior and ethics represent ideal standards.

A model of professional practice was presented as one way to conceptualize how all these terms might fit together in your actual practice as a counselor. In this model, both internal and external building blocks contribute to the development and maintenance of sound, professional practice.

Following are some of the key points about ethics and law in counseling that were made in this chapter:

- Principle ethics, which are based on the moral principles of the helping professions, and virtue ethics, which focus on traits of character, are two complementary ways of looking at the foundations of counselor ethics.
- Codes of ethics are vital resources in ethical decision making but they cannot answer every question that might arise in actual practice.
- It is critically important that counselors develop ethical decision making skills and that they have a model they can use to reason through the ethical dilemmas with which they are confronted.
- Almost all areas of counselor practice are affected by law.
- Counselors must know how to recognize when they are faced with a legal issue and know how to obtain legal advice.
- Although many resources exist to help counselors when they encounter difficult ethical or legal questions in their work, there is no substitute for professional judgment in these matters.

Professional Identity of Counselors

As has been noted, counselors are a relatively new professional group compared with other mental health professionals such as psychologists, social workers, and psychiatrists. Potential consumers of mental health services often are unaware that counseling is a distinct profession that can be clearly distinguished from similar mental health professions. Even counselors themselves sometimes find it difficult to describe the distinctions. Members of groups that are just beginning to establish themselves professionally often express confusion about their professional identity. Thus, a vital professional task for counselors is to adopt a strong professional identity and to be able to articulate that unique identity to others.

Professional identity is a rather nebulous concept, but it is vital to the long-term success of a profession. Individuals who have a strong professional identity can easily explain the philosophy that underlies the activities of their professional group, describe the services their profession renders to the public, describe the training programs that prepare them to practice their profession, explain their qualifications and the credentials they possess, and articulate the similarities and differences between members of their own profession and other similar groups. In addition, those with a strong professional identity feel a significant pride in being a member of their profession and can communicate this special sense of belonging to those with whom they interact.

We hope this chapter will help you clarify your professional identity as a counselor and will also help you tell others about the profession of counseling. It is also intended to help you understand and appreciate the history of the counseling profession, the professional associations that serve counselors, graduate program accreditation, and the credentials available to counselors.

PHILOSOPHY UNDERLYING THE COUNSELING PROFESSION

Counselors have a unique belief system regarding the best way to help people resolve their emotional and personal issues and problems. This belief system provides the foundation for the professional identity of counselors. Basically, counselors share the following four beliefs regarding helping others with their mental health concerns:

1. The best perspective for assisting individuals in resolving their emotional and personal issues and problems is the wellness model of mental health.
2. The issues and problems individuals face in life are developmental in nature, and understanding the dynamics of human growth and development is essential to success as a helper.
3. Prevention and early intervention are far superior to remediation in dealing with personal and emotional problems.
4. The goal of counseling is to empower individuals to resolve their own problems independently of mental health professionals and to teach them to identify and resolve problems autonomously in the future.

The Wellness Model

The first belief that counselors share is that the wellness model of mental health is the best perspective for helping people resolve their personal and emotional issues and problems. The primary model that other mental health professionals in the United States use to address emotional problems is the illness model, an approach that was created by physicians in caring for persons with physical illnesses.

In the illness model, the helper identifies the illness presented by the person asking for assistance. The diagnosis of the illness is always the first step in helping. This perspective assumes that the client is diminished in some significant way. The goal of the professional helper is to return the help seeker to the level of functioning enjoyed before the illness occurred. Once the illness has been isolated, the helper applies scientific principles in curing the illness. If the helper is successful and the illness is cured, the client then goes on about life. If another illness negatively affects the client's well being, the client returns to the helper to be cured again.

Psychiatrists, who are physicians, approach mental health issues in the manner described above. Other mental health professionals, including clinical and counseling psychologists, psychiatric nurses, and clinical social workers, also have adopted the illness model of mental health. Although many individual practitioners within these other mental health professions deviate from the illness model, the mental health professions as a whole have embraced this approach to helping people who are experiencing distress in their lives.

Counselors, on the other hand, have adopted the wellness model of mental health as their perspective for helping people. In the wellness model, a goal is established that includes positive mental health to the degree possible for each person. From a wellness perspective, mental health is seen as occurring on a continuum. At one end of the scale are individuals who are very healthy mentally. Maslow (1968) described people who are fully functioning mentally and emotionally as "self-actualizing." At the other extreme are persons who are dysfunctional because of mental problems. Such people might include persons with schizophrenia who do not respond to any kind of treatment or intervention.

In addition to this general continuum of mental health, the wellness orientation also views mental health as including a number of scales of mental and emotional functioning (see Fig. 2-1). These scales represent an individual's mental and emotional wellness in important areas of living. Counselors assess a client's functioning in each of these areas to determine where attention within counseling might best be focused to increase wellness. They include family relationships, friendships, other relationships (work/community/church,

```
┌─────────────────────────────────────────────────────────────┐
│                                                               │
│        Overall Functioning in Mental and Emotional Areas      │
│    ◄─ Dysfunctional                        Self-Actualized ─► │
│                        Specific Areas                         │
│                     Family Relationships                      │
│                         Friendships                           │
│        Other Relationships (Work/Community/Church, etc.)      │
│                          Career/Job                           │
│                         Spirituality                          │
│                       Leisure Activities                      │
│                       Physical Health                         │
│                      Living Environment                       │
│                          Financial                            │
│                          Sexuality                            │
│                                                               │
└─────────────────────────────────────────────────────────────┘
```

Figure 2-1   The Wellness Orientation to Mental Health

etc.), career/job, spirituality, leisure activities, physical health, living environment, financial status, and sexuality.

Counselors assess the client's current life situation and help determine which factors are interfering with the goal of reaching their maximum potential. Many persons are limited by physical disabilities or environmental conditions that cannot be changed. Keeping such limitations in mind, counselors assist their clients in becoming as autonomous and successful in their lives as is possible.

Mental health professionals who operate from the illness model might treat patients or clients in ways that appear similar to the way they would be treated by mental health professionals who embrace the wellness model. For example, mental health professionals who espouse either model would most likely provide individual or group counseling services, spend time talking with clients, take clinical notes, and even render a diagnosis of any mental disorders the person may have. Perhaps the primary differences between the two are in the attitude of the professional toward the client and the focus of the professional's clinical attention. Counselors see the client as having both the potential and the desire for autonomy and success in living, rather than having an illness that needs to be remediated. In addition, the goal of counseling is to help the person accomplish wellness, rather than cure an illness.

A Developmental Perspective

A second belief that counselors share is that many personal and emotional issues can be understood within a developmental perspective. As people progress through the lifespan, they meet and must successfully address a number of personal challenges. Counselors believe that most of the problems people encounter are developmental in nature, and therefore are natural and normal. Problems that other mental health professionals might view as pathological, and that counselors would see as developmental, include the following:

- a 5-year-old crying as if in terror when his mother drops him off for the first time at his kindergarten class

- an 11-year-old girl who seems to become obsessed with boys
- a teenager vigorously defying his parents' directives
- a 19-year-old girl becoming seriously depressed after breaking up with her boyfriend
- a young mother becoming despondent soon after the birth of a child
- a 35-year-old man beginning to drink so much he is getting into trouble after 15 years of social drinking
- a 40-year-old woman feeling worthless after her youngest child leaves home for college
- a 46-year-old man having an affair with a young woman after 23 years of a committed marriage
- a 65-year-old woman feeling very depressed as her retirement approaches
- an 80-year-old man forgetting so much that he is concerned that he is losing his mind

By studying the developmental stages in life and understanding tasks that all individuals face during their lives, counselors are able to put many problems that clients experience into a perspective that views these problems as natural and normal. Even problems viewed as psychopathological by other mental health professionals, such as severe depression, substance addiction, or debilitating anxiety can be seen as transitory issues that often plague people in our society and that must be dealt with effectively if individuals are to continue living in a successful fashion.

Prevention and Early Intervention

A third philosophical assumption of counselors is our preference for prevention of mental and emotional problems, rather than remediation. When prevention is impossible, counselors strive toward early intervention instead of waiting until a problem has reached serious proportions.

A primary tool that counselors use to prevent emotional and mental problems is education. Counselors often practice their profession in the role of teacher, using psychoeducation as a tool. By alerting clients to potential future areas that might cause personal and emotional distress and preparing them to meet such challenges successfully, counselors prevent problems before they arise. Just a few examples of prevention activities are parenting education programs, assertiveness training seminars, career exploration groups, and premarriage counseling.

When the time for prevention has already passed and a client is at risk of experiencing personal or emotional problems, counselors prefer seeing clients early in the process. Counselors believe that counseling is for everyone, not just for individuals who have mental illnesses or emotional disorders. By providing services to individuals when they begin to experience potentially distressing events in their lives, counselors hope to intervene early and therefore prevent problems from escalating. For instance, counselors would prefer to see a client who is beginning to have feelings of depression, rather than someone who could be diagnosed as having had an episode of severe depression. Counselors would encourage couples who are beginning to experience problems in their relationship to seek counseling, rather than waiting for their problems to escalate into serious marital discord.

Empowerment of Clients

The fourth belief that counselors share regarding the helping process is that the goal of counseling is to empower clients to problem-solve independently. Through teaching clients appropriate problem-solving strategies and increasing their self-understanding, counselors hope that clients will not need assistance in living their lives in the future. Realizing that individuals often need only transitory help, counselors also try to communicate to clients that asking for and receiving help is not a sign of mental or emotional weakness, but instead is a healthy response to life's problems in many circumstances.

It is quite easy for individuals to become dependent upon those who provide help to them. Some systems of mental health care seem to encourage a pattern of lifelong dependence. Counselors recognize this problem and encourage clients to assume responsibility for their lives and learn to live in a manner that allows them autonomy and independence. While some people may need assistance throughout their lives because of a physical or mental disability, all clients are helped to become as independent as their circumstances will allow. Counselors do not present themselves as experts in mental health who must be consulted when problems arise. Rather, counselors communicate the belief that clients are capable of developing the skills they need for independent living and wellness.

COUNSELING SERVICES

To achieve a strong professional identity as a counselor, it is essential that you understand the philosophy of helping we have just described. In addition, you need to be knowledgeable about the kinds of services that counselors provide to the public, even though the services counselors provide do not define the profession. Actually, counselors engage in a number of the same activities as do other professionals. The key to a strong professional identity is the philosophy underlying the services, not the services being rendered.

The basic service counselors provide is counseling—with individuals, couples, families, and groups. All other mental health professionals counsel patients and clients, too. A major difference between counselors and other mental health professionals who counsel is that counseling is the *primary* professional service counselors provide. By contrast, the primary service psychiatrists provide is the diagnosis and medical treatment of mental disorders as a physician, psychologists primarily provide assessment, psychiatric nurses provide management of mental health care within a hospital setting, and social workers link clients to community resources. For mental health professionals other than counselors, counseling is a secondary or ancillary service.

In addition, a number of other professionals outside the mental health field call the service they provide to clients counseling. For example, attorneys provide legal counseling, accountants offer financial counseling, and physicians offer counseling to their patients regarding their physical health. Counselors, in contrast to these non-mental health professionals, provide mental health counseling services to clients.

In conjunction with counseling, counselors also perform a number of other professional services. These services include assessment, teaching, diagnosing, and case management. Despite performing these other duties, the primary service provided by counselors is mental health counseling.

Counselors have a number of job titles, roles, and duties in their professional positions. In order to develop a strong professional identity, you must know when you are functioning as a counselor and when you are performing other roles in your professional position. You must also be able to identify the types of professional services counselors render to the public.

COUNSELOR TRAINING PROGRAMS

Ask lawyers what they were taught in law school, physicians what they were taught in medical school, and engineers what they were taught in engineering school, and they can easily and clearly describe the courses they were taught, the practical components of their educational experience, and the topics that were covered in their preparation programs. To develop a strong professional identity, it is vital that you are also able to describe your training program components. By describing the educational programs that prepare counselors, you summarize the essential nature of counseling as a profession and emphasize the basic knowledge required for becoming a counselor.

An essential aspect of counselor training is that the profession considers individuals to be professionals after they have completed a master's degree. While master's degrees are the required professional degree in both psychiatric nursing and clinical social work, psychiatry requires a medical degree and residency in psychiatry, and psychology requires a doctoral degree for the achievement of professional status. One of the primary differences between counseling psychology and the profession of counseling is that counseling psychologists must hold doctorates to be considered professionals, while counselors are considered professionals at the master's degree level.

In addition, counseling skills are the primary focus of the counseling master's degree training programs. While other subjects are taught, all of the training emphasizes competency in the areas of individual and group counseling. The other courses required in master's degree programs, such as research, assessment, multicultural counseling, and career counseling, are meant to strengthen the counseling skills of graduate students.

Counseling graduate programs generally are located in colleges of education within universities. The profession of counseling has its foundations in pedagogy and psychology, particularly in counseling psychology and human growth and development. All these fields have their roots in colleges of education, which is why counseling graduate programs are usually located there. Some counselor educators and counselors are concerned that this implies that counselors are being prepared to function only in educational settings, such as schools or colleges. They believe that the general public's perception is negatively affected when they think of all counselors as being prepared and practicing in the same way that school guidance counselors were prepared and practiced at the beginning of the school counseling movement in the 1950s. The reality is that the counseling process is educational in nature, and although counselors do not educate in formal classrooms like traditional teachers, counselors do educate their clients. Being located in colleges of education strengthens counseling graduate programs because the colleges emphasize pedagogy, human growth and development, applied research, and field placements as essential components of learning skills.

The counseling profession created the Council for Accreditation of Counseling and Related Educational Programs (CACREP) to set national standards for the preparation of master's and doctoral level counselors (CACREP, 1994). CACREP was begun during the 1960s under the leadership of Robert O. Stripling, a counselor educator at the University of Florida. CACREP began as a project of the Association of Counselor Education and Supervision (ACES), a division of the American Counseling Association (ACA), and now functions as a separate corporation that is affiliated with ACA (CACREP, 1994).

CACREP has established standards for the preparation of counselors (CACREP, 1994). These standards require a minimum of 2 years or 48–60 semester hours in master's degree programs that prepare counselors. In addition, the programs must include instruction in the following content areas: (a) human growth and development, (b) social and cultural foundations, (c) helping relationships, (d) group work, (e) career and lifestyle development, (f) appraisal, (g) research and program evaluation, and (h) professional orientation. CACREP requires that students complete a 100-hour practicum and a 600-hour internship. The CACREP standards also require that program faculty be counselors themselves, that programs have a laboratory for training, and that a number of other requirements for quality instruction be met.

Currently, of the approximately 1,510 master's and doctoral degree programs in counseling in the United States (Hollis, 1997), 315 are CACREP accredited (CACREP, 1998). Many programs that are not yet accredited have patterned their master's degree programs after the standards developed by CACREP. Although only about 21% of the counseling graduate degree programs in the United States are accredited by CACREP, it is accurate to say that CACREP standards have been accepted by the profession as the model curriculum for preparing master's and doctoral level counselors. Because graduation from a CACREP-accredited program is one type of credential that a counselor might possess, CACREP accreditation will be discussed further in the next section.

CREDENTIALING

One of the greatest challenges faced by those entering the profession is to understand counselor credentialing. A credentialed individual possesses some type of indicator that he or she is a legitimate professional. Credentialing comes in many forms, which is the basic reason people are so confused by it. Additionally, some credentials are essential to the practice of the profession, others are desirable but not necessary, and still others are of questionable value or even worthless.

This section contains a discussion of credentials and should assist you in conceptualizing and understanding counselor credentials. As mentioned previously, credentialing comes in many forms. Any indicator a counselor has that he or she is legitimate as a professional could be considered a credential. A major problem that causes confusion among counselors and the public is that terminology is not consistent within the area of credentialing. The major types of counselor credentials are degree, state license, state agency certification, national voluntary certification, and program accreditation.

Degree

The most obvious credential that counselors hold is the master's degree. Other degrees held, such as specialist or doctorate degrees, are credentials as well.

Counselors hold a variety of master's degree titles. A legitimate counselor might hold a Master of Education (M.Ed.), Master of Arts (M.A.), Master of Science (M.S.), Master of Divinity (M.Div.), or another, more unusual master's degree title. Most of the titles of master's degrees given in various universities were decided long ago and generally have little to do with any differences in the actual program content. The degree title in no way indicates whether a degree program requires a specified number of credits, includes a thesis, or has other specific requirements. In many universities, degree titles are politically decided among the various faculties. For example, a number of counseling master's degree programs award M.Ed. degrees because the degree programs are offered within university colleges of education.

While the basic credential for a professional counselor is a master's degree in counseling, many counselors hold higher degrees, including specialist's degrees, certificates of advanced study, and doctoral degrees. Doctoral degrees in counseling usually are either the Doctor of Education (Ed.D.) or Doctor of Philosophy (Ph.D.), although some doctoral programs have titles such as Doctor of Arts (D.A.) or Doctor of Divinity (D.Div.).

State License

In many states, a license issued by the state is required before a person is allowed to practice counseling in that state. This licensure affects private practice counseling most directly because most licensure statutes state that counselors who practice in many other settings are exempt from the licensure requirement. For example, in most states, counselors who practice in local, state, or federal agencies; in nonprofit corporations; or in schools or other educational institutions are exempt from the licensure requirement. Often when professions are first licensed, many exemptions are granted to the licensure requirement. This occurs because of a concern that, if licensure were required for all members of that profession, agencies that traditionally pay less for the professionals' services would not be able to attract employees. For example, when physicians were first licensed by states, physicians employed in a number of settings were exempt from licensure. Over the years, these licensure exemptions have been removed for physicians and now almost all physicians, no matter where they practice, must have a state license. The same removal of exemptions will most likely occur over time in the counseling field as well.

Unfortunately, counseling licensure statutes have various titles. In some states, counselors credentialed by the state are called licensed, and in other states they are referred to as certified. In some states, they are even called registered.

In the more general arena of state regulation of professions, the terms *licensed, certified,* and *registered* have separate and specific meanings. A licensure law is referred to as a *practice law,* which means that the professional must be licensed to practice that profession in that state. A certification law is what is known as a *title law,* which means that a person must be certified to use the title of *certified professional,* but that the practice of that profession is not regulated by the state. Finally, a registration law was intended to mean that a professional had to *register* with the state, but that no credentials would be required for registration. These terms, however, have been used interchangeably from state to state and profession to profession. For example, registered nurses in almost all states really are licensed. In addition, most current state registration laws do require that registered persons have some type of credentials before they will be added to the state registry.

Currently, in some states licensed counselors really function under title laws and some certified counselors really are operating under practice laws. As an individual counselor who wants to practice in a particular state, you should ascertain exactly what the state credential (whether it is a license, certificate, or registry) entitles the credentialed person to do. You do not have to fully understand the complexity of all state regulatory laws to understand what the particular law means in your state. Two ACA publications (1996, 1997) summarize the current state licensing laws for counselors. Almost all states and the District of Columbia now have laws that regulate the profession of counseling.

To add to the confusion, states have given a number of titles to counselors who are licensed. The most common title is professional counselor. However, other states use titles such as mental health counselor or clinical counselor. The individuals who proposed the counselor licensing laws in each state decided which title to use. In some cases, titles were chosen to satisfy political compromises that had to be made to obtain legislative support for the bills.

State Agency Certification

As the term is used here, state agency certification is different from state licensure. It was explained previously that in some states, counselors are certified rather than licensed. However, in this section, the term *certification* is used to refer to the process whereby official agencies of the state certify individuals as qualified to hold certain state jobs. In all states, this agency process is referred to as certification.

The most obvious state agency certification process is for school counselors. In each state the department of education determines which counselors may be certified as school counselors. Schools in that state must hire certified school counselors, just as they must hire only certified school teachers, in order to maintain their school accreditation. The requirements for being certified as a school counselor vary widely from state to state. For example, in some states, school counselors must first be certified, experienced school teachers before they can become certified as school counselors. This teacher certification requirement is being eliminated in most states. The requirements for state school counselor certification should be obtained from the state department of education in the state in which you wish to practice.

Another area in which counselors are certified by the state is in substance abuse counseling. Most states have different levels of certified substance abuse counselors, sometimes including counselors who hold less than a master's degree in counseling. State agencies that provide substance abuse treatment services are required to hire only certified counselors who meet state requirements for certification. Information regarding state requirements for substance abuse counselors can be obtained from the National Association of Alcoholism and Drug Abuse Counselors. See Appendix B for contact information for this association.

Rehabilitation counseling is another specialty area that involves varying state requirements. Although state rehabilitation agencies do not certify vocational rehabilitation counselors, they have established minimum requirements for rehabilitation counselors that vary from state to state. Information regarding the requirements for being hired as a vocational rehabilitation counselor can be obtained from each state's rehabilitation agency.

National Voluntary Certification

The two national certification agencies of the counseling profession are the National Board for Certified Counselors (NBCC) and the Council on Rehabilitation Counselor Certification (CRCC). National certification is voluntary in that there is no governmental requirement that a counselor be certified. Even though a counselor may be required to be licensed in a state to practice counseling, there is no legal need for that same counselor to be certified by NBCC or CRCC.

The counseling profession created the National Board of Certified Counselors (NBCC) in 1982 as the national agency to certify counselors who had met the minimum requirements of the profession (Stone, 1985). A National Certified Counselor (NCC) is an individual who has met the requirements set forth by NBCC. NBCC now functions as an independent corporation with its own board of directors. It was important for the profession to create NBCC so that the profession, rather than each individual state legislature, could determine the minimum requirements for being a professional counselor. In the same vein, it is important for counselors to support NBCC by becoming NCCs as soon as they are qualified to do so. In addition, counselors who hire other counselors should indicate that NCCs are preferred.

In order to become an NCC, a counselor must complete a master's degree in counseling, have 2 years of post-master's experience, and pass the National Counselor Examination. The 2 years of post-master's experience is waived for graduates of CACREP-accredited programs.

Every profession has national voluntary certification of specialists within that profession. NBCC has created specialty certification for the counseling profession. Although some believe that states should license counselors as specialists (Cottone, 1985; Emener & Cottone, 1989), Remley (1995) has argued that states should license counselors generally and NBCC should certify specialists. His position is that the role NBCC plays in certifying counselors as specialists within their chosen areas is vital to the success of the counseling profession. He believes that specialty designations should be voluntary and should be offered by a national body such as NBCC.

In order to become certified as a specialist by NBCC, a counselor first has to be an NCC. Currently, NBCC offers specialty certification in mental health, career, school, gerontology, and addictions counseling. The specific requirements for becoming specialty certified in one or more of these fields can be obtained by contacting NBCC (see Appendix B). In addition, NBCC has recently begun to offer an additional specialty certification, clinical supervision.

Rehabilitation counseling specialists began certifying rehabilitation counselors before NBCC was formed. As a result, that specialty certification is offered by a separate certifying agency, the Council on Rehabilitation Counseling Certification (CRCC). Contact information for CRCC is found in Appendix B.

In addition to NBCC and CRCC, there are a multitude of other national voluntary counselor certifications available to counselors. Some of these certifications have high standards and are multidisciplinary in nature. Others are simply designed to make money for the individuals who created them. If you are interested in a national certification for counselors offered by a group other than NBCC or CRCC, you should investigate the group's reputation among members of the counseling profession, the organizational structure of the group, and the general legitimacy of the credential.

Program Accreditation

In an earlier section in this chapter, the training of counselors was summarized. The standards for preparing counselors that have been agreed upon by the counseling profession are included in the accreditation standards of CACREP, detailed in the earlier section. The Council on Rehabilitation Education (CORE) accredits master's degree programs in the specialty area of rehabilitation counseling.

A counselor's graduation from a CACREP-accredited or CORE-accredited counseling graduate program is a credential. It distinguishes counselors as having completed a preparation program that meets the standards of excellence for the profession. Counselors can indicate on their resumes that they are CACREP-accredited or CORE-accredited program graduates. Many job announcements now indicate that CACREP-accredited or CORE-accredited program graduates are preferred.

The most comprehensive listing of graduate programs in counseling is found in a directory published by Hollis (1997). In the most recent edition of that directory, 1,072 master's level programs and 194 doctoral programs were listed. The master's degree programs focus on the following specialty areas: 193 in community counseling, 112 in marriage and family counseling/therapy, 104 in mental health counseling, 23 in pastoral counseling, 91 in rehabilitation counseling, 332 in school counseling, 100 in college counseling, and 117 in other specialty areas. The doctoral programs listed are divided into the following areas: 52 in counselor education and supervision, 70 in counseling psychology, 21 in marriage and family counseling/therapy, 17 in rehabilitation counseling, 6 in college counseling, 15 in pastoral counseling, and 13 in other specialty areas.

Only master's and doctoral degree programs offered by regionally accredited universities are listed in the Hollis (1997) directory. Nonaccredited universities also offer graduate degrees in counseling. However, individuals who graduate from these nonaccredited university degree programs often are unable to have their degrees recognized for the purposes of licensure, certification, or employment.

Accreditation of the university that offers degree programs in counseling, therefore, is essential for recognition. In addition to university accreditation, separate accreditation of counseling programs is important. Many state licensure statutes for counselors require the same preparation courses and field experiences as CACREP requires. In addition, NBCC has essentially the same preparation standards as CACREP.

Because the rehabilitation counseling specialty established a mechanism for accrediting master's degree programs before counseling in general began accrediting master's and doctoral degree programs, the counseling profession has two recognized program accreditation groups, CORE and CACREP. CORE accredits only master's degree programs in rehabilitation counseling. CACREP accredits master's degree programs in college, community, marriage and family, mental health, and school counseling, and doctoral programs in counselor education and supervision. Of the 1,072 master's degree programs that appear to be strictly in counseling in the Hollis directory (1997), 84 are accredited by CORE and 224 are accredited by CACREP. Of the 194 doctoral degree programs that appear, 29 are accredited by CACREP. This means that 744 master's degree programs and 165 doctoral degree programs in the Hollis directory are not accredited by either CORE or CACREP.

CORE and CACREP reflect the minimum preparation programs that have been agreed upon by the profession for master's and doctoral degree programs in counseling. If you want to determine whether programs that are not accredited by CORE or CACREP reflect these minimum standards, you could compare the degree requirements of these programs to the CORE or CACREP standards. Because counseling is a relatively new field, it will be some time before all programs are accredited by one of these two groups.

In mature professions such as medicine, law, and even psychology, all preparation programs are either accredited by their professional accreditation bodies or are actively pursuing accreditation. Graduates of nonaccredited programs in those professions are unable to obtain state licenses to practice or are unable to secure desirable jobs. It is likely that, eventually, all master's and doctoral degree programs in counseling will either be CORE or CACREP accredited.

Ethical Standards Related to Credentialing

Professional counselors are ethically required to present their credentials accurately. According to the ACA Code of Ethics (1995), professional credentials that may be claimed include the following: graduate degrees in counseling or closely related mental health fields, accreditation of graduate programs, national voluntary certifications, government-issued certifications or licenses, ACA professional membership, or any other credential that might indicate specialized knowledge or expertise in counseling (Standard C.4.a.).

As you acquire various professional credentials, you certainly will want to advertise them. Your professional association's code of ethics imposes very few restrictions on advertising, and those are limited to restrictions that can be clearly justified to protect the public. With respect to degrees held, counselors may advertise only the highest degree earned that is in counseling or a closely related field, and the degree must have been earned from a regionally accredited college or university. Some counselors hold a master's degree in counseling and a doctoral degree in another field. Counselors may only include their doctoral degrees on advertising materials if their doctorate is in counseling or a closely related mental health field (Standard C.4.e.).

Basically, advertising must be accurate and must not be false, misleading, deceptive, or fraudulent. When you become aware of any misrepresentation of your credentials that might be made by others, you are responsible for correcting the misinformation. Because many counselors hold multiple credentials, their business cards and advertising brochures can sometimes resemble a kind of alphabet soup. A counselor's degrees, licenses, certifications, and professional memberships might include, for instance, M.S. (Master of Science) from a CACREP-accredited counseling program, L.P.C. (Licensed Professional Counselor), NCC (National Certified Counselor), CCMHC (Certified Clinical Mental Health Counselor), CADAC (Certified Alcohol and Drug Abuse Counselor), and ACA Professional Member. It is important for counselors to make sure that the *meaning* of these credentials is clear to potential consumers of their services.

Finally, as a credentialed counselor, you must be careful not to attribute more to your credentials than the credentials actually represent, and you should not imply that other counselors are not qualified because they do not possess the same credentials as you do or because they lack certain credentials (Standard C.4.d.).

EVOLUTION OF THE COUNSELING PROFESSION

History is in the eye of the beholder. In other words, people view history from their own personal perspectives. A number of authors have attempted to summarize the history of the counseling profession and each summary is different (Hershenson, Power, & Waldo, 1996). Various authors emphasize different events and give their own interpretations to facts that have led them to various conclusions. The summary below represents a brief view of the history of the counseling profession that recognizes the input of others and adds our perspectives based on our observations as leaders and members of the profession.

Origins of the Profession

At the same time that the psychology profession was establishing the doctoral level as the requirement for professional status and that counseling psychology was developing as a specialty area within it, historical events were leading to the rapid development of school counseling programs and vocational rehabilitation counseling. Eventually, changes within counseling psychology, the school counseling movement, and federal funding of vocational rehabilitation counseling led to the emergence of the new profession of counseling.

Counseling Psychology

The counseling profession basically shares its history with the emergence of counseling psychology as a specialty within the psychology profession. Early leaders in the specialty of counseling psychology distinguished themselves from other psychologists by declaring that they were interested in the normal, healthy development of human beings, rather than illness and psychopathology. In counseling psychology, the focus was on developmental stages in people's lives and career concerns. World War I and the work of Frank Parsons on career classifications provided the impetus for the development of counseling psychology as a separate specialty within psychology.

Although the field of psychology has offered doctoral degrees for quite some time, at the beginning of its political movement to become a profession, psychology recognized individuals with master's degrees as professional psychologists. Several decades ago, the American Psychological Association (APA) declared that, in the future, only psychologists who held doctoral degrees would be recognized as professionals. The profession decided to continue to recognize all existing psychologists who held master's degrees and allow them to practice, but in the future to allow only individuals who held doctoral degrees in psychology into the profession. Licensure laws in psychology throughout the United States were changed to reflect this new political position.

Despite APA's declaration that only psychologists at the doctoral level would be recognized as professionals, universities throughout the United States continued to offer master's degrees in clinical and counseling psychology and still do today. Essentially, these master's degree programs in psychology have produced and are continuing to produce graduates who have limited or no professional recognition in psychology. Graduates of these master's degree programs most often seek and obtain licensure as counselors in states that have counselor licensure laws. When graduates of master's degree programs in clinical or counseling psychology become counselors through the process of state counselor licensure, the professional identities of both psychologists and counselors become blurred and the public becomes more confused about the differences between the two professions.

School Counseling

When the Russians launched the first spacecraft, Sputnik, on October 4, 1957, politicians in the United States feared that, because the Russians had exceeded our technology and beat us in the "race to space," they might overpower us politically as well. In response to this fear, Congress created substantial programs to encourage young people to seek careers in technical and scientific fields. Part of this effort included placing counselors in high schools to channel students into math and science courses. Throughout the United States, universities created summer institutes in which high school teachers were given basic courses that led to their placement in high schools as guidance counselors. In most instances, high school teachers were given two or three courses in "guidance" or "counseling," which then allowed them to be certified as school counselors and assume guidance counselor positions within schools. Since the primary purpose of this effort was to get students to take math and science courses, it did not seem necessary for counselors to be prepared beyond the training provided in these summer institutes.

In a very short time, school accreditation groups required that high schools have guidance counselors in order to receive or continue their accreditation. Today, middle and high school accreditation requires that these schools have counselors, and in some areas elementary schools are required to have counselors as well. Almost all states now require that certified school counselors have received the master's degree and have completed specified courses and an internship. For a school counseling program to achieve CACREP-accredited status, the master's degree must include a minimum of 48 semester hours.

Vocational Rehabilitation Counseling

In the 1950s, there was a recognition in the United States that citizens with physical and mental disabilities were not being given the help they needed to become productive members of society. As a result, legislation was passed that provided counseling and educational resources that were meant to rehabilitate persons with disabilities so that they could function as autonomously as possible.

A major component of this rehabilitation legislation was funding to prepare counselors to help disabled persons evaluate their disabilities, make plans to work, and find satisfactory employment. As a result of this funding, master's degree programs in rehabilitation counseling were developed and existing programs were expanded. State rehabilitation agencies created positions in rehabilitation case management and counseling for the graduates of these programs.

In summary, the dynamics around the creation of the specialty of counseling psychology, the decision within the psychology profession that professionals would be recognized only at the doctoral level, the emergence of school counseling, and the funding of vocational rehabilitation counseling programs led to the creation of counseling as a separate profession. Clearly, the origins of the profession lie in the convergence of several disparate forces, rather than in a unitary effort.

Counseling as a New Profession

There is an entire area of scholarly inquiry in the field of sociology that studies the emergence of new professions. Scholars within this field have identified the essential factors that define what a profession is and what steps a group must go through to establish itself as a legitimate, separate, and unique profession. In relation to other professional groups in general and to mental health professional groups in particular, counseling is a relatively new professional entity. Counseling may currently be viewed as a "semi-profession" (Etzioni, 1969) or "emerging profession" (Friedson, 1983), rather than a fully developed profession with all the rights and privileges that such status brings to a group.

Sociologists who study the development of professions have offered definitions of fully recognized professions. In order to understand some of the difficult problems that are facing the counseling profession today, it is important for counselors to compare counseling to other recognized professions and to recognize where we are in the process of becoming a fully recognized profession.

Toren (1969) defined a fully developed profession as one that has the following traits: a body of theoretical knowledge, members who possess competence in the application of this knowledge, and a code of ethics focused on the client's well-being.

A different concept of a profession has been offered by Hughes (1965). He has said that, compared to nonprofessions, emerging professions demand more independence, more recognition, a higher place, a clearer distinction between those inside and outside the profession, and more autonomy in choosing colleagues.

Six criteria for determining professional maturity have been described by Nugent (1981). According to Nugent, a mature profession and its members have the following characteristics:

- can clearly define their role and have a defined scope of practice
- offer unique services (do something that members of no other profession can do)
- have special knowledge and skills (are specifically trained for the profession)
- have an explicit code of ethics
- have the legal right to offer the service (have obtained a monopoly, through licensure or certification, over the right to provide the services)
- have the ability to monitor the practice of the profession (the profession can police itself)

By considering these traits, conceptualizations, and definitions of a mature profession, it is possible to see that the field of counseling meets the criteria in some areas and is lacking in others. Certainly counselors have a well-established code of ethics and have achieved societal recognition through state licensure. Areas that are still weak include identifying services that are uniquely offered by counselors, developing a body of knowledge that belongs specifically to counseling and does not borrow so heavily from psychology, and achieving a higher status within society.

Steps in Becoming a Profession

According to sociologists who have studied emerging professions within society (Abbott, 1988; Caplow, 1966; Dugan, 1965; Etzioni, 1969; Friedson, 1983; Hughes, 1965; Scott, 1969; Toren, 1969), there is a developmental process that professions must go through if they are to be successful in establishing themselves as fully recognized professions.

Caplow (1966) maintained that the steps whereby a group achieves professional status are quite definite, and that the sequence of steps is explicit. The first three steps toward professionalization are (a) forming associations, (b) changing names to reduce identification with the previous occupational status, and (c) developing a code of ethics. Certainly the counseling profession has accomplished these three steps. First, the ACA was chartered in 1952 from three long-standing subgroups. Second, the association's name was changed from the American Personnel and Guidance Association (APGA) to the American Association for Counseling and Development (AACD) and then to the American Counseling Association (ACA). Each change reduced the identification with words such as *guidance, student personnel,* and *student development* and embraced more fully the word *counseling.* Finally, ACA has had a code of ethics since 1961.

Caplow's fourth step in accomplishing the goal of becoming a profession is prolonged political agitation. Members of the occupational group obtain public sanction to maintain established occupational barriers. Counselors have been involved in substantial political agitation since the first counselor licensure law was passed in Virginia in 1976. That political activity has been continued since then as similar licensure laws have been passed in state after state. In addition, counselors have lobbied state legislators to mandate school counseling programs, to include counselors as providers in health care programs, and to ensure that the professional services of counselors are reimbursed by health care insurance companies. Caplow's prolonged political agitation certainly has begun for counselors and is continuing today.

A strong argument could be made that counseling is not a profession at all, but is what Etzioni (1969) has termed a "semi-profession." If doctoral-level counseling psychologists were compared to master's level counselors, many of the characteristics of Etzioni's semi-professions would seem to apply to counselors. When compared to actual professionals, Etzioni said the semi-professions require shorter periods of training, have less legitimate status, have a less established right to privileged communication with clients, maintain less of a specialized body of knowledge, and enjoy less autonomy from supervision or societal control. Counselors have been fighting hard and making a number of changes to overcome the deficiencies that have led to labels such as Etzioni's "semi-profession" being applied to counseling. Some of the changes that have taken place in the last 20 to 30 years in the field of counseling include the following: the length of most training programs has increased from 30 to 48, and even to 60 semester hours; efforts have been made to improve the professional status of counselors through credentialing and legislation; laws are continuing to be passed in states granting privileged communication to interactions between counselors and their clients; the body of knowledge is being increased through scholarly publications specifically in counseling, as distinguished from psychology; and counselor licensure laws have brought autonomy from being supervised by others to practice counseling.

Etzioni (1969) has identified a disturbing activity that often takes place within semi-professions. There is some evidence that counselors may be engaging in this negative practice. Etzioni maintained, ". . . a significant segment of the semi-professions aspire to a full-fledged professional status and sustain a professional self-image, despite the fact that they themselves are often aware that they do not deserve such a status, and despite the fact that they objectively do not qualify . . . ." (p. vi). He has suggested that, in their effort to identify with legitimate professionals, the semi-professionals often split their colleagues into two camps: those who approximate the professionals and those with fewer similarities to full-fledged professionals. According to Etzioni, this dissension weakens both groups. As a result, counselors who try to identify with psychologists and, in the process denigrate their counseling colleagues who have less resemblance to psychologists than they do, are behaving like "semi-professionals" and are weakening the entire counseling profession.

Progress Toward Professionalization

It is discouraging for graduate students who are preparing to enter the field to realize that counseling, despite its progress, still has some way to go before being recognized as a true profession within our society. On the other hand, it is encouraging to note that counseling is making progress toward recognition as a profession at a relatively fast rate when compared to the professionalization efforts in other fields. For example, as late as 1982, scholars within psychology wrote in one of their own profession's journals that they doubted that psychology could validly claim to be a profession (Phillips, 1982). The first law establishing psychologists as independent health practitioners was passed in 1968 in New Jersey (Dorken & Webb, 1980), and there are still some states that do not require a license to practice psychology. In comparison, the first counselor licensure bill was passed in Virginia in 1976, and already almost all states and the District of Columbia have passed licensure bills for counselors.

It is clear that significant progress has been made toward professionalization of counseling. However, counseling obviously lacks some of the accomplishments that indicate the establishment of a societally recognized profession. While counselors are continuing to work toward full professional status, we will continue to refer to ourselves as professionals and to our field as a profession.

PROFESSIONAL ASSOCIATIONS OF COUNSELORS

Professional associations are formed by professional groups for a number of reasons. First, associations provide a forum for professionals to gather to discuss issues and problems that exist within the profession. An association allows the members of a profession to address issues as a group, rather than work independently on behalf of the profession. Second, professional associations provide leadership by speaking for the profession on critical legislative issues that affect the profession at all levels of government. Professional associations also provide continuing education for their members. Earning a master's degree in counseling is only the beginning of the learning process for counselors. As new information becomes available, counselors must attend conferences and workshops to update their skills and expertise. Professional associations provide such learning opportunities and also publish scholarly journals, books, monographs, and other media resources for the continuing education of their members. Finally, professional associations publish and enforce a code of ethics for their members. Important hallmarks for professionals are having a code of ethics and policing themselves.

American Counseling Association (ACA)

The ACA, founded in 1952, has a number of divisions and state branches that represent the counseling profession and serve counselors in various ways.

You should join ACA when you begin your graduate degree program in counseling and maintain active membership throughout your career as a counselor. Students receive discounted membership. The contact information for ACA (including toll-free telephone number, address, fax number, and Web site address) is located in Appendix B. All members, including students, receive a subscription to the counseling professional journal, the *Journal of Counseling and Development.* In addition, members receive the monthly counseling newsletter, *Counseling Today,* which includes current political and professional news related to counseling as well as announcements of professional development opportunities, job openings, and advertisements for professional products. Other benefits of membership include the ability to purchase professional liability insurance policies, reduced registration fees for the national convention and national workshops, and discounted prices for books and media products published by ACA.

ACA Divisions

Currently, ACA has 17 divisions. ACA members, if they choose, may join one or more divisions in addition to their basic ACA membership. Division members receive scholarly journals from divisions that publish them, periodic newsletters, and from time to time information related to the divisions' special purposes.

There are two types of divisions within ACA, and all divisions are subgroups of ACA. One type of division has as members counselors who practice in various employment settings, such as schools, colleges, or mental health centers. The other has as members counselors who have special interests within counseling such as group counseling, multicultural counseling, or marriage and family counseling. Figure 2-2 provides a listing of the 17 ACA divisions with a description of their members.

ACA State Branches

All states plus the District of Columbia, the Virgin Islands, Puerto Rico, and Europe have ACA branches. Although these branches are chartered by ACA, they are separate, independent organizations. In order to join a state branch, you must contact that organization. Most branches offer discounted membership rates for graduate students. Telephone and address information for state branch associations can be obtained by contacting the ACA (see Appendix B). State

NAME OF ACA DIVISION	MEMBERSHIP INCLUDES
Association for Assessment in Counseling (AAC)	Counselors who are interested in testing
Association for Adult Development and Aging (AADA)	Counselors who have a special interest in counseling issues of adults and those who specialize in gerontology
American College Counseling Association (ACCA)	Counselors who work in college and university settings, including technical and community colleges
Association for Counselors and Educators in Government (ACEG)	Counselors employed by federal and state governments
Association for Counselor Education and Supervision (ACES)	University professors who teach in counseling graduate programs, supervisors of counselors, and individuals who specialize in counseling supervision
Association for Gay, Lesbian, and Bisexual Issues in Counseling	Counselors who have a special interest in providing counseling services to gay, lesbian, and bisexual clients
Counseling Association for Humanistic Education and Development (C-AHEAD)	Counselors who are oriented toward humanistic principles
Counselors for Social Justice (CSJ)	Counselors who are interested in the eradication of oppressive systems of power and privilege
	(Continued)

Figure 2-2   The 17 Divisions of the American Counseling Association

Association of Multicultural Counseling and Development (AMCD)	Counselors who have a special interest in multicultural issues in counseling
American Mental Health Counselors Association (AMHCA)	Counselors who practice in community mental health settings and who are in private practice
American Rehabilitation Counseling Association (ARCA)	Counselors who work in government and private vocational rehabilitation settings
American School Counselor Association (ASCA)	Counselors who practice at all levels of school counseling: elementary, middle, and secondary
Association for Spiritual, Ethical, and Religious Values in Counseling (ASERVIC)	Counselors who have special interests in spiritual, ethical, or religious values issues in counseling
Association of Specialists in Group Work (ASGW)	Counselors who have a special interest in group counseling
International Association of Addiction and Offender Counselors (IAAOC)	Counselors who work in substance abuse or prison settings
International Association of Marriage and Family Counselors (IAMFC)	Counselors who specialize in marriage and family counseling
National Career Development Association (NCDA)	Counselors who have a special interest in career counseling
National Employment Counseling Association (NECA)	Counselors who work in employment agency settings

Figure 2-2   (*Continued*)

branches hold annual conventions, represent counselors from their states in legislative matters, publish periodic newsletters, and sometimes provide publications and workshops for members.

Most state ACA branches have state branch divisions that parallel the national ACA divisions. So, in addition to a state ACA association, often there will exist, for example, state divisions for school counselors, mental health counselors, and counselors interested in multicultural counseling issues. When you join your state ACA branch, you will also have the opportunity to join any divisions that exist in your state that interest you.

Many important professional issues, such as licensure and school counselor certification, can be addressed only at the state level. In addition, it is very important for counselors to know and interact with their colleagues throughout the state in which they are practicing.

Therefore, counselors should belong to their ACA state branch in addition to belonging to ACA throughout their professional careers.

Other Associations

In addition to ACA and its national divisions and state branches, there are a number of national and international associations to which counselors belong. These associations represent a variety of interests. Associations consist of multidisciplinary groups of mental health professionals, professionals interested in specializations within the mental health field, special political purpose groups, and even associations that are in opposition to the professional and political interests of ACA and counselors. It might be beneficial for counselors to join multidisciplinary professional associations to gain from cross-disciplinary interactions and fresh perspectives on mental health issues. Counselors may also want to purchase materials developed by other associations or attend workshops these associations sponsor.

One association that was created as a result of ACA's success in the area of state licensure for counselors is the American Association of State Counseling Boards (AASCB). This group has as its members state boards that license counselors and individuals who have been appointed to or who administer those boards. The group meets annually to update members regarding developments in the area of counseling licensure.

Not all other mental health professional associations are supportive of counseling as a profession. Currently, two professional associations are in conflict with the efforts of counselors to establish themselves as separate, autonomous mental health professionals through the process of state licensure.

The American Psychological Association (APA) has opposed state licensure of counselors in the past and currently supports efforts to keep licensed counselors from passing legislation that would ensure that counselors' clients would receive third-party reimbursement from health insurance companies. In addition, APA has opposed attempts by counselors to specify in state legislation scope-of-practice language that would clarify that licensed counselors diagnose and treat mental disorders and administer and interpret psychological tests.

Many counselors oppose the licensure of specialties within counseling. The American Association of Marriage and Family Therapists (AAMFT) is committed to passing legislation in all states that would license marriage and family counselors/therapists separately from counselors. Although these efforts have been opposed philosophically by many counselors, AAMFT has been successful in getting licensure bills for marriage and family therapists passed in a number of states.

In addition to the national associations mentioned above, there are a number of associations that focus on special interests within mental health that include counselors, as well as other mental health professionals such as psychiatrists, psychologists, psychiatric nurses, and social workers. Some of these associations are listed in Appendix B.

CURRENT ISSUES RELATED TO PROFESSIONAL IDENTITY

One of your tasks as a graduate student preparing to enter the counseling profession is to develop a strong identity as a counselor. Yet, as we've seen, the profession itself seems confused about its identity. Identifying and discussing some of the current professional identity problems in the profession may help you acknowledge and put these problems in perspective as you develop your own professional identity as a counselor.

Specialties Versus One United Profession

Probably the most significant problem the counseling profession faces today is determining whether the profession will develop a strong identity as one united profession with a common philosophical foundation and knowledge base, or whether the specialties will emerge as the dominant force within counseling. If specialties prevail, counseling has little chance of becoming a unified and societally recognized profession.

The problems associated with the specialties within the counseling profession were discussed in the November/December, 1995 issue of the *Journal of Counseling and Development* (Myers, 1995). In that issue of the primary professional journal of the counseling profession, authors discussed the following established and emerging counseling specialties: career counseling (Engels, Minor, Sampson, & Splete, 1995), college counseling (Dean & Meadows, 1995), school counseling (Paisley & Borders, 1995), marriage and family counseling (Smith, Carlson, Stevens-Smith, & Dennison, 1995), mental health counseling (Smith & Robinson, 1995), rehabilitation counseling (Leahy & Szymanski, 1995), addictions counseling (Page & Bailey, 1995), and sports counseling (Miller & Wooten, 1995).

A complex profession needs to have specialties because no one practitioner can be proficient in all areas of the profession (Abraham, 1978; Kett, 1968; Napoli, 1981). Specialties are necessary to ensure that research, training, and improved practice occur in specialized areas of counseling that have unique needs and issues. If members of subgroups within a profession believe that their specialties are significantly different from the general profession, however, then those specialty groups will attempt to establish themselves as separate professions (Etzioni, 1969). This phenomenon seems to be occurring in counseling at this time, particularly within the specialties of mental health counseling, marriage and family counseling, school counseling, and career counseling. It would be wise for new counseling professionals to recognize that the specialty groups with whom they wish to affiliate may be working against the overall goal of establishing counseling as a strong, viable, and societally recognized mental health profession (Fox, 1994).

Our position on this issue is that counseling is our primary profession, and that counselors who are members of specialty groups should support the overall profession while paying attention to their special interests and needs within the counseling profession. When you enter the profession, you will have opportunities to voice your own position, and you will want to consider carefully the issues involved.

Organizational Structure of ACA

Historically, some specialty groups in counseling (school counselors, college counselors, career counselors, and counselor educators) came together to form the first professional association, which they named the American Personnel and Guidance Association (APGA) in 1952. The name was later changed to the American Association for Counseling and Development (AACD), and is now the ACA.

An unfortunate event occurred during the history of the association when, at some point, the divisions within ACA were incorporated as separate legal structures. This makes ACA appear to be a federation, or group of groups, rather than one unified organization with subgroups of specialties. The separate incorporation of the divisions within

ACA has led to many disagreements among association leaders as to whether ACA is a manager meant to serve the interests of the divisions, or whether the divisions are subgroups of individuals whose primary interest is in being members of a unified professional association.

These disagreements led the American College Personnel Association (ACPA) to disaffiliate from ACA in 1992 and become a separate, autonomous professional association. Currently, three additional ACA divisions are seriously discussing and taking actions that could lead to disaffiliation. They are the American School Counselor Association (ASCA), the American Mental Health Counselors Association (AMHCA), and the National Career Development Association (NCDA). Leaders and members of the association are spending their energy on the conflict rather than on the more important tasks of strengthening the counseling profession and ensuring that members' continuing professional development needs are met.

When ACPA left ACA, ACA immediately created a new division, The American College Counseling Association (ACCA), for members who worked in higher education settings. ACA leaders have stated their intent to do the same thing if the mental health counseling, school counseling, or career counseling associations disaffiliate from ACA. In the future, AMHCA, ASCA, NCDA, and perhaps others might disaffiliate from ACA and establish themselves as separate autonomous associations. If major divisions within ACA leave, ACA probably will create entities within ACA to replace them. In any eventuality, ACA members will be able to continue their affiliation with ACA and will have opportunities within ACA to affiliate with members who have their same speciality interests.

A basic aspect of human nature is that people tend to identify with the group they know best and with which they are the most familiar. Members and leaders within the specialty subgroups in counseling have naturally tended to create well-organized entities that represent their specialized interests. It also is clear that counseling is at a critical stage of development. Either the profession of counseling will find a way through its conflict and will emerge as a unified profession, or it will fragment and its various specialties will attempt to establish themselves as separate independent professions. Only time will reveal the outcome of the current struggles.

CACREP Accreditation of Specialties

Sweeney (1995) has pointed out that CACREP actually accredits master's degree programs leading to specialty degrees in counseling, rather than accrediting general master's degree programs in counseling. Currently, if a university that offers a master's degree program in counseling wants to obtain CACREP accreditation, the program must declare that it prepares master's level counselors for one or more of the following specialty areas: college counseling, community counseling, marriage and family counseling, mental health counseling, or school counseling. A core curriculum that includes basic instruction for all counselors is required for accreditation in any of the specialty areas, however.

This requirement that students specialize at the master's degree level does cause some professional identity problems for graduate students. While professors encourage graduate students to develop identities as counselors in general, these same graduate students are being told that they must choose and prepare for one specialty area within counseling.

Varying State Licensure and Certification Requirements

As explained earlier in this chapter, the states that license counselors vary significantly in requirements. Licensure statutes require from 30 to 60 hours of graduate course work and from 1 to 3 years of post-master's degree supervision, and they include a variety of requirements that are unique to the state (ACA, 1996, 1997). State requirements for certification as a school counselor also vary considerably from jurisdiction to jurisdiction.

These differences in licensure and certification standards reflect a profession that has not been able to establish an agreed-upon set of standards, and then get those standards accepted by political entities throughout the United States. Because of this lack of uniformity, individual counselors who move from state to state often find that they must take additional course work or even earn another master's degree in order to meet the new state's standards. Mature professions, such as law, medicine, and even psychology, have been able to establish licensing laws across the United States that are uniform and allow members of their professions to be licensed and practice no matter where they live. Eventually, the licensing and certification laws for counselors will become more uniform, but currently the lack of uniformity causes problems for counselors who relocate.

LEGAL AND POLITICAL ISSUES

In addition to the professional identity problems that currently exist for counselors, there are a number of legal and political issues with which you need to be familiar. The successful resolution of these issues is critical to the continued movement of counseling to establish itself as a legitimate societally recognized profession.

Challenges to the Scope of Practice of Counselors

Counselors believe that they are qualified to perform a number of professional services for clients, based on their training and expertise. Two areas in which counselors have been challenged by psychologists and other mental health professionals are in testing and in the diagnosis and treatment of mental and emotional disorders. Psychologists claim that they are adequately prepared to perform these professional services and that counselors are not.

There is an economic component to these issues. Counselors who test and who diagnose and treat mental and emotional disorders in their practices often compete in the marketplace with psychologists and social workers. Many health insurance companies and health maintenance organizations require that mental health professionals be qualified to perform these two tasks before they will reimburse their insured for the services of these professionals. Therefore, there is a significant economic advantage for psychologists and social workers to claim that counselors are not qualified in these professional practice areas.

This debate has taken place in the forum of state legislatures, in the form of arguments over the language in state statutes that license counselors for practice. In most states, counselors have been successful in inserting language into their licensing statutes that states they are competent and therefore qualified to test and to diagnose and treat mental and emotional disorders. There are some states, however, where these issues are still unresolved.

Testing   One of the core curriculum requirements for preparation of counselors is in the area of testing, or assessment. All counselor master's degree programs require at least one graduate course in testing principles that includes evaluating the validity and reliability of tests, selecting appropriate tests for clients, test administration, and interpretation of test results. Counselors have used tests in their practices since the profession was first established.

Of course, testing is a very broad area and there are a number of psychological tests that counselors might not be prepared at the master's degree level to administer and interpret, such as individual intelligence tests or projective tests. Psychologists have claimed that counselors should not be allowed to test at all within their practices, or only be allowed to use tests in a very limited fashion. Counselors, on the other hand, believe that they have the basic education needed to test and that each counselor should determine the particular tests he or she is qualified by education or experience to administer and interpret.

Some state licensure statutes give counselors broad testing privileges, while others either are silent on whether testing is part of a counselor's practice or are very restrictive in enumerating which tests a counselor may administer and interpret. In some states (Butler, 1998), counselors have been accused of practicing psychology without a license because of their testing activities. In states in which the testing practices of counselors are restricted, political activities are taking place to change the statutes to broaden the authority of counselors to test.

Diagnosis and Treatment of Mental and Emotional Disorders   Counselors are taught to diagnose and treat mental disorders as part of their specialized training. In most states, course work is required in this area of counseling for licensure. In addition, counselors are tested before they are licensed, to determine whether they are proficient in the diagnosis and treatment of mental and emotional disorders.

The *Diagnostic and Statistical Manual of Mental Disorders* (4th ed.) published by the American Psychiatric Association (1994) clearly states that many mental health professionals are engaged in the diagnosis and treatment of mental and emotional disorders and that the manual is meant to be a reference book for all of those professionals. The use of this standard manual is taught to counselors who wish to be licensed.

As with the testing issue, in many states the scope of practice of licensed counselors includes the diagnosis and treatment of mental and emotional disorders. In states in which the authority of counselors to diagnose and treat mental and emotional disorders is being challenged, efforts are being made to change the language of the licensure statutes to state clearly that counselors are qualified to perform this professional activity.

Job Classifications for Counselors

Positions for counseling professionals exist in many state and federal agencies. In some of these agencies, however, no job classification categories have been established for counselors. As a result, when counselors are hired, their job titles might be "psychologist I," "social worker I," or "mental health technician I." Although being hired into these positions gives counselors jobs and entry into agencies, counselors may be discriminated against later, because promotions might require a license in psychology or social work or a graduate degree in one of those fields.

As a result of this problem, efforts need to be made to have job titles established specifically for counselors. Convincing a state or federal agency that job titles or classifications need to be changed is not an easy task. Bureaucracies are very slow to change. Nonetheless, professional associations and leaders within the counseling profession need to address this problem if counselors are to be fully accepted as professionals within these agencies.

Third-Party Reimbursement

It is essential for counselors in private practice that their clients be able to access counselors' mental health services as part of the client's health care plan. If clients are participating in health maintenance organizations (HMOs) or preferred provider organizations (PPOs), then counselors must be on the list of eligible providers for the clients. If clients are part of an indemnity health care plan, then counselors must be acknowledged as qualified mental health care providers so that clients can be reimbursed for counselor services.

HMOs, PPOs, and health insurance companies can voluntarily acknowledge counselors as qualified mental health care providers, and most do. However, these health care organizations have a legal right to refuse to give their clients access to counselors unless there is legislation to the contrary. This type of legislation, called "freedom of choice legislation," requires health care providers to give access to licensed counselors for mental health care if they give access to other mental health care providers such as psychologists or social workers. Many states have passed freedom of choice legislation. In states that have not, counselors are active in trying to get freedom of choice legislation passed.

IDENTITY AND PROFESSIONALISM

Counseling and Other Mental Health Professions

As we noted at the beginning of this chapter, counselors are a relatively new professional group and counselors are often asked what they do. A weak answer would be that counselors do things that are similar to what psychologists do. A strong answer would be to describe the process of counseling, including its philosophical foundations, the services counselors provide, and the components of training programs that prepare master's level counselors. A counselor or prospective counselor with a strong professional identity will be able to describe the process of counseling without reference to other mental health professions.

The material that has been provided in this chapter should allow you to state clearly what a counselor does. However, a further challenge for counselors is to be able to describe objectively, accurately, and dispassionately the similarities and differences between counselors and other mental health professionals. Listeners should take away from a conversation with a counselor the conclusion that counselors have a clear and unique identity within the field of mental health and that the counselor with whom they have been talking takes pride in her or his chosen profession.

How are counselors similar to other mental health professionals, including psychiatrists, psychologists, psychiatric nurses, and social workers? We are all prepared at the master's degree level or higher, and we all provide mental health services for clients. All mental health professionals follow a similar process of assessing a person's mental health needs, developing a plan for assisting the person, and then providing mental health services consistent with the assessment and plan for treatment. All mental health professionals counsel clients in some fashion. Mental health professionals of all types can be found in agencies and institutions where mental health treatment is offered to individuals.

How are counselors different from other mental health professionals? The primary difference between counselors and other mental health professionals is that only counselors have adopted the wellness model of mental health instead of the illness model. The wellness model of mental health emphasizes helping people maximize their potential, rather than curing their illness. Counselors believe that human growth and development stages and processes make life's problems normal and natural, rather than pathological. Counselors emphasize prevention and early intervention, rather than remediation. Empowerment of clients is a goal of counselors. The training of counselors focuses on teaching counseling skills rather than skills in physical health care, psychopathology, assessment, or social service linkages.

The similarities to and differences from other mental health professionals, as summarized above, are easy to articulate. It is vital that counselors learn to state both the traits we share in common with our other mental health colleagues and the differences that make us unique as mental health care providers.

In addition to understanding differences and similarities, it is important to keep in mind that you will also have working relationships with other mental health professionals when you enter practice as a counselor. Many counselors work closely with other mental health professionals on a day-to-day basis, for example as members of multidisciplinary treatment teams in hospitals or as members of school teams that provide services to students with special needs. In the previous section we discussed some conflicts that currently exist between counselors and certain other mental health professional groups. Despite the likelihood that you and your colleagues will disagree about professional issues, in the practice environment these differences are always set aside in the interest of providing clients with the best possible mental health services. In addition, you have an ethical obligation to respect approaches to mental health treatment that are different from your own, and to know and take into account the traditions and practices of other professional groups with which you work (ACA Code of Ethics, 1995, Standard C.6.a.).

Pride in the Counseling Profession

In the introductory chapter, we defined professionalism as an internal motivation to perform at the level of "best practices" that represent the ideals of the profession, enhance its image, and promote its development. A crucial component of professionalism is having a sense of pride in one's chosen profession. Counselors who have strong professional identities are proud to be members of their profession. By understanding and appreciating the counseling profession's history, philosophical foundations, services that are offered to the public, training program contents, and similarities to and differences from other similar mental health professions, counselors with strong professional identities are satisfied with their chosen profession and communicate this pride to those with whom they come into contact.

It is important for members of a profession to be self-critical and to seek advancements in knowledge and improvements within the profession. At the same time, members of a profession must be comfortable with the career choice they have made in order to develop a professional identity that serves them and the profession well.

Counselors with strong professional identities express pride in their profession by defending the profession when inaccurate statements are made concerning the profession itself or members of the profession. In order to represent the profession vigorously to the public, counselors must be well informed regarding the information presented in this chapter. Individual counselors who provide quality counseling services are responsible for the positive reputation the counseling profession enjoys. Similarly, individual counselors who can articulate the strengths of the counseling profession are responsible for informing the public about the unique contribution to society that members of the counseling profession are making.

SUMMARY AND KEY POINTS

The aim of this chapter has been to help you clarify and strengthen your professional identity as a counselor. We hope that after reading the material in this chapter, you will have a clear sense of your professional identity and be able to:

- Explain the philosophy that underlies the activities of your professional group.
- Describe the services your profession renders to the public.
- Describe the components of your profession's preparation programs.
- Articulate the similarities and differences between members of your profession and other, similar professional groups.
- Communicate your pride in being a member of the counseling profession.

We began the chapter with a discussion of the philosophy underlying the counseling profession. This philosophy, which makes the counseling profession unique and distinguishes us from other mental health professions, includes the following four components: the wellness model of mental health, a developmental perspective, a strong preference for prevention and early intervention into problems, and a goal of empowerment of clients.

Other aspects of professional identity presented in this chapter include counselor training programs; credentialing; professional associations for counselors; and current professional, political, and legal issues A brief history of the counseling profession provided a foundation for a careful look at its present status as an emerging profession. Following are some of the key points of this chapter:

- A vital professional task for counselor trainees is to develop a strong professional identity and to be able to articulate that identity to others.
- Counselors have adopted the wellness model of mental health as their perspective for helping people. This distinguishes counselors from other mental health professionals, who espouse the illness model.
- Counselors take a developmental perspective to understanding people's personal and emotional issues and problems. From this perspective, problems that other mental health professionals might view as pathological are seen by counselors as natural and normal.
- Counselors believe that prevention of and early intervention into mental health problems is far superior to remediation.
- The goal of counseling is to empower clients so that they will be able, in the future, to resolve their problems independently of counselor assistance.
- For counselors, mental health counseling is the primary service they provide. By contrast, other mental health professionals provide counseling as a secondary or ancillary service.
- Counselors are considered to be professionals after they have completed the master's degree. Training programs emphasize the development of counseling skills and are generally located in colleges of education within universities.

- Credentialing in counseling is complicated and can be confusing. It is important that you are able to distinguish among state licensure, state certification, national voluntary certification, and program accreditation. It is also important that you plan your program of studies carefully so that you will qualify for the credentials you will need in order to practice effectively.
- Professional codes of ethics impose only a few restrictions, designed to protect the public, on advertising one's credentials in counseling. You will need to attend carefully to these restrictions as you prepare to practice and as you develop your business cards, brochures, or other advertising materials.
- The counseling profession emerged out of a convergence of several disparate forces, including counseling psychology, school counseling, and vocational rehabilitation counseling.
- The field of counseling meets some of the criteria that are generally accepted as constituting a mature profession and is making rapid progress toward becoming a fully recognized profession.
- The primary professional association for counselors is the ACA. This organization has various divisions and state branches that serve the particular needs and interests of its members. You should join ACA now, if you have not already done so.
- Currently, there are several professional identity problems with which the counseling profession is struggling. One issue presently being debated is whether counseling will develop as a united profession or as separate specialties. Another issue that is being decided is the organizational structure of ACA.
- Contemporary legal and professional issues include challenges to the scope and practice of counselors, particularly in the areas of testing and of diagnosis and treatment of mental disorders; job classifications for counselors; and third-party reimbursement for counseling services.
- Having a sense of pride in being a member of the counseling profession is essential both for your own internal satisfaction with your chosen career and for the continued progress of counseling toward being a societally recognized profession.

Diversity, Client Welfare, and Informed Consent

The following three vignettes illustrate therapeutic errors that counselors can make when they are not sensitive to cultural differences, are unaware of their own biases, or fail to secure fully informed consent from a client. As you read the vignettes, see whether you can discern the source of the counselors' errors. How do you think these mistakes could have been avoided?

Jack, a counselor intern, is working in a university counseling center. Mai-Ling, a freshman who came to the United States from mainland China with her parents 8 years ago, has come for her first session with Jack and has agreed to let him audiotape the session for his supervisor. She states that she has come for help in deciding whether to continue in her 2-year associate degree program or switch to a baccalaureate program in computer science. Jack, very much aware that his supervisor will be listening for reflections of feelings and other attending skills, asks Mai-Ling how she feels about being confronted with this decision. She responds by simply restating her problem. The session continues in this fashion, with Jack probing for the client's feelings and the client responding in a cognitive, content-oriented manner. After the session ends, Jack determines to ask his supervisor how to build rapport with this "difficult client."

Lynn has been counseling Elaine, a 30-year-old client. During this session, Elaine states that she wishes she could just walk away from her marriage, but she can't do it because it would traumatize the children. Lynn, herself a child of divorce whose father abandoned the family, further explores Elaine's fears for the children. At one point she says, "Well, yes, the statistics do show that a lot of kids lose touch with their fathers after a divorce. It would be really hard for them if that happened. It could even have repercussions well into their adult years."

Marsha, age 15, has been seeing her school counselor for several weeks. Although Marsha's parents and her teachers have been concerned about her erratic behavior, Marsha has asserted that she is "just moody." Now, she admits that she has been buying and using cocaine. After further exploration, the counselor believes that Marsha has been taking some serious risks, not only by using the drug, but also by making her purchases from various dealers in an unsafe area of the city. The counselor lets Marsha know that, because of the danger her behavior is putting her in, her parents will need to be informed. Marsha is outraged. Even though the counselor had told her that she couldn't uphold confidentiality if her behavior posed a danger to herself or others, Marsha insists it doesn't apply here. She says, "I know what I'm doing. I've been buying coke for months now and nothing bad has happened to me. I trusted you and now you've betrayed me. This is sure the last time I'll ever see a counselor!"

CLIENT WELFARE

In your work as a counselor, it is fundamental that you put client welfare first and foremost. The counseling profession attaches such importance to this principle that it is the very first ethical standard in the *ACA Code of Ethics* (1995). Standard A.1.a states that the "primary responsibility of counselors is to respect the dignity and to promote the welfare of clients." There are very few exceptions to this principle; these occur in rare circumstances when the good of others in society outweighs what might appear to be best for a particular client.

Counselors have with clients what is known in law as "fiduciary relationships." Although the exact meaning of fiduciary is debatable, it is agreed that an individual who is a fiduciary has a position of trust and confidence (Ludes & Gilbert, 1998). Clients rely on their counselor fiduciaries to act only in their best interests. The duties of fiduciaries are so strong that in any transaction between a fiduciary and the recipient of services in which the fiduciary benefits, the transaction is presumed to be fraudulent and void. It will be upheld only when the fiduciary can present clear and convincing proof that the transaction is legitimate (Ludes & Gilbert, 1998). Because of the law related to fiduciaries, counselors have a significant legal burden to protect the best interests of their clients and to avoid any interactions or transactions with clients that benefit the counselors themselves.

Safeguarding client welfare involves a number of considerations, including respecting diversity, being aware of one's own needs and values, and avoiding dependent relationships. In this section, we will explore each of these considerations in some depth.

Respecting Diversity

In our pluralistic society, honoring diversity is fundamental to counselors' efforts to promote the welfare and to respect the dignity of their clients. All counselors share the goal of practicing in a culturally sensitive manner. Mental health professionals have become increasingly aware that when counselors and clients are from different cultural groups, differences may exist between them related to values, perceptions of events, and communication styles. In fact, counselors must understand that even the counseling process may be uncomfortable or unacceptable to clients from some cultural backgrounds.

In the early years of its development, the counseling profession virtually ignored the impact of cultural diversity. Wrenn first introduced the concept of the "culturally encapsulated counselor" about 40 years ago (Wrenn, 1962). He suggested that culturally encapsulated counselors define reality according to one set of cultural assumptions and fail to evaluate other viewpoints, which renders them insensitive to cultural variations. They are trapped in one way of thinking and are bound by their own narrow perspectives.

Since then, a number of factors have worked to draw the attention of counseling professionals to diversity issues. Wehrly (1991) noted that the Civil Rights movement was occurring in the United States at the same time that Wrenn called for counselors to broaden their perspectives. One effect of the movement was that counselors began to recognize that cultural issues that had been ignored in society had also been ignored in counseling.

Demographic changes in American society have also been a major force. Sue (1995) has projected that groups of people who have been minorities will become a numerical majority between the years 2030 and 2050. As minority groups have increased in numbers, they have also increased in political and social power (Welfel, 1998).

The legal system has played a significant role in the changes that have occurred. The Civil Rights Act of 1964 and the Americans with Disabilities Act of 1990 are two examples of federal legislation that has recognized the rights of minority groups.

Finally, scholarship in multicultural counseling has blossomed. The prolific writings of major contributors to the field have helped counselors increase their recognition of and appreciation for cultural differences.

Although there are certainly some counselors practicing today who remain culturally encapsulated, counseling professionals now generally recognize that they must learn to practice in a diversity-sensitive manner. Our understanding of multiculturalism is based on the premise that all counseling can be viewed as multicultural when culture is broadly defined to include not only race, ethnicity, and nationality, but other cultural variables as well. Culture also includes gender, age, social class, sexual or affectional orientation, disability, place of residence, language, and religion (Das, 1995; Pedersen, 1994). Culture influences a person's view of reality and thus every aspect of life. A multicultural perspective in counseling recognizes that the client may hold values and beliefs that are different from those of the counselor. It seeks to provide a conceptual framework that recognizes the complex diversity of a pluralistic society while building bridges of shared concern that allow culturally different individuals to connect with one another (Pedersen, 1991).

Sue (1995) identified three goals of ethical multicultural practice. First, counselors need to become culturally aware of their own values, biases, and assumptions about human behavior. Second, they need to increase their awareness of the cultural values, biases, and assumptions of the diverse groups of clients with whom they work. Third, they need to develop culturally appropriate intervention strategies for assisting these diverse clients. The need for counselors to become multiculturally competent cannot be overemphasized. This will be explored in more detail in Chapter 6.

Multiculturalism and Ethical Standards

In its *Code of Ethics* (1995), the ACA conveys its commitment to multiculturalism in the Preamble, with the statement that members "recognize diversity in our society and embrace a cross-cultural approach in support of the worth, dignity, potential, and uniqueness of each individual." As Sue (1995) has observed, this statement suggests that multiculturalism should be valued rather than just tolerated and that culturally appropriate strategies must be developed in counseling. The code gives further guidance regarding nondiscrimination in Standard A.2.a., which states that "Counselors do not condone or engage in discrimination based on age, color, culture, disability, ethnic group, gender, race, religion, sexual orientation, marital status, or socioeconomic status." Additional standards regarding nondiscrimination and honoring diversity are included throughout the code in sections that address the counseling relationship, professional responsibility, relationships with other professionals, evaluation and assessment, teaching and supervision, and research and publication.

The code requires counselors and counselors-in-training to actively attempt to understand the diverse cultural backgrounds of the clients with whom they work. This includes learning how their own cultural and racial identity have an impact on their values and beliefs about the counseling process. Thus, counselors must engage in self-reflection and acknowledge their own biases and assumptions as a starting place. They must also seek out knowledge that will enhance their understanding of clients who are culturally different from them. If Jack, the counselor intern in the first vignette at the beginning of the chapter, had known that many Asian clients are very uncomfortable with the idea of discussing their feelings with a stranger, he might not have perceived his client as "difficult." His lack of understanding led him to make an error that is common among counselors who lack knowledge of different cultures—he blamed the client for his failure to establish a therapeutic alliance.

In seeking out knowledge about diversity, there is a limit to what can be learned through reading and taking courses. Experiential knowledge can be powerful. For example, Wehrly (1991) suggested that a White student can experience the discomfort and isolation often felt by members of minority groups by going alone to a function where the student is clearly in the minority, such as an NAACP or La Raza meeting or an African American church service. Serving one's practicum or internship at a culturally pluralistic site can provide invaluable learning experiences as well.

The guidelines found in the *Code of Ethics* can assist counselors to practice ethically in a culturally diverse society if, as Sue (1995) has pointed out, they are translated into meaningful action. The standards can be helpful, but they require thoughtful application in the day-to-day work of the counselor. With respect to cultural diversity, perhaps more than any other ethical issue, it is crucial that counselors attend to the *spirit* of the code. Although there are some specific sections of the *ACA Code of Ethics* that focus on diversity issues, we believe that all of the ethical standards are best seen as multicultural standards. Sensitivity to cultural diversity should be inherent in our interpretation of all our ethical obligations.

If cultural diversity is a theme that runs throughout the *Code of Ethics,* it is also a theme that runs throughout this book. In this and in each of the ensuing chapters that focuses on a specific ethical, legal, or professional issue, there is a section devoted to diversity issues that relate to that topic. For instance, some diversity issues that arise in informed consent are discussed later in this chapter. Diversity is far too important an issue in the professional practice of counselors to be limited to one section of this book.

Clients Who May Be Victims of Illegal Discrimination

The U. S. Constitution provided a foundation for making discrimination illegal through the Due Process Clause of the Fifth Amendment (*Adarand Constructors, Inc. v. Pena,* 1995), the Due Process and Equal Protection Clauses of the Fourteenth Amendment (*Truax v. Raich,* 1915), and First Amendment. Title VII of the Civil Rights Act of 1964 prohibits public and private employers, labor organizations, and employment agencies from discriminating on the basis of race, color, sex, religion, and national origin. After Title VII was enacted, federal laws were passed that prohibit discrimination on the basis of age (Age Discrimination in Employment Act of 1967) and disability (Title I of the Americans with Disabilities Act of 1990). The *ACA Code of Ethics* 1995, (Standards A.2.a., C.5.a., and D.1.i.) lists the groups counselors are admonished not to discriminate against and includes groups that are not protected from discrimination by the federal constitution or by federal statutes. The groups that are not legally protected include subgroups based on culture, sexual orientation, marital status, and socioeconomic status. Some states and local government entities, however, have passed nondiscrimination laws for some specific purposes related to these groups (Belton & Avery, 1999).

In our view, counselors are not responsible for ensuring that laws are followed in our society. Thus, counselors do not have a professional responsibility to expose those who they think may be illegally discriminating against protected groups or to encourage clients to assert their legal rights. On the other hand, counselors do have an obligation to assist clients in making decisions about whether to take action, and what action to take, if they are struggling with value conflicts or if they believe their legal rights have been violated, just as counselors would help clients make other types of important decisions in their lives.

When clients express concern that they may have been illegally discriminated against, counselors should first help the clients decide whether they want to take any kind of action. If they decide they want to assert their legal rights, counselors should refer them to an advocacy group for advocacy guidance or to an attorney for legal advice. Advocacy groups or attorneys will determine whether the client may have been a victim of illegal discrimination and, if so, the advocacy group or attorney will tell the client what options exist to address the wrong. The client may want to discuss these options with the counselor after speaking with an advocacy group representative or an attorney. Counselors can be very helpful in assisting clients to consider their options and the possible consequences, both positive and negative, regarding these options. It is important that counselors stay within their bounds in these situations and that they not render legal advice or promote their own political or moral agendas through the client.

Counselor Needs and Values

As a counselor, it is critically important for you to be aware of your own life issues, "unfinished business," areas of vulnerability, and defenses. If this self-awareness is lacking, there is a risk that you will inadvertently be working on your own issues in the counseling relationship, rather than the client's issues. This problem is evident in the second of the two vignettes presented at the beginning of the chapter. The counselor is interjecting her own feelings about paternal abandonment into the session. As Corey, Corey, and Callanan (1993) have noted, counselors who are unaware of their own issues are in a poor position to recognize the ways their personal lives are influencing their work with clients. This is particularly true when the client's problems or issues are similar to the unresolved issues of the counselor.

We are not suggesting that counselors do not have their own needs, or that it is unethical to get some of these needs met by choosing counseling as a profession. In fact, most counselors would probably say that they get a real sense of satisfaction or fulfillment from their work and from knowing that they have made a difference in the lives of others. Still, it is important for you to explore your own answers to the questions, "What do I get out of being a counselor? What needs of mine am I getting met?" Knowing your own needs system will help you identify potential areas of vulnerability and sources of therapeutic error.

To give some examples, if you have a strong need to nurture others, you may be tempted to encourage client dependency. If you have a strong need to be liked and appreciated, you may avoid confronting your clients. If you have a strong need to feel useful or prove your competence, you may want to rush in and give answers or advice. If you can recognize your potential problem areas, you will be better able to keep the best interests of your clients foremost and less likely to allow your needs to intrude into your work with clients. You will be better able to practice in accordance with Standard A.5.a., which cautions counselors to avoid actions that meet their personal needs at the expense of clients.

A closely related standard (A.5.b.) requires counselors to be aware of their own values, attitudes, beliefs, and behaviors and how they apply in a diverse society. Counselors must not impose their values on clients. This ethical obligation is easy to state, but it can be extremely difficult—if not impossible—to uphold in practice. A counselor's values will influence the counseling process in many ways, including what goals are considered appropriate or desirable in counseling, whether and how the client will be diagnosed, and what client issues will become the focus of therapy. Even the theory from which the counselor operates can influence the counseling process in value-laden ways. Certain theories promote certain values. For instance, the Adlerian approach emphasizes the development of social interest as a benchmark of mental health, while the existential approach emphasizes individual freedom and responsibility.

Both the client and the counselor enter the relationship with their own set of values that they have acquired through years of experience and exposure. Values issues may never become a a problem in counseling when the value systems of the client and counselor are similar or compatible. When the value systems of the counselor and client differ, however, particularly around emotionally charged issues, these differences can become problematic. Some issues that might cause problems include the following:

- abortion
- assisted suicide and the right to die
- beliefs and behaviors of members of cults
- beliefs and behaviors of gang members
- child or elder neglect or abuse
- genetic engineering
- interracial dating and marriage
- premarital sex or extramarital sex
- sexual identity

Undoubtedly, you can think of many more issues that might be added to this list. When issues of conflicting values arise in counseling, a counselor might consider disclosing his or her values to the client, if it can be done in a manner that conveys to the client that these values may be accepted or rejected without risking the relationship (Cottone & Tarvydas, 1998). It might then be possible for differences to be discussed and new understandings to be incorporated into the working alliance. For example, a counselor who is a strong feminist might find it difficult to work with a client whose religious beliefs dictate subservience to her husband. The counselor might share her belief system with the client while framing their differences as a learning experience. Once the counselor has disclosed her values, it is hoped that she would find that she was no longer so concerned about inadvertently imposing them. It would be easier for the counselor to keep in mind that it was not her job to convert the client to feminism, but rather to assist the client in finding her own way.

Huber (1994) described four key assumptions that might guide counselors as they struggle with values issues:

1. There is no such thing as an absolute value that exists objectively or factually. Rather, values are developed over time as a result of a person's experiences and interpretations of those experiences.
2. Each person must take responsibility for choosing, interpreting, and holding his or her own values. No one is responsible for anyone else's values.

3. Counselors must acknowledge their tendency to pathologize clients as a way to sidestep the role of their own values in the counseling process.
4. Counselors must accept clients as they are, rather than judge them to be sick, deviant, or immoral because their beliefs and behaviors do not conform to the counselor's values.

Cottone and Tarvydas (1998) have pointed out that values issues that arise between counselor and client have the potential to enrich the counselor and the client, and their relationship if they are addressed directly. When values remain unexamined and unchallenged, there is increased potential for counselors to unethically impose their values on clients.

Client Dependency

The *ACA Code of Ethics* states that counselors must avoid fostering dependent counseling relationships (Standard A.1.b.). Clients have a right to expect that the counseling process will help them move toward increased autonomy and independence. In counseling, clients learn new skills for living including an increased ability to make decisions without the counselor's help.

Earlier we mentioned the possibility that some counselors might encourage client dependency on them. There are a number of ways this could happen to you if you are not alert to the potential problem. During your internship you will need to complete a certain number of contact hours with clients, and you might be tempted to keep some clients in counseling longer than necessary in order to fulfill your requirement. Or, you might do so in hopes of demonstrating to your supervisors that your clients keep coming because you are being so helpful to them. After you graduate and are in practice, temptations to foster dependency might arise out of a need to feel needed, a need to nurture others, a need to feel that you are important or even indispensable to your clients, or even a need for income from client fees if you are in private practice.

Sometimes it is not the counselor's needs but rather the client's needs that work to foster a dependent relationship. Some clients may attempt to maintain or even increase their dependency on the counselor. They may request more frequent sessions, have a new crisis every time the counselor suggests that they may be nearing the end of their work together, or engage in other strategies to avoid progress toward autonomy. For these clients, remaining dependent on the counselor is less risky than having to live autonomously. Counselors will need to find ways to balance ongoing support for them with encouraging independence and risk taking.

The dramatic increase in the number of clients who participate in managed care health plans has had an impact on this issue. Managed care plans limit clients to a certain number of sessions and require counselors to justify any requests for additional sessions. Thus, it is much more difficult for counselors to unnecessarily prolong a counseling relationship. Nonetheless, counselors are obligated to work toward client autonomy regardless of whether the motivation for doing so comes from an external source such as managed care or from an internalized sense of responsibility to promote client welfare.

Counseling Techniques

Another consideration in promoting client welfare is the counselor's obligation to select appropriate counseling strategies or techniques. In recent years, the mental health professions have worked to develop guides for treatment planning that match client concerns with the strategies that research has demonstrated to be the most effective in treating those concerns. Lambert and Cattani-Thompson (1996) reviewed studies on counseling effectiveness and found that some specific techniques seemed to be more efficacious with certain symptoms and disorders. They cautioned, however, that successful client outcome is determined in large part by client characteristics such as motivation, locus of control, and severity and duration of symptoms.

As a counselor, your selection of techniques will depend on a number of factors, including your theoretical orientation and your training. Corey et al. (1993) put it best when they advised that your strategies should fit your counseling style and be tailored to the specific needs of your client. If you use any techniques that could be considered experimental or unusual, you should do so very cautiously. The client should be fully informed about the potential risks and benefits and should consent to your use of such techniques. Before attempting them, you should be sure that you are adequately trained and have a sound clinical rationale for their use. Think about how you would justify your procedures if a complaint were filed against you with a licensing board or in a court of law.

Counselors have an ethical responsibility to work jointly with clients to devise treatment plans that offer reasonable promise of success (*ACA Code of Ethics,* Standard A.1.c.). As we have mentioned, managed care organizations typically limit the number of sessions for which a client will be reimbursed and require counselors to justify any requests for additional sessions. Counselors will be more successful in making such requests when they can present empirical support for their clinical judgments. Managed care organizations demand accountability from their providers, and counselors must be able to present data that demonstrate their efficacy (Glosoff, Garcia, Herlihy, & Remley, 1999).

INFORMED CONSENT

As an ethical obligation, the rationale for informed consent is simple—clients have a right to know what they are getting into when they come for counseling. Counselors believe that obtaining consent from clients before counseling begins constitutes best practice and is the proper and ethical way to proceed. In addition, there are concepts in law that require informed consent be obtained from clients before counseling relationships are initiated. Some state counseling licensing laws or regulations require that licensed counselors provide written documents to clients (e.g., La. Rev. Stat. Ann. 5 37:1101–1115 (West, 1999)) and these written documents constitute informed consent (Madden, 1998). Counselors must provide prospective clients with information that will enable them to make wise choices. This includes deciding whether or not to enter into a counseling relationship and if so, choosing the mental health professional who seems best suited to their needs and the type of counseling they will receive. Providing clients with information about how the counseling process works helps demystify counseling and makes clients active partners in defining the counseling relationship.

Contract Law

Contract law is complex. Counselors do not need to understand the technical principles of contract law such as offer, acceptance, and consideration (Calamari, Perillo, & Bender, 1989) in order to appreciate their contractual obligations to clients.

Generally, relationships with professionals who provide services are contractual in nature (Murphy, Speidel, & Ayres, 1997). In the terms of contract law, a professional in a private practice offers services to a recipient for a fee. The professional says to the client that services will be provided that will benefit and not harm the recipient if the recipient will pay the professional the amount of money required. Once the client accepts the professional's offer of services, a legal contract is formed and all of the laws of contract govern the relationship. The process that leads up to professional services being rendered to a recipient does not look at all like a contractual process to nonlawyers. Because of the fiduciary duty owed to clients of professionals, and because clients must trust professionals to treat them appropriately, the idea of signing a contract before accepting services from a professional seems almost contradictory. If you trust someone, why would you need a contract?

Some contracts, such as real estate deals, must be in writing (Murphy, Speidel, & Ayres, 1997). Contract law does not generally require, however, that contracts be in writing to be valid and enforceable. As a result, most contracts for professional services are not in writing. Although written contracts are generally not necessary under the law, many parties choose to execute them. The reason for reducing to writing the terms of a contract is to ensure that both parties understand exactly what they are agreeing to (i.e., the terms of the contract).

If two parties enter into a contractual arrangement, nothing goes wrong, and both are satisfied with the result, a written contract was not needed. However, written contracts allow the parties to ensure they both understand the specifics in the agreement they have reached. In addition, written contracts often anticipate changes or problems that might occur and set forth the agreement in the event such things happen. Agreements that are complex or need to anticipate changes, therefore, should be in writing to protect both parties.

Informed Consent in Medicine

The process of informing recipients of professional services and obtaining their consent to receive such services is a relatively new legal concept. The requirement that health professionals obtain informed consent from their clients before rendering services began in medicine (Appelbaum, Lidz, & Meisel, 1987).

Until recently it probably rarely occurred to physicians that they should explain to patients what they knew about their medical conditions. Physicians probably never thought that they should tell their patients about various treatment options or allow their patients to decide which option to choose. Perhaps consumers of medical services were once less educated or less aware of their right to receive information. In any event, the idea of informed consent for medical patients is relatively new.

As far back as 1767, a court in England determined that physicians had a responsibility to obtain consent from their patients before touching or treating them (*Slater v. Baker & Stapleton*). Originally this obligation to obtain consent was based on the basic tort principle of battery that held that members of a society have a right to personal privacy, which includes not having their bodies touched by others unless they have given permission.

It has only been in the last half-century that courts have created the concept that patients must be educated or informed regarding their medical treatment options and consequences before they are able to give valid consent to treatment that is legally binding. The first case in the United States that took this position was *Salgo v. Leland Stanford Jr. Univ. Bd. of Trustees* (1957).

However, because there have been very few lawsuits alleging that physicians failed to obtain informed consent from patients before rendering treatment that led to harm, courts and physicians currently are unclear as to exactly what constitutes valid informed consent from patients (Appelbaum, Lidz, & Meisel, 1987). Katz (1977) has suggested that the Salgo case did nothing more than add confusion to an already vague area of the law.

The Salgo case provided the essential elements that physicians must give to patients. According to Appelbaum, Lidz, and Meisel (1987, p. 41), these elements are, ". . . disclosure of the nature of the ailment, the nature of the proposed treatment, the probability of success, and possible alternative treatments." *Canterbury v. Spence* (1972), a later case, took a different position on informed consent. It found that physicians were required to disclose information about a proposed treatment that a reasonable person, such as the patient being treated, would find necessary to make a decision to either accept or refuse treatment.

After considering the case law on informed consent, Berner (1998) has argued that there are two elements to the informed consent legal standard. These elements are professional and materiality. The professional element is defined as information that a reasonable physician would have provided to a patient under similar circumstances. Materiality, on the other hand, is defined as the amount of information the average patient would consider adequate in deciding whether or not to accept treatment. If Berner is correct, then courts will most likely require that physicians provide basic information to all patients *and* require that physicians ensure that the particular patient they are dealing with understands the information.

Although legal decisions have been rendered in the area of informed consent and a great deal has been written about the requirement in the professional literature, whether all of this activity has had an impact on the actual practice of physicians is questionable. Lidz, Meisel, Zerubavel, Sestak, and Roth (1984), in an empirical study of informed consent activities in psychiatric units of hospitals, concluded that if informed consent is being obtained from mental patients, it certainly is not occurring in hospitals.

Informed Consent in Mental Health

At present, there have been no appellate legal cases involving the responsibility of mental health professionals to obtain informed consent from their clients. But like other legal areas in mental health, most of the precedents and rules are created first with physicians, and later become verified for other mental health professionals through cases involving psychologists, counselors, and social workers.

It is probably safe to conclude that counselors do have a legal obligation to obtain informed consent from their clients before they begin treatment with them. Further, the informed consent should include information that would be given to the client by other reasonable professionals, and should be delivered in a way that the client being served understands. Counselors should provide information that, at a minimum, discloses the client's diagnosis, the type of treatment being proposed to address the problem, the probability of success in treating the problem, and possible alternative treatments.

Unless written consent is required by state law or licensing regulations, the process of obtaining informed consent may be oral. However, in our opinion, providing clients with written information is recommended for best practice.

Model Written Disclosure Statements

A number of model written contracts that counselors might use in various circumstances are included in this chapter (see Figures 3-1 through 3-5). In mental health, such contracts are commonly referred to as *disclosure statements.* These documents disclose to clients the nature of the counseling relationship they are entering into. Disclosure statements are also legal contracts. Often, they are signed by both the client and the counselor. Figures 3-1 and 3-2 include model disclosure statements for counselors who are providing counseling services to clients in a private practice and for employed counselors who are providing counseling services to clients in an agency or mental health center, respectively. Also included are model disclosure statements that counselors might use who are evaluating individuals for some purpose (Fig. 3-3), who are counseling involuntary clients (Fig. 3-4), and who are providing counseling in a school setting (Fig. 3-5). Because special issues are associated with evaluations, involuntary clients, and clients in school settings, these model disclosure statements are covered in more detail in Chapters 8 and 10 in this book.

The model counseling disclosure statements for private practice (Fig. 3-1) and agencies or mental health centers (Fig. 3-2) are similar in many ways. However, fee issues and some other aspects of the disclosure statements are quite different.

The *ACA Code of Ethics* (1995) spells out in considerable detail in Section A.3. the elements that ethically need to be included in securing informed consent. Therefore, these elements should be included in counseling disclosure statements:

- the purposes, goals, techniques, procedures, limitations, potential risks, and benefits of proposed counseling services
- the implications of diagnosis and the intended use of tests and reports
- information about fees and billing information
- confidentiality and its limitations
- clients' rights to obtain information about their case notes and to participate in ongoing counseling plans
- clients' rights to refuse any recommended services and be advised of the consequences of refusal

In addition to the elements addressed by the code, various writers have recommended that these additional topics be included:

- a description of the counselor's *qualifications,* including relevant degrees held, licenses and certifications, areas of specialization, and experience (Haas & Malouf, 1995)
- a description of the counselor's *theoretical orientation,* in lay language that the client can understand (Corey et al., 1993), or a brief statement of the counselor's *philosophy* (how the counselor sees the counseling process)
- information about *logistics* of the counseling process, such as length and frequency of sessions, procedures for making and canceling appointments, policies regarding telephone contact between sessions, how to reach the counselor or an alternative service in an emergency (Haas & Malouf, 1995)
- information about *insurance reimbursement,* including the fact that any diagnosis assigned will become part of the client's permanent health record; what

**CLIENT INFORMATION AND AGREEMENT FOR
COUNSELORS IN PRIVATE PRACTICE**
_____, M. Ed., NCC
Licensed Professional Counselor (LPC)

I am pleased you have chosen me as your counselor. This document is designed to inform you about my background and to insure that you understand our professional relationship.

I am licensed as a Professional Counselor by the _____ Board of Examiners for Licensed Professional Counselors. Only licensed mental health professionals may provide counseling services in this state. In addition, I am certified by the National Board of Certified Counselors, a private certifying agency that recognizes counselors who have distinguished themselves through meeting the board's standards for education, knowledge, and experience.

I hold a Master's (M.Ed.) degree in counseling from the University of _____. The graduate program I completed is accredited by the Council on Accreditation of Counseling and Related Educational Programs (CACREP).

I have been a counselor since _____. I provide services for clients in my private practice who I believe have the capacity to resolve their own problems with my assistance. A counseling relationship between a Professional Counselor and client is a professional relationship in which the Professional Counselor assists the client in exploring and resolving difficult life issues. I believe that as people become more accepting of themselves, they are more capable of finding happiness and contentment in their lives. Self-awareness and self-acceptance are goals that sometimes take a long time to achieve. While some clients may need only a few counseling sessions to feel complete, others may require months or even years of counseling. Clients are in complete control and may end our counseling relationship at any point and I will be supportive of that decision. If counseling is successful, clients should feel that they are able to face life's challenges in the future without my support or intervention.

My counseling services are limited to the scheduled sessions we have together. In the event you feel your mental health requires emergency attention or if you have an emotional crisis, you should

Figure 3-1 Disclosure Statement Example A

report to the emergency room of a local hospital and request mental health services.

Although our sessions will be very intimate, it is important for you to realize that we have a professional, rather than a personal, relationship. Our contact will be limited to the paid session you have with me. Please do not invite me to social gatherings, offer gifts, or ask me to relate to you in any way outside our counseling sessions. You will be best served if our relationship stays strictly professional and if our sessions concentrate exclusively on your concerns. You will learn a great deal about me as we work together during your counseling experience. However, it is important for you to remember that you are experiencing me only in my professional role.

My counseling practice is limited to adolescents and adults and includes career, personal, couples, marriage, and group counseling. I also am available for divorce mediation.

I will keep confidential anything you say to me with the following general exceptions: you direct me to tell someone else, I determine you are a danger to yourself or others, or I am ordered by a court to disclose information.

In the event you are dissatisfied with my services for any reason, please let me know. If I am not able to resolve your concerns, you may report your complaints to the State of _____ Licensed Professional Counselors Board of Examiners, (address, telephone number). I hold license # _____.

In return for a fee of $ _____ per session, I agree to provide counseling services for you. Session are 50 minutes in duration. It is impossible to guarantee any specific results regarding your counseling goals. However, I assure you that my services will be rendered in a professional manner consistent with accepted ethical standards.

The fee for each session will be due and must be paid at the conclusion of each session. Cash or personal checks are acceptable forms for payment. I will provide you with a monthly receipt for all fees paid.

In the event you will not be able to keep an appointment, you must notify me 24 hours in advance. If I do not receive such advance notice, you will be responsible for paying for the session you missed.

Figure 3-1   *(Continued)*

If you are a member of a HMO, PPO, or some type of managed health care plan, I can tell you if I am an authorized provider of services under that plan. If I am an authorized provider, services will be provided to you under the terms of that plan's contract. Fees will be billed and collected according to the requirements of that plan. If I am not an authorized provider, you may still receive services from me for a fee, but your plan will not reimburse you for the cost of any of my services. Plans often will reimburse for only a limited number of visits per year. If you exceed that limit, you may still receive services from me, but your plan will not reimburse you for the cost of services that exceed their maximum number of visits.

If you wish to seek reimbursement for my services from your health insurance company, I will be happy to complete any necessary forms related to your reimbursement provided by you or the insurance company. Since you will be paying each sessions for my services, any later reimbursement from the insurance company should be sent directly to you. Please do not assign any payments to me.

Most health insurance companies will reimburse clients for my counseling services, but some will not. Those that do reimburse usually require that a standard amount be paid by you before reimbursement is allowed and usually only a percentage of my fee is reimbursable. You should contact a company representative to determine whether your insurance company will reimburse you and the schedule of reimbursement that is used.

Health insurance companies usually require that I diagnose your mental condition and indicate that you have an illness before they will agree to reimburse you. In the event a diagnosis is required, I will inform you of the diagnosis I plan to render before I submit it to health insurance company.

If you have any questions, feel free to ask. Please sign and date both copies of this form. You keep one and give the other copy to me.

_____   _____
Your Signature   Your Client's Signature

_____   _____
Date   Date

Figure 3-1   *(Continued)*

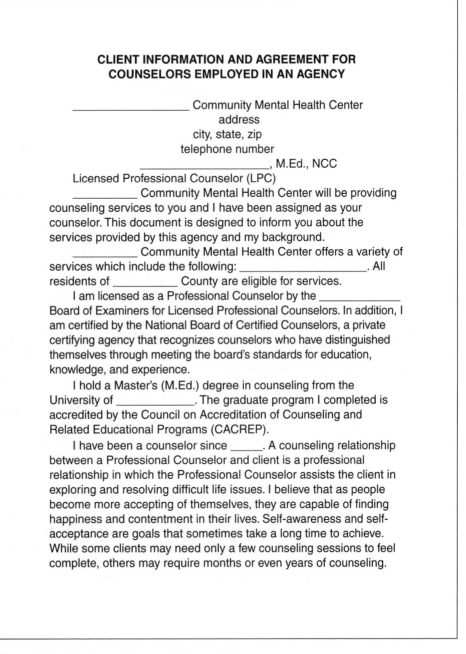

**CLIENT INFORMATION AND AGREEMENT FOR
COUNSELORS EMPLOYED IN AN AGENCY**

_____ Community Mental Health Center
address
city, state, zip
telephone number
_____, M.Ed., NCC
Licensed Professional Counselor (LPC)

_____ Community Mental Health Center will be providing counseling services to you and I have been assigned as your counselor. This document is designed to inform you about the services provided by this agency and my background.

_____ Community Mental Health Center offers a variety of services which include the following: _____. All residents of _____ County are eligible for services.

I am licensed as a Professional Counselor by the _____ Board of Examiners for Licensed Professional Counselors. In addition, I am certified by the National Board of Certified Counselors, a private certifying agency that recognizes counselors who have distinguished themselves through meeting the board's standards for education, knowledge, and experience.

I hold a Master's (M.Ed.) degree in counseling from the University of _____. The graduate program I completed is accredited by the Council on Accreditation of Counseling and Related Educational Programs (CACREP).

I have been a counselor since _____. A counseling relationship between a Professional Counselor and client is a professional relationship in which the Professional Counselor assists the client in exploring and resolving difficult life issues. I believe that as people become more accepting of themselves, they are capable of finding happiness and contentment in their lives. Self-awareness and self-acceptance are goals that sometimes take a long time to achieve. While some clients may need only a few counseling sessions to feel complete, others may require months or even years of counseling.

Figure 3-2 Disclosure Statement Example B

Clients are in complete control and may end our counseling relationship at any point and I will be supportive of that decision. If counseling is successful, clients should feel that they are able to face life's challenges in the future without my support or intervention. My counseling services are limited to the scheduled sessions we have together. In the event you feel your mental health requires emergency attention or if you have an emotional crisis, you should report to the emergency room of a local hospital and request mental health services.

Although our sessions will be very intimate, it is important for you to realize that we have a professional, rather than a personal, relationship. Our contact will be limited to the paid session you have with me. Please do not invite me to social gatherings, offer gifts, or ask me to relate to you in any way outside our counseling sessions. You will be best served if our relationship stays strictly professional and if our sessions concentrate exclusively on your concerns. You will learn a great deal about me as we work together during your counseling experience However, it is important for you to remember that your are experiencing me only in my professional role. My counseling practice is limited to adolescents and adults and includes career, personal, couples, marriage, and group counseling. I also am available for divorce mediation.

I will keep confidential anything you say to me with the following general exceptions: you direct me to tell someone else, I determine you are a danger to yourself or others, or I am ordered by a court to disclose information. In the event you are dissatisfied with my services for any reason, please let me know. If I am not able to resolve your concerns, you may report your complaints to _____, my supervisor here at the _____ Community Mental Health Center.

The general fee for services at _____ Community Mental Health Center is $75 per session. However, if you apply for a reduction in fees for services based on your family's income, you may be eligible for a reduction in fees. If you are granted a reduction in fees, United Way, a local charitable organization pays the portion

Figure 3-2   *(Continued)*

of the fees that you cannot afford. Based on your application for a reduction in fees for services, your fees have been established at $ _____ per session.

Sessions are 50 minutes in duration. It is impossible to guarantee any specific results regarding your counseling goals. However, I assure you that my services will be rendered in a professional manner consistent with accepted ethical standards.

The fee for each session will be due and must be paid at the conclusion of each session. Cash or personal checks are acceptable forms for payment. I will provide you with a monthly receipt for all fees paid.In the event you will not be able to keep an appointment, you must notify me 24 hours in advance. If I do not receive such advance notice, you will be responsible for paying for the session you missed. If you are a member of a HMO, PPO, or some type of managed health care plan, I can tell you if this agency is an authorized provider of services under that plan. If this agency is an authorized provider, services will be provided to you under the terms of that plan's contract. Fees will be billed and collected according to the requirements of that plan. If this agency is not an authorized provider, you may still receive services from me for a fee, but your plan will not reimburse you for the cost of any of my services. Plans often will reimburse for only a limited number of visits per year. If you exceed that limit, you may still receive services from me, but your plan will not reimburse you for the cost of services that exceed their maximum number of visits.

If you have any questions, feel free to ask. Please sign and date both copies of this form. You keep one and give the other copy to me.

_____   _____
Your Signature   Your Client's Signature

_____   _____
Date   Date

Figure 3-2   *(Continued)*

**CLIENT INFORMATION AND AGREEMENT FOR
COUNSELORS WHO EVALUATE INDIVIDUALS**

The purpose of our relationship is for me to gather information from you and to evaluate you so that I will be able to render an opinion regarding the best custody situation for your minor child. This process will work best if you are cooperative in providing me with the information I need and if we maintain a professional relationship throughout the evaluation.

Nothing that we discuss will be confidential. I will be required to give a written opinion to the judge who appointed me to your case. I may use any information in that report that you give to me during the duration of our relationship. In addition, I may be required to testify under oath at legal proceedings regarding interactions we have had and opinions I have rendered.

I guarantee you that I will be fair and unbiased in rendering my opinions in this case. The best interest of your child will guide my decisions.

In the event you feel I am acting in an unfair or biased manner, please have your attorney notify the judge who is presiding in this case and request that the judge determine whether my actions have been unprofessional.

Although I am a Licensed Professional Counselor in this state, I am not serving as your counselor. In the event you feel a need for counseling, I will be happy to refer you to agencies or individuals who might be able to assist you.

If you have any questions, feel free to ask. Please sign and date both copies of this form. You keep one and give the other copy to me.

_____   _____
Your Signature   Signature of Individual
                                                        Being Evaluated

_____   _____
Date   Date

Figure 3-3   Disclosure Statement Example C

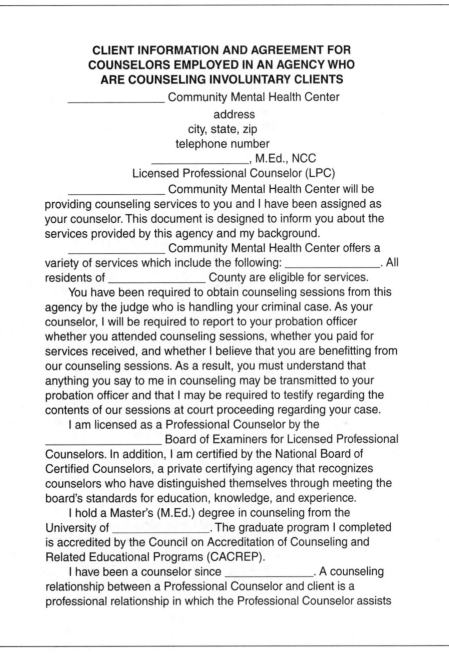

CLIENT INFORMATION AND AGREEMENT FOR COUNSELORS EMPLOYED IN AN AGENCY WHO ARE COUNSELING INVOLUNTARY CLIENTS

_____ Community Mental Health Center

address

city, state, zip

telephone number

_____, M.Ed., NCC

Licensed Professional Counselor (LPC)

_____ Community Mental Health Center will be providing counseling services to you and I have been assigned as your counselor. This document is designed to inform you about the services provided by this agency and my background.

_____ Community Mental Health Center offers a variety of services which include the following: _____. All residents of _____ County are eligible for services.

You have been required to obtain counseling sessions from this agency by the judge who is handling your criminal case. As your counselor, I will be required to report to your probation officer whether you attended counseling sessions, whether you paid for services received, and whether I believe that you are benefitting from our counseling sessions. As a result, you must understand that anything you say to me in counseling may be transmitted to your probation officer and that I may be required to testify regarding the contents of our sessions at court proceeding regarding your case.

I am licensed as a Professional Counselor by the _____ Board of Examiners for Licensed Professional Counselors. In addition, I am certified by the National Board of Certified Counselors, a private certifying agency that recognizes counselors who have distinguished themselves through meeting the board's standards for education, knowledge, and experience.

I hold a Master's (M.Ed.) degree in counseling from the University of _____. The graduate program I completed is accredited by the Council on Accreditation of Counseling and Related Educational Programs (CACREP).

I have been a counselor since _____. A counseling relationship between a Professional Counselor and client is a professional relationship in which the Professional Counselor assists

Figure 3-4 Disclosure Statement Example D

the client in exploring and resolving difficult life issues. I believe that as people become more accepting of themselves, they are more capable of finding happiness and contentment in their lives. Self-awareness and self-acceptance are goals that sometimes take a long time to achieve. While some clients may need only a few counseling sessions to feel complete, others may require months or even years of counseling. If counseling is successful, clients should feel that they are able to face life's challenges in the future without my support or intervention.

My counseling services are limited to the scheduled sessions we have together. In the event you feel your mental health requires emergency attention or if you have an emotional crisis, you should report to the emergency room of a local hospital and request mental health services.

Although our sessions will be very intimate, it is important for you to realize that we have a professional, rather than a personal, relationship. Our contact will be limited to the paid session you have with me. Please do not invite me to social gatherings, offer gifts, or ask me to relate to you in any way outside our counseling sessions. You will be best served if our relationship stays strictly professional and if our sessions concentrate exclusively on your concerns. You will learn a great deal about me as we work together during your counseling experience However, it is important for you to remember that you are experiencing me only in my professional role.

My counseling practice is limited to adolescents and adults and includes career, personal, couples, marriage, and group counseling. I also am available for divorce mediation.

In the event you are dissatisfied with my services for any reason, please let me know. If I am not able to resolve your concerns, you may report your complaints to _____, my supervisor here at the _____ Community Mental Health Center.

The general fee for services at _____ Community Mental Health Center is $75 per session. However, if you apply for a reduction in fees for services based on your family's income, you may be eligible for a reduction in fees. If you are granted a reduction in fees, United Way, a local charitable organization pays the portion of the fees that you cannot afford. Based on your application for a

Figure 3-4 *(Continued)*

reduction of fees for services, your fees have been established at
$_____ per session.

Sessions are 50 minutes in duration. It is impossible to guarantee any specific results regarding your counseling goals. However, I assure you that my services will be rendered in a professional manner consistent with accepted ethical standards.

The fee for each session will be due and must be paid at the conclusion of each session. Cash or personal checks are acceptable forms for payment. I will provide you with a monthly receipt for all fees paid.

In the event you will not be able to keep an appointment, you must notify me 24 hours in advance. If I do not receive such advance notice, you will be responsible for paying for the session you missed.

If you are a member of a HMO, PPO, or some type of managed health care plan, I can tell you if this agency is an authorized provider of services under that plan. If this agency is an authorized provider, services will be provided to you under the terms of that plan's contract. Fees will be billed and collected according to the requirements of that plan. If this agency is not an authorized provider, you may still receive services from me for a fee, but your plan will not reimburse you for the cost of any of my services. Plans often will reimburse for only a limited number of visits per year. If you exceed that limit, you may still receive services from me, but your plan will not reimburse you for the cost of services that exceed their maximum number of visits.

_____ Community Mental Health Agency does not participate in any type of health insurance reimbursement. If you have a health insurance policy that allows reimburses you for mental health services, it is suggested that you seek a provider who is qualified to render those services to you. If you receive services from me at this agency, you will be responsible for the fees for all services received.

If you have any questions, feel free to ask. Please sign and date both copies of this form. You keep one and give the other copy to me.

_____   _____
Your Signature   Your Client's Signature

_____   _____
Date   Date

Figure 3-4   *(Continued)*

**CLIENT INFORMATION AND AGREEMENT FOR COUNSELORS
EMPLOYED IN A SCHOOL**

Include a statement similar to the one below in a letter to parents at the beginning of the year, orientation materials, etc. The statement could be easily modified to be addressed to students themselves and included in a student handbook.

"I'm Your Child's School Counselor"

The counseling program at _____ school is designed to assist your child make the most of his or her educational experiences. As your child's counselor, I am concerned about his or her emotional well-being, academic progress, and personal and social development.

I have a master's degree in school counseling from the University of _____. My graduate program is accredited by the American Counseling Association's Council for the Accreditation of Counseling and Related Educational Program (CACREP), the nationally recognized accrediting agency for counseling graduate programs. I am a National Certified Counselor (NCC), National Certified School Counselor (NCSC), and a Licensed Professional Counselor (LPC) in _____. In addition, I am certified as a school counselor by the state of _____. Before beginning my duties as a counselor at _____ school, I held the following positions: _____. I currently serve as President of the _____ School Counselor Association.

The following specific activities are offered by the counseling program:
1. Periodic classroom lessons related to positive personal growth and development.
2.
3.
etc.

Reasons that I might contact parents regarding their child include, but are not limited to, the following:
1. Assistance is needed from parents in specific areas to help their children achieve success in school.
2.
etc.

Unfortunately, I am not able to provide the following services to your child or to parents:
1. Testifying in court in child-custody matters.
2. Providing intensive long-term counseling services when they are needed by a child.
3.
etc.

Your child will be participating in the school counseling program on a regular basis. In the event you have questions about the counseling program, please call me at _____. I sincerely look forward to working with you in the coming year to help your child have a successful experience in our school.

Figure 3-5   Disclosure Statement Example E

information will be provided to insurance carriers and how this limits confidentiality (Welfel, 1998); and, if applicable, a description of how the *managed care* system will affect the counseling process (Corey et al., 1993; Glosoff et al., 1999)

- information about *alternatives to counseling,* such as 12-step groups or other self-help groups, books, medications, nutritional or exercise therapy, or other services (Bray, Shepherd, & Hays, 1985)
- if applicable, a statement that sessions will be *videotaped or audiotaped,* along with the information that the client's case may be discussed with a supervisor or consultant (Corey et al., 1993)
- the client's *recourse if dissatisfied with services,* including names and contact information for supervisors, and addresses and telephone numbers of licensing boards and professional organizations (Welfel, 1998)

Beyond the informed consent areas required by the *ACA Code of Ethics* and areas suggested by others, some legal concerns need to be addressed in disclosure statements. The following informed consent areas are particularly sensitive and could lead to legal problems if not handled properly. Examples of problems that could arise are included. A client might have the basis for a lawsuit against a counselor if the client believed, for some reason, that the counselor had done any of the following:

1. **Guaranteed an outcome as a result of counseling.** Example: A wife believed when she reluctantly agreed to enter marriage counseling with her husband that by agreeing to engage in counseling, she was guaranteed that her marriage would not end. She says that the counselor told her that counseling was "the only thing that would save her marriage." She feels betrayed by the counselor when, after five sessions, her husband moves out of their home and files for divorce. The wife sues the counselor for breach of contract, conspiracy, and alienation of affection.
2. **Guaranteed privacy with no exceptions.** Example: A new client expresses concern to his counselor that others might find out what he tells the counselor in their sessions. To reduce the client's anxiety, the counselor explains her ethical and legal responsibilities to protect his privacy. The client believes that his counselor told him that she would never, under any circumstances, reveal to anyone else information given to her in counseling sessions. Later the counselor informs the client's wife, over his objection, that he has expressed suicidal ideas and that she believes he should be evaluated to determine whether he is at risk. He sues the counselor for breach of contract, malpractice, and intentional infliction of emotional distress.
3. **Agreed to fee arrangements different from what was intended.** Example: A counselor begins a counseling relationship with his client, charging the client his standard rate of $75 per hour. After 3 months of sessions once a week, the counselor tells his client that his fees will be increased in one month to $90 per hour. The client objects, saying that he feels that the new hourly rate is too high. The counselor replies that he is not willing to provide further counseling services to the client unless the client agrees to pay the new rate. The client sues the counselor for breach of contract and abandonment.

4. **Touched without implied or actual permission.** Example: In the course of a group counseling experience, a counselor asks group members who are blindfolded to allow themselves to fall backwards into the arms of another group member to demonstrate the difficulty of trusting another person. A female group member reluctantly participates and is caught by a male group member. The female group member is very upset after the exercise and leaves the session visibly shaken. The female client sues the counselor for breach of contract, breach of fiduciary duty, assault, battery, and sexual assault.

5. **Misrepresented credentials.** Example: A client begins counseling sessions with a master's level licensed counselor. The client tells his family members and friends that he is seeing a psychologist for therapy. The client makes out his checks to "Dr.____," notes on the checks that he is paying for "psychological services," and gives the checks each week to the office receptionist, who deposits them. At the ninth session, the client calls the counselor, "Dr. ____," and she corrects him. He then says, "You are a psychologist, aren't you?" He is very upset when he realizes that she is a master's level licensed counselor. The client sues the counselor for breach of contract and fraudulent misrepresentation.

6. **Failed to communicate the nature of counseling.** Example: A client has taken a new job in which she is required periodically to give presentations to small groups of potential clients. She is very anxious about speaking before groups and has sought counseling to overcome her anxiety. The counselor believes that her anxiety is the result of low self-esteem and focuses on positive reinforcement of the client's positive attributes. After five sessions, the client complains that she is still as anxious as she was when she began counseling. She tells the counselor that she had expected to be taught how to give presentations without being anxious and she does not understand why the counselor has not given her books to read, given her advice on how to be less anxious, or practiced speaking with her. The client sues the counselor for breach of contract and malpractice.

7. **Neglected to warn client about possible stigma.** Example: After the first session with a new client, the counselor completes an insurance form at the client's request. The counselor indicates on the form that the client has had a single episode of depression and assigns the appropriate DSM-IV diagnosis. The counselor counsels the client for 10 sessions, terminating when the client moves to a new city hundreds of miles away. Two years later the client contacts the counselor and complains that he has been denied a security clearance for a job he has applied for because she diagnosed him, without his knowledge or agreement, with a mental disorder. He sues the counselor for breach of contract, malpractice, and defamation.

These seven unfortunate situations illustrate the importance of ensuring that counselors and their clients have the same understanding regarding their relationship before counseling begins. All of these problems could have been avoided if the counselors had fully informed the clients regarding the counseling relationship and then offered the clients a written agreement to read and sign.

In the process of having clients sign counseling disclosure statements, counselors should attempt to ensure that clients know what they have read and what was in the document being signed. If questions arise later about what counselors may have said, a signed written document demonstrates the intent of the parties much more clearly than does a statement of what someone says they intended. In addition, counseling disclosure statements can be used to correct misunderstandings on the part of clients before counseling begins.

You may be thinking that a lot of information has to be included in a disclosure statement and, indeed, this is true. In order for clients to give truly informed consent, they need to have considerable information before deciding whether or not to enter into a counseling relationship. This may raise your concern that inundating prospective clients with information will overwhelm them and give the impression that the counseling relationship is nothing more than a complex, contractual business arrangement. It is difficult for counselors to achieve the delicate balance between giving clients too little information and giving them so much information that they feel overwhelmed or intimidated. Written disclosure statements allow counselors to provide detailed information. Oral exchanges between counselors and potential clients can then focus on areas the counselor wishes to emphasize or that cause particular concern for clients.

If there is a danger in giving too much information, there is also a risk in giving too little. The third vignette that was presented at the beginning of the chapter is a case in point. Although the teenage client's counselor had informed her of the duty to report dangerous behavior, apparently they had not discussed their respective ideas about what behaviors might be considered dangerous. Thus, when the counselor determined that she had a duty to tell the client's parents about her drug use, the client felt betrayed. Each counselor will need to take a number of factors into account in determining the amount and types of information that will work best with their particular clientele, and the best ways to present the information.

As noted earlier, every counselor should have a professional disclosure statement that can be given to clients. A complete signed disclosure statement will fulfill a counselor's legal obligation to obtain informed consent from a client. Keep in mind, though, that disclosure statements are necessary but not sufficient strategies for securing genuine informed consent. They cannot serve as a substitute for dialogue with the client. We cannot rely on standard forms, no matter how well they are written, to do our work for us (Pope & Vasquez, 1991). Prospective clients are likely to have many questions and some of these are best addressed in face-to-face conversation. Such a dialogue gives clients an opportunity to clarify any information that seems confusing to them and gives counselors the opportunity to gauge the extent to which the clients comprehend the information. At the outset of the relationship, informed consent discussions present a mutual opportunity for the client and the counselor to ensure that they understand their shared journey.

It is impossible to predict which clients will need what information and when they will need it, so it is best to be as thorough as possible in a written disclosure statement. Then later, in a face-to-face discussion, issues that arise frequently in one's practice can be emphasized and rare events can be given less attention. For example, Weinrach (1989) has suggested that the two most common problems for private practitioners concern fees and billing, and late cancellations or no-shows. Thus, it behooves counselors in private practice to be clear with their clients about methods of payment and policies regarding missed appointments.

Some counselors make it a practice to give clients not only a disclosure statement, but also a written statement of client rights and responsibilities. The NBCC has developed such a statement (see Fig. 3-6) that counselors may wish to give to their clients.

From an ethical perspective, ensuring informed consent is not a one-time event. Rather, it is a recurring process that begins with the initial contact between client and counselor and

Your Rights As A Consumer
- Be informed of the qualifications of your counselor: education, experience, and professional counseling certification(s) and license(s).
- Receive an explanation of services offered, your time commitments, and fee scales and billing policies prior to receipt of services.
- Be informed of the limitations of the counselor practice to special areas of expertise (e.g. career development, ethnic groups, etc.) or age group (e.g. adolescents, older adults, etc.).
- Have all that you say treated confidentially and be informed of any state laws placing limitations on confidentially in the counseling relationship.
- Ask questions about the counseling technique and strategies and be informed of your progress.
- Participate in setting goals and evaluating progress toward meeting them.
- Be informed of how to contact the counselor in an emergency situation.
- Request referral for a second opinion at any time.
- Request copies of records and reports to be used by other counseling professionals.
- Receive a copy of the code of ethics to which your counselor adheres.
- Contact the appropriate professional organization if you have doubts or complaints relative to the counselor's conduct.
- Terminate the relationship at any time.

Your Responsibilities As A Client
- Set and keep appointments with your counselor. Let him or her know as soon as possible if you cannot keep an appointment.
- Pay your fees in accordance with the schedule you preestablished with the counselor.
- Help plan your goals.
- Follow through with agreed upon goals.
- Keep your counselor informed of your progress towards meeting your goals.
- Terminate your counseling relationship before beginning with another counselor.

What To Do If You Are Dissatisfied With The Services Of A Counselor
Remember that a counselor who meets the needs of one person may be wrong for another. If you are dissatisfied with the services of your counselor:
- Express your concern directly to the counselor if possible.
- Seek the advice of the counselor's supervisor of the counselor is practicing in a setting where he or she receives direct supervision.
- Terminate the counseling relationship if the situation remains unresolved.
- Contact the appropriate state licensing board national certification organization, or professional association if you believe the counselor's conduct to be unethical.

Figure 3-6   National Board for Certified Counselors Consumer Rights and Responsibilities

continues throughout the counseling relationship. According to Pope and Vasquez (1991), informed consent procedures must fit the situation and setting; conform to standards of professional associations, state licensing boards, and laws; and be sensitive to the client's ability to understand, particularly when clients are minors, developmentally disabled, referred by a third party, court-mandated, or suffering from a severe thought disorder.

Managed care arrangements present some new considerations in informed consent. Glosoff (1998) has suggested that counselors need to expand the information they provide to clients being served by managed care systems, as compared to other clients. Clients often do not understand how their health plans affect the duration of their treatment, the implications of diagnosis, or the extent to which their insurance providers require counselors to provide them with information about treatment plans and counseling progress. Thus, Glosoff (1998) has suggested that it is incumbent on their counselors to fully understand the requirements of each client's managed care company and to discuss with the client the impact their plan will have on the length of treatment, types of treatment available, limits to confidentiality, development of treatment plans, and how diagnoses will be made and used. See Chapter 11 for further discussions regarding managed care.

Research supports the wisdom of securing informed consent. Studies have suggested that clients want information about their prospective counselors (Braaten, Otto, & Handelsman, 1993; Hendrick, 1988); that they perceive counselors who provide informed consent information as being more expert and trustworthy (Walter & Handelsman, 1996); and that clients who have received appropriate information are more likely to follow their treatment plans, to recover more quickly, to be less anxious, and to be more alert to possible negative consequences (Handler, 1990). In addition, some legal problems can be avoided by the use of disclosure statements. If allegations do arise that a counselor did not fully explain the counseling relationship to a client, a disclosure statement signed by a client often can go a long way toward vindicating an accused counselor who has done no wrong.

Diversity Issues in Informed Consent

It is important for us to question whether the individualism inherent in our concept of informed consent is truly respectful of people of all cultures. We need to be aware that the full and truthful disclosure that counselors value may be at variance with some clients' cultural beliefs about hope and wellness, that autonomous decision making may run counter to family-centered or group-centered values, and that uncoerced choices may contradict cultural norms about obedience to the wishes of elders or spouses (Gostin, 1995). Following are two examples that illustrate these points.

Joseph, a Navajo Indian who espouses the traditions of his culture, is your prospective client. During the initial interview, you want to secure his informed consent, which would include giving him information about the implications of diagnosis and the potential risks associated with counseling. You might make a statement like, "Sometimes clients in counseling seem to feel worse before they feel better." You might tell Joseph that, based on the symptoms he has described, he seems to be suffering from depression. In traditional Navajo culture, it is believed that language has the power to shape reality and control events. Thus, in following your standard informed consent procedures, you could be *creating* the reality for Joseph that he is depressed and will feel worse for a while.

Soo Jung is a 22-year-old Korean American who is brought to the counseling center by her husband. During the intake interview, she tells you that she has been having crying spells, has lost her appetite, and is not sleeping well. She gave birth to her first child two months ago. When you suggest to Soo Jung that she may be experiencing post-partum depression, she becomes very upset and says, "Why are you telling me this? You need to talk to my husband." Because the counselor did not include her husband in this discussion, the client may be interpreting the counselor's action as attempting to undermine her marital relationship.

Joseph and Soo Jung illustrate the fact that there are communities of clients in our pluralistic society who do not claim dominant values as their own (Carrese & Rhodes, 1995). Had you known about Navajo belief systems, or known that Korean Americans are significantly more likely than European Americans and African Americans to hold a family-centered model of decision making about health issues (Blackhall, Murphy, Frank, Michel, & Azen, 1995), you might have proceeded differently with these two clients.

What is important in this discussion of informed consent and cultural diversity is that we remember to put the client's needs first. Weinrach and Thomas (1996) suggest that counselors identify, and then focus on, the frame of reference or belief and value system that is central to the client, as one way to remain sensitive to differences. Expanding our frame of reference regarding informed consent does not mean that we must abandon our commitment to client autonomy, but it does encompass respect for the cultural values that our clients bring with them to counseling.

INTERRUPTIONS AND TERMINATION

Once a counselor has accepted a client and begins providing services, there is an assumption that those services will continue on a regular basis until the client no longer needs counseling. In reality, however, counselors sometimes have to interrupt counseling services for a period of time. In addition, counseling relationships are occasionally terminated by counselors before clients are prepared to discontinue counseling services. From both an ethical and a legal perspective, counselors must be careful to protect the best interests of clients when services have to be interrupted or prematurely terminated.

Interruptions in Services

Counselors are no different from other workers in that they take vacations, go out of town to attend conferences, and do other things that cause interruptions in the weekly rhythm of the therapeutic relationship. Clients sometimes have strong and even puzzling reactions to their counselor's absence, so it is important that the counselor give clients adequate notice and ensure that clients know whom to contact in a crisis or emergency.

If a counselor believes that a client is at risk for harm to self or others, the counselor should refer the client for an evaluation. Counselors should not have at-risk clients in their practices who are not also under the care of other professionals who have accepted responsibility for the well-being of the clients. As a result, all clients should be able to tolerate absences of their counselors for reasonable periods of time.

There is truth in Pope and Vasquez' (1991) wry observation that both counselors and clients tend to find comfort in the fantasy that the counselor is invulnerable. The reality is, however, that counselors fall seriously ill, have accidents, or are called away by family emergencies. Counselors need to plan ahead for emergency absences by developing procedures to safeguard their clients' welfare. Anticipating that unexpected events might occur, counselors should have plans in place regarding who will notify the clients, who has access to client records, and how the transfer of clients to another counselor will be handled.

Termination

Proper termination of the counseling relationship is an important ethical consideration that also has serious legal consequences if done poorly. Clients should be able to expect that their counseling sessions will end when they have received what they were seeking from counseling or when they have realized the maximum benefit from the services (*ACA Code of Ethics,* 1995 Standard A.11.c.). Because counselors always anticipate termination as a phase or stage in the counseling relationship, they need to raise and discuss the issue of termination with the client well in advance of the final session. This allows ample time to plan for the client's transition to functioning without the counselor and to deal with the natural and appropriate issues of separation and loss. It is best if the timing of the termination is mutually agreed upon, although the ultimate decision might be made independently by either the counselor or the client depending upon the circumstances.

Premature Termination

In an ideal world, all counseling relationships would end smoothly by mutual agreement. In reality, however, circumstances can arise that allow the counselor to terminate the counseling relationship even against a client's wishes. In addition to routine terminations, it is ethically permissible (*ACA Code of Ethics,* 1995 Standard A.11.c.) for counselors to terminate counseling relationships under the following circumstances:

- It is clear that the client is no longer benefitting from counseling.
- Clients do not pay the fees charged.
- Agency limits do not allow services to continue.

When counselors are unable to be of continued assistance to clients or decide to end the relationship over the client's objection, counselors must give adequate notice and give the client time to secure another mental health care provider (Hilliard, 1998). In addition, counselors should suggest an appropriate referral and do all they can to facilitate a smooth transition to the new mental health professional. If the client is unable to continue to pay the counselor's fee, an appropriate referral can be made to free services or to an agency that uses a sliding fee scale, if such alternatives are available. If a client refuses to accept the idea of a referral, the counselor is not obligated to provide free or meaningless services. The *Code of Ethics* specifies that counselors may discontinue the relationship if the client declines the referral (Standard A.11.b.).

Abandonment

Ethical guidelines (Standard A.11.a.) and legal decisions related to physicians (*Allison v. Patel,* 1993; *Manno v. McIntosh,* 1994) prohibit counselors from abandoning their clients. Once a counseling relationship has been established, the counselor cannot arbitrarily end it if the client will be put at risk as a result.

Hilliard (1998), an attorney who represents mental health professionals who are sued by their clients, has observed the events that lead individuals to sue their mental health providers. As a practical consideration, Hilliard has recommended that mental health care providers never terminate a professional relationship over a client's objection when the client is angry or when the client is in a serious crisis situation. Taking the time to address a client's distress is very important to avoid unresolved angry feelings that could lead to a lawsuit. Also, a judge or jury probably would not support a mental health professional's decision to end a relationship in the midst of a crisis (*Allison v. Patel,* 1993; *Manno v. McIntosh,* 1994).

Of course, counselors may always refer an at-risk client to a psychiatrist or health care facility that evaluates individuals for suicide or danger to themselves or others. This referral does not always lead to a transfer of that client to another professional or termination. In many circumstances, counselors continue to provide services to a referred client in collaboration with another mental health professional. It is very important, however, when a referral of an at-risk client is made that the counselor informs all parties whether the referral is a transfer of the client to another professional, or whether the counselor will be providing services in conjunction with another professional.

To protect mental health professionals from being held accountable for abandonment of their clients, Hilliard (1998) and Macbeth, Wheeler, Sither, and Onek (1994) have developed the following guidelines for mental health professionals to use when they are terminating clients in adverse circumstances:

- Honestly discuss with the client your intention to terminate and the specific reason for the your decision.
- Give the client an opportunity to make changes that would be necessary to continue the relationship.
- Give written notice to the client that the relationship will be terminated.
- Offer the client one to three termination sessions.
- Give your client up to three good referrals.
- Give your client places to contact in the event of emergencies.
- Place a summary of your interactions with the client around the termination issue in the client's file. Do not transfer that document to another individual or entity without an express written request from the client.
- Give the client plenty of time to find another mental health professional. If more time is requested, allow it.
- Transfer records to the new mental health professional promptly.

SUMMARY AND KEY POINTS

This chapter addressed three vitally important and interrelated ethical and legal issues in counseling: respect for diversity, client welfare, and informed consent. Following are key points regarding client welfare and respecting diversity:

- Counselors are ethically responsible for putting client welfare first and foremost in their work.

- Counselors have a fiduciary relationship with their clients, which means that they have a legal obligation to protect their clients' best interests and to avoid interactions that benefit themselves.
- Respecting diversity is fundamental to protecting client welfare and promoting client dignity in our pluralistic society.
- In recent years, the counseling profession has given much more recognition to cultural differences. Cultural variables include not only race, ethnicity, and nationality, but also gender, age, social class, sexual or affectional orientation, disability status, place of residence, language, and religion.
- Goals of multicultural practice include counselors becoming culturally aware of their own biases, values, and assumptions; increasing their awareness of other cultural groups; and developing culturally appropriate intervention strategies for assisting diverse clientele.
- Although the *ACA Code of Ethics* contains a number of standards that specifically address cultural diversity, counselors are advised to view all of the standards as being multicultural in spirit and intent.
- The U.S. Constitution and various statutes prohibit discrimination. When counselors work with clients who believe they have suffered illegal discrimination, counselors can assist these clients to consider their options and the possible consequences of the options.
- It is vital for counselors to be aware of their own life issues, unfinished business, areas of vulnerability, and defenses, so that they will not inadvertently be working on their own issues in the counseling relationship, rather than on the client's issues.
- Counselors must avoid fostering client dependency. They have an obligation to promote client autonomy and independence.
- Counselors have an obligation to select appropriate counseling strategies or techniques and to make clients active partners in treatment decisions.

The following are key points regarding informed consent in counseling:

- As an ethical obligation, informed consent is based on the rationale that clients have a right to know what they are getting into when they come for counseling.
- Counselors should understand that counseling services are contractual in nature. Agreements should be put in writing in an informed consent document.
- The requirement that health professionals inform prospective recipients of services and obtain their consent to treatment originated in the field of medicine. More recently, it has been applied to the mental health field. As shown in Figures 3-1 through 3-5, a number of model disclosure statements are available to assist counselors who work in various settings with a variety of clientele.
- Informed consent in counseling involves a number of elements that are required by the code of ethics, recommended by various writers, and suggested as a means to address legal concerns.
- Counselors should be aware of at least seven areas of informed consent that, if not handled properly, could lead to legal problems.
- It can be difficult to achieve a correct balance between providing prospective clients with too little information and giving them so much information that they

feel overwhelmed or intimidated. Informed consent is an ongoing process that should be conducted both orally and in written form.

- It is important for counselors to be sensitive to the fact that informed consent as traditionally conceptualized may not be respectful of people of all cultures.
- Counselors must protect the best interests and welfare of clients when counseling services have to be interrupted or terminated prematurely.
- It is unethical, as well as illegal, for counselors to abandon their clients. Although there are valid reasons for a counselor to end a counseling relationship, care must be taken not to put the client at risk when doing so. Several guidelines were offered for counselors to use when they are terminating counseling relationships in adverse circumstances.

Confidentiality and
Privileged Communication

Confidentiality is one of the most fundamental of all professional obligations in counseling. It is also one of the most problematic duties to manage in day-to-day practice. Consider, for instance, what you would do in each of the following situations.

> You have been seeing Pete, age 28, who came for counseling to resolve some family-of-origin issues that he believes are creating problems in his relationship with his partner, Jacob. During your last session together, Pete tearfully revealed that before he met Jacob, he had a series of casual sexual encounters and that he was terrified that he might have contracted the AIDS virus through these encounters. He comes to today's session with the news that he has been fully tested and is confirmed to be HIV-positive. He says he cannot tell Jacob, because he is sure Jacob will leave him if he knows.

As Pete's counselor, are you obligated to keep his secret? Or do you believe you have a duty to inform Jacob of Pete's condition, even though this would involve breaching his confidentiality? Suppose Pete tells you, after further discussion, that he realizes he must tell Jacob but needs some time to gather his courage. Would you be willing to keep his secret under this circumstance? For how long?

> As a high school counselor, you have been conducting a group for freshman and sophomore girls. The focus of the group is on building self-esteem and making wise choices. During the fourth session today, the group members begin discussing boyfriends and whether to "just say no" to sex. Marlee, a 15-year-old freshman, shares that she and her boyfriend are having sexual relations and that she thinks its okay because they are really in love. She mentions, almost in passing, that her boyfriend is 20 years old and that her parents would "kill her" if they found out about him.

As Marlee's counselor, can you keep her disclosure in confidence, or must you notify Marlee's parents? If you breach confidentiality, what are the risks to your relationship with Marlee? To the group process, to the trust that other group members may have come to feel toward you, and to your reputation for trustworthiness among the student population in general? Are these risks greater than the risks posed by keeping Marlee's relationship with her boyfriend a secret from her parents?

You are a student intern in a university counseling center. You have informed your client, Susan, that you are an intern working under supervision and that you are audiotaping the counseling sessions so that your supervisor can listen and give you feedback. Susan has had no objections to these procedures. Today, though, she says, "I'm about to get into something really personal. Can you turn off the tape recorder, please? I can't talk about this if anyone else might hear . . ."

Should you honor Susan's request? How might you respond to her concern? What do you think your supervisor would say if you were to ask how to handle the client's request?

After pondering your responses to these scenarios, you may not be surprised to learn that counselors encounter dilemmas of confidentiality more frequently than other types of ethical dilemmas and find them the most difficult to resolve (Hayman & Covert, 1986). Questions surrounding confidentiality can be very complex and often involve legal as well as ethical considerations.

A useful starting place may be to clarify the distinctions among three terms—privacy, confidentiality, and privileged communication. These terms are sometimes used interchangeably by counselors, but the concepts have important differences. Both confidentiality and privileged communication arise from our societal belief that individuals have a right to privacy. *Privacy* is the broadest of the three concepts and refers to the right of persons to decide what information about themselves will be shared with or withheld from others. Confidentiality and privileged communication both apply more specifically to the professional relationship between counselors and clients. *Confidentiality* is primarily an ethical concept that refers to the counselor's obligation to respect the client's privacy, and to our promise to clients that the information they reveal during counseling will be protected from disclosure without their consent. *Privileged communication* is the narrowest of the three terms and is a legal concept. Privileged communication laws protect clients from having confidential communications with their counselors disclosed in a court of law without their permission (Shuman & Weiner, 1987). For a communication to be privileged, a statute must have been enacted that grants privilege to a category of professionals and those whom they serve.

In this chapter, we first explore confidentiality as an ethical issue, and then discuss privileged communication. Later, we look at the numerous exceptions that exist, both to confidentiality and to privilege.

CONFIDENTIALITY

Origins of Confidentiality

Helping professionals assume that an assurance of confidentiality is an indispensable requirement for effective therapy, and that without this assurance, many clients would not feel safe to discuss openly the intimate and personal aspects of their lives or would not seek counseling. Actual studies, however, show only mixed support for this assumption. Some studies have supported the belief that privacy assurances are essential (McGuire, Toal, & Blau, 1985; Merluzzi & Brischetto, 1983; Miller & Thelen, 1986), while other studies have indicated that such assurances have little effect on encouraging disclosures (Muehleman, Pickens, & Robinson, 1985; Shuman & Weiner, 1982; Schmid, Appelbaum,

Roth, & Lidz, 1983), or that limits to confidentiality matter only to some clients in some circumstances (Taube & Elwork, 1990; VandeCreek, Miars, & Herzog, 1987). Despite this lack of unequivocal evidence, confidentiality has become such an internalized norm in the counseling profession that it is rarely questioned. A brief look at some of the historical origins of the profession may be helpful in understanding how this norm developed.

Counseling represents the fusion of many diverse influences. One of these influences was the emergence of the field of psychiatry in the treatment of mental illness. Almost until the beginning of the 19th century, mental illness was viewed as mystical and demonic. These early times are associated with images of "lunatics" in chains in asylums. It was not until the 1800s that significant strides were made in the understanding of mental illness, and not until the 1960s that the deinstitutionalization of the mentally ill brought these individuals back into contact with society. Another force that bears mentioning is the emergence of psychoanalysis in the early to middle years of this century. Patients of Freudian analysts were expected to work through their socially unacceptable urges, sexual fantasies, and repressed feelings and thoughts, and to do so in a society that held Victorian social mores! Our early notions about mental illness, and our impressions about the nature of personal material discussed in analysis, helped to create a social stigma. In this climate, it is understandable that the patient's need for absolute privacy was assumed and that people would want to hide any information related to their having sought and received treatment.

It was not until the second half of this century that other, countervailing influences emerged in the mental health field. Carl Rogers' humanistic views, theorists who emphasized the natural developmental life stages that all individuals pass through, and the career guidance movement all helped to shift our thinking away from counseling as a service only for the mentally ill or the sexually repressed. Concurrently, as we began to discover the biological bases for some mental disorders and to find medications that could alleviate conditions formerly thought to be untreatable, the stigmatization associated with mental illness and psychotherapy began to decrease. Nonetheless, even in today's society, a notion stubbornly persists that there is something shameful about seeking the services of a mental health professional. Note, for instance, the language used by the U. S. Supreme Court in its 1996 decision in *Jaffee v. Redmond,* a case we will describe later:

> Because of the sensitive nature of the problems for which individuals consult psychotherapists, disclosure of confidential communications made during counseling sessions may cause *embarrassment or disgrace* [emphasis added]. (*Jaffee v. Redmond,* 1996, p.8)

The Rationale for Confidentiality

Whatever its origin, confidentiality is universally viewed today as being essential to the counseling relationship. Clients need to know that they can trust their counselors to respect their privacy, and the counselor's confidentiality pledge is the cornerstone on which this trust is built (Herlihy & Corey, 1996). Counselors believe that effective therapy depends on an atmosphere of confidence and trust, in which clients are able to tell their stories freely, and honestly disclose their feelings, fears, thoughts, memories, and desires.

Confidentiality is a strong moral force that helps shape the manner in which counselors relate to their clients. Bok (1983) has suggested that confidentiality is based on four premises. The first two premises relate to respect for client rights in counseling. The principle of *autonomy* (which was described in the introductory chapter) means that counselors respect their clients' ability to be self-determining and to make their own choices. Applied to confidentiality, it also means that counselors honor the rights of clients to decide who knows what information about them and under what circumstances. The second premise is *respect* for human relationships and for the secrets that certain types of relationships entail. In the professional relationship, the intimate context in which these secrets are shared is seen as essential to counseling. The third premise has to do with the counselor's obligation that arises from autonomy and respect. Bok contends that an additional duty is created by a *pledge of silence,* which is the offer of confidentiality extended by the counselor to the client. Counselors are bound to this pledge both in word and deed; when they have given their word, they are obligated to actively work to protect clients' secrets from disclosure. The final basis for confidentiality is its *utility.* The rationale here is that confidentiality in counseling relationships is useful to society, because clients would be reluctant to seek help without an assurance of privacy. Society gives up its right to certain information and accepts the risks of not knowing about some problems and dangers in society in exchange for the benefit that is gained when its members improve their mental health. Stadler (1990) has cogently summarized the essential meaning of these four premises for counselors:

> The duties to respect autonomy, respect relationships, keep a pledge of silence, and reinforce its utility are *each* of great importance in counseling. When they are combined in support of the principles of confidentiality, they develop a powerful moral claim on counselors' actions. I believe the power of that claim makes confidentiality a compelling duty for counselors, more compelling than each of the duties taken separately. (p. 104)

Respect for autonomy is only one of the moral principles upon which confidentiality rests. Another is fidelity, which means being faithful and keeping promises, as we described in the introductory chapter. Certainly, one of the most important promises that counselors make to clients is that they will keep the secrets shared in counseling. One perspective on fidelity is that confidentiality is based on a covenant between counselor and client (Driscoll, 1992). In ancient sacred scriptures and myths, covenants were hallmarks of a special and intimate relationship among peoples or between peoples and their gods. In the modern world, covenants are created when one person offers another person a relationship and the offer is reciprocated. Because the basic dynamic of a covenant is trust, maintaining a covenantal relationship requires a pervasive fidelity. Any breach of confidentiality violates the bond of trust between counselor and client and breaks the covenant.

Today, confidentiality is an issue of consumer rights as well as an issue of counselor belief systems. An equally important basis for confidentiality is that clients in counseling are involved in a deeply personal relationship and have a right to expect that what they discuss will be kept private (Corey et al., 1993). Our culture has placed increasing emphasis on the rights of service recipients, and clients are more likely to hold an expectation that their privacy will be maintained by the professionals whose help they seek. This expectation of privacy has important legal as well as ethical implications, as you will discover later in the chapter.

Counselor Practices and Confidentiality

How well do practicing counselors deal with confidentiality issues? There is some evidence to suggest that counselors feel confident of their ability to make sound ethical judgments about confidentiality issues. Gibson and Pope (1993) surveyed a large national sample of counselors regarding their beliefs about a wide range of ethical behaviors. They asked respondents to rate each behavior as ethical or unethical and then to indicate on a scale of 0 (no confidence) to 10 (highest confidence) how certain they were in making these judgments. Twenty-nine percent of the items for which the confidence rating was very high (at least 9.0) concerned confidentiality.

Counselors' confidence in their ethical judgments may be well founded. Complaints made against helping professionals for violations of confidentiality are not as common as one might expect. Various studies have shown that only 1–5% of complaints made to the ethics committees and state licensing boards of counselors and psychologists involve violations of confidentiality (Garcia, Salo, & Hamilton, 1995; Garcia, Glosoff, & Smith, 1994; Neukrug, Healy, & Herlihy, 1992; Pope & Vetter, 1992; Pope & Vasquez, 1991). It appears that mental health professionals take seriously their pledge to maintain their clients' confidentiality and are diligent in honoring their responsibilities in this regard.

Complacency should be avoided, however, because statistics regarding formal complaints may not accurately reflect the actual frequency of breaches of confidentiality. According to one study, 61.9% of psychologists reported that they had *unintentionally* violated their clients' confidentiality (Pope, Tabachnick, & Keith-Spiegel, 1987b). Clients may not have been aware of these unintentional breaches. Although it may be startling to think that the majority of practitioners may have violated their clients' confidentiality, it is somewhat understandable when we pause to consider the myriad ways that an inadvertent or careless breach could occur. A few examples will illustrate this point:

New technologies present many challenges to counselors. Most counselors make some use of computers in their work and those who are not computer literate might be unaware of the special precautions needed to keep any information stored on computers secure. Sampson (1996), in the ACA *Ethical Standards Casebook,* presents an interesting (and frightening) case study involving a computer hacker on a college campus who gained access to the records of one of the clients of a counselor in the university counseling center. This hacker bragged about his accomplishment, and eventually the client learned that confidential information she had shared in her counseling sessions was known by fellow students. When the upset client confronted her counselor about this violation, the counselor was not only appalled but was at a complete loss to understand how it could have occurred.

On a related note, counselors routinely use other modern communications devices. It is important to remember that faxes, e-mail, and cellular phones are not secure means of communication and that confidential information should not be exchanged using these systems. Answering machines present another set of pitfalls. Counselors must not play back accumulated messages within earshot of others, and if the answering machine is at home, special measures need to be taken to ensure that family members and friends do not retrieve or overhear messages from or about clients.

Counselors do not always have the luxury of having a separate entrance and exit for their clients to use. When clients who are leaving their sessions must pass through a waiting area, counselors need to take special precautions to guard their clients' privacy. We know one very conscientious counselor in private practice who routinely left 15-minute intervals between the end of one scheduled appointment and the beginning of the next, and who avoided scheduling consecutively any clients from the same part of town. Nevertheless, one day she ran late with a client, who exited into the waiting room and ran into a friend from church. Both clients appeared uncomfortable to have encountered each other in this way.

Counselors are encouraged to consult with each other regarding clients who present challenges to them, and most consultations can be managed without revealing a client's identity. However, it is important not to obtain a colleague's advice while walking through the halls of an agency or institution, at a restaurant over lunch, or in another public place. Pope and Vasquez (1991) related the story of a therapist who was consulting a colleague about a particularly "difficult" client while they were on a crowded elevator. The therapist did not mention the client's name but gave enough detail that the client, who happened to be standing only a few feet behind them in the elevator, was able to ascertain that he was the subject of the discussion and to listen with intense interest and dismay.

Clearly, it is easy for even seasoned practitioners to violate a client's privacy unintentionally. Students in counselor training programs also need to take special care to maintain client confidentiality. Although it may be tempting to share with family, friends, or fellow students your excitement about what you are learning in a practicum, a practice session with a peer "client," or an experiential group, it is important to keep in mind that the ethical obligations of students are the same as those of practicing counselors. Your conversations must not reveal any information that could conceivably allow listeners to ascertain the identity of a client. Case notes, test protocols and interpretations, audiotapes, and videotapes of work with clients must not be left in places where they might be seen by anyone other than authorized supervisors or professors. It is a good idea to get into the habit of zealously safeguarding client confidentiality from the very beginning of your graduate studies.

Ethical Standards and Confidentiality

Confidentiality is the only specific ethical issue to which an entire section of the *ACA Code of Ethics* (1995) is devoted. (See Appendix A.) *Section B: Confidentiality* emphasizes the client's right to privacy in the counseling relationship. Exceptions and limitations to confidentiality are addressed and, because exceptions to confidentiality may be mandated by legal as well as ethical considerations, the standards are carefully written to minimize conflicts between law and ethics. This section addresses special circumstances in counseling minors, families, and groups, and offers guidelines for maintaining confidentiality when consulting or conducting research.

The first standard in this section is the most general. It states that, "Counselors respect their clients' right to privacy and avoid illegal and unwarranted disclosures of confidential information" (Standard B.1.a.). The next standard reminds counselors that confidentiality belongs to the *client,* not the counselor, and may be waived by the client or the client's authorized representative (Standard B.1.b.). Sometimes counselors, in their zeal to protect a client's privacy, mistakenly believe that they should maintain a client's confidentiality even when the client asks them to share information with others (Herlihy & Corey, 1996). When clients request that information be disclosed, counselors should honor these requests. If the counselor believes that releasing the information might be detrimental to the client's best interests, these concerns should be discussed with the client, but the ultimate decision belongs to the client. In many instances, client requests for disclosure are not particularly problematic for counselors, such as when clients move and later request that their records be sent to their new counselor. Other situations may cause counselors some discomfort, such as when clients ask to see their own records. It is important to realize that records are kept for the benefit of clients and that counselors are obligated to provide clients with access to their records, unless the records contain information that may be misleading or harmful to the client (Standard B.4.d.).

One of the reasons that confidentiality is such a difficult ethical issue is that *confidentiality is not absolute.* Although counselors should make every effort to avoid inadvertent breaches, there are other times when confidentiality *must* be breached. Counselors need to inform clients at the outset that there are limitations to their confidentiality. It is important to discuss thoroughly these limitations and to identify foreseeable situations in which confidentiality must be breached (Standard B.1.g.). Prospective clients may not be aware at the time they seek your services that confidentiality is not absolute. In one survey of the general public, 69% of respondents believed that everything discussed with a professional therapist would be held strictly confidential, and 74% thought that there should be no exceptions to maintaining confidential disclosures (Miller & Thelan, 1986). Counselors may be hesitant to explain the exceptions to confidentiality to new or prospective clients, for fear that clients will feel constrained in discussing their problems. However, some researchers have found very little evidence that explaining in detail the limits of confidentiality actually inhibits client disclosures. Others have concluded that the advantages of informing clients about limits outweigh any disadvantages in terms of inhibited disclosure (Baird & Rupert, 1987; Muehleman et al., 1985).

There are numerous exceptions to confidentiality. We have identified at least 15 types of situations in which compromising a client's confidentiality might be permissible or required. Because most of these exceptions to confidentiality have both a legal and an ethical basis, we will explore them in more detail after we have discussed the legal counterpart to confidentiality—privileged communication.

PRIVILEGED COMMUNICATION

At the beginning of the chapter, we noted that privacy is a broad concept that provides the underpinnings for both confidentiality and privileged communication. The right to privacy is guaranteed to all citizens by the Fourth Amendment to the U. S. Constitution, which prohibits government searches without warrants. This privacy right is not absolute, however. When the interests of society outweigh the individual's right to privacy, the privacy right is compromised in the interest of preserving a stable societal structure. The U. S. Supreme Court has never addressed the question of whether the Fourth Amendment supports the concept that some relationships are privileged because of this constitutional right to privacy. State and lower federal courts have been mixed in their results on the issue (Knapp & VandeCreek, 1987).

Basically, privileged communication means that a judge cannot order information that has been recognized by law as privileged to be revealed in court. The concept of withholding any relevant evidence is antagonistic to the entire system of justice in our country, since legal procedures demand that all evidence relevant to a case be presented to a judge or jury. The legal system also demands that the opposing side in a court case have access to the evidence before the trial takes place, through a process called discovery. As a counselor, you will surely want to guarantee that the information clients give you will be kept confidential. The idea that information and secrets revealed in a counseling session might someday be disclosed in court is very unsettling for counselors. However, the idea that a judge or jury might have to decide the outcome of a court case without the benefit of essential privileged information is very unsettling to judges.

A good question to ask, then, is, "Why did the idea of privileged communication emerge in our legal system in the first place?" According to Slovenko (1966), "A trial is only as good as the evidence presented to the court." Despite the strong belief that all evidence should be available to the judge or jury who will decide the outcome of a case, federal and state legislators have realized that the requirement to make available all evidence compromises many important interactions in our society. These legislators have been convinced that, without a guarantee of absolute privacy for conversations between citizens and certain professionals, it would be impossible for the professionals to provide necessary assistance to those who seek their help. As a result, legislators have passed statutes that specifically exempt certain conversations between citizens and professionals from the general rule in law that all relevant evidence will be presented in a court case. These laws are called privileged communication statutes.

Origins of Privileged Communication

According to Shuman and Weiner (1987), the first reference to courts recognizing a legal privilege between professionals and the citizens they served was in early Roman law. This privilege was based on the duty of servants (attorneys) to their masters (clients), rather than on the modern principle of a right to privacy.

Under the English common law, the foundation upon which the legal system in the United States is based, there was no need for privileged communication. In early England, truth during trials was determined by various modes including ". . . trial by oath or oath helpers, trial by ordeal, trial by battle, and trial by witnesses" (Shuman & Weiner, 1987, p. 50). Even when witnesses were used in trials, they were the jurors themselves who relied on information they had gathered as members of the community. Individuals who were not jurors who volunteered information were viewed as meddlers and could be sued for interfering with the legal process.

About 1450, English equity courts began recognizing subpoenas for nonparty witnesses, and started using them in law courts in 1562 (Wigmore, 1961). Yet, few communications were privileged under the English common law. Other than government secrets, the common law recognized as privileged only attorney-client and husband-wife relationships (Knapp & VandeCreek, 1987).

Once the English legal system allowed compelling witnesses to testify at trials, a question arose as to whether certain information obtained by professionals should be excluded from testimony for one reason or another. Wigmore (1961), the leading authority on evidence, described four requirements for a relationship to be privileged under the law:

1. The communications must originate in a *confidence* that they will not be disclosed.
2. This element of *confidentiality must be essential* to the full and satisfactory maintenance of the relation between the parties.
3. The *relationship* must be one that, in the opinion of the community, ought to be sedulously *fostered.*
4. The *injury* to the relationship that disclosure of the communications would cause must be *greater than the benefit* gained for the correct disposal of the litigation.

State and federal legislatures have used these requirements as criteria in considering whether to grant privilege to relationships between citizens and various categories of professionals. The question of which professional relationships meet these criteria and, therefore, should be accorded privilege has been a source of controversy that continues to this day. Some legal scholars have criticized all statutes that have been passed by legislatures granting privilege to relationships with professionals (Chafee, 1943; Cleary, 1984; Curd, 1938; Morgan, 1943; Purrington, 1906; Wigmore, 1961). The attorney-client relationship was the first professional relationship to be recognized under the English common law, during the reign of Queen Elizabeth I. The first recorded case that recognized the attorney-client privilege was decided in 1577 (Wigmore, 1961). In the United States today, the attorney-client privilege is universally recognized (Rice, 1993).

Physicians, on the other hand, have been less successful at obtaining legal privilege with their patients. According to Shuman and Weiner (1987), most legal scholars agree that the concept of a physician-patient privilege fails Wigmore's test. Every jurisdiction in the United States, except South Carolina and West Virginia, now has privileged communication statutes for physician-patient interactions (Shuman & Weiner, 1987). However, many of the statutes include a multitude of exceptions, including criminal cases, workers compensation proceedings, will contests, cases where the condition for which treatment or diagnosis was sought is raised by the patient to support a claim or defense, or cases in which the parent-child relationship is at issue.

According to Knapp and VandeCreek (1987), the clergy-communicant privilege is unique because it has its roots in the common law, but is now protected by statute. Every state except West Virginia now has a clergy-communicant privilege statute (Gumper, 1984). These statutes were passed to ensure that confessions by penitents to priests would be absolutely confidential. The clergy, in persuading legislators to pass such statutes, stressed that there was a substantial societal benefit in ensuring citizens that their confessions would never be repeated by priests or members of the clergy outside the confessional. The clergy argued that unless citizens were absolutely convinced that their confessions would remain confidential, they would not confess their sins and this could cause serious disruption to the framework of society. They asserted that the need for privacy in the confessional far outweighed the need for all evidence to be presented in a trial. The notion of extending the clergy-communicant privilege to include counseling has been criticized by Knapp and VandeCreek (1987). They argue that the privilege for recipients of mental health services should apply only when citizens have relationships with professionals with specialized training in counseling or psychotherapy, and that only a few specially trained pastoral counselors have such qualifications.

Once citizens had been granted privileged communication with attorneys, physicians, and clergy, a variety of other professionals, including mental health professionals, began arguing successfully for privileged communication statutes for the benefit of their clients. Remember, though, that any exception to the general rule that all evidence will be presented in court is compromised by privileged communications statutes. Each time such a statute is passed, the legislators have to be convinced that making an exception to the rule is vital to the well being of society, and that an individual citizen's need for privacy outweighs the need for evidence in court cases.

The earlier scholars who argued for a mental health professional-client privilege (Cottle, 1956; Fisher, 1964; Guttmacher & Weihofen, 1952; Heller, 1957; Slovenko, 1960; Slovenko & Usdin, 1961) did not base their arguments on the physician-patient privilege. Instead, they contended that citizens who sought the services of mental health professionals required more privacy than patients needed with physicians (Knapp & VandeCreek, 1987). Because of physicians' status in our society, you might think that physician-patient privilege could be considered more important than mental health professional-client privilege. However, some legal scholars (Guttmacher & Weihofen, 1952; Louisell & Sinclair, 1971; Slovenko, 1960; Wigmore, 1961) have concluded that it is more important to protect the privacy of clients of mental health professionals than it is to protect the privacy of physicians' patients because of the unique nature of the psychotherapeutic relationship.

Prior to World War II, no state had a privileged communication statute for mental health professionals, although some psychiatrists were covered under physician-patient privilege statutes (Knapp & VandeCreek, 1987). State legislative bodies meet annually, changing statutes each time they meet, and sections affecting privileged communication statutes might be found in obscure places in state statute volumes. Therefore, it is impossible to give a completely accurate picture of privileged communication statutes for counselors and other mental health professionals. However, it is true that all 50 states and the District of Columbia have enacted some type of privileged communication statute for mental health professionals and their clients (*Jaffee v. Redmond,* 1996).

Statutes making relationships between mental health professionals and their clients privileged vary substantially from state to state in their language and construction. States have taken four approaches in formulating privilege laws for relationships between clients and their mental health providers (Knapp & VandeCreek, 1987). Some privilege statutes are modeled on attorney-client privilege laws. Others take the approach of the proposed, but rejected, Rule 504 of the Federal Rules of Evidence. This rule has advantages over the attorney-client privilege laws because the proposed rules specified the extent and limitations of the privilege with great precision. A third approach provides for a privilege, but allows judicial discretion in its waiver. Finally, the last group of statutes are idiosyncratic and do not follow any special pattern.

The Rationale for Privileged Communication in Counseling Relationships

Over the past few decades, counselors have been working to convince state legislators to enact privileged communication laws that protect their relationships with clients. Many of the arguments used to justify passage of these statutes were accepted and repeated by the U. S. Supreme Court (Remley, Herlihy, & Herlihy, 1997) when *Jaffee v. Redmond* (1996) was decided in favor of the existence of such a privilege under the Federal Rules of Evidence.

Counselors have argued that society benefits when individuals seek counseling to help them lead more productive lives as citizens. Mental health professionals have argued that because clients must reveal personal secrets that could be embarrassing, sensitive, or against their best interests, clients must be assured that the content of their counseling sessions will not be revealed without their permission. Society benefits when clients receive counseling that allows them to be more independent and productive, and these benefits outweigh the negative consequences of some evidence being privileged and therefore unavailable in court cases.

However, after an extensive review and analysis of empirical research studies related to confidentiality and privileged communication in the mental health professions, Shuman and Weiner (1987) concluded that while confidentiality is important in therapeutic relationships, privilege is not. Among their more interesting findings were (a) few lay persons know whether privilege exists in their states, (b) many mental health professionals indicate that clients are reassured by their disclosure or threat of disclosure of potential harm to self or others, and (c) judges do not find privilege a great impediment to finding the truth at trials. The first two findings argue against privileged communication statutes that protect relationships with mental health professionals, while the last one would seem to support the existence of such statutes.

Another argument used to get counselor privileged communication statutes passed is that the evidence lost to courts because of privilege statutes would never have been produced in the first place if the statutes did not exist. Clients would not go to counselors and reveal their secrets if they did not have the protection of legal privilege. As a result, society does not lose important evidence in lawsuits by granting privilege to counselor-client relationships because the evidence would never have come into existence if there were no privilege.

Psychiatrists, psychologists, and social workers have been successful in their efforts to have statutes enacted that grant privileged communication to their relationships with clients. Counselors have argued that their services are similar to those of other mental health professionals, and that they are as deserving of the protection.

Recent studies have indicated that counselor-client privilege of some type existed in all except one of the states that license counselors (Glosoff, Herlihy, & Spence, in press) and that psychologist-client privilege statutes existed in all 50 states (Glosoff, Herlihy, Herlihy, & Spence, 1997). These statutes vary, ranging from some that protect counselor-client relationships to the fullest extent allowed by law to others that are quite weak. Professional counselors in jurisdictions where there are no counselor-client privileged communication statutes, or where existing ones are weak, are continuing in their efforts to get such laws passed or strengthened.

Privileged communication statutes are not always limited to interactions between clients and licensed professional counselors. In some states, school counselors, substance abuse counselors, or other designated categories of counselors have privilege. You will need to investigate the statutes of the state in which you practice to determine whether your interactions with clients enjoy privilege.

If you practice in a state that does not offer statutory privilege, you should inform your clients that you will keep confidential the content of your counseling sessions with them, but that one of the exceptions would be if a judge orders you to disclose information. You must include the same exception even if you practice in a state that does include a counselor-client privileged communication statute, but it is much less likely that a judge will order disclosure in a state with such a statute.

Occasionally, counselors will be involved in court cases heard in federal rather than state courts. A recent U.S. Supreme Court ruling, *Jaffee v. Redmond* (1996), has interpreted the Federal Rules of Evidence to mean that there is a licensed psychotherapist-patient privilege in some cases heard in federal courts (Remley, Herlihy, & Herlihy, 1997). In the Jaffee case, the psychotherapist was a social worker. It seems probable, but not guaranteed, that a similar privilege would be acknowledged for licensed counselor-client relationships in future cases.

Counselors struggle with deciding the exact language to use when writing disclosure statements for clients or when informing clients orally regarding the confidentiality and privilege that might exist in the relationship. On one hand, counselors want to fully inform clients of the exceptions that exist to confidentiality and privilege, so that clients will be able to give truly informed consent to entering the counseling relationship (see Chapter 3 on Informed Consent). On the other hand, counselors do not want to be so technical and detailed in describing exceptions to confidentiality and privilege that clients become confused or lose confidence in the privacy of the counseling relationship. Suggested disclosure statements regarding confidentiality and privilege are included in Figures 3-1 through 3-5 in Chapter 3.

Asserting the Privilege

A statutory privilege belongs to clients rather than to counselors. If you or your records are subpoenaed or if you are asked during a legal proceeding to disclose privileged information, it is up to your client to assert the privilege so that you will not have to disclose the information. However, sometimes the client cannot be located or is not present when counselors are asked to disclose privileged information. In these circumstances, the counselor has an obligation to assert the privilege on behalf of the client. Counselors should secure the advice of an attorney if they are put in the position of asserting a client's privilege, since legal procedures and questions regarding privilege are quite technical.

Responding to Subpoenas

Subpoenas are legal documents that might require counselors to produce copies of records; appear for a deposition, court hearing, or trial; or appear and bring their records with them. Subpoenas are official court documents and cannot be ignored. Counselors who do not respond appropriately to subpoenas can be held in contempt of court and could be fined or jailed until they comply. Unless you deal with subpoenas on a regular basis in your work, legal advice should be obtained before responding to a subpoena. Methods of obtaining legal advice were discussed in Chapter 1.

An attorney will review a subpoena for you and will advise you in how to respond. You should inform the attorney advising you if you believe there is a privileged communication statute that might protect the counseling relationship or records. In addition, you should tell the attorney if you think it would violate the client's privacy for you to reveal information regarding the counseling relationship.

Attorneys might assist you in a number of ways. For example, they could ask the attorney who issued the subpoena to withdraw it, file a motion to quash the subpoena, or advise you to comply with the subpoena. After you have done your best to explain to your attorney your reasons for not wanting to comply with a subpoena, you should follow the attorney's advice. In the event you violate some legal rights of your client by complying with a subpoena, and the client wants to hold you accountable, you can in turn hold your attorney accountable for giving you inaccurate or inappropriate legal advice.

If you must appear at a deposition, hearing, or trial as a result of a subpoena, you should ask your attorney to prepare you for what to expect and advise you about how you should conduct yourself. If possible, the attorney should go with you so you could be given advice throughout the proceeding. It is especially important that you have your own legal advisor with you when you attend depositions, because a judge will not be present.

Suits for Disclosure

When counseling relationships are privileged under state or federal laws, clients have a right to expect counselors to keep information from their sessions private. With or without the privilege, counselors have a legal duty to maintain the privacy of their clients. Clients enter the counseling relationship with assurances of privacy and with very high expectations that information they disclose will not be revealed.

If a counselor discloses confidential information and the disclosure does not qualify as one of the exceptions to confidentiality and privilege, a client could sue the counselor for malpractice. The client would be required to prove the elements of a malpractice suit that are explained in Chapter 6. Clients who could show that they were harmed by the counselor's disclosure might prevail in such lawsuits and collect damages from the counselor. Thus, it is crucial that you understand the exceptions to confidentiality and privileged communication and know how to apply these exceptions in your practice.

EXCEPTIONS TO CONFIDENTIALITY AND PRIVILEGED COMMUNICATION

The general rule that counselors must keep their clients' disclosures confidential is easy to understand and follow. The exceptions to this general rule, however, occur frequently in the course of counseling, and counselors must understand them and be able to apply them to real situations.

To facilitate understanding, we have organized the exceptions into clusters according to the purposes they serve. First, we discuss client waiver of the privilege or right to privacy and exceptions that deal with sharing information with subordinates or other professionals in order to improve the quality of services. Next, we turn to exceptions that involve protecting clients or others who may be in danger. Then we look at ways that confidentiality and privileged communication are different when working with multiple clients as opposed to individuals, and with minor clients as opposed to adults. Finally, we note some exceptions that are legally mandated.

Client Waiver of the Privilege

Confidentiality and privilege belong to clients, not to counselors. As a result, clients can waive their privacy. This occurs most often when clients explicitly ask counselors to give information regarding the counseling relationship to third parties. Usually, clients who waive the privilege have an understanding that their secrets will be revealed. In some circumstances, however, clients may unknowingly waive the privilege by their actions (Knapp & VandeCreek, 1987). For example, clients might implicitly waive the privilege by filing a lawsuit seeking damages for emotional distress caused by an accident or by filing a malpractice lawsuit against a mental health professional, as discussed later in the section on exceptions. In *Cynthia B. v. New Rochelle Hospital* (1982), the court found that the client had responsibility for any embarrassment or inconvenience that resulted from the disclosure of privileged mental health information in a lawsuit she had filed.

Death of the Client

According to Cleary (1984), the common law doctrine is that privilege does not end with the death of a person. In some states, statutes specifically state how privilege is controlled after an individual dies. When there is no statutory language dealing with privilege and the death of the holder, then the common law practice of allowing a legal representative of the deceased person to assert the privilege generally is followed (Knapp & VandeCreek, 1987). An executor of an estate is not always recognized by a court as a deceased person's legal representative for the purposes of privilege (*Boling v. Superior Court,* 1980). If you believe that a deceased client's privilege needs to be asserted or waived, you should contact his or her family members, probate attorney, or executor to determine whether a legal representative is available to deal with the matter.

Sharing Information with Subordinates or Fellow Professionals

In some situations, the "umbrella" of confidentiality can be extended to cover others who assist or work with the counselor in providing services to clients. While these situations do not involve a breach of the client's confidentiality, they do constitute exceptions to the general rule that only the counselor and client are privy to information shared in sessions. Sharing information with others in order to provide the best possible services to clients is permissible when (a) clerical or other assistants handle confidential information, (b) counselors consult with colleagues or experts, (c) counselors are working under supervision, and (d) other professionals are involved in coordinating client care.

Clerical or Other Assistants may Handle Confidential Information

It is routine business practice for many types of professionals, including physicians and attorneys as well as counselors, to have clerical assistants, employees, and other subordinates who handle confidential client information. Some state statutes that grant privilege to counselor-client relationships may also specifically extend the privilege to communications when assistants are present or when assistants see privileged information, but such specific language is rare. Knapp and VandeCreek (1987) have concluded that common law principles most likely would extend privilege to unprivileged assistants who are involved in activities that further the treatment of the client.

Counselors should be aware, however, that they are ethically responsible for any breach of confidentiality by someone who assists them. Standard B.1.h. alerts counselors to "make every effort to ensure that privacy and confidentiality of clients are maintained by subordinates including employees, supervisees, clerical assistants, and volunteers." Counselors may also be held legally responsible for breaches of confidentiality by their subordinates. Under the general legal principle of *respondeat superior,* employers are held responsible for the acts of their employees. Counselors, then, can be held accountable for assistants who breach confidentiality through the doctrine of vicarious liability. It is important for counselors to impress upon their employees the importance of keeping information confidential and to supervise them in such a way as to ensure they are complying with this requirement.

There are some precautions that counselors can take to help ensure that their subordinates understand both the importance of confidentiality and the procedures for maintaining it. Counselors are obligated to determine whether individuals they may hire are trustworthy. Counselors could be held accountable if they hired persons who were notorious for disregarding the privacy of others, if these persons later disclosed confidential client information. Further, we suggest that counselors take an inventory periodically of everyone who may handle confidential information about their clients. This might include answering service personnel, an office receptionist, clerical assistants, billing service staff, counselor interns or supervisees, and paraprofessionals. The counselor can conduct training sessions for these employee groups to ensure that they understand the importance of confidentiality and they know how the counselor wants them to handle confidential material.

Counselors may Consult with Colleagues or Experts

Counselors are encouraged to consult with peers or experts whenever they have questions about their ethical obligations or professional practice (Standard C.2.e.). If the questions have to do with clinical practice, counselors should seek consultation from a practitioner who has experience or expertise in the particular area of concern. If an ethical question is involved, it is a good idea to consult a fellow mental health professional who has expertise in ethics. In a particularly perplexing ethical dilemma that involves a difficult judgment call, it is wise to seek more than one opinion. Counselors should take care not to choose consultants who would be put in a conflict of interest situation if they were to give their opinion or advice regarding a particular situation or case (Standard D.2.a.).

Consultation need not involve a breach of confidentiality, because consultations can be managed without revealing the identity of the client. The ACA *Code of Ethics* gives some guidance in this respect. Standard B.6.a. states that "written and oral reports present data germane to the purposes of the consultation, and every effort is made to protect client identity and avoid undue invasion of privacy." Sometimes, because of the nature of a particular situation or because the identity of the client might be obvious, it is impossible to avoid revealing the identity of the client. In these instances, the client should be informed that you are planning to consult and the identity of the consultant should be revealed to the client.

Finally, counselors should choose consultants who have the appropriate expertise for the question at hand. If you have an ethical or clinical question, consult with a professional colleague. If you have a legal question, ask an attorney.

Confidential Information may be Shared when the Counselor is Working under Supervision

While you are a counselor-in-training, your work with actual clients will be supervised by experienced professionals. During your practicum, internship, and other field experiences, university supervisors and on-site supervisors will review your counseling sessions with you and provide you with feedback about your performance. After graduation, if you are planning to obtain a credential such as a license, your initial post-master's counseling work will also be under supervision. Some day, when you are an experienced counselor yourself, you may want to provide supervision to beginning professionals, or you may need to work under supervision while you are acquiring skills in a new specialty area of practice. Supervision is likely to be a part of your experience throughout your professional career.

Supervision situations are like consultation, in that information about clients is shared with other professionals who subscribe to your ethic of confidentiality. But in supervision, unlike consultation, the client's identity cannot be concealed. Supervisors may observe actual counseling sessions from behind a one-way mirror, review videotapes or audiotapes of sessions, and review your case notes and counseling records. Supervisors have the same obligations as you do; they must keep information revealed in counseling sessions that they are supervising confidential. Nonetheless, your clients have the right to know that you are working under supervision. According to Standard A.3.a., *Disclosure to Clients,* you have an ethical obligation to inform your clients that their confidentiality is limited because your supervisor will have access to information about them. When you are involved in group supervision, clients have the right to know that a group of your fellow practicum students or interns may also be discussing their cases.

You may feel some reluctance to divulge to your clients that you are working under supervision, or to explain to them all the circumstances under which information about them might be shared. You may be concerned that clients will have less confidence in your professional abilities, or that they will feel constrained about revealing personal information. These concerns must be set aside in the interest of your clients' right to informed consent. It is best to inform your clients about the limits to confidentiality in a straightforward manner and to do so at the very outset of the counseling relationship. Clients can be told that the purpose of supervision is to help you do a better job and that the focus of the supervision will be on you and your performance, rather than on them and their problems. Sometimes clients will be unnerved by the idea of a supervisor, who is a faceless stranger to them, sitting behind the mirror. In these cases, it is a good idea to arrange for the client to meet the supervisor and have the opportunity to express concerns and ask questions directly. In our experience as supervisors, we have seen that clients typically forget their initial concerns once they become engaged in the counseling process. You may be pleasantly surprised to find that this will happen for you, too.

Generally, the relationships between counseling students who are in supervision and their clients is not privileged. As a result, students would be forced to reveal the contents of counseling sessions if ordered to do so by a judge in a legal proceeding. Some counselors who are being supervised, however, could have privileged relationships with their clients because the counselors are licensed or because a statute in the state specifically states that such relationships are privileged. In those circumstances, the privileged counselors' supervisors would be treated under the law the same as counseling assistants, and the privilege of clients probably would not be lost due to the supervisory relationship.

Other Professionals may be Involved in Coordinating Client Care

In some settings, such as inpatient units in hospitals, treatment teams routinely work together in caring for patients. Although the benefits of coordinating the efforts of various professionals are obvious, as an ethical matter clients need to be told what information about them is being shared, with whom, and for what purposes (Herlihy & Corey, 1996). According to Standard B.1.i., when client care involves a continuing review by a treatment team, the client must be informed of the team's existence and composition.

There are numerous other situations in which you might want to share confidential client information with fellow professionals in order to ensure coordination or continuity of care. A client might be receiving psychotropic medications from a physician while seeing you for counseling. A client might be seeing you for individual counseling while being in group counseling with another therapist. Clients might move and later request that you send their records or communicate by telephone with their new therapist. In all these situations, it is ethically appropriate for you to communicate with the other professionals *when the client has given permission for you to do so.* Several standards in the ACA *Code of Ethics* address these kinds of circumstances. Standards A.4. and C.6.a. both speak to the need for mental health professionals to work cooperatively. When clients are receiving services from another mental health professional, the code directs counselors to obtain client consent and then to inform the other professional and develop clear agreements to avoid confusion and conflict for the client. Two standards relate to the transfer of records: B.4.e. requires counselors to obtain written permission from clients to disclose or transfer records to legitimate third parties, and B.4.e. and B.6.b. remind counselors that they are required to work to ensure that receivers of their records are sensitive to and able to protect the client's confidentiality.

From a legal perspective, situations in which counselors function in treatment teams or coordinate client care are similar to situations in which counselors' assistants or supervisors learn confidential information about clients. If the relationship between a counselor and a client is privileged, then it is likely that the privilege will continue to exist when confidential information is discussed in treatment teams or with other professionals when coordinating client care.

Protecting Someone Who Is in Danger

Situations sometimes arise that require the counselor to breach confidentiality in order to warn or protect someone who is in danger. Certain of these situations also involve a duty to report the dangerous situation to responsible authorities. These three types of duties— to warn, to protect, and/or to report—constitute some of the most stressful situations you will encounter as a practicing counselor.

Because these exceptions require that you make a deliberate decision to breach a client's confidentiality, there must be a compelling justification for doing so. Winston (1991) suggests that breaching a confidence can be justified by the concept of vulnerability. A duty to protect from harm arises when someone is especially dependent on others or in some way vulnerable to the choices and actions of others. Persons in a vulnerable position are unable to avoid risk of harm on their own and are dependent on others to intervene on their behalf. When counselors, through their confidential relations with clients, learn that a vulnerable person is at risk of harm, they have a duty to act to prevent the harm. This is a higher duty than the duty to maintain confidentiality.

Counselors must Take Action when They Suspect Abuse or Neglect of Children or Other Persons Presumed to have Limited Ability to Care for Themselves

Although the ACA *Code of Ethics* does not specifically address child or elder abuse reporting, we have seen that counselors do have a general ethical duty to protect vulnerable persons from harm. It appears that many mental health professionals do not routinely report child abuse and that confidentiality is the crucial variable that causes them to fail to make such reports (Corey et al., 1993; MacNair, 1992). Counselors may be reluctant to report for several reasons. These include their desire to avoid betraying a child's trust, fear that a child protective services investigation will be poorly handled, or hope of maintaining the counseling relationship with the family so that the abusing adults can be helped to learn more appropriate parenting skills. Nonetheless, in cases of abuse, the need for absolute confidentiality in counseling is not as great as the need to protect children.

The duty to report suspected physical, sexual, or emotional child abuse or neglect is a legal requirement as well. Some statutes include a requirement to protect the elderly, developmentally disabled, residents of institutions, or other vulnerable adults. This reporting obligation is clear, but counselors still must exercise clinical judgment in making a determination that some vulnerable person has been abused or is being abused.

All states and U.S. jurisdictions now have mandatory reporting statutes of some type in the area of child abuse. It is vital for counselors to know the exact language of statutes that require them to make reports of suspected abuse. These statutes can be found in any public library. Reference librarians can help you locate the statutes for your state and the index for the statutes will lead you to abuse reporting laws. The exact language of the statute in your state is important because the laws vary significantly. It is important to determine whether reports must be made only for suspected child abuse or for suspected abuse of elders, disabled persons, or vulnerable citizens in other categories.

In addition, counselors need to know which categories of professionals must make suspected abuse reports and whether reports must be made only for suspected current abuse, or for suspected past abuse as well. Reporting statutes protect mandatory reporters from lawsuits that might be filed against them by those who have been reported, but only if the report is mandated by law. If reports of suspicions of past abuse are not mandated by law, then counselors making reports of past abuse would not be protected. Where counselors work, their job titles, their licensing status, and other such factors may determine whether they are mandated by statute to make suspected abuse reports. The protective clauses of mandatory abuse reporting laws protect counselors who make suspected abuse reports in "good faith." In other words, as long as counselors sincerely believe that abuse may have occurred or is occurring, they will be protected from lawsuits that might be filed against them by individuals who have been reported.

Before counselors determine that they have a legal obligation to file a report, they must form a clinical opinion that a possibility exists that a child has been or is being abused. Suspicion regarding abuse might arise as the result of something a counselor observes, such as seeing marks on children or observing behavior that indicates abuse, or something someone says in a counseling session. Also, clients may reveal that they have been abused or that they have perpetrated abuse on others. If you are unsure whether you have enough information to form a suspicion that abuse is involved, consult with colleagues.

The language of the statute in your state also tells you who must make an actual suspected abuse report and where and how the report must be filed. In some states, counselors can fulfil their legal obligation by telling their supervisors that they suspect abuse, and then it is the supervisors' legal obligation to file the report. In other states, the counselor who suspects abuse has the legal obligation to personally file the report. Some statutes require oral reports only; others demand that written reports be filed as well within certain time frames. Five mandatory abuse reporting statutes from various U.S. jurisdictions are included in Appendix C to demonstrate how they differ in details. You are encouraged to locate and read carefully the mandatory abuse reporting statutes in your jurisdiction.

In addition to following statutory requirements in making mandatory suspected abuse reports, counselors also must follow any procedures in effect in their employment setting. For example, a school district might require that a building principal be notified and a written report be filed before a report is made to state authorities, even when the counselor is mandated by law to make the report personally.

It is important that counselors not forget their professional obligations to clients in fulfilling their legal obligations to make suspected abuse reports (Remley & Fry, 1993). Abuse reports are very disruptive to families. The lives of victims, perpetrators, and family members can be changed significantly when suspected child abuse reports are made. While making a report of suspected abuse may end your legal duties, your responsibilities as a counselor in the situation may continue for a long period of time.

Counselors must Take Action when a Client Poses a Danger to Others

The duty to warn an identifiable or foreseeable victim of a dangerous client arose out of the landmark *Tarasoff v. Regents of University of California* (1976) court case, which established the following legal concept in California.

. . . when a psychotherapist *determines,* or pursuant to the standards of his profession *should determine,* that a patient presents a serious danger or violence to others, the therapist incurs an obligation to use reasonable care to protect the foreseeable victim from such danger (*McClarren*, 1987, p. 273).

Although the Tarasoff doctrine has not been accepted or applied in every jurisdiction in the United States, counselors have chosen to incorporate it into their *Code of Ethics* (American Counseling Association, 1995) and generally assume that the concept is a national legal requirement.

The facts in the Tarasoff case are important in understanding the duty that has been imposed on counselors. Prosenjit Poddar was a 26-year-old graduate student at the University of California at Berkeley. In the course of a session with his counselor, Poddar confided his intention to kill his girlfriend, Tatiana Tarasoff. His counselor was Dr. Lawrence Moore, a psychologist in the university counseling center. Because Moore believed that Poddar might be serious regarding his threat, Moore initiated proceedings to have Poddar committed for psychiatric evaluation. Moore orally notified two campus police officers of his intentions to commit Poddar and then sent a letter to the police chief requesting assistance from the police department. The police took Poddar into custody, but released him when he promised not to contact Tarasoff. Poddar never went to see Moore again. Neither Moore nor the police notified Tarasoff of Poddar's threat. Two months later, Poddar stabbed and killed Tarasoff on the front porch of her parents' home. Tarasoff's parents sued Moore in a wrongful death action for not confining Poddar and not warning Tarasoff of the threat against her life.

Decisions subsequent to the Tarasoff case throughout the United States have interpreted the holding of the case differently. Many courts have limited application of it to situations in which the victims are readily identifiable. Other courts, however, have extended the duty to all persons who are endangered by the patient's condition or threats (McClarren, 1987). In *Lipari v. Sears, Roebuck & Co.* (1980), a federal court held that a psychotherapist has a duty to warn and protect unknown victims, as well as those who are readily identifiable. This case extended a counselor's duty to those persons who are foreseeably endangered by a client's conduct.

A Washington state court, following the Lipari decision, held that a psychiatrist could possibly be held responsible for injuries sustained by a traffic accident victim. The victim was hurt when a drug-abusing patient, released by the psychiatrist, ran a red light while under the influence of drugs (*Petersen v. State,* 1983). Two California cases expanded the Tarasoff doctrine by no longer requiring that a psychotherapist be able to readily identify the patient's victim (*Hedlund v. Superior Court of Orange County,* 1983; *Jablonski v. United States,* 1983).

In a Vermont case, the supreme court held that a mental health professional has a duty to take reasonable steps to protect a third party from threats of damage to property posed by a patient (*Peck v. Counseling Service of Addison County, Inc.,* 1985). In the Peck case, the court found that a counselor could be held responsible for property damage when a client burned down a barn. The client told the counselor he intended to do so, and the counselor did not warn the owners of the barn.

Originally, the Tarasoff holding imposed a duty to warn only if the victim was specifically identifiable. Subsequent decisions have extended that duty to include warning persons who are unknown, persons who are unintentionally injured by a patient, whole classes of persons of which the victim is a member, bystanders who might be injured by a patient's negligent act, and individuals whose property a client has threatened to destroy (McClarren, 1987).

Decision making for counselors around the Tarasoff legal requirements is complex. First, you must decide whether a particular client has the potential of harming another person, or perhaps even an individual's property. Making this decision is difficult, since there is no scientific basis for such decisions. If you do determine that a client is a danger to another person, then you must take the steps necessary to prevent harm. This includes warning intended victims, whether or not their identity is known. In making these difficult decisions, it is essential to consult with other mental health professionals and to include supervisors to the extent possible.

What began as a legal requirement has now evolved into an ethical duty as well. Standard B.1.c. of the ACA *Code of Ethics* states that the counselor's confidentiality requirement "does not apply when disclosure is required to prevent clear and imminent danger to the client or others." This particular exception to confidentiality has caused considerable confusion and consternation among helping professionals, not only because it involves breaching confidentiality but also because it demands that counselors be able to predict dangerousness. Human behavior is not always predictable, and counselors may find themselves caught on the horns of a dilemma, both ethically and legally, in determining whether to breach a client's confidentiality in order to warn an intended victim. Think about how you might react if you were counseling a client who made a threat to harm someone else. If you were to decide that the client was only venting anger and was not likely to act on the threat, and then later the client carried out the threat, you would have acted ethically in trusting your professional judgment and in preserving confidentiality and the counseling relationship. That would be little solace, however, if someone were killed or seriously injured. Also, the question might arise before an ethics committee or in a court as to whether you could have acted, or should have acted, to avert that harm. On the other hand, if you were to decide that the danger was in fact clear and imminent and you were to issue a warning, no harm would be done to a third party. If the client did nothing, however, you would have erred in labeling the client dangerous and your actions probably will destroy the counseling relationship. You could be accused of misdiagnosis, defamation of character, or violating confidentiality (*Hopewell v. Adebimpe,* 1982). It is no wonder that counselors view these as no-win situations and might be tempted to simply avoid working with dangerous clients. Yet, it would be ethically questionable to close the doors of the counseling profession to a group of individuals who clearly need our help (Herlihy & Sheeley, 1988).

Research indicates that it is impossible to predict whether a particular person is going to harm someone else, yet the law and our ethical standards require counselors to determine whether a client is dangerous. How can this legal and ethical duty be fulfilled? First, it is important to learn as much as you can about the warning signs of persons who commit violent acts against others. For example, it appears that the best predictor of violence is past violent behavior (Litwack, Kirschner, & Wack, 1993; McNiel & Binder, 1991; Megargee, 1979; Meloy, 1987; Monahan, 1995; Mulvey & Lidz, 1995; Slovic & Monahan, 1995; Truscott, Evens, & Mansell, 1995).

Once you have determined that a client is indeed dangerous and might harm another person, the law then requires that you take whatever steps are necessary to prevent the harm, and further, that the steps you take are the least disruptive (Rice, 1993). You have choices that range from the least intrusive action (obtaining a promise from your client not to harm anyone else) to the most intrusive (having the client involuntarily committed to a psychiatric facility). There are numerous possibilities in between these two extremes, such as notifying the client's family members and getting one of them to take responsibility for keeping the client under control, persuading the client to be voluntarily committed to a residential facility, notifying the police, or calling the client periodically. There certainly are no right formulas for action when you determine that your client is dangerous. If at all possible, consult with other mental health professionals and use their input in making your decision. One thing is clear, however. Because of the Tarasoff case, when you determine that a client might harm an identifiable or foreseeable person, you must directly or indirectly warn that individual of the danger.

Counselors must Take Action to Protect Clients who Pose a Danger to Themselves

When clients threaten to commit suicide, an ethical duty arises to protect the client from harm to self. The ethical standard that applies to clients who pose a danger to others applies to suicidal clients as well: confidentiality requirements are waived when disclosure is required to "prevent clear and imminent danger to the client or others" (Standard B.1.c.). Evaluating and managing suicide risk is one of the most stressful situations that you will encounter in your work (Corey et al., 1993). You will need to be prepared to take measures to prevent a suicide attempt. These begin with a thorough risk assessment and then, depending on the level of danger, might include involving the client's family or significant others, working with the client to arrange for voluntary hospitalization, or even initiating the process that leads to an involuntary commitment of the client. All of these interventions are disruptive and compromise the client's confidentiality. Ethically, it is important to disclose only information you consider essential in order for someone else to help prevent a suicide attempt (Standard B.1.f.).

Similar to situations in which clients threaten harm to others, the counselor's first responsibility is to determine that a particular client is in danger of attempting suicide. There is no sure way to determine this, but experts agree that individuals who commit suicide generally give cues to those around them in advance (Capuzzi, 1994; Capuzzi & Golden, 1988; Curran, 1987; Davis, 1983; Hafen & Frandsen, 1986; Hussain & Vandiver, 1984; Johnson & Maile, 1987). Further, in most circumstances, a counselor's determination of a client's level of risk must be based on clinical observations, not on test results.

As noted above, determining that a client is at risk of committing suicide leads to actions that can be exceptionally disruptive to the client's life. Just as counselors can be accused of malpractice for neglecting to take action to prevent harm when a client is determined to be suicidal, counselors also can be accused of wrongdoing if they overreact and precipitously take actions that violate a client's privacy or freedom when there is no basis for doing so. As a result, counselors have a legal duty to evaluate accurately a client's potential for suicide. Counselors can be held liable for overreacting and for underreacting. So, how should a determination be made as to whether a client is suicidal?

First, no matter where you work as a counselor, you are likely to provide services to individuals who might express suicidal thoughts. Therefore, it is necessary for all counselors to know the warning signs that indicate that a particular person is more at risk for committing suicide than are other individuals. An old legal case (*Bogust v. Iverson*, 1960) held that a college counselor was not a mental health professional and therefore had no duty to assess a client's risk of suicide. Since then, however, counselors have established themselves as mental health professionals, and the law imposes on counselors practicing in all settings the responsibility of knowing how to accurately determine a client's risk of suicide (Bursztajn, Gutheil, Hamm, & Brodsky, 1983; Drukteinis, 1985; Howell, 1988; Knuth, 1979; Perr, 1985).

There is much help available in the professional literature, including research studies and articles that provide information about warning signs of future suicidal behavior (Berman & Cohen-Sandler, 1982; Cantor, 1976; Meneese & Yutrzenka, 1990; Sudak, Ford, & Rushforth, 1984). Today's counselors must know how to make assessments of a client's risk for suicide and must be able to defend their decisions at a later time.

The law does not require that counselors always be correct in making their assessments of suicide risk, but the law does require that counselors make those assessments from an informed position and that they fulfill their professional obligations to a client in a manner comparable to what other reasonable counselors operating in a similar situation would have done. Because of this standard of care to which counselors are held, the very best action you can take if you are unsure whether a client is at risk for a suicide attempt is to consult with other mental health professionals who are similar to you. It also is important to look for consensus among your consultants and certainly to follow their advice in making your final decision about what to do in a particular case.

When you make a decision that a client is a danger to self, you must take whatever steps are necessary to prevent the harm, and your actions must be the least intrusive to accomplish that result. Again, consulting with colleagues could be very helpful. Many counselors require a possibly suicidal client to submit to an evaluation by a mental health professional who has particular expertise in the area of suicide. For example, you might demand that your client see a psychiatrist who is on the staff in the facility where you work, if that is an option. Or you might require your client to submit to a mental evaluation at a local hospital where psychiatric services are available. Of course there are other, less intrusive, options available. But you should choose a less intrusive option only if you are sure the client is not at imminent risk.

Counselors Need to Determine Whether to Breach Confidentiality when a Client has a Fatal, Communicable Disease and the Client's Behavior is Putting Others at Risk

The advent of AIDS has placed mental health professionals in a quandary. Do therapists have an ethical duty to warn when a client is HIV-positive or AIDS-confirmed and could be putting others at risk through such behaviors as unprotected sex or needle sharing? According to Standard B.1.d., *Contagious, Fatal Diseases,* of the ACA *Code of Ethics,* when a counselor receives information confirming that a client has a disease commonly known to be both communicable and fatal, the counselor is "justified in disclosing information to an identifiable third party, who by his or her relationship with the client is at a high risk of contracting the disease."

Note that, according to ethical guidelines, counselors are *justified* in disclosing, but are not necessarily *required* to disclose, information to an endangered third party. You will need to weigh a number of factors and determine your own stance regarding arguments that have been offered both for and against breaching confidentiality in working with AIDS clients. Some writers (Driscoll, 1992; Melton, 1991; Perry, 1989) have made the following arguments in favor of maintaining confidentiality. Breaches of confidentiality are especially countertherapeutic when working with clients who have a high level of mistrust due to discrimination against them (for instance gay men, prostitutes, and intravenous drug users). Exposure to HIV does not carry the same level of risk as a homicidal client who threatens to use a lethal weapon; not every exposure to HIV results in harm. Individuals who have consented to unsafe sex practices or sharing needles that could be contaminated must take responsibility for their own choices. If the client's confidentiality is compromised, the client is likely to discontinue therapy, and the problems that contribute to continuation of high-risk behavior (such as fear of abandonment and loss of control) will be exacerbated.

Other writers have argued for disclosure (Cohen, 1997; Erickson, 1993; Gray & Harding, 1988), pointing out that confidentiality is not an end in itself and that the need to protect someone who may be at risk of contracting a fatal disease creates a higher duty. They suggest that, with AIDS having reached epidemic proportions, mental health professionals have an obligation to do their part to protect the health and welfare of society at large when AIDS clients are putting others at risk. These writers also argue that, although it is an injustice that clients with AIDS suffer from discrimination, the protection of others must take precedence over the possibility of discrimination.

It is crucial that you use your clinical judgment in these cases and that you evaluate each AIDS confidentiality dilemma on a case-by-case basis (Harding, Gray, & Neal, 1993; Kain, 1989). To be in compliance with the ethical standards, it is imperative that you do not act hastily to breach confidentiality. First, you should ascertain that your client really does have AIDS or actually is HIV positive. Often, a consultation with the client's physician is necessary. You should obtain your client's permission for such a consultation. Since AIDS/HIV status is a medical condition, in many circumstances informing the client's physician of your concern about the client endangering others will transfer the obligation of protecting others to the physician.

If you believe you must take responsibility because a physician is not available, then you must determine whether your client has already informed the partner or other third party or is intending to do so in the immediate future. It is preferable that clients make their own disclosures, so you might continue to work with the client in exploring the client's willingness to assume this responsibility, or you might involve the partner in the counseling process.

In some jurisdictions, specific statutes have been passed that address the issue of AIDS and the duty to warn. When your clients who have AIDS or who are HIV positive refuse to disclose their condition to an endangered third party and you believe that you must do so, you will need to be aware of any applicable state laws that might restrict or guide your reporting options. Without a doubt, keeping abreast of legal and ethical obligations related to HIV/AIDS will continue to pose real challenges for counselors as more is learned about ways to transmit, prevent, and eventually, cure the disease.

To summarize, your work with clients who are dangerous to themselves or others will be fraught with ethical and legal complexities. It is important to keep up with the literature in this area and to familiarize yourself with guidelines for practice regarding the duty to warn, such as those offered by Costa and Altekruse (1994). Whenever possible, you should consult with fellow professionals (Standard B.1.c.) if you are in doubt about whether you have a duty to warn, protect, or report in a given situation.

Counseling Multiple Clients

Unique confidentiality problems arise when working with multiple clients. Generally, when your client and one or more additional persons are in the room, confidentiality is compromised and privilege often is waived. Although you can make your own pledge not to disclose certain information, you cannot guarantee the behavior of others such as group participants or family members. Despite the fact that others in the room might not keep a client's secrets, a counselor's responsibility is not diminished by the presence of additional persons in a counseling session.

Confidentiality cannot be Guaranteed in Group Counseling

Confidentiality is a particularly difficult ethical issue in group counseling. Although confidentiality certainly is as important in group counseling as it is in individual counseling, it is difficult to enforce. Group counselors frequently encounter problems with maintaining confidentiality among group members who are not bound by the same professional standards. They may inadvertently breach confidentiality or yield to the temptation to discuss group experiences with family or friends. The ACA *Code of Ethics* gives some specific guidance for dealing with confidentiality in groups. Standard B.2. states that "counselors clearly define confidentiality and the parameters for the specific group being entered, explain its importance, and discuss the difficulties related to confidentiality involved in group work." This standard also requires you to clearly communicate to group members the fact that confidentiality cannot be guaranteed. A significant portion of the ethical guidelines of the Association for Specialists in Group Work (ASGW, 1989) is devoted to confidentiality among group members. This is an especially helpful resource with which you will want to familiarize yourself.

A few states specifically provide for privilege to extend to group counseling situations, but most privileged communication statutes are silent on this issue (Knapp & VandeCreek, 1987). It is important, then, that you read the privileged communication statute in your state (if one exists for counseling relationships) to determine whether group counseling sessions are privileged. In states where group counseling situations are not mentioned, at least one court has found privilege to exist (*State v. Andring,* 1984). As a result of the Andring case, it is possible that group counseling sessions would be found by courts to be privileged even if statutes do not specify that privilege exists for group counseling clients.

Confidentiality cannot be Guaranteed in Couples or Family Counseling

When the focus of counseling shifts from the individual to the family system, new ethical issues arise and existing ones become more complicated. Counselors who provide services for couples and families encounter some unique confidentiality concerns, such as how to deal with family secrets. For example, what would you do in the following situation?

> A husband and wife are seeing you for marriage counseling. The husband shared during one of his individual sessions with you that he is having an affair, but his wife doesn't know, he doesn't plan to tell her, and he doesn't want you to tell her.

This scenario points up the importance of informed consent procedures. You would need to make clear to both marital partners at the outset how you will handle confidentiality issues. According to Standard B.2.b., in family counseling, "information about one family member cannot be disclosed to another family member without permission." Therefore, you would be ethically bound to keep the husband's secret unless you had established ground rules to deal with such a situation. For instance, you might have told the couple initially that, if either of them had a secret they were withholding from the other that would interfere with the goals or process of counseling, and if they refused to discuss that secret, you would not be able to continue to work with them as a couple.

Counseling couples or families can also lead to very difficult legal questions regarding confidentiality and privilege. Under general legal principles, any statutory privilege that exists between a counselor and client is waived if there is a third party present when information is being disclosed. However, privilege laws in some states specifically cover relationships between counselors and married couples or between counselors and family members (Knapp & VandeCreek, 1987). In these states, it is clear that a counseling relationship will be privileged despite specific additional persons being present during the counseling session. In states without such statutes, it is unclear whether an individual who is being counseled with a spouse or other family members present could assert the privilege. Appellate court decisions are split as to whether a privilege that otherwise would exist by statute would be extended to sessions that include a married couple (*Clausen v. Clausen,* 1983; *Ellis v. Ellis,* 1971; *Sims v. State,* 1984; Virginia Court, 1979; *Wichansky v. Wichansky,* 1973; *Yaron v. Yaron,* 1975).

A very difficult dilemma for counselors is posed when one spouse demands that the counselor not reveal information related in a marital counseling session, and the other spouse demands that the counselor reveal it. Situations like this often arise when a married couple enters counseling because of marital problems and then later engage in divorce proceedings.

The spouse who does not want the contents of the counseling sessions revealed should assert the privilege through his or her attorney. Of course, a counselor never wants to reveal in court private information that was related in a counseling session. Counselors generally will cooperate with the spouse and attorney as arguments are made to maintain the privilege of the client who does not want the private information revealed. Counselors are quite vulnerable legally in these situations because revealing privileged information inappropriately could lead to a malpractice lawsuit. On the other hand, refusing to disclose information that is not privileged could lead to being found in contempt of court. If you find yourself in a situation like this and are unsure of your legal responsibilities, you should consult your own attorney who will advise you regarding your legal obligations and rights.

Counseling Minor Clients

When Clients are Minor Children, Counselors Cannot Give the Same Assurances of Confidentiality as They Give to Adult Clients

Conflicts between law and ethics arise very clearly in situations where the client is a minor. Every child, regardless of age, has a moral right to privacy in the counseling relationship. From a philosophical viewpoint, many counselors would argue that children should have the same rights to confidentiality as adult clients. The legal rights to confidentiality and privilege of minors are more limited, however. Basically, counselors have an ethical obligation of privacy to minor clients, and a legal obligation to the parents or legal guardians of those same minor clients to keep their children safe.

Generally, the law regarding parent-child relationships would lead to the conclusion that parents determine the need for counseling for their children, that parents have access to information obtained within the counseling relationship, and that parents control the release of information resulting from counseling relationships with their children (Knapp & VandeCreek, 1987). Statutes in some states provide for minors to obtain counseling independent of their parents' permission (Weinapple & Perr, 1979). This might lead to an argument that minors who do not have to have parental permission to enter counseling should be able to protect their privacy interests from their parents, but this argument has not been accepted by any courts up to this point.

As a counselor, you should respect your minor clients' right to control access to personal information, to the extent that it is possible for you to do so. Minor clients should have some control over the release of information that results from their choosing to engage in the counseling process (Huey, 1996). Answers to confidentiality questions may vary, depending on the age of the client and the setting in which the counseling takes place. Very young children are often not nearly as concerned about confidentiality as the counselor is, while these concerns may be paramount for adolescent clients. According to Hendrix (1991), community mental health counselors tend to favor giving minors the same confidentiality rights that adults have, while school counselors (particularly those at the elementary school level) feel more responsibility to release information to parents.

Counselors who work with minor clients need to respect parents' rights and responsibilities for their children, yet they want to honor the confidentiality rights of their clients. These two demands need not necessarily be in conflict. While the code of ethics requires counselors to act in their minor clients' best interests and take measures to safeguard confidentiality, the code also states that "parents or guardians may be included in the counseling process as appropriate" (Standard B.3.). This standard reinforces the fact that the relationship between parent and counselor need not be adversarial. In fact, parents can be valuable allies in the counseling process (Huey, 1996). Counselors should understand that any time they decide to withhold information from a parent, they assume responsibility if that information later leads to injuries for the client. Examples of such potentially injurious information include minors disclosing that they are using controlled substances, engaging in sexual activity, breaking laws, or engaging in other risky behavior that their parents do not know about.

Sometimes parents request information that you believe is not in the child client's best interests to divulge. In these instances, we suggest that you approach the problem in the following sequential manner:

1. Discuss the request with the minor to determine whether the child is willing to disclose.
2. If the child is unwilling, try to educate the adult about the nature of the counseling relationship, assure the adult they will be informed if the child is engaged in any behavior that might lead to harm, and attempt to persuade the adult that the child's interests are not served by disclosure.
3. If the parent continues to demand disclosure, schedule a joint session with the adult and the child and hope they resolve the matter between themselves.
4. If none of these interventions works, finally inform the child before making the disclosure over the child's objection.

To avoid situations in which parents demand information and minor clients refuse to authorize you to provide it, it is wise to have a thorough understanding with all parties regarding the issue of confidentiality before the counseling relationship is initiated. The use of written agreements among counselors, their minor clients, and the parents of minors would be helpful to avoid misunderstandings.

Generally, a parent or guardian has a legal right to assert the privilege that would belong to a minor. However, in some circumstances courts have found that parents did not have the best interests of the child in mind and have refused to allow the parents to assert a child's privilege (*People v. Lobaito,* 1984). Courts have also appointed a *guardian ad litem* to determine the best interests of a child related to privilege (*Nagle v. Hooks,* 1983).

All of the issues related to minor clients apply equally to any adult clients who have been legally adjudicated mentally incompetent or who have had legal guardians appointed based on their diminished capacity (such as elderly, physically disabled, or developmentally disabled individuals). Although these clients have a right to privacy, their legal guardians have the right to determine what is in their best interests.

Court Ordered Disclosures

Counselors must Disclose Confidential Information when Ordered to Do so by a Court

There will be instances when counselors are called to testify in court, and their clients will ask them not to reveal information shared in counseling sessions. If the relationship is privileged, either the client or the counselor will assert the privilege. In cases where no privilege exists, counselors should ask the court not to require the disclosure and explain the potential harm that could be done to the counseling relationship (Standard B.1.e.). If the judge still requires the disclosure, only essential information should be revealed (Standard B.1.f.). Counselors who are ordered by a judge to reveal confidential information should not worry that clients may sue them for violating their privacy. Complying with a judge's order is a defense to any charge of wrong doing (Prosser, 1971). Remember though, that a subpoena may not be valid. Confidential or privileged information should not be revealed in response to a subpoena until an attorney representing the counselor has advised that course of action.

Legal Protections for Counselors in Disputes

Counselors may Reveal Confidential Information when it is Necessary to Defend Themselves against Charges Brought by Clients

When ethical or legal complaints are filed against counselors by their clients, the concepts of confidentiality or privilege could become problematic for counselors who must defend themselves. It would be odd if a client could claim that a counselor had done something wrong in a counseling relationship, and then the same client could claim that confidentiality or privilege prevented the counselor from explaining the details of the counseling relationship in presenting his or her defense. As a result, the law of privileged communication requires that clients waive their privilege when they bring complaints or malpractice lawsuits against their counselors (Knapp & VandeCreek, 1987).

Other Legal Exceptions

Clients Waive their Privilege when They Bring Lawsuits Claiming Emotional Damage

If clients claim emotional damage in a lawsuit, then the law automatically waives their privilege associated with counseling relationships (Knapp & VandeCreek, 1987). It would be unfair to allow individuals to claim in court that they had been emotionally damaged, and then to prohibit the counselor who had treated the person for the damage from testifying. The person accused of damaging the client must be given an opportunity in a court proceding to cross-examine the counselor regarding the nature and extent of the damage.

Nonetheless, most courts have held that suits for normal distress or physical injuries arising out of a physical trauma do not automatically waive a plaintiff's right to privilege in counseling relationships (*Ideal Publishing Corp. v. Creative Features,* 1977; *Roberts v. Superior Court,* 1973; *Tylitzki v. Triple X Service, Inc.,* 1970; *Webb v. Quincy City Lines, Inc.,* 1966). Only when individuals bringing lawsuits claim that they were emotionally damaged and that damage required them to seek mental health treatment will their therapeutic privilege be waived.

Privilege is Generally Waived in Civil Commitment Proceedings

Privilege is usually waived by law for individuals who are being evaluated by a court to determine whether they should be involuntarily committed to a psychiatric hospital. Obviously, the contents of an evaluation conducted for the purpose of rendering an opinion to a court concerning the advisability of a commitment will not be privileged. Evaluators should carefully explain the nature of the interview to individuals who are being evaluated to ensure that the individual does not misconstrue the relationship as involving mental health treatment (Knapp & VandeCreek, 1987). When a mental health professional seeks a commitment of a client who initiated treatment voluntarily, privilege may also be waived by the client by law (*Commonwealth ex rel. Platt v. Platt,* 1979), although in *People v. Taylor* (1980) a Colorado court refused to waive the privilege. Individuals who are involuntarily committed do not have privileged relationships with their treating mental health professionals at a judicial review of that commitment (*State v. Hungerford,* 1978; *State v. Kupchun,* 1977). The important distinction to remember is that evaluation interviews are different from counseling interviews in terms of privilege. Evaluation interviews conducted to help determine whether a client should be committed to a residential facility are not privileged.

See Figure 4-1 for a summary of the exceptions to confidentiality and privileged communication that were just covered.

SUMMARY AND KEY POINTS

After reading this chapter, we expect that you have developed a healthy appreciation for the complexities of the ethic of confidentiality and its legal counterpart, privileged communication. We also expect that you have a clearer understanding of why counselors encounter dilemmas of confidentiality more frequently than they encounter other types of dilemmas and find them the most difficult to resolve. The considerable amount of information contained in this chapter should be helpful. These dilemmas, nevertheless, will challenge you to use your clinical judgment, and your skills in ethical reasoning and in researching the current status of professional knowledge and the law. We hope we have emphasized how important it is that you do not try to go it alone when you encounter questions about confidentiality and privileged communication, but rather that you seek consultation from colleagues or an attorney. Following are some of the key points made in the chapter:

- Both confidentiality and privileged communication are based in the client's right to privacy. Confidentiality is an ethical concept, and privileged communication is a legal term.

Sharing information with subordinates or fellow professionals is permissible under the following circumstances:

- Clerical or other assistants handle confidential information.
- A counselor consults with colleagues or experts.
- The counselor is working under supervision.
- Other professionals are involved in coordinating client care.

Protecting someone who is in danger may require disclosure of confidential information when the following conditions exist:

- The counselor suspects abuse or neglect of children or other persons presumed to have limited ability to care for themselves.
- A client poses a danger to others.
- A client poses a danger to self (is suicidal).
- A client has a fatal, communicable disease and the client's behavior is putting others at risk.

Confidentiality is compromised when counseling multiple clients, including the following:

- Group counseling
- Counseling couples or families

There are unique confidentiality and privileged communication considerations when working with minor clients:

- Counseling minor clients

Certain exceptions are mandated by law, including the following:

- Disclosure is court ordered.
- Clients file complaints against their counselors.
- Clients claim emotional damage in a lawsuit.
- Civil commitment proceedings are initiated.

Figure 4-1   Exceptions to Confidentiality and Privileged Communication

- Although research does not clearly support the notion that assurances of privacy are essential to clients' willingness to disclose, counselors view confidentiality as a strong moral force and a fundamental ethical obligation.
- In general, counselors seem to do a very good job of protecting their clients' confidentiality. It is easy for an inadvertent breach to occur, however, and counselors need to be zealous in safeguarding client privacy.
- Privileged communication means that a judge cannot order a counselor to reveal information in court that has been recognized by law as privileged. Because privileged communication is antagonistic to the entire U.S. system of justice, courts and legislatures have been reluctant to extend privilege to relationships between mental health professionals and their clients.
- Except for cases heard in federal courts, privileged communication in counseling is determined by state statutes. It is essential that you learn your state laws regarding privileged communication in counseling relationships.
- Confidentiality and privilege both belong to the client, not the counselor, and clients can waive their privacy.
- There are at least 15 exceptions to confidentiality and privileged communication. You will need to understand each exception and be able to apply exceptions to real situations you encounter in your practice.
- It is permissible to share information with subordinates and fellow professionals in order to provide the best possible services to clients.
- The duties to warn, protect, and/or report when a client's condition poses a danger to self or others pose some of the most excruciating dilemmas faced by counselors.
- Confidentiality cannot be guaranteed when counseling couples, families, groups, or minor clients.
- Certain exceptions to confidentiality and privileged communication are legally mandated.
- When in doubt about your obligations regarding confidentiality or privileged communication, consult!

Records, Technology, and Subpoenas

Although records were mentioned in the previous chapter in relation to counselors' responsibilities regarding confidentiality and privileged communication, records are such an important (and somewhat complex) area of a counselor's practice that we are making them the focus of this separate chapter. In this chapter, we also discuss recent advances in technology that have necessitated the development of relatively new methods of creating, storing, and transferring records. In addition, records are often subject to being subpoenaed, and counselors must be prepared to respond to legal demands for their records.

RECORDS

Records are any physical "recording" made of information related to a counselor's professional practice. When you consider what kinds of records counselors create and maintain, you probably think of the notes that counselors take concerning sessions with clients. These types of records are referred to as *clinical case notes* in this chapter. Others that might come easily to mind are administrative records related to clients, such as appointment books, billing and payment accounts, copies of correspondence, intake forms, or other routine papers. Additional records that are often generated are audio or video recordings of sessions with clients. These recordings usually are used for supervision purposes, but might also be created for clients to review or by counselors for the purpose of training other counselors. Unusual records generated in counseling practices might include records of clients logging on to computerized information systems, telephone bills indicating clients' numbers called, computerized records that clients had used parking or building passes, or video recordings of clients entering or leaving a counseling office. All the items listed above are records and the privacy of clients could be compromised if these records were not kept confidential.

While records are a necessary part of a counselor's practice, it is important that counselors balance their need to keep documents with their obligation to provide quality counseling services to clients. Counselors who find themselves devoting inordinate or excessive amounts of time creating and maintaining records probably need to reevaluate how they are spending their professional time and energy.

In today's litigious environment, many administrators and lawyers who represent counseling agencies are requiring counselors to keep voluminous records to protect the agencies in the event a lawsuit is filed. While counselors are wise to document actions they take when they are fulfilling an ethical or legal obligation (such as protecting an intended victim against a client's threat of harm), it is not appropriate for counselors to neglect their counseling services to clients in order to produce excessive amounts of records that are self-protective. Counselors, their administrators, and the lawyers who advise them must balance the need to protect themselves in the event of legal claims against their duty to provide quality counseling services. It is possible to keep adequate records *and* provide quality counseling services. From both a legal and an ethical standpoint, this should be the goal of counselors and counseling agencies. In this chapter, we first discuss the ethical issues and standards related to counseling records, and then turn to legal requirements.

Ethical Issues and Standards Related to Records

Section B.4 of the ACA *Code of Ethics* includes five standards that specifically address counseling records. The first of these standards (B.4.a.) states that counselors maintain records necessary for rendering professional services to their clients. From an ethical perspective, this is the primary purpose of keeping records—to assist you in providing clients with the best possible counseling services. Unless you have perfect recall, you will find that the clinical case notes you have recorded will help you to refresh your memory prior to sessions. They will allow you to review progress toward goals that you and the client have jointly determined, to know when and under what circumstances important decisions and actions were taken, and to maintain an overall perspective on the content and process of the entire counseling relationship.

Keeping good records allows counselors to stay on track by documenting what kinds of treatment were undertaken and why. As Jagers (1998) has noted, counselors are by nature prone to drift in the direction of abstraction. It is helpful to us, our clients, and the therapeutic process when we work to maintain a clear conceptualization of counseling goals and our progress toward those goals. Good records can assist us in helping clients measure their change and growth. We can use our notes to reference and affirm significant turning points and successes in our clients' work.

Clinical case notes can be particularly important when a client decides to resume counseling with you after an extended break. It would be a daunting task to try to remember details of a client's life and concerns after months or even years have passed, during which so many other clients' lives and concerns have consumed your attention. If you can use your notes to refresh your recollections about former issues and events that occurred during the counseling process, you will take a significant step toward reconnecting with your returning client.

Continuity of care is a consideration when a client is referred from one mental health professional to another, as well. Notes should be written with enough clarity that another helping professional, by learning what did and did not help the client, can provide continuation of counseling. The receiving counselor can get attuned to the meaningful aspects of a client's work if records clearly describe goals, treatment strategies, and progress that was made. If you are the receiving counselor, you will particularly appreciate these records.

Standard B.4.b. addresses confidentiality of records, stating that counselors are responsible for securing the safety and confidentiality of any counseling records they create, maintain, transfer, or destroy. This caveat includes records that are written, taped, computerized, or stored in any other medium. In the previous chapter, we discussed at some length how easy it can be for a counselor to inadvertently breach a client's confidentiality. That discussion is as pertinent to counseling records as it is to other aspects of the counseling relationship.

Standard B.4.c. addresses the issue of informed consent and requires counselors to obtain client permission before they electronically record or observe sessions. Recording and observing sessions are common practices in supervision, which we discuss in more detail later in this chapter.

Standard B.4.d. alerts us to the fact that we have an ethical obligation to provide competent clients with access to their records, unless the records contain information that might be misleading or detrimental to the clients. This standard also provides guidance on a trickier situation that occurs when clients have been seen in the context of group or family counseling. In situations involving multiple clients, counselors limit access to records to those parts of the records that do not include confidential information related to another client.

Finally, Standard B.4.e. requires counselors to obtain written permission from clients to disclose or transfer records to legitimate third parties unless exceptions to confidentiality exist. Interestingly, this standard also makes counselors responsible for taking steps to ensure that receivers of counseling records are sensitive to the confidential nature of those records. It is not possible for a counselor to guarantee anyone else's behavior, including that of a fellow mental health professional who receives records. However, one step that can be taken to promote professionally appropriate transfer of records is to include a cover letter that explains the confidential nature of any transferred records.

Legal Requirements

The ACA *Code of Ethics and Standards of Practice* provisions regarding records do not conflict with any legal requirements regarding counseling records. In fact, one ethical standard (Section B.4.e.) goes beyond legal requirements and indicates that written permission should be obtained from clients before records are transferred, unless specific exceptions exist. It is interesting to note, however, that the corresponding Standard of Practice (SP-15) requires client consent to disclose or transfer records, but does not require *written* consent. The law does not require that counselors obtain written permission from clients to give copies of their records to third parties. Some federal laws, state statutes, and agency policies may have such written permission requirements, however. In addition, it is generally advisable for counselors, in order to protect themselves, to obtain written authority from clients before transferring records to third parties. If a client later denies that such permission was given or a client is not available to say whether oral permission was granted, the counselor will have a document as evidence that permission was obtained. Counselors should use the client request for records forms created by the agency in which they work. If the agency does not have a standard form, or if a counselor in private practice does not have such a form, the sample form provided in Appendix D can be used.

There is no common law principle nor are there any general federal or state statutes that require counselors to keep clinical case notes. Nonetheless, there are a number of legally related reasons why counselors do keep various types of records. For example, counselors in private practice must keep administrative records regarding their expenses and income for federal and state income tax purposes. As is discussed later, there are also some specific federal statutes that require counselors to handle records in particular ways if counselors work in settings in which these statutes apply. Additionally, lawyers always advise counselors to document carefully everything they do so they can protect themselves if their actions or judgments are later questioned in a lawsuit.

All counselors in all types of practices keep records of some kind. It is important that counselors approach their record keeping responsibilities in both an ethical and legal manner.

Confidentiality and Privileged Communication Requirements

All the points made in Chapter 4 regarding the confidentiality and privileged communication responsibilities of counselors apply to records to the same degree they apply to oral comments regarding the privacy of clients. However, since records have physical properties, whereas "information" may not, it is important to consider carefully the responsibility of counselors to handle records appropriately.

Purposes of Records

Counseling records are created for a number of reasons (Corey, Corey & Callanan, 1998). Some of these reasons benefit clients, while others benefit counselors or their employers.

Overall, clinical health care records are seen as being created to benefit the person who is receiving the services. In fact, legal principles view the contents of the records about a particular client as belonging to that client, even though the paper or recording instrument belongs to someone else (*Claim of Gerkin,* 1980; *People v. Cohen,* 1979). Records can benefit clients in a number of ways.

Records are used to transfer the information one health care provider has about a client's condition to another health care provider. This efficient method of exchanging information can be very beneficial to clients.

Health care records also create a history of a client's diagnosis, treatment, and recovery. Health care providers can render better services when they have access to information regarding a client's past that is more thorough and accurate than a client's oral recall.

Clinical case notes benefit the client because they allow the counselor to summarize each interaction with the client and record plans for future sessions. The work of counselors can be more consistent, precise, and systematic when accurate and thorough notes are kept.

Counselors also keep clinical case notes for their own benefit (Schaffer, 1997). Counselors document any steps they have taken in an emergency or critical situation. Later, if counselors are accused of not having provided competent services, the records serve as evidence of their thinking and the notes document any actions taken.

Counselors keep a number of business records associated with their counseling practice for their own purposes. Counselors who work within agencies or other facilities that provide counseling services often need to document the number of persons who have been served, the categories of services rendered, and other types of information. Counselors in private practice have to keep business records to justify tax deductions they take in relation to their counseling business. Regardless of whose purpose is being served in creating records, it is the privacy of clients that dictates how records must be handled.

Types of Records Kept by Counselors

Some think it is unfortunate that there is no agreed-upon listing of the types of records counselors should keep or the manner in which these records should be created or maintained.

Section B.4.a. of the ACA *Code of Ethics* simply says, "Counselors maintain records necessary for rendering professional services to their clients and as required by laws, regulations, or agency or institutional procedures." This is an excellent standard in that it allows each counselor to determine which types of clinical case notes are needed to render professional services. The standard also acknowledges that many record keeping requirements are imposed on counselors by laws, regulations, and procedures.

It may be helpful for counselors to receive more instructions about the record keeping responsibilities that will be a part of most of the jobs they will hold. However, it would not be wise for the profession or the Code of Ethics to tell counselors what types of records they must keep, the contents of such records, and the ways in which those records should be created. It is best for counselors to determine the kinds of records they need based on their position, and the kinds of clinical notes they need to create in order to be effective practitioners. Keeping in mind that there will be variations depending on a counselor's style and the requirements imposed by employment settings, we offer some general guidelines regarding three types of records: administrative records, recordings, and clinical case notes.

Administrative Records

All settings that provide counseling services keep some type of administrative records. The type of agency and external pressures determine how many and what types of records are kept. When counselors accept employment in an agency, school, hospital, or other setting, they agree to conform to agency rules and procedures, which include record keeping requirements.

Administrative records are any types of records that would not be considered recordings or clinical case notes. Administrative records include appointment books, billing and payment accounts, copies of correspondence, intake forms, or other routine papers that are created as a result of providing counseling services to clients. In most businesses, records of these types are not considered confidential. The very fact that someone has applied for or received counseling services is a private matter, however. Therefore, business records that reveal the identity of individuals who have had contact with the agency must be treated as confidential and must be protected in the same way as clinical case notes are protected.

Recordings

Clinical supervision of counseling services takes place in some form in most settings. Agencies often accept practicum or internship students who must record their sessions with clients for the purposes of clinical supervision. Mental health professionals, after they have received their graduate degrees, usually have to practice under clinical supervision for two to three years before they can become licensed themselves. In addition, many practicing counselors continue supervision throughout their careers and might record sessions for supervision purposes.

Counseling sessions could be recorded when counselors want clients to listen to or view their own behavior or interpersonal interactions during sessions. Although this therapeutic use of client session recordings is not unusual, a few cautions should be mentioned. Counselors should emphasize to their clients that these recordings would compromise their privacy if the clients did not keep them secure or erase them after using them. Counselors also should make sure clients know that until these recordings are erased or destroyed, they would be available for subpoena in some lawsuits that could arise. We suggest that counselors who give recordings of sessions to their clients for any purpose have their clients sign a form to ensure that they understand the problems that might arise and their responsibility for their own privacy protection.

There are a number of procedures that need to be followed when recordings of client sessions are created. Clients must know that recordings are being made and must agree to the process. The tapes, once they are created, must be kept as secure as any confidential record within the agency is kept. Once the recordings have been used, they must be erased or destroyed.

Section B.4.c. of the ACA *Code of Ethics* and ACA *Standard of Practice 14* require that consent of clients be obtained prior to recording sessions. The consent of clients must be "informed" in that clients must understand the reason the recordings are being made and who will have access to them. It would be a violation of privacy if sessions were recorded without a client's knowledge, or if consent was given and then the recordings were used for purposes not agreed to or accessed by persons unknown to the client.

Although there is no ethical or legal requirement that the client's permission be obtained in writing, counselors often obtain written permission from clients to record counseling sessions in order to protect themselves. This self-protection would be necessary if a client later claimed that permission had never been given for the recording or that the client did not fully understand how the recording would be used. In addition, many agencies require written permission before client counseling sessions may be recorded. If such policies exist, counselors must comply. If you wish to obtain a client's permission to record a session for supervision and your agency does not have a standard form to use, a form is provided in Appendix D. Any signed form of this type obtained from a client should be placed in the client's folder and kept until the record is destroyed.

Our experience is that once audiotapes or videotapes of counseling sessions are made, graduate students, counselors, and supervisors tend to be somewhat lax in keeping these recordings secure. Perhaps the reason for this problem is that tapes do not look like confidential records. In any event, it is imperative that graduate students or counselors who make tapes take responsibility for delivering them to their supervisor, retrieving them once the supervisor has reviewed them, and erasing them. Clinical supervisors bear the responsibility of handling recordings appropriately during the time that tapes are in their possession. Supervisors must also return tapes to counselors after reviewing them.

We recommend that tapes of counseling sessions be labeled simply, so that the counselor and supervisor can recognize their contents, but in a manner that does not bring attention to the fact that they are confidential records. A good method of labeling the tapes is to put the counselor's name and telephone number on the tape along with the date of the counseling session. There is no need to write the client's name on the tape or to indicate that the tape contains a counseling session. Tapes labeled in this manner can be returned to the counselor if they are misplaced or lost, and those who come into contact with them will not be tempted to listen to or view them. Also, when a new session is recorded over a previous session, the only thing on the label that will need to be changed is the date of the session.

Counselors who record counseling sessions must also ensure that tapes are erased after they have been used for supervision or any other purposes. Most counselors record new sessions over previously recorded sessions. This method works well. If more than one tape is used for supervision tapes, it would be important to keep track of the tapes and, particularly when supervision sessions are terminated, to purposefully erase or record over them. Magnetic devices that erase the contents of audio or videotapes are available commercially and are recommended for university and agency settings where a number of tapes are recorded and erased on a continuing basis.

Clinical Case Notes

The records that concern counselors and clients most are the clinical case notes that counselors keep regarding their sessions with clients. These notes contain detailed information about the content of counseling sessions. They often include specific details clients have told counselors, counselors' clinical impressions of clients, and generally very sensitive and personal information about clients.

A problem with clinical case notes is that counselors often think of them as being personal notes to themselves that will be seen only by their eyes in the future. However, the reality of clinical case notes is much different, and we have found that even seasoned counselors are sometimes surprised to learn how many people have a right to access their clinical case notes. Counselors must be aware of how these notes are viewed by clients, agencies, and the law.

We often have heard the suggestion that counselors simply should not take clinical case notes, so that they will not have to worry about the notes being subpoenaed or being seen at a later time by the client or any other person. This is not sound advice. In the first place, it seems to be general practice today for mental health professionals, no matter what their credentials or orientation, to routinely create and use clinical case notes in their practices. If counselors were to fail to create these notes, it is likely that they would be accused of unprofessional practice and probably would be called upon to explain how they could render quality counseling services without taking clinical case notes (Anderson, 1996). Second, not having clinical case notes would not keep a counselor from having to reveal confidential information orally from memory if someone had a legal right to that information. Finally, counselors should take the clinical notes they need in order to function effectively as professionals. Counselors should not feel inhibited about creating clinical case notes just because the notes may later be seen by clients themselves or by third parties.

Assume Notes Will Be Read. Counselors never know whether others will read the clinical case notes they create. Thus, counselors should assume that notes they write will become public information at some later date. Counselors who make this assumption will be very cautious in deciding what to include in their notes. At the same time, counselors should write whatever they need to render quality counseling services to their clients.

Situations in which the clinical case notes of counselors appropriately and legally are read by others are discussed below. It is important for you to remember the following sobering information when you are writing clinical case notes:

- Your clients have a legal right to review the notes and to obtain copies of them.
- Your clients have a legal right to demand that you transfer copies of those clinical case notes to other professionals, including other mental health professionals, attorneys, physicians, and even accountants.
- Your clients can subpoena the clinical case notes when they are involved in litigation.
- Other parties can legally subpoena the clinical case notes when involved in litigation situations involving the client, sometimes over the client's objection and even when the records are privileged.

- The legal representatives of deceased clients have the same rights to clinical case notes as the clients had when they were alive.
- Clinical case notes sometimes do become public information and get published in the media.

Appropriate Content of Clinical Case Notes.   Unfortunately, very little instruction occurs in counseling graduate programs regarding the purposes and the actual creation of clinical case notes (Cottone & Tarvydas, 1998). In other professions, such as medicine, nursing, and social work, a heavy emphasis is placed on how to write health records, what information should and should not be included, and proper ways of creating such clinical notes. Most health records, however, are passed from one professional to another and professionals rely on each other to record information so it can be used in the care and treatment of a patient. Counseling clinical case notes, on the other hand, generally are written by a counselor for the counselor's own use. There are times, however, when these records are read by others and even when counselors offer such records to prove they acted professionally. Piazza and Baruth (1990), Mitchell (1991), and Snider (1987) have provided suggestions for keeping records. The guidelines developed by the American Psychological Association (1993) are included in Appendix E. We are offering some recommendations here regarding the creation of clinical case notes to assist counselors in their practices.

You should never lose sight of the purposes of clinical case notes. There are two basic reasons to keep notes: (a) to provide quality counseling services to clients, and (b) to document decisions you have made and actions you have taken as a counselor. Both of these purposes are legitimate and reasonable.

It is critical that you take your notes either during sessions or immediately after. It does no good to write clinical case notes long after the counseling session occurs. The whole purpose of the notes is to record on paper what your memory will not hold. If you wait too long, you will be relying on your memory, which is what you are trying to avoid.

Your own personal style should dictate whether you take notes during a counseling session or after it is over. There are advantages and disadvantages to both approaches. Taking notes during sessions allows you to record accurate information immediately without having to rely on your memory as to what was said. Some counselors can take notes unobtrusively during sessions. Other counselors may have trouble taking notes and listening to clients at the same time. Clients could be distracted or inhibited by your note taking during sessions, if it is not done easily. Some counselors find that waiting until after the session is over is the best way for them to take clinical case notes. We suggest that you try both methods and adopt the approach that works best for you.

As we have emphasized, the first purpose for creating clinical case notes is to render quality counseling services. It would be impossible for you to see a number of clients over a relatively short period of time and remember all the information that clients revealed to you and all your thoughts regarding the clients' situations. You should take clinical case notes to remember what was said by clients, to record your own clinical impressions, and to plan future interactions with your clients.

A very important part of writing clinical case notes is to separate objective information (what was said by anyone or observed by you during the session) from your clinical impressions (hypotheses or conclusions you developed as a result of what was said or observed). Quite often, you will review notes to determine what a client actually said during a session. You must be able to separate what was actually said from what you thought about as a result of what was said. In addition, there may be times when your notes are used as evidence in a legal proceeding and being able to determine what was actually said by a client could be critical. A common format for clinical case notes is the use of "SOAP" notes, which include four separate sections:

Subjective: information reported by the client

Objective: results of the counselor's tests and other assessments administered

Assessment: the counselor's impressions generated by the data

Plans: diagnosis and treatment plan, along with any modifications to them

The second purpose for keeping clinical case notes is to document decisions you have made or actions you have taken (Woody, 1988b). Such documentation would be important when you determine that a client is a danger to self or others, and take some actions to prevent harm. Documentation is also important when you consult with others regarding a client's situation. When you make decisions that clients may not like, you should also document your actions in your clinical case notes. If you decide to terminate counseling over a client's objection, instruct a client to take some action the client is reluctant to take, or impose limits to a client's interactions with you outside of sessions, it is wise to document how and why you did these things and the client's reactions.

When you document decisions or actions in your case notes, you are doing that to protect yourself in the event such decisions or actions are questioned later by anyone else (Mitchell, 1991). As a result, it is important to provide as much detailed information as possible. For example, listing the exact time a conversation took place could be vital. When you are talking to people other than your client, it is important to include the person's name, title, and contact information; date and time the conversation took place; and any other information that might be needed later. Recording exact words you used and exact words of others often can be important as well. When documenting to protect yourself, it is essential that you do so immediately after conversations take place. If you write notes hours, days, or weeks after conversations have occurred, such notes will be much less helpful to you if you are trying to prove that you made the decisions or took the actions you are claiming to have taken in your notes.

It would be impossible to write a summary of every action you take as a counselor or to make an audiotape or videotape of every counseling session. Excessive documentation can take away valuable time that might be spent providing counseling services. On the other hand, there are circumstances in which counselors should document their actions to create a record showing that they have done what they should have done.

Guidelines for documenting for self-protection are included in Figure 5-1.

Another important part of note taking is to write notes that are legible, at least to you. For notes to be useful in the future, you must be able to read and understand them. If your notes are transferred to a client or to a third party at a later date and they cannot read them, you will be called upon to explain what you wrote. This can be very inconvenient for you, because it occurs in a court after you have been subpoenaed and put under oath to tell the truth. It is much better to write your notes so that others can read them than to have to interpret them later. It is definitely not a good idea to purposefully write notes so that they cannot be read by others or to use symbols that only you can understand. If clients or third parties try to read those notes, they often become irritated. You can be put in a difficult

1. Documentation should be undertaken in circumstances in which a counselor's actions or inaction may be later reviewed by an ethics panel, licensure board, or administrator, or within the context of a legal proceeding.

2. Some of the situations in which some level of documentation is called for include the following:
   - Someone accuses a counselor of unethical or illegal behavior.
   - A counselor reports a case of suspected child abuse.
   - A counselor determines that a client is a danger to self.
   - A counselor determines that a client is a danger to others.
   - A client who is being counseled is involved in a legal controversy that could lead to the counselor being forced to testify in court. Such controversies include counseling a child whose parents are arguing about custody in a divorce case, a husband or wife who is involved in a contentious divorce case, a couple who are contemplating a divorce, or a person who is involved in a personal injury lawsuit.

3. Documentation efforts should begin as soon as counselors determine they are in a situation in which documentation is important.

4. When documenting for self-protection, as much detail as possible should be included. Dates, exact times events occurred, and exact words spoken should be included to the degree details are remembered. Only factual information should be included. Thoughts, diagnoses, and conclusions of counselors should be avoided when documenting. If these need to be written down, they should be included in clinical case notes rather than records kept for documentation.

5. The best documentation is created very soon after a conversation or event has occurred. Indicate the date and time anything is written. Never back date anything that is written. In other words, do not imply or state that something was written on an earlier date than it was actually written.

6. In the event counselors realize that documentation should have been occurring sooner, they should write a summary of what has happened up to that point in time. Include as much detail as can be remembered. The date and time the summary was written should be included on the summary.

7. Maintain a documentation file that includes the originals of notes written to counselors, copies of notes written by counselors to others, copies of relevant papers counselors cannot keep for themselves, and other papers that might be relevant to the situation.

8. Records kept for documentation should be kept secure in a locked file drawer or cabinet. If counselors agree to provide copies of their files, they should never release originals of their records, only copies.

Figure 5-1   Documentation Through Records for Self-Protection

position, because it appears that you are not cooperating with people who have a legal right to review the notes.

Client Access to Records

It would never occur to most health care providers to have concerns about patients having access to copies of their records. Mental health care is different from physical health care in many respects. Some mental health care professionals feel that it is not appropriate for patients or clients to have information about the diagnoses of mental disorders, treatment approaches being taken, or clinical impressions that have been formulated by the professional. In fact, some mental health care professionals might argue that it could be harmful to individuals who are being treated to have such information from their records.

The legal perspective on health care records is that they are kept for the benefit of the patient, and therefore, the patient should have access to them and must receive copies if requested (*Claim of Gerkin,* 1980; *People v. Cohen,* 1979). Further, the patient has the right to demand that one health care provider transfer the records to another health care provider. Mental health care is not seen as different from physical health care concerning patient or client records. It is important, then, for counselors to assume that clients will have access to clinical case notes created and that clients have a right to copies of those notes and have a right to request that copies of the notes be transferred to other professionals.

In the event a client requests a copy of your clinical case notes and you have any reason to think that it would be best if the client did not see your notes, there are steps you can take. You could explain to your client why you believe it would not be best to see your notes and your client might accept your explanation and withdraw the request. You also could suggest that it might be more helpful for the client or for the person to whom the client wants the records transferred if you were to create a summary of your notes, rather than copying the notes themselves. You might explain that the notes were written for your own clinical purposes, and that others probably would be more interested in summaries than in day-to-day notes.

If you were to refuse to show a client your clinical case notes regarding treatment or refuse to provide copies for the client or for a third party the client has designated, the client probably could take legal steps to compel you to comply with the demand. It would appear that the law would support the client's rights to the records (*Application of Striegel,* 1977).

In some circumstances, your clinical case notes may contain information about other parties involved in sessions in which the client was counseled. Such situations could arise in couples, family, or group counseling. If your clinical case notes contain information that would compromise another person's privacy if they were given to a client or to someone designated by the client, you might try to convince your client to withdraw the request or you might suggest that you provide a summary for your client. If your client insists, however, on having copies of your original records, then you should copy what you have written, eliminate references to others, and provide your client with the portions of the records that deal only with that client.

Federal Laws Affecting Counseling Records

It would be impossible to reference every federal law or regulation that contains requirements for counseling records. Most federal statutes related to mental health records apply only to programs that are funded by federal tax money. Counselors who work in settings that are administered by the federal government or in agencies that receive federal funding should ask their employers whether there are any federal laws or regulations that affect the counseling records they keep as part of their jobs. Many private agencies as well as state and local government programs receive federal funding. Two federal laws affect a number of counselors—the Family Educational Rights and Privacy Act of 1974 (FERPA; 20 U.S.C. §1232g, 1997) and the Comprehensive Alcohol Abuse and Alcoholism Prevention, Treatment and Rehabilitation Act of 1972 (42 U.S.C. §290dd-2, 1997).

Family Educational Rights and Privacy Act

The Family Educational Rights and Privacy Act of 1974 (FERPA), which is sometimes referred to as the "Buckley Amendment," affects all public educational institutions and any private or parochial educational institution that receives federal funding in one form or another. Almost all private and church sponsored educational institutions receive some type of federal funding. The penalty for violating provisions of FERPA is the loss of all federal funding, which could be devastating for many educational institutions. Individuals cannot bring lawsuits under FERPA (*Tarka v. Franklin,* 1989; *Fay v. South Colonie Cent. School Dist.,* 1986).

This legislation basically says that parents of minor students (and students who are 18 or older or who are in college) have two rights: (a) to inspect and review their education records and to challenge the contents to ensure the records are not inaccurate or misleading, and (b) to have their written authorization obtained before copies of their education records can be transferred to any third party.

After students are 18 years old or are attending a postsecondary institution, the legal rights under this legislation are vested in them. However, parents or guardians of dependent students may be given copies of the records of such students without the student's consent. Dependent students are defined as children or stepchildren, over half of whose support was received from the taxpayer the previous tax year (26 U.S.C. §152). As a result of this definition, most educational institutions give access to student records to parents who can show they claimed their child as a tax dependent the previous year.

Education records are defined in the federal legislation as records kept by educational institutions regarding students. The law specifically exempts from the right to inspect and review, any records that "are in the sole possession of the maker" [20 U.S.C. §1232g(a)(B)(i)]. To qualify under this exemption, counselors in schools and other educational institutions should keep their case notes separate from other records and should not let anyone else have access to those records. Treatment records "made or maintained by a physician, psychiatrist, psychologist, or other recognized professional or paraprofessional" are also exempt [20 U.S.C. §1232g(a)(B)(iv)]. As a result of these exemptions, clinical case notes kept by counselors in educational institutions do not have to be shown to students, parents, or guardians under FERPA requirements.

Schools are not required by FERPA to obtain written permission from parents or students to release a student's records to "other schools or school systems in which the student intends to enroll" [20 U.S.C. §1232g(b)(1)(b)]. Nonetheless, when copies of records of transfer students are forwarded to other schools, parents must be notified of the transfer and must be given copies of the transferred records if they desire copies.

These access exemptions to inspect and review one's records under FERPA do not in any way diminish a person's rights to counselors' records under a subpoena in relation to a lawsuit. A valid subpoena for records must be complied with under all circumstances. When an educational institution intends to release records pursuant to a subpoena, the institution must notify parents and students in advance of the release [20 U.S.C. §1232g(b)(2)(B); *Rios V. Read,* 1977; *Mattie T. v. Johnston,* 1976], although notification is not required if the subpoena orders that the existence of the subpoena not be disclosed [20 U.S.C. §1232g(b)(J)(i–ii)].

In an emergency situation, an amendment to the act has given permission to release private information without parent or student written permission. The information must be "necessary to protect the health or safety of the student or other persons" [20 U.S.C. §1232g(a)(1)(I)]. This provision would allow counselors to release their records on students to medical personnel or law enforcement authorities without violating FERPA, if they determined that a student was a danger to self or others.

Educational institutions may release to an alleged victim of any violence the results of any disciplinary proceeding conducted against the alleged perpetrator with respect to that specific crime [20 U.S.C. §1232g(b)(6)]. FERPA also allows institutions to include in education records any disciplinary action taken against students and to disclose such action to school officials in other schools [20 U.S.C. §1232g(h)].

There is no general legal principle that requires counselors to obtain *written* authorization from clients to transfer records to third parties. Oral permission is legally adequate, but obtaining written authorization is always recommended. Under FERPA, however, written authorization is required to transfer records.

Federally Funded Substance Abuse Programs

The federal government funds a multitude of substance abuse prevention and treatment programs. Private and public agencies apply for federal funds to operate many of these programs. Programs that receive federal funds must comply with federal laws related to substance abuse treatment.

A federal statute (42 U.S.C. §290dd-2) declares that records kept by any facility that is "conducted, regulated, or directly or indirectly assisted" by the federal government are confidential. Disclosure of records of individuals receiving substance abuse services (including education, prevention, training, treatment, rehabilitation, or research) is permitted only in a few circumstances. Exceptions to the nondisclosure of records requirement include the following: (a) when the person gives prior written consent, (b) medical emergencies, (c) audits or evaluations, and (d) to avert substantial risk of death or serious bodily harm if a court order is secured. Records cannot be used for criminal charges or investigations [42 U.S.C. §290dd-2(c)]. However, a counselor's direct observations are not a record and can be used in criminal proceedings against clients or patients (*State v. Brown,* 1985; *State v. Magnuson,* 1984).

The statute related to federal substance abuse programs does not prohibit exchange of information between the military and the department of Veterans Affairs. The statute also permits the reporting of suspected child abuse and neglect under state laws.

Unlike FERPA, the violation of this statute or the regulations that implement it can result in criminal charges and a fine. As a result, clients may file criminal complaints against counselors in federally supported substance abuse treatment programs who violate their rights to privacy, although individuals whose confidentiality rights are violated cannot file civil lawsuits for damages (*Logan v. District of Columbia,* 1978).

Other Federal Statutes

Additional federal statutes prohibit or limit the disclosure of counseling records for the following clients who are served by federally assisted programs: (a) runaway and homeless youth (42 U.S.C. §5731), (b) individuals with sexually transmitted diseases [42 U.S.C. §247c(d)(5)], (c) voluntary clients in federal drug abuse or dependence programs [42 U.S.C. §260(d)], (d) older persons [42 U.S.C. §3026(d); 42 U.S.C. §3027(f)(1)], and (e) victims of violence against women [42 U.S.C. §14011(b)(5)]. On the other hand, privacy is sometimes expressly limited by statutes. A federal statute specifically denies confidentiality to individuals who are examined by a physician in civil commitment proceedings due to drug abuse (42 U.S.C. §3420).

Handling, Storing, and Destroying Records

Creating counseling records is an important process, but maintaining and ultimately getting rid of them are crucial matters for counselors as well. The privacy of clients and the self-protection of counselors both have an impact on the manner in which records are handled, stored, and destroyed.

Because counseling records are so sensitive, agencies should develop written policies regarding how these records will be handled on a day-to-day basis. Typically, counselors create and keep their own clinical case notes. These notes should be kept in locked drawers or cabinets. In offices with more than one person, an individual should be designated as the records manager. Generally, this person would be a clerical or administrative employee. The records manager should have the responsibility of ensuring that counseling records are kept secure, checked out and back in properly, stored safely, and finally, eliminated according to a set schedule and policy.

Everyone who handles counseling records should make sure the records are not left unattended so that unauthorized persons can read them. Care should be taken to promptly return counseling records to their proper place after they have been used.

There are no general laws that dictate how long a particular counseling record must be kept (Woody, 1988b). You should be aware, however, that some federal or state statutes require that certain types of records created for certain purposes be kept for a definite period of time. For instance, some state counselor licensure laws dictate that counselors' records be kept for a certain number of years. Attorneys who advise counseling agencies should be asked to review statutes and regulations to determine whether there are any requirements regarding records, including the length of time they must be maintained.

Many agencies have determined that they want to keep their counseling records for a set period of time. Generally, agencies also have rules and guidelines regarding how records should be handled, stored, and eliminated. Counselors should always inquire as to whether the agency in which they work has such requirements. All rules and regulations should be followed by counselors.

Counseling records often are affected by agency accreditation rules as well. Many counseling centers, hospitals, and treatment facilities are accredited by private agencies such as the Joint Commission on Accreditation of Healthcare Organizations (JCAHO), the International Association of Counseling Services (IACS), and the Commission on Accreditation of Rehabilitation Facilities (CARF). See Appendix B for contact information for these organizations. These accreditation agencies have specific requirements regarding counseling records, and many require that records be kept for a set period of time. Counselors who work in agencies that are accredited should ask about record keeping requirements.

If there are no laws, agency rules, or accreditation standards that require records to be kept for a specific length of time, then counselors should encourage their agency to establish a written policy and to destroy counseling records on a periodic basis. There are a number of reasons for not keeping counseling records indefinitely. Practically speaking, it is expensive to keep records locked away and to keep up with logging them in and out. In addition, confidential records that exist could be compromised in some way, while confidential records that are destroyed cannot be seen by unauthorized persons.

It is wise to establish a record destroying policy stipulating that certain categories of records will be destroyed on a specific date each year unless one of the following applies: (a) there is reason to believe the records may be subpoenaed in a current or future lawsuit; or (b) the records contain documentation of actions taken by counselors that need to kept longer than the usual period of time. There are no guidelines about whether individuals "believe they may be subpoenaed." Common sense should dictate this determination. If records are purposefully destroyed when someone knows or should have reasonably known that those records would be subpoenaed later, the person destroying them can be charged with a serious crime (Woody, 1988a). Records documenting actions that counselors have taken to protect themselves probably should be kept longer than counseling records normally would be kept.

Voluntarily Transferring Records

Clients often request that their counseling records be provided to another professional who is rendering services to them. In addition, professionals often request your clients' counseling records when they begin treating your current or former clients. After clients have requested or given permission in writing that their counseling records be transferred to a third party, counselors have an obligation to comply. A form is provided in Appendix F for clients to sign when they wish to have their records transferred.

Counselors should make sure the written request of the client is followed precisely and that only records the client authorizes for transfer are actually sent. In addition, counselors should never send originals of records, only copies. Finally, records located in client files from other professionals or agencies should never be transferred to a third party. If clients want those records sent, they must contact the agency that created the records and authorize that agency to forward them.

The written and signed authorization from the client should be filed in the client's folder. In addition, a notation should be entered in the client's file that indicates which records were sent and when, the method of transfer (U.S. mail, courier service, personal delivery, etc.), to whom they were sent, and to what address.

TECHNOLOGY

Technological advances in our society have had a significant impact on the profession of counseling. The various forms of technology that have been developed and are still being developed all have the same basic purpose—to facilitate the transfer of information. In this transfer process, situations are inevitably created in which sensitive or confidential information might be accessed by inappropriate persons. Every form of technology discussed in this section creates records or recordings of information that, if not treated carefully, could lead to the privacy of clients being compromised.

Certainly, counselors want to maximize their effectiveness by utilizing as many forms of technology as possible. It is imperative that counselors educate themselves regarding the subtle ways in which their clients' privacy might be affected by the use of technology (Cottone & Tarvydas, 1998). In the following discussion, we identify a number of areas in which technology is having an impact on the counseling process, and we provide guidelines for ensuring that the privacy of clients is protected.

Telephones

Although telephones have become such an essential means of communicating in our society that we seldom even think of them as technology, the use of telephones raises a number of significant issues for counselors. Some of the more important concerns related to telephone use and client privacy will be outlined below. The following technological inventions related to telephone use will be discussed as well: (a) answering machines and answering services, (b) pagers, and (c) cellular telephones.

Counselors must be cautious in discussing confidential or privileged information with anyone over the telephone. There is no way to ensure that the person you are talking to on a telephone is the person he or she claims to be. Also, there are many ways that telephone conversations can be monitored or intercepted without you realizing it. Even when you talk to individuals frequently and know their voices well, you still are taking a chance when you assume that you know who you are talking to or that your conversation is private. As a result of these problems, counselors are advised to be very careful when talking about confidential information over the telephone.

Counselors should follow the guidelines listed in Figure 5-2 when using the telephone. In addition, counselors must ensure that the staff members in the agency in which they work are educated regarding proper telephone use.

Answering Machines, Voice Mail, and Answering Services

Many counseling offices in community mental health centers, hospitals, schools, and other settings use answering machines, voice mail, or answering services in order to conduct their business. In fact, because of the high cost of secretarial or reception services, most counseling agencies and counselors in private practice have answering machines or services. Many clients also have answering machines or answering services in their homes or at their places of employment.

Counselors must strive to protect the privacy of their clients both when receiving messages and when leaving messages for clients. Counselors who use answering machines in their offices should not allow unauthorized persons to use their offices when they are not present to ensure that no one hears answering machine messages as they are being left or retrieves messages inappropriately. The audio option on answering machines should be turned to the off position when counselors are not present in their offices. In addition, counselors should not retrieve messages when people are present in their offices who should not hear confidential information.

Counselors who use voice mail or answering services must ensure that their access codes to their messages are not disclosed to unauthorized persons. It is unwise to write access codes in personal books that could be misplaced or stolen. It is also important that answering

1. Never acknowledge that clients are receiving services or give out information regarding clients to unknown callers. Explain that in respect for the privacy of clients, such information is not given out unless clients first sign authorizations. Explain how authorizations from clients may be obtained.

2. Make efforts to verify that you are talking to the correct person when you receive or make calls in which confidential information will be discussed.

3. Keep in mind the possibility that your conversation is being recorded or monitored by an unauthorized person.

4. If you discuss confidential information regarding a client on the telephone, be professional and cautious throughout the conversation. Avoid becoming friendly or informal, or saying anything off the record.

5. Remember that a record will exist at the telephone company that this telephone call was made or received.

6. Do not say anything during the conversation that you would not want your client to hear or that you would not want to repeat under oath in a legal proceeding.

Figure 5-2   Guidelines for Counselor Telephone Use

service personnel be educated regarding the confidential nature of messages taken for counselors so that they can avoid inadvertently compromising the privacy of clients.

It is common practice for counselors to make written notes as they listen to their messages from answering machines, voice mail, or answering services. Such written messages to themselves could contain confidential information and must be handled as carefully as any other confidential record.

Two important factors should be considered when using answering machines or voice mail. First, a recording is being created that will exist until it is erased or destroyed. And second, there is no way to ensure that the intended person will be the one who retrieves a message that is left. The fact that others may hear the message when answering machines or voice mail are being used requires that counselors never reveal anything that is confidential when leaving such messages. Since the fact that a person is a counseling client is itself confidential information, counselors must be very cautious when leaving messages for clients.

From a practical perspective, counselors often have to reach their clients by telephone. Appointments sometimes have to be canceled or rearranged, forms need to be signed, and other matters come up that need to be handled by telephone. It is wise for counselors who leave messages for their clients to identify themselves by name and state their message in such a manner that a third person would not hear anything that the clients would not want them to hear. Remember that clients often have others present when they retrieve their messages and that messages left at their homes could be retrieved by other family members.

Telephone Pagers

Telephone pagers have become popular today both for professionals and for private individuals. Counselors who carry pagers must ensure that messages received from clients are kept confidential. Since pager messages can be received in public places, counselors must exercise caution in retrieving their pager messages.

Counselors who send pager messages to clients must be careful to ensure their clients' privacy, exercising the same caution they would when sending answering machine, voice mail, or secretarial service messages.

It is important for counselors to know that companies supplying pagers to individuals keep records of all calls received. It is not possible, then, to receive a pager message from a client or to send a message to a client without a record being created of the pager telephone contact.

Cellular Telephones

Cellular telephones operate just like telephones connected by wires, except that conversations are transmitted by airwaves. As a result, there may be more chance of a conversation on a cellular telephone being accidentally or purposefully intercepted by an unauthorized person.

In addition, cellular telephones are carried around wherever individuals go. As a result, persons with cellular telephones often have conversations in public places or in their automobiles. When talking to a client with a cellular telephone, it is wise to assume that the person is not in a private place.

Office Security

Many modern offices have security systems designed to protect the individuals who work there. These security systems can include cameras that film each person who enters the building, guards who require identification from visitors, or voice systems that require those who wish to enter to request that a door be unlocked for them. All these measures could compromise the privacy of a counseling client. Counselors who practice in environments where security measures are used should make efforts to minimize the intrusive nature of these systems. Also, clients should be informed of security measures being used that may not be readily observed.

Computer Storage

Records, once they are created in any form, are never totally secure. It is always possible for an unauthorized person to gain access to records, or for mistakes to occur in which the privacy of records is compromised. Just as files filled with papers can be seen by unauthorized persons, so can records kept on a computer.

Keeping counseling records on computers is becoming a more common practice. An advantage for counselors is that, by avoiding hard copies of records, they do not have to make storage space available or worry about securing physical files and file cabinets. A disadvantage is that, in some respects, computers may not be as secure as a locked file cabinet kept in a locked room.

The preferred method of storing information in agencies and offices today is through computers. File cabinets and hard copies of documents will eventually become obsolete since computers allow incredible amounts of information to be contained on a single disk. Computers have made business environments more efficient and cost-effective and will become more heavily utilized in the future.

Counselors usually think in terms of locks and keys when they consider methods of keeping confidential information secure. With so much data being stored on computers in modern counseling settings, it is important that counselors understand security problems and solutions associated with keeping information on computers (Swensen, 1997).

Access to confidential computer files is one of the first issues to consider. It is possible to set up computers so that a password must be used to access sensitive files. One of the problems with using passwords, however, is the danger that the passwords will become known to unauthorized persons. Password holders tend to be anxious about the possibility of forgetting their password. As a result, they make notes to themselves with the password on them and the notes are sometimes seen by others. Some people have even been known to post their password directly on their computer. Offices often will change passwords from time to time to help with security. But, again, this makes computer users nervous about forgetting their passwords, so they record them in a way that leads to their disclosure. Counselors who practice in offices in which computer passwords are used for confidential computer files should be careful not to disclose the passwords to unauthorized persons and not to record the passwords in places where they might be seen by others. In addition, counselors should train office personnel about the importance of password security and alert staff members to the problems that exist in keeping passwords secure.

Printing hard copies of documents from confidential computer files can also cause problems. Printed confidential information should be filed in locked cabinets or destroyed when no longer needed.

Disposing of confidential computer files also is a problem area. Most people believe that when they delete a file in a computer, they have destroyed that information. In reality, most deleted computer files can be retrieved by computer experts. Counselors should understand that all information entered into a computer has the potential of eventually being seen by unauthorized persons, even after the information has been deleted. As in creating any type of record, counselors should assume that what they have written will someday become public information, despite their best efforts to keep the record confidential or to delete or destroy it.

Steps should be taken to prevent confidential counseling records kept on computers from being compromised. Listed below are some suggestions for counselors who use computers for their records:

- Use passwords for accessing the files in the computer. Keep the passwords secure, limit the number of individuals who know the passwords, and change the passwords periodically.
- Any time a confidential record is printed from the computer, ensure that it is handled as other confidential materials would be.
- Avoid placing computers with monitors in public areas where unauthorized persons might accidentally see confidential information.
- Limit access to computer equipment that is used to enter and retrieve confidential records.
- Delete computer stored records on the same basis that traditional records would be destroyed in the agency or office. Keep in mind, though, that deleted files usually

can be retrieved by computer experts from a computer's hard drive even after they have been deleted.

- When confidential information is downloaded from a computer's hard drive to a disk, or transferred electronically, make sure that confidential material is not accidentally included.
- Be careful in networking a computer used for confidential information. The more separate computers that can access information, the greater the chance that confidential information will be compromised.

Electronic Mail Communications

Electronic mail, commonly referred to as *e-mail,* is fast becoming a preferred method of communication by those individuals who have access to personal computers in their work or home environments. E-mail allows individuals to send and receive messages on their computer. These messages seem secure because a secret password must be used to send or read messages. Messages are typed, but written documents, video images, or audio messages may be attached to e-mail messages that are sent to another person.

Usually, messages are sent between individuals with periods of time passing between communications. This type of interaction resembles a letter writing exchange. However, it is possible to send and receive messages instantly if both persons are at the computer at the same time. Instant communication by e-mail simulates a conversation.

A primary advantage of e-mail is that it is free once access to an e-mail system is secured through a subscription that usually involves a service fee. Many employers provide e-mail access to their employees. Other advantages to e-mail over other methods of communication are that individuals can retrieve their messages at their convenience rather than being interrupted by telephone calls, printed copies of messages can be easily created, and messages can be returned quickly and efficiently.

Disadvantages of e-mail communication, when compared to telephone conversations, are the following:

- Communication usually is one-way—it is not interactive.
- Each message is recorded in computers, often in several.
- Communication is not complete until the recipient actually accesses the messages and reads them.
- Once sent, messages cannot be retrieved.
- The quick nature of the communication can lead to sending messages that are not well conceptualized.
- Recipients may misinterpret messages and do not have the benefit of asking for clarification or of noting a person's tone of voice or inflection.
- It is easy to make errors and send messages to the wrong person or to many persons at once.
- Messages can easily be forwarded to others.
- Messages can be altered before being sent on to another person.
- The ease of using e-mail seems to encourage an informality that may not be well-suited for professional communications.

The use of e-mail can be deceptive. Those who use e-mail type their message, press a button, and it disappears. Although it appears to be private between the message sender and the receiver, in reality there are a number of opportunities for e-mail messages to be intercepted or read by others.

The primary legal concern for counselors who use e-mail is that a record exists in computers for every message that is sent or received. Each message is recorded in several computers and can be retrieved. As a result, an e-mail message creates a record that is vulnerable to exposure. Although an e-mail message record is secured by the passwords of the sender and the receiver, it can be retrieved by individuals who operate the computer systems through which the message is sent. Further, the message can be forwarded easily and can be altered before being forwarded. As a result of the many ways e-mail messages can be accessed or compromised, counselors who use e-mail should be extremely cautious about disclosing confidential information to clients or other professionals through e-mail communications and should warn their clients about the possibility that e-mail messages could be compromised.

Counselors sometimes belong to e-mail communication groups. When a message is sent by an individual, it is received by all persons in the group. Counselors should understand that the increased number of individuals receiving such messages increases the possibilities of a message being sent to others or becoming public (Berge, 1994; Sampson, 1996). Also, belonging to such groups increases the possibility of mistakes in which a private message intended for an individual is sent instantly to a very large group of people.

Use of the Internet

The Internet as a Source of Information for Clients

Counselors sometimes ask clients to read or review materials relevant to the issues they are discussing in counseling. The explosion of information that is available over the World Wide Web is phenomenal. To take just one example, Dedden and James (1998) found 9,000 sites that offered career counseling and reviewed several Internet sites that they believed offered positive and helpful career resources.

Counselors who send their clients to the Internet for information must understand the nature of the materials found there. First, sites on the Internet are not monitored for content or quality. As a result, clients must be cautioned to keep in mind that what they are reading or reviewing may not be accurate or helpful to them. In addition, sites that counselors have reviewed can be changed and may be different by the time they are viewed by clients.

Internet Counseling

The traditional process for counseling involves a counselor and one or more clients meeting face to face in a professional office. Since the Internet has come into existence, some individuals have begun offering counseling by e-mail or through fee-for-service sites. The practice of providing counseling services over the Internet is controversial. There are several advantages to this approach: (a) increased accessibility of services for those who would otherwise find it difficult to receive services, such as low-income clients, the frail elderly, individuals who are severely physically disabled, home-based women, and rural or isolated individuals; (b) perceived anonymity may decrease client anxiety, thus encouraging people to ask for help and increasing the extent to which clients are willing to share intimate issues; (c) greater freedom in scheduling; and (d) the medium facilitates improved preparation by allowing better choice of written words over spoken ones (Sampson, Kolodinsky, & Greeno, 1997; Wilson, Jencius, & Duncan, 1997). On the other hand, a number of concerns have been raised, including the following: (a) the possibility that counselors may operate from erroneous assumptions due to the absence of visual and auditory cues, (b) lack of security of communications could lead to breaches of confidentiality, (c) a relationship-building human presence between counselor and client is lacking, (d) effectiveness of counseling non-White clients may be reduced because the counselor may have difficulty attending to the high-context communication style of a population, and (e) issues that are interpersonal in nature cannot be addressed effectively using this medium (Wilson, Jencius, & Duncan, 1997). Some of these potential problems may be resolved as new technologies, such as videoconferencing and encryption devices that increase the security of transmitted messages, are more widely used. Maintaining confidentiality of client records will continue to be problematic for some time, however, due to the ease with which unauthorized access can be gained and to unresolved questions regarding the number of individuals, agencies, and government entities who might make a case for having a right to access Internet databases.

The current ACA *Code of Ethics* does not address Internet counseling and, therefore, does not expressly prohibit the practice. Because Internet counseling is already occurring, the NBCC has issued guidelines to assist counselors and clients who are engaged in the activity. These guidelines are included in Appendix G.

A major legal question is whether Internet counseling is permitted in states in which counselors must be licensed to practice. A further question arises as to where Internet counseling takes place—in the location of the counselor, the location of the client, or both. Which laws govern the counseling process related to issues such as reporting abuse is another question. Since Internet counseling is so new, these questions will not be addressed until lawsuits are filed in which Internet counseling was used.

Counselors who consider offering counseling services through the Internet should ensure that they are not violating state laws (in the state of the counselor or of the client) that require counselors to be licensed. Counselors should also adhere to the ACA *Code of Ethics* when they provide counseling services in such an unconventional environment.

SUBPOENAS

Subpoenas are legal documents that might require counselors to produce copies of records; appear for a deposition, court hearing, or trial; or appear and bring their records with them (Cottone & Tarvydas, 1998). Subpoenas are official court documents and cannot be ignored.

Receiving a subpoena can be an intimidating, and even frightening, experience for a counselor. Unless counselors deal with subpoenas on a routine basis in their work, there is some justification for this reaction. Dealing with a subpoena places a counselor in the legal arena—into a system that is adversarial in nature and that operates by a different set of rules than those to which counselors are accustomed. If you should receive a subpoena, the information that follows will help guide you through the process of responding to it.

In Chapter 4, one of the exceptions to confidentiality and privileged communication that was noted was a court order. Court orders might be issued in hearings or trials at which judges are present and give verbal orders, or they might be issued when judges sign written orders in their official capacity. All citizens must obey court orders. The sanctions for not obeying orders issued by judges are imprisonment, fines, or both. The only alternative to obeying a court order is to appeal to a higher court. Such appeals must be filed immediately by a lawyer. Although a subpoena is a type of court order, counselors should always consult with their own attorneys before turning over records or appearing at a deposition, hearing, or trial in response to a subpoena.

Discovery in Litigation

Lawyers who are representing parties in lawsuits are members of the bar in the jurisdiction in which they are practicing. Therefore, they are considered official officers of the court. One of the privileges extended to officers of a court is to issue valid subpoenas for information related to cases they are litigating.

One of the concepts in lawsuits of any kind is that attorneys representing the parties are entitled to "discovery." Discovery is the process whereby attorneys have the right to ask for and receive information relevant to their case before the case is tried (Swensen, 1997). The idea is that there should be no surprises during trials. Instead, each side in a lawsuit should know all the information that will be entered into evidence during the trial, before the actual trial begins.

Subpoenas are used extensively during the discovery or pretrial phase of lawsuits. Attorneys from both sides ask potential witnesses to respond in writing to written questions (interrogatories), to provide copies of records they are entitled to see, and to come to their offices for depositions. In addition, witnesses can be subpoenaed to testify at hearings before the judge presiding over the case, and finally, at the trial as well.

Validity of Subpoenas

The records of counselors might be subpoenaed or counselors themselves may be subpoenaed for their oral testimony at depositions, hearings, or trials. Also, written questions may be submitted with a demand for written answers. Counselors might also be subpoenaed to appear at a legal proceeding and instructed to bring records with them. In the event you receive a subpoena to appear at a legal proceeding, but no mention is made of records, do not take records with you unless you are instructed to do so by your own attorney. If a subpoena is issued to you by an attorney, your first step is to consult your own lawyer to determine whether the subpoena is valid and whether you must respond to it (Woody, 1988a). Guidelines for obtaining your own legal advice, whether you are an employee or are in private practice, were provided in Chapter 1.

An attorney will review a subpoena for you and will advise you regarding the proper manner in which to respond. Attorneys might assist you in a number of ways. For example, they could ask the attorney who issued the subpoena to withdraw it, file a motion to quash the subpoena, or advise you to comply with the subpoena.

Attorneys who are litigating cases may not issue subpoenas for records or for witnesses to testify if the attorneys know they do not have a right to the information. However, because material may be privileged without attorneys realizing it, you could receive a subpoena that is not enforceable because of privilege. Subpoenas could be unenforceable or invalid for other reasons as well. You must obtain legal advice regarding your response to any subpoena you receive. If you refuse to respond to a valid subpoena, you could be held in contempt of court and either imprisoned or fined. On the other hand, if you provide information in response to an invalid or unenforceable subpoena, you could be held legally accountable to a client or former client for any damages suffered.

When you receive a subpoena, you should take action immediately, because most subpoenas must be completed within a fixed number of hours. Many counselors mistakenly believe that subpoenas must be personally handed to them to be valid and enforceable. In fact, if you have knowledge through any means that a subpoena has been issued to you, you should take the steps listed below immediately.

Your first step, if you are employed, should be to notify your immediate supervisor that you have received a subpoena and to request legal advice regarding your response to it. In the event your employer does not provide you with access to a lawyer, then follow the directives of your supervisor. If you are in an independent private practice, your first step should be to call your own practice attorney.

Your lawyer or supervisor should be informed if you think the information being requested might be privileged. You should also inform your attorney or supervisor if you believe testifying or producing records regarding the matter would compromise the privacy of a former or current client, even if the relationship was not privileged by law. Feel free to openly discuss the situation with a lawyer because your relationship with the lawyer is privileged. Often it is necessary to explain to your lawyer the general concepts of counseling, the nature of your relationship to the parties involved in the lawsuit, and the details regarding clients who are involved or affected by the litigation. You should give complete information to your lawyer and answer any questions regarding the situation.

Once your attorney or supervisor understands the situation and has given you advice, follow the instructions precisely. If you have doubts or questions, discuss them with your attorney or supervisor, but ultimately you must follow the advice given to you.

Generally a subpoena received from the attorney of your client or former client will not be problematic, because the individual waives privilege, if it exists, by calling you as a witness. Nonetheless, legal advice in such situations still is needed to ensure you are proceeding properly.

Interrogatories

One of the easiest types of subpoenas to deal with is a subpoena that involves interrogatories. Included with the subpoena will be a set of written questions with a requirement that you respond to each question in writing. You must sign an oath that your answers are truthful.

If you receive a set of interrogatories and your attorney informs you that you must respond to them, you should discuss each question and your proposed answer with your attorney before you begin writing. After composing your answers, you should ask your attorney to review your answers before you submit them. Take your attorney's advice about changes or rewording of your answers.

Appearances at Proceedings

In the event you are directed by your attorney or supervisor to appear at a legal proceeding, ask that you be told what to expect. Ask your attorney or supervisor to explain in detail how such events take place. Also, request that the attorney tell you what questions you might be asked and ask for advice on responses you think you should make to the anticipated questions. Request that the attorney accompany you to the proceeding if possible.

Depositions usually take place in the office of the lawyer who has issued the subpoena. While the judge will be present at hearings and trials, the judge does not attend depositions. Generally, depositions are attended by the attorney who issued the subpoena, the attorney representing the other party involved in the lawsuit, a court reporter, and the witness being deposed.

It is important to have your own attorney present at your deposition if possible. During a hearing or trial, the judge will rule on controversies and will instruct witnesses whether to answer questions. With no judge present at depositions, you need your own attorney there to tell you how to proceed and to protect you from being pressured by the other attorneys.

Testimony Under Oath

Testimony you give at any legal proceeding will be under oath, which means that you will be required to swear to tell the truth. Once an oath has been administered, false statements usually are considered perjury, which is a serious crime. You might be instructed by your attorney not to answer questions at a deposition, but you should always, under all circumstances, answer questions truthfully when you do respond.

Turning Over Records

In the event your attorney or supervisor directs you to turn over your records in response to a subpoena, you should follow the advice you have been given. Sometimes attorneys who issue subpoenas will accept summaries of notes rather than case notes themselves, or other similar compromises may be needed. Your attorney will negotiate appropriately on your behalf.

You should never forward the originals of your records. Instead, make copies and deliver the copies. Sometimes records of other individuals are mixed in with records that must be turned over. In that situation, sometimes it is permissible to obliterate private information related to other parties. Again, follow the advice of your attorney in this situation.

If your records include records you have received from other professionals, such as physicians, other mental health professionals, or hospitals, do not copy and forward those records. If the attorney issuing the subpoena wants copies of those records, the individual or entity that created them will have to be subpoenaed.

SUMMARY AND KEY POINTS

This chapter familiarized you with the complexities of counseling records and discussed new issues that have been created by developments in technology. Subpoenas were also addressed in this chapter, because records are often subject to being subpoenaed.

With respect to **records,** some key points made in the chapter include the following:

- Counselors keep records for two legitimate reasons: to provide the best possible quality of services to clients, and for their own self-protection.
- Keeping good records can benefit clients in several significant ways. Some benefits to clients include continuity of care when client information is transferred from one mental health professional to another, or when a former client returns to counseling after an extended absence; helping clients measure and affirm their growth and change; and the creation of an accurate history of a client's diagnosis, treatment, and recovery.
- Records can also serve to protect counselors. In the event that your decisions are ever challenged, it is essential that you have documented decisions you have made and actions you have taken.

- Counselors keep three major types of records: administrative records, recordings, and clinical case notes. It is important for you to understand what is involved in keeping each of these kinds of records, and that you follow sound procedures for keeping them secure and protecting the privacy of your clients.
- Many counselors are surprised to learn how many people can have access to their records. You should always make records with the assumption that they will be seen by others, including clients who have the right to access their records.
- Two important federal laws that affect counseling records are the FERPA and a statute related to federally funded substance abuse programs. If you work in an educational institution or in an agency that receives federal funds to provide substance abuse treatment, you will need to understand the major provisions of these laws.
- When you begin working with clients, you will need to have clear and consistent policies and procedures for creating, maintaining, transferring, and destroying your records. While your personal style and preferences may play some role, many of these policies and procedures will be dictated by your employer, laws, and accreditation standards.

Advances in **technology** have had a significant impact on the practice of counseling. Although you certainly will want to use as many forms of technology as you can to maximize your effectiveness, it is imperative that you are aware of subtle ways that the use of technology can affect your clients' privacy.

- Remember to be very cautious about discussing confidential information over the telephone.
- Messages sent and received via answering machine, voice mail, answering services, pagers, and cellular phones are particularly vulnerable to unauthorized intrusions into privacy. You will need to keep in mind the various ways in which confidential information can be compromised when you use these means of communication.
- Although computers can help make your work more efficient and cost-effective, you must be able to restrict access, secure stored information, transfer information, and dispose of files appropriately.
- E-mail communication has many advantages over telephone conversations, but there are many ways e-mail messages can be accessed or compromised. Again, you will need to have enough knowledge of how this medium works to be able to avoid inadvertent breaches of your clients' privacy.
- The Internet holds promises and pitfalls for use both as an information resource and as a counseling medium. Advances in Internet technology have outpaced the ability of mental health professionals to ensure that clients receive high-quality services.

The thought of receiving a **subpoena** might make you quite anxious. Subpoenas are official court documents that you cannot ignore. Unless you deal with subpoenas on a routine basis in your work, you should consult your supervisor (if you are employed) or your practice attorney (if you are in private practice) whenever you receive a subpoena. Your attorney will be an invaluable resource in helping you respond appropriately to subpoenas and deal with legal proceedings such as interrogatories, depositions, and trials. Always seek the counsel of your supervisor or attorney and follow the advice you are given.

Competence and Malpractice

When clients come for counseling, they invest a great deal of trust and reliance in their counselors. The client's role in the therapeutic relationship, which involves dependency, self-disclosure, vulnerability, and expectations of finding relief and solutions to problems in a safe environment, underscores the counselor's obligation to provide competent services. "When clients put their trust in us as professionals, one of their most fundamental expectations is that we will be competent" (Pope & Vasquez, 1991, p. 51).

Counselors are neither totally competent or totally incompetent, although legal arguments during malpractice lawsuits might imply otherwise. In discussing the competency of lawyers, Cramton (1981) distinguished between "the ability to perform a task at an acceptable level" and "the reality of actually doing so in a particular situation" (p. 161). From Cramton's perspective, competency is not an abstract concept; instead, it is based on performance. Neither is competency a dichotomous concept; there is a continuum of professional expertise with gross negligence at one end and maximum effectiveness at the other extreme.

COMPETENCE AS AN ETHICAL AND LEGAL CONCEPT

As was discussed in Chapter 1, the difference between law and ethics is that law demands a minimum level of practice from counselors, and ethics encourages counselors to approach the ideal in their level of practice. Competency is a parallel concept in that external forces require counselors to demonstrate minimum competency for professionals, while an internal force demands that counselors strive for ideal practice. For example, state licensure boards set the *minimum* requirements that counselors must meet to practice in that state, and counseling graduate programs require *minimum* levels of performance in order to be granted a degree. On the other hand, counselors are constantly striving to attain *maximum* knowledge and skills, and national voluntary credentialing organizations such as the NBCC certify counselors who have distinguished themselves beyond the minimum in the field.

So, as we discuss competence in this chapter, keep in mind that competency is not an *either/or* concept. Rather, competency is a complex concept with many possible levels along a continuum.

Competency in counseling involves both ethical and legal considerations. From an ethical perspective, the moral principle that is most salient to its consideration is nonmaleficence—do no harm. Incompetence is often a major factor in causing harm to clients. Counselors rarely intend to harm their clients, but harm *can* occur if the counselor is not knowledgeable, skillful, and capable.

The most basic ethical standard related to competence in the ACA *Code of Ethics* is that counselors "practice only within the boundaries of their competence" (Standard C.2.a.). How can a counselor determine just where these boundaries lie? It is difficult to answer this question because counseling is an exceptionally broad profession. Just as attorneys and physicians could never be competent to practice in every area within law and medicine, counselors could never be competent to offer counseling services in all areas of practice or to everyone who seeks their services. A counselor who is qualified and experienced in working with children might not be competent to work with a geriatric population. Expertise in counseling basically healthy clients who are having difficulty coping with life transitions does not qualify a counselor to work with clients who suffer from severe, clinical depression. Competence in individual counseling does not necessarily translate into competence to lead a therapy group or to counsel families.

Competence is also a legal issue, because society expects professionals to be competent and holds them to this standard through licensing boards and the courts. Legal issues relating to competence include state licensure and the law of malpractice. When a client is harmed, the counselor could be sued for malpractice and be held legally responsible in a court of law. Many lawsuits brought by plaintiffs alleging that they were harmed as clients focus on competence.

In this chapter, we first explore methods of developing and assessing competence to *enter* the counseling profession. Next we focus on ways to *maintain* competence during one's professional career. Finally, we address issues that arise when a counselor's competence is *questionable* or is called into question. These issues include malpractice, one of the most frightening of all legal issues for counselors, and impairment.

TRAINING ISSUES

Competence is based on "education, training, supervised experience, state and national professional credentials, and appropriate professional experience" (ACA *Code of Ethics*, Standard C.2.a.). Training is obviously a basic component in developing competence to counsel; the process of becoming competent to enter professional practice begins with education and training.

The initial responsibility for producing competent practitioners lies with those who do the training—counselor educators and supervisors. They must select and admit individuals to training programs who are likely to succeed at developing the skills, knowledge, and characteristics needed to become effective counselors. Academic ability is one important factor. Selection criteria typically include grade-point averages and scores on standardized tests such as the Graduate Record Examination (GRE) or Miller Analogies Test (MAT). It is entirely possible, however, for a student to have strong intellectual abilities and still not possess the personal characteristics that are needed to be a "therapeutic person." Characteristics such as self-awareness, tolerance for ambiguity, and a willingness to explore one's own biases, values, and personal issues have been shown to be related to the ability to develop effective therapeutic relationships. Although these characteristics are difficult to measure, most training programs rely on a personal interview, written essay, or other subjective criteria in selecting candidates for admission into training programs.

Once candidates have been selected and admitted into a graduate program, the next question that arises is "What does a training program need to include, in order to produce competent counselors?" As we described in Chapter 2, CACREP has developed standards for training counselors, and the CORE has set forth similar standards for rehabilitation counselors. CACREP and CORE accredit training programs that have undergone a rigorous review, so it can be reasonably assumed that graduates of approved programs possess certain competencies (Herlihy & Corey, 1996). It should be noted, however, that the majority of counselor training programs are not CACREP or CORE accredited, and that many competent counselors are trained in programs of sound quality that have not sought this accreditation. Another approach to ensuring adequacy of training programs is regional accreditation of universities. Graduation from a regionally accredited institution is a requirement set forth in the *Code of Ethics*. Standard C.3.a. states that counselors may advertise only their highest degree in counseling or a related field "from a college or university that was accredited when the degree was awarded by one of the regional accrediting bodies recognized by the Council on Postsecondary Education."

While these approaches to ensuring quality of training are both necessary and helpful, the reality remains that successful graduation from an accredited training program does not guarantee competence. Much depends on the individual student's motivation and ability to learn, the quality of instruction, the breadth and extent of supervised experience in working with clients that is provided by the training program, and the quality of supervision received. In our own experience as counselor educators, we have found that most students who are about to graduate are keenly aware that they have only just begun to develop competence as practitioners. As a novice counselor, you need not be hobbled by a concern over your limitations and lack of experience. Nonetheless, a healthy awareness can help you avoid exceeding your boundaries of competence in your eagerness to begin practicing your new profession.

CREDENTIALING

Credentialing is a "method of identifying individuals by occupational group" (Sweeney, 1995, p. 120). As was discussed in Chapter 2, two important types of credentialing that are found in counseling are certification, which takes various forms, and licensure. These credentials provide a tangible indicator of certain accomplishments and, as such, they have implications for assessing the competence of the credential holder.

The terms, *licensure, certification,* and *registration,* have many different meanings but sometimes are used interchangeably, which causes a great deal of confusion. As was explained in depth in Chapter 2, the strict use of the terms in governmental regulation of a profession is as follows: (a) licensure refers to the most rigorous form of regulation in that only those who are licensed may practice the profession in a state; (b) certification is the term used when a title, such as "professional counselor," can be used only by those who are certified, but anyone can practice the profession without being certified; and (c) registration is the form of governmental regulation in which members of a profession must "sign up" with the government if they practice the profession in the state, but anyone may sign the registry without a review of their credentials (Anderson & Swanson, 1994). National private organizations, such as NBCC, offer national *certification,* which is a credential that is voluntary (not required by a government for practice). In addition, state departments of education require *certification* of school counselors employed in public school districts. In this chapter, we are using the term *licensure* to refer to state regulation of a profession generally, and the term *certification* to refer to national voluntary credentials and state department certification of school counselors.

Licensure

Licensure is the most powerful type of credentialing and is established by state law. When state legislators determine that the public's best interests are best served by creating a license to practice a particular profession, the minimum standards for practice of that profession in that state are established through a political process. State governments would rather not be involved in regulating the practice of professions. Legislators agree to license a professional group only when it can be shown that members of the public (a) do not have the ability to determine who is competent to practice within a particular profession, and (b) could be harmed by incompetent practitioners. Currently, most of the 50 states and the District of Columbia license counselors (Harris, 1997).

When a state legislature passes a statute that establishes counselor licensure or passes amendments to an existing licensure statute, part of that statute specifies the minimum standards for becoming licensed to practice in that state. When counselor licensure bills or amendments are introduced, political pressures are put on politicians. Economists oppose counselor licensure, arguing that licensing of professions is self-serving, restricts entry into professions, and causes fees for services to rise unreasonably (Rottenberg, 1980). Organizations whose purpose it is to limit the role of government in citizens' lives also oppose licensure statutes. They often are joined in their opposition by other mental health professionals (including psychologists, psychiatrists, and social workers) who do not want to see other professional groups licensed to provide mental health services. When these groups of related mental health professionals realize that a bill or amendment is going to be passed over their objection, they often demand very high standards for licensure to keep as few individuals as possible from being licensed. All these groups put political pressure on legislators to set the minimum standards for licensure very high.

On the other side, there are pressures to set the minimum standards very low. For instance, individuals who are already practicing counseling in a state when counselor licensure statutes are being considered or amended often lobby for statutes that include very low standards so that they will not lose their status and will be entitled to licenses.

As a result of these various political pressures, states now have differing standards. According to Harris (1997), licensing statutes for counselors range from a low of 30 required graduate credits to a high of 60 credits. In addition, the number of required post-master's degree supervised hours range from 2,250 to 4,000. Some statutes specify a significant number of required courses; others require very few specific courses.

Although there is variation from state to state, all licensed counselors have completed at least a master's degree, have had post-master's supervised experience, and have successfully completed an examination or other form of screening. Thus, when clients select licensed professionals as their counselors, they can be assured that their counselors have demonstrated certain knowledge, skills, and abilities to the satisfaction of those professionals who evaluated them. Nonetheless, as is true of other approaches, there are limitations to what licensing can accomplish in terms of ensuring competence. Some writers have questioned whether there is evidence that licensure actually ensures general competence, protects consumers, or promotes higher standards of practice (Keith-Speigel & Koocher, 1985; Pope & Vasquez, 1991). Hogan (1979) contended that there is no evidence that the quality of services of psychotherapists has improved since licensing laws have been enacted, and that challenging the practices of unlicensed counselors is often aimed at attacking competition rather than eliminating incompetence. Despite Hogan's position that the licensing of mental health professionals is self-serving and has little to do with protecting the public, the licenses of mental health professionals are revoked regularly for incompetent practice (Morris, 1984).

Corey et al. (1993) have pointed out that the possession of a license does not ensure that practitioners will competently *do* what their license permits them to do. The counselor license is a generic one. This leaves it up to licensed counselors, as individuals, to discriminate between professional titles and the professional *functions* they are competent to perform. Too, while licensure boards can restrict or terminate the practice of incompetent practitioners against whom they have received complaints, they are not in the business of monitoring the practices of counselors about whom they have received no complaints.

Clearly, licensing of counselors is an attempt to ensure competent practice. Government regulation of the counseling profession may have a positive influence on competency within the profession, but it falls short of accomplishing its objective of ensuring competence. In reality, the standards set for licensure are often the result of political compromises rather than standards that have been set by the profession for minimum competency.

Certification

In addition to becoming licensed, counselors can offer evidence that supports their competence by becoming certified. Some types of certification are mandatory for practicing in certain settings and occur at the state level. For instance, public school counselors must be certified by the states in which they practice. There are also national, voluntary certifications, such as those offered by the NBCC. National Certified Counselors, like licensed counselors, have received training in specific content areas and clinical instruction, have had supervised counseling experience, and have passed an examination.

Specialties

In addition to generic certification as an NCC, NBCC offers several specialty certifications including school, mental health, career, gerontological, and addictions counseling. Specialty certifications are another means of establishing a counselor's competence to work with certain types of clients, in certain settings, or in specialized areas of counseling. There are also a host of other, more narrow specialty certifications offered by various groups in such areas as hypnotherapy, biofeedback, or sex therapy.

Specialty training is a controversial issue in counseling. Some have argued that only practitioners who have specialized training should be allowed to practice that specialty. Some have called for specialty *licensing* (Cottone, 1985), while others (Remley, 1995) strongly oppose it. Specialty *accreditation* of counselor education programs is another approach to establishing that certain counselors are qualified to practice in specified areas. This is the approach that is currently being taken (Sweeney, 1995).

There appears to be tension between proponents of two schools of thought regarding specialty training. Some counselors believe that establishing competence boundaries should be left up to individual professionals, who then would be accountable to licensure or certification boards if they exceeded those boundaries to the detriment of a client. Others believe that counselors should be prevented by licensure boards from practicing within specialty areas unless they have received specific training in the form of graduate courses or supervision. The issues of specialty training, and specialty licensing and certification will likely be debated within the counseling profession for some time.

MAINTAINING COMPETENCE

Once counselors have completed their formal training and are licensed or certified to practice, the burden of determining competence shifts away from trainers and supervisors and onto the counselors themselves. Counselors are autonomous professionals, responsible for monitoring their own effectiveness. One of the indicators of a profession, that distinguishes it from a semiprofession or a nonprofession, is that the members of the profession practice autonomously. In return for this privilege of independence, professionals must limit themselves to practicing within the areas in which they are competent. Professionals individually determine the limits of their competence and practice accordingly.

Continuing Education

Although competence can certainly be enhanced by the skillful application on a day-to-day basis of the knowledge gained in a formal training program, experience alone is no guarantee against errors. Considering the constant contributions new research makes to knowledge in the field, as well as significant, ongoing changes in the environment in which counseling is practiced, we doubt that a counselor could retain even a modicum of professional competence over a 30- or 40-year career without further training. The code of ethics states that counselors recognize the need for continuing education to maintain awareness of current scientific and professional information (Standard C.2.f.), and most counselor licensure boards have established continuing education requirements for maintaining one's license. As Herlihy and Corey (1996) have noted, however, there are limits to what continuing education requirements can accomplish. "It is difficult to monitor the quality of continuing education offerings or their relevance to a particular counselor's needs. The number of clock hours obtained may have little relationship to how much the counselor has actually learned and integrated into practice" (p. 219).

There are many other questions that could be raised regarding what constitutes a legitimate effort to maintain competence. For instance, is attending a seminar commensurate with teaching one? Is writing an article for a professional journal an indicator of continuing competence? What is the relative value of reading books and scholarly articles about new techniques and theories? Can counselors who regularly but informally consult with colleagues about their cases be considered to be as diligent in working to maintain competence as counselors who attend formal seminars? There may be no way to objectively assess whether a counselor has maintained competence over time. External criteria such as continuing education credits earned are not sufficient to ensure continuing competence. Perhaps more important are counselors' own efforts, as autonomous professionals operating at the aspirational level of ethics, to remain aware of their own limitations, to recognize that these limitations can increase over time, and to seek to keep skills current by both formal and informal means (Keith-Spiegel & Koocher, 1985).

PEER REVIEW

Peer review is an approach to monitoring competence that we believe can be very effective. Peer review is "an organized system by which practitioners within a profession assess one another's services" (Corey et al., 1993, p. 186). Peer consultation or peer supervision groups are useful for counselors at all levels of experience and offer many benefits to counselors. They include mutual support; objective feedback in dealing with countertransference issues; information on therapeutic techniques, new research, and referral sources; and help in dealing with difficult cases, stress, and the isolation often experienced by private practitioners. Ideally, peer consultation or supervision groups would meet on a regular, scheduled basis to discuss practice issues and ethical issues, with a flexible agenda determined by the needs of the members (Greenburg, Lewis, & Johnson, 1985). Borders (1991) has suggested that a structured peer group provides the procedure and tasks needed for participants to benefit from peer feedback and a mechanism for counselors to contribute to their own professional development as well as that of their colleagues. Independent private practitioners are expected to seek peer supervision (ACA *Code of Ethics,* Standard C.2.d.) and this is a strategy we recommend for counselors in all work settings. Remley, Benshoff, and Mowbray (1987) have developed a model for peer supervision that can be used by counseling practitioners.

Intercultural Counseling Competence

Recognizing diversity in our society and developing intercultural counseling competence are essential to ethical practice. The demographic landscape of the United States is changing rapidly; it is projected that racial/ethnic minorities will become a numerical majority between the years 2030 and 2050 (Sue, 1995). Increasingly, counselors will come into contact with clients who are culturally different from themselves.

When you think of your own future practice, keep in mind that if you are not trained and competent to work with culturally diverse clients, you might be practicing unethically if you attempt to provide services to these clients. Counselors have an ethical obligation to actively attempt to understand the diverse cultural backgrounds of their clients and to learn how their own cultural/racial/ethnic identities impact their values and beliefs about the counseling process (ACA *Code of Ethics,* Standard A.2.b.). They are also required to keep current with the diverse and special populations with whom they work (Standard C.2.f.) and are encouraged to stretch their boundaries of competence by gaining knowledge, personal awareness, sensitivity, and skills for working with diverse client populations (Standard C.2.a.).

Information Technologies

The cyberspace phenomenon presents counselors with a myriad of opportunities for keeping current and improving their competence as practitioners. New information technologies are developing at such a rapid pace that any attempt we might make to describe them would be obsolete almost immediately. We can, however, highlight a few key resources. The counseling profession has established a solid presence on the Internet. This offers opportunities to access virtual libraries for researching the latest information on client problems and effective counseling techniques, as well as to collaborate and consult with other professionals around the world. Many of ACA's divisions, NBCC, and CACREP have home pages on the World Wide Web (WWW), so you can communicate quickly and directly with professional groups that are working to strengthen counseling as a profession. Videoconferencing on the Internet enables you and counselors everywhere to obtain further training and even supervision without having to travel great distances. You can subscribe to mailing lists that allow you to share experiences, ask questions, and exchange information and ideas.

These new technologies present many exciting opportunities, but they also have created problems related to assuring competence of services. Some counselors have begun to provide direct counseling services over the Internet. The fact that counseling is taking place over the Internet before the profession has fully considered the ethical implications is cause for concern. There is no reliable method of regulating the services offered, of ensuring the competence of the providers, or of protecting consumers from ill-advised Internet-based services (Wilson, Jencius, & Duncan, 1997).

Making Referrals

Ethical counselors recognize that they will often need to refer a client, when accepting or continuing to work with that client would exceed their boundaries of competence. Sometimes it can be difficult for counselors to acknowledge that they are not competent to take on every client who might request their help. There are many sources of temptation to accept clients who might be better served by a referral. These might include a reluctance to disappoint a valued source of referrals, financial pressures to increase your client load when business has been slow, or the ego-enhancing nature of requests from clients who hold exaggerated beliefs about your talents and abilities to help them. To succumb to these kinds of temptations would be unethical and would not be in the clients' best interest.

Another type of challenge is posed when counselors need to refer a client with whom they are already engaged in a counseling relationship. Despite the best efforts of counselors to accept only those clients whom they believe they can provide with competent services, the course of therapy is unpredictable. A client's presenting problem may be well within the counselor's scope of competence, and the counselor might in good faith begin working with that client, only to discover as therapy progresses that the client has unanticipated therapeutic needs. The case described below is an example.

Marianne, an LPC in private practice, began working with Ellen, a young woman who came for counseling to deal with what at first appeared to be moderate anxiety. Ellen described herself as a perfectionist and sought counseling to learn to "stop being so hard on myself." It was only after several counseling sessions that Ellen felt safe enough in the counseling relationship to reveal to Marianne that she was so fearful of becoming "fat" that she regularly engaged in self-induced vomiting after meals, abused laxatives, and exercised excessively. Marianne recognized these behaviors as symptoms of anorexia nervosa or bulimia nervosa (American Psychiatric Association, 1994), a problem area with which she had no experience.

Marianne's ethical obligation at this point is clear. She must either refer Ellen to a specialist or to another therapist who is competent to work with clients who suffer from eating disorders, or she must ensure that she provides quality counseling services to Ellen by obtaining educational experiences and consultation, or supervision from experts. This may not be as simple as it seems. What if Marianne practices in an isolated, rural community and a local referral resource, or expert consultants or supervisors are not available? What if Marianne is able to find a suitable referral source but Ellen refuses, stating that she has complete faith in Marianne's ability to help her? Marianne will need to invest the effort required to meet Ellen's needs. Without the needed competence or expert assistance, Marianne cannot in good conscience continue to work with a client who may have an illness that can be life-threatening.

Other situations that might raise the question of referring a client are less clear-cut. As Corey et al. (1993) have noted, even the most experienced counselors will at times seriously wonder whether they have the personal and professional abilities to work with some of their clients. Difficulty in working with some clients does not, in itself, imply incompetence. In fact, counselors who refer all clients with whom they encounter difficulties will probably have few clients. Instead, counselors can extend their boundaries of competence through reading, participating in workshops and other professional development opportunities, consulting, co-counseling with colleagues who have expertise in a needed area, and working under supervision. The key is to keep a careful balance. Counselors can avoid stagnation, and can continue to learn and grow as professionals by taking on clients who present new concerns and issues, thus extending their scope of competence. In fact, it would be impossible to develop expertise in a new counseling specialty area without eventually accepting a client with an issue in that area. At the same time, care must be taken that clients are not harmed while the counselor is in the process of learning new skills and developing new competencies. You will need to make careful judgments regarding when to refer and when to keep new clients when you are preparing to provide services in a new area.

COUNSELOR INCOMPETENCE

Stress, Burnout, and Impairment

The counseling profession has been slow to recognize the problem of impairment among its members. Although concern has increased in recent years, counselor impairment still has not been clearly defined (Emerson & Markos, 1996). The terms *distressed, burned out,* and *impaired* have been used somewhat interchangeably in the counseling literature. However, they might be better viewed as ranging along a continuum from the least to most serious in terms of their impact on competent professional performance.

Counseling can be stressful work, and this stress occasionally takes its toll on practitioners. Ironically, the counseling relationship itself can be a source of stress. In other interpersonal relationships, such as friendships, there is give and take and a reciprocal meeting of needs. This balance does not exist in a counseling relationship. Counselors make a "loan of the self" to the therapeutic relationship (Squyres, 1986), receive little in return, and sometimes doubt the effectiveness of counseling. Of therapists surveyed by Farber and Heifetz (1982), 74% saw "lack of therapeutic success" as the most stressful aspect of their work, and 55% felt depleted by the nonreciprocated attentiveness, giving, and responsibility that the therapeutic relationship demands. Stress can lead to distress, and most counselors probably could be described as *distressed* at some time during their professional lives. In fact, results of one survey indicated that 82% of psychotherapists had experienced at least one episode of psychic distress (Prochaska & Norcross, 1983). Distressed counselors may experience anxious and depressed moods, somatic complaints, lowered self-esteem, and feelings of helplessness, but they are not necessarily impaired in their professional functioning. They know at some subjective level that something is wrong, and distress is usually a transitory and temporary condition.

When distress remains unalleviated, however, it can lead to *burnout,* which has been described as "physical, emotional, and mental exhaustion brought on by involvement over prolonged periods with emotionally demanding situations and people" (Pines & Aronson, 1988). Burned out counselors, exhausted and depleted, have little energy left for their clients. They tend to manifest negative attitudes toward self and work. Some writers have suggested that few counselors can expect to stay immune from burnout, and even that burnout may be nearly inevitable after 10 years in the field (Grosch & Olsen, 1994; Kottler, 1993). Burnout is not so much a state or condition as it is a process that, if not corrected, can lead to impairment.

While it would be a rare counselor who never experiences a frustrating week, a difficult client, an emotional overload, or occasional symptoms of burnout, counselors who are functioning well can put these experiences into perspective. *Impaired counselors,* by contrast, are unable to transcend periods of stress (Stadler, 1990). Their therapeutic skills have diminished or deteriorated to the point that they are unable to perform their responsibilities appropriately (Emerson & Markos, 1996; Guy, 1987). The medical profession has described impairment as "the inability to deliver competent patient care" (Stadler, Willing, Eberhage, & Ward, 1988, p. 258). Substituting "client" for "patient," this definition can be applied to counseling, and incompetence raises the risk that clients might be harmed. Impairment is often associated with alcohol and other drug abuse, and with the blurring of therapeutic boundaries that can lead to sexual exploitation of clients.

Why do some counselors become impaired, while others manage to bounce back from periods of distress or burnout? Sometimes environmental factors can play a key role. A counselor may experience the death of a loved one, divorce or desertion, rape, the severe physical illness of a family member, or other personal loss or trauma. These events can unbalance anyone's emotional equilibrium. If the counselor takes time off work, goes for counseling, or in some other overt way takes control and works toward a return to full functioning, this type of impairment is usually transitory and need not be a cause for ongoing concern about the counselor's competence (Emerson & Markos, 1996).

In other instances, preexisting conditions may put the counselor at risk. Some individuals enter the helping professions in order to work through their own unresolved problems. Personal difficulties that have led some counselors to enter the profession may be exacerbated by the practice of the profession. The practice of counseling can reactivate early experiences, open old wounds, and reawaken unresolved issues. Counselors with a history of or vulnerability to substance abuse seem to be predisposed to problems after entering the profession (Guy, 1987). Studies indicate that a significant number of impaired counselors experience alcoholism or other substance abuse problems (Deutsch, 1985; Thoreson, Nathan, Skorina, & Kilberg, 1983). Depression is also a common preexisting condition among impaired professionals; 57% of female psychologists who responded to one survey (Deutsch, 1985) reported that they had experienced more than one episode of depression. For these at-risk professionals, the connection between depression and suicide is a particular cause for concern. The death-by-suicide rate among female psychologists has been reported to be four times that of White women in general (Preski in Scott & Hawk, 1986).

The ACA *Code of Ethics* provides clear guidance regarding impairment. Counselors are required to refrain from offering professional services "when their physical, mental, or emotional problems are likely to harm a client or others. They are alert to the signs of impairment, seek assistance for problems, and, if necessary, limit, suspend, or terminate their professional responsibilities" (Standard C.2.g.). Burnout and impairment can be prevented when individual counselors monitor their own vulnerabilities and are aware of the ethical ramifications of practicing when they are unable to function effectively (Witmer & Young, 1996). Many resources and strategies are available to counselors when they recognize that they need to make changes in their lives if they are to remain competent practitioners. Some of these are (a) seeking counseling for themselves, (b) seeking supervision, especially of their work with clients who are difficult and tend to drain their personal resources, (c) taking a break or vacation from practice, and (d) joining a peer support group.

It is crucial that you develop self-monitoring skills so that you can stay psychologically and emotionally healthy as a counselor. Because graduate school is often stressful, now is a good time to learn and practice these skills. It will be helpful for you to know the symptoms of burnout, to familiarize yourself with various wellness models, and to periodically take the time to assess how you are managing the stressors in your life.

MALPRACTICE

Malpractice involves professional misconduct or unreasonable lack of skill, and has been defined as follows:

> Failure of one rendering professional services to exercise that degree of skill and learning commonly applied under all the circumstances in the community by the average prudent reputable member of the profession with the result of injury, loss or damage to the recipient of those services or to those entitled to rely upon them. It is any professional misconduct, unreasonable lack of skill or fidelity in professional or fiduciary duties, evil practice, or illegal or immoral conduct (Black, 1990; p. 959).

Although malpractice includes intentional wrongdoing, the role of competency of the professional involved in malpractice is clear in this definition. "Unreasonable lack of skill" and "failure . . . to exercise . . . skill" are both indicators of incompetence that can form the basis of malpractice lawsuits against counselors. The concept of competency might be extended so that a counselor who is guilty of "professional misconduct," "evil practice," or "illegal or immoral conduct" also could be defined as incompetent.

Malpractice is a type of civil lawsuit that can be filed against professionals for practicing in a manner that leads to injury to a recipient of their services. Professionals have a legal obligation not to harm individuals who come to them for professional services. Although the law cannot restore people who have been injured to their former state of existence, it can require the person who harmed them to compensate them financially for their damages. If clients believe they have been harmed by their counselors, they can file a malpractice lawsuit against the counselors. Counselors who are sued must then defend themselves against the lawsuit before a judge or jury. Although there is widespread belief that juries favor plaintiffs in professional malpractice suits against health professionals, evidence has demonstrated that juries' findings follow what physicians themselves consider to be negligence, and probably even favor the professionals (Vidmar, 1995).

In order for a client plaintiff to prevail in a malpractice lawsuit against a counselor, the plaintiff must prove the following elements (Prosser, Wade, & Schwartz, 1988):

- The counselor had a duty to the client to use reasonable care in providing counseling services.
- The counselor failed to conform to the required duty of care.
- The client was injured.
- There was a reasonably close causal connection between the conduct of the counselor and the resulting injury (known as "proximate cause").
- The client suffered an actual loss or was damaged.

Proximate cause is a difficult legal concept to understand. *Actual cause* means that a person actually caused the injury of another person. *Proximate cause* has to do with whether the individual would have been injured had it not been for the action or inaction of the other person. Cohen and Mariano (1982) explained that "an intervening cause which is independent of the negligence absolves the defending negligent actor of liability" (p. 121). In other words, just because professionals are negligent does not make them responsible for an injury. It must be proven that some other intervening event did not, in fact, cause the injury. Foreseeability is important in determinations of proximate cause (Cohen & Mariano, 1982). Foreseeability has to do with whether the professional knew or should have known that the professional's actions would result in a specific outcome.

Counselors have become increasingly concerned about being sued for malpractice. While malpractice lawsuits against mental health professionals have increased dramatically over the past decade, the total number of these lawsuits is relatively small. Hogan (1979) concluded that few malpractice lawsuits are filed against counselors, because it is difficult for plaintiffs to establish an adequate case. It is not easy to prove that a counselor deviated from accepted practices and that the counselor's act or negligence caused the harm that a client suffered.

A Hypothetical Malpractice Case

To illustrate how a malpractice case might be considered against a counselor, we will analyze a typical situation in which a counselor might be sued. Suppose that a teacher has come to Monica, a high school counselor, with a concern about Mark, an 11th grade student. Mark has written a paper for English class in which he discusses taking his life because he is upset about his parents' recent divorce. Monica calls Mark into her office and talks with him about the paper. She asks him if he has seriously considered taking his life. After a thorough discussion with Mark, Monica determines that he is not suicidal.

That same day, after school, Mark shoots himself with his father's rifle and kills himself. Mark's mother, Sheila, finds out about the teacher's referral and files a malpractice lawsuit against Monica, claiming that Monica's incompetence caused her son's death. Sheila's attorney probably would name as respondents in the lawsuit Monica individually, each of her direct supervisors up through the school superintendent, the school board, and any other individuals or groups who might be responsible for Monica's actions or failure to act. If Monica had her own independent professional liability insurance policy, her insurance company would hire a lawyer who would represent Monica individually in the case. If Monica did not have her own liability insurance policy, she probably would not be able to afford to pay an attorney to represent her. She would have to rely for her defense on the school system lawyers, who ultimately represent the school system, not her. The school system would have its lawyers, or the lawyers provided by the school system's liability insurance company, file a legal response to the case. Monica's lawyer, if she had one, and the school system lawyers would work together in defending the lawsuit.

Sheila's attorney, in presenting her case in court, would first have to prove that Monica owed a duty of reasonable care in providing counseling services to Mark. This would not be difficult to prove since Monica is a counselor in the school and called Mark in for a counseling session. When a counselor accepts a person as a client, the counselor then has a duty to provide the client with professional care that meets accepted standards within the profession. Counselors have a fiduciary relationship with clients, which is a relationship that fosters the highest level of trust and confidence (Anderson, 1996). Clearly, Monica owed Mark a duty of care.

After establishing that a duty of care was owed to Mark, Sheila's attorney then would have to prove that Monica breached that duty and failed to conform to the required standard of care. Most experts would agree that counselors must assess whether a client is suicidal, even though studies have shown that it is impossible to scientifically predict suicidal behavior (Coleman & Shellow, 1992). If it is determined the client is in danger, action must be taken to prevent the impending suicide (Ahia & Martin, 1993; Austin, Moline, & Williams, 1990). The question in this situation is whether Monica was reasonable in her assessment of Mark's risk. The only way to prove that Monica made an error in her professional judgment is for Sheila's attorney to bring in one or more expert witnesses who will testify that a competent counselor would not have done what Monica did. The expert witnesses must compare the actions Monica took to the actions that a reasonable counselor with Monica's same background and training, practicing in the same locality, would have taken in the same set of circumstances. This is the legal standard of care to which counselors are held. Monica's attorney would arrange for a different set of experts to testify that Monica did act reasonably in this particular situation. The judge or jury would have to decide which expert witnesses to believe.

After offering evidence through expert witness testimony that Monica breached her duty of care, Sheila's attorney would have to prove that Mark was injured as a result of this breach. It would not be difficult to prove that harm occurred, since Mark killed himself.

Next, Sheila's attorney would have to prove that there was a close causal connection between what Monica did, or failed to do, and Mark's suicide. Sheila's attorney would have to prove that Sheila knew or should have known that her actions would result in Mark's death. The attorney would argue that Monica was the proximate cause of Mark's death because she failed to take actions that would prevent him from committing suicide. On the opposing side, Monica's attorney would argue that a number of other intervening factors led to Mark's suicide, and that a reasonable counselor would not and could not have predicted that Mark would take his life, given the circumstances in this situation. Further, Monica's attorney would argue that even if Monica did act negligently in this situation, Mark's suicide cannot be blamed on her failure to take action. Other factors "caused" his suicide—factors such as his father leaving his gun out so that Mark had access to it, no one being at home to supervise him after school, or his distress over his parents' contentious behavior during the divorce. The judge or jury would have to decide whether Monica's failure to act to prevent Mark's suicide was the proximate cause of his death, or whether other factors caused him to take his life.

If Sheila's attorney was successful in convincing the judge or jury that Monica was responsible for Mark's death, then the damage to Sheila, expressed in financial terms, would have to be determined. If a person is damaged with a financial loss, such as a loss in the stock market or investing in a deal that has no value, then it is easy to determine how much money the person needs to be "made whole again." However, when a person has a physical injury, or loses a loved one through death, then it is very difficult to determine how much money it would take to compensate the person for the loss. In fact, these are losses that cannot be compensated with money, but the law requires that there be a financial compensation.

Damages in this situation would be determined by expert witness testimony on Mark's life expectancy, his earning potential, and the anticipated benefit of earnings that would go to his mother, Sheila. Since the loss of a life was involved in this situation, the damages could be hundreds of thousands or several million dollars. Judges or juries have wide discretion in setting the value in these kinds of cases.

If Sheila received a judgment in her favor, the school system's professional liability insurance carrier would most likely pay the judgment. Monica's professional liability carrier might be responsible for paying a portion of the judgment, as well. Both the school's and Monica's insurance companies would pay the attorneys' fees and other costs of litigation, which could be as much as several hundred thousand dollars.

At this point, you probably are wondering how often lawsuits are based on client suicide and how often family members prevail and collect judgments. Although client suicide is not the only possible basis for a malpractice lawsuit against counselors, it is undoubtedly one of the most painful types of suits for both plaintiffs and defendants. In the following section, we review some actual cases related to client suicide.

Real Malpractice Cases

In 1960, a college counselor was sued for the wrongful death of a student who had committed suicide. The student had seen the counselor in a professional capacity (*Bogust v. Iverson*). The holding in that case was that the college counselor was not a therapist and therefore had no duty to detect or prevent a suicide of a client. Since 1960, however, the counseling profession has evolved substantially and counselors in all settings are considered mental health professionals. A similar case today would probably have a different result.

A case that is similar to *Bogust v. Iverson* and the hypothetical case of Monica was decided in Maryland in 1991. In *Eisel v. Board of Education of Montgomery County,* Dorothy Jones and Deidre Morgan, school counselors at Sligo Middle School in Maryland (along with their school board, principal, and superintendent) were sued in a wrongful death action by Stephen Eisel, the father of Nicole Eisel.

Nicole Eisel was a 13-year-old student at Sligo Middle School. Nicole and another 13-year-old girl consummated an apparent murder-suicide pact on November 8, 1988. The complaint filed in the lawsuit was summarized in the case report:

> The amended complaint avers that Nicole became involved in satanism, causing her to have an "obsessive interest in death and self-destruction." During the week prior to the suicide, Nicole told several friends and fellow students that she intended to kill herself. Some of these friends reported Nicole's intentions to their school counselor, Morgan, who relayed the information to Nicole's school counselor, Jones. Morgan and Jones then questioned Nicole about the statements, but Nicole denied making them. Neither Morgan nor Jones notified Nicole's parents or the school administration about Nicole's alleged statements of intent. Information in the record suggests that the other party to the suicide pact shot Nicole before shooting herself. The murder-suicide took place on a school holiday in a public park at some distance from Sligo Middle School (pp. 449–450).

Attorneys for the school board and its employees argued that school guidance counselors had no duty to recognize or prevent an adolescent's suicide. A motion for summary judgment in favor of the school board and its employees was granted, which means that the court, without even hearing the evidence in the case, found that the counselors were not responsible. Eisel appealed to the Maryland Court of Appeals. The Court of Appeals reversed the summary judgment and required that the case go back to the trial court so that a judge or jury could determine whether the counselors would be held responsible for Nicole Eisel's death.

In coming to this decision, the Maryland Court of Appeals held that "school counselors have a duty to use reasonable means to attempt to prevent a suicide when they are on notice of a child or adolescent student's suicidal intent" (p. 456). The decision noted that the counselors could have determined that Nicole was in danger of committing suicide even though she denied it when asked, that the school board had a policy requiring counselors to notify parents despite any confidentiality concerns, and that the school had a formal suicide prevention program in place. The decision stated, ". . .the relationship of a school counselor and pupil is not devoid of therapeutic overtones" (p. 452). The appeals court did not decide that the two school counselors were responsible for Nicole Eisel's suicide, but it did decide that a judge or jury could determine that the facts were such that they could be held responsible.

It is almost impossible to determine how many lawsuits of a particular nature are filed in court. Many lawsuits are settled without a judgment being rendered or are determined at the trial court level and are not appealed. Only cases that are appealed are reported in case books. However, from the cases that are appealed, it appears that very few lawsuits are filed against counselors due to client suicide, and few of those filed result in judgments against the counselors. Nonetheless, counselors certainly hope to avoid experiencing the double trauma of having a client commit suicide and being named as a defendant in a lawsuit resulting from that suicide. In fact, if you practice competently, the chances are good that you will never have to respond to a malpractice lawsuit.

SUMMARY AND KEY POINTS

Counselor competence is an important concept, even though it is difficult to define from an ethical viewpoint and difficult to demonstrate in a court of law. It is best viewed as being based on performance and as existing along a continuum from gross negligence to maximum effectiveness. Some of the key points made in this chapter include the following:

- The law demands a minimum level of practice from counselors, while ethics encourages counselors to aspire to an ideal level of practice.
- Counselors must practice within their boundaries of competence. It can be difficult to determine just where these boundaries lie.
- The development of competence begins with training and education, and the initial responsibility for producing competent practitioners rests with counselor educators and supervisors.
- Training standards established by accrediting bodies help to ensure that graduates of accredited programs possess certain competencies. Nonetheless, graduation from an accredited training program does not guarantee competence.

- Licensure is a legal process that establishes minimum standards for a counselor to practice in a given state. Because licensure is a political process, counselor licensure requirements are not uniform across the states.
- It is questionable whether licensure actually accomplishes the goals of ensuring competence, protecting consumers, and promoting high standards of practice.
- Certification is another approach to attempting to ensure competence.
- Specialty training, licensure, and certification are controversial issues in the counseling field.
- Once counselors begin to practice, they are responsible for determining their own competence.
- Counselors are required to seek continuing education in order to maintain their competence. Peer review is an effective approach to monitoring competence.
- It is essential in today's society that counselors possess intercultural counseling competence.
- Many new information technologies exist and offer counselors resources for maintaining and increasing their competence.
- Counselors must know when and how to refer clients when they are not able to provide competent services to these clients.
- Counselors must exercise care while stretching their boundaries of competence to include client populations and concerns with which they have little or no experience.
- When counselors are experiencing stress, burnout, or impairment, they need to take steps to protect clients from harm and to restore themselves to their full level of functioning.
- Malpractice lawsuits arise from claims of counselor incompetence. It is difficult to prove all five elements of malpractice that must be proved for a malpractice case to succeed.
- Some lawsuits have been filed against counselors for failing to prevent a client's suicide. Counselors are being held to a higher standard of care in these cases.
- Few malpractice lawsuits are filed against counselors, and few of those filed result in judgments against the counselors.

CHAPTER 7

Boundary Issues

Perhaps no ethical and legal issue has caused more controversy among helping professionals than determining the boundaries of the therapeutic relationship. Although the term *boundary* is part of the everyday language of counseling, it has rarely been defined in the literature (Hermanson, 1997). Therefore, we will define *boundaries* and the related term, *dual or multiple relationships,* before we explore what makes them so controversial.

A boundary can be conceptualized as a frame or membrane around the therapeutic dyad that defines a set of roles for the participants in the therapeutic relationship (Smith & Fitzpatrick, 1995). Viewed this way, boundaries help us understand the parameters of the relationship. Although counseling can involve a great deal of emotional intimacy, it is a professional relationship and, therefore, it has certain limits that might not apply to a personal relationship. To give just a few examples, there are limits on physical contact between counselor and client, on time and place for counseling (counseling takes place during regularly scheduled appointments and in a particular setting), on the amount and types of self-disclosure made by the counselor, and on the exchange of gifts. Boundaries help provide structure to the therapeutic relationship. Katherine's (1991) definition of a boundary as a "limit that promotes integrity" (p. 3) nicely captures the purpose of boundary setting. Boundaries serve to protect the welfare of clients who are in a vulnerable position in the therapeutic relationship.

Boundary issues are usually framed as questions of dual or multiple relationships. According to Herlihy and Corey (1997), dual or multiple relationships occur when helping professionals take on two or more roles simultaneously or sequentially with a help seeker. Stated another way, dual or multiple relationships occur whenever helping professionals have another, significantly different relationship with one of their clients, students, or supervisees. Dual relationships can involve combining the role of counselor with another professional relationship (such as teacher, supervisor, employer, or business partner) or with a personal relationship (such as friend, relative, or lover).

Much of the early attention to boundary issues in therapeutic relationships was focused on sexual intimacies between therapist and client. Later in this chapter, we will discuss in more detail the harm done to clients and the ethical and legal ramifications for counselors who become sexually involved with their clients. First, we will focus on a variety of nonsexual dual relationship issues, exploring the complexities that make them so problematic for practitioners.

NONSEXUAL DUAL RELATIONSHIPS

The codes of ethics of all major mental health professions address the issue of dual relationships in similar ways. The ACA *Code of Ethics* states

> Counselors are aware of their influential position with respect to clients, and they avoid exploiting the trust and dependency of clients. Counselors make every effort to avoid dual relationships with clients that could impair professional judgment or increase the risk of harm to clients. (Examples of such relationships include, but are not limited to, familial, social, financial, business, or close personal relationships with clients.) (Standard A.6.a.)

This standard seems clear and straightforward and you may be wondering why the dual relationship issue has been so controversial. In reality, boundary questions can be complex and ambiguous. First, you should note that the code of ethics does not prohibit *all* dual relationships per se. Rather, it cautions counselors to avoid those dual relationships that *could impair professional judgment or increase the risk of harm to clients.* How does one distinguish among dual relationships that might be acceptable and those that could cause harm? A beginning step is to understand the factors that create the potential for harm.

The Potential for Harm

In determining the risk of harm in a dual relationship, Kitchener and Harding (1990) suggested that counselors should consider three factors: incompatible expectations, divergent responsibilities, and the power differential. We will discuss each of these in turn, using the following example:

> Cora is the director of a university counseling center and Eileen is a secretary in the center's main office. Eileen has been an excellent employee for many years and Cora has come to count on her to help keep the center functioning smoothly. One day Cora comes out of her office and notices that Eileen's eyes are red and puffy and that she seems sad. When Cora expresses her concern, Eileen begins to cry. She tells Cora that she is having some personal problems and adds, "Can I just step into your office for a minute while I pull myself together?" Cora agrees to this request and they both go into Cora's office and close the door. Eileen begins to tell Cora about her personal problems. Cora listens as Eileen tells her story. After nearly an hour she suggests that Eileen might want to seek counseling. Eileen demurs, saying that she feels better now and thinks she can handle things.
>
> Several weeks go by, during which time Eileen's work is not up to her usual high standards. She makes careless errors and forgets things. Cora calls her into her office twice to address this problem. Each time Cora spends about 30 minutes listening to Eileen's personal problems. At the end of each conversation, Eileen insists that she is "getting a grip on things." When the time comes for Cora to complete her quarterly evaluations of her counseling center staff, she gives Eileen a low rating on a number of the items on the form. When Eileen receives the evaluation, she is hurt and angry. She confronts Cora, saying, "How could you—of all people—do this to me! You know I'm a good employee but am just going through a rough time. You know what's going on in my life. I expected you to understand."

It is likely that Eileen's hurt and anger have resulted from the incompatible expectations she held for Cora. On the one hand, Cora has been a caring and sympathetic listener.

Even though Cora did not intend to enter into a formal therapeutic relationship with Eileen, she has behaved as a counselor. Eileen has come to expect her to be understanding, accepting, and nonjudgmental while Eileen is working through her personal problems. She also expects Cora to respect her privacy and keep confidential everything she has told her. Given this set of expectations, the evaluation feels like a punishment and a betrayal. On the other hand, she has been a secretary in the center for several years and is accustomed to receiving quarterly evaluations from her supervisor. As an employee, she realizes that her work has not been up to par and in that role she would expect to receive a fair and accurate evaluation. Her expectations for Cora as a supervisor are incompatible with what she expects from Cora as a sympathetic listener/counselor.

Cora is faced with two divergent responsibilities in this situation. Because she has stepped into a counselor role, she needs to be accepting and supportive of Eileen, as well as patient, while she works through her problems. As a supervisor, however, it is her responsibility to evaluate her employees and to do so accurately. It is impossible for her to evaluate Eileen and be nonjudgmental at the same time.

Finally, there is a power differential in the relationship between Cora and Eileen. Cora is in a position of power because she is Eileen's supervisor who evaluates her work. Eileen is in a less powerful position as an employee and has made herself even more vulnerable by revealing her personal problems. It is Cora's professional responsibility to avoid misusing her power and to ensure that the more vulnerable individual in the relationship is not harmed. Certain characteristics of the therapeutic relationship place counselors in a position of power over clients. When clients come for counseling, they are in an emotionally vulnerable state. In the counseling relationship, the counselor learns much about the client's innermost thoughts and feelings, while the client learns little about the counselor. Additionally, in most societies power is traditionally ascribed to healers (Smith & Fitzpatrick, 1995).

This unfortunate problematic situation between Cora and Eileen could have been avoided if Cora had not appeared to assume the role of counselor for Eileen. Counselors who are asked to counsel others with whom they have other relationships are put in a difficult situation, and it happens quite often. When persons with whom you have other relationships (relative, friend, employee, etc.) know that you are a counselor and ask you to counsel them, you need to be prepared to respond in both a caring and professionally appropriate manner. A good approach would be to acknowledge their distress and empathize with them. It would be good to state that you cannot function as their counselor because of your other relationship with them and offer to help them locate a good counselor. If you then proceed to listen to their situation, it is wise to remind them periodically that you are listening as a relative/friend/supervisor rather than as a counselor.

According to Kitchener and Harding (1990), three postulates regarding the potential for harm can be derived from the risk factors. First, the greater the incompatibility of expectations in a dual role, the greater the risk of harm. Second, the greater the divergence of the responsibilities associated with dual roles, the greater the potential for divided loyalties and loss of objectivity. Third, the greater the power differential between the two parties involved in a dual relationship, the greater the potential for exploitation of the individual in the less powerful position.

Considering these risk factors will help you make wise decisions when you are faced with potential dual relationships. It may also be helpful for you to understand the problematic nature of dual relationships and how they have been debated by helping professionals.

The Problematic Nature of Dual Relationships

Herlihy and Corey (1997) have identified four characteristics of dual relationships that make them so problematic. First, *potential dual relationships can be difficult to recognize.* They can evolve in subtle ways. There is no "danger sign" that marks the point at which a professional relationship crosses the line into behavior that could lead to an inappropriate relationship. It is not difficult for a counselor, or a counselor educator or supervisor, to innocently enter into a form of extraprofessional relationship. A counselor might accept a client's invitation to attend a special event that has meaning for the client. A counselor educator might find a friendship developing with a student whom the educator is mentoring. A supervisor might feel attracted to a supervisee, and think about dating the supervisee as soon as the formal supervision is completed.

When dual relationships are sequential rather than simultaneous, it can be particularly difficult to foresee potential problems. As Pope and Vasquez (1991) have pointed out, the mere fact that two roles are sequential rather than clearly concurrent "does not, in and of itself, mean that the two relationships do not constitute a dual relationship" (p. 112). Some of the questions with which conscientious professionals struggle are whether a former client can eventually become a friend, how a smooth transition can be made from a supervisory relationship to a collegial relationship once supervision is completed, and what factors need to be considered in determining whether a former therapeutic relationship can become a personal relationship of any kind.

A second complicating characteristic of dual relationships is that *their potential for harm ranges along a wide continuum from extremely harmful to benign,* as can be seen in the following two examples.

> Dorothy, age 23, seeks counseling from Gerard, an LPC in private practice. Her goal is to work through issues related to the sexual abuse by her stepfather that she had endured when she was a child. After two months of counseling, Gerard initiates a sexual relationship with Dorothy. He rationalizes his behavior by telling himself that she can benefit from having a "healthy" sexual relationship. Dorothy feels guilty, confused, and isolated by this betrayal of her trust. She wants to end the sexual relationship but has become so dependent on Gerard that she feels trapped. She begins to have thoughts of suicide.

> Fiona has been coming to see Elizabeth, her counselor, for nearly a year. Through counseling, Fiona has gained the self-esteem and confidence to return to college and complete the last four courses she needed in order to graduate. She asks Elizabeth to attend the graduation ceremony. She says that Elizabeth's attendance would mean a great deal to her because she credits the counseling process for making it possible for her to achieve her goal. Elizabeth agrees to attend the ceremony.

As these examples illustrate, at one extreme are sexual dual relationships that can cause severe harm to clients. Gerard's behavior is exploitive, and he is causing harm by revictimizing his client. Near the other end of the continuum are situations in which a counselor chooses to engage in a form of dual relating in order to benefit a particular client. Elizabeth's choice to attend the graduation ceremony has a low risk of causing harm.

Third, *with the exception of sexual dual relationships, there is very little consensus among mental health professionals regarding the propriety of dual relationships.* Hedges (1993), presenting a psychoanalytic viewpoint, has argued that there is an essential dual relatedness in psychotherapy in that transference, countertransference, resistance, and interpretation all rest de facto upon the existence of a dual relationship. Hedges urged counselors to remember that, viewed from this perspective, all beneficial aspects of therapy arise as a consequence of a dual relationship. Tomm (1993) has suggested that when counselors actively maintain interpersonal distance, they highlight the power differential and promote an objectification of the therapeutic relationship. Tomm believed that dual relating invites greater authenticity and congruence from counselors and can actually improve their professional judgments because dual relationships make it more difficult for them to hide behind the protection of a professional mask.

Other writers have taken an opposing stance. St. Germaine (1993) has reminded counselors that the potential for harm is always present in a dual relationship due to the loss of objectivity that accompanies that relationship. Bograd (1993) noted that the power differential between counselor and client makes it impossible for the client to give truly equal consent to an extraprofessional relationship. It is possible that counselors may unintentionally or unconsciously exploit or harm clients who are in a vulnerable position in the relationship. Pope and Vasquez (1991) cautioned that counselors who engage in dual relationships may rationalize their behavior in an attempt to evade their professional responsibility to find acceptable alternatives to dual relationships.

Obviously, there is no consensus among professionals about dual relationships. You will need to give considered thought to developing your own stance toward this issue. As you ponder the risks and benefits of dual relationships, we believe it may be helpful to keep in mind Tomm's (1993) point that it is not dual relating in itself that creates an ethical problem. Rather, it is the counselor's personal tendency to exploit clients or misuse power. Thus, simply avoiding dual relationships will not prevent exploitation. There are many ways that counselors can misuse their power and influence over clients even when they are not occupying more than one role with them.

The fourth and final characteristic that makes boundary issues so complicated is that *some dual relationships are unavoidable.* This reality is acknowledged in the ACA *Code of Ethics* in Standard A.6.a., which state that, "When a dual relationship cannot be avoided, counselors take appropriate professional precautions . . . to ensure that judgment is not impaired and no exploitation occurs." Most of the literature regarding unavoidable dual relationships has centered on rural practice. Counselors in isolated, rural communities or very small towns may find it impossible to avoid some overlap among roles. Imagine a situation in which the local banker, beautician, auto mechanic, grocery store checkout clerk, and owner of the dry cleaners are all clients of a particular counselor who practices in a small town located a two-hour drive from a major city. Would you expect that counselor to make a four-hour round trip to receive all the routine services these clients provide, in order to avoid any possible overlapping of roles?

Rural and small-community practitioners face the additional problem of dealing with the effects overlapping relationships have on their own families (Schank & Skovholt, 1997). Consider the following scenario:

> Marianne has been a client in counseling with Paula for several weeks. Marianne's husband and Paula's husband both serve on the advisory board for a charitable organization and they begin to develop a friendship. They decide that they would like for their wives to meet and that the two couples should go out to dinner together. How should Paula respond when her husband suggests this social contact?

There is no easy answer to this question. As most ethical situations evolve, the answer really depends upon the personalities and unique circumstances of the individuals involved. Factors that should be considered before Paula decides whether to agree to a dinner party with Marianne and her husband include the following: Does Marianne's husband know that she is in counseling? Does he know that Paula is her counselor? Is the marriage a compelling issue in the counseling? Does Marianne have a high need for privacy? How does Marianne relate to Paula currently—is she extremely deferential or more peer-like in her interactions? Would Paula feel uncomfortable? All these (and others) are factors that might be carefully considered before Paula could make a good decision regarding this boundary issue.

Similarly, if the children of a client become friends with the children of the counselor, then the counselor and client will need to relate to each other as fellow parents, in addition to dealing with the effects of this added relationship on their therapeutic relationship. Without question, counselors in rural and small-town practice face dual relationship and role overlap dilemmas more frequently than most other practitioners.

It is important to recognize that, in addition to rural practice, there are other "small worlds" that can exist even in an urban environment. People's political affiliations, ethnic identities, sexual orientations, and substance dependence recovery status can all lead to dual relationships, because clients often seek counselors with similar values (Lerman & Porter, 1990).

Some gay and lesbian counselors specialize in counseling gay and lesbian clients. These counselors might find it impossible to participate in many social or political activities in the gay community without encountering their clients. Would you expect these counselors to constrict their social lives and forgo political activities in order to avoid chance meetings with clients?

Similar issues arise in substance abuse counseling. Many substance abuse counselors are themselves in recovery. What if there is only one 12-step program in the area where a counselor practices? Would you expect that counselor to jeopardize recovery by avoiding the meetings for fear a client might be in attendance?

Kain (1997) posed some questions regarding a counselor who is HIV-positive and who works with clients who are HIV-positive or are living with AIDS. What if there is only one HIV support group in the area? What if there is only one physician who specializes in treating HIV and AIDS? Would you expect this counselor to sacrifice the need for a support group or for quality medical care, in order to avoid role overlap?

Sometimes cultural factors can create "small world" dilemmas. For instance, imagine a counselor who immigrated from Vietnam to a city in the United States 20 years ago. He has earned his master's degree in counseling and continues to live and work in a section of the city where the population is primarily Vietnamese. Many residents of the area seek him out as a counselor, because he speaks their native language and because they believe he will be able to understand their cultural values. Many of these prospective clients are people with whom he is acquainted or are even distant relatives. Would you expect this counselor to deny his services to these clients?

At this point in your reading, you have a feel for some of the complexities of dual relationships. They pose many questions but very few absolute answers. You may be uncertain regarding your own stance toward some of the issues we have raised. If it is any comfort, many seasoned practitioners are also uncertain. Gibson and Pope (1993) surveyed a large national sample of counselors regarding a range of behaviors. Fully 42% of the items on their survey found to be controversial (with at least 40% judging the behavior as ethical and at least 40% judging it as unethical) described some form of nonsexual dual relationship.

Compounding the confusion around this issue is the fact that counselors may engage in some behaviors with clients from time to time that have a *potential* for creating a dual relationship but are not in themselves dual relationships. These behaviors have been described as "boundary crossings" to distinguish them from ongoing dual relationships.

Boundary Crossings Versus Boundary Violations

Several writers (Gabbard, 1995; Gutheil & Gabbard, 1993; Simon, 1992; Smith & Fitzpatrick, 1995) have attempted to distinguish between boundary crossings and boundary violations. A boundary crossing is a departure from commonly accepted practice that is done to benefit a client. In a crossing, the boundary is shifted to meet the needs of a particular client at a particular moment. By contrast, a violation is a serious breach that causes harm.

An example of a boundary crossing was given earlier in the chapter, in the scenario involving a counselor (Elizabeth) who decided to attend her client's college graduation ceremony. This counselor's behavior did not constitute an ongoing dual relationship and, arguably, it has the potential to enhance the therapeutic relationship. You should be aware, though, that not all counselors would agree with Elizabeth's decision. When Borys (1988) surveyed a large sample of mental health professionals regarding their beliefs about the ethics of certain boundary-crossing and dual relationship behaviors, she found very little agreement about most of the behaviors. We have adapted some of the survey items described in a later article (Borys & Pope, 1989) into a questionnaire (see Figure 7-1). We encourage you to complete the questionnaire, and then discuss your responses with fellow class members or with colleagues. Think about the rationale you would offer for your responses, should a class member or colleague challenge your decisions.

One factor that the survey does not address, and that probably will influence your decisions regarding whether you are willing to engage in occasional boundary crossings in your practice, is that each client is unique. Some clients will have generally clear interpersonal boundaries, and an occasional crossing during your relationship with them may have no further repercussions. Other clients present a real challenge to maintaining therapeutic boundaries. Clients with borderline personality traits or disorder, for example, are often adept manipulators who will try to draw their counselors into a "special" relationship (Gutheil, 1989; Simon, 1989). You will want to be very firm and consistent in maintaining the therapeutic frame with them.

In general, from an ethical standpoint, occasional boundary crossings probably can be justified when there is benefit to the client and very little risk of harm. Counselors must take care, however, not to let these crossings become routine. As Herlihy and Corey (1997) have noted,

> Interpersonal boundaries are not static and may be redefined over time as counselors and clients work closely together. Nonetheless, even seemingly innocent behaviors . . . can, if they become part of a pattern of blurring the professional boundaries, lead to dual relationship entanglements with a real potential for harm (p.9).

As small, well-intended boundary crossings become more frequent in a therapeutic relationship or in a counselor's practice in general, it has been suggested (Gutheil & Gabbard,

For each item below, place an X in the box that best represents your opinion.					
How ethical is it for a counselor to:	Never Ethical	Rarely Ethical	Sometimes Ethical	Usually Ethical	Always Ethical
1. Barter with a client for goods or services?					
2. Invite a client to a personal party or social event?					
3. Provide counseling to a friend who is in crisis?					
4. Accept a gift from a client if the gift is worth less than $10?					
5. Accept a gift from a client if the gift is worth more than $50?					
6. Accept a client's invitation to a special event?					
7. Go out for coffee with a client after a counseling session?					
8. Become friends with a client after termination of the counseling relationship?					
9. Give a home phone number to a client?					
10. Share personal experiences as a member of a self-help group when a client is in attendance?					
11. Occasionally hire a client to babysit?					

Figure 7-1   Boundary Issues Survey of Opinion

1993; Pope, Sonne, & Holroyd, 1993; Sonne, 1994) that the "slippery slope phenomenon" may come into effect. That is, the gradual erosion of the boundaries of the professional relationship can take counselors down an insidious path toward serious ethical violations.

As we discuss next, reasoning about boundary crossings from a legal perspective leads to similar conclusions.

The Legal Perspective on Boundary Crossings

Counselors who are accused of wrongdoing for any reason may have their peers investigate complaints against them, or may even have to defend themselves in an ethics hearing or criminal court (see Chapter 15 on responding to charges of wrongdoing generally). Once you have been accused of having done something wrong, it is too late to undo any small indiscretions from your past. Often in the area of boundary issues, counselors will think, "Well, maybe just this one time it will be all right to ask my client to babysit for my daughter," or "This client is particularly mature, so I'm sure we can have lunch together after our session today."

Unfortunately, these small and seemingly insignificant boundary crossings can be the very evidence that causes an ethics panel, judge, or jury to find against you when you have been accused of having done something wrong. When people judging you consider the small boundary crossings that you have committed, they may come to the conclusion that you are incapable of understanding your profession's prohibition against engaging in multiple relationships that are harmful to clients. Whether you have been falsely accused or even have been accused of something you wish you had not done, it is best if you have very few boundary crossings in your past.

Specific Boundary Issues

In this section of the chapter, we explore some specific issues that are associated with nonsexual dual relationships and boundaries. These issues include bartering, social and business relationships with clients, accepting gifts from clients, the limits of counselor self-disclosure, and touching or hugging a client.

Bartering

Bartering with a client for goods or services is not prohibited by the ethical standards of the counseling profession, although it is discouraged as a routine practice. There is no consensus among counseling practitioners as to whether they consider bartering to be ethical. In Gibson and Pope's (1993) survey, 53% rated accepting services and 63% rated accepting goods in lieu of payment as ethical. Counselors who enter into bartering arrangements with clients usually are motivated by a desire to provide services to clients whose financial resources are limited and who could not afford counseling without some sort of alternative arrangement for payment. This intention is admirable and you may find yourself tempted to enter into bartering agreements with clients from time to time in your professional career. However, you should be aware of the problems that are inherent in this practice.

One form of bartering involves the exchange of services. For example, a client might be a self-employed interior decorator who is having difficulty paying for continued counseling because his business has been slack lately. His counselor's office suite needs new paint and wallpaper, so they agree to exchange counseling services for redecorating services. It is possible that an arrangement like this could work smoothly, but there are a number of potential pitfalls. For one thing, most services that clients can offer do not have monetary value equal to an hour of counseling (Kitchener & Harding, 1990). Unless clients can devote considerable time each week to holding up their end of the agreement, they are likely to fall further and further behind in the amount owed. They can become trapped in a kind of indentured servitude and come to feel resentful.

In addition to the question of quantity of bartered services, the issue of quality of services provided can be problematic. To take the example of the decorator, what if the counselor thinks the client is doing a sloppy and inferior job of painting and wallpapering the office suite? What if the redecorating work is excellent, but the decorator is not satisfied with the counseling services? Feelings of resentment that build up in the counselor or in the client are bound to have a negative effect on the counseling relationship.

Another form of bartering involves the exchange of goods for counseling services. For example, a client who is an artist might wish to pay for counseling services by giving the counselor an oil painting. The issues of quality that arise in bartering of services apply to this type of bartering as well. In addition, the issue of how many hours of counseling are equivalent to the value of the painting needs to be addressed. What criteria should be used to make such a determination?

All these potential problems are acknowledged in the ACA *Code of Ethics,* which states that counselors "ordinarily refrain from accepting goods or services from clients in return for counseling services because such arrangements create inherent potential for conflicts, exploitation, and distortion of the counseling relationship" (Standard A.10.c.). Nonetheless, a blanket prohibition against bartering is not made. Instead, the code offers guidelines for counselors to help them determine whether a potential bartering arrangement might be acceptable. The code states that counselors may participate in bartering only if three criteria are met: the relationship is not exploitive, the client requests it, and bartering is an accepted practice among professionals in the community (Standard A.10.c.).

If you establish your practice in a rural community, you may find that bartering is common among local physicians and other professionals. In such a setting, it would be acceptable for you to engage in bartering if your clients initiate the request and if you believe you and the client can work out fair and equitable terms of agreement. We believe it would also be wise for you to consider other alternatives to bartering with clients who cannot pay your full fee. Some of these alternatives, which are further explored in Chapter 11 in a discussion of private practice, might include using a sliding scale fee or providing a set amount of pro bono services.

Social Relationships with Clients

Individuals who choose to become professional counselors do not cease to be members of their communities, nor are they expected to forgo their social lives in order to avoid all nonprofessional contacts with clients (Glosoff, 1997). Some social contact with clients is difficult to avoid for counselors who share "small worlds" with their clients. Even when extraprofessional contacts with clients can be avoided with relative ease, however, counselors can find it tempting to develop social relationships and even friendships with their clients.

As Glosoff (1997) has noted, individuals ordinarily look to work as one setting where they can gratify certain psychological and social needs. For many people, their work environment is a place to meet others with whom they can socialize and form friendships. Choosing to become a counselor can limit these opportunities. Almost all counselors will have some clients who are likable and who would make nice friends, but a friendship and a therapeutic relationship cannot exist simultaneously. The therapeutic relationship is like a friendship in that it involves emotional intimacy, but it is different in a significant way. In a therapeutic relationship, the intimacy is one way. Friendships are coequal relationships in which personal disclosures, support, challenge, and other interpersonal dynamics are re-ciprocal. For a counselor to seek a friendship with a client would be to look for reciprocity in a relationship that is not, by its nature, reciprocal (Hill, 1990).

Short of an ongoing friendship, there are many possibilities for more limited types of social contact with clients, and a counselor's stance toward these contacts may depend on several factors. The counselor's theoretical orientation might make a difference. Borys (1988) suggested that a psychodynamically oriented counselor might be quite strict about out-of-the-office social contacts with clients, because psychodynamic theory stresses the importance of "maintaining the frame of therapy" and attention to transference and coun-tertransference issues. In contrast, relationship-oriented counselors or those who espouse systems theory might be more willing to interact with clients outside the therapeutic set-ting. Another factor may be the nature of the social function. Of the respondents in Borys' (1988) study, only 33% thought it was never or only rarely ethical to accept a client's invi-tation to a special occasion, while 92% disapproved of inviting a client to a personal party.

Although there has been much debate in the literature, our opinion is that counselors have an ethical obligation to keep their professional and personal/social lives as separate as they reasonably can. Counselors should not get their social needs or personal needs for friendship met through interactions with their clients.

Counselors and clients do, however, meet each other in social contexts without prior planning on either person's part. Therefore, it is essential that counselors discuss with their clients how they might be affected by encountering the counselor outside the office and how these chance meetings should be handled.

A closely related issue that has also been debated in the literature is the question of post-termination friendships with clients. Counselors are often aware of clients' attributes that would make them desirable friends. Clients, for their part, may hope to continue the intimacy they felt and the caring attention they received during the therapeutic relation-ship. The code of ethics offers no guidance regarding post-termination friendships with clients, and there is no consensus among helping professionals regarding the advisability of such relationships.

Several risks in post-therapy friendships have been identified. Vasquez (1991) noted that many clients consider reentering counseling with their counselors, and that if a friend-ship develops this option is closed. Other writers have argued that therapeutic gains are jeopardized when a friendship follows a therapeutic relationship, because a post-termination friendship may disrupt a healthy resolution of transference issues (Gelso & Carter, 1985; Kitchener, 1992). The power differential that existed during the therapeutic relationship is not automatically negated when the counseling is terminated. As Salisbury and Kinnier (1996) have noted, "Unreciprocated knowledge of a former client's most sensitive weak-nesses and most intimate secrets can render a client particularly vulnerable" (p. 495) in a friendship with a former counselor.

Despite these risks, there is some evidence that most counselors find the development of friendships with former clients to be ethically acceptable. Fully 70% of counselors surveyed by Salisbury and Kinnier (1996) believed that a post-therapy friendship with a client could be acceptable. Approximately one-third of them actually had engaged in this behavior. The fact that a substantial number of counselors condone or engage in a practice does not necessarily indicate that the practice is ethical, however. You should avoid a tendency to reflexively accept "prevalence" arguments as a justification for dual relationship behaviors (Pope & Vasquez, 1991).

There are a number of factors that you should consider before pursuing a friendship with a former client. These include the time that has passed since termination, transference and countertransference issues, the length and nature of the counseling, the client's issues and diagnosis, the circumstances of the termination, the client's freedom of choice, whether any exploitation might have occurred in the professional relationship, the client's ego strength and mental health, the possibility of reactivation of counseling, and whether any harm to the client's welfare can be foreseen (Akamatsu, 1988; Kitchener, 1992; Salisbury & Kinnier, 1996). It would be difficult to demonstrate that none of these factors was at play if a counselor were challenged by a licensing board or in court. We believe counselors would be wise to avoid developing friendships with both current and former clients.

Business or Financial Relationships with Clients

Business and financial relationships with clients have received little focused attention in the literature, perhaps because the issues are much the same as those raised by personal and social dual relationships. For instance, counselors who work in rural settings may be more likely to have business-related encounters with clients. Schank and Skovholt (1997) described a situation in which a counselor took his car to a shop to be serviced. He thought the bill was rather high for the services performed, but was reluctant to question the charges when he realized that one of his clients had done the work. Of course, such unintended encounters can happen in urban and suburban practice. A counselor might have an electrical or plumbing problem at home, and have a client who is employed by the electric company or plumbing contractor show up to do the work. These occurrences, while awkward, can be handled through an open discussion during the next counseling session.

Anderson and Kitchener (1996) asked therapists to describe critical incidents involving post-therapy relationships with clients. Business or financial relationships were second only to personal or friendship relationships in the frequency with which they were related. Their respondents identified two types of situations that could apply equally to relationships with current clients. The first involved the therapist paying for a client's expertise or assistance. Examples might include hiring a client or former client to perform clerical work or to cater a party at the counselor's home. The second involved a therapist and client joining areas of expertise to produce income, such as going into business together. It appears that counselors regard going into business with a current client as unethical; only 9% of respondents in Gibson and Pope's (1993) survey rated this behavior as ethical. When the question was one of going into business with a former client, however, the percentage rose to 46%.

Other types of dual relating that involve financial considerations occur when a counselor patronizes a client's place of business, or when a counselor sells goods (such as a relaxation tape or a book) to a client. In the former situation, the client could feel pressured to give the counselor a discount or some kind of special services. In the second instance, the client might feel coerced to buy the counselor's product. Only 16% of the counselors who participated in Gibson and Pope's (1993) study rated selling goods to a client as ethical.

Although the practice of entering into business or financial relationships with clients needs further study, our own recommendation is that counselors should avoid entering into these relationships with current or former clients. Whenever a counselor is making a monetary profit from a secondary relationship with a client, that counselor's self-interest is clearly involved.

Accepting Gifts from Clients

When clients offer gifts to their counselors—even small, token gifts—it can make counselors feel uncomfortable. They may be torn between wanting to decline the gift in order to keep the relationship within proper boundaries, yet wanting to accept the gift so that the client will not feel hurt or rejected. The best way to minimize such conflicts is to have a general policy that you do not accept gifts from clients and to include a statement to that effect in your informed consent document. This procedure will not solve completely all potential problems, however. Clients may vary in how they interpret the idea of a gift, or they may forget or choose to ignore that you have a policy. For your part, you probably will not want to interpret your own policy too rigidly. It is difficult to imagine an elementary school counselor refusing to accept a child client's offering of a handmade Valentine, for instance.

It is certainly possible that a client may sometime offer you a gift. It is wise for you to think through how you plan to handle this event. One strategy is to consider what criteria you might use in determining whether to accept or refuse a gift.

The monetary value of the gift is one obvious consideration. When you responded to the Boundary Issues Survey, did you answer the fourth item differently than you answered the fifth? If so, a gift's monetary value played some part in your decision making process. Apparently, many mental health professionals would reason similarly. When Borys (1988) asked these same two questions in her survey, only 16% of her respondents answered that they believed it was "never" or "only rarely" ethical to accept a gift worth less than $10, but the percentage jumped to 82% when the gift was worth more than $50.

It may be useful to consider the client's motivation for offering the gift. A client might offer a small gift as a way of expressing appreciation. This seems different from a gift that the counselor perceives to be a form of manipulation or an attempt to buy loyalty or friendship. Sometimes a client's need to offer gifts can become a useful therapeutic tool. For example, we know of a client who came to each of her first three sessions bringing a small home-baked item such as a brownie or a loaf of banana bread, saying that she had just finished baking and thought the counselor might like to sample the result. She was an excellent baker, and the counselor accepted the first two offerings with pleasure. When the client came to the third session with a treat, the counselor used this as an entree to exploring the client's motivations. Through this exploration, the client became aware of her need to "make herself welcome" everywhere she went because she believed that she could not possibly be valued just for herself. This became a very productive session.

It may be equally useful to consider the counselor's motivation for wanting to accept or decline the gift. For example, assume that your client has an extra ticket to a championship sports event and asks you to go along. You are a great sports fan and have been unable to get a ticket to the game. If you find yourself tempted to accept the ticket, keep in mind that you have a fiduciary relationship with your client (see Chapter 3) and that you must not benefit from the relationship. If would also be useful to think about the implicit messages you would be sending to the client, who may think it is now acceptable to call you at home or invite you to future social functions. What if you are not really a sports fan but find yourself thinking that going to the game would be more enjoyable than sitting home alone? In this case, consider your obligation to avoid using clients to meet your own social needs. When you are determining whether to accept a gift from a client, your reasoning must be based on consideration for the client's welfare.

Related to the issue of motivation is the question of when the gift is offered. A client might bring a small gift to a mutually agreed-upon termination session as a way of saying "thank you" to the counselor. Accepting such a gift might not be problematic. By contrast, accepting a gift during the early stages of counseling before a stable therapeutic relationship has been established could set in motion a blurring of boundaries that could become problematic down the road.

Cultural factors also need to be considered, because gift giving has different meanings in different cultures. For instance, giving gifts is a common practice in many Asian communities as a means of showing gratitude and respect (Sue & Zane, 1987). Counselors responding from a European-American perspective might politely refuse an offered gift without realizing the great insult and cultural meaning of their refusal for the client (Sue, 1997). Counselors need to take care that their own discomfort at being presented with a gift does not overshadow their sensitivity to what the gift means to the client.

Self-Disclosure

The extent to which counselors engage in self-disclosure depends in large measure on their theoretical orientation, and their skill and comfort in using this technique. Psychodynamically oriented counselors, whose tradition includes Freud's belief that the therapist should remain anonymous, are not likely to engage in much self-disclosure. Counselors who view the therapeutic relationship as co-equal, such as feminist therapists and existential therapists, place more value on self-disclosure. As a technique, counselor self-disclosure can be a powerful intervention that can strengthen the therapeutic alliance. It is important that you learn the skill of self-disclosure and be able to articulate your rationale for using it in the counseling process. It is equally important that you understand self-disclosure as an ethical issue.

Counselor self-disclosures that are ethically appropriate are done for the client's benefit within the context of the therapeutic process (Smith & Fitzpatrick, 1995). Self-disclosures are considered unethical when they are used to meet the counselor's own needs for intimacy or understanding. Counselors in independent private practice may be particularly vulnerable to using self-disclosure as a way to counter feelings of isolation (Glosoff, 1997). Self-disclosure, used improperly or excessively, can lead to a role reversal in which the client becomes the emotional caretaker of the counselor. Topics that are not considered appropriate for counselors to disclose are details of current stressors, personal fantasies or dreams, and their social or financial circumstances (Borys, 1988; Gutheil & Gabbard, 1993; Simon, 1991).

Self-disclosure has become an area of increasing ethical concern as more research has demonstrated that when treatment boundaries become blurred, they usually erode gradually over time. Inappropriate therapist self-disclosure, more than any other kind of boundary violation, is likely to precede therapist-client sexual intimacy (Simon, 1991).

Guidelines for distinguishing appropriate from inappropriate self-disclosure may seem fairly clear as you read about them, but judging what may benefit the client can be very difficult in practice (Smith & Fitzpatrick, 1995). Cultural factors need to be taken into consideration. For example in Asian culture, self-disclosing to strangers (counselors) is considered a violation of familial and cultural values. Some Asian clients believe that personal matters are best discussed with intimate acquaintances or friends (Sue, 1997). Counselor self-disclosure might facilitate the establishment of the close personal relationship that these clients need in order to feel comfortable in sharing their concerns.

Self-disclosure is a complex issue. You will need to think about whether to self-disclose, and how and when, in working with each of your clients. When you choose to self-disclose, your primary reason must be that you believe the disclosure will benefit the client.

Physical Contact with Clients

The boundary question of whether counselors should touch or hug their clients is not easy to resolve. For certain clients, at certain times, a reassuring touch or a gentle hug can be facilitative. Yet, counselors who engage in these behaviors risk having their gestures misinterpreted as sexual advances or as violations of the client's personal space.

Smith and Fitzpatrick (1995) have noted that the issue of therapeutic touch has an interesting history. When "talk therapy" first began in the Freudian era, physical contact with clients was prohibited because of its presumed negative effect on transference and countertransference. Later, in the 1960s and 1970s, touching became an accepted practice within the human potential movement. One study (Holroyd & Brodsky, 1977) found that 30% of humanistic therapists, as compared to only 6% of psychodynamic therapists, believed that touching could be beneficial to clients. A decade later Pope, Tabachnick, and Keith-Spiegel (1987) investigated the beliefs of mental health professionals regarding three types of physical contact. Their respondents believed that the most unethical type was kissing a client (with 85% stating that is was never or only rarely ethical), followed by hugging (with 44% disapproval), and finally by handshakes, which were deemed ethical by 94%.

In today's litigious climate, it appears to us that the pendulum of opinion has swung back nearly to its starting point. Generally, counselors are now trained to be cautious about making physical contact. They are often advised to hug a client only when the client requests it or, at the very least, when the counselor first secures the client's permission. Certainly, professional liability insurance carriers have become concerned that clients might bring suit against their counselors for even well-meaning instances of physical contact. Some applications for malpractice insurance directly ask the question, "Do you ever touch a client beyond a routine handshake?" Counselors who answer "yes" must attach an explanation.

When you begin to practice as a counselor, you will need to determine your own stance toward physical contact with your clients. There are many factors that might be considered, such as the age of the client. Routinely hugging elementary school children is probably more acceptable than giving frequent hugs to adult clients. With teens and adults, you will want to assess the likelihood that the client may sexualize or misinterpret your touch. Cultural variables also may be important factors. For example, people from some European countries routinely kiss each other on both cheeks as a way of greeting, and these clients might think you are cold and distant if you avoid physical contact with them. The client's diagnosis and history may also be relevant. For instance, hugging or touching a client who has been sexually abused is contraindicated. As with most other boundary questions, it comes down to assessing the risks and benefits and deciding accordingly.

Multicultural Considerations

Cultural factors are often important variables in ethical decision making regarding therapeutic boundaries. In this chapter, we have noted that bartering, gift giving, self-disclosure, and therapeutic touch are viewed differently in different cultures. A consideration of multicultural factors goes beyond differing interpretations of various counselor behaviors, however. The multicultural counseling movement has challenged the traditional roles that counselors play and has encouraged counselors to take a fresh look at the concept of multiple roles and relationships.

Traditionally, counseling has been conducted in an office environment, has had remediation as its goal, and has been a one-to-one process (Sue, 1997). Writers in the multicultural arena (Atkinson, Thompson, & Grant, 1993; Atkinson, Morten, & Sue, 1993; Lee & Richardson, 1991; Sue, 1997) have urged counselors to take on different, more active roles in order to be effective helpers when working with minority clients. These writers have suggested that counselors need to function as advocates for their clients, particularly those whose acculturation to the majority culture is minimal and who need help in resolving problems that have resulted from discrimination and oppression. They have further suggested that counselors should function as change agents by using their political power to confront and make changes in societal systems that create and perpetuate many problems. When counselors include considerations of oppression and discrimination in their work with ethnic minority clients, there will be a shift in their thinking. They will move away from a tendency to look for intrapsychic causes of client problems and toward examining factors in the environment that may be contributing to these problems.

Multiculturally sensitive counselors are aware that many clients who adhere to African American, Hispanic or Latino(a) American, or Asian American cultural norms may expect to receive suggestions and even advice, because they perceive counselors as being experts with higher status and special knowledge (Sue, 1997). Sensitive counselors recognize that clients with an African world view value connectedness and see the group or community rather than the individual as the basic unit of their existence. The concern about dual relationships may not be widely shared in the African American community, where helpers typically play multiple roles (Parham, 1997). Multiculturally sensitive counselors know that for many minority clients, the idea of seeking traditional counseling is foreign, and that these clients are often more comfortable turning to social support systems within their own community. They may be more likely to put their trust in healers who are a part of their culture such as shamans, folk healers, acupuncturists, or cueranderos(as).

Counselors who work with ethnic minority clients need to be flexible and willing to take on different roles, such as advocate, change agent, advisor, and facilitator of indigenous support systems, if they are to effectively assist these clients. They need to balance their understanding of and adherence to their codes of ethics with their understanding of and sensitivity to the values and world views of minority clients.

An Ethical Decision Making Model

Herlihy and Corey (1997) have offered a decision making model to assist counselors who are faced with potential dual or multiple relationships. In their model, the first step is to determine whether the potential dual relationship is avoidable or unavoidable. If it would be possible to avoid entering into the dual relationship, an important next step is to have a full and open discussion with the client, exploring the possible problems and benefits. Third, counselors must judge whether the benefits outweigh the risks or whether the reverse is true. They need to consider the factors that create a potential for harm, including differences in the client's expectations of the counselor in the two roles, the counselor's divergent responsibilities in the two roles, and the power differential in their relationship.

If the counselor believes that the risk of harm to the client is greater than the potential benefits, the counselor should decline to enter the dual relationship and refer if needed. An explanation should be given so the client understands the rationale for not proceeding with the problematic part of the dual relationship.

If the counselor believes that the potential benefits to the client are great and the risk of harm is small, or if the potential dual relationship cannot be avoided, then the dual relationship can be initiated and the following safeguards put in place:

- Secure the client's informed consent to proceed with the dual relationship. The counselor and client should discuss the potential problems and reach an understanding regarding how they want to handle these problems if they arise.
- Seek consultation. Because one of the most intransigent problems in managing dual relationships is the counselor's loss of objectivity, it is important for the counselor to seek ongoing consultation for help in monitoring the relationship and the risk for harm.
- Engage in ongoing discussion with the client. As we discussed in Chapter 3, informed consent is not a one-time matter. The counselor can involve the client in a mutual, ongoing monitoring of the relationship and can discuss any potential problems that they might foresee and attempt to resolve any problems that do arise.
- Document and self-monitor. Although we have heard of instances in which counselors were advised to keep any mention of a dual relationship out of their case notes, we think this is unwise. If a dual relationship ever became an issue in a complaint proceeding before a licensure board or in a court of law, behavior that appears as if the counselor is trying to hide something will not be seen favorably by the parties adjudicating the complaint. It is much better for counselors to be able to demonstrate that they were aware of dualities, that they considered the risks and benefits for the client, and that they took steps to protect the client.
- Obtain supervision. If the risks in a dual relationship seem high, if the relationship is particularly complex, or if the counselor is concerned about the ability to assess the situation objectively, seeking consultation may not be sufficient. In these instances, counselors are wise to engage a fellow mental health professional in ongoing supervision of their work throughout the dual relationship.

In concluding this section of the chapter, we want to emphasize that boundary issues and dual relationships pose some complex and difficult questions. Counselors will struggle with boundary setting throughout their professional careers. There are few certainties regarding this issue. In the absence of absolute answers, counselors will need to think carefully about the consequences of their decisions, have a clear rationale for any boundary crossings, be open to discussing the issues with their clients who are equally affected by any decisions, and consult with colleagues.

SEXUAL DUAL RELATIONSHIPS

Without doubt, the problem of sexual relationships between therapists and their clients has existed for many decades, even though it remained unacknowledged in the professional literature through the 1970s. Therapist-client sexual intimacy was the "problem with no name" (Davidson, 1977) because helping professionals were reluctant to confront the issue. The reluctance was so pervasive that Pope (1988) concluded that helping professionals had engaged in "massive denial" (p. 222) of the problem. It was through the pioneering work of a few researchers, such as Gartrell and her colleagues (Gartrell, Herman, Olarte, Feldstein, & Localio, 1987) in psychiatry, and Pope (Pope, 1986,1988) in psychology and counseling, that helping professionals were made aware that such violations were occurring, and in startling numbers.

Although the limitations of self report data make it difficult to gauge how commonly therapist-client sexual intimacies actually occur, in various studies 8.7% to 13% of male therapists and 2% to 3% of female therapists reported sexual relationships with their current or former clients (Akamatsku, 1988; Borys, 1988; Holroyd & Brodsky, 1977; Pope & Bouhoutsos, 1986; Pope, Sonne, & Holroyd, 1993; Pope, Tabachnick, & Keith-Speigel, 1987; Salisbury & Kinnier, 1996; Thoreson, Shaughnessy, & Frazier, 1995; Thoreson, Shaughnessy, Heppner, & Cook, 1993). It is safe to state that these estimates are probably conservative. When Pope (1986) surveyed patients rather than therapists, as many as 20% of them reported having had sexual contact with their therapists. One hopeful note among these statistics was provided by Anderson and Kitchener (1996). They reviewed studies that had been conducted since 1977 and concluded that the frequency of sexual contact between therapists and current clients is decreasing.

The Offending Therapist

Therapists who engage in sex with their clients have not been well studied, but the male therapist/female client dyad clearly dominates. It appears that most offenders are repeat offenders. Holroyd and Brodsky (1977) found that 80% of psychologists who reported sexual contact also reported that they had been sexually intimate with more than one client. Pope and Bouhoutsos (1986) described several typical scenarios and rationalizations used by offending therapists:

- In a reversal of roles, the wants and needs of the therapist become the focus of the treatment.
- The therapist claims that sexual intimacy with the client is a valid treatment for sexual or other problems.
- The therapist fails to treat the emotional closeness that develops in therapy with professional attention and respect, claiming that the dual relationship "just got out of hand."
- The therapist exploits the client's desire for nonerotic physical contact (e.g., a need to be held).
- The therapist fails to acknowledge that the therapeutic relationship continues between sessions and outside the office.
- The therapist creates and exploits an extreme dependence on the part of the client.

Although offending therapists do not fit a single profile, the portrait that emerges from the scant literature is one of a professionally isolated, male therapist who is experiencing distress or crisis in his personal life (Simon, 1987; Smith & Fitzpatrick, 1995). He shares many characteristics with other impaired professionals, including professional burnout and a pattern of attempting to meet his own personal needs though his clients. Not all offenders will fit this description, however. Golden (in Schafer, 1990) and Schoener and Gonsiorek (1988) described a wide range of professionals who become sexually involved with their clients. At one end of the range are those who are naive and uninformed about ethical standards. At the other extreme are professionals who suffer from sociopathic, narcissistic, or borderline personality disorders and the attendant inability to appreciate the impact of their behavior on others.

It is natural to feel compassion for those naive offenders who feel remorse for their behavior, but it is important to remember that ignorance is never a valid excuse, nor is blaming the client for being "seductive." It is always the responsibility of the helping professional to ensure that sexual intimacies do not occur.

Harm to Clients

We believe that sexual relationships with therapists are extremely detrimental and sometimes even devastating to clients. The harm is deep, lasting, and occasionally permanent. At least 90% of clients who have been sexually involved with a therapist are damaged by the relationship, according to their subsequent therapists (Bouhoutsos, Holroyd, Lerman, Forer, & Greenberg, 1983).

Pope (1988) suggested that clients are likely to suffer from "therapist-patient sex syndrome," with reactions similar to those of victims of rape, spouse battering, incest, and post-traumatic stress disorder. He described a range of associated symptoms. Clients often experience a deep *ambivalence* toward the offending therapist. They are trapped between extreme dependency on and fear of separation from the therapist, and a longing to escape from his power and influence. Like many victims of incest and battering, clients vacillate between wanting to flee from the abuser and wanting to cling to and protect him.

Clients often suffer from feelings of *guilt,* believing that they are to blame for the relationship. They may think that they did something to invite the therapist's behavior. Although they may be deeply angry at the therapist, their rage remains suppressed due to the therapist's continuing power, their feelings of ambivalence, and their sense of guilt. This guilt and rage, when turned inward, leads to an *increased risk of suicide.*

Because the offending therapist insists that the client keep their sexual relationship secret, clients feel *isolated,* alone, and cut off from the normal world of human experience. Not surprisingly, many victims manifest a profound *confusion* about their sexuality and about appropriate roles and interpersonal boundaries. When roles are reversed and the client becomes the therapist's emotional caretaker, the client does not know where safe and appropriate boundaries lie.

Therapy involves a high degree of trust, and violation of that trust can have lifelong consequences. Clients' *impaired ability to trust* often prevents them from seeking help from other therapists and may impair their ability to form other close relationships.

Finally, many clients display symptoms similar to those experienced by victims of post-traumatic stress disorder. These symptoms include difficulties with attention and concentration, re-experiencing of overwhelming emotional reactions when they become involved with a sexual partner, and nightmares and flashbacks.

The harm to clients caused by sexual intimacies with their therapists is now well recognized. The ethical standards of all mental health providers' professional organizations, including the ACA *Code of Ethics,* prohibit sexual relationships with clients. There are no credible voices in the profession arguing that sexual relationships with clients should be allowed.

Legal Consequences for Offending Counselors

Civil Law Suits

The impropriety of sexual intimacies with clients is universally recognized. As a result, clients who sue counselors for having been sexually involved with them have an excellent chance of winning their lawsuits, if the allegations are true. These lawsuits are civil, which means that one citizen has to sue another for action to be taken against a person who does something wrong.

For example, clients who were sexually victimized by their counselors and who are ashamed, uneducated, or lacking in self-confidence might choose not to file formal complaints or file civil lawsuits against their perpetrators. When that happens, counselors who violate our ethical standards and violate the rights of their clients are never held accountable. In fact, many believe that the lack of accountability often encourages offending counselors to sexually violate other clients. When some counselors observe that others are getting away with having sexual relationships with clients, they may be inclined to do so as well.

Counselors who engage in sexual relationships with their clients may be sued on a number of grounds. Jorgenson (1995) has listed the following causes of action that victimized clients might allege in their lawsuits: malpractice, negligent infliction of emotional distress, battery, intentional infliction of emotional distress, fraudulent misrepresentation, breach of contract, breach of warranty, and spouse loss of consortium (love, companionship, and services). As discussed in Chapter 6, one of the elements a client must prove in a malpractice suit is that a counselor behaved in a manner that breached the standard of care expected or required of counselors.

To encourage clients who are victimized by their mental health professionals to sue, some state legislatures have now passed laws that automatically make it negligence for certain categories of mental health professionals to have sexual relationships with their clients [e.g., Cal. Civ. Code sec. 43.93, West, 1993; Ill. Ann. State. Ch. 70, secs. 801–802, Smith-Hurd, 1992; Minn. Stat. Ann. Sec. 148A, West, 1993; Texas Senate Bill 210, engrossed May 22, 1993; Wis. Stat. Ann. Sec. 895.70(2), West, 1992]. Those who sue must still prove they were harmed as a result of the sexual relationships, but harm can be emotional and financial as well as physical.

Some of these statutes have unusual and forceful components. For example, the Wisconsin statute [Wis. Stat. Ann. sec. 895.70(5), West, 1992] forbids accused mental health professionals from settling their cases without public disclosure. In other words, mental health professionals (or their professional liability insurance companies) who are sued by their clients for having engaged in sex with them cannot agree to an out-of-court settlement that is never reported to the public.

Criminalization of Sex with Clients

Our society has become so convinced that therapist-client sexual relationships are wrong that some states have now passed statutes that make it a crime for mental health professionals to engage in sex with their clients. Losing a civil lawsuit for having sex with a client can be distressing for counselors, but going to jail for the same thing is a much more dramatic result.

Between 1983 and 1992, 13 states enacted legislation that criminalized sexual relationships between mental health professionals and their clients. Kane (1995) reported that the following states had passed such statutes at the time the review was conducted: California, Colorado, Connecticut, Florida, Georgia, Iowa, Maine, Michigan, Minnesota, New Mexico, North Dakota, South Dakota, and Wisconsin. Each state statute varies in language, but the following professionals have been included in some of the laws: psychotherapists, counselors, marriage and family therapists, clergy, social workers, psychiatrists, and psychologists.

Some of these criminal statutes take unusually tough positions with mental health professionals. For example, the Colorado statute [Colo. Rev. Stat. secs. 12-43-708 (b&c), 1988] permits prosecutors to file injunctions that will put a mental health professional out of business even before the individual has been found guilty, if it can be proven that the professional presents a risk to clients by continuing to practice.

Roberts (1995), in giving a history of the passage of the Colorado statute, reported that the law was passed in 1988 over a great deal of objection from mental health professionals. Proponents had to compromise and exclude clergy from the bill before it could be passed. Roberts summarized the law as stating, in essence, that "any psychotherapist who perpetrates sexual penetration or intrusion on a client commits a felony (p. 340)." The law does not allow accused mental health professionals to use consent of the client as a defense.

Although Kane (1995) believes that the laws criminalizing sexual relationships between mental health professionals and their clients have had a deterrent effect, it appears that they do not totally solve the problem. In Colorado, 8 years after the law had been passed, Roberts (1995) reported that victims were still treated poorly during the investigation process, and that many prosecutors were unwilling to proceed with cases because they did not understand abuse generally.

Post-Therapy Sexual Relationships

Ethical standards of the various mental health professions are divided on the issue of whether it is ethical for professionals to have sexual relationships with former clients. Social workers are forbidden from ever having a sexual relationship with an individual after a professional relationship has been established (National Association of Social Workers, 1997). However, counselors (American Counseling Association, 1995) and psychologists (American Psychological Association, 1982) have determined that after a set period of time following termination, sexual relationships may be permissible with former clients. These codes should not be interpreted as blanket permission, however. Counselors who consider entering into romantic or sexual relationships with former clients, even after several years have passed, still have an ethical responsibility to ensure that no harm is done. Not only do all the risk factors for post-termination friendships apply to post-termination sexual relationships, but because of the severity of potential harm, it is even more important to put safeguards in place. Herlihy and Corey (1997) recommended, for instance, that the counselor and former client go for a counseling session together before becoming sexually involved, to examine transference and countertransference issues, to clarify expectations, and to try to anticipate any problems that might arise.

Just as professional associations disagree about whether sexual relationships are acceptable after a waiting period, scholars are also divided on the issue. While Friedman and Boumil (1995) have struggled with the arguments for and against the idea, Simon (1998) has recommended never having a sexual relationship with a former client. Apparently there is no consensus among counseling practitioners, either. In two studies that surveyed ACA members, 63.5% of male counselors believed sexual contact with former clients was unethical (Thoreson et al., 1993), and 45% of female counselors believed that this behavior was harmful and constituted misconduct (Thoreson et al., 1995). As Herlihy and Corey (1997) noted, whether sexual relationships with former clients are ever acceptable probably will be a subject of continuing debate for some time to come. In our opinion, sexual relationships with former clients are not appropriate under any circumstances.

Counseling Clients Who Have Been Abused by Previous Therapists

Counselors who provide services to individuals who have been sexually abused by mental health professionals are put in awkward positions. Most counselors feel obligated to take some action to bring attention to the wrongdoing of a fellow mental health professional. These counselors are afraid if they do not take some action, more clients may be abused.

We caution you though, if you are ever put in this situation, to be respectful of your client's wishes in the matter. Clients have to be willing not only to allege that a mental health professional has abused them, but they also will have to testify at formal hearings, will probably be cross-examined in a hostile and accusing manner, and will have to deal with the emotional strain of the process.

Your role, as a counselor, is to assist your client in meeting the counseling goals the two of you establish together. If the client decides to proceed against the perpetrator in some manner, you can be very helpful in assisting the client deal with a very difficult situation.

It does no good for you to file an ethics complaint against another mental health professional if the victim refuses to participate. Not only will you be violating your client's privacy if you disclose the client's identity, but most licensure boards, criminal prosecutors, or certification groups will not proceed in a case without a witness who was a victim.

Your role as a counselor is not to push your client toward accusing the mental health professional. Your job is to provide appropriate counseling services, to avoid imposing your own values, and to assist clients in meeting their personal goals.

To avoid becoming inappropriately involved if a client is trying to decide whether to accuse a former mental health professional of inappropriate sexual activity, you might consider referring the client to an advocacy group. There are many such groups that assist clients in making the initial decisions and then support them once the process begins. Biele and Barnhill (1995) and Schoener (1988) have listed such advocacy groups in their publications.

SUMMARY AND KEY POINTS

Therapeutic boundaries and dual relationships are among the most controversial of all ethical issues. A boundary can be conceptualized as a frame around the therapeutic relationship that defines the participants' roles in that relationship. Counselors enter into dual relationships whenever they take on two or more roles, simultaneously or sequentially, with their clients.

Codes of ethics discourage dual relationships but do not prohibit them completely. The only type of dual relationship that is absolutely forbidden is sexual intimacy with a current client. There are a number of factors that counselors need to consider when they are contemplating entering into a nonsexual dual relationship, to determine the potential for harm to the client.

Most counselors occasionally engage in boundary crossings, which are departures from usual practice that are made to benefit a particular client at a particular time. For instance, a counselor would not routinely meet all clients at out-of-the-office functions but might choose to attend a client's graduation or other special occasion. From a legal perspective, counselors who develop a pattern of frequent boundary crossings are at risk.

Several specific boundary issues were discussed in this chapter. These included bartering, social and business relationships with clients, post-termination friendships, accepting gifts from clients, counselor self-disclosure, and physical contact with clients. Throughout the discussion of these issues, multicultural considerations were highlighted. Guidelines for ethical decision making completed the first section of the chapter. Key points with respect to nonsexual dual relationships are as follows:

- Codes of ethics caution counselors to avoid those dual relationships that could impair professional judgment or increase the risk of harm to the client.
- Factors that should be considered in assessing the risk of harm are incompatible expectations on the part of the client, divergent responsibilities on the part of the counselor, and the power differential between the two parties.
- Potential dual relationships can evolve in subtle ways and can be difficult to recognize.
- Dual relationships can be relatively benign but can also be extremely harmful to clients.
- With the exception of sexual dual relationships, there is very little consensus among counselors regarding the propriety of various types of dual relationships.
- Some dual relationships are unavoidable, particularly when counselors practice in rural communities or other types of "small worlds."
- There are a number of counselor behaviors that do not by themselves constitute dual relationships but have the potential to create dual relationships. These behaviors can be termed *boundary crossings*.
- From both an ethical and a legal perspective, counselors are well advised to avoid developing a pattern of frequent boundary crossings with clients.
- Although bartering with a client for goods or services is fraught with potential problems, it is ethically permissible when the client requests it, when exploitation can be avoided, and when bartering is a common practice among professionals in the community.
- Although counselors may be tempted to develop social relationships or even friendships with current or former clients, counselors should not get their own social needs met through their interactions with clients.
- Business or financial relationships with clients should be avoided.
- Generally, counselors should not accept gifts from their clients, although there may be instances when accepting a gift is appropriate. There are a number of factors that counselors should consider when deciding whether to accept or refuse a gift from a client.

- Appropriate self-disclosure on the part of counselors is therapeutic, but when it is used inappropriately or excessively it can create a role reversal in which the client becomes the counselor's emotional caretaker.
- The issue of physical contact with clients is difficult to resolve and, again, there are many factors to consider. Today's legal climate tends to discourage counselors from the practice of therapeutic touch.
- Multicultural factors are often important variables in ethical decision making regarding dual relationships and professional boundaries.
- An ethical decision making model is available to assist counselors in deciding what actions to take when faced with a potential dual relationship.

The second section of the chapter focused on sexual dual relationships. Sexual intimacies with clients are probably the most harmful of all types of dual relationships. Although estimates of the prevalence of sexual relationships between therapists and their clients seem to vary, it is clear that male therapists are more frequent offenders than are female therapists. Pope has described the harm to clients as a "therapist-patient sex syndrome" that is similar to post-traumatic stress disorder. Legal consequences for offending therapists can be severe. They can be prosecuted in civil court and, in some states, in criminal court as well. Although there is universal agreement among mental health professionals that sexual intimacies with current clients are unethical, the question of post-termination sexual relationships is the subject of some debate. Counselors who provide services to clients who have been sexually abused by their former therapists face some difficult decisions. They must keep in mind that their role is to assist these clients in meeting goals that are chosen by the clients themselves.

Child and Adolescent Clients

Assume that the counselor depicted in each of the following vignettes has asked you to consult regarding the situation. What advice might you offer? How would you explain your rationale for that advice?

> Mary, age 16, reveals to her school counselor that she occasionally smokes marijuana with her friends on the weekends. She states that she has never tried any other drugs and insists that she knows better than to "get hooked on the hard stuff." She also insists that the counselor must not tell her parents and that to do so would be a betrayal of her trust.

> As a result of a play therapy session, Leslie, an elementary school counselor, has come to suspect that Arielle, a second grader, is being physically abused by her father. Leslie realizes that the law in her state requires her to report the suspected abuse within 24 hours. She is hesitant to do so, however, because her experience with the children's protective services agency is that they are ineffective in responding to such reports. Leslie fears that the agency social worker will visit Arielle's home but take no further immediate action. Her concern is that the father will escalate the abuse, placing Arielle in even greater danger.

> Jeffrey is a high school counselor who is well liked and respected by his student clients. He has a reputation among them for being willing to go out of his way to help them. One morning at 2:00 A.M., 16-year-old Edmund, who is a member of one of the groups that Jeffrey conducts at school, shows up at Jeffrey's home. Edmund claims that he has been kicked out of the house by his parents and that he has nowhere else to go. He begs Jeffrey to let him stay there for just one night and promises that he will call his parents in the morning.

As we have noted several times in this book, legal and ethical requirements regarding counseling generally do not conflict with one another. Exceptions to this rule occur when counselors work with minor clients, however. Counselors who work with children and adolescents under the age of 18 may be more likely than any other counselors to experience conflicts between what they consider to be their ethical or moral obligations and what the law dictates that they must do. These conflicts often concern confidentiality of client disclosures made during counseling sessions. The legal perspective is that counselors are obligated to parents or guardians when counseling minor children. Child psychiatrists acknowledge in their ethical standards that decisions regarding treatment of minors usually reside with parents or legal guardians (Enzer, 1984). Counselors, in contrast, often believe that their primary ethical obligations are to the minor clients. This discrepancy between the legal and the ethical perspectives causes problems, especially in the area of privacy (Orton, 1997).

In this chapter, we explore these problems and suggest ways to resolve them. Because many of the same issues that arise with minor clients also apply when working with dependent and involuntary clients, this chapter includes a discussion about working with these clients as well. Counselors who provide services to minors and to others who lack legal competency must pay attention to the legal rights of parents and guardians. When individuals are forced to participate in counseling, counselors must ensure that their involuntary clients understand the nature of their relationship and the limited amount of privacy clients have in such situations.

COUNSELING MINOR CLIENTS

Confidentiality

As was discussed in detail in Chapter 4, one of the basic tenets upon which the counseling relationship rests is that clients have a right to expect confidentiality in the relationship. The promise of confidentiality is assumed to be essential in creating a climate of trust and safety in which the client feels free to disclose information that is necessary to successful counseling outcomes. Counselors are also committed to promoting the autonomy and freedom of choice of their clients.

Every child, regardless of age, has an *ethical* right to privacy and confidentiality in the counseling relationship. Thus, ethically conscientious counselors work hard to respect the rights of minor clients to control access to information divulged during counseling, to the extent that this is possible. It is important to remember that confidentiality is not absolute for clients of any age. One legal consideration that limits the confidentiality of minors is that confidentiality and freedom of choice are both predicated on the ability of the client to give voluntary, informed consent.

Clients who cannot comprehend what is being requested in a consent for disclosure or who are unable to make a rational decision are not able to give valid informed consent (Huey, 1996). The law stipulates that clients under the age of 18 are not adults and, therefore, are not competent to make fully informed, voluntary decisions (Davis & Mickelson, 1994). Although counselors may argue that many minor clients are developmentally capable of making these decisions for themselves, the law does not support this belief. The privacy rights of minor clients legally belong to their parents or guardians. Because counselors often find it difficult to accept this legal reality, we will briefly explain its history and current status.

Legal Status of Minors

When the United States was established as a separate country, the government adopted the English common law as its legal foundation. The common law holds that minors must exercise through their parents any legal rights they may have and that minors have no legal standing to contract or bring lawsuits (Kramer, 1994).

The law with respect to minors has seen significant changes in the past two centuries. Prior to legal reforms, children were seen as property of their parents (especially the father) and the government seldom interfered with the control and authority of parents over their children. In Massachusetts during the 1600s, children could be executed if found to be "stubborn and rebellious" (Kramer, 1994). Reforms have included laws that prohibit child labor, require compulsory school attendance, and, more recently, require suspected child abuse reports by professionals.

Today, even though minors have more governmental protection and are beginning to be recognized by courts as individuals with their own legal rights, the law still favors biological parents' rights over their children. It usually requires that children assert any legal rights they have through their parents or guardians.

Rights of Parents to Private Information

Parents or guardians probably have a legal right to know the contents of counseling sessions with their children, although a court may hold otherwise because of specific state statutes or legal precedent in that jurisdiction. Of course, it would be complicated and expensive for parents to enforce their rights, but given the state of the law regarding parent and child relationships, they probably do have the right.

On the other hand, counselors want to offer an appropriate degree of privacy to children they counsel. They want them to feel free to disclose aspects of their lives that trouble them, in an atmosphere of trust and confidentiality. It may be helpful for counselors to consider the following facts about children and privacy:

1. Younger children do not have an understanding of confidentiality or a need for privacy, which is a socially learned concept. Young children are often not nearly as concerned about confidentiality as the counselor is (Huey, 1996).
2. Preadolescents and adolescents may have a heightened desire for privacy that is related to the confusion regarding self and others that is appropriate to their developmental stage of growth.
3. Some children may not be concerned about their privacy. It is inappropriate to assume that children do not want their parents or guardians to know information they have told counselors.
4. Children sometimes tell an adult about their concerns hoping that the adult will act as an intermediary in telling their parents.
5. The reasoning capacity of children is limited and they may not be able to make decisions that are in their best interest because of their age.

When the ACA *Code of Ethics* last underwent a major revision in 1995, some statements were added that were intended to help counselors bring their ethical and legal obligations toward minors into closer alignment. The previous ACA ethical standards said, "when working with minors or persons who are unable to give consent, the member protects these clients' best interests." Huey (1996) described the difficulties this wording seemed to have caused:

> This reinforced the idea for some counselors that the best interest of the client was to protect from disclosure any information received because no mention was made of any ethical responsibilities to the parent or guardian. For other counselors, perhaps more in tune with liability issues, disclosing information to parents upon request was always considered to be in the minor client's best interest. It certainly was viewed by these counselors as being in their own best interest (p. 242).

The current standards clarify that counselors, in addition to protecting minor clients' best interests and taking measures to safeguard confidentiality, may include parents or guardians in the counseling process as necessary (Standard B.3). Further, counselors recognize that families are often important forces in clients' lives and strive to enlist family understanding and involvement as a positive resource when appropriate (Standard A.1.d.). These new guidelines acknowledge that it is often helpful to establish cooperative relationships with parents and other family members when working with minor clients. The guidelines allow counselors more latitude to use their professional judgment in determining whether and when to involve parents or guardians in the counseling process (Huey, 1996).

Many professionals who counsel children report that they have never faced situations in which a parent or guardian demanded to know the contents of counseling sessions, when the child felt strongly that the parent or guardian should not be told. If you are ever presented with such a situation and decide that the child's desire that the parent or guardian not be told is reasonable, we suggest you consider following these steps:

1. Discuss the inquiry with the minor and see if the minor is willing to disclose the content of the counseling session to the adult. Sometimes counselors are more concerned than a child about privacy. If that doesn't work go to step 2.
2. Try to persuade the adult that the child's best interests are not served by revealing the information. Attempt to educate the inquiring adult about the nature of the counseling relationship, and assure the adult that information will be given if the child is in danger. If that doesn't work, go to step 3.
3. Schedule a joint session with the adult and the minor. Assume the role of a mediator at this session. Hope that the adult's mind will be changed about wanting the information or that the minor will be willing to disclose enough information to satisfy the adult. If that doesn't work, try step 4 or step 5.
4. Inform the child ahead of time and then disclose the content of the session to the inquiring adult. If the adult is not a parent or guardian, inform the parent or guardian before disclosing the information. Remember that the adult may have a legal right to the information.
5. Refuse to disclose the information to the inquiring adult. Secure approval from your direct administrator before doing this. Remember that the adult may have a legal right to the information.

A minor client's confidentiality might need to be breached due to parental demands. Other times, it will be the counselor who determines that parents or guardians must be given information that a child has disclosed in counseling sessions. If counselors determine that a child is at risk of harm (to self or others), they must inform the child's parents. There is a difficult judgment to make, however, in deciding whether a child is at risk. Consultation with other counselors is recommended when difficult decisions must be made. If a counselor always tells parents every time a child engages in any risky behavior, children will not be willing to disclose important information to that counselor. On the other hand, if a counselor decides not to inform a parent when a child is engaged in risky behavior, that counselor could be held legally accountable if the child is later harmed or harms someone else.

When such situations arise, counselors should make efforts to maintain the counseling relationship with their clients who are children. Steps that might help in that regard would be having the children tell their parents themselves, telling parents with the children present, or at a minimum, informing the child before telling the parents.

The first vignette presented at the beginning of the chapter involves a teenager who is smoking marijuana on the weekends. It is an example of a situation that requires a counselor to make a judgment call about informing parents. Of course, if the counselor's school system has a policy that parents must be informed in situations like this, the counselor would be unwise to ignore the policy. If no such policy exists, however, the counselor must weigh the risks involved. How serious is the danger involved in the weekend use of marijuana? Is it better to honor the client's wishes and not tell the parents in the hope of maintaining a trusting counseling relationship in which the problem can be further explored? Or is informing the parents a wiser choice? There are no easy answers to these questions. The counselor would be well advised to consult with other school counselors who are likely to have dealt with situations like this one. If he were to consult with us, we would ask him to check out any values issues involved. Is his decision making process being influenced by his own liberal attitudes toward marijuana use, for instance? What are the prevailing standards and attitudes in the community? We would ask him to consider a number of factors, including the age and maturity of the student involved, his judgment about whether the parents' response would harm the student if the parents were told, the student's willingness to consider informing her parents in the near future, any applicable school policies, and any relevant ethical standards and laws. If he decides that the parents must be informed, we would recommend that he let the client know that he cannot keep this particular secret and try to negotiate a procedure for informing the parents that will be acceptable to the client.

Confidentiality in Institutions

Many counselors who provide services for children work in schools, treatment facilities, or social services agencies. Staff members often must consult with each other for the benefit of the children being served. It is important for counselors to educate other non-mental health staff members that they must keep confidential any personal information they learn about children as a result of their professional positions. If professionals disclose confidential information outside the institution and the reputations of parents or guardians are damaged, they could have the basis for a lawsuit.

Privacy is only one of the many legal concerns that counselors who provide services to minors face. We believe that legal issues challenge counselors of children more often than any other mental health professionals.

Parental Permission

Because of their legal status in our society, children are not able to enter into contracts. Since the counseling relationship is contractual in nature, minors cannot legally agree to be counseled on their own. Many states have enacted statutes that lower the legal age for obtaining health or counseling services to an age lower than 18. Reppucci, Weithorn, Mulvey, and Monahan (1984) have taken the position that not all children are equally capable from a legal or psychological perspective. A model statute has been developed by the Institute of Judicial Administration and the American Bar Association. It proposes that minors 14 years old or over be allowed to have three sessions for a believed mental or emotional disorder for the purposes of diagnosis and consultation without parental consent (Mnookin & Weisberg, 1995).

Unless there is a federal or state statute to the contrary, school counselors do not have a legal obligation to obtain parental permission before counseling students. When parents enroll their children in school, they know or should know that their children will be participating in a number of obligatory and optional services, and one of those optional services is counseling in most schools. School systems or school principals who require counselors to obtain parental permission to counsel students are imposing that requirement because they feel it is an appropriate or "politically correct" thing to do, not because it is required by law.

However, since most counseling services are not required of all school students, parents who object to their child's participation in counseling probably have a right to do so. In extreme circumstances, school counselors should consider whether a child might be a victim of abuse or neglect when the parents object to their child's participation in counseling.

Counselors outside of school settings need to obtain informed consent to counseling forms that are signed by the parent or guardian of a minor. The form that is included in Chapter 3 should be modified to indicate that a minor is the client and a parent or guardian is verifying that he or she is the legal parent or guardian and consents to the counseling relationship. For therapeutic rather than legal purposes, counselors may also want to obtain the minor's signature on the form, depending on the minor's level of development and ability to understand the meaning of the release.

Enzer (1984) has noted that child psychiatrists are expected by their ethical code to inform children or seek their agreement to activities that affect them even though this is not required by law. Corey, Corey, and Callanan (1998) have suggested that counselors also have an ethical obligation to provide information to children and adolescents that will help these clients be active partners in their treatment. These authors pointed out that counselors demonstrate respect for client autonomy when they involve minor clients in defining counseling goals and choosing among treatment alternatives. Such a cooperative approach might also help to minimize some of the reluctance or resentment that minor clients often feel when they are sent to a counselor by their parents, their teachers, or other adults in authority.

Counselors in schools might consider publishing information about their services found in Chapter 3 in the documents given to parents when they enroll their child in the school. A modified version of the information addressed to students might be published in student handbooks as well.

Suspected Child Abuse

Every state now has a statute that requires counselors and other professionals to report cases of suspected child abuse to a governmental agency (Jones, 1996; Kemp, 1998). In addition, many states now have laws requiring reports of suspected abuse of elderly persons, incompetent persons, or individuals who are dependent for any reason on others for their well-being.

The actual wording of the requirements for reporting abuse varies significantly from state to state. Counselors are advised to read the statute requiring abuse reports and then to ask for interpretations from an attorney if there is something they do not understand. Most university and public libraries have copies of the current state statutes available for patrons.

Basically, the statutes require abuse reports to be made if counselors have reason to believe a child may be abused or neglected, or in some cases, if a child was abused or neglected in the past. The statutes also protect reporters from liability as long as reports are made in good faith. This means that lawsuits against a reporter for defamation of character or some other type of tort would not prevail as long as the counselor really believed that abuse might have occurred, even if it was later proven that no abuse had existed. In the event a counselor has been involved in a conflict on some other matter with a suspected perpetrator, it would be wise to ask another professional to gather evidence of the suspected abuse directly and make the report.

Important language in the statutes includes the following: (a) who must make the report to the governmental agency (the person with the suspicion or the supervisor); (b) when the report must be made (immediately, within 24 hours; 48 hours, etc.); (c) whether the oral report must be followed by a written report; (d) what specific information is required when the report is made (age of the child, name and address of the child, specifics of cause of suspicion, name and address of parents, etc.); (e) whether past abuse must be reported; and (f) which suspected perpetrators must be reported (parents or guardians only, caretakers, siblings, other).

Statutes vary in reporting requirements for past abuse when the victim is no longer in danger. The statute may say specifically that past abuse must be reported, or that only currently abusive situations must be reported, or it may be silent on the issue. Some statutes mandate that only suspected abuse by parents or guardians must be reported. However, all statutes allow nonmandated reports to be made as well. In the event that more than one person is involved in suspecting abuse and that all of those involved are mandated reporters, the person making the report should indicate that the report is being made on behalf of others as well and ask that their names also be recorded as reporters.

Employed counselors need to determine whether their employer requires internal reports in addition to the reports to the governmental agency. An employed counselor should always inform the supervisor before or immediately after making a report, even if supervisor notification is not required by policy.

Although most statutes allow suspected abuse reports to be made anonymously, professionals should give their names when they make reports. In addition, to protect themselves, reporters should always make a note to themselves indicating the date and time they called in the report and the name of the person who took the report, along with a written summary of what was said when the report was made.

The procedural aspects of making suspected abuse reports are important from a legal perspective. However, counselors always must exercise their professional judgment before and after making such reports. They should have several goals in mind, which include (a) maintaining, to the extent possible, any counseling relationship they have with the parties involved; (b) being concerned about the welfare of the alleged victim before and after the report (Remley & Fry, 1993); (c) helping the parties deal with the process that follows reports; and (d) fulfilling their statutory legal obligations.

Counselors must first exercise their judgment as to whether they suspect that abuse or neglect might be occurring or might have occurred in the past. Responsible counselors would consider the following factors in exercising their judgment: (a) the credibility of the alleged victim, (b) prevailing standards for discipline in the community, and (c) information that is known about the alleged victim and alleged perpetrator. Consultation with colleagues is recommended in difficult situations.

After making a report, counselors must again exercise their professional judgment in determining whether to tell the alleged victim that a report has been made; whether to tell the alleged perpetrator; and how to interact with the alleged victim, parents or guardians, and the alleged perpetrator after the report has been made.

State agency personnel or police officers may contact the reporter after a report has been made to gather information. These individuals have investigatory powers and have a right to question witnesses. Agency personnel or police officers need to determine whether an abuse report reflects actual abuse and the degree to which a child may be in danger (Kemp, 1998). Counselors should not discuss the case with unknown persons on the telephone. They should ask to see credentials of investigators, and they should be cooperative. Counselors may request that interviews be scheduled at times that are convenient for them. If investigators want to speak to alleged victims, the director of the agency or principal of the school should respond to such requests.

State agencies that investigate suspected abuse reports often are inundated with reports and are understaffed. They must decide which cases are the most severe and usually pay particular attention to those situations. Whenever counselors are frustrated because they do not believe the state agency handles investigations properly or they believe children are put at risk after reports are made, they should report additional incidents and should request a meeting with governmental agency representatives to discuss the perceived problems.

For example, consider the case of Leslie, the elementary school counselor depicted in the second vignette that introduces this chapter. This counselor suspects that her second-grade client is being physically abused by her father. The counselor is reluctant to make a report because she fears that doing so might put the client in greater danger. If we were to help Leslie reason through her dilemma, we would emphasize the importance of compliance with the law that requires her to report. We would explore with her any actions she might take to help ensure the child's safety. These might include enlisting the assistance of the child's mother or other relatives and teaching the child self-protection strategies. She might also emphasize her concerns for the child's safety to the children's protective services personnel and request that they take steps to protect the child. We would also recommend that she document her contact with the agency and that she inform her principal (or other immediate supervisor) of the situation.

Dual or Multiple Relationships

Ethical dilemmas can be created by the job description and work environment of school counselors (Huey, 1996). School counselors play multiple roles, and there are inherent conflicts in some of these roles. Sometimes counselors are expected to serve, along with teachers, in duty assignments such as bathroom monitor, lunchroom supervisor, or chaperone at extracurricular events. If counselors must carry out the disciplinary functions that accompany these duties, this will compromise their ability to function effectively as personal counselors with their students. It would be unreasonable to expect students to trust and confide in a counselor who assigned them to detention or reported their misbehavior to the principal.

School counselors sometimes voluntarily take on additional roles such as coach for an athletic team or club sponsor. Counselors can justifiably argue that these extra roles provide them with opportunities to know their student clients better outside the formal setting of the counselor's office. They should also be cognizant, however, that there is potential for misunderstandings and conflicts because these roles involve evaluation and supervision.

Occasionally, school policies exist that impinge on counselor effectiveness. If policies require counselors to inform parents about details of counseling sessions involving issues of birth control, pregnancy, abortion, sexually transmitted diseases, or other sensitive matters, some students will avoid discussing these issues with their counselors (Herlihy & Corey, 1997).

School counselors, especially those who work in small towns and rural communities, are likely to have friends who are teachers and friends who are parents. Both of these situations can lead to uncomfortable dual role conflicts. Friendships between teachers and counselors seem inevitable, given their shared interest in children's welfare, their daily contacts, and the fact that many school counselors were teachers before they became counselors. Teachers are accustomed to the sharing that occurs among colleagues and they value open communication with other school personnel regarding students with whom they all work. Counselors, on the other hand, come from a position of honoring the confidentiality of their child clients. This "clash of cultures" complicates the work of the school counselor (Welfel, 1998).

School counselors are equally likely to have friends who are parents, and it is possible that a friend's child might also be a student client of the counselor. In these instances, counselors must be careful to keep boundaries around the professional relationship with the child and the personal relationship with the child's parents. This can pose difficult challenges (Herlihy & Corey, 1997).

Finally, there is great potential for dual role conflicts when counselors deal with child abuse. Counselors are required to report suspected abuse, yet their role is rarely limited to that of reporter. They are often asked to perform many other functions, including that of school system employee, court witness, liaison with social services, and counselor to the victim, perpetrator, and family (Remley & Fry, 1993). Because most children are left in their parents' custody after a report is made, the school counselor is likely to have the ongoing task of providing counseling for the child. Treatment of abuse victims is an intense and lengthy process that can strain a counselor's resources, during a period when the counselor must also remain involved with the court system. The counselor will need to work with caseworkers from the children's protective services agency, with police and prosecutors, and perhaps with other attorneys. These simultaneous, multiple roles can severely test a counselor's ability to handle conflicting demands.

It is a challenge for caring counselors to maintain appropriate professional boundaries when they work with children who have been abused or who, for other reasons, are clearly in need of help. The counselor in the third vignette at the beginning of the chapter is a case in point. This high school counselor was confronted with a student who showed up on his doorstep at 2:00 A.M. claiming that he had been kicked out of the house by his parents and had nowhere else to go. The counselor might well be tempted, at that hour of the night, to invite the boy into his home where the boy would be safe until morning. This crossing of the professional boundary could have serious consequences, however. A worst case scenario would be that the boy might later claim that the counselor had sexually abused him while he was in a vulnerable emotional state. The counselor would be well advised to find an alternative arrangement that would ensure the boy's safety without putting himself at risk.

INCOMPETENT CLIENTS

All of the legal issues applying to children apply to individuals who are declared incompetent by courts, as well. Very few individuals are declared by courts to be legally incompetent. Adults who are developmentally disabled, critically ill, seriously injured, mentally ill, or elderly could be declared incompetent by a court. If such individuals are declared incompetent, the court appoints a legal guardian who has the same legal powers over the individual that a biological parent or a legal guardian would have over a child.

Counselors must be careful to distinguish between adult clients who have actually been declared incompetent and those who still maintain their legal rights, but who are dependent on others. Dependent adults maintain their legal rights until a court, upon a petition filed by some party, declares them incompetent and appoints a guardian.

INVOLUNTARY CLIENTS

Involuntary clients usually are required to sign a waiver of their privacy rights when they begin a counseling relationship. Because they are being required to participate in counseling and would suffer some type of negative consequences if they refused, the person or entity requiring the counseling also requires some type of report regarding the participation of clients in the counseling process.

The legal issue involved in these situations is to ensure that involuntary clients know that reports must be made and understand the types of information that will be included in the reports. As much specificity as possible should be included in the privacy waiver form that involuntary clients sign. Since different individuals and entities require that different types of information be reported, the form should allow for detailed information to be added. A model agreement form for involuntary clients that includes a waiver of privacy is included in Appendix H.

When counselors write reports on the progress of involuntary clients in counseling, they must follow the guidelines outlined in Chapter 10 regarding evaluators. Reports should be written with concrete information provided for each conclusion in the report.

Counselors who provide services to involuntary clients actually function in a dual role that is not ideal. They are both counselors and evaluators. Because of this dual role, it is vital that clients complete an information agreement and that they understand its contents.

SUMMARY AND KEY POINTS

This chapter has focused primarily on legal and ethical considerations in working with minor clients. There are discrepancies between legal and ethical perspectives regarding certain issues in counseling minors, such as privacy and confidentiality rights. These discrepancies pose some difficult challenges for counselors. Many of the same issues that arise in working with minor clients also apply when providing services to dependent and involuntary clients.

Some of the key points made in this chapter include the following:

- Minor clients have an ethical right to privacy and confidentiality in the counseling relationship, but the privacy rights of minors legally belong to their parents or guardians.
- Parents or guardians probably have the legal right to know the contents of counseling sessions with their children.
- Counselors should not automatically assume that all minor clients do not want their parents to know information they have shared with their counselors. The stance that minor clients take toward privacy will vary according to their age, developmental stage, and motivation for sharing information with the counselor.

- The ACA *Code of Ethics* allows counselors latitude to use their professional judgment in determining whether and when to involve parents or guardians in the counseling process.
- Counselors can follow a sequence of steps in resolving a situation in which a parent or guardian demands information and the minor client feels strongly that the parent or guardian should not be told.
- When counselors determine that a minor client is at risk of harm to self or others, they must inform the client's parents or guardians. Determining when a minor client is sufficiently at risk to justify such a step is a difficult judgment to make. The counselor should make every effort to maintain the counseling relationship with the client.
- Although counselors who work in institutional settings often share information about clients for the benefit of clients being served, these counselors must take appropriate steps to maintain client confidentiality.
- Counseling is a contractual relationship into which minors cannot legally enter, on their own. Nonetheless, school counselors do not have a legal obligation to obtain parent permission before counseling student clients. On the other hand, parents who object to their child's participation in counseling probably have the legal right to demand that services be discontinued.
- For legal purposes, informed consent to counsel a minor should be obtained from the parents. As an ethical matter, the child client should be actively involved in giving consent and determining treatment goals and strategies.
- Counselors are required by law to report suspected child abuse. Counselors need to be very familiar with reporting requirements in the state where they practice, because statutes vary considerably from state to state.
- The reporting of suspected child abuse requires counselors to exercise their professional judgment before and after making a report. A host of factors need to be taken into consideration throughout the process.
- School counselors often play multiple roles. Conflicts can occur between the role of counselor and other roles such as bathroom/lunchroom monitor, coach or club sponsor, and friend to teachers and parents of student clients. Difficult challenges are posed by the need to maintain appropriate boundaries around dual professional roles or simultaneous personal and professional roles.
- All of the legal issues that apply to minor clients apply to individuals who have been declared by courts to be legally incompetent. Counselors need to be careful to distinguish between legally incompetent clients and clients who are dependent on others but retain their legal rights.
- Because counselors who work with involuntary clients function in a dual role as both counselor and evaluator, it is crucial to secure fully informed consent from these clients.

Counseling Families and Groups

Ethical and legal issues can be complex when counselors work with more than one client at a time, as they do in family counseling and group counseling. The issues that apply to counseling individuals often are more complicated to resolve when more than one client is involved.

This chapter begins with a focus on counseling families. Some familiar topics are revisited, but are examined from a family systems orientation. These topics include informed consent, protecting client welfare, privacy and confidentiality, the role of counselor values, and counselor competence. The section also examines some special considerations that often arise in family counseling such as preserving a marriage versus divorce, child custody, family secrets, and ethical questions posed by domestic violence.

The second portion of the chapter focuses on group work. The issues of client welfare and informed consent, protecting clients from harm, privacy and confidentiality, dual relationships, the role of counselor values, and counselor competence take on new dimensions when applied to group counseling. Additional ethical and legal rights and responsibilities must be addressed when conducting group counseling, such as freedom to exit a group, screening potential members, protecting confidentiality with minors in groups, and dealing with outside-of-group socializing among group members.

FAMILY COUNSELING

Family counselors use a systems perspective in working with their clients. From this viewpoint, the family provides the context for understanding its individual members and their problems. Family counselors believe that actions taken by any family member will influence the other members and that their reactions will in turn have a reciprocal effect on the individual (Corey et al., 1998). Counselors often work with couples, parents and children, nuclear families, families of origin, extended families, and nontraditional families. Therefore, the first question that the counselor needs to answer is, "Who is the client?" Although family counselors see the entire family system as their client, the answer to this seemingly basic question is not that simple. If the counseling goals of one family member are different from or even antithetical to the wishes of another member, whose interests does the counselor serve?

One of the areas of law that is in conflict with mental health is their different perspectives on the family. Family counselors often view the family system as their client and treat the family, as opposed to treating individual members of a family. The law, on the other hand, always views family members as having separate and distinct rights and responsibilities that are individual in nature. To further complicate the situation, the law states that any minor or legally incompetent family member can exercise rights only through parents or legal guardians. This poses problems when one family member wants a family counselor to uphold confidentiality, while another family member demands that the counselor reveal in court conversations that took place during counseling sessions. A family counselor generally favors the family member who wants privacy, while the law usually favors the family member who wants the information revealed. This problem is discussed in greater depth later in this chapter.

Sometimes counseling begins as individual work, with the family included later. You will remember from Chapter 8 that the ACA ethics code encourages counselors to recognize that families are usually important forces in clients' lives. They should enlist family understanding and involvement, when doing so would be of therapeutic benefit (Standard A.1.d.). When counseling begins with an individual client and then includes family members, to whom does the counselor have primary responsibility—the individual family member who originally sought counseling or the family as a whole?

The ACA *Code of Ethics* (1995) recognizes that problems can arise when these questions are not resolved at the outset of the counseling relationship. The code states that counselors who provide services to two or more persons who have a relationship, such as wife and husband or parents and children, need to clarify at the outset which person or persons are clients. They also need to explain the nature of the relationships they will have with each involved person (Standard A.8.). This standard raises the issue of who gives informed consent to counseling when there are multiple clients.

Informed Consent

The issue of informed consent when working with families goes beyond the usual matter of descriptive adequacy (Lakin, 1994). Not only must the counselor attempt to ensure that consent to counseling is given freely after clear and sufficient information has been provided, but family counseling also presents additional challenges. Some of the questions that need to be addressed include the following:

- Who gives consent on behalf of the family?
- Who in the family is seeking counseling and who is a reluctant participant? Can family members who feel pressured to join in the counseling process give truly free consent?
- What happens when one of the adults in the family refuses to give consent for family counseling?
- How capable are potential participants, particularly children, of understanding what they are getting into?
- How can counselors adequately address the reality that there will be changes in the family system, as well as in individual members, as a result of counseling?

Obtaining informed consent from all members of a family sometimes is not possible. In marriage and family counseling the desired procedure is to have all adults and legally competent family members give consent to counseling. A difficult situation arises if one such individual refuses to do so. In these cases, Cottone and Tarvydas (1998) have suggested that the autonomy of the individual probably should override the consensus of the other family members and counseling should not take place. In some circumstances, however, some members of a family may wish to enter counseling, even when an individual member refuses, or families may enter counseling because they are mandated by courts to do so. In such situations, individual family members may refuse to participate, but counseling still should be made available for those who desire counseling or who are required to attend.

The issue of what to do about nonparticipating family members raises some difficult questions from the standpoint of ethical practice. A controversial procedure used by some family counselors is to withhold services until all family members agree to participate in counseling. The problem with this practice is that the counselor thereby cooperates with the resistant family member by keeping the rest of the family from receiving counseling. Willing family members are then put in an unfair position of being denied services (Haas & Alexander, 1981). Of course, coercion of reluctant family members could be considered unethical, but some family counselors are comfortable exerting some pressure on a resistant family member to participate in one or two sessions. These counselors hope that the resistance can be overcome when they see that they are not going to be scapegoated or blamed for the family's problems (Welfel, 1998).

Although children cannot legally give informed consent, counselors are wise to involve them in the decision making process. It is hard to imagine that family counseling would be successful if it included a resistant, resentful teenager who felt left out of the decision to engage in the process. Counselors need to be able to communicate with adolescents and children in a way that enables them to understand their role in the counseling process, and then request their consent to participate (Goldenberg & Goldenberg, 1996).

Just as counselors have an ethical obligation to alert individual clients to life changes that might occur as a result of counseling, family counselors must describe potential changes in family relationships as well as adaptations that individual family members might make in conjunction with shifts in the family system (Herlihy & Corey, 1996). It can be very difficult to anticipate directions that these reciprocal changes might take. Nonetheless, family counselors have an obligation to explain that the family system will be the focus of the counseling process and that no one family member will be treated as the "identified patient" who is the source of the family's problems (Corey et al., 1998).

Client Welfare

Family counseling gives priority to the good of the family and, thus, may not be in the best interests of an individual in the family. Ethical practice demands that family counselors make every effort to minimize the risks to individuals (Hare-Mustin, 1980). One way to accomplish this is to encourage family members to question how counseling relates to their needs and goals as well as to those of the family. This kind of discussion should take place as part of the informed consent process and throughout counseling, as needed.

Although family counselors may consider the family as a whole to be their client, the law would demand that all clients within a family group be able to rely on the counselor to act in a manner that furthers their best interest and protects them from harm. Legal problems might arise, for example, if a client in family counseling were financially harmed after a counselor encouraged the family to make decisions that excluded the family member from the financial support of the family.

The changing nature of families raises another legal concern for family counselors. Few families seeking counseling today consist of a biological mother and father, and their children. Instead, families reflect a number of societal trends: single parents are raising children; a step-parent is in the family; single parents have partners to whom they are not married living with the family; close friends are intimately involved with the family; extended family members such as grandparents, adult siblings, uncles, aunts, or cousins reside with the family; and gay and lesbian couples are raising children. Family counselors must keep in mind, when working with nontraditional families, that only biological parents or court-appointed guardians have legal rights of control and authority over children. Often, one or more biological parents who are not present in a family have legal rights that must be considered when family decisions regarding children are made.

Risky Techniques

Any time counselors use techniques that are out of the ordinary, they must ensure that clients are protected. If a client is harmed as a result of a nontraditional or unusual technique, counselors' colleagues may claim that they were operating outside the scope of accepted practices in the field.

Family counselors who subscribe to the systemic family counseling model sometimes become quite active in directing family members to take or refrain from taking certain actions. Directives given by counselors are sometimes called *prescriptions* (Carlson, Sperry, & Lewis, 1997). A professional who prescribes behavior must ensure that no one is harmed as a result of the directives.

A controversial technique used by some family counselors is known as paradoxical directives or interventions. The concept behind the technique is that if authorities instruct persons to do things that are against their best interests, they will defy the counselor and correct the behavior on their own (Goldenberg & Goldenberg, 1998). When paradoxical directives are used in the strategic family counseling model, according to Carlson et al (1997), "The therapist assigns tasks in which success is based on the family defying instructions or following them to an extreme point and ultimately recoiling, thus producing change" (p. 63). As an example, assume that a teenaged daughter is in an inappropriate role reversal situation with her parent. The parent is acting like a teenager and the daughter is acting like a disapproving parent. The family counselor tells the daughter to work harder at correcting her parent's irresponsible behavior and to take on even more household responsibilities. In this situation, the counselor would hope that the daughter would recoil, defy the counselor's directive, and recognize that she was taking on a parenting role that was inappropriate for her.

Ethical concerns have been raised regarding this technique. One objection to paradoxical directives is that they are manipulative and deceptive. Even though the counselor may ultimately debrief the target of the intervention (the daughter in the above example), the counselor delivers the intervention without revealing these intentions. Haley (1976) has argued that such a procedure is a "benevolent lie," but many writers question whether techniques that involve deception can ever be considered ethically permissible (Lakin, 1994; Welfel, 1998).

A second concern involves the risk of negative outcomes. Some applications of this technique that are potentially dangerous are (a) a parent who is overly strict is told to become more strict in disciplining the children and (b) an employee who is frantically worried about not performing up to an employer's expectations is told to be more concerned about pleasing the boss. In these two examples, it is clear how problems could manifest themselves. The parent could physically harm the children and the employee could become so distressed as to lose the job.

Paradoxical techniques are not the only type of powerful intervention used in family counseling. Family sculpting also can have powerful and unpredictable effects. Other interventions that evoke strong feelings or uncover feelings that have been kept secret in the family can leave clients vulnerable to harm. As a result, family counselors must carefully consider the ramifications of such interventions (Welfel, 1998). They must ensure that no one is harmed, and they should not risk a lack of support from colleagues who do not believe that such techniques are appropriate.

Family Violence

Some scholars, and feminist therapists in particular, have been critical of the idea of applying systems theory to abusive relationships. They note that 95% of victims of physical abuse are women and they assert that blaming the relationship or relationship dynamics for the abuse is inexcusable. They believe strongly that the male abuser must be held responsible for his behavior.

Welfel (1998) has described the difficulties inherent in attempting to conduct family counseling with couples when abuse is occurring in their relationship. When one partner in a relationship is being abused by the other, the foundation for successful counseling is absent. The partner being abused cannot express feelings honestly in counseling sessions nor risk behavior change. The perpetrator can evade personal responsibility when the problem is framed as a family issue. For these reasons, most writers recommend that family counselors see the partners individually at first. Family therapy should be avoided when there is ongoing abuse (Houskamp, 1994). Later, when the perpetrator has taken responsibility for the abuse and has begun to change behavior, joint sessions are more feasible.

Of course, some counselors believe that couples counseling should be selected as the approach when dealing with some physically abusive relationships. Each situation is evaluated given the personalities of the individuals involved and the nature of their relationship. There is no empirical evidence that one approach is more effective than the other.

Privacy and Confidentiality

When counselors counsel more than one person at the same time, they can guarantee confidentiality only on their own parts. They must encourage confidentiality but make it clear that it cannot be guaranteed on the part of family members. You might review the statement regarding privacy in family situations that is included in the client information and agreement found in Chapter 3, to see how this might be accomplished.

Privileged Communication

The legal counterpart to the ethic of confidentiality is privileged communication. The general rule regarding privileged communication is that privilege is waived if a third party is present (Knapp & VandeCreek, 1987). Exceptions to waivers usually exist when the third party is another professional with whom the client would have privilege or when the third party is an assistant to the professional and under the professional's control and authority

(Knapp & VandeCreek, 1987). Most licensed counselors practice in jurisdictions where privilege exists between counselors and their clients, but where there is no specific guarantee of privilege for family situations. In these circumstances, clients who wish to bring family members into counseling sessions need to be told that the privilege that normally would exist between the counselor and the client probably would be lost.

Some privilege statutes that have been enacted more recently specifically grant privilege to family members individually and to their counselor (Arthur & Swanson, 1993; Huber & Baruth, 1987; Kearney, 1984). In these situations, an individual client could prevent a counselor from being forced to testify as to what occurred in the sessions, but probably would not be able to prevent other family members from testifying if they were inclined to do so. As a result, counselors should assure clients that they would not willingly disclose information from their sessions, but should inform clients that other family members do not have the same obligation to keep the relationship confidential (Jacobs, Masson, & Harvill, 1998).

Counselors who provide professional services for married persons are often confronted with a problem related to privileged communication and married couples. In a typical scenario, the couple comes to the counselor because they are experiencing problems in their marriage. In the course of the counseling relationship, a number of stressful topics are discussed and either the husband or wife admits negative behaviors such as excessive drinking, infidelity, abusive behavior, or violent acts. Later, the couple decides to divorce. One of the parties wants the counselor to repeat in a legal deposition or hearing the admissions the other party made in the course of the counseling sessions. The other party, for obvious reasons, wants the counselor to keep the information confidential.

The situation described above occurs frequently. When counselors find themselves in such dilemmas, they need to consult an attorney where they are employed or a private practice lawyer if they are private practitioners. If the counselor refuses to testify at a deposition after a subpoena has been issued, and the spouse who made the negative admissions had legally waived privilege under state law, the counselor could be held in contempt of court. If, on the other hand, the counselor does testify and the relationship with the spouse who made the negative admissions was privileged under state law, the counselor could be legally accountable to that person for violating the spouse's privacy. Reading the state statute on privilege is not sufficient because legal arguments could be made for and against disclosure whether or not a privilege statute exists and regardless of the wording in the statute. This is a situation in which counselors must seek legal counsel and must follow the advice of their attorneys. Of course counselors should tell their attorneys whether they want to testify and their reasons for feeling that way. This will help the attorney review the situation from the counselor's perspective.

One-third of the children in the United States live in some type of stepparenting situation (Jones, 1996). Stepparents, nonmarried partners, grandparents, other relatives, and friends have no legal rights to confidential information or to other privileges held by biological parents.

Family Secrets

A confidentiality issue that emerges frequently in family counseling is how to deal with family secrets—information that one family member has shared with the counselor but has withheld from a spouse, children, or other family members. Following is a fairly typical scenario:

> Bob and Rhonda have been engaged in marriage counseling for two months. Their counselor generally sees them jointly but occasionally will spend a portion of a session working with one of them individually. Today, Bob is in an individual session and reveals that he has been having an extramarital affair. He adds that he really is committed to saving his marriage and realizes he has to end the affair. He says that Rhonda must not learn about the affair as it would devastate her and ruin any chance of making the marriage work.

There has been considerable debate over whether counselors should keep in confidence such revelations (Margolin, 1982). One position is that secrets should be kept. A rationale for this stance is that the counselor, by agreeing to uphold the confidentiality of individual family members, will be more likely to obtain honest and complete information. This will help the counselor better understand family dynamics and conduct an accurate assessment.

A second position has been that counselors should refuse to keep secrets. In this view, secrets are seen as being counterproductive to the open and honest communication that is necessary for family counseling to be successful. Additionally, by refusing to keep secrets, the counselor can prevent triangulation. This is a kind of subgrouping created when the counselor and the family member with the secret collude in withholding information from the other family member(s).

Still others have argued a third, middle ground, position. They stress the need for flexibility and propose that counselors should exercise their professional judgment, divulging or maintaining a confidence in accordance with the greatest benefit for the family. They argue that the criterion should be the effect on therapeutic progress and family welfare.

In 1995, the ACA, in its *Code of Ethics,* took a position in agreement with the first of these arguments. The code states that, "In family counseling information about one family member cannot be disclosed to another member without permission. Counselors protect the privacy rights of each member" (Standard B.2.b.). As an ACA member, you are obligated to follow the guidance of the code in dealing with family secrets. In the event, however, that you believe that no secrets should be allowed within the context of family counseling, you could include in your disclosure statement that each individual gives permission to the counselor to disclose to other family members anything said in any interactions between family members and the counselor.

You should keep in mind that your promise to uphold confidentiality is not absolute. When securing informed consent from the family members, tell them that if you learn about activities going on in the family that put family members in danger (such as spouse battering, child abuse, or incest) you may need to take steps to prevent further harm. You will also need to let your family clients know that you must breach confidentiality when you are required by law to do so.

Divorce and Child Custody

Because it appears that half the marriages in the United States end in divorce and that 60% of second marriages fail (Jones, 1996), many children are affected by divorce. It is important for counselors to understand the nature of child custody so that they will not be tempted to involve themselves inappropriately in custody battles. Some basic information regarding custody is offered here to give you some sense of the difficulties involved in trying to make decisions regarding your role.

Generally, a custody order by a court defines the nature of the rights and responsibilities of two parents who are separated or divorced, in relation to a child or children. Mnookin and Weisberg (1995) have distinguished between physical and legal custody, stating that, "Legal custody carries with it the right and obligation to make long range decisions involving education, religious training, discipline, medical care, and other matters of major significance concerning the child's life and welfare" (p. 846). They also stated that when the parent who was not granted legal custody has physical possession of the child, that parent usually has the authority to make decisions concerning the child's welfare.

The primary components of a custody order specifically define which parent has physical possession of a child at which times and orders child support payments when appropriate. Unless a parental right is specifically altered, modified, or terminated in a custody order, a parent maintains that right, even without the right to physical custody. As a result, noncustodial parents might have a right to receive correspondence that schools send to parents, to review their child's school record, to contract for counseling for the child, to demand that a child discontinue counseling services, and to take other actions that a custodial parent would have a right to take.

Whether a child's preferences will be considered in making custody decisions varies greatly from court to court. Appellate courts have done everything from allowing judges to base custody decisions entirely on the expressed preferences of the child to allowing judges to disregard those preferences entirely. Most judges will consider the wishes of a child regarding custody, particularly if the child is older (Kramer, 1994).

Awarding joint custody to both parents is a controversial practice. Some experts believe joint custody is a positive concept in that it allows natural parents to participate equally in raising their children. Others believe that joint custody is usually detrimental to children because children suffer when parents disagree and no one seems to be in charge. In Nebraska, a court has said that joint custody is not favored and should be avoided (*Petrashek v. Petrashek,* 1989). By contrast, a court in Montana has determined that joint custody is in the best interests of a child (*In re marriage of Kovash,* 1993). Kramer (1994) has reported that about half the states allow joint custody arrangements by statute.

It is difficult for nonlawyers to determine whether a parent has a legal right to possession of a child at any given moment. Parents often agree between themselves to modify the times that they have possession. Some custody orders even stipulate that the parties may mutually agree to modifications. If parents are in conflict over who should have possession of a child, counselors should insist that administrators, lawyers, or even the police become involved in resolving the dispute, rather than trying to resolve it themselves.

Courts sometimes though rarely issue an order terminating parental rights. This order severs the legal relationship between a child and the biological or legal parent. Custody and termination of parent rights orders vary greatly in their structure and language, and must be drafted to comply with state law. Court orders should always be interpreted by attorneys if there is a question regarding their meaning.

Mrs. Jones brings her 12-year-old daughter to school and enrolls her mid-year. As she is enrolling her daughter, Mrs. Jones produces a legal document that she says gives her full legal custody of her daughter and terminates all of her husband's parental rights. She instructs school officials that if her former husband inquires about his daughter, they should give him no information and that they certainly should not allow him to see or pick up her daughter from the school. What should the school officials do?

First, the officials should read the court order to determine what the language actually says regarding Mrs. Jones' custody rights and the rights of her former husband. If the language is technical or is unclear, the school officials should ask the school district lawyer to read the document and inform them of its technical and legal meaning. Termination of all parental rights is rare. Usually, a custody order giving custody to a mother does not terminate all parental rights of the father. School officials should inquire as to what rights exist for noncustodial parents if it is determined that the father's parental rights have not been terminated. School officials should also ask the school board lawyer how to handle the situation if a noncustodial parent shows up at their school and demands to see his child or take the child away from the school.

Generally, courts give custody preference to natural parents over others who have an interest in obtaining custody. For a caretaker who is not a biological parent to obtain custody over the objections of a natural parent, usually a court would have to find the natural parent unfit (Kramer, 1994).

Couples who are divorcing sometimes attempt to get counselors to take one side or the other in child custody battles. This can happen after two individuals have come together for relationship counseling and have decided to separate or divorce, or when one of the parents has been in individual counseling. Counselors should not offer to testify for their clients in child custody proceedings. Unless the counselor has served in the capacity of child custody evaluator—an involved process that entails home visits, interviews with both parents, and the use of formalized assessment instruments—the counselor is in no position to make a judgment as to who is the better parent.

In the event counselors are subpoenaed to testify after refusing to do so voluntarily, their position should be that they do not have sufficient information to form a judgment about which party is the better parent or who should get custody. Usually, counselors know only what has been told to them in counseling sessions and do not know the truthfulness or accuracy of the information. If they have counseled only one parent, they have no direct knowledge of the other parent.

Counselor Values

The personal values of counselors undeniably have an influence on how they conduct individual counseling. The role of counselor values may be particularly critical in the practice of marriage and family counseling (Corey et al., 1998; Huber, 1994). Very few family counselors deliberately attempt to impose their own values on clients. Yet, it is impossible for counselors to avoid using their influence in subtle ways—sometimes without being aware that they are doing so. Marriage and family counseling often deals with some of the most value-laden issues in our society. Following are just a few examples:

- cohabitation, marriage, and divorce
- marital fidelity and extramarital affairs
- parenting and disciplining of children
- birth control, abortion, and adoption
- relationships between couples of different races or cultures
- gay and lesbian relationships
- sex roles and gender roles

Counseling is never value free, and all family counselors have their own definitions of healthy and dysfunctional families, effective and ineffective ways of communicating, and affirming and destructive relationships. As Welfel (1998) has so aptly pointed out, no therapeutic work could take place without these definitions. It is not unusual for couples and family clients to espouse values that are different from those of the counselor, and it is in these instances that counselors are the most challenged to avoid imposing their own agendas. To illustrate, as you read the following scenario try to be aware of the assumptions and values that have entered your thinking about the case.

George and Victor are a homosexual couple who have sought counseling to help them decide whether to make a big change in their lives. A number of years ago, George was married and had a son with his wife. He has been divorced and in a committed relationship with Victor for 5 years. George has been thinking about seeking joint custody of his son who is now 12 years old and with whom he has maintained a parental relationship. Victor is generally supportive of the idea but admits to some apprehension about having to share George's affection and attention.

What assumptions do you hold that might influence how you work with George and Victor? Do you hold certain ideas about the morality of homosexuality? About how enduring homosexual and heterosexual relationships are likely to be? About what makes a "healthy" role model for a 12-year-old boy? About the impact that a homosexual or heterosexual partner's jealousy or possessiveness might have on child rearing?

One issue of counselor values that has received increased attention in recent years is gender bias. Feminist therapists in particular have contended that family counselors are far from immune to the sex role stereotyping that exists in our society. When counselors do not challenge traditional assumptions about gender roles, they are likely to expect women to be the ones to change in counseling (Nixon, 1993). They may be vulnerable to certain other biases such as (a) placing less importance on the demands of a woman's career than on a man's, (b) encouraging couples to accept the belief that raising children is primarily the mother's responsibility, (c) seeing a woman's extramarital affair as more serious than a man's, and (d) assuming that marriage is the best choice for a woman (Guterman, 1991; Margolin, 1982; Sekaran, 1986). On the other hand, feminist therapists have been accused of having their own biases when they encourage counselors to help women to define themselves rather than be defined by others, to set their own standards rather than try to meet the expectations of others, and to nurture themselves as much as they nurture others.

Family counselors need to work to achieve a balance with respect to gender and therapeutic change. They are likely to cause harm to both partners in a relationship if they urge change in gender-prescribed roles solely because they believe such changes are needed. Conversely, it is equally irresponsible to condone through silence emotional abuse or intimidation (Wendorf & Wendorf, 1992). Of course we are exposing our own biases when we suggest that some goals worth striving for, in your work with couples and families, might include: (a) practicing in a gender-aware manner, (b) being open to nontraditional roles and relationships, (c) helping family members identify ways that their views on gender roles may be contributing to their problems, and (d) continually monitoring your own behavior for unintended bias, such as looking more at the wife when discussing child rearing and more at the husband when discussing financial issues.

You probably have identified some of your values and assumptions as you reflected on the issues we raised in this section. Over the course of your career as a counselor, you will inevitably encounter couple and family clients whose values, lifestyles, and choices are very different from your own. It will be important for you to be aware of your own values and biases and keep clearly in mind that it is not your role to decide how couples or families should change. You will be better able to make informed ethical decisions when you know your own values, and understand and respect the values of the families with whom you are working.

Counselor Competence

Marriage and family counseling is based on a theoretical perspective that is philosophically quite different from the foundations of individual counseling (Cottone, 1992). Thus, developing competence in marriage and family counseling requires more than the completion of one or two specialized courses. The AAMFT has established educational requirements that are quite extensive and include, in addition to academic training, supervised experience in working with couples and families, work in one's own family of origin, and personal therapy. The CACREP has also promulgated a set of core competencies that are considered necessary for counselors who practice marriage and family counseling.

There is debate among helping professionals as to whether marriage and family counseling is a separate discipline or a specialty area of counseling. Marriage and family counselors in most states have succeeded in getting separate licensure bills passed that set them apart from licensed professional counselors. This diversity of opinion is reflected in the ethics arena. The AAMFT has a code of ethics, as does the International Association for Marriage and Family Counseling (IAMFC), which is a division of the American Counseling Association. We recommend that you familiarize yourself with both of these specialized codes for family counselors. They provide guidance more specific to working with couples and families than does the ACA code, which is focused primarily on individual counseling. For example, the AAMFT code (1991) explicitly states that counselors must clearly advise their clients that decisions on marital status are the responsibility of the client (Section 1.4). The ACA code does not address the issue of whether counselors can ethically advocate for the preservation of a marriage or for divorce.

We believe that counselors who are trained generically as professional counselors can appropriately include family counseling in their practices. More specific training in marriage and family counseling is recommended. Additional training could include specific coursework, supervised experience, and some personal work on understanding one's own family of origin issues. The bottom line is that professional counselors must stay within the boundaries of their competence in providing services to couples and family clients.

GROUP COUNSELING

Most of the ethical and legal issues that were discussed in relation to family counseling apply to group counseling as well. This portion of the chapter addresses the issues of informed consent, client welfare and protection from harm, privacy and confidentiality, dual relationships, counselor values, and competence as they pertain to group work. Included in the discussion are some ethical and legal considerations that are unique to group counseling, such as freedom to exit a group and screening potential members.

Informed Consent

Potential members of a counseling group have the same rights to informed consent as do prospective clients who are seeking individual counseling. See Chapter 3 for a review of these rights. Because the group format differs in some significant ways from individual counseling, counselors need to address additional elements of informed consent for group participation, preferably in a pregroup interview. According to Corey (2000), these elements include the following:

- the purpose of the group, and its format, procedures, and ground rules
- the psychological risks involved in group participation
- what services can and cannot be provided within the group setting
- the division of responsibility between leader and participants
- the rights and responsibilities of group members
- freedom to leave the group if it does not turn out to be what a member wants or needs
- consultation with the group leader if a crisis should arise as a direct result of participation in the group, or a referral to other sources of help
- freedom from undue group pressure or coercion regarding participation, decision making, personal disclosures, and suggestions from other members

The purpose of counseling is an issue that needs to be addressed in individual as well as group counseling, but clients in a group setting have less freedom to determine the topics or process of counseling. Typically, group leaders have already established a general theme or purpose for the group such as adjustment to divorce, assertiveness training, or succeeding in college. Therefore, the aim in discussing the group's purpose is to help prospective members determine whether their goals in seeking counseling have a reasonable chance of being met within a group context, and if so, whether the particular group is compatible with their goals and needs.

There are psychological risks involved in individual counseling as well as in group participation, but in group counseling the risks are increased because the group leader has less situational control over events. Therefore, informed consent needs to include a full discussion of this topic. Group pressure or coercion is one such risk that has received considerable attention from specialists in group work. Risks will be discussed further in the next section on client welfare.

Although group workers consider it an ethical imperative to give members the freedom to exit a group at any time during the life of the group, they have debated the delicate matter of how such an event should be handled. When a member drops out of a group, it can cause disruptions in the process for the remaining members. If they are concerned that they have said or done something to cause the departure, the trust and cohesion of the group will be affected. For this reason, many group leaders believe that members who are considering leaving the group should be encouraged to raise the matter in a group session rather than simply notify the leader of their decision to withdraw. Corey (2000) believes that group members have a responsibility to the leaders and other members to explain why they want to leave. The member who wants to exit the group may feel pressured or coerced to remain, however, rather than have to submit to such a process. The ethical question in these situations is whether the comfort and wishes of the individual member or of the group as a whole should take precedence.

Both counselor and client need to fulfill certain responsibilities in order for counseling to be successful. In a group setting, regular attendance and being on time for sessions are particularly important client responsibilities, because other members and the group as a unit are negatively affected when an individual does not meet these obligations. In individual counseling, clients can choose to share information they have discussed in sessions, but in group counseling they have a responsibility to maintain the confidences of other members. Taking interpersonal risks and giving feedback to others are further responsibilities that pertain to group counseling participants.

Screening

Leaders should secure informed consent of potential group members prior to implementing a counseling group. They should also screen potential members to determine whether any of them should be excluded. The ACA *Code of Ethics* requires that counselors screen prospective group participants and do their best to select members whose needs and goals are compatible with the goals of the group. Members must be selected whose well-being will not be jeopardized by participating and who will not impede the group process (Standard A.9.a.). The primary criteria for inclusion should be whether potential members are likely to contribute to the group and whether they are likely to be compatible with each other.

Unless the group has a very specific purpose, it is much easier to decide who to exclude than it is to decide who to include. Prospective participants who generally should be excluded are those who are likely to dominate or monopolize group time, are hostile or aggressive in their style of interacting with others, are in a state of severe crisis, are suicidal, are lacking in ego strength, are acutely psychotic, and are highly suspicious or paranoid (Corey, 2000). Individuals diagnosed with certain personality disorders such as narcissistic or antisocial are considered poor candidates for group counseling (Yalom, 1995).

Generally, highly motivated clients who have interpersonal problems will profit most from a group experience (Yalom, 1995). Of course, the purpose of the group will be an important factor in determining whether prospective members will be included or excluded.

Client Welfare and Protection from Harm

Participating in a counseling group, like any catalyst for personal change, can pose psychological risks. Group counselors have an ethical responsibility to take precautions to protect group members "from physical or psychological trauma" (ACA *Code of Ethics,* Standard A.9.b.). They need to have a solid understanding of the forces that operate in groups and how to mobilize those forces in a constructive manner (Corey, 2000). Four potential dangers to which group leaders need to be alert are scapegoating of members, members being subjected to undue pressure, the misuse of confrontation, and injury resulting from group exercises or activities that involve physical contact.

Sometimes an individual member of a group is singled out as a scapegoat and this person is made the object of the group's frustration or hostility. When this happens, it is the responsibility of the group leader to take firm steps to stop this behavior.

The Association for Specialists in Group Work (ASGW), in its *Ethical Guidelines for Group Counselors* (1989), states that it is essential for group counselors to differentiate between the "therapeutic pressure" that is part of any group and "undue pressure" that is not therapeutic. The guidelines remind group counselors that the purpose of a group is to help members find their own answers rather than to be pressured into doing what the group thinks is appropriate. Group counselors have an ethical responsibility to avoid coercing participants into changing in directions that are not chosen by the participants themselves, and to intervene when members use undue pressure or coercion.

Confrontation is a valuable and powerful tool in a group, but it can be misused by members who have not developed the skill of confronting constructively. When members are inappropriately confrontive, it is the group counselor's responsibility to intervene. It is critical that group counselors model appropriate confrontation.

Although the possibility of a group member being physically harmed by another group member is remote, it could happen with some populations and in particular settings. Counselors who conduct group counseling sessions are expected to ensure the safety of members. Group members who have the potential for harming others should either be excluded from group sessions or should be monitored carefully. Warning signs for potentially dangerous clients were outlined in Chapter 4.

Some group counseling approaches involve group members interacting with each other physically. The law of assault and battery requires that individuals not be touched or put in apprehension of being touched without their permission (Swenson, 1997). Counselors who use group exercises that involve touching should explain in their disclosure statements to clients that touching among members will take place. They should avoid touching that might be considered offensive or sexual, and they should not use any activity that might result in a physical injury.

Privacy and Confidentiality

As was noted earlier in the chapter, counselors can guarantee only their own behavior with respect to upholding confidentiality. Counselors must inform clients that they cannot guarantee confidentiality on the parts of group members. According to the ASGW *Ethical Guidelines* (1989), group counselors define confidentiality clearly, explain why it is important, and discuss the difficulties involved in enforcement. The *Guidelines* offer several specific suggestions to assist group counselors in dealing with confidentiality in groups:

- Define the limits of confidentiality and when working with minors, specify the particular limits that apply.
- Stress the importance of maintaining confidentiality before the group begins and at various times during the group.
- Set a norm of confidentiality.
- Provide members with examples of how confidentiality might be breached inadvertently.
- Inform members about the potential consequences of intentionally breaching confidentiality.
- Make participants in a mandatory group aware of any reporting procedures that are required.

Privileged Communication

Privileged communication may exist for relationships between counselors and clients in your jurisdiction, but this privilege generally is considered to be waived when you are counseling more than one person. A few privileged communications statutes grant privilege to individual group counseling members and their counselor (Arthur & Swanson, 1993: Huber & Baruth, 1987; Kearney, 1984). Read and understand provisions of the privileged communication statute in your state to determine whether group counseling situations are covered.

Confidentiality with Minors

The ethical and legal complexities of conducting groups with minors are illustrated in the following vignette:

A high school counselor is conducting a group for sophomore girls. The purpose of the group is to foster self-esteem and to help in making wise choices. During the fifth session, the topic is boyfriends and whether to "just say no" to sex. Megan, a 15-year-old, shares that she and her boyfriend are sexually active and that she thinks its okay because they are really in love. She mentions that her boyfriend is 18 years old. She adds that her parents "would kill him" if they found out and would throw her out of the house.

This scenario raises a number of ethical and legal questions. Must Megan's parents be notified? Or can the counselor keep Megan's disclosure in confidence? If the counselor does so, what are the risks? Does the fact that Megan's boyfriend is a legal adult make a difference in terms of the counselor's obligations? If the counselor breaches confidentiality, what are the risks to her relationship with Megan and with the group? What will be the likely effects on the group process and on the counselor's reputation for trustworthiness among the student population in general?

If the counselor in the vignette does not inform Megan's parents of her sexual activity, the counselor risks being held accountable by the minor's parents in the event Megan is harmed as a result of the relationship (gets pregnant, contracts a venereal disease, becomes HIV positive, etc.). On the other hand, if the counselor does inform Megan's parents, then other students most likely will be reluctant to be truthful in future counseling relationships. There is no answer as to how this situation should be handled. The counselor will assess the situation, given all that is known about Megan and her family and what is known about the sexual activity Megan is involved in. Consultation with other counselors before making a decision would be the best course of action for the counselor.

The case points up the importance, when working with minors, of discussing confidentiality and its limits before the group begins and throughout the life of the group. If counselors reiterate confidentiality limits whenever sensitive topics are broached during group sessions, they will have a better chance of avoiding dilemmas like the one described in the scenario.

Dual Relationships

Although dual relationships between counselors and their clients, including members of counseling groups, are generally to be avoided, relationships between group members and leaders will vary somewhat depending on context. When task groups are held within a work environment, for instance, casual contact between leaders and group members may be inevitable. In therapeutic groups, however, outside-of-group contact between leaders and individual members can be inappropriate and counterproductive for the group as a whole (Gladding, 1995).

If the group counselor has a personal or social relationship with one of the members, this can lead to charges of favoritism. The counselor might avoid confronting this member or might be reluctant to explore in group some interpersonal issues that are problematic in the social relationship with the member. Group counselors should not use group clients to meet their personal needs for social relationships or friendships. The role of group counselors is to help members meet their goals, not to help counselors meet their own needs.

Just as group counselors should not develop friendships with group members, they should not admit friends or close acquaintances to groups they are conducting. In the same way that preexisting personal relationships are problematic in a group context, prior professional relationships can cause difficulties. Some counselors make it a routine practice to form their groups largely from their former clients in individual counseling (Herlihy & Corey, 1997). This is not unethical, although there are potential problems. Members of a group who have been counseled individually and who are accustomed to having the counselor's full attention for the entire session may find it difficult to share their counselor with other group members. Additionally, members who are not former individual clients of the counselor may feel disadvantaged because they have not had the same opportunity to form a bond with their group counselor.

There are limits to counselor self-disclosure in group counseling as well as in individual counseling. As a group leader, you will need to monitor your self-disclosures so that you are aware of what you are saying and your rationale for sharing any personal information. Although it is not your role to use group time to work on your own issues, you can self-disclose appropriately in several ways. You can let members know that you are personally affected by what they are sharing, you can express your persistent reactions to members and offer feedback, and you can model appropriate and timely self-disclosure by expressing how you are affected in the moment by what is going on in the group (Herlihy & Corey, 1997).

Socializing Among Members

Group work specialists have taken varying positions on the question of whether socializing among group members facilitates or hinders the group process. As is true of leader-member contact outside of group sessions, much depends on the context in which the group occurs. In 12-step groups, socializing between members outside the meetings is common and one member might serve as another member's sponsor. In hospitals, schools, and other institutional settings, it is inevitable that members will encounter each other between sessions. Many group leaders avoid making strict rules about socializing and personal relationships among members because these rules are impossible to enforce (Jacobs, Harvill, & Masson, 1994).

Although the group counselor cannot control members' lives outside the group, there are some good reasons for discouraging the members from forming friendships or social relationships with each other during the group's duration. If cliques or subgroupings form, this is detrimental to the group process. If some group members meet outside the group context and discuss matters that are best dealt with in group sessions, hidden agendas will develop and impede group progress. Members who meet outside the group in this way have a responsibility to bring information about their meetings into the group, but they may avoid doing so. Yalom (1995) has made the point that counseling groups teach people how to form intimate relationships but do not provide these relationships. Thus, group leaders have a responsibility to discuss with members the reasons why it is inadvisable for them to socialize between group sessions. If members recognize the pitfalls and understand the rationale for avoiding outside-of-group socializing, they are more likely to honor the counselor's request to refrain from this activity.

Counselor Values

It is not at all unusual for value-laden issues—such as divorce, sexuality, religion, family of origin issues, and honesty versus deceit in relationships—to be brought into a group. Corey (2000) has noted that a group can be an ideal place for members to assess the degree to which their interpersonal behavior is consistent with their values, through receiving feedback from others. The group counselor's role in this process is to make the group a safe place where members can feel free to explore values issues that are troubling to them.

The ASGW Best Practices Guidelines (1998) remind group counselors of the importance of sensitivity to cultural differences. It is crucial that you, as a group leader, are aware of how your own cultural background, attitudes, values, and beliefs influence the way you work with a group. You will need to be alert to issues of oppression, sexism, and racism as you work with diverse group members. You should not impose your values on group members or operate as though all members share your world view or cultural assumptions. Rather, you will want to understand and respect the roles of family and community, religion and spirituality, and ethnicity and culture in the lives of group members.

Certain values are inherent in the group process, such as self-disclosure, risk-taking behaviors, communicating openly and directly, and increasing awareness and autonomy. Group counselors must be cognizant that some of these values may run counter to the values of group members. For example, striving for personal autonomy may be an alien concept for group members who come from certain cultures (Herlihy & Corey, 1996).

Counselor Competence

Because many, if not most, counselors will conduct group work as part of their professional practices, training standards are written to ensure that counselors have adequate knowledge and experience in leading groups. CACREP (1994) requires that graduate programs in counseling include training in group work that incorporates the study of group dynamics, group leadership, theories of group counseling, methods of group counseling, types of group work, and ethical considerations. The CACREP standards also require the development of group work skills under supervision as part of the requirements for practicum and internship training.

ASGW has published *Professional Standards for the Training of Group Workers* (1992) that describes two levels of competencies for group counseling. The first level specifies core knowledge and skill competencies that provide a foundation for specialized training. Areas of knowledge include awareness of personal strengths, weaknesses, and values; characteristics associated with typical stages of group development; facilitative and debilitative member roles and behaviors; therapeutic factors of a group; group and member evaluation; and ethical issues special to group work. Skill competencies include opening and closing group sessions, modeling appropriate behavior, self-disclosing appropriately, giving and receiving feedback, helping members attribute meaning to the group experience, helping members integrate and apply learnings, and demonstrating the ability to apply ethical standards in group practice.

According to ASGW (1992), after counselors-in-training have mastered the core knowledge and skills, they can develop a group work specialization in one or more of the following areas: (1) task facilitation groups, (2) psychoeducation groups, (3) counseling groups, and (4) psychotherapy groups. Developing competence in both the basic and the specialized levels of practice requires participation in planning and supervising small groups, and clinical experience in leading groups under careful supervision.

Different groups require different leader competencies. For example, a counselor may be qualified to facilitate adolescent groups but be ill-prepared to conduct reminiscence groups for elderly residents of a nursing home. You will need to continually evaluate the match between the types of groups you are considering conducting and your level of training and experience. As you prepare to include group work in your professional practice, you will find that you need specific training and supervised experience for each type of group you intend to lead (Corey, 2000).

It is equally important that you continue to update and expand your skills and knowledge. Lakin (1994) has expressed concern that many counselors fail to monitor their own competence in the wide range of group modalities and varied clientele to be served. Both continuing education and peer supervision can be useful in this regard. Gladding (1995) has suggested that peer supervision groups can be particularly helpful for increasing one's knowledge as well as one's awareness of even minor misconduct or misjudgments in group leadership.

SUMMARY AND KEY POINTS

When counselors work with multiple clients, as they do in family and group counseling, ethical and legal issues can be more complicated to resolve. Family counselors often work from a systems perspective that is quite different from the theoretical underpinnings of individual counseling. They view the entire family system, rather than its individual members, as their client.

Key points with respect to family counseling include the following:

- The issue of informed consent in family counseling presents some unique challenges, such as determining who in the family gives consent and how to deal with situations in which one family member is reluctant to participate or refuses to participate in the process.
- When one adult, legally competent individual in the family refuses to give consent for the family to participate, counseling cannot take place with all family members.
- Although reluctant family members cannot be forced or coerced into participating in family counseling, some family counselors encourage these resistant members to attend one or two sessions.
- Children cannot give legal informed consent; nonetheless, they should be included in the process.
- Counselors must be aware of legal questions created by the changing nature of families, particularly with respect to the rights of biological parents versus other family members who may wish to be involved in family counseling.

- Family counseling involves some powerful techniques. One such technique about which ethical concerns have been expressed is paradoxical directives. Such techniques must be used with caution so that no harm is caused.
- Whether family counseling should be avoided when there is ongoing abuse in the family should be carefully considered.
- Counselors must make it clear to family clients that there are special limits to confidentiality; counselors can guarantee confidentiality only on their own parts.
- Privileged communication generally is waived if a third party is present in the counseling situation.
- Some more recently enacted privileged communication statutes extend privilege to family clients and group member clients. Counselors should consult with an attorney regarding how to interpret these statutes.
- Family counselors take differing positions on how to handle the issue of family secrets.
- Divorce and child custody issues can be particularly problematic for counselors and counselors should take care to avoid involving themselves inappropriately in custody disputes.
- Counselor values have a strong impact on how counselors conduct family counseling. Counselors must be vigilant so that they do not inadvertently impose their own values and assumptions, particularly regarding culture and gender roles.
- Developing competence in family counseling requires specialized coursework, supervised experience, and experience in the counselor's own family of origin work.

Group counseling is another modality that involves multiple clients. Ethical and legal issues have different implications in the group context than they do in individual counseling. Key points regarding group counseling include the following:

- Informed consent to participate in group counseling involves a number of issues in addition to the standard elements of informed consent for individual counseling.
- Group leaders must balance the rights of the individual against the needs of the group when a member wants to exit the group prematurely.
- It is good practice to screen potential members of a group to exclude those who are unlikely to benefit from the experience, and to select those who are most likely to contribute to the group and be compatible with each other.
- Group counselors have a responsibility to protect group members from harm and to be alert to the dangers inherent in scapegoating, undue pressure, inappropriate confrontation, and injury resulting from activities that involve physical contact.
- As is true in family counseling, confidentiality is difficult to enforce in group settings, and counselors should make a special effort to ensure that group members understand the importance of confidentiality and how to avoid inadvertent breaches.
- Privileged communication may not exist in group counseling situations unless the state statute specifically extends privileged communication to group counselors and their clients individually.
- There are additional limitations to confidentiality when groups are composed of clients who are minors.

- Group counselors should make every effort to avoid dual relationships with members of their counseling groups.
- Generally, members should be discouraged from socializing with one another between group sessions.
- Counselors need to be aware of the impact of their personal values, and of the effect of the values that are inherent in the group process, as they conduct groups.
- Specific guidelines for developing competence in group counseling have been published by CACREP and by ASGW.
- Counselors need to take steps to maintain their competence in group work. These steps include continuing education and peer supervision.

Evaluation, Testing, and Diagnosis

Evaluating, assessing, testing, and diagnosing individuals are activities that are a critical part of the counseling process, but they are not counseling as it is usually conceptualized. Before beginning the counseling process with a client, the counselor must assess the circumstances of the individual and determine the goals of the relationship. Assessment is a collaborative process to which both the counselor and the client contribute with the aim of gaining a better understanding of the client's problems. An accurate assessment of the problems, in turn, increases the likelihood that the problems will be resolved successfully in counseling.

Counselors usually complete this preliminary step in the counseling process during the initial interview with a client. Sometimes, a more extensive assessment is needed, and counselors decide that formal evaluations are required. The ethical and legal pitfalls in the areas of evaluation, assessment, and diagnosis are numerous (Welfel, 1998), and an entire section (Section E) of the ACA *Code of Ethics* is devoted to this topic. We begin this chapter with a discussion of ethical requirements and related legal issues in evaluation and assessment generally. Then we focus on two types of assessment—testing and diagnosis. Multicultural issues in evaluation, assessment, testing, and diagnosis are examined along with other issues.

EVALUATION AND ASSESSMENT

Objectivity in Evaluation

Evaluations can be simple or complex, and might be completed by counselors or by other mental health professionals. When the counselor who is also going to treat the client completes an assessment, the sole purpose should be to provide information to allow the counselor and client to understand the problems and establish appropriate counseling goals. Dual roles should be avoided. For example, a counselor who is a parent's individual counselor should never evaluate that parent in a child custody situation. Child custody evaluations require that unbiased and objective recommendations be made to a judge (Gould, J.W., 1998). An evaluator must be objective and dispassionate. Counselors always have the best interests of their clients in mind and, therefore, could not be objective evaluators if the findings might negatively affect their clients.

Client Welfare and Informed Consent

When an assessment or evaluation is completed, the assessment itself is the end product. A counselor or any number of other individuals might then use the assessment report for purposes other than counseling. Clients who are being assessed need to understand that the process is different from counseling, what the process entails, what the final product will be, and how the assessment is intended to be used. They also need to understand that it could be used by others. According to the ACA *Code of Ethics,* counselors promote client welfare when they respect the client's right to know the results of assessment techniques, the interpretations made, and the basis for conclusions drawn and recommendations made by counselors (Standard E.1.b.).

Counselors have a responsibility to secure their clients' informed consent to evaluation procedures. Before they conduct an assessment, they need to explain its nature and purposes in language that the client can understand. This obligation applies whether the counselor, an assistant, a computer, or an outside service conducts the assessment (Standard E.3.a.). The client disclosure form found in Chapter 3 contains a paragraph that explains that an assessment is the initial step in a counseling relationship and gives information about the assessment process. The disclosure statement also sets forth information about the process that takes place when an assessment is being conducted by a mental health professional other than a client's counselor.

Competence in Evaluation

Counselors have the education necessary to conduct certain types of evaluations. Some counselors have jobs in which they conduct evaluations on a regular basis, and some have private practices in which they conduct evaluations occasionally or exclusively. In order to conduct an evaluation, a counselor should have expertise in the area that is being evaluated and must be prepared to serve as an expert witness in court.

Counselors commonly conduct evaluations to determine the following:

- what type of custody arrangement would be in the best interests of a child
- the extent of an individual's disability and the potential for future employment
- whether an individual has a substance abuse problem and, if so, the type of treatment that is needed
- whether a person is at risk for abusing children in the future
- whether a person is at risk for harming others
- whether a person is at risk for suicide
- whether a person has a mental disorder that needs treatment
- whether a person would perform well in a particular job

The Counselor as Expert Witness

Counselors should avoid conducting evaluations that cast them in the role of expert witness unless they have agreed to do so. If your job requires that you conduct evaluations or if you complete evaluations in your private practice, you must be prepared to testify in court as an expert witness. There is a good chance that eventually you will be subpoenaed and ordered to explain and defend your conclusions and recommendations.

An expert's testimony in court usually supports one side in a legal controversy and damages the other side. As a result, the attorney for the side that is damaged has a professional obligation to minimize the impact of the expert's testimony. The attorney will do this in one or more of the following ways: (a) object to the expert's credentials, arguing that the counselor is not expert enough to give an opinion in court; (b) attack the process the counselor used in completing the evaluation, claiming it was not adequate; (c) attempt to get the counselor to contradict statements, hoping that the judge or jury will give less credibility to a witness who is not consistent; and (d) offer another expert witness's testimony that contradicts the counselor's conclusions and recommendations, hoping the judge or jury will give more credibility to the other expert's testimony.

Counselors who agree to provide expert testimony in the belief that judges, attorneys, and juries will listen respectfully to the counselor's opinions and be appreciative of their input are in for a big surprise. Hagan (1997) has argued that all mental health expert testimony is a fraud. She has taken the point of view that mental health, as a science, is too inexact to allow its opinions as evidence. Ziskin (1995) has produced a three-volume set of books designed to assist lawyers in discrediting the testimony of mental health expert witnesses.

Counselors who plan to serve as expert witnesses should take courses to prepare themselves, observe other experts testifying over a period of time, and read written materials (e.g., Becker, 1997; Gould, J.W., 1998; Strasburger, 1998).

TESTING

Although formal tests are only one type of assessment that counselors use, they are particularly vulnerable to abuse (Welfel, 1998). There are a multitude of tests available. Perhaps at least partly for these reasons, the ACA *Code of Ethics* addresses testing in a number of ethical standards. Counselors use tests in various ways. Occasionally they may be involved in developing new tests, but more often they select existing tests, administer them, and interpret them for their clients.

Developing and Publishing Tests

When counselors develop and publish testing instruments, they have an ethical obligation to use established scientific procedures, relevant standards, and current professional knowledge for test design (Standard E.12.). To learn more about test development, consult the standards for testing (American Educational Research Association, 1999) that have been developed jointly by the American Educational Research Association (AERA), the American Psychological Association (APA), and the National Council on Measurement in Education (NCME).

Designing, developing, validating, and marketing a new test requires specific knowledge and skills and is a complex and lengthy process. These factors undoubtedly deter many counseling practitioners from undertaking the task. Even if you are never involved in constructing a test, however, you should understand the ethical responsibilities of test producers. In essence, these responsibilities are to use the best scientific methods in devising their instruments and to have client welfare as their first priority (Welfel, 1998). They must produce and market tests that have demonstrated validity and reliability; appropriate norms; and a manual that clearly explains how to use the test, the clientele for whom it is and is not suitable, and its strengths and limitations. They need to provide information that will help users interpret the results accurately.

There are some ethical considerations in marketing tests. Test publishers should make their tests available only to professionals who are qualified to use them. Typically, test publishers require those who wish to purchase their tests to state their degrees, licenses, graduate courses in testing, and training in the use of the specific test. If you ask to use tests as part of your graduate thesis or a research project, you probably will be required to supply the qualifications of your supervisor.

Test Security

Counselors have both ethical and legal obligations to protect the security of tests from improper usage, copying, or dissemination. Almost all tests depend on the user being unfamiliar with the test items. Therefore, counselors must keep testing materials safely locked away when not in use to prevent unauthorized users from gaining access to them.

Counselors also have a responsibility to appropriately supervise the test-taking process, unless the test is specifically designed to be self-administered. Do you see any problems with the counselor's behavior in the following scenario?

> Kathleen has sought counseling from Aaron, a licensed professional counselor. Her job situation is tentative because the company where she has worked for the past 12 years is downsizing. She is experiencing a number of somatic complaints related to anxiety along with a general feeling of apprehension. By the end of their second session together, Aaron believes that Kathleen may be experiencing depression as well as anxiety. Because her company's managed health care plan allows them only six sessions, he doesn't want to use precious time for assessment activities. He gives Kathleen a standardized depression scale and tells her to complete it at home.

If Aaron's decision seems reasonable to you, you are not alone in your thinking. Gibson and Pope (1993) found that 26% of counselors did not deem the practice of sending a test home with a client to be ethically problematic. There are any number of things that could happen that would produce invalid results in such a situation, however. In Kathleen's case, she might misread or misunderstand the directions, exceed the time limits for completing the test, try to complete the test while watching TV or being otherwise distracted, or become alarmed if she becomes aware as she responds to the items that she is indeed depressed.

Copyright Laws

A second problem related to test security occurs when counselors and other professionals break the law by violating copyrights of tests held by test authors and publishers. The general principles of copyright law are reviewed in Chapter 14. Once a test has been created, the author (or a publisher if the author transfers the rights) owns the test for 75 years from the date of first publication or 100 years from its date of creation, whichever date expires first (Henn, 1991).

Tests that are published by commercial testing companies must be purchased. Materials include answer sheets, question booklets, report forms, manuals, and other items related to the test. Computer software of all types related to testing is copyrighted and may not be duplicated or used without permission of the publisher. Some commercial testing companies are aggressive in protecting their copyrights because their business profits are negatively affected by violations.

Some tests have never been published by the author or may have been published in a journal. Such tests are not available from a commercial testing company. However, permission must be obtained from the copyright holder before counselors can use the tests either to administer to clients or for research.

Competence to Test

Counselors generally do not use testing as much as psychologists do in their practices. The preparation master's level counselors receive in testing usually includes the following: (a) a three-credit assessment course, (b) some testing principles in a research class, (c) testing information in courses such as career counseling and diagnosis of mental disorders, and (d) supervised practice of the use of tests in practicum and internship. Because of the limited use counselors generally make of tests and the educational level of counselors in the area of testing, it is important both ethically and legally for counselors to administer and interpret only tests for which they have been adequately trained.

At first glance, testing procedures might seem to be fairly simple and straightforward. Test manuals give detailed step-by-step instructions for administration and many tests can be scored and interpreted by a testing service. In reality, considerable knowledge and professional judgment are needed to select the right test for the intended purpose and clientele, to administer the test properly, and to interpret the findings to the client. Anastasi (1988) has stated that professional judgment is required to select tests that are *relevant* to the needs of the particular client. In order to select wisely, counselors must have a solid knowledge of the various tests that are available, what they measure, and their limitations. Anastasi also has reminded counselors of their ethical responsibility to use *multiple criteria* for decision making. This means that counselors should never use a test as the sole criterion for making clinical or educational decisions. Returning to the case of Kathleen to illustrate this point, let us begin by assuming that Aaron reconsidered his plan and had Kathleen complete the depression scale in his presence. Even though the results are now more likely to be valid, Aaron should not use only her score on the scale to determine whether a diagnosis of depression is warranted. He will also need to consider his clinical impressions and Kathleen's behavioral indicators, consult the diagnostic criteria for depression in the *Diagnostic and Statistical Manual, Fourth Edition* (1994) (DSM-IV), and perhaps (with Kathleen's permission) interview her spouse.

There is no absolute standard for adequate preparation to use particular tests. In addition, formal educational experiences such as for-credit courses and internships are not the only methods of training. Counselors could become proficient in testing through workshops, supervised practice, and independent study as well. The amount of training needed to develop proficiency varies greatly depending on the test. Developing competence to use complex personality tests such as the Minnesota Multiphasic Personality Inventory-2 requires extensive training (Pope, Butcher, & Sheelen, 1993). There are many tests, however, that counselors can learn to use through the instruction and supervised practice provided in a typical master's degree program. Competence to use a test always depends on the individual counselor's training and experience with the particular test.

In some states, counselors are restricted to certain testing activities by the statutes and regulations that license counselors. For example, some states prohibit counselors from using projective tests, and at least one state statute requires licensed counselors to be further "privileged" to test (Louisiana Licensed Mental Counselor Licensing Act, 1999). Counselors should review their licensing statute and regulations to determine whether there are any tests they cannot legally administer and interpret. If licensed counselors exceed their statutory authority to test, they could be accused and found guilty of practicing psychology without a license. This happened to a Licensed Professional Counselor in Louisiana (*State of Louisiana v. Atterberry,* 1995).

Counselors should regulate themselves in the practice of testing; that is, counselors should test only in areas in which they are qualified by education, training, or experience. In states that limit the testing activities of counselors in the counselor licensing statute, counselor professional associations usually make efforts to change the restrictive language through the legislative process. In most states, testing is listed as an appropriate professional activity of counselors, and no restrictions are placed on that activity. That type of statutory language is the goal in states where testing activities of counselors are restricted in some way.

Debate continues within some professions, such as psychology and counseling, and in multiprofessional organizations regarding who should decide whether a particular professional is competent to administer and interpret certain tests. Anastasi (1988), the leading scholarly authority on testing, has taken the position that testing is appropriately used by many professionals who should be properly prepared to test. Some argue that only mental health professionals with the highest level of training (i.e., doctoral level psychologists) should be allowed to test. Most professionals agree, however, that many different professionals test and that professionals themselves should decide whether they are competent to use a particular test in their practices.

Release of Testing Records

Records of test results are the same as other counseling records. In Chapter 5 it was explained that counselors must ensure that testing records stored in computers are kept secure. A discussion of circumstances under which testing records of clients can be released to third parties was also included. Counselors who receive test results for clients they have been counseling should never transfer those records to another person. In the event testing records received from another professional are requested or subpoenaed, counselors should refer the individual asking for the records to the professional who originally created them.

Counselors should not release test data to anyone who is not qualified to receive the information. The ACA ethical standards state that counselors should release test data "only to persons recognized by counselors as competent to interpret the data" (Standard E.4.b.). Counselors may be uncomfortable asking someone who requests test records to verify their qualifications, but releasing test data to unqualified individuals carries such a high risk to client welfare that counselors must stand firm on this point (Welfel, 1998).

Providing Explanations to Clients

Clients have the right to make an informed choice about whether they want to participate or refuse to engage in testing procedures. They can also expect to receive an explanation of the results of any test they take.

The code of ethics clearly indicates that informed consent applies to testing. Before counselors test, they must explain the nature and purposes of assessment and the specific use of the results in language the client can understand (Standard E.3.a.). It is particularly important that clients understand what uses will be made of their test results. They have a right to know in advance if tests will be used as a factor in employment decisions, as a criterion for placement in a special educational program, as a device for screening potential members of a psychotherapy group, or as a means of making other decisions that will affect their lives.

The ACA *Code of Ethics* includes one other client right that must be attended to before testing takes place. The code requires counselors to tell examinees what conditions produce the most favorable test results. For example, if being well rested has been shown to improve performance on a test, test takers need to be given that information.

After clients have participated in testing procedures, they have a right to receive feedback about the results. It is essential that counselors communicate this feedback directly to their clients. A number of commercial services exist that score and interpret psychological tests. Counselors appreciate these services because they save time and relieve them of the task of scoring the tests, but they should avoid overreliance on such services. Interpretations generated by commercial services cannot, by themselves, provide sufficient feedback to clients. They do not take into account the individual characteristics of the test taker and they may not generate enough alternative explanations of results (Matarazzo, 1986). Counselors need to exercise their professional judgment and personal knowledge of the client in using reports provided by test interpretation services.

A face-to-face conversation with the client regarding test results can serve additional purposes. Clients sometimes view test results—particularly elaborate, computer-generated score reports—as being infallible. Counselors need to educate clients about the limitations of tests and to keep these limitations prominent in their own thinking. This will help them avoid any tendency to present results in absolute language. Additionally, a dialogue with the client can shed light on any unclear or unexpected test results.

For some clients, taking a test is an anxiety-producing event, and they may worry until they see their results. Counselors should keep in mind that some clients have had negative experiences with test taking. Finally, feedback can have therapeutic value. Finn and Tonsager (1992) found that clients who received feedback on their Minnesota Multiphasic Personality Inventories (MMPI) found the feedback to be a positive experience and actually showed a reduction in symptoms.

In practice, counselors often struggle with the question of how much feedback or explanation of test results they should give their clients. They want to be thorough, without overwhelming the client with detail. For many counselors, the pressures of time-limited counseling relationships imposed by managed care are also a factor. Welfel (1998) has suggested that the criteria for deciding how much time to devote to test interpretation should include the following: (a) clients' satisfaction that they understand the meaning and implications of the results, (b) the counselor's assessment that feedback has clarified any confusion or unclear results, (c) a mutual agreement about ways the test results should influence the counseling process, and (d) implications of releasing the findings to others if the client has agreed to such a release.

Multicultural Issues in Testing

Counselors must be cautious in using tests with culturally diverse clients. They need to select tests carefully to avoid inappropriate testing that may be outside the socialized behavioral or cognitive patterns of cultural minorities (ACA *Code of Ethics,* Standard E.6.). Often, special populations are not represented in the norm group on which a test was standardized, and, therefore, the test results may be less valid for them. When you use tests, you need to be knowledgeable about the characteristics of the norm group and recognize the limitations of the test with other populations.

The ethical standards require counselors to recognize the effects of age, color, culture, disability, ethnic group, gender, race, religion, sexual orientation, and socioeconomic status on test administration and interpretation. Especially when working with culturally diverse clients, test results need to be placed in perspective with other relevant factors (Standard E.8.).

No test is completely culture-free. The use of educational and psychological tests, in the school setting in particular, has been challenged. There is evidence that these tests tend to discriminate against African-American and Hispanic children (Walsh & Betz, 1995). Academic placement or advancement decisions should never be made on the basis of test data alone.

In addition to knowing about the norm groups on which tests are standardized, counselors should examine tests for content bias. When some items in a test refer to experiences that are not familiar to certain populations, the test is content-biased. For example, an item on a test that refers to milking cows may make no sense to an urban child who lives in an impoverished socioeconomic environment. There is evidence that content bias of tests of cognitive abilities, in particular, is partly responsible for lower scores among cultural minorities (Lonner & Ibrahim, 1996). Disparities between the average scores of African-American and White children on tests of intellectual ability are at least partly attributable to African-American students' lack of exposure to White middle-class culture (Axelson, 1993).

Counselors need to be alert to the passage of laws that affect testing practices. Two examples are the Education for All Handicapped Children Act (1975) and the Americans with Disabilities Act (1990). The Education for All Handicapped Children Act requires that tests be in a child's language and be appropriate for the intended use. It also requires that parents give their consent to testing and that they be given access to test protocols after testing has been completed. The Americans with Disabilities Act mandates that testing be appropriate for the individual being tested, that reasonable accommodations be made in testing, and that results may not be used to discriminate in employment choices for people with disabilities.

In summary, counselors need to be alert to cultural bias in tests and in test interpretation, and must use caution in interpreting results with minority clients. A good resource for developing competence in assessment with culturally diverse clients is *The Handbook of Multicultural Assessment* (Suzuki, Meller, & Ponterotto, 1996).

DIAGNOSIS

Counselors are often uncomfortable with the idea of diagnosing mental disorders. Diagnoses usually are made using the APA's *Diagnostic and Statistical Manual of Mental Disorders, Fourth Edition* (DSM-IV) (1994), which is the world's most thorough and widely used system for identifying and describing mental disorders (Wylie, 1995). This system of diagnosis is based on the medical model and runs counter to the wellness philosophy that counselors espouse.

When clients want to use their health insurance to help pay for mental health care, counselors usually must assign a diagnosis in order for their services to be reimbursable. Counselors may have conflicting feelings about this situation. They want to serve their clients by helping them receive reimbursement for counseling services, yet their philosophical objections make them reluctant participants in diagnosis. Discomfort with diagnostic labeling can lead to problems. Some counselors may try to diagnose most or even all of their clients as having an adjustment disorder, which is the mildest and least stigmatizing type of disorder. Some might assign a more serious diagnosis than is clinically warranted so that a client can qualify for health insurance reimbursement. When counselors' diagnoses are dishonest and inaccurate, clients can be harmed by the diagnostic process, and the counselors are on shaky ground both ethically and legally.

If you use the DSM-IV system in your work as a counselor, it is vital that you use it appropriately. A first step is to clarify your own stance toward diagnosis. Diagnosis involves much more than assigning labels to clients. It is best conceptualized in context, as a part of the overall process of assessment that helps counselors understand their clients. Sleek (1996) has likened the diagnostic process to working a jigsaw puzzle, in that it involves putting together pieces of information about the client to build an overall picture of the person. The primary purpose of diagnosis is to facilitate effective treatment. The relationship between diagnosis and treatment is like a driving trip and a road map (Seligman, 1986; Welfel, 1998). The diagnosis is a map that helps travelers develop a plan for reaching their destination. Diagnosis should point the way to treatment planning and to the selection of effective treatment strategies for identified disorders.

Diagnosis serves other important functions. First, an accurate diagnosis can help counselors make a prognosis or predict the course of a disorder. Second, the original diagnostic system in mental health care was developed to facilitate communication among professionals (Kutchins & Kirk, 1987). The current DSM system continues to provide a common language and shared frame of reference for mental health professionals. Third, it helps counselors identify conditions that may require the attention of a physician, such as organic disorders or medical conditions that are contributing to psychological problems, so that a referral can be made. Finally, the diagnostic system provides a framework for research. Clinical outcome studies build our knowledge base regarding the effectiveness of various treatment approaches.

While keeping in mind all the useful functions of diagnosis, you should be aware of the risks involved, even when it is done honestly and accurately. For clients, learning their diagnosis can be a double-edged sword. It can be comforting for clients to learn that their condition has a name, that they are not alone in what they are experiencing, and that they are not "going crazy." On the other hand, clients may feel embarrassed or ashamed of their diagnosis, or feel stigmatized by a diagnostic label and refuse treatment rather than have the diagnosis become part of their record. There is also a possibility that a diagnosis can lead to a self-fulfilling prophecy; for instance, a client who is diagnosed with depression may become even more deeply depressed. Counselors need to be sensitive to the powerful effect that diagnosis can have on clients.

Diagnosis can affect not only clients' feelings and self-concepts, it can affect their lives in significant ways. Severe diagnoses can have harmful effects far into a client's future, including having difficulty obtaining certain kinds of employment, having difficulty obtaining health insurance, or having their diagnosis used negatively in child custody proceedings. Under managed care, some diagnoses can "shadow a client's life like hounds from hell" (Wylie, 1995, p. 32).

The process of diagnosing a client's condition can have effects on the counselor as well as the client. Studies have shown that the very availability of diagnostic labels can bias counselors in favor of using them, even when a client's condition does not warrant a DSM-IV diagnosis (Langer & Abelson, 1974; Rosenhan, 1973). Particularly when a client's eligibility for health insurance coverage depends on a diagnosis, counselors may be tempted to "pathologize" behaviors that are developmentally normal. A rebellious adolescent might be diagnosed as having "oppositional defiant disorder" or "conduct disorder." A very shy young adult might be diagnosed as having an avoidant personality disorder. As Welfel (1998) has stated, "Counselors who jump ahead to naming a problem before they have verified that one exists are showing a bias inconsistent with the profession's ethics" (p. 218).

Counselors who use diagnosis must take care to avoid losing sight of the uniqueness of each client. Even while using a system that is focused on mental disorders and pathology, they must maintain the wellness perspective that is unique to their profession. This can be a challenging task.

Some ethical issues that arise for counselors when they use diagnosis are securing the client's fully informed consent, working with physicians, and having the qualifications to diagnose. Multicultural considerations are also important in diagnosis. Following is a discussion of these issues as well as legal issues related to accurate diagnosis.

Informed Consent

Some clients do not understand the stigma that might be associated with being diagnosed with an emotional or mental disorder. Others may be very concerned about the implications of diagnosis for their future employment or for health care insurability. While it would be inappropriate to overemphasize the possibility that a client may be discriminated against in the future as a result of receiving a diagnosis, counselors do have a responsibility to raise the issue with clients.

As part of the informed consent process, counselors must "take steps to ensure that clients understand the implications of diagnosis" (ACA *Code of Ethics,* Standard A.3.a.). When clients are participants in managed care plans, there is an increase in the information that needs to be discussed (Applebaum, 1993; Glosoff, 1999; Haas & Cummings, 1991). Clients must understand the impact that their insurance policy may have on the types and length of treatment that will be reimbursed. They need to be aware that third-party payment might end before they believe they have met their counseling goals. They also need to know what and how much information will be released to managed care companies.

So that clients cannot later claim that they did not even realize they might receive a diagnosis of an emotional or mental disorder, counselors should include a phrase regarding diagnosis in their client disclosure statement (see sample disclosure statement in Chapter 3). We also recommend that, whenever possible, counselors should disclose to clients (or their parents or guardians) their diagnosis when the diagnosis is recorded. If an initial diagnosis is changed after the counseling process has begun as a result of a counselor's reassessment of the client's condition, of course this change should also be discussed with the client.

Working with Physicians

Since mental health is one dimension of health care, counselors have a responsibility to understand that some client behaviors or reported thoughts and feelings could have a physical basis. Counselors are wise to determine the physical condition of their clients when they begin the counseling process. Intake forms or interview protocols need to ask clients whether they have any negative health conditions, and if so, the details regarding their treatment. Counselors also need to know if their clients are taking any medications and, if so, the purpose of the medications and the effects and side-effects the medications produce. When clients have not had a physical exam in a long time, or if a possibility exists that a problem may be physical in nature, counselors should recommend that clients have a physical exam and ask the clients to report the results to them.

When clients have physical complaints that obviously might be related to medical problems (such as headaches, dizziness, or chest pains), counselors must insist that these clients have physical examinations as a condition to their continued mental health treatment. Mental health professionals who overlook or ignore the obvious need for a referral to a physician could be held negligent if a client's supposed mental condition later turned out to be caused by a physical problem.

The symptoms of some mental disorders can be alleviated by psychotropic medications. For example, lithium has been demonstrated to be effective in reducing symptoms of bipolar disorder (formerly called manic depression) in many sufferers. When counselors diagnose conditions that can be helped by taking medication, they must make clients aware of this option. Counselors can then refer clients who are willing to consider taking medication to a psychiatrist. With the client's permission, the counselor and psychiatrist can work cooperatively in assisting the client.

Qualifications to Diagnose

An issue that has been controversial is whether counselors are qualified to diagnose mental disorders. Of course, counselors should not assign a diagnosis of an emotional or mental disorder unless they have had adequate training to do so, but there is no absolute standard for determining adequate training. In terms of academic preparation, most contemporary programs that prepare counselors for mental health or community agency practices require counselors to complete a course in diagnosis of emotional and mental disorders. Counselors should also have had supervised experiences in diagnosing as part of their practicum or internship in their master's degree programs, and should continue to gain supervised experience in diagnosis while they are working toward their licenses. Diagnostic criteria are updated periodically and new research about effective treatments is appearing constantly, so counselors must continue to learn in order to stay current.

In some states, licensed counselors have been challenged and accused of practicing outside their scope of authority when they have diagnosed emotional and mental disorders. This is an example of a "turf issue" that can pit counselors against other mental health professionals who have traditionally endorsed the medical model, such as psychiatrists, psychologists, and social workers. The issue is very important because if mental health professionals are unable to render diagnoses of emotional and mental disorders, health care providers and health insurance companies may refuse to employ them or may not reimburse their clients for mental health services they provide

Counselors have responded to this problem by introducing legislation that amends the scope of practice in their state licensure statutes. The amendments specifically indicate that licensed counselors may diagnose and treat emotional and mental disorders. In states that do not have such specific language in their counselor licensure statutes, counselors still diagnose emotional and mental disorders. However, they must argue that doing so is part of the counseling process in general that is covered in other language in their counselor licensure statutes.

Multicultural Considerations

Counselors must keep in mind whenever they are dealing with diagnosis that "mental disorders" are defined in a cultural context. Behaviors that may seem bizarre in one culture may be considered perfectly normal in another. The work group that created the DSM-IV attempted to incorporate into the manual an awareness of the culturally diverse populations in the United States and the world. Descriptions of each disorder include a discussion of associated culture, age, and gender features, which is a step in the direction of multicultural sensitivity. The DSM-IV only *describes* mental disorders, however. It does not ask, for instance, why twice as many women as men are diagnosed with Major Depressive Disorder. It could be because women are more prone to depression than men, because it is generally more acceptable in our society for women to express sadness and to ask for help for symptoms of depression, or because women are more likely as an oppressed group to experience feelings of hopelessness and depression. Several studies have demonstrated gender bias against women among mental health professionals. These studies have been an outgrowth of a well-known study by Broverman and colleagues (Broverman, Broverman, Clarkson, Rosencrantz, & Vogel, 1970). These researchers found that mental health professionals used nearly identical adjectives to describe a "healthy male" and a "healthy adult" but a different set of adjectives to describe a "healthy female."

A number of studies have also demonstrated that members of minority groups tend to receive more severe diagnoses than members of the majority culture for the same symptoms. Counselors must be alert to the fact that Americans who are members of various minority groups will assign different cultural meanings to such traits as assertiveness, emotional expressiveness, and obedience. The DSM-IV cautions mental health professionals that, if they are unfamiliar with the nuances of a client's cultural frame of reference, they may incorrectly judge as psychopathological the normal manifestations of behavior, beliefs, and experiences particular to that client's culture. This ethical responsibility is addressed in the ACA *Code of Ethics* in the statement that "counselors recognize that culture affects the manner in which clients' problems are defined. Clients' socioeconomic and cultural experience is considered when diagnosing mental disorders" (Standard E.5.b.).

Legal Issues

Earlier in this section, we made the point that when counselors decide to render a diagnosis, the diagnosis must be accurate and honest despite any philosophical uneasiness or cognitive dissonance they may be experiencing. We noted that some mental health professionals record what they consider to be less serious disorders than what they believe the client has in an effort to avoid stigma for the client. At the other end of the spectrum, they sometimes assign diagnoses that are more serious than warranted so that their clients will receive third-party reimbursement for counseling services. These practices are not uncommon. Inappropriate use of a diagnostic category to obtain insurance reimbursement is the type of financial misconduct that is most frequently brought before ethics committees, licensing boards, and courts (Peterson, 1996).

In Chapter 11, we identify such practices as insurance fraud, which can expose counselors to both civil and criminal liability. A client could bring a civil malpractice suit against the counselor, and a prosecutor could bring criminal charges against the counselor based on the fraud. A client who was assigned a false diagnosis would have an excellent foundation for a successful malpractice suit against the counselor if the client later lost a job, was denied a license, or was denied a security clearance because of the false diagnosis. If it could be shown that a mental health professional knew or should have known that a client had a serious disorder but recorded a less serious disorder, and that the client received inadequate treatment that led to harm, or was denied health insurance reimbursement because of the false diagnosis, the mental health professional could be found to have committed malpractice. Obviously, you want to avoid ever having to face such a situation. It is crucial that you do not get caught up in the practice of assigning a diagnosis to fit insurance companies' criteria for reimbursement.

SUMMARY AND KEY POINTS

This chapter discussed activities that are not counseling per se, but are an essential first step in the process of helping clients resolve their problems. Assessment is a collaborative process between counselor and client during which they work to gain a better understanding of the client's problems. An accurate assessment then guides the treatment planning.

Testing and diagnosis are two specific types of assessment that are particularly vulnerable to ethical and legal problems. Multicultural considerations are vital in both testing and diagnosis. Key points made in the chapter regarding evaluation and assessment include the following:

- Evaluations must be objective and for this reason counselors should avoid taking on dual roles such as counselor and child custody evaluator.
- Clients have a right to understand what an assessment process will involve, what its purposes are, and the uses to which it will be put.
- Counselors are competent to conduct many types of evaluation.
- When counselors conduct evaluations, they must be prepared to serve as expert witnesses in court.

Counselors may be involved in developing, selecting, administering, and interpreting various tests. Some key points with respect to testing include the following:

- Although counselors are unlikely to be very much involved in developing new tests, they need to understand the ethical responsibilities of test producers.
- Test publishers must use the best scientific methods available in devising their instruments; must keep client welfare foremost; and must publish materials that describe the test's development, standardization, and instructions for use.
- Counselors are responsible for maintaining the security of tests that they use and for appropriately supervising the test-taking process.
- Counselors must be aware of copyright laws and must be careful not to violate such laws.
- Counselors are competent to administer and interpret many tests, but they should keep in mind that some tests require specific training in their use.

- In order to be competent in using a test, a counselor should have completed formal coursework and have had supervised experience in using the test.
- Other mental health professionals in some states have attempted to prohibit counselors from using certain kinds of tests.
- Counselors must use caution in releasing test records to third parties and should release the records only to those individuals who are qualified to receive them.
- Clients have the right to receive a full explanation of their test results.
- Counselors must be cautious in using tests with culturally diverse clients. Many tests have been shown to be culturally biased, and minority groups often are not represented in the norm groups on which the tests were standardized.
- Counselors need to be knowledgeable about laws that affect testing practices.

Counselors are often uncomfortable with diagnosing mental disorders because the prevalent diagnostic system is based on the medical model. There are many good reasons for counselors to participate in diagnosis, however. Counselors who choose to participate need to clarify their own values with respect to diagnosis and its application within a wellness philosophy. Key points with respect to diagnosis include the following:

- Clients must understand the implications of any diagnosis that might be assigned to them.
- Counselors must be prepared to work cooperatively with physicians when clients may have a physical condition that is contributing to their mental or emotional problems or when they could benefit from taking medications for their condition.
- A controversial issue has been whether counselors are qualified to diagnose.
- Multicultural considerations are of paramount importance in diagnosis because all mental disorders occur in and are defined by a cultural context.
- Counselors must be alert to sources of bias against women and minority group members in the diagnostic process.
- Counselors are guilty of insurance fraud when they do not diagnose honestly and accurately, and they can be subject to both civil and criminal liability.

Professional Relationships, Private Practice, and Health Care

PROFESSIONAL RELATIONSHIPS

Counselors who practice in all settings interact regularly with other professionals. Counselors must be able to establish and maintain appropriate relationships with mental health and other professionals (such as physicians, law enforcement officials, and teachers) in order to render quality mental health services to their clients. They must also be alert to ethical and legal considerations that relate to their interactions with other professionals.

Just as it is essential to establish appropriate personal boundaries with clients, students, and supervisees, it is equally important to establish appropriate boundaries with other professionals. Counselors must continually determine their precise role when they are interacting with other professionals. This role depends on the circumstances. Therefore, counselors must understand that they have many roles and responsibilities and often must clarify their position to others with whom they interact. Two examples may help to illustrate this point.

Example One A psychiatrist in private practice has diagnosed a patient with a mental disorder and has prescribed medication. The psychiatrist refers the person for counseling services to a counselor in private practice. In this situation, the psychiatrist and counselor function as co-equal partners in treating the individual. They consult and relate to each other in that fashion.

Example Two A psychiatrist is employed as director of a public mental health center. The psychiatrist assigns a client to a staff counselor for treatment and specifies that the counselor should have five sessions with the client related to proper parenting skills development. The psychiatrist is the counselor's administrative supervisor and the counselor is in the role of an employee carrying out the directives of a superior. Of course the counselor has an obligation to exercise judgment in the case, but the dynamics between the two professionals will be much different than in the first situation.

The ethical and legal issues that are important to counselors as they interact with other professionals include the following: (a) employer/employee relationships, (b) confidential information, (c) referrals, and (d) respect for other professionals.

Employer/Employee Relationships

Most counselors practice their profession as employees of agencies and entities such as schools, hospitals, mental health centers, and rehabilitation agencies. At some time in their careers, most counselors also supervise others in organizational settings, which requires them to function in the role of employer.

As a result, it is important that counselors understand the basic legal principles of employment law. Counselors also need to be prepared to address some of the tensions experienced by professionals who have obligations both to clients and to employers.

Counselors as Employees

When a counselor applies for, is offered, and accepts a job, the counselor then becomes an employee and must function within the legal framework that guarantees certain rights to employees and also imposes upon them a number of obligations.

Employed counselors have a legal right guaranteed by the U. S. Constitution or federal statutes (Title VII of the Civil Rights Act of 1964; Age Discrimination in Employment Act of 1967; Title I of the Americans with Disabilities Act of 1990) to be free in the workplace of discrimination based on race, color, sex, religion, national origin, age, and disabilities (Belton & Avery, 1999). In some states or localities, discrimination based on other traits such as sexual orientation may be prohibited by statute as well. For example, in Florida, in addition to the federally protected categories of individuals, it is also illegal to discriminate in employment matters based on political affiliation or marital status (Fazio, 1997).

Also, employees do not have to submit to any supervisor's directive that constitutes a crime. If a directive is unethical, it might also be illegal. Because most ethical issues are debatable, a directive probably would have to be clearly unethical and put clients at substantial risk for a court to support a professional who refused to follow a supervisor's directive.

Although a few employees have contracts with their employers that specify the details of their relationship, most employees work without contracts. This means that they are employed at the pleasure of their employer and that the employer may terminate the arrangement at any point without giving a reason.

Originally, under the common law that was inherited from England, employees worked for employers under what is known as the "at will" doctrine. According to Perritt (1998), this concept held that employers could fire employees "at any time for a good reason, a bad reason, or for no reason at all" (p. 3). The pure "at will" doctrine has eroded over time in the United States. However, there is still a general concept in law that employees do not have a right to employment, and a presumption that employers have a right to dismiss employees without giving any reasons.

Perritt (1998) has explained that when employees who do not have employment contracts are fired, the legal burden is on them to prove that their dismissal was wrongful and should be overturned by a court. There are three legal theories that might lead courts to conclude that a dismissal was wrongful: (a) the employer promised that the employee would have employment security, (b) the dismissal offends some important public policy, or (c) the termination was "unfair" or done "in bad faith."

In many large businesses and governmental settings, policies and procedures exist that govern employer/employee relationships without contracts being signed. When such policies and procedures exist, they must be followed.

Labor unions generally negotiate employment contracts for their members. Unions provide leverage for employees that they would not normally have when disputes arise between employee and employer. If an employment contract has been negotiated either individually by an employee or by a union, then the exact terms of the contract will dictate the employer/employee relationship.

When disputes arise between employees and employers, the law generally favors the employer (Perritt, 1998). Individuals are not forced to work and certainly they do not have to work for a particular employer. Because employees are free to resign from their jobs if they are dissatisfied, employers cannot be forced to comply with the preferences of an employee.

By accepting a job, an employee agrees to perform the tasks assigned. These tasks can be any that the employer wishes, unless there is an employment contract or internal policies and procedures to the contrary. If an employee refuses to carry out the directives of a supervisor, this constitutes insubordination. An employee can be legally dismissed for insubordination. The only defenses to refusing to carry out the directives of a supervisor would probably be that a directive (a) was in violation of an employment contract, (b) was in violation of internal policies or procedures, (c) illegally discriminated against a protected category of individuals, or (d) constituted a crime.

Many counselors who are also employees are concerned about being in a situation in which they believe they have an ethical obligation to act or refrain from acting, and their employer issues a directive to the contrary. The ACA *Code of Ethics* does not require counselors to "fall on their swords" and resign if they believe an organization demands actions that pose a conflict with the code. Instead, they should address their concerns directly with their employer and work toward change in the organization (Standards D.1.l. and H.2.c.). Although counselors may be uncomfortable working in a conflictual situation, it is acceptable from both an ethical and a practical standpoint for them to secure employment elsewhere before resigning their position.

Most employers understand that licensure laws and codes of ethics guide the behavior of the professionals they employ, even though the employers may not be members of the same profession. Nonetheless, there are many disagreements among experts and professionals regarding what constitutes ethical and unethical behavior. Most often, when disputes arise in ethical areas between professionals and their employers, it is because the parties disagree as to what is ethical and unethical.

Following are some examples of situations in which professionals and their employers might disagree about an ethical issue:

1. A physician believes that an operation would be in a patient's best interest, but the health maintenance organization determines that a different, less expensive form of treatment is acceptable.
2. An attorney who is an associate in a law firm believes that a potential client has no chance of winning a lawsuit against a former employer because of the facts and the law. The attorney recommends that the firm decline to represent the potential client, but a senior partner directs the associate to take the case and to pursue it vigorously.
3. An associate accountant in an accounting firm believes that some business dealings within an organization the firm is auditing constitute a breach of fiduciary duty and wants to note an exception in the audit. A senior partner disagrees and

orders the accountant not to even mention the business dealings in the audit report.

4.   A psychologist who is employed by a prison believes that many of the inmates that are evaluated are in need of medical care due to their mental conditions. The supervisor, who is a psychiatrist, disagrees and says that the psychologist should just conclude that the inmates do not need medical care.

These situations illustrate that any professional who is employed could face problems of ethical decision making. The case presented below describes a counselor who has a disagreement with an employer regarding an ethical issue.

Jason has been a counselor in a community mental health center for two years. A new director has been hired recently. The director holds a master's degree in business, and she has never worked in a mental health facility before. Other counselors tell the director that Jason is an ineffective counselor, that he becomes inappropriately involved in the personal lives of clients, and that he does not follow center policies. The director wants to ensure that Jason is performing his job responsibilities adequately. Therefore, she directs Jason to show her his case notes at the end of each day and to summarize his work with each of his clients. Jason refuses, based on his requirement to keep his conversations with his clients confidential. The director fires Jason.

This situation describes a difficult problem for counselors and for those who supervise mental health professionals but are not mental health professionals themselves. The counseling center director in this case study certainly has an obligation to ensure that her employees are performing their jobs adequately. The director is legally responsible for the work of her employees. On the other hand, professionals have a confidentiality obligation to clients.

A better approach for the supervisor would have been to assign another, perhaps senior, mental health professional to supervise Jason's work for a period of time. On the other hand, Jason could have responded differently and perhaps saved his job. He could have tried to accommodate his supervisor's concerns in some way and at the same time preserved the privacy of his clients. He could have engaged in a conversation with his supervisor to determine why the supervisor was concerned about his job performance. Through that conversation, Jason could have presented his side of the story. He could have offered to be supervised by a senior counselor for a period of time to assure his supervisor of his competency. Trying to work with a supervisor is much better than defying the supervisor's order.

At some time in your professional career, you may be faced with a situation in which you and your employer disagree about what is ethical. Listed below are the steps we recommend that you take if you believe your employer is forcing you to act in what you consider to be an unethical manner:

1.   Avoid discussing the situation with co-workers in casual conversations or in staff meetings. Consult with outside experts and colleagues in a confidential manner regarding the issue, and ask them to keep your conversations confidential. If there is a consensus that the action is unethical, go to step 2. If time allows, a request could be made to the ACA Ethics Committee for an

interpretation of the ACA *Code of Ethics*. There is a formal process for requesting interpretations (See Chapter 15) and it takes a number of months to receive an interpretation. If experts and colleagues do not agree that the action is unethical, you could argue internally for change, but should follow the directives of your supervisor.

2. Schedule an appointment with your supervisor to discuss the matter. Tell your supervisor which provisions in the ACA *Code of Ethics* you believe are being violated and ask that you not be directed to act in what you consider to be an unethical manner. If your supervisor requests additional information or support for your position, offer to provide it to the extent possible.

3. If step 2 does not lead to a satisfactory resolution of the issue, you must decide whether to stay in the organization and work toward change or whether to look for a different job that does not force you to compromise your beliefs about your ethical obligations. If you decide to stay in the organization, go to step 4. If you decide to leave, update your resume and begin your search. For practical purposes, keep your present job while you are searching, if possible. Many employers are suspicious that unemployed professionals may be poor employees, and many employers do not favor applicants who left previous jobs because of disputes with their employers.

4. Ask your supervisor to schedule a three-way appointment with you and his or her supervisor to discuss the situation. If your supervisor refuses, inform your supervisor that you are going to talk with his or her supervisor. Then, ask that supervisor directly for an appointment to discuss the matter.

5. If step 4 does not resolve the issue (and you still have your job), determine whether organizational policies could be created or changed that would resolve the dilemma in a manner that would be ethically acceptable to you. If so, suggest that a policy or procedures be created or changed following the procedure used to make suggestions within your organization. To try to preserve your working relationship, inform your supervisor of your activities, if possible. Try to avoid the appearance that this issue is a struggle between you and your boss that one of you will win and the other will lose. Instead, present the issue as important to the organization and to your profession and advocate for change in a professional manner.

Counselors as Employers

Counselors who are in private practice or who own their own businesses naturally will hire employees from time to time to assist them with their work. In addition, counselors who become supervisors in the agencies in which they are employed become members of the management team and agents of their employer. Such supervisor-counselors function as employers as well.

Employed counselors should realize that they must assume the role of employer any time they have one or more persons who report to them administratively. Sometimes administrative lines within organizations are blurred. It is vital for counselors to clarify, if they are unsure, whether they are the supervisors for individuals with whom they work. Generally, a supervisor assigns work responsibilities to another employee and evaluates that person's performance. In addition, supervisors generally make final decisions or final recommendations about whom to hire for positions that report to them. Supervisors also have significant influence and responsibility in disciplining and dismissing employees who report to them.

Employed counselors may have clerical or professional staff members who report to them. Employees want their supervisors to be clear in communicating expectations and directives. All counselors—whether they are in a supervisory, subordinate, or collegial relationship with employers and employees—have an ethical obligation to make expectations clear and to establish working agreements that are known to all parties. The ACA *Code of Ethics* specifies that these working agreements should address counseling relationships, confidentiality, adherence to professional standards, distinctions between public and private material, handling of records, work load, and accountability (Standard D.1.b.).

Employees also want their supervisors to be fair and just in dealing with them. As an ethical requirement, counselors do not commit or condone practices that are inhumane, illegal, or unjustifiable in hiring or promotion. They do not discriminate on the basis of age, color, culture, disability, ethnic group, gender, race, religion, sexual orientation, or socioeconomic status (Standard D. 1.i.) even when the law in their jurisdiction might not protect some of these categories of persons.

It is very important that counselors who supervise others avoid favoritism or the appearance of favoritism among employees. Consider what could happen if a friendship or personal relationship developed between a supervisor and a supervisee. When the supervisor later disciplined or dismissed another employee or gave some type of benefit or promotion to the friend, the supervisor would be vulnerable to a complaint of favoritism, or perhaps even illegal discrimination.

As a result, it is recommended that counselors who supervise others maintain a personal distance between themselves and those they supervise. Organizational environments, however, often promote employee friendships through a friendly climate or social gatherings that sometimes even extend to family members. If a friendship or personal relationship does develop between a supervisor and employee, the counselor should be careful to avoid personal interactions with the employee at work and must self-monitor carefully to ensure that the employee is not being given favorable treatment. See additional discussions of multiple relationships in Chapter 7 and consider the following case.

> When Margaret was promoted to director of the local mental health center, one of the first personnel decisions she made was to hire one of her best friends, Beth, as a staff counselor. Margaret knew that Beth was an excellent counselor with many years of experience who would perform well as an employee for the center. Now, after a year, Beth has indeed performed her job in an exemplary manner. However, because Beth is very focused on work and is highly productive in the work environment, she has alienated most of the other employees at the center. They see her as unfriendly, abrupt in interpersonal communications, and self-centered. Margaret and Beth have maintained their friendship and frequently socialize together on the weekends. A unit supervisor has recently resigned, and Margaret must appoint someone to take his place. The two top candidates for the job are Beth and another staff counselor who is very popular among his peers. However, he is not as capable as an administrator, in Margaret's opinion. Margaret wants to promote Beth to the supervisory position, but she is worried that other staff members will be very upset with her if she does.

This case demonstrates how difficult it can be for a supervisor who has a personal relationship with a supervisee. If Margaret promotes Beth, surely most of her staff members will believe she is biased and promoted Beth because of their personal friendship. If Margaret promotes the other staff member instead of Beth, Margaret will worry that she is being unfair to Beth and to the organization. There is no easy solution to a problem like this. No matter what she decides, Margaret should work with Beth to help her improve her interpersonal relationships with other staff members. However, Margaret's attempt to do that may have a negative effect on her personal relationship with Beth. To avoid situations such as this, it is best to avoid personal relationships with supervisees, if possible.

Employed counselors who serve as administrative supervisors must thoroughly familiarize themselves with the policies and procedures of the organization and with the contract terms of anyone who is employed through either a personal or union contract. It is essential that administrative supervisors follow, in detail, all written procedures. A common problem for administrative supervisors is having their decisions overturned either within the organization or by courts because they have failed to follow written procedures. Administrative supervisors who disapprove of organizational policies, organizational procedures, or contract clauses should work within proper channels to get them changed. Supervisors must follow such policies and procedures or contract clauses precisely while they are still in effect.

Confidential Information

In the context of relationships with other professionals, counselors must often share information about clients that is confidential or even privileged. In Chapter 4, sharing information with other professionals was identified as an exception to confidentiality and privileged communication requirements.

It is best to obtain written permission from clients to transfer private information to others. Although written permission generally is not a legal requirement, state licensure laws or regulations for counselors could require that permission be in writing. Also, the ACA *Code of Ethics* requires that written permission be obtained to transfer records (Standard B.4.e.). A model client waiver form is included in Chapter 3.

The ACA *Code of Ethics* also requires counselors to try to ensure that receivers of their records are sensitive to the confidential nature of the records. Counselors are not expected to conduct an investigation of the policies and procedures for maintaining confidentiality of every individual, agency, or institution that receives their records. What good practice dictates is that counselors ensure that the client's fully informed consent has been given to transfer the records and that they clearly mark as "confidential" any records that they send.

Referrals

The ethical requirements and general legal principles regarding referrals from one professional to another come to the same conclusions. The ACA *Code of Ethics* has specific standards related to referrals. The first of these standards (C.3.d.) prohibits counselors from using their places of employment or institutional affiliations to recruit clients for their own private practices. A second standard (D.3.b.) prohibits counselors from accepting a referral fee from other professionals.

The law regarding referrals is based on professionals' fiduciary responsibilities to their clients. The law requires that professionals not do anything that would benefit themselves at the expense of a client or that would harm a client in any way. Fiduciaries are not allowed to enter into arrangements with clients that benefit the fiduciary in any way (Ludes & Gilbert, 1998). Obviously, counselors would benefit if they referred clients to either their own practice or to the practice of someone who compensated them for the referral.

Many counselors worry about how to make a referral. They are concerned that referring a person to a particular counselor is either unethical or illegal. It is neither unethical nor illegal. There is a misperception among counselors that such referrals are wrong because many agencies, particularly agencies that are publicly funded, have policies either prohibiting referrals altogether or requiring that counselors refer to a specified minimum number of individuals. Agencies have developed these policies in an attempt to avoid furthering the business interests of some mental health professionals to the detriment of other mental health professionals who practice in the community. To avoid complaints from professionals that others are being favored by the agency, many agencies adopt policies that require no referrals or multiple referrals.

Ethical guidelines require counselors to be knowledgeable about referral resources so that they can "suggest appropriate alternatives" to clients (Standard A.11.b.). Perhaps it is the use of the plural "alternatives" that has led some counselors to believe mistakenly that they must always provide clients with more than one referral source. The intent of this standard is to stress that counselors need to be familiar with the resources in their community that provide mental health and related services. If a counselor believes that a client would be well served by a referral to any of a number of other professionals, then it is good practice to give all these choices to the client. If a counselor believes that a client would be best served by a particular mental health professional whose specialty area matches the client's needs, then the counselor should feel free to recommend that particular resource.

Generally, a counselor would not be held accountable for the malpractice of a professional to whom an individual had been referred. However, if the counselor making the referral had some reason to know or should have known that a particular professional had a notoriously negative reputation in the professional community, then the counselor might be held accountable for harm suffered by the person who was referred.

John's best friend, Mike, is a local physician. Mike recently lost a malpractice case that was filed against him based on failure to diagnose a life-threatening illness. In addition, Mike has told John that there are three similar current complaints filed against him with the medical board. John routinely refers many of his counseling clients to physicians for physical examinations as they begin counseling. John is wondering whether he should continue to refer clients to his friend Mike.

Situations such as this are rare because professionals who are grossly incompetent usually lose their licenses or lose their jobs, if they are employed. In this case, because John has personal knowledge that Mike may not be competent as a physician, he should not refer counseling clients to Mike for medical services. Certainly if John were to refer a client to Mike, he would have to inform the client of the situation regarding the lost lawsuit and pending complaints. If John referred a counseling client to Mike and that counseling client suffered harm as a result of services rendered by him, the client might successfully sue John for breach of his fiduciary duty.

Respecting Other Professionals

Counselors must be careful to avoid saying or writing comments that might damage the reputation of another professional. If counselors repeat rumors that are inaccurate, or purposefully make false oral or written statements, such actions could damage the reputations of other professionals, and those individuals could sue for libel or slander. Libel is written dishonesty; slander is oral.

Generally, the law of libel and slander requires that persons who believe they were harmed by the words of another prove "special harm" (Robertson, Powers, & Anderson, 1989). Injured persons usually have to prove actual pecuniary loss, as opposed to humiliation or general harm to their reputations. However, accusing persons of being unfit for their profession falls under the category of libel or slander "per se," which means that "special harm" does not have to be proven. Because professional reputation is so important to a career, it is assumed in law that persons are harmed if their reputation is damaged by lies or deceit.

Prosser et al. (1988) have listed the following defenses to accusations of libel or slander: truth, retraction, absolute privilege, and qualified privilege. If you were accused of defaming another person, you could argue that what you said or wrote was true. You also could publicly retract what you said or wrote. Judges have absolute privilege and cannot be sued for what they say in their official capacity. If you are defending yourself, you have a "qualified privilege" to repeat what you have heard if you must do so to protect yourself.

As an ethical consideration, counselors need to be aware that their opinions regarding other professionals, particularly other mental health professionals, carry more weight with the general public than do the opinions of others. Counselors must be respectful of other professionals even if they personally have negative feelings about their approaches to practice. Our relationships with fellow mental health professionals should be based on respect, honesty, and fairness (Welfel, 1998). We noted in Chapter 2, in our discussion of professional identity, that counselors sometimes have philosophical and practical differences regarding therapeutic approaches, as well as turf wars, with other mental health professionals. A counselor and a psychologist might find themselves, on Monday, testifying at the state legislature on opposite sides of a mental health provider issue. On Tuesday, they might meet as members of a treatment team to work for the best interests of their shared clients. The key to managing such situations is to keep professional disagreements in the political and philosophical realms and to stringently avoid bringing them into our work with clients.

The ACA *Code of Ethics* (Standard C.6.a.) requires that counselors respect mental health approaches that are different from their own. Also, counselors should not imply that other counselors are not qualified because they do not possess certain credentials (C.4.d.). Standards like these would be considered if a counselor was accused by another professional of libel or slander.

PRIVATE PRACTICE

The ethical issues regarding private practice discussed earlier in this chapter revolve around the responsibilities of counselors to ensure that they are treating clients and other professionals fairly. Many counselors-in-training idealize private practice and have a goal of owning their own independent counseling practice some day. They may not have considered that by owning a private practice they will be running a business and that opening a practice involves all the promises and pitfalls of starting any small business. Most counselors do not have training or experience in business administration, so it is important that they consider the following issues before deciding whether to go into private practice.

Taxes and Business Licenses

If counselors generate any income at all outside of their salary, they are in business and have a private practice. Depending on the state statute and the nature of the services rendered, counselors may need to be licensed by their state counselor licensing board. In most states, counselors may conduct educational workshops, produce professional written products, and engage in other counseling-related activities that produce an income without being licensed.

Counselors who generate income outside of wages or salaries must file a separate federal income tax form for income produced from a business. In states that have income taxes, similar forms sometimes must be filed at the state level as well.

There are numerous federal, state, and local requirements that must be addressed when counselors open their private practices. Haynsworth (1986) has listed the following possible steps that might need to be taken:

- A federal tax identification number has to be obtained if there might be any employees.
- A professional license has to be obtained in some states.
- A business license must be applied for and obtained.
- Worker's compensation insurance or unemployment compensation insurance may have to be purchased.
- Employee bonds may be required.
- Liability, property damage, or other types of insurance may be needed.
- A fictitious or assumed name statute may need to be complied with.
- Other public filing requirements may exist.

Counselors with businesses must purchase a business license from their local jurisdiction's office, which is usually located in a city hall or county courthouse (Alberty, 1989). Purchasing a business license involves listing a business address. In most jurisdictions, zoning laws prohibit or limit in some way, clients (or customers) coming to a residence. So, if a residence is listed as the place of business, the counselor must indicate that no clients or customers come there for services. Each year, when a business license is renewed, counselors must report the amount of their gross income and pay a tax to the city or county. This tax is minimal until substantial income is generated. Few jurisdictions actively pursue those who violate business license laws. Violations could become important, though, if a counselor were accused of wrongdoing at some point.

Counselors who generate income and fail to report it on federal and state income tax forms, or who fail to purchase and renew business licenses each year, are committing crimes. A number of counselors who are unaware of tax and business license requirements are in violation of these laws. Ignorance of legal requirements does not excuse those who violate them.

Business Form

Businesses are structured in a number of ways. Most professional private practices are known in law as sole proprietorships. The individual professional owns the private practice and no other professional has a financial interest in it. This is the simplest form of business ownership and the one chosen by most private practitioners in counseling. In our opinion, it is usually the best option for counselors who engage in private practice.

The second most popular business form for counselors is a partnership. Generally partnerships should be chosen only if a partnership is required to obtain financing for a new business or if there is a significant advantage in the commercial market for a partnership over a sole proprietorship.

Many counselors seem to choose partnerships because they are anxious about beginning a business venture on their own, or because they want the social benefits of affiliating with friends or colleagues. These are not good reasons for forming a partnership. There are many arguments against forming partnerships that should be carefully considered before one is established: (a) total agreement on all business decisions is required, (b) each partner is fully liable for the acts of omissions of each other partner, (c) there is a presumption of equality of partners regarding liabilities and profits, (d) personal assets are not protected from business debts, and (e) dissolutions of partnerships can be contentious and very expensive if problems cannot be resolved amicably, and one or more partners hire lawyers to represent their interests.

A corporation is a third possible business form. Generally, individuals are motivated to form corporations if the business involved is very risky and if the owner has substantial personal assets (Alberty, 1989). Most states have what is known as professional corporations, in which individual professionals essentially incorporate their individual private practices. Although professional corporations were very popular in the past, tax advantages have been reduced through legislation (Hamilton, 1990). Corporations are complicated and difficult to keep current, and as a result, professional corporations have fallen out of favor. Weil (1983) has pointed out, however, that professional corporations are still being formed by some individuals and has listed the following advantages that still exist: (a) accumulation of capital, (b) transferability of ownership, (c) flexible fiscal year, (d) employee benefits, (e) some reduction in liability, and (f) management structure.

A professional's primary motivation for choosing any type of corporate form for a private practice would be to protect personal assets in the event that the business failed or a judgment was rendered against it. However, a reason for not forming a corporation is that adequate professional liability insurance can be purchased to avoid losing the business and personal assets because of a lawsuit or judgment. Other problems with corporations include the following: (a) they are very expensive to form, (b) meetings have to be held periodically and annual reports have to be filed or the corporation will cease to exist legally, (c) income is taxed to the corporation and is taxed again when it is distributed to owners, and (d) accountants and lawyers must be retained on a continuous basis to ensure the corporation is functioning properly.

Some counselors choose to form nonprofit corporations as the basis of their practice. Essentially, counselors form a nonprofit corporation and then pay themselves a salary from the proceeds of the entity. Such corporations have favorable tax laws (Hamilton, 1990) and might be eligible for certain grants. The significant problem with nonprofit corporations is that the counselor does not own or control them. In order to qualify as a nonprofit corporation, the charter of the entity must include a board of directors. While counselors might originally form boards that will support them as directors, it is possible that board members may begin to assert themselves or that replacement board members may not support the counselor. A nonprofit corporation board has the authority to remove the counselor as the director and to take over the business entity.

Fees for Services

Counselors in private practice must set fees for their services, and they struggle with establishing their fee structures. They are in business, so they must generate enough income to cover their business expenses. In addition, if their private practice is their only source of income, they want to generate enough income above expenses to allow them to have a comfortable lifestyle. If their fees are too high, clients will go elsewhere for services. If their fees are too low, clients may not value the services they are receiving, or they may choose a practitioner who charges higher fees in the belief that the fee reflects the quality of services offered. Although most professionals seek to establish the highest fee the market will tolerate, counselors, like lawyers, are in a fiduciary relationship with clients. Therefore, they must set fees within a framework of basic fairness (Smith & Mallen, 1989).

The ACA *Code of Ethics* (Standard A.10.b.) states that in establishing fees, counselors should consider the "financial status of clients and locality." The standard probably was intended to encourage counselors to set fees that reflect the economy in the locality. However, it could be misinterpreted to mean that counselors should charge clients according to their ability to pay, which could result in serious legal problems for counselors in private practice. Legally, counselors and other professionals may set any fees for their services that they wish. They can even charge different clients different amounts for the same service as long as they do not discriminate based on protected categories of persons.

Some counselors establish the same "sliding scale" fee structure in their private practices that is used by counseling centers supported by public funds or private charitable funds. A sliding scale fee structure sets the fee for services based on objective criteria such as amount of income, size of family, etc. With sliding scales, individuals with more income and less financial burden pay more for the same services as those with less income and more financial burden. Although a sliding scale seems more appropriate for a nonprofit agency than it does for a private practice from a business perspective, counselors can adopt this method, too. However, if counselors take clients who receive health insurance reimbursement for services, they must apply the sliding scale formula precisely for all clients, regardless of whether the client has health insurance that reimburses for the counselor's services or not. See the last section of this chapter that deals with health insurance issues.

An important part of charging fees is the process of collecting them. Many counselors are uncomfortable taking money from their clients, but collecting fees is a necessary part of maintaining a successful private practice. Counselors who avoid the collection of fees probably should consider working in an agency where they do not have to collect client fees, rather than operating a private practice.

The trend today is for all professionals to collect fees as services are rendered. In other words, counseling clients probably should be expected to pay for each session at the time the session is held. An exception, of course, would be clients whose payments will be made by another entity, such as an indemnity health insurance company, PPO, employee assistance program, or governmental agency. Counselors in private practice should develop clear policies regarding fee payment, and these policies should be spelled out specifically in the counselor's disclosure statement (See Chapter 3). It is unwise to make any exceptions.

In the event a counselor does allow a client to develop a large bill for services, the counselor should never threaten a client in any way if payment is not made, and certainly should never sue the client. If a counselor demanded payment from a former client for past services rendered, the former client could take the position that the services were inferior and could countersue or file a complaint with the counselor's licensure board, certifying agency, or professional association (Smith & Mallen, 1989). In our opinion, it is better just to forget client bills that are never paid and, in the future, to avoid allowing any bills to develop.

Attorney and Accountant Services

Counselors who are employed can expect their employer to provide them with legal consultation when needed. Counselors in private practice must pay for the services of attorneys when they are needed. Employed counselors are not required to keep business financial records, but counselors in private practice must retain the services of an accountant on an ongoing basis.

As a counselor in private practice, you will need the services of attorneys for a variety of issues. Listed are some of the more common situations:

- You are considering forming a partnership and need to know the legal implications.
- You have been presented with a lease to sign for your office space and you do not know much about leases.
- You receive a subpoena for a client's records and the client tells you not to release them.
- A health insurance company notifies you that they are denying claims made by one of your clients because they do not believe you rendered the services you said you rendered.
- An investigator for a suspected child abuse case you reported is very aggressive in dealing with you.
- You and your partner have decided to dissolve the partnership and your partner is being very unreasonable.

Legal issues arise regularly in a private practice, as this list illustrates. Advice regarding identifying and establishing a relationship with an attorney is provided in Chapter 1 in the section on "Obtaining Legal Advice."

Most counselors in private practice do not have the expertise or time to handle all the financial obligations of their business. As a counselor in private practice, you would retain an accountant or an accounting firm to perform the following tasks for you:

- Set up a system for recording income and expenses.
- Develop a retirement program for you and your employees.
- Handle your payroll, including deducting income taxes and social security payments.
- File annual tax returns for you.

The expenses for the services of attorneys and accountants are substantial and are a part of the overhead for a counselor's private practice. Avoiding legal or financial advice because of the expense involved can lead to substantial problems later.

Professional Liability Insurance

Professional liability insurance is essential for counselors in private practice. If a counselor's private practice accumulates debts that exceed the assets of the practice, which could happen if a counselor were sued, a counselor's personal assets might be taken. A counselor's personal assets are always at risk when a private practice is opened. Even if the practice is incorporated, personal assets can sometimes be accessed in a lawsuit.

Therefore, it is essential that counselors purchase professional liability insurance for their practices. Counselors in private practice should purchase the best professional liability insurance available to them and should request the maximum coverage available. If possible, a policy should be purchased that pays for attorneys' fees and judgments, legal representation if ethical complaints are filed against the counselor, claims made for actions that occurred during the time the policy was in effect, and claims against partners or employees.

Counselors in private practice also need insurance that covers injuries that might occur on their office premises (Schutz, 1990), acts of omissions by employees they may be supervising, and any other claim that may arise as a result of their business. This type of insurance is relatively inexpensive.

Counselors who are considering going into private practice should assess their ability to handle financial uncertainties. These include an initial period of struggle that may last 3 to 5 years while the practice is getting established, financial losses incurred by cancellations and no-shows, and income that fluctuates from month to month. Personal stressors, such as isolation and dealing with suicidal clients, should also be given some thought. For counselors who can manage the stressors and who enjoy the independence that self-employment allows, private practice can be very rewarding.

HEALTH CARE PLANS

It has been estimated that 14% of the nation's income is spent each year on health care (Randall, 1994a). Private insurance pays 37% of health care bills, government programs pay 42%, and individuals pay 21% (Randall 1994b). Health care plan assistance is a necessity for many individuals who receive mental health services, because they could not afford the services without this help. It is important for counselors to have a basic understanding of how health care plans function, particularly in the area of providing mental health services.

Individuals pay for health care plans because the cost of some of their health care needs could easily exceed their financial resources. When people enter into contracts with health care companies, the health care plan agrees to provide them with health care in return for a premium they pay on a regular basis.

As a fringe benefit, employers often provide health care plans for their employees free of charge, or more commonly, they subsidize the cost of the plans for their employees. Individuals who are unemployed, who own their own businesses, or who work for employers who do not provide health care plans must purchase their own. Indigent persons or disabled individuals who cannot purchase their own insurance may receive health care assistance in the form of Medicaid (42 U.S.C. § 1396, 1982) from the government. Older persons receive Medicare from the federal government.

Unfortunately, a number of persons in the United States have no health care plan at all. These individuals must pay for medical services as they are rendered to them or they simply do not receive medical care. Howe (1999) has suggested that most of the people who do not have health care plans belong to the "working poor." These are people who produce income that exceeds the eligibility limits for Medicaid, have jobs that do not provide health care plans as a fringe benefit, and cannot afford to purchase health care plans on their own. There are millions of individuals in the United States who do not have health care plans to assist them in paying for mental health services. In addition, many of the health care plans that people do have pay for no mental health services or services that are extremely limited.

State Insurance Laws

Each state or jurisdiction in the United States has different laws governing health care plan contracts that may be sold in that state. These laws require that health care plan companies offer certain health benefits to be allowed to sell plans in that state. In addition to benefits that are mandated by state law, health care companies can offer additional benefits as an incentive for individuals to purchase plans from them rather than from other companies.

A state may also mandate by statute which categories of professionals are eligible to render the health care services that are reimbursable. Physicians are always listed as acceptable providers of health care services. State legislation can require that other health care providers, such as chiropractors, nurses, or physical therapists, be eligible to provide health care services under all insurance plans sold in the state. This type of statute is called "freedom of choice" legislation. It allows consumers of health care services to choose the provider they prefer, rather than allowing health care companies to designate categories of approved providers, thereby excluding other providers. In some states, freedom of choice statutes exist that require licensed counselors to be allowed to provide mental health services if those services are reimbursed by health care companies. In other states, where such legislation does not exist, health care companies can determine for themselves whether they will reimburse for services if they are rendered by licensed counselors.

In most circumstances, health care companies will voluntarily reimburse their plan members for the reimbursable mental health services of licensed counselors. If a health care company refuses to allow licensed counselors to provide mental health services to their plan holders and there is no statute in that state to the contrary, plan members or licensed counselors cannot force them to allow licensed counselors to be providers. See Chapter 2 for a review of how counselors can become active in legislative issues affecting their profession.

Types of Health Care Plans

Health care companies offer many different types of plans to the public. The most common kinds available today include health maintenance organizations (HMOs), preferred provider organizations (PPOs), and traditional indemnity health insurance policies. Of course, many other types of health care plans exist, such as exclusive provider organizations (EPOs)(Carabillo, 1986), managed care organizations (MCOs), and individual practice associations (IPAs)(Randall, 1994a). Combinations of two or more types are occasionally formed, and sometimes what appears to be an HMO is called a PPO. However, three basic types of health care plans —HMOs, PPOs, and indemnity health insurance plans—are the most common today.

When individuals purchase health care plans from an HMO, they agree to go to the HMO for all their health care needs, and they agree to accept the provider of the health care services assigned to them by the HMO. While most HMOs offer some flexibility in choosing providers within the organization, members cannot go outside the organization for their health care. HMOs hire providers of health care. Members do not pay for services and then get reimbursed. Instead, they receive health care services from the HMO for no fee or for copayments they have agreed to in their contracts.

Individuals who purchase health care plans from a PPO agree to go to providers who have been preapproved by the organization for all of their health care needs. PPO policy members can choose their providers, but only from the list of approved providers given to them by the PPO. PPOs do not hire providers of health care. The approved providers on their list usually are in private practice or work for a separate health care agency. PPO members pay for health care services and are then reimbursed by the PPO.

Indemnity insurance works in a similar fashion to PPOs, but individuals who purchase indemnity health insurance do not have to go to providers who have been preapproved by the organization. Policy holders can choose their health care provider, as long as the provider is in a category of providers the insurance company recognizes. Persons insured by indemnity health insurance companies pay for services and are then reimbursed by the insurance company.

Managed Care

Managed health care is a relatively new concept that has had a significant impact on mental health care services. Basically, managed care means that people are not given all health care services that they want or that their provider wants for them. Instead health plan members are given the services that the health care plan company has determined are appropriate and necessary. The idea is to lower the cost to the company for health care by "managing" the care provided.

These companies have policies regarding the type of care they will provide for preventive procedures or for various illnesses. They also use a procedure known as utilization review, in which a physician or panel of physicians reviews requests for services from the treating service providers to determine whether the services will be allowed (*Wickline v. State of California,* 1986). If plan members or their providers want services that exceed those allowed under a managed care system, they have to request exceptions from the company.

The controversy regarding managed care revolves around whether health care companies are indeed containing health care costs appropriately by eliminating unnecessary procedures and limiting services that are allowed, or whether health care companies are simply increasing their profits at the expense of health care recipients. Many health care providers are dissatisfied with managed care systems because administrators make decisions about health care services that professionals believe they should make themselves.

Most health care companies today limit the number of outpatient visits for mental health concerns that members are allowed each year. The idea of limiting counseling services to a set number of visits is objectionable to many mental health care providers. They would rather have health care companies allow clients as many visits as the professional believes is necessary to resolve a mental health concern. In reality, members will be reimbursed only for the number of visits that their health care plan allows. Of course, clients who are plan members could have more visits, but they would have to pay the fees themselves.

Counselors as Service Providers

Some counselors or counseling agencies refuse to accept clients who plan to use their health care plan to assist them with fees. The position of these counselors and agencies is that dealing with health care plans or insurance companies is too time-consuming or is objectionable philosophically. The clients of such counselors and agencies are directly responsible for any fees charged for the services rendered to them.

In contrast, many agencies that employ counselors require that they become providers for health care plans. In addition, most counselors in private practice find that they must become providers in order to have enough paying clients to maintain their businesses.

Becoming a provider for a PPO is not an easy process. Counselors must first determine which PPOs exist in their community, and then apply to become a provider separately for each one. Sometimes the application process is difficult and time-consuming. PPOs purposefully limit their lists of preferred providers. Not all eligible mental health professionals in the community will be accepted by a PPO. They can accept or reject any application they receive, as long as they do not illegally discriminate against a professional. In order to become a provider for a particular PPO, a counselor may have to apply many times over a long period. Once a counselor has been accepted by a PPO as a provider or when a counselor has accepted a client who has indemnity health insurance that will reimburse the client for the counselor's services, it is important that the counselor complete health plan forms in an appropriate and professional manner.

Most health care plans demand accountability from their providers. Plans may require counselors to submit detailed justifications for their diagnoses. In addition, most health care plans expect providers of mental health services to develop objective and measurable goals as a part of each client's treatment plan. Some plans even send auditors to providers' offices to determine whether the provider is offering a professional setting for rendering services, is keeping confidential information secure, is accessible to clients for services, and is keeping records appropriately. If providers do not comply with a health care plan's requirements, the plan has the option of removing them as providers. In fact, to avoid liability, health care plans need to remove providers from their lists who are ineffective professionally (Corcoran, 1989).

It is vital for counselors to request detailed information from each health care plan for which they provide services regarding the plan's expectations from providers. Each plan is unique and requests different types of information in a multitude of formats. In order to maintain provider status, counselors must comply with the requirements of each health care plan.

Counselors who serve as providers must be prepared to deal with a number of ethical and legal issues that are unique to managed care and other types of health plans. These issues include client privacy, proper diagnosis, receiving payment for services, continuing treatment and denial of services, and avoiding fraud.

Client Privacy

When clients contract with health care plans, they sign forms that give health care providers permission to provide information regarding their health care to their health care plan administrators. Generally, clients agree that providers may release any information regarding their treatment that the administrators request.

Many mental health professionals feel uneasy about providing detailed information regarding their clients' diagnoses and treatment to administrators who usually are not mental health professionals. Yet if counselors wish to be providers, they will have to provide this information. When counselors become providers for PPOs, they should request a copy of the privacy waivers that PPO members routinely sign. If a counselor is ever unsure whether a client wants the counselor to provide information requested from a health care plan administrator, it would be best to ask the client to sign a waiver giving permission for the information to be sent.

In our opinion, it is fruitless for an individual counselor to challenge the idea that health care providers inappropriately invade the privacy of their clients. If a counselor believes that a health care plan policy should be changed, the counselor should communicate directly with a company representative regarding the policy. Counselors who believe laws or regulations should be changed should work through the state or national counseling association to seek legislative changes. The ACA belongs to a coalition of mental health organizations that are working to influence national legislation. Glosoff (1998) has suggested that counselors might take additional steps, such as increasing their role in the decision making processes of managed care companies and working with companies to establish clearly structured appeals processes.

Diagnosis

In the previous chapter, we noted that using the *Diagnostic and Statistical Manual, Fourth Edition* (DSM-IV) creates conflicts for counselors who espouse a wellness or developmental orientation. Managed care organizations require that mental health professionals assign a DSM-IV diagnosis to their clients in order to qualify for reimbursement of services. Most companies limit in some way the diagnoses for which they will pay benefits. Some companies will not reimburse for V-code conditions, typical developmental transitions, exclusively Axis II diagnoses, adjustment disorders, or family or couples counseling.

Counselors are sometimes caught in a conflict because they want to promote client welfare by helping clients to receive reimbursement and, at the same time, want to provide accurate diagnoses. Some counselors may succumb to playing a game of "diagnosing for dollars" in which diagnoses are tied to the chance of being reimbursed by health care companies (Wylie, 1995). Such practices are unethical and, as will be discussed later in this section, constitute a type of insurance fraud as well. Rather than yield to these temptations, counselors can improve the chances that their treatment plans will be approved by assessing thoroughly, setting realistic treatment goals, and complying with health care companies' recommended treatment protocols (Hoyt, 1995).

Receiving Payment for Services

Most PPOs pay providers directly for services rendered to the PPOs' members. These fees are sent to providers after they have completed necessary forms that document the services rendered. This arrangement means that counselors often receive payment long after services have been rendered.

When counselors provide services to indemnity health insurance policy holders, counselors can handle payment in one of two ways. Counselors may require that the client pay for services as they are rendered and then file for reimbursement. Counselors may also allow clients to assign their reimbursement to the counselors, so that the payment comes to the counselor from the insurance company. With either method, counselors must verify to the insurance company that they provided services for the client and must provide all the information regarding the services requested by the insurance company.

Usually, both PPOs and health insurance companies require clients to pay a portion of the professional's fees directly. This amount is called a copayment. It is vital that counselors collect copayments from clients when such payments are a requirement of the PPO or indemnity health insurance company.

After counselors have succeeded at becoming approved providers under managed care plans, they confront some ethical issues. Most managed care companies approve only brief mental health treatment as one cost containment measure. The average length of treatment under managed care ranges from 2.5 to 6.6 sessions (Miller, 1996). Thus, counselors must be prepared to provide brief therapy for many of their clients who want their health care plans to pay for services. Many counselors have not been trained in the brief therapies. Only recently have counselor training programs recognized the need to teach not only the traditional approaches, but brief therapy models as well. Programs are just beginning to prepare students to meet the clinical and ethical challenges created by managed care. Therefore, practitioners whose training did not adequately prepare them must seek continuing education in the brief therapies and seek supervision and consultation while developing their competencies (Glosoff, 1998).

Counselors who participate in managed care plans must be able to assess which clients will be well served in a time-limited context. They must be knowledgeable about referral resources for clients whose needs cannot be met under the limitations of their health care plans. They must also be skilled at appealing health care companies' decisions to deny reimbursement when clients need more sessions than their plan allows.

Continuing Treatment and Denial of Services

Although counselors may do their best to accept clients who can be well served by time-limited therapy, inevitably there will be clients who will need more sessions than their health care plan allows or approves. In these situations, counselors may be caught between the need to uphold their ethical standards and their need to remain financially viable in private practice. They have ethical obligations to avoid abandoning clients, to ensure appropriate termination, and to help clients find alternative resources for continued treatment. At the same time, they cannot be expected, except in emergency situations, to continue to see clients without receiving payment for their services.

Lawsuits have been filed when patients suffered injuries after their health plans refused to cover services that were requested (*Wickline v. State of California,* 1986; *Wilson v. Blue Cross,* 1990). In these cases, the health plans argued that their denial of payment or reimbursement for services was not a denial of care. They argued that the treating health care provider had the final responsibility for appropriate care. The courts in these cases held that health plans could be held liable if they were negligent in denying health care services that were necessary to avoid a patient being injured. As Mihaly (1991) has pointed out, many patients have no choice but to forgo treatment when payment or reimbursement is denied.

In Wickline, the court also found that the physician should have protested the health plans' denial of care that he requested. It was the court's position that a health care provider is not liable if a health plan refuses to provide necessary care, but that the provider does have a responsibility to protest if the recommendation for care is not accepted.

Mental health services under managed care probably present more challenges to providers than do physical health care services. First, mental health care often is limited to levels that seem inappropriate to mental health care providers. For example, a health care plan may allow only five reimbursed counseling sessions a year. Or worse, the plan may require that a member have a diagnosis of a serious mental or emotional disorder while severely limiting the services that may be provided under the plan.

The court cases discussed previously provide a foundation for making some recommendations to counselors providing services to clients covered by managed health care companies. These recommendations will help you protect yourself from legal liability:

- If you believe that a client requires counseling services beyond what has been approved by a managed health care company, request the additional services on behalf of the client. If the request is denied, file a written protest or complaint with the company.
- Instruct the client regarding the right to appeal a decision that denies additional services (Hilliard, 1998).
- If the client is a danger to self or others or is in a crisis and cannot afford to pay for your services directly, continue providing services for the client until care can be transferred to another professional or to a facility that provides mental health care.

Avoiding Fraud

Counselors who complete the forms required by PPOs or health insurance companies must be careful to avoid fraudulent practices. Fraud occurs when counselors misrepresent to health care companies any facts regarding their services so their clients will receive payment or reimbursement for the counselors' services. If fraudulent practices are discovered, health care companies can file civil lawsuits to recover payments or reimbursements made inappropriately, and can even cause prosecutors to file criminal charges against counselors, since fraud is a crime.

Mayfield (1996) found that many counselors do not know what constitutes health care fraud. It is possible for counselors to commit fraud without realizing they are doing so if they do not understand which practices are fraudulent. New counselors should be careful not to pattern their behavior after that of seasoned practitioners because some things that mental health professionals have been doing for years are actually fraudulent.

We believe that counselors sometimes engage in health care fraud activities because they are motivated to help their clients receive mental health care services that are paid for or reimbursed by health plans. Counselors report inaccurate information to health care plans so that their clients will be able to begin or continue counseling. Unfortunately, counselors also benefit from fraudulent practices, in that health plans pay for their services based on inaccurate information they have provided. Therefore, it appears to outside observers that counselors are being very self-serving when they give false information to health care plans. Consider the following situation:

Danielle has just been licensed and has decided to open a private practice. She knows from talking to other licensed counselors in her state that the major PPOs and health insurance companies in her state do not pay or reimburse clients for the services of licensed counselors. Danielle's good friend, Monique, is a licensed clinical psychologist. Monique's clients do receive payment or reimbursement for her services. Monique agrees to sublease office space to Danielle for Danielle's private practice. In addition, Monique agrees to "sign off" on PPO and health insurance forms, indicating that she is the client's therapist, even though Danielle is the one seeing the clients. Monique and Danielle meet weekly and review each of Danielle's cases to ensure that Monique is comfortable with her treatment of clients. All clients are told that Monique is supervising Danielle. In exchange for Monique's assistance, Danielle agrees to give Monique 25% of all fees she collects from PPO and health insurance clients.

This arrangement between Danielle and Monique appears to be one that serves everyone's purposes well. Monique is helping out her friend and realizing extra income through subleasing her office space, supervising Danielle, and receiving 25% of the PPO and health insurance client fees that Danielle collects. Danielle is able to see clients who normally would not be able to see her, because their health care plans will pay or reimburse as long as Monique continues to supervise her and sign off. Clients are pleased that their health care plans are paying for their counseling services. This may seem like a perfectly reasonable arrangement and mental health practitioners have long been involved in these kinds of arrangements.

The problem is that Monique and Danielle are fraudulently misrepresenting their services to the PPOs and health insurance companies. Although Monique, Danielle, and Danielle's clients may feel that it is unfair that health care plans do not reimburse licensed counselors for their services, health care plans in their state do have the right to refuse to pay for the services of licensed counselors.

Danielle and Monique may continue their arrangement for years without health care plans ever finding out. However, if a company does discover what they are doing, the company could sue Monique, Danielle, and Danielle's clients for fraud, and perhaps collect all of the fees they paid out to them plus other damages. In addition, the company could request that the local prosecutor file criminal fraud charges against all the parties, and might also file ethics complaints against Monique and Danielle with their licensure boards.

Actually, there is nothing wrong with licensed counselors affiliating with other mental health professionals such as licensed psychologists or licensed physicians. If the counselor is going to provide the direct service to clients, then PPO and insurance forms must be completed to reflect the actual situation. For example, in the case study above, there would have been no fraud involved if Monique had indicated on forms that Danielle, a licensed counselor, was providing the direct service, and she, the licensed psychologist, was supervising Danielle's work. A PPO or health insurance company might have refused to pay or reimburse for services provided under such an arrangement (which they would have a legal right to do), but most likely payment or reimbursement would have been approved. Then, the entire arrangement between Danielle and Monique would have been acceptable. There is nothing illegal or unethical about fee splitting under arrangements such as theirs, as long as there are no misrepresentations to PPOs or health insurance companies.

Listed are a number of fraudulent practices in which mental health professionals sometimes engage that could lead to serious trouble. Counselors commit fraud when they report the following to PPOs or health insurance companies:

- that an approved professional is providing direct services to a client when the services actually are being provided by a counselor who is not approved for payment or reimbursement
- that a client has a DSM-IV diagnosis that is approved for payment or reimbursement when the counselor actually does not believe the diagnosis is accurate
- that the counselor's fee is a specified amount, when actually the counselor charges a sliding scale for clients without health care plans and charges the full fee only to clients who have health care plans that will pay or reimburse for mental health services

- that the counselor is seeing a client for individual counseling (which is reimbursable) when actually the counselor is providing couples, family, or group counseling (which is not reimbursable)
- that the counselor is collecting a required copayment from a client when actually the counselor is waiving the copayment
- that counseling services were rendered on a specific date when actually the client missed the session but the counselor billed for the missed session anyway
- that the counselor may be a physician by signing forms in the space marked "physician's signature," without noting that the counselor is a licensed counselor rather than a physician
- that the counselor is beginning a counseling relationship with a client for the first time when actually they are involved in an ongoing counseling relationship, because health care providers often will not pay or reimburse for "pre-existing conditions"
- that the client is requesting payment or reimbursement from only one health care plan, when the counselor knows that the client is requesting payment for the same services from two or more plans

A couple of these fraudulent practices are so prevalent that they need further discussion. Counselors seem particularly susceptible to diagnosing improperly to satisfy health care plan requirements and to using sliding scales.

As discussed in Chapter 2, many counselors object to diagnosing their clients with an emotional or mental disorder before beginning the counseling process because of their wellness orientation and their rejection of the medical model. Health care payment and reimbursement are based on the medical model. Generally, only treatment for illnesses is paid for or reimbursed. If clients want their health care plans to pay or reimburse for their mental health treatment, they will have to be diagnosed with an emotional or mental disorder. Counselors who are willing and properly trained to diagnose emotional and mental disorders have an ethical and legal obligation to diagnose according to accepted standards in the mental health field.

If a counselor determines that a client does not have a DSM-IV disorder for which a health care plan will pay or reimburse, then the counselor must not assign such a disorder just to allow a client to obtain health care plan financial assistance. Some counselors assign what they consider to be the most benign condition, "adjustment disorder," to satisfy a health care plan's requirements for payment or reimbursement, even when they do not believe the client's symptoms or behaviors warrant such a diagnosis. Such counselor actions would be considered unethical, and could even lead to legal problems. Health care plans could accuse these counselors of fraud. Clients who receive such diagnoses could later be stigmatized in some harmful way and accuse the counselors of malpractice.

Generally, counselors and agencies should not offer sliding-scale fees to clients who do not have health care plans for mental health services if they also accept clients who do have such plans. It is fraud for a counselor or agency to indicate to a health care plan that their fee for services is a set amount, when that amount really is charged only to clients with health care plans and lesser amounts, based on a sliding scale, are charged to clients without health care plans.

If counselors or agencies insist on offering sliding scales for services, then the only way to avoid fraud is to apply the sliding scale to all clients, whether or not they have health care plans. However, problems sometimes arise with health care plans when the same counselor is charging differing fees to each client. Administrators may suspect fraud and investigate when they see that one client of the counselor is paying $100 per session and another one is paying only $25 per session for the same services.

Changing Nature of Health Care Plans

We have summarized the current types of health care plans available and the issues they raise for mental health providers. Health care plans have changed substantially over the past decade and are expected to continue to change as legislators and the public discuss and change health care delivery systems in the United States. It is important for counselors who provide services for clients with health care plans to constantly monitor changes in the health care industry. What may be an acceptable practice today may be prohibited tomorrow.

SUMMARY AND KEY POINTS

This chapter focused on three interrelated topics—professional relationships, private practice, and health insurance. Counselors who practice in any settings interact regularly with other professionals and must conduct themselves in an ethically and legally appropriate manner. Although private practice is idealized by many counselors-in-training, private practice is a business that carries associated risks and requires knowledge of business practices. Many counselors in private practice and in agency or institutional settings want to participate as approved providers under their clients' health insurance plans. Health care plans raise a host of legal and ethical considerations.

Key points regarding professional relationships include the following:

- Counselors will take different roles depending on the circumstances of their interactions with other professionals.
- Because most counselors function at various times as employees and as employers, it is important that they understand the basic principles of employment law.
- Counselors as employees have the right to be free of discrimination in the workplace and to refuse to follow a supervisor's directive if it constitutes a crime.
- Counselors as employees do not have a right to employment and under all but limited circumstances can be dismissed from their jobs.
- Counselors and their employers sometimes disagree about what is ethical, and several steps can be taken to attempt to resolve these disagreements.
- Counselors as employers need to be clear about their roles and their expectations of those whose work they supervise.
- Counselors as employers should avoid close personal relationships or friendships with their employees.
- Counselors should obtain client permission and must work to preserve client confidentiality when transferring private information about clients.
- Although counselors cannot make referrals in ways that might benefit the counselors themselves, they may make referrals to other professionals as dictated by client welfare or the policies of their employers.

- Relationships between counselors and other mental health professionals are characterized by respect, honesty, and fairness.
- Counselors must avoid making statements about other professionals that could be libelous or slanderous.

Private practice is a business. Counselors who wish to start their own practices need to understand certain aspects of business practice. Key points regarding private practice include the following:

- Counselors who wish to start their own practices must be knowledgeable about taxes and business licenses, and about the various forms of businesses including sole proprietorships, partnerships, and corporations.
- Private practitioners must set fees that are reasonable by community standards.
- Counselors must understand the appropriate and inappropriate uses of a sliding scale fee.
- Counselors should collect payment at the time they render their services.
- Counselors in private practice need the services of attorneys and accountants to assist them in managing their businesses.
- It is vitally important that counselors carry adequate professional liability insurance.
- Private practice is not for every counselor. The risks and benefits must be carefully weighed before a decision to enter private practice is made.

Most individuals today have some type of health insurance that is paid for or subsidized by their employers or by the government. There are several types of health insurance plans that raise complex issues for counselors who wish to become approved providers of mental health services. Key points regarding health insurance include the following:

- Each state in the United States has different laws that govern which health care plan contracts may be sold in that state.
- There are a number of types of health care plans, including HMOs, PPOs, and traditional indemnity plans.
- Managed care has been a controversial development that has had a significant impact on mental health care services.
- With some perseverance, counselors can often become providers for managed care companies.
- Ethical and legal issues raised by managed care and other types of health plans include maintaining client privacy, rendering appropriate diagnoses, receiving payment for services, continuing treatment after benefits end and the problems caused by denial of services, and avoiding insurance fraud.

Issues in Counselor Education

In this chapter and the next chapter, we will explore some of the complex issues that arise in counselor training, supervision, and consultation. All three of these functions involve relationships that are tripartite; that is, they involve at least three parties. Professionals who serve as counselor educators, supervisors, or consultants share common ethical and legal concerns in that they are responsible for the welfare of counseling clients, but in an indirect fashion. These professionals have obligations to graduate students, supervisees, and consultees. At the same time, they are responsible to the clients who are being served by those they train and supervise and with whom they consult. These multiple responsibilities can complicate ethical, legal, and professional decision making.

This chapter focuses on issues in counselor education. In Chapter 13, we will consider issues in supervision and consultation that are in many respects similar to considerations in counselor training but take on different meanings according to the context in which they arise.

COUNSELOR EDUCATION PROGRAMS

Informed Consent

Just as clients have the right to know what they are getting into when they come for counseling, students have the right to know what will be expected of them before they choose to enter a graduate program in counseling. In keeping with the spirit of informed consent, prospective students need to be provided with enough information to enable them to make wise choices about their graduate studies.

In the ACA *Code of Ethics,* an entire section is devoted to teaching, training, and supervision (Section F). Standard F.2.a. lists quite explicitly the information that must be provided to prospective students before they enter a program. This information includes the following:

- the type and level of skill acquisition required for successful completion of the training
- subject matter that will be covered
- basis for evaluation
- training components that encourage self-growth or self-disclosure as part of the training process

- the type of supervision settings and requirements of the sites for clinical field experiences
- student and supervisee evaluation and dismissal policies and procedures
- up-to-date employment prospects for graduates

It is evident that prospective students can expect to receive an orientation to program expectations, skills development, evaluation criteria and procedures, and their potential for employment as counselors after they graduate. Application materials given to applicants should be thorough and current.

You learned in Chapter 3 that informed consent is a legal as well as an ethical matter. The law of informed consent requires that individuals be properly "informed" before their "consent" is valid. Before graduate students can appropriately agree to enter a program into which they have been accepted, and subsequently meet the program's requirements for graduation, they must be informed of all of the requirements. In addition, they must be presented in sufficient detail to allow entering students to fully understand their obligations.

When program requirements are modified in a substantial manner, or graduation requirements are increased, current students should be exempted from the changes. Entering students must be informed of the changes as well.

Admissions

Counselor educators want to admit individuals into training programs who are likely to succeed at developing the knowledge, skills, and characteristics needed to become effective counselors. Academic ability is one important criterion, and relevant work experience might also be considered. Some graduate programs list minimum criteria for admission, which might include a minimum Graduate Record Examination (GRE) score or Miller Analogy Test (MAT) score, a minimum undergraduate or graduate grade point average (GPA), or a minimum number of years of work experience. From a legal perspective, graduate programs should indicate that preference is given to applicants who meet the criteria. They should not publish that the minimum criteria are absolute, unless they plan to apply the requirements without any exceptions. Generally, courts will defer to educators in making admissions decisions if the educators have not discriminated against a protected category of students.

Which prospective students are in these protected categories? Counselor education programs are prohibited from negatively discriminating against any category of students that is protected by the U.S. Constitution or federal statutes and their implementing regulations. These categories include race, sex, disability, age, residence, and alien status (Kaplin & Lee, 1995). Programs can give special consideration to applicants whose characteristics are underrepresented in the program or in the profession of counseling. Affirmative action is an attempt to consider how past discrimination may have negatively affected a category of individuals and to give them special consideration when they apply to a graduate program. Although it appears that the government has the right to refuse to implement affirmative action programs, universities still may apply affirmative action principles to their admissions process if they choose to do so [*Bakke v. Regents of the University of California* (1978); *DeFunis v. Odegaard* (1973/1973/1974); *DeRonde v. Regents of the University of California* (1981); *McDonald v. Hogness* (1979)].

Nondiscrimination is an ethical as well as a legal consideration. Counselor educators have an ethical responsibility to ensure that counselor education programs reflect the cultural diversity of our society. According to Standard F.2.i. of the ACA *Code of Ethics,* counselor educators need to be responsive to their program's recruitment needs for training students with diverse backgrounds and special needs.

Demonstrated academic ability and nondiscrimination against protected categories of applicants usually are relatively straightforward criteria to apply. Admissions decisions become more difficult when we consider that learning to be a counselor involves more than mastery of academic content. Counselor educators must attempt to ensure that students have the emotional stability and temperament to succeed as counselors (Welfel, 1998). As we noted in an earlier chapter on competence, it is possible for a student to have strong intellectual abilities and still not possess the personal and interpersonal characteristics to be an effective counselor. The personality of the counselor is at least as important as knowledge and skills (Cavanagh, 1982; Rogers, 1961). Therefore, counselor educators attempt to select students for training programs who possess characteristics that have been shown to be associated with counseling effectiveness, such as empathy, emotional insightfulness, cultural sensitivity, and flexibility (Ford, Harris, & Schuerger, 1993; Guy, 1987). As you can imagine, it is difficult for counselor educators to assess whether program applicants have these personal and interpersonal attributes. Many programs attempt to gather some information by requiring applicants to submit letters of reference or a personal statement or essay. The admission process also might include a personal interview.

Admissions decisions for applicants are usually based on a review of several factors. These are considered in relation to the number of individuals the program can accommodate and the credentials of other applicants. Counseling graduate programs should make it clear that they make admissions decisions in this manner. University administrators and judges generally would not substitute their judgment for that of faculty members unless it was clear that an applicant had been unfairly discriminated against or that the faculty had failed to follow procedures that they had established.

Counselor educators must also be careful to adhere to deadlines for application materials to be submitted and to follow any procedures they have established for the admissions process. If exceptions are made for one applicant regarding deadlines or procedures, rejected applicants might claim that they were discriminated against because a similar exception was not made for them.

Curriculum Issues

In Chapter 2, we discussed in some detail the curricular components that a counselor education program must contain in order to be accredited by CACREP. CACREP standards are generally accepted by the profession as a model curriculum for master's level preparation of counselors. Here, we will highlight some of the ethical responsibilities of counselor educators in delivering the curriculum, and explore one of the most ethically sensitive components of training—self-growth experiences.

First, counselor educators must make students aware of the ethical standards of the counseling profession and their responsibilities to the profession (ACA *Code of Ethics,* Standard F.2.d.). In some programs, ethics is taught as a separate course while, in others, it is not. We believe that all programs, whether or not they offer an ethics course, should infuse ethical, legal, and professional issues throughout the curriculum. Students who are just beginning their studies in this area may look at these issues one way. Later, as they encounter a variety of situations during their practicum and internship, their views are likely to evolve.

Second, counselor educators are obligated to provide information about the scientific bases of professional practice and to present varied theoretical positions so that students can make comparisons and develop their own theoretical stances (Standard F.2.f.). Counselor educators have not always agreed on the need to present varied theories in an equitable manner. In the past, some programs espoused a particular orientation, such as behavior therapy or humanistic philosophy. Currently, there is consensus that students need to be exposed to a wide range of viewpoints. We believe it is also important for counselor educators to present not only the long-established, traditional theories, but also alternative positions such as multicultural counseling theory and feminist therapy theory that apply to diverse client populations. Additionally, counselor educators would be remiss if they did not include training in the brief therapies for students who intend to work in managed care environments. Because many counselor educators were not trained in the brief therapies or other new approaches themselves, they have an obligation to seek continuing education to keep current (Glosoff et al., 1999).

Counselor education programs must also integrate academic study and supervised practice. Typically, training programs present students with a graduated series of opportunities to practice the skills they are learning, beginning with an introductory skills or techniques course and progressing through a supervised practicum and internship.

Self-growth experiences in counselor education programs have been the subject of considerable debate, particularly among educators who teach group counseling courses and skills classes in which students practice counseling with each other (Forester-Miller, 1997; Merta, Wolfgang, & McNeil, 1993; Pierce & Baldwin, 1990; Schwab & Neukrug, 1994). The issue is how counselor educators can balance students' rights to privacy against the need to provide effective training that helps students increase their understanding of interpersonal dynamics and their awareness of self and others.

Over the past decade, there seems to have been a shift in thinking about this issue. The previous ACA ethical standards, published in 1988, prohibited professors who had any administrative, supervisory, or evaluative authority over students from offering students self-growth experiences. Additionally, the 1988 standards required counselor education programs to offer students alternatives to self-growth experiences without penalty or prejudice. This set of guidelines, which certainly protected students' privacy rights, allowed for the possibility that a student could go through an entire training program without participating in a self-growth experience.

The current code, adopted in 1995, requires counselor education programs not only to integrate academic studies and supervised practice (F.2.b.), but also seems to acknowledge that self-growth experiences are expected to be a part of counselor training. The current standards caution counselor educators to carefully use their professional judgment when designing and conducting training experiences that require student self-growth or self-disclosure. Informed consent and nonevaluation of self-disclosure are the mechanisms required to protect student rights (Standard F.3.b.). Evaluation must be independent from the student's level of self-disclosure; that is, students cannot be graded on their self-disclosures. Students also must be made aware of the possible ramifications of self-disclosures they make. Students should know, for instance, that if they disclose information that would cause a counselor educator to seriously question their fitness for the profession, the counselor educator has an ethical obligation to follow up on this concern. Counselor educators serve as gatekeepers to the profession. A counselor educator who had strong reservations about a student's ability to provide effective counseling services, and who allowed that student to progress through and graduate from the program, would be doing a disservice both to the student's future clients and to the counseling profession.

To summarize, the current guidelines allow counselor educators to provide students with opportunities to identify and explore personal issues and interpersonal dynamics that are related to their potential effectiveness as counselors. At the same time, they must provide safeguards for students. As Welfel (1998) has aptly stated, the successful inclusion of self-growth experiences in counselor training "depends on adequate informed consent, on a boundary between materials subject to grading and the type or quality of self-disclosure in the experience, and on an agreement that the faculty member acts in all possible ways to respect the dignity of the student" (p. 292).

Evaluation Issues

Evaluation of Skills

Effective counseling requires counselors to apply techniques and behaviors that are accepted as desirable in the professional literature. In addition, they must know when to engage in which behaviors, and how to acknowledge, in the counseling process, the unique personalities of the counselor and the client. Counseling includes scientific principles that are artfully applied; therefore, evaluation of a student's counseling skills requires counselor educators to exercise judgment that is less objective than in tests of academic performance that have scores or numbers.

Counselor educators who teach counseling skills must define effective counseling in specific and concrete terms so that students can become proficient in their skill development. Students who are not performing well in counseling skills classes have a right to know their deficiencies, so they can take steps to improve their performance.

If an evaluation or grade is challenged, counselor educators have to explain to peers, and later perhaps to a judge or jury, the criteria they used to evaluate a student's counseling skills performance. Steps that counselor educators should take to help students understand their requirements in a counseling skills course include the following:

- Indicate the skills to be learned in the course in terms that are as specific and behavioral as possible.
- Give students periodic, specific feedback regarding the development of those skills.
- Develop methods of transferring evaluations into numbers or grades that can be justified.

In other disciplines in which skills must be mastered by students, such as medicine and nursing, courts defer to the judgment of professors, unless established procedures are violated or professors are clearly unfair in rendering their evaluations (*Connelly v. University of Vermont* (1965). In the Connelly case, the judges explained why courts defer to professors on academic matters:

> The reason for this rule is that, in matters of scholarship, the school authorities are uniquely qualified by training and experience to judge the qualifications of a student, and efficiency of instruction depends in no small degree upon the school's faculty's freedom from interference from other noneducational tribunals. It is only when the school authorities abuse this discretion that a court may interfere with their decision to dismiss a student. (p.160.)

Although this particular case was related to an academic dismissal, the same reasoning probably would be used by judges any time a professor's evaluation of a student's academic work was challenged.

Evaluations of Field Experience Performance

Just as evaluating the development of counseling skills can be difficult, evaluating students' performance in their practicum and internship experiences is an area in which evaluations or grades can be challenged. It is important for counselor education programs to have specific and understandable procedures for entering and completing field experiences. Developing practicum and internship sites, communicating with on-site supervisors, and orienting everyone involved is a complex task for counselor educators, yet these responsibilities are clearly delineated in the ACA ethical standards. According to Standard F.2.g., counselor educators must develop clear policies regarding field placement and other clinical experiences, and they must provide clearly stated roles and responsibilities for students, site supervisors, and program supervisors. Counselor educators must also confirm that site supervisors are qualified to provide supervision and are informed of their ethical and professional responsibilities as supervisors.

During field experiences, graduate students are evaluated by a number of professors and on-site supervisors. If a student's performance is evaluated negatively, counselor educators must ensure that the evaluations are fair. To avoid having negative evaluations successfully challenged, counselor educators must follow all the procedures that have been established by the program for field placements.

Retention, Dismissal, and Endorsement

Professional preparation programs such as medicine, nursing, and counseling have a responsibility to society to ensure not only that graduates have the knowledge necessary to practice successfully, but also that they have the ability to apply that knowledge in a manner that leads to effective professional practice. Because mental health professionals address the personal issues of their clients, they must be able to manage their own personal issues so that they do not interfere with those of their clients. In addition, graduates of counseling programs must be able to work cooperatively within agency and institutional settings if they are to be successful practitioners.

Counselor educators share a strong commitment to giving students every possible opportunity to succeed in their studies and to keeping students informed of their progress. As we have seen, the integration of academic and experiential learning places some special burdens on counselor educators. They provide students with "periodic performance appraisal and evaluation feedback throughout the training program" (Standard F.2.c.). It is hoped that students will use this feedback to build on their strengths and to remediate problem areas or deficiencies.

This process does not always work in the desired way, however. Sometimes, even after counselor educators have identified problems and have assisted a student in securing remedial assistance, the student is still unable to demonstrate mastery of the required skills or knowledge. At other times, students may deny the feedback they receive, so that growth and change do not take place. When efforts at remediation fail, counselor educators are obligated to dismiss students from the training program who are unable to provide competent counseling services.

Counselor educators never take lightly a decision to dismiss a student from a training program. The care that is taken in such decisions is reflected in the ethical standards. They state that counselor educators must use ongoing appraisal to become aware of academic and personal limitations of students that might impede performance. When limitations are identified, counselor educators seek professional consultation and document their decisions to refer students for assistance or to dismiss them from the program. Students must be provided with the opportunity to appeal such decisions (Standard F.3.a.). The CACREP also addresses the issue of dismissal of students for nonacademic reasons, requiring that when evaluations indicate that a student is inappropriate for a counseling program faculty "assist in facilitating the student's transition out of the program and, if possible, into a more appropriate area of study" (CACREP, 1994, p. 48).

Counselor educators should develop clear guidelines for reviewing students' performance in nonacademic areas. A U.S. Supreme Court case, *Horowitz v. Board of Curators of the University of Missouri* (1978), has established that professional programs have the right to dismiss students who have excellent academic records but poor performance in applied areas. In this case, a medical student, who had excellent grades on written examinations, was dismissed for deficiencies in the areas of clinical performance, peer and patient relations, and personal hygiene. Because there has been litigation in the area of dismissing students for nonacademic reasons, counseling graduate programs should ask that their policies and procedures be approved by their university attorney before they are implemented.

No hearing is required if a student is dismissed for academic or performance reasons. However, if a student is dismissed for misconduct, a hearing is required. Due process probably requires that a student be informed of inadequacies, and their consequences on academic standing (Kaplin & Lee, 1995). As a result, it is important that faculty members avoid mixing misconduct charges with academic or performance reasons if they discipline or dismiss students (*Horowitz v. Board of Curators of the University of Missouri,* 1978; *Regents of the University of Michigan v. Ewing,* 1985).

Although negative decisions or recommendations can be difficult for counselor educators, they must not endorse a student for employment or for any credential (such as a graduate degree, certification, or licensure) if they believe that student is not qualified (Standard F.1.h.). Remember that counselor educators are gatekeepers to the profession, and they have responsibilities not only to their students, but to the future clients of their students and to the profession as a whole. Consumers' trust in the profession is violated if counselors are not adequately prepared for the challenges of their work (Donigian, 1991; Stadler, 1990).

FACULTY AND STUDENT ISSUES

Faculty Competence

Competence is not an issue that applies only to students. Counselor educators must also be able to provide competent services. The ACA ethical standards require counselor educators to be skilled as teachers and practitioners. They must be knowledgeable regarding the ethical, legal, and regulatory aspects of the profession and they have an obligation to make students aware of their responsibilities. They conduct counselor education programs in an ethical manner and serve as role models for the profession (Standard F.1.a.).

As role models, counselor educators must "practice what they preach," and make ongoing efforts to ensure their own continuing competence. Reading and attending workshops and conferences to stay up to date on developments in the field, working a few hours a week at a counseling agency in the community to keep their skills as practitioners sharp, paying serious attention to student evaluations of their teaching and courses and implementing recommended improvements, and conducting and publishing their own research are just a few of the strategies counselor educators might use to keep themselves on their "growing edge."

Student-Faculty Research Collaboration

Counselor educators are often subject to the same pressures felt by their colleagues in other disciplines when they work in a "publish or perish" environment. These pressures may tempt counselor educators to become overly concerned about the number of their publications and to neglect considerations of quality or their actual contributions to a study (Welfel, 1998). Nonetheless, ethically conscientious counselor educators are careful to avoid exploiting their students who may be eager to contribute to a professor's research study or who may feel honored to be asked to assist. They must give credit to students who contribute to research and scholarly projects in a manner that is in accordance with the students' contributions. Substantial student involvement might deserve coauthorship, while less extensive assistance might merit an acknowledgment (ACA *Code of Ethics,* Standard F.1.d.). To avoid misunderstandings, it is wise for a student and professor who wish to undertake a collaborative research project to carefully work out, in advance, the arrangements regarding their respective contributions, deadlines, and publication credit for the completed work.

In doctoral programs, faculty members often work with students to help them publish material from their dissertations. When an article is substantially based on a student's dissertation or thesis, the ethical standards state that the student is listed as the principal author (Standard G.4.c.).

Personal Relationships Between Counselor Educators and Students

Counselor educators are obligated to clearly define and maintain ethical, professional, and social relationship boundaries with their students (ACA *Code of Ethics,* Standard F.1.b.). They should not seek to meet their personal needs for affiliation or sex through relationships with students. In Chapter 7 we examined issues surrounding dual relationships between counselors and clients. The relationships between counselor educators and students are both similar to and different from the relationships between counselors and clients. Thus, the dual relationship issues in counselor education programs are in some ways similar and in some ways unique. A similarity is that both dyads involve a power differential in an inherently unequal relationship in which one person is seeking a service—counseling or education. Throughout a graduate degree program, and even after a degree is earned, faculty members must evaluate students. Evaluative responsibilities create a power differential. The power of educators goes far beyond grades; counselor educators can provide students with introductions that create networking opportunities, sponsorship to professional associations, opportunities for research experience and publications, and letters of recommendation for scholarships, assistantships, internships, and jobs (Moore, 1997).

Faculty-student relationships are different from counselor-client relationships in some significant ways. Faculty-student relationships are usually characterized by multiple and overlapping roles (Kitchener, 1988). The roles in the relationship between counselor and client are fixed, in that the client never becomes the counselor nor does the counselor become the client. Whether these roles can be shifted after termination of a therapeutic relationship is a subject of debate. Some counselors believe, "once a client, always a client." To assert "once a student, always a student" would be foolish, however. The roles in the educator-student relationship are always in transition as students progress through the program, first as beginning students, next as advanced students and interns, then as graduates, and finally as colleagues and professional peers of their trainers. Students can differ considerably in levels of maturity as well, and this has implications for how faculty relate to them (Biaggio, Paget, & Chenoweth, 1997).

It has been argued that students are in an even more vulnerable position than clients with respect to dual relationships. While clients can terminate their relationships with their counselors, students do not have the same option. Furthermore, students engaged in dual relationships with educators risk not only damage to themselves personally, but also damage to their professional careers (Blevins-Knabe, 1992; Keith-Spiegel & Koocher, 1985).

Relationship boundaries in counselor education are somewhat fluid because good teaching, especially at the graduate level, often involves mentoring and opportunities for faculty and students to interact in professional and social settings such as colloquiums, receptions, and special events (Keith-Spiegel, 1994). Mentoring is typically viewed in the literature as a positive kind of dual relationship that is encouraged in academia because of its potential benefits to students. Nonetheless, even mentoring involves potential risks, such as personal disillusionment with the relationship, professional repercussions when the mentoring relationship falters, and the possible sexualization of the relationship which is particularly associated with the male mentor-female protégée dyad (Gilbert & Rossman, 1992; Haring-Hidore & Paludi, 1989; Kitchener & Harding, 1990; Rosenbach, 1993).

Despite these complicating factors, there are some steps that counselor educators can take to maintain healthy boundaries with students. First, they should avoid accepting close relatives as students (Standard F.1.e.). As Herlihy and Corey (1997) have noted, this restriction could pose problems when counselor educators teach in universities located in rural or isolated areas and have a spouse, or son or daughter, who wants to pursue a degree in counseling. These situations might be resolved through careful planning to ensure that the student takes all courses with other instructors. It might also involve some personal sacrifice such as commuting a significant distance to pursue graduate studies at another university.

In order to maintain healthy boundaries, it is important that counselor educators not become counselors to their students. Standard F. 3.c. spells out faculty responsibilities, stating that counselor educators "do not serve as counselors to students . . . over whom they hold administrative, teaching, or evaluative roles unless this is a brief role associated with a training experience." Although counselor educators should not enter into formal, therapeutic relationships with students, the very nature of counselor training presents many opportunities for professors to get to know students at a personal level. Students may self-disclose personal issues during a live demonstration of counseling, a dyadic practice session in which one student is serving as the counselor and the other as a client, or an experiential component of a group counseling course. This could also happen when a counselor educator is exploring a practicum student's difficulties in working with a particular client, or in courses in which students are encouraged to explore any personal biases, prejudices, or values that might interfere with their ability to counsel effectively. Each of these situations could be considered to fall within the bounds of a "brief role associated with a training experience." Students who engage in self-exploration do so in the belief that their professors will not violate their trust. Thus, counselor educators have a special responsibility to be trustworthy recipients of the knowledge they gain about students' personal lives, and personal and interpersonal struggles. This trustworthiness is as important in the student-educator relationship as it is in the client-counselor relationship.

It is clear that certain kinds of dual relationships are inevitable in counselor training programs. There is no universal agreement regarding how these situations can best be handled. Bowman, Hatley, and Bowman (1995) surveyed students and faculty in counselor education programs and found a wide range of opinions regarding how ethical it was for faculty to hire students to babysit, to have a friendship with a current student, or to socialize with students, among other behaviors. These authors suggested that dual relationships should be evaluated in terms of how the faculty member and student *behave* in the relationship, rather than assuming that the very existence of a dual role is unethical. Welfel (1998) and Lloyd (1992) have expressed similar sentiments, arguing that when faculty take a rigid stance against all forms of dual relationships with students, they are probably overreacting to the risks. They may also be sidestepping their obligation to confront the struggles of making responsible decisions that will foster maximum student development. When counselor educators develop a "dual relationship phobia," no one is well served. Welfel (1998) offers the following thoughtful guidelines for counselor educators:

- Avoid using students as confidants about personal matters or about frustrations with colleagues.
- Ensure that the bulk of time spent with students focuses on professional issues.
- Decline repeated one-on-one social engagements in favor of group events.
- Make mentoring activities available to a variety of students, clarify the parameters of mentoring relationships at the outset, and allow students who want to withdraw from such relationships to do so with dignity and without retribution.
- To receive external feedback, consult with colleagues about issues of relationships with students.

The issue of sexual dual relationships between counselor educators and students merits separate consideration. The ethical standards explicitly forbid counselor educators from engaging in sexual relationships with students or subjecting them to sexual harassment of any kind (Standard F.1.c.). It is illegal as well as unethical; Title IX of the Education Amendments of 1972 prohibits sexual harassment, which occurs when students are pressured by unwanted sexual overtures or acts.

Consensual sexual relationships between adult students and professors are not prohibited by law. Whether such sexual relationships should be allowed has been debated in the professional legal literature (Chamallas, 1988; DeChiara, 1988; Keller, 1988). Those who believe they should be prohibited have argued that because of the differential in power between students and professors, truly consensual sexual relationships could never be possible. Those who argue that such relationships should be allowed have contended that prohibiting such relationships would infringe on constitutional rights of free association, would inappropriately invade the privacy of faculty and students, or would infantilize or disempower adult students by denying them the right to make their own choices. Historically, concern about the harm caused by sexual relationship has been a concern primarily of faculty in counseling and psychology programs, but there is some indication that this concern is spreading. Several universities have implemented policies that forbid all professors and administrators from dating students they teach, mentor, or supervise (James, 1996; Leatherman, 1993).

Lawsuits brought by students against college and university professors because of consensual personal relationships probably would not be successful, because these relationships are not prohibited. However, because teaching counseling skills requires personal reflection on the part of students and requires counselor educators to assess students in personal as well as academic areas, an argument could be made that professor/student personal relationships in counseling programs have more potential for harm than such relationships in other academic disciplines. In addition, the specific sections in the ACA *Code of Ethics* that prohibit personal (Standard F.l.b.) and sexual relationships (Standard F.l.c.) with students would seem to give students a foundation for prevailing in a lawsuit when they believe they have been harmed by a professor who had a personal relationship with them.

The question of whether a sexual relationship between a counselor educator and student can truly be consensual and noncoercive takes on some new dimensions when viewed from an ethical framework. Most of the research studies that have examined faculty-student sexual relationships have focused on psychology students and professors and have found that sexual contact occurs most frequently between male professors and female graduate students. Studies of sexual intimacies between counselor educators and students have also found that the male professor-female student is the predominant dyad, and that these intimacies occur at a prevalence rate of 6–7% (Miller & Larrabee, 1995; Thoreson, Morrow, Frazier, & Kerstner, 1990). Studies also indicate that the attitudes of women who have been involved in these relationships change over time. Although they may have believed that the relationship was truly consensual at the time, in retrospect they view the experiences as more coercive, more of a hindrance to the working relationship, and more damaging to their professional careers (Glaser & Thorpe, 1996; Miller & Larrabee, 1995). These studies challenge the argument that adult students are able to consent freely to such relationships and raise questions about how prepared the students were to deal with the ethics of such intimacies at the time. Gilbert and Scher (1987) view sexual dual relationships as an example of sexism and suggest that these relationships in academia promote a climate of male entitlement that perpetuates the problem.

Biaggio et al. (1997) have suggested guidelines for maintaining ethical relationships between faculty and students. First, the professor's position of power and authority over students needs to be acknowledged, and dual relationships should be carefully monitored. Second, a flexible frame that includes a core set of norms for ethical relationships should be utilized to evaluate dual relationships between faculty and students. Finally, a climate for ethical behavior should be fostered. The importance of an ethical climate cannot be overemphasized. Counselor educators function as role models for the profession. Studies have indicated that dual relationships between educators and students increase the likelihood that students will later judge dual relationships between counselors and clients as being ethical, and thus foster the continued occurrence of unethical behaviors (Moore, 1997; Pope, Levinson, & Schover, 1979; Vasquez, 1988). Students learn about dual relationships not only from explicit ethics education but from their own experiences. Counselor educators have a crucial responsibility to model ethical management of relationships with students, if they hope to foster ethical attitudes and behaviors in students.

Blevins-Knabe (1992) has suggested some questions that are helpful when trying to determine whether a dual relationship between a faculty member and a student is appropriate.

You might ask yourself the following questions when considering having a dual relationship with a counselor educator:

- Has my professor fully discussed with me the potential risks and benefits of our dual relationship? Do we have a clear working agreement?
- What am I learning in this relationship? Am I becoming more competent, or more dependent on a "special" relationship?
- What are my fellow students learning? Are they learning about equitable treatment, or about special privilege?
- Do I have a choice? Do I feel the freedom to refuse requests the professor might make or to withdraw from the relationship without penalty?
- Do I believe the professor has maintained the capacity to evaluate me objectively?

Relationships Between Students

When counselor education programs offer the doctorate degree as well as the master's degree, advanced students frequently are involved in supervising the skills development of beginning students. This practice offers many advantages. When motivated and enthusiastic doctoral students assist with supervision, master's students receive more supervision and high-quality supervision. These doctoral students may have more focused energy and effort to devote to supervision, compared with faculty members who have many other responsibilities. Students learn to give and receive corrective feedback and to manage multiple roles (Remley et al., 1998). At the same time, this practice creates the potential for problematic dual relationships between students. The ACA *Code of Ethics* addresses this concern by requiring counselor educators to take steps to ensure that students placed in supervision roles "do not have personal or adverse relationships with their peers" and that they fully understand their ethical obligations (Standard F.2.e.). Faculty need to carefully supervise the student supervisors to ensure that dual relationship problems between students are avoided when possible and resolved when they do occur.

Responsibilities of Students

Reading this chapter has made you aware that students have many rights. For example, you are entitled, under the law, to due process and freedom from discrimination. The ACA *Code of Ethics* contains numerous standards concerning the duties of counselor educators to ensure that your welfare is safeguarded. Along with your rights come certain responsibilities. According to the ACA *Code of Ethics,* students preparing to become counselors must adhere to the code and have the same obligations to clients as do counselors who have already completed their training (Standard F.3.e.). You must be familiar with codes of ethics; lack of knowledge or misunderstanding of an ethical responsibility is not a defense against a charge of unethical conduct (Standard H.l).

Therefore, it is crucial that you practice ethical behaviors and decision making while you are still a student. Your time as a graduate student can be well spent by developing good professional habits such as carefully handling client records and consulting when you are uncertain about how to deal with a situation. Following are some strategies to enhance the development of your professional identity and learn more about your legal, ethical, and professional responsibilities:

- Join and actively participate in student organizations such as Chi Sigma Iota, if your university has a chapter of this honorary society for counselors, or other campus organizations for counseling students.
- Join professional organizations such as ACA and its divisions that represent your specialty interests, as well as your state and local counseling organizations. Student membership rates are generally much lower than regular dues.
- Attend professional workshops and conferences that deal with ethical, legal, and professional issues.
- Join an Internet list-serve such as COUNSGRADS to learn more about current issues.

SUMMARY AND KEY POINTS

This chapter has explored a number of complex ethical and legal issues that arise in the counselor training process. Counselor educators' ethical and legal responsibilities to students begin before students enter a graduate program and continue even after students graduate. Students have many rights—to give informed consent to enter a program, to expect admissions decisions to be equitable, to receive high-quality training, to be able to count on fair evaluations and opportunities to remediate deficiencies, to receive credit for their contributions to research, and to have appropriate boundaries maintained in their relationships with faculty and peers. With these rights come a number of concomitant responsibilities.

Some of the key points in this chapter include the following:

- Students have the right to know what will be expected of them before they select a graduate program in counseling. Counselor education programs have a responsibility to provide students with enough information to make wise decisions.
- Admissions criteria for counselor education programs typically include demonstrated academic ability as well as more subjective measures. These are designed to assess whether applicants possess personal and interpersonal characteristics associated with the ability to counsel effectively.
- It is illegal to discriminate in admissions decisions against protected categories of applicants. These categories include race, sex, disability, age, residence, and alien status.
- Counselor educators are responsible for making students aware of the ethical standards of the counseling profession. Students have the same obligations to uphold standards for ethical behavior as do counselors who have already completed their training.
- Counselor educators must be competent practitioners and teachers. They must provide students with information about the scientific bases of professional practice and present varied theoretical positions.
- Counselor education programs integrate academic study and supervised practice. Self-growth experiences that involve student self-disclosure are an integral part of the training process. Counselor educators strive to balance students' rights to privacy against the need to provide effective training that helps students increase their understanding of interpersonal dynamics and their awareness of self and others.

- It is difficult to assess the development of a student's counseling skills and to evaluate field experiences. Although evaluation may be subjective, courts defer to professors on academic matters.
- Counselor educators, as gatekeepers to the profession, must ensure that students who are unable to provide competent counseling services are not graduated from the program or endorsed for any professional credential. Counselor educators never take lightly a decision to dismiss a student from a training program, and students are given every opportunity to remediate their deficiencies as well as the opportunity to appeal the decision.
- When students collaborate with faculty on research projects, and when faculty assist students in publishing the students' theses or dissertations, credit is given to each person in accordance with the contributions made.
- Dual relationship issues in counselor training are complex. Faculty-student relationships are characterized by multiple and overlapping roles, and best practice does not require that all dual relationships be avoided but that these relationships be carefully managed. Counselor educators can maintain healthy boundaries with students by declining to accept close relatives as students, by not entering into formal therapeutic relationships with students, by assiduously avoiding sexual harassment and sexual intimacies with students, and by maintaining a thoughtful awareness of their potency as role models for students.

Supervision and Consultation

Before you begin reading about legal, ethical, and professional issues that occur in supervision and consultation, consider how you would answer the questions posed in the following scenarios.

Dr. Jones has been supervising Marla's work as a practicum student. Marla has demonstrated very good skills as a counselor thus far in her first semester of working with real clients. Dr. Jones has just watched one of Marla's sessions from behind the one-way mirror at the practicum clinic and was surprised to see Marla falter midway through the session and continue to give a poor performance. After the session, Dr. Jones sits down with Marla for a supervision session and shares her surprise that Marla's counseling skills in the session had fallen so far short of her usual abilities. Marla responds by bursting into tears and stating that her personal life is falling apart and she is under incredible stress. As Marla's supervisor (not her counselor), what should Dr. Jones do now?

Raymond, a counselor in a mental health center, approaches Allison, another counselor at the center, and asks her to consult with him regarding a client with whom he is having some difficulty. As Raymond describes his work with the client, Allison has a hunch that the client may have borderline personality traits that Raymond has not recognized. She is hesitant to enter into a consultation with him, however, because she knows that clients diagnosed with borderline personality disorder can be difficult to counsel. What if Raymond doesn't do an adequate job in working with this client? If she gives him advice, can she be held accountable?

Supervision has been practiced for as long as counseling and psychotherapy have been in existence. Only in recent years, however, has supervision been given much attention as a process that is distinct from education, counseling, and consultation. The term *supervision* can involve a number of processes, ranging from one counselor having direct control and authority over another to one counselor simply giving input to a colleague involving a specific case. Bernard and Goodyear (1992) define supervision as "an intervention that is provided by a senior member of a profession to a junior member or members of that same profession" (p. 4). Supervision involves multiple roles, including teacher, mentor, coach, evaluator, adviser, and consultant. Supervision also involves multiple responsibilities. Depending on the circumstances, supervisors may be responsible, not only for the welfare of their supervisees, but also in an indirect way for the welfare of the clients served by their supervisees. Additionally, a supervisor may have an obligation to the agency or other setting where the supervised practice occurs to ensure that quality services are provided. Finally, supervisors, like counselor educators, sometimes serve as gatekeepers to the profession.

Consultation, like supervision, involves a tripartite relationship among at least three parties: the consultant, the consultee, and the consultee's client or client system. Consultation has become increasingly common among mental health professionals in community agencies, schools, and other settings (Dinkmeyer, Carlson, & Dinkmeyer, 1994; Dougherty, 1990). Dougherty's (2000) definition of consultation is widely accepted. He describes consultation as

> . . . a process in which a human services professional assists a consultee with a work-related (or caretaking-related) problem with a client system, with the goal of helping both the consultee and the client system in some specified way (p. 9).

Counselors frequently are the recipients of services from consultants, and they often function in the role of consultant themselves. When consulting, they apply their professional expertise to the questions, needs, or concerns of those who have sought their services.

Many of the issues we raised regarding counselor education in Chapter 12 are equally pertinent to supervision and consultation. In this chapter, we discuss them as they apply to the specific triad involved (supervisor-supervisee-client or consultant-consultee-client or client system).

SUPERVISION

The professional literature in mental health supervision recognizes that there are two basic types of supervision for counselors—administrative and clinical (Borders & Leddick, 1987). Administrative supervision occurs when direct-line administrators give direction, or supervision, to counselors who are their employees. Clinical supervision, on the other hand, is the process whereby the work of counselors is reviewed by other mental health professionals, usually with the goal of increasing the counselors' effectiveness.

The purpose of administrative supervision is to ensure that counselors who are employed are performing their jobs appropriately. Administrative supervisors usually have direct control and authority over those who are being supervised. Generally, the purpose of clinical supervision is to help counselors increase their skills and satisfy themselves that they are serving their clients appropriately. Clinical supervisors usually have no direct control and authority over the counselors they supervise, unless they happen to be the counselors' administrative supervisor as well. Counselors who are receiving clinical supervision often are completing field experiences for their graduate program, or post-master's supervised experience for state licensure or national certification. Most of our discussion in this chapter focuses on clinical supervision rather than administrative supervision. Keep in mind, though, that the law treats the relationships differently because the purposes of the two types of supervision generally are quite different. When there is a legal question regarding supervision, the issue of direct control and authority is important.

Fair Evaluation

Fair evaluation in supervision has to do with supervisee rights. Legal due process rights derive from the Fourteenth Amendment to the U.S. Constitution. Supervisees who work in public institutions and those who work in private organizations that have policies stipulating due process rights can expect to be protected from unfair or arbitrary decisions that affect them negatively. According to Bernard and Goodyear (1992), the most blatant violations of supervisees' fair evaluation rights occur when a supervisee is given a negative final evaluation or is dismissed from an internship or job without having been given warning that performance was inadequate along with reasonable opportunity to improve.

What this means for supervisors is that they need to provide supervisees with ongoing feedback, periodic evaluation, and opportunities to correct their deficiencies. When evaluation is negative, the changes that the supervisee needs to make should be communicated in specific, behavioral terms. Bernard and Goodyear (1992) suggest that supervisees should be given a specific description of what constitutes inadequate performance, what behaviors constitute improvement, and what degree of improvement is expected.

Counselors who supervise sometimes create problems because they are uncomfortable with evaluation and avoid giving clear feedback to a supervisee about deficiencies they observe. Supervisees will then be justifiably upset and angry when they receive a negative final evaluation or when the supervisor declines to endorse them for licensure or another professional credential. Supervisors should provide formative as well as summative feedback to supervisees. Evaluation needs to be ongoing and given both orally and in writing.

Informed Consent

Informed consent for supervision must be obtained both from the client and from the supervisee. *Clients* of supervisees need to know that their counselor is working under supervision and to understand what this supervision will mean for them. For instance, will their sessions be observed, or audio- or videotaped? Who will be involved in supervision? Will supervision be conducted by just one person, or will the client's case be discussed with a supervision group? What does this all mean in terms of the client's confidentiality? These questions need to be clearly addressed with clients, and their written consent should be obtained before clients agree to enter into the counseling relationship.

Sometimes counselors will minimize the need for supervision and gloss over the details of the arrangement, in an attempt to make themselves and their clients more comfortable. As a counselor working under supervision, you may be concerned that your clients will not believe you are competent to provide services and may not develop trust and confidence in you. These concerns must not inhibit you from fully informing your clients about supervision, however. If a client expresses reservations about a third party being privy to sensitive information that might be shared, a solution might be to arrange for the client to meet the supervisor face to face and raise any concerns directly with the supervisor.

Just as the supervisee has a responsibility to secure the client's informed consent, the supervisor is obligated to ensure that the *supervisee* understands and consents to the conditions of supervision. Several writers (Borders & Leddick, 1987; Cohen, 1979; McCarthy et al., 1995) have suggested points that should be discussed between the supervisor and supervisee before they enter into a formal working relationship. These points include the following:

- *Purposes of supervision.* The purposes of supervision are varied. The goal of a supervision arrangement could be to foster the supervisee's professional development and protect the welfare of clients while a supervisee is in the process of developing the competence to work independently. Although an important benefit of supervision could be that the supervisee accrues the supervised hours to fulfill requirements for an internship or licensure, simply acquiring a certain number of hours is not the purpose of supervision. When a supervisor and supervisee undertake their relationship with the intent of having the supervisor "sign off" on the required hours, there is little chance that supervision will be a growth-producing experience for the supervisee.

- *The logistics of supervision.* An understanding should be reached regarding how frequently the supervisor and supervisee will meet, where they will meet, and for how long. If the supervisee is under the direct control and authority of the supervisor in a work setting, the supervisee should know how to contact the supervisor, who to contact in case of an emergency, and what to do if the supervisor or the designee is unavailable. Supervisors and supervisees should discuss the various forms of documentation required by licensing boards, or in the case of student interns, by the university and the internship site, and who will be responsible for completing the paperwork.

- *Information about the supervisor.* Supervisors need to know that their supervisors are qualified by training, experience, or credentials to provide them with competent supervision. To help supervisors and supervisees determine whether there are any differences in perspective that might need to be negotiated, supervisors should explain their theoretical orientations and describe their supervisory styles to potential supervisees.

- *Expectations, roles, and responsibilities.* These should be made clear for each party in the relationship. For instance, is the supervisee expected to bring audio- or videotapes to the supervisory sessions, present cases for discussion, or prepare in some other specific way? If the supervisor is charging a fee, what are the arrangements for payment? What is the nature of the supervisory relationship, and how does it differ from a counseling relationship or a consulting relationship? What are the boundaries of the relationship?

- *Evaluation.* It is best practice to explain to supervisees the processes and procedures for evaluating their performance.

- *Ethical and legal practice.* Supervisors should not simply assume that supervisees have been instructed and that they know all they need to know about legal and ethical issues. Supervisors protect themselves and safeguard the welfare of their supervisees and the supervisees' clients when they ascertain at outset of the supervisory relationship areas of ethical and legal practice in which the supervisee may need further instruction or clarification.

Supervision Agreements

Written agreements are recommended for counselor-client relationships, and these agreements are also important for supervisory relationships. Generally, written agreements are not necessary in administrative supervision because such relationships are dictated by the job descriptions of both the supervisor and supervisee. The types of supervisory arrangements in clinical supervision vary substantially among dyads. While one clinical supervisor may require payment for services and weekly audiotapes of sessions, another clinical supervisor may not charge a fee and may prefer to observe sessions. A written agreement can articulate a supervisory relationship in detail to avoid later misunderstandings. It can also serve to formalize the relationship, educate the supervisee regarding the nature of supervision, provide a model of how to approach informed consent with clients, and provide security for both parties by structuring the relationship (McCarthy et al., 1995).

An example of a supervision agreement is included at the end of the chapter. This particular agreement is designed for a licensed counselor to provide supervision for a counselor who is accruing post-master's supervised experience required for licensure. Sections of this agreement could be modified easily to fit a number of other clinical supervision situations. This agreement covers very important understandings between the supervisor and supervisee. Note that the clinical supervisor gives deference to the administrative or on-site supervisor, and that the agreement includes several statements meant to limit the clinical supervisor's responsibilities for the counselor's day-to-day activities.

Supervisor Competence

At the beginning of this chapter, we stated that being a competent practitioner does not necessarily mean that one is also a competent supervisor. In fact, being a skilled counselor is only one prerequisite for competence as a supervisor. It also requires specific training in the knowledge and skills involved in supervision. Licensure boards in some states now require those who supervise candidates to be trained and licensed not only as counselors, but also as supervisors. The NBCC offers a separate supervisory credential.

The ACA *Code of Ethics* (1995) states that "counselors who offer clinical supervision services are adequately prepared in supervision methods and techniques" (Standard F.1.f.). The ACES Standards for Counseling Supervisors (1990) provide a detailed description of the characteristics and competencies of effective supervisors in 11 core areas. Briefly, the standards state that competent supervisors have the following characteristics:

- They are effective counselors themselves.
- They have attitudes and traits consistent with the supervisory role, such as sensitivity to individual differences, motivation and commitment to supervision, and comfort with the authority inherent in the supervisory role.
- They are familiar with and can skillfully apply the ethical, legal, and regulatory dimensions of supervision.
- They understand the professional and personal nature of the supervisory relationship and the impact of supervision on the supervisee.
- They understand the methods and techniques of supervision.
- They appreciate the process of counselor development and how it unfolds in supervision.
- They are skilled in case conceptualization and management.
- They can evaluate a supervisee's counseling performance fairly and accurately and provide feedback to facilitate growth.
- They are knowledgeable about oral and written reporting and recording.
- They have a solid grasp of the rapidly expanding body of theory and research concerning counseling and counselor supervision.

Supervisors must be cognizant of the need for continuing education. Bernard and Goodyear (1992) have commented that, because of "the tremendous influence that supervisors have on future practitioners, it is frightening to consider the supervisor who is not actively engaged in continuing education" (p. 143). Supervisors need to keep current in their own specialty areas and be aware of advances that are being made in the general area of clinical supervision.

Recent literature on supervision has emphasized the importance of recognizing and appreciating cultural diversity in supervision (Bernard & Goodyear, 1992; Leong & Wagner, 1994; Williams & Halgin, 1995). If supervisors are not adequately prepared to deal with diversity, they are likely to inadvertently reinforce the biased attitudes and behaviors of their supervisees. Effective cross-cultural supervisors are sensitive to diversity issues in the client-supervisee and supervisor-supervisee relationships. They understand that their own world views may differ from those of their supervisees.

Supervisees sometimes want to gain experience working in specialty areas or with client populations in which the supervisor has limited training or experience. In these cases, supervisors must decide whether they have the necessary skills to adequate supervise. Supervisors need to be clear about the kinds of cases they would not supervise (such as substance abuse, genetic counseling, or sexual abuse), the kinds of settings that are outside their scope of expertise (e.g., an agency counselor who works with adults not feeling competent to supervise an elementary school counselor), and the kinds of cases they would supervise only when they are working under supervision themselves or in conjunction with a consultant. In fact, because supervision is such a complex and demanding responsibility, supervisors would be wise to have a consultant or consultation group with whom they meet regularly to monitor their performance. The ACES Ethical Guidelines for Supervisors (1993) recommend that supervisors be active participants in peer review and peer supervision procedures (3.03).

Confidentiality Concerns

As a counselor working under supervision, you will have access to sensitive information about clients that must be kept confidential. In some circumstances, this information may be privileged by statute. At the same time, you will be required to share information about your clients with your supervisor. As a general rule, sharing confidential and privileged information with professionals who have a need to know for professional purposes, such as supervision, is acceptable and does not destroy legal privilege (Cleary, 1984). You will need to know how to apply the general principles of confidentiality to your specific situation. If you are working in a community agency, the agency is likely to have policies and regulations regarding release of client information and you must know and abide by these regulations.

What would happen if your site supervisor were to inappropriately disclose confidential or privileged information? Because you may have had no control over who would be your supervisor, you probably would not be held accountable. Nonetheless, you do have a professional and legal responsibility to address concerns you may have regarding an untrustworthy supervisor. This can be extremely difficult, because you are in a vulnerable position. If you are a practicum student or intern in a counselor training program, you should bring your concern to the attention of your university supervisor, who will help you determine how to proceed. If possible, it is best for you to resolve the concern directly with the site supervisor involved. Counselors who have graduated from a training program and are working under supervision toward their licensure should also attempt first to resolve the concern directly with the supervisor. If this approach is not feasible or is unsuccessful, they should consult with their supervisor's administrative supervisor.

Supervisory Relationships

Supervision occurs at multiple levels and involves a number of parties including a client, a counselor/supervisee, and one or more supervisors. Within a counselor training program, both a university supervisor and a site supervisor typically oversee the work of the student who is completing a field-based practicum or internship. An advanced doctoral student who is learning applied supervision might also provide some of the supervision, and this doctoral student supervisor will be supervised as well. When relationships involve clients, a supervisee, a university supervisor, a site supervisor, a supervisor who is a doctoral student, and the supervisor of the doctoral student supervisor, sorting out the roles and responsibilities can be a difficult task.

Supervision also occurs at the post-master's level. The counselor licensure movement has produced another group of supervisors—those who work with licensure applicants (Borders, Cashwell, & Rotter, 1995). Obviously, there are multiple roles and relationships to consider in supervision.

All of the guidelines in the ACA *Code of Ethics* regarding dual relationships between counselor educators and students apply equally to the supervisory relationship. In addition, the ACES has published a set of ethical guidelines for counseling supervisors (ACES, 1993). Boundaries in supervisory relationships must be carefully managed because supervisors have considerable power in the relationship. In their gatekeeping function, they hold the key to the supervisee's entrance into the profession. Their supervisees look to them as models of professional behavior. Additionally, because the supervisory relationship can involve a strong emotional connection, transference and countertransference reactions are common.

Supervision is a complex process that can be further complicated when supervisors have multiple roles with their supervisees, such as teacher, clinical supervisor, and administrative supervisor. In these instances, the ACES guidelines suggest that these roles be divided among several supervisors, if possible (2.09). According to the ACA ethics code, supervisors should not serve as both site supervisor and training program supervisor for a student (Standard F.2.h.).

In more general terms, both the ACA *Code of Ethics* and the ACES guidelines caution supervisors to avoid dual relationships with supervisees that might impair their objectivity and professional judgment. The ACES guidelines add that supervisors should not engage in any form of social contact or interaction that would compromise the supervisor-supervisee relationship (2.10). Although supervisors will probably encounter their supervisees in social settings and community activities, such as workshops or meetings of professional associations, socializing or friendships with supervisees could make it difficult, if not impossible, for the supervisor to make an objective evaluation. As we noted in the previous chapter, counselor educators and supervisors can be tempted to relax the boundaries as students near completion of their training programs. As they make the transition to becoming their supervisors' professional peers, their interactions take on an increasingly collegial tone. Nonetheless, supervisors must remember that their position requires them to evaluate their supervisees and perhaps recommend them for licensure or future employment.

Business relationships between supervisors and supervisees are ill-advised, although they may not be unusual. Slimp and Burian (1994) believe that it is not uncommon for interns in field placements to be hired as staff members' employees in roles ranging from house sitting or babysitting to assisting in research or consulting activities. These authors point out that transference issues, the power differential, and the intern's developmental needs all make it difficult for an intern to resist supervisors' requests for such services. If supervisors are not satisfied with the services, the quality of supervision is likely to be affected, and the supervisor's evaluation is likely to be influenced.

Just as counselor educators should not become counselors to their students, a supervisor should not establish a therapeutic relationship with a supervisee as a substitute for supervision. The ACES guidelines direct supervisors to address personal issues in supervision "only in terms of the impact of these issues on clients and on professional functioning" (2.11). The distinctions between the therapeutic aspects of the supervisor's role and the role of the counselor are not always clear. Supervisors play multiple roles, functioning as teachers, counselors, or consultants to supervisees at various times in the supervisory relationship. Herlihy and Corey (1997) have argued that when supervisors are overly cautious in trying to avoid the counselor role, they may do their supervisees a disservice. Effective supervision includes a focus on the impact of the counselor on the counseling process, and when supervision focuses exclusively on client cases or problem-solving strategies for working with clients, opportunities for supervisee growth may be lost. Research studies have indicated that supervisees value and feel comfortable in sessions that focus on their personal issues (Sumerel & Borders, 1996), that supervisees experience less role conflict when the emotional bond between supervisor and supervisee is strong (Ladany & Friedlander, 1995), and that counselors prefer a supervisor who is collegial and relationship oriented over one who is task oriented (Usher & Borders, 1993). At the same time, a personal-issues focus should not slide beyond appropriate boundaries and become a therapeutic relationship. When supervisors become counselors to their supervisees, these dual relationships model inappropriate behaviors that the supervisees may later perpetuate when they become supervisors themselves (Tyler & Tyler, 1994).

There is a delicate balance to be maintained in the supervisory relationship. In your work as a practicum student or intern, your own unresolved personal issues occasionally may be triggered by a client and this may interfere with your counseling effectiveness. You can expect your supervisor to help you identify what is occurring and to understand the issues involved. Your supervisor might even suggest that you seek counseling to help resolve the issues, but the focus of your supervisory sessions should remain on your work and should not become personal therapy sessions for you.

There is clear consensus in the counseling profession regarding the impropriety of sexual dual relationships between supervisors and their supervisees. Both the ACA *Code of Ethics* and the ACES ethical guidelines state that sexual intimacies between supervisors and supervisees are unethical. Bowman et al., (1995) survey of faculty and graduate students in CACREP-accredited programs included a scenario that depicted a romantic relationship between a practicum student and the professor who was supervising her. All faculty and 99% of students believed this was unethical. Despite this belief system, sexual relationships still do occur in supervision. One survey (Miller & Larrabee, 1995) found that about 6% of female ACES members reported sexual experiences with educators or supervisors during their graduate training. Less than one-third of these encounters, however, were with supervisors.

Although sexual intimacies seem to occur in only a small percentage of relationships between supervisors and supervisees, it is probably much more common for feelings of sexual attraction to develop between them. When this happens, several actions could be taken to resolve the problem. The supervisee could be transferred to a different supervisor, if this could be done without having a negative impact on the supervisee's clients or the supervisee's professional growth. If circumstances prevent a transfer, the supervisory relationship should be carefully documented by both the supervisor and the supervisee. The supervisor should, at a minimum, request regular consultation and obtain a second opinion when evaluating the supervisee's abilities. It would be prudent to involve another supervisor who would monitor the supervisory relationship.

The manner in which issues of sexual attraction are handled by a supervisor can have a potent modeling effect for the supervisee. Feelings of sexual attraction to a client are likely to occur for the first time when counselors are still novices working under supervision. Therefore, supervisors must do more than admonish their supervisees to avoid sexual intimacies with clients. They must create an ethical climate for supervisee self-exploration (Bartell & Rubin, 1990). It is crucial that the supervisor develop a relationship of trust that encourages supervisees to honestly discuss their feelings of sexual attraction to a client without fear of being judged negatively.

Accountability and Responsibility

Supervisors have a number of parties to whom they are directly and indirectly accountable. Although their primary responsibilities are to facilitate the growth of supervisees and to protect clients, they also have a larger scope of responsibility that includes parties who are indirectly involved.

The supervisor is indirectly responsible to the field setting in which the supervisee is working to ensure that clients who are served by the supervisee receive quality care. Community agencies, schools, hospitals, and other settings that accept and provide site supervision to practicum students and interns take on an additional responsibility that requires considerable time and effort. In return, university supervisors feel an obligation to ensure that these students make a positive contribution to the setting and do so in a professional manner.

Supervisors, like counselor educators, serve as gatekeepers to the profession. If supervisee incompetence is not addressed, the counseling program's reputation in the community will suffer, and the counseling profession itself will be diminished. Supervisors must not endorse supervisees for graduation from a training program or for a professional credential if the supervisees are not able to provide effective counseling services. In a broad sense, the supervisor functions to protect future consumers of counseling services. Figure 13-1 depicts the multiple layers of responsibility and accountability of supervisors.

Supervisors are not only accountable for the work of their supervisees in an ethical and professional sense, but they can also be held legally liable for supervisee incompetence. This legal responsibility, which occurs under the principle of vicarious liability, will be discussed next.

Vicarious Liability

The legal principle known as "respondeat superior" or "vicarious liability" holds that individuals who have control and authority over others will be held accountable for their negligence (Christie, Meeks, Pryor, & Sanders, 1997). Generally, an employer will be held accountable for the negligence of an employee who is acting within the scope of employment (*John R. v. Oakland Unified School District,* 1989; *Lisa M. v. Henry Mayo Newhall Memorial Hosp.,* 1995). "Respondeat superior," a Latin term that means "let the master answer," is the basis for an English legal concept known as "master/servant." The

Figure 13-1   Responsibilities of Supervisors

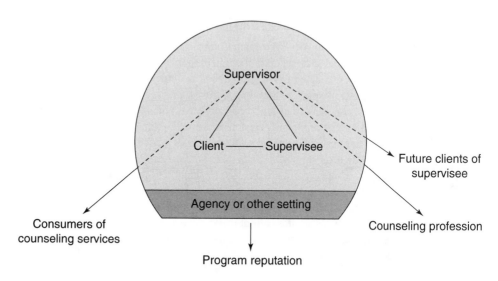

legal reasoning has been that one who has the authority to direct the activities of another (the "master") should be held accountable for the negligence of the person who has submitted to such authority (the "servant"). In the mental health arena, counselors who work for others or who volunteer their services, such as they usually do in an internship, would be the "servants." The administrative supervisor would be the counselor's "master." From a practical standpoint, a person who has been injured by a servant (or employee) has a better chance of being compensated by a master (or employer) because masters tend to have more resources than servants.

The principle of vicarious liability was applied to the mental health professions in the famous Tarasoff case. (See Chapter 4 for a review of the events that occurred in this lawsuit.) In this case, not only was a precedent set for a mental health professional's duty to warn potential victims of a violent client, but liability for the harm that was done was extended to the professional's supervisor.

When a counselor who is under the control and authority of another person harms a third person, giving rise to a lawsuit, the amount of control that the counselor's administrative and clinical supervisors have over the counselor probably will determine the degree to which each supervisor will be held responsible for the counselor's negligence. For example, a counselor intern's on-site supervisor who is physically present each day, assigns work to the intern, and monitors the counselor's activities would most likely be held accountable by a court for the intern's negligence. A court would be less likely to hold a university supervisor responsible who meets weekly for an hour with the intern and discusses issues brought to the supervisor's attention by the intern. Of course, the liability of the supervisors would depend upon the exact facts in the situation and the extent the supervisors knew or should have known about the counselor's negligent acts. Lack of awareness of a supervisee's behaviors that caused harm to a client is not, in itself, an adequate legal defense for a supervisor. Borders and Leddick (1987) stated that

Ironically, if the supervisor is aware of the case, but makes an incorrect judgment regarding the case, the supervisor probably will not be found to be liable. The law does not ask the supervisor to be infallible, but rather, to be involved (p. 55).

Obviously, supervision can be a risky undertaking. Snider (1985) has offered some guidelines for supervisors to help them reduce their likelihood of being named as a codefendant in a malpractice lawsuit. These guidelines offer protection to supervisees as well. First, it is important to maintain a trusting relationship in which supervisees feel comfortable in sharing their doubts and concerns. Second, supervisors need to keep up to date with legal issues that affect supervision and mental health practice in general. Third, supervisors must recognize the need for competent legal advice and ensure that an attorney is available to provide legal support. Finally, both supervisors and supervisees should carry liability insurance.

Supervisors are advised to document their supervisory sessions, not only because of the liability issues involved, but also to improve evaluation and to monitor client care. This documentation should include (a) meeting date and time, (b) a listing of cases discussed, (c) notes regarding client progress, (d) recommendations made to the supervisee, (e) issues to be followed up in future meetings, and (f) a plan for remediating any significant supervisee deficiencies that are identified (Harrar, VandeCreek, & Knapp, 1990; Welfel, 1998).

Supervisor and Supervisee Rights and Responsibilities

It should be evident from your reading thus far that supervision is a serious responsibility that is not undertaken lightly by your supervisor. For the process to facilitate your maximum professional growth, both you and your supervisor must understand your roles and responsibilities and work conscientiously to fulfill them.

You have the right to expect certain behaviors from your supervisor. In accordance with the ACES guidelines (1993), you can expect your supervisor to provide you with regular face-to-face supervision (2.07). If you are a student in a CACREP-accredited training program, you will receive a minimum of one hour per week of individual supervision and one and one-half hours per week of group supervision during your practicum and internship. Your supervisor may require you to bring audio- or videotapes to your supervisory sessions, or may even wish to have direct interaction with clients. Simply reviewing your case notes is not a viable alternative to these direct activities, although it may be a fairly common practice (Navin, Beamish, & Johanson, 1995).

You can expect supervisors to give you their full attention during your agreed-upon supervision time. Your supervisory sessions should be reasonably free from interruptions, and your supervisor should not have taken on an excessive number of supervisees. Although some agencies have policies limiting the number of supervisees for whom their employees may be responsible, not all state licensure boards stipulate a maximum number of supervisees (Welfel, 1998).

You can expect your supervisor to thoroughly explain the supervision process to you and secure your informed consent, to possess competencies in the 11 core areas described earlier in the chapter, to be skilled at managing the boundaries of the supervisory relationship, to provide you with ongoing feedback about your performance, and to safeguard the confidentiality of information exchanged.

For your part, it is important that you are open to receiving feedback and are willing to work to implement suggestions that will help you improve your effectiveness as a counselor. Although you may be hesitant at times to admit your uncertainties, confusion, or lack of knowledge about various aspects of your professional functioning, it is much better that you bring your concerns to your supervisory sessions and ask for assistance. Remember that supervision is a developmental process. Each time you master a new skill or add new knowledge and understanding to your repertoire, you become more competent to one day practice independently.

CONSULTATION

Counselors must assume a variety of roles as they perform their work responsibilities, and each role demands different perspectives, attitudes, and behaviors. The professional role that counselors engage in at any given moment determines their behavior and, in many instances, their responsibilities to the individual with whom they are interacting. Consultant and consultee are two roles that counselors take on regularly.

As we have noted several times, the very best step a counselor can take when faced with a difficult ethical decision or with a legal question is to consult. Consulting with peers and other mental health professionals is best for ethical dilemmas. Consulting with supervisors and attorneys is necessary for legal problems.

Counselors regularly consult with others for the benefit of their clients and to further their knowledge of a particular area of counseling. Counselors use the following consultants: other mental health professionals when making clinical or ethical judgments; other professionals, such as physicians, social workers, nurses, and psychologists, who are also treating their client; family members and friends, for the benefit of clients; administrators in their employment setting, regarding their job responsibilities or when seeking direction in difficult situations; and attorneys, when they have legal questions.

Counselors also find themselves in the role of consultant in a number of situations. Another counselor may be having difficulty making a clinical or ethical decision. Another professional who is treating one of their clients may request a consultation. Or, a client's family member or friend (or teacher in the case of a child client in a school setting) might ask for information about a client. In all of these examples, the consultation takes place between two individuals (a consultant and a consultee) for the benefit of a third person (a client). These consultation relationships are not formalized and generally are limited to a single discussion or a brief series of discussions. We will refer to this type of consultation as *peer consultation*. By contrast, counselors sometimes function as consultants to organizations such as businesses, agencies, or schools. These consultation relationships are usually more long-term and are formalized in some manner, often through a contract. This type of consultation is known as *organizational consultation*.

Both peer and organizational consultations are primarily aimed at work-related concerns as opposed to the consultee's personal problems. However, the consultation relationship may resemble the counseling relationship in that it is a temporary process aimed at helping the consultee or consultee system function more independently.

Accountability

Generally, a consultant does not have power and control over the person who is the recipient of the consultant's advice. Exceptions exist when a consultant is a counselor's boss or clinical supervisor. As explained earlier in the chapter, a supervisor who has control over a counselor's actions probably has some degree of legal liability for the negligence of the counselor.

In most situations, however, consultants do not have control and authority over the person who is receiving the benefit of their consultation. Consultants essentially are giving advice. Once individuals receive advice from a consultant, they are free to accept or ignore the advice they have been given. When consultants have no control over the actions taken by individuals who have received their advice, they cannot be held accountable legally for an individual's negligence. Even if consultants give inaccurate or wrong information or give bad advice, they generally will not be held legally liable for harm caused by it, because they had no control over the person who made the final decision. It is possible, however, that an individual who retains a consultant may have a legal cause of action against a consultant who gives wrong or poor advice based on contract principles.

After you have begun your counseling practice and you need to consult, you should choose consultants carefully with the understanding that you, as the individual who is seeking advice, will be held accountable. You should choose consultants who are knowledgeable, trustworthy, and reputable. When you are serving as a consultant to others, you should listen carefully, apply the information and knowledge that you possess, and offer the best advice possible given the limitations of the information you have regarding the situation.

Consultation Contracts

In organizational consulting and in some other situations, consultants enter into long-term agreements with others to provide advice in a particular manner. A clinical supervisor who provides supervision over a two-year period for a counselor who is gathering experience for licensure or certification, is a consultant. Just as a supervision agreement is recommended for supervisory relationships, a written contract is recommended for counselors who consult.

The following recommendations have been offered for contracts that are prepared by consultants:

- Clearly specify the work to be completed by the consultant.
- Describe in detail any work products expected from the consultant.
- Establish a time frame for the completion of the work.
- Establish lines of authority and the person to whom the consultant is responsible.
- Describe the compensation plan for the consultant and the method of payment.
- Specify any special agreements or contingency plans agreed upon by the parties (Remley, 1993).

Counselors who take on consulting roles need to understand the legal principles involved in accountability and contracts. They also want to fulfill those roles in an ethical manner. Unlike counselors who function as supervisors (who have the ACES ethical guidelines to assist them), consultants are at somewhat of a disadvantage. There is no code of ethics specifically for consultants, and the ACA *Code of Ethics* contains only two subsections (B.6 and D.2) that address consultation directly. This paucity of ethical standards, along with the fact that not all counselors are adequately trained in consultation (Brown, 1993; Newman, 1993), raises some cause for concern that counselors may not be well prepared to resolve the ethical dilemmas they encounter when they are functioning as consultants. Writers in the field of consultation (Dougherty, 2000; Newman, 1993) have identified several ethical issues that consultants frequently face. These include (a) the influence of culture and values on the consulting process; (b) consultant competence; (c) consultee rights, including due process and confidentiality; and (d) the consulting relationship.

The Influence of Values and Culture

Consultants, like counselors, must be aware of the ways in which their values influence the process and outcomes of their work. As Newman (1993) has stated, "To ignore or deny the central role of values in the practice of consultation is naive at best, and from an ethical perspective, dangerous" (p. 151). The consultant, consultee, and client or members of the client system all have values formed by their life experiences, and these values will have a mutual influence in the consulting process. Therefore, consultants must possess a reflective understanding of their values and how they influence the process of consultation, and make a commitment not to impose them on consultees (Dougherty, 2000). Additionally, consultants need to understand diverse world views and be aware of differences in reasoning and communication patterns. They need to be aware of how their own culture and gender affect their work as consultants.

Value conflicts may be inevitable in organizational consulting, because the process involves multiple parties who have diverse and often competing interests and priorities. Conflicts can occur in peer consultations as well, particularly when the consultant and consultee have differing world views. For example, Pete, a Native American counselor, has asked Judy, a traditionally trained Anglo counselor, to consult with him regarding a client with whom he is working. Pete believes that the client would be well served by bringing members of the client's family into the counseling process. Judy disagrees, believing that this would diminish the client's autonomy and violate the client's confidentiality. In this case, the consultant and consultee have very different ideas, formed by their world views, regarding how the client can best be helped. Judy is operating from EuroAmerican notions of individualism and autonomy. For Pete, including the client's family would be consistent with the tradition of honoring the wisdom of tribal elders, which is part of his cultural background. Consultants need to be honest with themselves in determining whether they can be objective enough to work with a consultee whose values or world views differ significantly from their own.

Consultant Competence

Competence to provide services is an important ethical issue in consultation, just as it is in counseling and supervision. The ACA *Code of Ethics* cautions counselors to be reasonably certain that they have the necessary competencies and resources for giving the kinds of consulting services needed (Standard D.2.b.). Before they agree to enter into a consultation relationship, they need to assess whether their personal and professional competence is adequate for the task (Dougherty, 2000). When you become an experienced counselor, and are asked to consult with peers, you should ask for a description of the potential consultee's problem and then determine whether you possess the expertise needed to be of assistance. For example, if you have worked for several years in a clinic that specializes in treating individuals with eating disorders, you will probably feel confident that you can serve as a consultant to a high school counselor who is wondering whether one of her student clients suffers from anorexia. By contrast, assume that you are approached by another counselor in the clinic where you work. She tells you that she needs a consultation because she is concerned that one of her teenaged clients' parents might sue her for malpractice. This colleague has a legal problem, and you should refer her to the clinic supervisor.

When counselors are asked to perform organizational consultation, they should present their professional qualifications clearly to avoid misrepresenting themselves. Prior to entering into an agreement to provide services, they should gather enough information to ensure that the organization has the resources to provide the needed assistance (Standard D.2.b.). It is essential that consultants know their own limitations as well, and they should make an appropriate referral when they are unable to provide the requested services. The ability to carefully self-monitor one's own boundaries of competence is particularly critical because so few counselors have received formal training in consultation. Welfel (1998) has stated that counselors tend to make the same mistake regarding competence to consult as they make regarding competence to supervise—they assume that clinical skills are sufficient. She cautions counselors that when they present themselves as skilled consultants, they must be prepared to demonstrate the sources of their knowledge and to be ethically responsible for any harm their interventions might cause. Without a contract, consultants may not be legally responsible for the outcomes of interventions they suggest, but they do have a professional and ethical obligation to carefully consider the implications of actions that may be taken based on their advice.

Safeguarding Consultee and Client Rights

Due to the triadic nature of consultation, the client does not employ the consultant or sometimes even know that a consultant is involved. Welfel (1998) reminds counselors who consult to be attuned to the ramifications of their work for these rather invisible participants. Newman (1993) raises a similar caution, noting that consultants need to be sensitive to the effects of their work on all parties involved and to avoid situations in which their work could be used to the detriment of clients or client systems. Following is an example of such an event.

Jerry was hired by an administrator in a large organization to conduct a series of conflict resolution workshops with an employee group. Part of the agreement was that Jerry would conduct a pre- and post-assessment of the participants' conflict resolution skills, to assess what they had learned. Jerry included the results of these assessments in his final report to the administrator. Later, the administrator used this information as one basis for determining which of the employees would be let go when the organization downsized.

This scenario raises two crucial ethical issues—informed consent and confidentiality. Obviously, Jerry failed to negotiate how his report would be used by the administrator who hired him. The unfortunate outcome could have been avoided if Jerry had adhered to his ethical obligation to develop with his consultee "a clear understanding of problem definition, goals for change, and predicted consequences of interventions. . . ." (ACA *Code of Ethics,* Standard D.2.c.).

Informed consent is an important consultee right that also extends to clients and client systems involved. In peer consultation, informed consent is a relatively straightforward matter. As we have suggested in earlier chapters, it is sound ethical practice for counselors to inform a client that they plan to consult about the client's case, explain their rationale, and obtain consent to proceed.

Informed consent is much more complicated in organizational consulting. Oftentimes, administrators or executives hire consultants and make decisions about the work they want the consultant to do. Employee-clients may have little or no input into this decision and the consultation process will be negatively affected if they feel coerced to participate. Therefore, consultants must be sensitive to the hierarchical nature of organizations and work skillfully with all the parties involved to make consent as informed and voluntary as possible (Welfel, 1998). Consultants will need to discuss the goals and purposes of the consultation, potential benefits and risks, and desired outcomes with those who will be affected by the consultation. Dougherty (2000) suggests that consultants should mentally put themselves in the consultees' position and ask themselves what they would like to know at the outset. Consultants also need to remember that informed consent is an ongoing process, so the issues identified above may need to be revisited periodically.

The ACA *Code of Ethics* (1995) offers these guidelines for protecting confidentiality in consultation: (a) information is discussed for professional purposes only with persons clearly concerned with the case, (b) reports present data that is germane to the purposes of the consultation, (c) every effort is made to protect client identity and avoid undue invasion of privacy, and (d) counselors work to ensure that when they share information with other agencies that serve their clients, those agencies have policies that protect client confidentiality (Standards B.6.a. and B.6.b.). In peer consultations, confidentiality issues are not particularly difficult to manage. It is usually possible for a counselor to consult without revealing the identity of the client who is the subject of the consultation. Even if the consultant were to ascertain the client's identity, the consultant understands the professional obligation to keep information confidential.

In organizational consulting, it is important that those who participate in the process have a clear understanding of the limits of confidentiality. Corey, Corey, and Callanan (1998) describe a situation in which a consultant would have to break confidentiality. In their example, a consultant working in a residential care facility for the elderly is ethically required to report certain incidents in order to protect the residents from abuse. It is hoped that the consultant would have established the limits of confidentiality during contract negotiations.

Managing confidentiality is particularly complicated when consultation is aimed at organizational change (Newman, 1993). If disgruntled employees share information about their boss with the consultant, will the consultant keep their disclosures confidential? Dougherty (2000) suggests that employing the concept of anonymity—sharing the information but protecting its source—might be a useful strategy in such situations. He also suggests that complex questions about confidentiality should be posed at the outset of consultation, consensus on the answers reached, and the consensus publicized.

The Consultation Relationship

Because the consultant-consultee-client relationship is very complex, consultants need to be particularly careful to maintain appropriate boundaries. Dougherty (2000) identifies three issues that relate to consultation relationships: work-related focus, dual relationships, and freedom of choice.

The focus of the consultation relationship should be on work-related problems, not on the personal problems of the consultee. As is the case in supervisory relationships, there is a fine line to be drawn and it can be difficult to distinguish between professional concerns and personal issues. For example, assume you are a school counselor who has been approached by a teacher who wants help in dealing with a difficult student. During the consultation, the teacher says, "You're helping me see that the student's behavior isn't all that much out of line. If I weren't in the midst of a painful divorce, he wouldn't be getting under my skin this way." You would need to be careful to avoid converting the consultation into a counseling relationship that centers on the teacher's personal problems.

Dual relationships in consultation create conflicts of interest as well as role conflicts. The two most common dual roles in consultation are combining the role of consultant with that of counselor or supervisor (Dougherty, 2000). The blurring of boundaries that leads consultants into the counselor role often occurs when a consultant determines that the basis for a work-related concern resides more in the consultee than in the client. In these instances, the consultant should refer the consultee for assistance.

When a consultant has supervisory or administrative experience, it can be easy to incorporate supervision into a consulting relationship. This is inappropriate because consultation is essentially a peer relationship, while supervision involves evaluation and a power differential. Dougherty (2000) notes that the use of supervision in consultation allows the consultant to build an illegitimate power base, creates potential conflicts of interest, and violates the consultation contract. Dual relationships in consultation should be avoided.

Freedom of choice is the final important relationship issue to consider in consultation. Consultees should feel comfortable that they have the freedom to do whatever they choose to do with the consultant's recommendations. Freedom of choice is diminished when a dependency on the consultant is created. The ACA *Code of Ethics* (1995) addresses the consultant's obligation to encourage and cultivate consultee adaptability and growth toward self-direction (Standard D.2.d.). Consultants need to avoid coercing, pressuring, or manipulating consultees into taking actions that the consultant might advocate. Having a clear understanding at the outset about the parameters of the relationship can help prevent later problems caused by blurred boundaries.

SUMMARY AND KEY POINTS

Supervision and consultation are two types of tripartite relationships that involve complex ethical considerations. Legal issues in supervision and consultation have to do primarily with fair evaluation, accountability, and contracts. Supervision is an intervention that an experienced member of a profession provides to a novice member of that profession. Consultation is a process in which a counselor assists a consultee with a work-related problem related to a client or client system.

Key points regarding supervision include the following:

- There are two types of supervision—administrative and clinical—that differ in the amount of control or authority that the supervisor has over the supervisee.
- Supervisors need to be sensitive to the due process rights of their supervisees, especially with respect to the obligation to provide ongoing feedback and evaluation of supervisee performance.
- Informed consent for supervision must be obtained from both the client and the supervisee.
- Points that should be discussed between a supervisor and supervisee before they enter into a working relationship include the purposes of supervision; the logistics

of supervision; information about the supervisor's qualifications and supervisory style; the expectations, roles, and responsibilities of both parties; evaluation; and ethical and legal practice.

- Written supervision agreements are recommended in order to avoid misunderstandings and to articulate the nature of the supervisory relationship.
- The major components of supervisor competence have been described in the ACES Standards for Counseling Supervisors (1990). Supervisors need to possess the competencies described in this document, to be aware of the need for continuing education in supervision, to develop cross-cultural supervision skills, and to self-monitor the boundaries of their competence.
- The requirements to keep client information confidential in counseling relationships apply equally to supervision relationships.
- Boundaries in the supervisory relationship must be managed carefully. Supervisors should not engage in close personal or social relationships with their supervisees, nor should they enter into business relationships with them or establish a counseling relationship as a substitute for supervision. Of course, sexual intimacies between supervisors and supervisees are unethical.
- Supervisors have a large scope of responsibility and a number of parties to whom they are accountable. Under the legal principle of "vicarious liability," to the extent that supervisors have direct control and authority over their supervisees, they may be held liable for their negligence.
- Both the supervisor and the supervisee have certain rights and responsibilities in the relationship. It is crucial that both parties understand these rights and responsibilities in order for supervision to work in facilitating supervisee growth while protecting client welfare.

Counselors frequently take on the roles of consultant and consultee. Two types of consultation discussed in this chapter are peer consultation and organizational consultation. Key points regarding consultation include the following:

- Because consultants generally do not have direct control and authority over those who receive their services, they cannot be held accountable legally for the negligence of the consultee.
- When counselors enter into long-term agreements to provide consultation services, they should negotiate a written contract for the services.
- Consultants need to be aware of the ways in which their values and their cultural backgrounds influence the consulting process and outcomes.
- Counselors need to ensure that they have the needed competencies before they agree to take on a consulting role with a peer or with an organization.
- Consultants must take care to safeguard the informed consent and confidentiality rights of consultees and clients.
- Consultation focuses on work-related problems, not on the personal problems of the consultee. Maintaining this work-related focus, avoiding the dual relationship problems that are created by blending consultation with counseling or supervision, and ensuring consultee freedom of choice are all important consultant obligations.

Research and Publications

This chapter explores ethical and legal issues involved in the scholarly activities of research and publication. If you are a full-time counseling practitioner or a master's level graduate student, you may be thinking that this chapter has only minimal relevance to what you do or intend to do. Generally, counselors think of themselves as consumers of scholarly information rather than as producers of research. They view research and publication as activities that are performed by their professors, by doctoral level graduate students, or by counselors whose employment depends on governmental or private funding sources that demand research to show that their dollars are well spent. You should be aware that current economic and societal trends are challenging these assumptions (Welfel, 1998).

Counselors in schools and agencies are experiencing increased demands for accountability. More and more, counselors are being required to demonstrate that they are making a difference in the lives of children and adults. They are being asked to show that their services are having an effect on societal concerns such as school shootings, teen suicide, school failure and dropping out, unemployment, and the spread of sexually transmitted diseases. Managed care companies are demanding accountability from counselors as well. They are requiring counselors whose services they are reimbursing to demonstrate that their treatments are effective with the clients served. These trends suggest that more counselors will be involved in conducting research and disseminating the results.

CONDUCTING RESEARCH

Research Roles

Perhaps the first question that should be addressed in a discussion of research procedures is this: Who conducts the research and who is responsible for ensuring that it is carried out in an ethical and legally appropriate manner? The APA (1982) has described several roles in research. The first is the *principal investigator* who conceptualizes, designs, and plans the study. If the principal investigator carries out the research alone, of course the ethical and legal responsibilities fall to this one individual. More often, though, the principal investigator has one or more persons who assist in the data collection, statistical analysis, or other components of the research study. In these instances, a second role is that of *research assistant*. In academia, students often play this role when they assist their professors with research. When this is the case, both the principal investigator and the research assistant(s) are responsible for proper behavior, but the principal investigator, as the supervisor, has the ultimate responsibility for any breaches of ethics or law that might occur.

A third role is that of *research supervisor.* This person advises and oversees the research of someone else. In an academic setting, this typically would be a professor who supervises the doctoral dissertation or master's thesis research of a student. These relationships are based on mutual respect and are more co-equal because graduate students are knowledgeable researchers who have been trained in research procedures and in ethics.

A discussion of roles raises the issue of potential dual relationships. Professors who supervise thesis or dissertation research often have other relationships with the students involved. They may be simultaneously supervising students' clinical work in an internship, teaching them in formal courses, mentoring them toward their transition into the world of work, copresenting with them at professional conferences, interacting with them as peers at meetings of local professional organizations, and writing letters of recommendation for their future employment. Most of these roles have an evaluative component, thus giving the professor considerable power over the student who is conducting the research.

Because of this power differential and the resultant potential for exploitation, counselor educators must attend carefully to ethical issues when they involve their students as research subjects or research assistants. Students' participation as research subjects should be voluntary. Certainly, professors should not require students to participate in their research as part of the student's grade or evaluation. Beyond that minimal requirement, they also must realize that students can feel pressured or even coerced to serve as subjects for professors' research.

When students volunteer or are asked to serve as research assistants, a full discussion needs to take place before the students agree to participate. In this discussion, the counselor educator should provide (a) assurance that there will be no penalty to the student who declines to participate, (b) a clarification of expectations regarding who will do which parts of the work, (c) a time line for completion of the various tasks, (d) an agreement about the type of acknowledgment that the student(s) will receive when the research is published, and (e) an agreement about the process that will be followed if any problems or misunderstandings should occur.

Research Design

Research studies must be rigorously and carefully designed. Rosenthal (1994) has argued that poorly designed research is unethical because it wastes the time of the participants and makes people skeptical about the value of participating in research studies. Researchers must remain aware that voluntary research participants are providing a valuable service and should "take reasonable precautions to avoid causing disruptions in subjects' lives" (ACA *Code of Ethics,* Standard G.1.e.).

Even when research is of high quality, experimental design raises some ethical considerations. Some researchers use a control group that does not receive the potential benefits of the treatment being investigated. If a delay in receiving treatment increases subject discomfort, or if the emotional conditions of control group members deteriorate while they are participating in the study, client welfare is at issue. The conundrum is that whether or not the experimental treatment is indeed beneficial cannot be known without conducting the study. One way to reduce risk to control group participants is to compare the experimental treatment with other treatments that are known to be effective, if such an option is available and viable. If the experimental treatment is found to be effective, the researcher has an ethical obligation to offer it to control group participants as soon as possible after the experiment is completed.

Good research design also pays attention to issues of diversity. Researchers should not generalize their results to populations not represented in their sample. If a study's participants were only men, the researcher cannot make generalizations to both genders. If the participants were primarily White and middle-class the researcher must acknowledge the limitations of the study with respect to race, ethnicity, and socioeconomic status. ACA's ethical guidelines note that "counselors are sensitive to diversity and research issues with special populations" (Standard G.1.f.).

Protecting Research Participants from Harm

In every research project that involves human subjects, there is some risk to the participants. Although counseling research rarely poses physical risks, there may be psychological risks because participation can cause discomfort, stress, anxiety, or distress. The ACA ethical standards remind counselors who conduct research that they are responsible for the participants' welfare and must "take reasonable precautions to avoid causing injurious psychological, physical, or social effects" to the participants (Standard G.1.c.). Risks to participants must be minimized to the extent possible. Three ways to accomplish this goal are to (a) ensure that participation is voluntary, (b) secure participants' informed consent, and (c) protect the confidentiality of participants.

Voluntary Participation

Ethical standards encourage researchers to make participation in their research voluntary. There should be no penalty for declining to participate. Involuntary participation should be avoided if possible, but if it is essential to the investigation the researcher must demonstrate that participation will have no harmful effects on subjects (ACA *Code of Ethics,* Standard G.2.c.).

Researchers must be particularly careful to protect the rights of subjects who may not be participating voluntarily or who may be vulnerable to abuse, including prisoners, hospital patients, residents of institutions, or individuals who are not competent to give consent. Children should be given the opportunity to assent to participation, although legally their parents or guardians must give informed consent (Welfel, 1998).

Informed Consent

The ACA ethical standards go into great detail regarding what informed consent for research should entail. Participants have a right to receive a full explanation of the following, in language that they understand.

- The purpose of the research and procedures to be followed. Researchers need to explain to participants what they will be expected to do and how long it will take.
- Any procedures that are experimental or relatively untried.
- Discomforts and risks involved.
- Benefits that might be expected. There are many possible benefits, but basically they can be considered to be external, such as money, or internal, such as learning something new, or making a contribution to science (Wilkinson & McNeil, 1996).

- Appropriate alternative procedures that might be advantageous for subjects.
- Their right to have their questions answered regarding the procedures.
- Any limitations on confidentiality. For example, if a participant showed signs of suicidal ideation, confidentiality concerns would be secondary to concerns for ensuring the person's safety.
- Their freedom to withdraw their consent and discontinue their participation at any time.

A troublesome issue in informed consent is that of concealment or deception. There can be some very good reasons for researchers to withhold certain information from participants. For example, if participants know the goals of the study, their desire to perform in socially desirable and helpful ways can skew the data. Some measure of concealment can often be justified.

Deception is a more difficult matter. Researchers should be cautious about deliberately misinforming participants about the purpose of the study. The ACA guidelines state that counselors do not conduct research involving deception "unless alternative procedures are not feasible and the prospective value of the research justifies the deception." If deception is used, the researcher is obligated to give participants an explanation as soon as possible (Standard G.2.b.). The ethical guidelines for psychologists are even more explicit about deception. They specify that researchers never deceive participants about significant aspects that would affect their willingness to participate, such as physical risks, discomfort, or unpleasant emotional experiences. Additionally, any deception must be explained to participants as early as feasible, preferably at the conclusion of their participation but not later than at the conclusion of the research. During the explanation, the researcher is obligated to try to correct any misperceptions that participants may have (APA *Ethical Principles of Psychologists and Code of Conduct,* 1992, Standards 6.15 and 6.18).

Confidentiality

The third consideration in minimizing risks to research participants is confidentiality. Information obtained about research participants during the course of a study must be kept confidential (ACA *Code of Ethics,* Standard G.2.d.). Researchers can ensure confidentiality in several ways. During data collection or in scoring protocols, a coding system rather than participants' names can be used. Any material collected (such as written reports, test scores, or audiotaped interviews) that includes identifying information about participants must be securely kept in a locked file to which only the investigators and their assistants have access.

When results are reported, participants' names are not used. The ACA *Code of Ethics* requires that the identity of research participants be disguised unless participants have specifically authorized otherwise (Standard G.3.d.). When reporting case studies or other descriptive information about research participants, all identifying details are disguised. Information is never disclosed to a third party without the prior consent of the participant, unless an exception to confidentiality (such as danger to self or others) applies. The bottom line is that people who participate in research studies have a right to expect to have their anonymity protected.

Institutional policies often require researchers to guarantee anonymity to participants when their informed consent is obtained. Once a researcher has guaranteed that a participant's identity will not be revealed, the researcher must take care to avoid disclosure (Wilkinson & McNeil, 1996). If a lawsuit were filed claiming damages for disclosure of a research participant's identity, courts probably would try to determine whether the researcher had made reasonable efforts to ensure anonymity after promising to do so. Careless disclosure of research participants' identities could cause legal problems for those who engage in counseling research.

Welfel (1998) has raised an ethical concern about research that does not involve the actual participation of clients but instead reviews client records. Securing the informed consent of the clients may seem unnecessary because they are not put at risk or inconvenienced, but it would be ethically questionable to proceed on such an assumption. Unless the clients were told when they entered counseling that their records would be utilized in a research study, Welfel believes that the researcher should attempt to contact the clients and request their permission to review the records. If this is not feasible, the counselors who produced the records might eliminate any identifying data from the records before giving the researcher access to them.

Institutional Review Boards

Many of the ethical mandates regarding the protection of research participants are legal requirements as well. The National Research Act of 1974 requires institutions that receive any federal funds to establish committees to review research proposals to ensure that human participants are protected (Maloney, 1984). National Research Act regulations have been developed with specific requirements for researchers (45 Code of Federal Regulations 46). The penalty for violation of the requirements would be removal of federal funds from the institution, which would be devastating for both public and private institutions because almost all receive substantial federal support.

Universities and other research institutions have Institutional Review Boards (IRBs) that approve and oversee research involving human subjects. All investigators connected with an institution must have their research approved by an IRB, also sometimes called a Human Subjects Committee. This applies to graduate students who conduct research as well as to faculty. IRBs, which have considerable power, typically require researchers to submit detailed proposals describing informed consent procedures, the voluntary nature of participation, and the protection of confidentiality of information collected (Welfel, 1998). If the proposals are not judged to be adequate, IRBs will either reject them and prevent them from proceeding, or more commonly, mandate that changes be made. If you plan to conduct research during your graduate studies, your university will have a standard protocol for submitting your proposed research to its IRB. You will need to obtain this protocol, complete it carefully, and have it reviewed by your major professor before you begin your research study. If you are collecting data from more than one source (e.g., students at several universities) you may be required to obtain approval from all of the IRBs. When you apply for approval to conduct a research project, you must guarantee to the IRB that you will take a number of steps to protect human participants. If you fail to do the things you have promised, you could be held legally accountable by the institution and by any participant who was harmed.

Reporting Results

Once researchers have collected and analyzed the data from a study, they have three additional ethical obligations. They need to give feedback to their research participants, report their results honestly and accurately, and make their data available to other researchers who request it.

Feedback to Participants

In research parlance, the process of providing feedback is sometimes called debriefing. Two standards in the ACA *Code of Ethics* address this process. According to Standard G.2.g., counselors must provide participants with full clarification of the nature of the study after the data has been collected. A primary purpose is to clarify any misconceptions that might have developed during participation. This is particularly important when the researcher has withheld information about the purpose of the study out of concern that disclosure would invalidate the results.

If you plan to conduct research, you will need to consider (a) when you will give feedback to your participants, (b) how you will give it, and (c) what you will tell them. In terms of timing, the feedback should be given as soon as is feasible after the data are collected. You may decide to provide it to your participants individually or in groups. You will also need to decide how much information you want to share about such aspects as the research purpose, hypotheses or research questions, the sample, and the contribution you hope the study will make.

A second standard that relates to feedback requires counselors to honor all commitments they make to research participants. Some evidence seems to suggest that providing feedback may be a frequently neglected commitment. McConnell and Kerbs (1993) found that more than 30% of researchers failed to provide the feedback they had promised to their participants. When this happens, not only are the participants left hanging with respect to the particular study, they are likely to be less enthusiastic about participating in future research studies.

Honest and Accurate Reporting of Results

Counselors are responsible for reporting research accurately and in a manner that minimizes the possibility that results will be misleading. They are prohibited from engaging in fraudulent research, distorting or misrepresenting data, or deliberately biasing their results (Standard G.3.b.).

Unfortunately, these practices may not be uncommon (Swenson, 1997). In the academic setting, pressures to "publish or perish" can be strong for assistant professors who are nearing their tenure decisions. Sometimes doctoral students, having become emotionally invested in producing a study with significant results, are tempted to ignore contrary findings or manipulate data to fit their expectations. The push for productivity can also be strong in research environments where continued funding depends on demonstrating that grant funds are being well spent. Miller and Hersen's (1992) book on research fraud cites numerous examples of the kinds of research misconduct that occur when a researcher's self-interest takes precedence over ethical standards.

ACA ethical standards provide some specific guidance regarding the full and accurate reporting of research results. First, counselors cannot ignore findings that run contrary to their hopes or expectations. They must explicitly mention all known variables and conditions that may have affected the outcome of a study or the interpretation of data (Standard G.3.a.). They must also provide a thorough discussion of the limitations of their data and alternative hypotheses (Standard G.3.b.). Finally, they must communicate the results of any research judged to be of professional value, even if it reflects unfavorably on institutions, programs, services, prevailing opinions, or vested interests (Standard G.3.c.).

Cooperating with Other Researchers

The ultimate aim of research in counseling is to improve the practice of the profession. As a body of evidence accumulates about the effectiveness of a counseling process or treatment strategy, it will be more widely applied and more clients will be better served. Replication studies are one vital process through which this goal is accomplished. Thus, counselors have an ethical duty to "make available sufficient original research data to qualified professionals who may wish to replicate the study" (Standard G.3.e.).

What this means for you, as a researcher, is that you have an obligation to keep your raw data for a number of years so that other researchers can have access to it. As Welfel (1998) has pointed out, this is not such an onerous duty now that voluminous data can be stored on computer diskettes. If you receive a request for your data, you would be wise to follow the dictates of the *APA Ethical Principles* (1992), which require you to release the data when "other competent professionals . . . seek to verify the substantive claims through reanalysis and . . . intend to use such data for that purpose, provided that the confidentiality of the participants can be protected and unless legal rights concerning proprietary data preclude their release" (Section 6.25).

PUBLICATIONS

Ethical issues related to publication include giving credit to others for their work and following appropriate procedures for submitting work for publication consideration. Giving credit to others is a legal as well as an ethical issue. Other legal issues such as observing copyright laws, signing contracts, and reporting income derived from research, presentations, or publications are important to counselors who engage in all types of scholarly activities.

Giving Credit to Contributors

Earlier in this chapter we mentioned the pressure to "publish or perish" that can exist among university faculty. This pressure can affect the behavior of professors and can also have a negative impact on their students.

The practice of evaluating professors for tenure, promotion, and merit pay increases based largely on their records of scholarly publications has fostered an atmosphere that is more competitive and self-interested than would be ideal. Sometimes counselor educators who are outstanding teachers are denied tenure for lack of sufficient publications and are forced to leave their university positions, to the dismay of their students and the professors themselves. Others are challenged to uphold their scholarly integrity under reward systems that give more credit for sole authorship than for cooperative research endeavors, for being listed as first author on a publication, and for producing publications in quantity with little consideration for quality. These factors, while they do not excuse inappropriate behavior, probably do contribute to such practices among professors as publishing student work under their own names or usurping first authorship for work that was more the student's than their own.

The ACA *Code of Ethics* addresses these practices in several ways. First, in publishing, counselors must be familiar with and give recognition to previous work on a research topic and give full credit to those who deserve the credit (Standard G.4.a.). Second, they must give credit through "joint authorship, acknowledgment, footnote statements, or other appropriate means to those who have contributed significantly" to their work, in accordance with such contributions (Standard G.4.b.). Third, there are guidelines for determining the order and types of acknowledgment to be given when more than one person has contributed to research. The principal contributor is listed first, while minor technical or professional contributions are acknowledged in notes or introductory statements (Standard G.4.b.). A student is listed as the principal author on an article that is substantially based on the student's dissertation or thesis (Standard G.3.c.). This standard arose because students have sometimes felt taken advantage of by their professors.

It is important for you to be familiar with these guidelines if you are involved or are planning to be involved in research activities during your graduate studies. The professor with whom you are collaborating or whom you are assisting should have a conversation with you before you begin the research endeavor regarding the work you will do and the type of acknowledgment you will receive. If you will be contributing substantially to the project, your professor should discuss with you and any other coauthors the order in which names will be listed, since the first author listed is generally assumed to have contributed the most to a collaborative project, and the last author listed is assumed to have contributed the least. The order of names should be open to negotiation throughout the project and all authors must be in agreement by the time the product is published. If your professor does not offer to have a discussion with you about these matters, you should feel free to request it.

We turn now to the legal arena as it applies to the issue of giving credit to others. One source of litigation involves conflicts among multiple authors of scholarly work. Because individuals legally own the ideas that are reflected in written materials, multiple authors may argue over who owns which ideas.

Counselors who contribute to a scholarly work have legal rights regarding that work. When more than one person is involved, each author has some independent legal rights and some legal rights that require full agreement of all the involved authors (Leaffer, 1989). Each joint author has the full right to use the work or to allow others to reproduce it. However, agreement among all the joint authors is required to grant exclusive rights to the work or to transfer ownership rights of the work to a nonauthor. Authors must agree on an equitable manner of sharing income derived from the product as well.

Financial compensation for written works usually occurs in conjunction with a contract signed by the author(s) and a publisher. The terms of such contracts vary substantially and should always specify the amount of compensation that will be paid to each author individually.

Problems occur in multiple authorship of scholarly works when counselors do not discuss issues such as percentage of ownership, order of listing of author names, and other joint authorship matters. If one of the authors believes that he or she has not received adequate recognition or financial compensation, the individual may have legal ownership rights that could be pursued.

Submitting Work for Publication Consideration

The primary ethical standard regarding the process of submitting work for publication has to do with duplicate submission. Counselors must submit their manuscripts for publication consideration to only one journal at a time. Counselors who publish in academic areas outside the social sciences may discover that other fields (such as law) allow multiple submissions of a manuscript to several refereed journals at one time. The social sciences rule requiring submission to only one journal at a time can be frustrating for authors, because the time that lapses between the original submission and the publication of a manuscript can be lengthy. There is always concern that the material will be outdated by the time it is published or that someone else may publish something similar in the interim. There is no alternative to this system, however.

If you conduct research with your professors, you will experience the frustrations of "the waiting game." It is likely that you will need to rewrite and resubmit your manuscript, maybe more than once. Or, it may be rejected by the first journal to which you have submitted it. You and your professor will then need to rewrite it and submit it to another journal. This process takes many months, at best, and can take years. Patience is a necessary virtue if you intend to be active in conducting and publishing research.

Copyright Laws

Counselors involved in research, presentations, or publishing need to be aware of basic legal principles involving copyright. Essentially, a copyright acknowledges legally that individuals "own" ideas once they have created them.

Authors of original written materials have a copyright immediately when the documents are produced (General Revision of the Copyright Law). Materials do not have to be registered with the U.S. Copyright Office to be protected from infringement. However, individuals who do register their materials might qualify for an award of attorney's fees and substantial statutory damages if someone "steals" their ideas (Patry, 1986).

Authors who wish to announce that they are protective of their work usually insert at the end of the document either the symbol © or the letters, "Copr.," followed by the year of first publication, with the author's name listed underneath (Carroll, 1994). This © symbol indicates that authors are aware that their work is protected legally, but does not necessarily indicate that the work has been registered (Henn, 1991).

Most written materials are legally protected from the time they are created and continue to be protected until 50 years after the author's death. In the case of multiple authors, the copyright lasts until 50 years after the death of the last author. Copyright protection of tests, corporate products, or anonymous works lasts for 75 years from the date of first publication or 100 years from its date of creation, whichever date expires first.

When authors publish their work in a book or journal, they often assign or transfer their copyright to the publisher. As a result, a publisher, rather than the authors themselves, may own a copyright to a particular written work. The fact that a publication may no longer be available for purchase, or may be "out of print," does not affect the author's or publisher's legal copyright protection. Permission to reproduce the work must still be obtained from the copyright owner.

Some publishers have become rather aggressive in protecting their copyrighted materials. Publishers sell the materials they produce for a profit, so they are naturally concerned when individuals duplicate their published materials and they lose income as a result. Cases against businesses that duplicate materials (Henn, 1991) have demonstrated that some publishers will bring lawsuits to protect their copyrighted materials.

Counselors who are involved in scholarly activities generally do not register their written materials with the U.S. Copyright Office because of the time and expense involved.

However, when you produce materials that are unique, have a potential for a high commercial value, or might be susceptible to being illegally duplicated, you may wish to consider registering them.

Counselors also must ensure that they do not infringe on the legal rights of others by duplicating protected materials without permission. Before duplicating any material, you should obtain permission from the copyright owner, either the author or the publisher (Johnson & Roark, 1996). Most duplicating businesses, university printing operations, and publishers are familiar with the process of obtaining permission to duplicate copyrighted materials.

Contracts

Counselors who engage in scholarly activities sometimes enter into contracts with publishers, entities that fund research projects, or organizations that pay for presentations. Generally, when there are no financial dealings involved, such as pay, honoraria, or reimbursement of expenses, no contract is signed by the parties. When counselors benefit in some way financially from the scholarly activity in which they are engaged, a contract often is signed by all of the parties involved. Letters of agreement that are signed by two parties usually are legal contracts as well.

The legal assumption made when a contract is signed by two or more parties is that the written contract represents an agreement reached among the individuals involved after they have carefully considered all the options and after open negotiations have occurred. Another important assumption regarding contracts is that the written document covers all the issues that were important to the parties. These two assumptions generally are not true when counselors sign contracts related to their scholarly work, and this can cause problems for counselors at a later time.

The reality is that counselors generally sign, without questioning, contracts that are presented to them by the entities with whom they will be working. Most entities that contract with counselors for services use preprinted contract forms that usually have been prepared by the attorneys representing the entities. They are the result of years of experience in contracting with authors, presenters, and researchers. Specific terms are filled on blank lines. Attorneys who prepare contract forms naturally include terms that are favorable to their clients. As a result, such contract forms protect the rights of the entities who are buying the counselors' services, but do not favor the counselors who will be signing them.

A further reality is that most counselors who produce scholarly works and who contract with entities for their services do not believe they have the financial resources to have contracts reviewed by their own attorneys. In addition, counselors may not have a favorable position in the negotiations process. The entities contracting with them can often go to other counselors for the same services if they cause problems in the negotiations process. These entities may be unwilling to alter their contract form for one individual.

The result is that most counselors engaged in writing, presenting, or conducting research usually sign the contract presented to them and hope for the best. Sometimes the only area that can be successfully negotiated with preprinted contracts is the amount of compensation or reimbursement. Most counselors sign very few contracts and have neither the position nor resources to do anything more than read contracts presented to them, ask for clarification of terms they do not understand, negotiate basic financial matters, and finally sign them.

Of course, counselors who have unique credentials or talents have more negotiating power and can be more aggressive in the contract negotiations process. If substantial compensation is involved or if the publications could have a significant impact on their careers, they probably should hire an attorney to either negotiate contracts for them or at least advise them as they negotiate contracts for themselves. Beren and Bunnin (1983) have developed a guide for authors that includes advice on locating attorneys who specialize in publications law.

When a counselor is employed and the contract for a research project is between the institution and the funding entity, the contract usually is negotiated directly between the institution's representatives and the funding entity. A counselor may apply for external funding, but the contract goes to the counselor's employer.

When counselors receive funding that is external to their institution, it is important that they comply with the terms of their funding contract. The person who applies for a grant and receives the funding usually is responsible for ensuring that the money is spent properly.

The funded project's manager must sign all expenditure authorizations. Occasionally project managers engage in fraudulent practices that can lead to civil and criminal charges against them. Diverting project funds to other purposes, falsifying reimbursement requests, and failing to follow required bidding for service procedures are some of the fraudulent practices that may cause problems.

Reporting Income

When counselors receive any payment for their services, they must report it for income tax purposes. It does not matter whether the payment is called a fee, charge, payment, or even an honorarium. It is considered income by the Internal Revenue Service and must be reported.

In fact, counselors who receive income for their scholarly activities are in "private practice" and should conform to all of the legal requirements for private practices that are discussed in Chapter 11. A city or county business license should be purchased, and professional liability insurance should be secured.

Generally, the type of practice can be listed as "consultant," and counselors are not required to be licensed as mental health professionals by their state to engage in many types of scholarly activities, such as writing, presenting workshops, or conducting research. State laws should be consulted to determine whether a license is required.

SUMMARY AND KEY POINTS

This chapter dealt with ethical and legal considerations that are important for counselors who conduct research and report their findings in scholarly publications. Due to current demands for accountability of counselors in all settings, more counselors than ever before will probably be involved in conducting research and publishing their findings. The process of conducting research involves understanding the various roles that are involved, knowing how to design good studies, and protecting participants from harm. The process of reporting the results entails giving feedback to the participants, reporting honestly and accurately, and cooperating with other researchers. Some key points regarding research include the following:

- The principal investigator conceptualizes, designs, and plans a research study and has the primary responsibility for seeing that ethical and legal requirements are followed.
- Students sometimes serve as research assistants when they help with a professor's research project.
- The professor who supervises the master's thesis or doctoral dissertation of a graduate student is the research supervisor who shares ethical and legal responsibilities with the student investigator.
- Counselor educators must carefully manage dual roles with their students who are involved with them in research projects.
- Poorly designed research is actually unethical because it wastes the time of participants and erodes the esteem in which research is generally held.
- Researchers must attend to the rights of control group members as well as the needs of participants in an experimental group.
- Good research pays attention to issues of cultural diversity.
- Participating in a research study involves some level of risk to human subjects; therefore, they must be protected from harm.
- Ways to protect participants are to ensure that their participation is voluntary, secure their fully informed consent to participate, and protect their confidentiality.
- Proposed research studies must be approved by Institutional Review Boards who are quite rigorous in evaluating research that involves human subjects.
- After a study is completed, researchers must debrief or give feedback to everyone who participated in the study.
- Despite the existence of many pressures to publish, counselors must report the results of their studies with complete honesty and accuracy.
- Researchers are required to keep their raw data and make it available to other researchers who might want to replicate the study.

There are both ethical and legal issues related to publications. One ethical issue is knowing the procedures for submitting one's work for publication. Legal issues include observing copyright laws, signing contracts, and reporting income. The issue of giving credit to others who have contributed to a research study has both ethical and legal dimensions. Some key points regarding publications include the following:

- Pressures to "publish or perish" that exist in academia can make it challenging for counselor educators to uphold their scholarly integrity.
- When publishing research, authors must give credit to all others who have contributed to the study, in accordance with their level of contribution.
- Counselors who produce scholarly works have legal rights regarding those works; when problems occur they are usually due to multiple authorship.
- Counselors must not submit manuscripts for publication consideration to more than one social sciences journal at a time.
- Counselors need to know the basic principles of copyright law.
- Counselors generally are not very adept at understanding contracts, although they may enter into contracts with publishers, entities that fund research, and organizations that pay them for giving presentations.
- All income received for scholarly activities must be reported to the Internal Revenue Service.

Resolving Legal
and Ethical Issues

In Chapter 1, ethical and legal decision making were discussed. A model for ethical decision making was suggested to help you identify key points to consider when you are faced
with an ethical dilemma. Reasoning through a dilemma before taking action to resolve it
can prevent later problems, such as being accused of unethical behavior. This chapter, by
contrast, focuses on how to deal with suspicions or accusations of unethical conduct when
they do occur.

Chapter 1 also presented a process for identifying legal issues when they arise and
ways to request legal advice as an employee or as a counselor in private practice. It is one
thing to understand rationally how to recognize legal issues and obtain legal advice, but it is
quite another thing to feel the distress of dealing with legal issues when they actually arise.

This chapter is aimed at helping you deal with situations that directly involve you in
ethical and legal challenges that come before ethics committees, licensure or certification
boards, and courts of law. After legal and ethical decision making are briefly reviewed, two
kinds of situations are addressed: (a) what to do when you are accused of unethical or illegal behavior, and (b) what to do if you suspect that a professional colleague is behaving unethically or illegally. The chapter concludes by suggesting some guidelines for avoiding
ethical and legal problems and maintaining your professional vitality.

Personal Legal Decision Making

It is impossible for counselors to understand all aspects of the law. As a result, you will
have to rely on the advice of attorneys from time to time as you practice. You must make
every effort to fully explain a situation to your legal advisors and educate them, to the extent possible, regarding the counseling process and the counseling profession. You can then
follow the legal advice you have been given without worrying about whether or not it is
correct. Of course, you should raise questions if you believe you are being given incorrect
advice, but you can rely on the advice you have been given. Lawyers are required to stand
behind the advice they render. You can sue your lawyers if you are harmed as a result of relying on their incorrect advice. D. Gould (1998) represents mental health professionals
when they are sued. He has stated that the best advice he can give to those who are involved in litigation and are trying to protect themselves from attacks is to listen to their
lawyer and do what the lawyer says.

Most legal issues faced by counselors involve acting as witnesses in litigation concerning other people. Unless you are being sued for malpractice or have had a complaint of improper conduct filed against you, it is important to remember that you are not being accused of wrongdoing. Reporting what you know in legal proceedings can be a simple matter if you have been advised to do so by your attorney. It is important to avoid getting emotionally involved in your client's lawsuits or in legal proceedings that affect others. If you lose your objectivity and professional distance, it is easy to get inappropriately involved in legal matters that do not affect you.

Personal Ethical Decision Making

No doubt it has become evident to you, after reading the previous chapters, that ethical questions rarely have a single, clearly correct answer. Oftentimes, counselors' ethical problems are existential dilemmas. The decisions they make when attempting to resolve an ethical issue become the "right" decisions only because they were taken. It is impossible to guarantee in advance that actions, no matter how carefully considered, will have the desired outcome.

Ethical decision making is a complex process, even in the abstract. It can be even more difficult when it is you who must make a decision when you are unsure about the ethics of your behavior or when you suspect that a colleague is behaving unethically. Of course, when you have an ethical question, you should consult with fellow counselors, just as counselors who have a legal question should consult with an attorney. As was noted in the previous section, when a counselor asks an attorney for advice, the attorney becomes responsible for the advice given. In a parallel fashion, sometimes a counselor with an ethical question will have a clinical supervisor to whom the responsibility for decisions can be passed. Often, though, this option will not be available. When you have an ethical question, you can—and should—consult with colleagues, but the consultants are not responsible for your decisions or actions. Although an attorney can help you defend your actions later before an ethics committee or a licensing board, if that becomes necessary, an attorney cannot advise you about an ethical dilemma. You must decide.

RESPONDING TO ACCUSATIONS OF UNETHICAL OR ILLEGAL BEHAVIOR

Individuals react in various ways to accusations of unethical or illegal behavior. Emotions such as fear, panic, and anger are common. It is natural to have a strong reaction, but you must keep your emotions under control so that you can handle the situation effectively. Chauvin and Remley (1996) have recommended that you seek personal support by expressing your emotions regarding the accusation to clinical supervisors, family members, friends, or your personal counselor. However, you should avoid talking to them about the facts of the situation.

Despite the denial, embarrassment, or distress you may feel, you should immediately report any threatened or completed accusation of professional misconduct to your immediate administrative supervisor, if you are employed, and to your personal professional liability insurance carrier. If you fail to notify your insurance company, you could jeopardize the policy's providing legal representation for you or paying off possible judgments. When you tell your supervisor about the accusation, you should ask the supervisor to keep the information confidential and not discuss it with anyone other than the administrative supervisor or the organization's attorney.

In reality, it is not unusual for counselors to be threatened with ethical complaints or malpractice lawsuits. Counselors engage in many activities that could result in ethical claims against them. They must report cases of suspected child or elder abuse, and they often counsel individuals who are embroiled in legal conflicts with others. Sometimes counselors must take actions their clients do not wish them to take, such as informing family members, over a client's objection, if the client is at risk for suicide. As a result, individuals occasionally are angry with counselors and make threats. Some counselors serve as child custody evaluators. There is always a disappointed—and often angry—parent when a child custody recommendation is made to a judge. Some parents who are upset file ethics complaints against child custody evaluators, accusing them of being biased and unfair.

It appears that clients who sue other people may be more inclined to sue their counselors as well.

A counselor who is dealing with an angry client should respond directly to the person making the threat, if that is possible. If you can calm the person down and listen to the concerns, you might be able to resolve the problem immediately or through additional conversations. You should be careful, though, not to admit to wrongdoing and not to say anything you would not want repeated or would not want to repeat yourself under oath at a later time.

If you receive notice from a licensure or certification board or from a professional association ethics committee that you have been accused of unprofessional conduct, you need immediate legal counsel. The professional liability insurance policy offered to members of the ACA provides legal counsel to policy holders who have complaints filed against them.

Licensure boards, professional association ethics committees, and counselor certification boards have adopted procedures for processing complaints against those who are licensed or certified by their boards or who are members of their association. Each set of procedures is different; however, they have many common steps. The general process that boards and committees use in processing complaints is summarized (Chauvin & Remley, 1996):

- Generally, all investigations and the processing of complaints are confidential.
- First, a board will determine whether it has jurisdiction over the counselor against whom the complaint is being made. If the board does not have jurisdiction, they notify the person making the complaint that they do not have jurisdiction and the case is closed. If the individual is licensed or certified by the board (or is an applicant for a license or certification), then the board generally has jurisdiction.
- Once jurisdiction has been established, the board determines whether the counselor may have violated the board's code of ethics, if the allegations against the counselor are true. If the action (or inaction) of the counselor would not have constituted a violation, the case is closed. When the allegation, if true, might be a violation of the board's code of ethics, the board then begins an investigation of the complaint.
- Investigations might range from actions that are as expensive and complicated as sending investigators to talk to witnesses or the accused counselor, to actions as simple as asking written questions of the accuser or the accused.
- Often, if a violation is found, informal negotiations between the board and accused counselor occur. A settlement of the matter may be reached on a voluntary basis that satisfies both parties.

- If a settlement is not offered by the board or is refused by the counselor, a hearing is generally held. Members of the board (or their designees) sit as a jury. A representative of the board prosecutes the case and the accused counselor, or the counselor's representative, defends. Usually witnesses are called to testify, including the accuser.
- After the hearing, the board determines whether the counselor violated the code of ethics. If violations are found, the board may impose sanctions. Sanctions vary but could include a written reprimand only; probation; suspension; or revocation of license, certification, or association membership.
- If the counselor who has been found in violation of the code of ethics is not satisfied with the result, the counselor can appeal. Usually, there are internal appeals in which the board reviews the case again. Once the internal appeals are exhausted, the counselor can sue the board in a court of law if the counselor believes the treatment was unfair.

If you receive official notice that a malpractice lawsuit has been filed against you, of course you need to notify your employer and your professional liability insurance carrier immediately.

An emotional response to being accused of wrongdoing is natural. It may help to keep in mind that many formal complaints and lawsuits filed against mental health professionals are either dismissed or result in a finding in favor of the professional (Anderson & Swanson, 1994). In most formal complaint or lawsuit situations, the individuals being accused wish they had done or said some things differently. This is natural as well. To avoid making mistakes that might be detrimental to your case, Chauvin and Remley (1996) and Herlihy and Corey (1996) have advised that you take the following steps if you are accused or sued:

- Maintain composure and respond at all times in a professional and unemotional manner.
- Notify your employer and professional liability insurance carrier immediately.
- Once you have a lawyer, follow the lawyer's advice precisely.
- Respond carefully to the charges. Remember that the members of the board or committee who will be deciding the outcome of the complaint do not know you and will base their decision only on material they have received. Write your response as deliberately and dispassionately as you can and address each of the specific charges that have been made. For instance, if you have been accused of misapplying a technique, you should submit case notes or other records that show how you deliberated and decided to use the technique, how you were trained to use it, when you consulted about it, and any other steps you took to prevent harm to the client. Do not submit any responses until your attorney has reviewed them.
- Even if you are surprised and hurt that a client or colleague has filed a complaint against you, do not attempt to contact the complainant directly. Doing so could be interpreted as an attempt to coerce or unduly influence the client or colleague (Crawford, 1994).
- Seek emotional support from colleagues, friends, or family members, but focus your interactions on dealing with your emotions. Avoid discussing details of the case except with your attorney.

- Seek professional counseling if being accused results in distress that interferes with your personal or professional functioning.
- If you are guilty of having breached the code of ethics, seek assistance to help you avoid future breaches. This assistance could take the form of professional counseling, continuing education, supervision, or a combination of these resources.

WHEN YOU SUSPECT A COLLEAGUE IS ACTING UNETHICALLY OR ILLEGALLY

Unethical Behavior

In our opinion, the primary purpose of the ACA *Code of Ethics* is to guide our own behavior, not to judge the behavior of others. We cannot turn our heads and ignore unethical behavior on the part of others, however. It is our responsibility to society and to the profession to address in an appropriate manner the behavior of other mental health professionals that appears to be unethical. Generally, mental health professionals have been reluctant to confront the unethical behavior of a colleague. The role of "policeperson" can be very uncomfortable and runs contrary to who we are as counselors and to our commitment to accepting and helping others rather than judging and punishing them. Nonetheless, we must recognize that unless we police our own profession, the courts will step in and do it for us. Even more importantly, Herlihy and Corey (1997) have asserted

> . . . public confidence in a profession is based in large measure on the extent to which the public believes that the profession holds its members accountable to acceptable standards of behavior. A public perception that members of a profession "protect their own," and close ranks to protect an unethical or incompetent practitioner, diminishes the profession. Counseling is a relatively young profession; this presents us with a unique opportunity to deal with unethical behaviors in a way that enhances the trust that our clients and society have invested in us (p. 53).

The ACA *Code of Ethics* states, (in Section H.2.) "When counselors possess reasonable cause that raises doubts as to whether a counselor is acting in an ethical manner, they take appropriate action" (Standard H.2.a.). Two phrases in this standard require careful consideration. First, what is "reasonable cause"? And second, what constitutes "appropriate action"?

In determining whether there is reasonable cause to suspect that a colleague is acting unethically, we caution you against making a rush to judgment. You may hear rumors from colleagues that a fellow mental health professional engages in inappropriate behaviors such as sexually harassing clients or billing insurance companies for services that are not actually provided. While you would be justified in feeling concerned, it would be unwise for you to take on the role of detective and investigate whether the rumors are true. Instead, urge the persons who are telling you the rumors to talk *to* the professional who is supposedly behaving inappropriately rather than talking *about* the individual. At other times, a client might tell you directly about unethical behavior on the part of a former counselor. In these instances, your role can be one of assisting the client to decide whether to take action, if the client has been harmed by the former counselor's behavior. Only when you have direct knowledge of unethical behavior on the part of a fellow mental health professional should you feel obligated to take action.

With respect to what constitutes "appropriate action," the code of ethics provides guidance. According to Standard H.2.d., counselors should "attempt to first resolve the issue informally with the other counselor if feasible, providing that such action does not violate confidentiality rights that may be involved." It is entirely possible that taking this step will resolve the problem. Consider what you might do if you were the counselor in the following scenario.

> Ramona is a counselor educator. At her university, the counseling program is housed within a larger department that includes counseling, educational administration, and school psychology. One day Ramona is visiting an intern at a United Way funded agency. She notices a flyer on the bulletin board that announces that "John Doe, Ph.D., will be forming a counseling group for men who are divorced." John is a colleague in her department at the university. He has a master's degree in counseling but his Ph.D. is in educational administration. She realizes that his advertising himself on the flyer as holding a Ph.D. is a violation of the ACA *Code of Ethics.*

If Ramona were to decide to report John's behavior to their supervisor (such as their department chairperson) or to the ACA Ethics Committee, she would be creating problems—probably unnecessarily—for John and for their ongoing relationship as colleagues. Her first action should be to seek informal resolution by talking directly with John. If she were to talk with him, she might point out that Standard C.4.e. in the ACA ethical standards is of concern. John may reply that he was unaware of this standard and had no idea that his advertisement was a breach of the code. Although it is true that "ignorance is no excuse," Ramona's goal should be to correct the problem, not to punish John for his error. She might talk with him about what he can do to correct the situation. This might include taking down the flyers and printing new ones, being sure to clarify his credentials during the pregroup screening interview with potential group participants, and carefully reading the ACA *Code of Ethics.* If John is willing to do these things, Ramona can consider that the problem has been satisfactorily resolved.

You will find that an informal resolution will not always be possible. The offending colleague may be unwilling to discuss your concern, or you may not be able to raise your concern without violating the confidentiality of an involved party. In that case, you should consult with colleagues who are uninvolved and who will not be able to ascertain the identity of the subject of the consultation. If someone has been harmed or is being harmed by the unethical behavior, and if your consultants agree that you must take action, you will need to go forward. These circumstances will be rare. We suggest that counselors report suspected ethics violations of other counselors to licensure and certification boards, and to association ethics committees only when the following conditions have been met.

- It is impossible to resolve the issue directly with the counselor because of the nature of the circumstances, or because attempts at resolution have been unsuccessful.
- You are certain and have direct knowledge that a serious ethics violation has occurred.
- Colleagues with whom you have consulted agree that a report must be made.
- You are willing to participate in a hearing and testify against the counselor if a hearing is held.
- You are prepared to defend yourself if you have a counterclaim filed against you.

The last two items on the list come as a surprise to many counselors, but are understandable when the ACA Ethics Committee's policies and procedures for dealing with complaints are taken into consideration. The committee accepts only written complaints that are signed by complainants. The committee does not accept anonymous complaints. If you believe you must file a complaint, you should write a letter to the Ethics Committee outlining the nature of the complaint, sign it, and send it in an envelope marked "confidential." If the person against whom you are making the complaint is an ACA member or was a member when the alleged violation took place, the committee will send you a formal complaint that identifies all the ACA ethical standards that might have been violated, if the accusations are true. You will be asked to sign the complaint (after suggesting modifications, if needed) and a release-of-information form. The accused member then will receive copies of the formal complaint and any evidence or documents you have submitted to support your complaint. (For more complete information, see the ACA Ethics Committee Policies and Procedures for Processing Complaints of Ethical Violations contained in Appendix A.)

It is very distressing for counselors to have ethics charges filed against them by professional colleagues. Rarely does an accused counselor simply admit wrongdoing. Instead, the counselor often makes accusations of unprofessional behavior against the accuser. Usually, a long period of time passes while the complaint is being investigated and considered. The aftermath of the filing of an ethics complaint is stressful for both the accused and the accuser.

If you ever decide to file a complaint, you should request formal complaint forms from appropriate entities and follow precisely the instructions for filing the complaints. It is recommended that you consult with an attorney and follow the attorney's advice (Austin et al., 1990; Crawford, 1994). In many instances, depending upon the circumstances and credentials of the counselor being accused, multiple complaints may be appropriate. Complaints may be filed at the same time with all of the following entities:

- all state licensure boards that have licensed the counselor
- all national certification boards that have certified the counselor
- ethics committees that accept complaints of all professional counseling associations in which the counselor holds active membership
- the counselor's employer

Licensure boards, certification boards, and professional associations will tell individuals, who inquire, whether an individual comes under their jurisdiction and whether they accept ethics complaints against members. In the counseling profession, complaints are filed with and processed by national associations rather than with local or state chapters. When local chapters, state branches, regions, and divisions of the ACA receive ethical complaints against members, they refer them to the national ACA Ethics Committee. On the other hand, the National Association of Social Workers and the APA process ethics complaints against members on a local or state level. If an association processes complaints at the local level, information on the proper way to file complaints is available from the association's national office.

Illegal Behavior of Others

Individuals in our society, who know of illegal acts by others, are not violating any laws if they choose not to report such activities. In the same manner, counselors who know of illegal acts of other counselors generally do not have to report those illegal acts. A citizen in our country cannot be charged with a crime for refusing or failing to report the criminal act of another person. However, some illegal acts by counselors would be unethical or might violate state licensure statutes or regulations as well. The section above discusses how to proceed if you believe another counselor is acting unethically.

Counselors might become aware of the following illegal activities by other counselors:

- lying to health care companies so that clients will get reimbursement for the counselors' services
- purposefully not reporting income to the Internal Revenue Service
- engaging in a sexual relationship with a minor
- smoking in a building in which smoking is prohibited
- speeding while driving a car

Obviously, you might decide to report some of these illegal activities even though you are not legally obligated to do so. Some activities might fall into a "gray" area, and you would not even think of reporting others.

Counselors do not have an affirmative duty to report illegal activities of others. However, if they are questioned by police investigators or subpoenaed, they have to answer questions regarding the matter truthfully. Counselors cannot assist individuals who have broken the law if they are attempting to avoid being questioned, arrested, or convicted of a crime they have committed.

Guidelines for Avoiding Problems

No matter how carefully you practice or how conscientious you are as a professional, there is always a possibility that someone will accuse you of unethical or illegal behavior. Guidelines that have been suggested by Chauvin and Remley (1996) for avoiding problem situations follow:

- Restrict your practice of counseling to your areas of competence (Daniluk & Haverkamp, 1993; Gilbert, 1992).
- Never sue clients for unpaid fees (Woody, 1988a). Those who are sued by you may, in turn, complain about your competency. If you avoid allowing clients to run up bills with you, collecting fees from them will never become an issue.
- Utilize a thorough and complete client disclosure statement in your practice (Beamish, Navin, & Davidson, 1994; Hendrick, 1988; Epperson & Lewis, 1987).
- Never guarantee or imply a guarantee of outcomes (Woody, 1988a).
- Establish and maintain firm professional boundaries between you and your clients.
- Always use supervision for your practice, even if it is peer supervision (Remley, et al., 1987).

We suggest and briefly discuss a few additional guidelines:

- Stay connected with your fellow mental health professionals. Attend meetings of professional organizations and continuing education workshops. Join a peer consultation group that meets regularly. Counselors who are isolated from their colleagues are more prone to burnout and to inappropriately trying to meet their own needs through their relationships with clients.

- Monitor your self-disclosures made in counseling relationships. Check to make sure that you are self-disclosing for the benefit of your clients rather than to have your own needs met. This is one important way to avoid a subtle slide into blurred boundaries and inappropriate dual relationships.

- Keep current with developments in law and ethics. A case in point is John, whose inadvertent breach of ethics was described in the scenario presented earlier. He was not aware of a new standard in the most recent revision of the ACA *Code of Ethics*. Laws related to the practice of counseling and ethical standards for the profession are not static. It is vital that you keep abreast of changes in requirements for practice, and advances in knowledge in the field.

- To reiterate advice we have offered many times throughout this book, when in doubt, consult. As we have noted, decisions made in isolation are rarely as sound as those made in consultation with others. Choose your consultants wisely—fellow mental health professionals for ethical questions, and attorneys for legal questions—and follow their advice.

- Continually monitor your own effectiveness as a counselor. You have an ethical duty to do this (ACA Code of Ethics, Standard C.2.d.), as well as a moral responsibility. Recall the discussion of virtue ethics presented in Chapter 1. Virtuous counselors have such an abiding commitment to the ethical values of the profession that they hold themselves accountable even when others do not (Meara et al., 1996).

Taylor (1995) has suggested that the following are keys to professional behavior: (a) authentic caring; (b) willingness to examine our own motivations; (c) willingness to tell the truth to ourselves, our peers, and our clients; and (d) willingness to ask for help and to learn. These seem to us to be excellent touchstones for maintaining an ethically and legally sound counseling practice.

A further suggestion is to take care of your own mental and emotional health. In our view, it is often the most conscientious counselors who fall prey to mental and emotional exhaustion. It may help to keep in mind that sound practice is not about achieving perfection; rather, it is about taking responsibility for one's actions and keeping client welfare foremost (Welfel, 1998). At the same time, we believe that there is an ethic of self-care. As Corey et al. (1998) have stated, a key to retaining your vitality as a person and a professional is to realize that you do not have an unlimited capacity to give without replenishing yourself. Attending to your own wellness is fundamental to your ability to assist your clients in achieving emotional health and wellness.

Counselors must take care of themselves legally as well. Professionals who are sued or accused of wrongdoing are not able to function to their maximum potential. We owe it to our clients to protect ourselves legally as we practice, to seek legal advice when it is needed, and to maintain professional liability insurance. By protecting ourselves legally, we are able to help others as professional counselors.

American Counseling Association
Code of Ethics and Standards of Practice

As Approved by Governing Council, April 1995. Effective July 1, 1995.

PREAMBLE

The American Counseling Association is an educational, scientific and professional organization whose members are dedicated to the enhancement of human development throughout the life span. Association members recognize diversity in our society and embrace a cross-cultural approach in support of the worth, dignity, potential, and uniqueness of each individual.

The specification of a code of ethics enables the association to clarify to current and future members, and to those served by members, the nature of the ethical responsibilities held in common by its members. As the code of ethics of the association, this document establishes principles that define the ethical behavior of association members. All members of the American Counseling Association are required to adhere to the Code of Ethics and the Standards of Practice. The Code of Ethics will serve as the basis for processing ethical complaints initiated against members of the association.

SECTION A: THE COUNSELING RELATIONSHIP

A.1. Client Welfare

a. Primary Responsibility.

The primary responsibility of counselors is to respect the dignity and to promote the welfare of clients.

b. Positive Growth and Development.

Counselors encourage client growth and development in ways that foster the clients' interest and welfare; counselors avoid fostering dependent counseling relationships.

c. Counseling Plans.

Counselors and their clients work jointly in devising integrated, individual counseling plans that offer reasonable promise of success and are consistent with abilities and circumstances of clients. Counselors and clients regularly review counseling plans to ensure their continued viability and effectiveness, respecting clients' freedom of choice. (See A.3.b.)

d. Family Involvement.

Counselors recognize that families are usually important in clients' lives and strive to enlist family understanding and involvement as a positive resource, when appropriate.

e. Career and Employment Needs.

Counselors work with their clients in considering employment in jobs and circumstances that are consistent with the clients' overall abilities, vocational limitations, physical restrictions, general temperament, interest and aptitude patterns, social skills, education, general qualifications, and other relevant characteristics and needs. Counselors neither place nor participate in placing clients in positions that will result in damaging the interest and the welfare of clients, employers, or the public.

A.2. Respecting Diversity

a. Nondiscrimination.

Counselors do not condone or engage in discrimination based on age, color, culture, disability, ethnic group, gender, race, religion, sexual orientation, marital status, or socioeconomic status. (See C.5.a., C.5.b., and D.1.i.)

b. Respecting Differences.

Counselors will actively attempt to understand the diverse cultural backgrounds of the clients with whom they work. This includes, but is not limited to, learning how the counselor's own cultural/ethnic/racial identity impacts her/his values and beliefs about the counseling process. (See E.8. and F.2.i.)

A.3. Client Rights

a. Disclosure to Clients.

When counseling is initiated, and throughout the counseling process as necessary, counselors inform clients of the purposes, goals, techniques, procedures, limitations, potential risks and benefits of services to be performed, and other pertinent information. Counselors take steps to ensure that clients understand the implications of diagnosis, the intended use of tests and reports, fees, and billing arrangements. Clients have the right to expect confidentiality and to be provided with an explanation of its limitations, including supervision and/or treatment team professionals; to obtain clear information about their case records; to participate in the ongoing counseling plans; and to refuse any recommended services and be advised of the consequences of such refusal. (See E.5.a. and G.2.)

b. Freedom of Choice.

Counselors offer clients the freedom to choose whether to enter into a counseling relationship and to determine which professional(s) will provide counseling. Restrictions that limit choices of clients are fully explained. (See A.1.c.)

c. Inability to Give Consent.

When counseling minors or persons unable to give voluntary informed consent, counselors act in these clients' best interests. (See B.3.)

A.4. Clients Served by Others

If a client is receiving services from another mental health professional, counselors, with client consent, inform the professional persons already involved and develop clear agreements to avoid confusion and conflict for the client. (See C.6.c.)

A.5. Personal Needs and Values

a. Personal Needs.

In the counseling relationship, counselors are aware of the intimacy and responsibilities inherent in the counseling relationship, maintain respect for clients, and avoid actions that seek to meet their personal needs at the expense of clients.

b. Personal Values.

Counselors are aware of their own values, attitudes, beliefs, and behaviors and how these apply in a diverse society, and avoid imposing their values on clients. (See C.5.a.)

A.6. Dual Relationships

a. Avoid When Possible.

Counselors are aware of their influential positions with respect to clients, and they avoid exploiting the trust and dependency of clients. Counselors make every effort to avoid dual relationships with clients that could impair professional judgment or increase the risk of harm to clients. (Examples of such relationships include, but are not limited to, familial, social, financial, business, or close personal relationships with clients.) When a dual relationship cannot be avoided, counselors take appropriate professional precautions such as informed consent, consultation, supervision, and documentation to ensure that judgment is not impaired and no exploitation occurs. (See F.1.b.)

b. Superior/Subordinate Relationships.

Counselors do not accept as clients superiors or subordinates with whom they have administrative, supervisory, or evaluative relationships.

A.7. Sexual Intimacies With Clients

a. Current Clients.

Counselors do not have any type of sexual intimacies with clients and do not counsel persons with whom they have had a sexual relationship.

b. Former Clients.

Counselors do not engage in sexual intimacies with former clients within a minimum of two years after terminating the counseling relationship. Counselors who engage in such relationships after two years following termination have the responsibility to thoroughly examine and document that such relations did not have an exploitative nature, based on factors such as duration of counseling, amount of time since counseling, termination circumstances, client's personal history and mental status, adverse impact on the client, and actions by the counselor suggesting a plan to initiate a sexual relationship with the client after termination.

A.8. Multiple Clients

When counselors agree to provide counseling services to two or more persons who have a relationship (such as husband and wife, or parents and children), counselors clarify at the outset which person or persons are clients and the nature of the relationships they will have with each involved person. If it becomes apparent that counselors may be called upon to perform potentially conflicting roles, they clarify, adjust, or withdraw from roles appropriately. (See B.2. and B.4.d.)

A.9. Group Work

a. Screening.

Counselors screen prospective group counseling/therapy participants. To the extent possible, counselors select members whose needs and goals are compatible with goals of the group, who will not impede the group process, and whose well-being will not be jeopardized by the group experience.

b. Protecting Clients.

In a group setting, counselors take reasonable precautions to protect clients from physical or psychological trauma.

A.10. Fees and Bartering

(See D.3.a. and D.3.b.)

a. Advance Understanding.

Counselors clearly explain to clients, prior to entering the counseling relationship, all financial arrangements related to professional services including the use of collection agencies or legal measures for nonpayment. (A.11.c.)

b. Establishing Fees.

In establishing fees for professionals counseling services, counselors consider the financial status of clients and locality. In the event that the established fee structure is inappropriate for a client, assistance is provided in attempting to find comparable services of acceptable cost. (See A.10.d., D.3.a., and D.3.b.)

c. Bartering Discouraged.

Counselors ordinarily refrain from accepting goods or services from clients in return for counseling services because such arrangements create inherent potential for conflicts, exploitation, and distortion of the professional relationship. Counselors may participate in bartering only if the relationship is not exploitive, if the client requests it, if a clear written contract is established, and if such arrangements are an accepted practice among professionals in the community. (See A.6.a.)

d. Pro Bono Service.

Counselors contribute to society by devoting a portion of their professional activity to services for which there is little or no financial return (pro bono).

A.11. Termination and Referral

a. Abandonment Prohibited.

Counselors do not abandon or neglect clients in counseling. Counselors assist in making appropriate arrangements for the continuation of treatment, when necessary, during interruptions such as vacations, and following termination.

b. Inability to Assist Clients.

If counselors determine an inability to be of professional assistance to clients, they avoid entering or immediately terminate a counseling relationship. Counselors are knowledgeable about referral resources and suggest appropriate alternatives. If clients decline the suggested referral, counselors should discontinue the relationship.

c. Appropriate Termination.

Counselors terminate a counseling relationship, securing client agreement when possible, when it is reasonably clear that the client is no longer benefiting, when services are no longer required, when counseling no longer serves the client's needs or interests, when clients do not pay fees charged, or when agency or institution limits do not allow provision of further counseling services. (See A.10.b. and C.2.g.)

A.12. Computer Technology

a. Use of Computers.

When computer applications are used in counseling services, counselors ensure that: (1) the client is intellectually, emotionally, and physically capable of using the computer application; (2) the computer application is appropriate for the needs of the client; (3) the client understands the purpose and operation of the computer applications; and (4) a follow-up of client use of a computer application is provided to correct possible misconceptions, discover inappropriate use, and assess subsequent needs.

b. Explanation of Limitations.

Counselors ensure that clients are provided information as a part of the counseling relationship that adequately explains the limitations of computer technology.

c. Access to Computer Applications.

Counselors provide for equal access to computer applications in counseling services. (See A.2.a.)

SECTION B: CONFIDENTIALITY

B.1. Right to Privacy

a. Respect for Privacy.

Counselors respect their clients' right to privacy and avoid illegal and unwarranted disclosures of confidential information. (See A.3.a. and B.6.a.)

b. Client Waiver.

The right to privacy may be waived by the client or their legally recognized representative.

c. Exceptions.

The general requirement that counselors keep information confidential does not apply when disclosure is required to prevent clear and imminent danger to the client or others or when legal requirements demand that confidential information be revealed. Counselors consult with other professionals when in doubt as to the validity of an exception.

d. Contagious, Fatal Diseases.

A counselor who receives information confirming that a client has a disease commonly known to be both communicable and fatal is justified in disclosing information to an identified third party, who by his or her relationship with the client is at a high risk of contracting the disease. Prior to making a disclosure the counselor should ascertain that the client has not already informed the third party about his or her disease and that the client is not intending to inform the third party in the immediate future. (See B.1.c. and B.1.f.)

e. Court Ordered Disclosure.

When court ordered to release confidential information without a client's permission, counselors request to the court that the disclosure not be required due to potential harm to the client or counseling relationship. (See B.1.c.)

f. Minimal Disclosure.

When circumstances require the disclosure of confidential information, only essential information is revealed. To the extent possible, clients are informed before confidential information is disclosed.

g. Explanation of Limitations.

When counseling is initiated and throughout the counseling process as necessary, counselors inform clients of the limitations of confidentiality and identify foreseeable situations in which confidentiality must be breached. (See G.2.a.)

h. Subordinates.

Counselors make every effort to ensure that privacy and confidentiality of clients are maintained by subordinates including employees, supervisees, clerical assistants, and volunteers. (See B.1.a.)

i. Treatment Teams.

If client treatment will involve a continued review by a treatment team, the client will be informed of the team's existence and composition.

B.2. Groups and Families

a. Group Work.

In group work, counselors clearly define confidentiality and the parameters for the specific group being entered, explain its importance, and discuss the difficulties related to confidentiality involved in group work. The fact that confidentiality cannot be guaranteed is clearly communicated to group members.

b. Family Counseling.

In family counseling, information about one family member cannot be disclosed to another member without permission. Counselors protect the privacy rights of each family member. (See A.8., B.3., and B.4.d.)

B.3. Minor or Incompetent Clients

When counseling clients who are minors or individuals who are unable to give voluntary, informed consent, parents or guardians may be included in the counseling process as appropriate. Counselors act in the best interests of clients and take measures to safeguard confidentiality. (See A.3.c.)

B.4. Records

a. Requirement of Records.

Counselors maintain records necessary for rendering professional services to their clients and as required by laws, regulations, or agency or institution procedures.

b. Confidentiality of Records.

Counselors are responsible for securing the safety and confidentiality of any counseling records they create, maintain, transfer, or destroy whether the records are written, taped, computerized, or stored in any other medium. (See B.1.a.)

c. Permission to Record or Observe.

Counselors obtain permission from clients prior to electronically recording or observing sessions. (See A.3.a.)

d. Client Access.

Counselors recognize that counseling records are kept for the benefit of clients, and therefore provide access to records and copies of records when requested by competent clients, unless the records contain information that may be misleading and detrimental to the client. In situations involving multiple clients, access to records is limited to those parts of records that do not include confidential information related to another client. (See A.8., B.1.a., and B.2.b.)

e. Disclosure or Transfer.

Counselors obtain written permission from clients to disclose or transfer records to legitimate third parties unless exceptions to confidentiality exist as listed in Section B.1. Steps are taken to ensure that receivers of counseling records are sensitive to their confidential nature.

B.5. Research and Training

a. Data Disguise Required.

Use of data derived from counseling relationships for purposes of training, research, or publication is confined to content that is disguised to ensure the anonymity of the individuals involved. (See B.1.g. and G.3.d.)

b. Agreement for Identification.

Identification of a client in a presentation or publication is permissible only when the client has reviewed the material and has agreed to its presentation or publication. (See G.3.d.)

B.6. Consultation

a. Respect for Privacy.

Information obtained in a consulting relationship is discussed for professional purposes only with persons clearly concerned with the case. Written and oral reports present data germane to the purposes of the consultation, and every effort is made to protect client identity and avoid undue invasion of privacy.

b. Cooperating Agencies.

Before sharing information, counselors make efforts to ensure that there are defined policies in other agencies serving the counselor's clients that effectively protect the confidentiality of information.

SECTION C: PROFESSIONAL RESPONSIBILITY

C.1. Standards Knowledge

Counselors have a responsibility to read, understand, and follow the Code of Ethics and the Standards of Practice.

C.2. Professional Competence

a. Boundaries of Competence.

Counselors practice only within the boundaries of their competence, based on their education, training, supervised experience, state and national professional credentials, and appropriate professional experience. Counselors will demonstrate a commitment to gain knowledge, personal awareness, sensitivity, and skills pertinent to working with a diverse client population.

b. New Specialty Areas of Practice.

Counselors practice in specialty areas new to them only after appropriate education, training, and supervised experience.

While developing skills in new specialty areas, counselors take steps to ensure the competence of their work and to protect others from possible harm.

c. Qualified for Employment.

Counselors accept employment only for positions for which they are qualified by education, training, supervised experience, state and national professional credentials, and appropriate professional experience. Counselors hire for professional counseling positions only individuals who are qualified and competent.

d. Monitor Effectiveness.

Counselors continually monitor their effectiveness as professionals and take steps to improve when necessary. Counselors in private practice take reasonable steps to seek out peer supervision to evaluate their efficacy as counselors.

e. Ethical Issues Consultation.

Counselors take reasonable steps to consult with other counselors or related professionals when they have questions regarding their ethical obligations or professional practice. (See H.1)

f. Continuing Education.

Counselors recognize the need for continuing education to maintain a reasonable level of awareness of current scientific and professional information in their fields of activity. They take steps to maintain competence in the skills they use, are open to new procedures, and keep current with the diverse and/or special populations with whom they work.

g. Impairment.

Counselors refrain from offering or accepting professional services when their physical, mental or emotional problems are likely to harm a client or others. They are alert to the signs of impairment, seek assistance for problems, and, if necessary, limit, suspend, or terminate their professional responsibilities. (See A.11.c.)

C.3. Advertising and Soliciting Clients

a. Accurate Advertising.

There are no restrictions on advertising by counselors except those that can be specifically justified to protect the public from deceptive practices. Counselors advertise or represent their services to the public by identifying their credentials in an accurate manner that is not false, misleading, deceptive, or fraudulent. Counselors may only advertise the highest degree earned which is in counseling or a closely related field from a college or university that awarded by one of the regional accrediting bodies recognized by the Council on Postsecondary Accreditation.

b. Testimonials.

Counselors who use testimonials do not solicit them from clients or other persons who, because of their particular circumstances, may be vulnerable to undue influence.

c. Statements by Others.

Counselors make reasonable efforts to ensure that statements made by others about them or the profession of counseling are accurate.

d. Recruiting Through Employment.

Counselors do not use their places of employment or institutional affiliation to recruit or gain clients, supervisees, or consultees for their private practices. (See C.5.e.)

e. Products and Training Advertisements.

Counselors who develop products related to their profession or conduct workshops or training events ensure that the advertisements concerning these products or events are accurate and disclose adequate information for consumers to make informed choices.

f. Promoting to Those Served.

Counselors do not use counseling, teaching, training, or supervisory relationships to promote their products or training events in a manner that is deceptive or would exert undue influence on individuals who may be vulnerable. Counselors may adopt textbooks they have authored for instruction purposes.

g. Professional Association Involvement.

Counselors actively participate in local, state, and national associations that foster the development and improvement of counseling.

C.4. Credentials

a. Credentials Claimed.

Counselors claim or imply only professional credentials possessed and are responsible for correcting any known misrepresentations of their credentials by others. Professional credentials include graduate degrees in counseling or closely related mental health fields, accreditation of graduate programs, national voluntary certifications, government-issued certifications or licenses, ACA professional membership, or any other credential that might indicate to the public specialized knowledge or expertise in counseling.

b. ACA Professional Membership.

ACA professional members may announce to the public their membership status. Regular members may not announce their ACA membership in a manner that might imply they are credentialed counselors.

c. Credential Guidelines.

Counselors follow the guidelines for use of credentials that have been established by the entities that issue the credentials.

d. Misrepresentation of Credentials.

Counselors do not attribute more to their credentials than the credentials represent, and do not imply that other counselors are not qualified because they do not possess certain credentials.

e. Doctoral Degrees From Other Fields.

Counselors who hold a master's degree in counseling or a closely related mental health field, but hold a doctoral degree from other than counseling or a closely related field do not use the title, "Dr." in their practices and do not announce to the public in relation to their practice or status as a counselor that they hold a doctorate.

C.5. Public Responsibility

a. Nondiscrimination.

Counselors do not discriminate against clients, students, or supervisees in a manner that has a negative impact based on their age, color, culture, disability, ethnic group, gender, race, religion, sexual orientation, or socioeconomic status, or for any other reason. (See A.2.a.)

b. Sexual Harassment.

Counselors do not engage in sexual harassment. Sexual harassment is defined as sexual solicitation, physical advances, or verbal or nonverbal conduct that is sexual in nature, that occurs in connection with professional activities or roles, and that either: (1) is unwelcome, is offensive, or creates a hostile workplace environment, and counselors know or are told this; or (2) is sufficiently severe or intense to be perceived as harassment to a reasonable person in the context. Sexual harassment can consist of a single intense or severe act or multiple persistent or pervasive acts.

c. Reports to Third Parties.

Counselors are accurate, honest, and unbiased in reporting their professional activities and judgments to appropriate third parties including courts, health insurance companies, those who are the recipients of evaluation reports, and others. (See B.1.g.)

d. Media Presentations.

When counselors provide advice or comment by means of public lectures, demonstrations, radio or television programs, prere-corded tapes, printed articles, mailed material, or other media, they take reasonable precautions to ensure that (1) the statements are based on appropriate professional counseling literature and practice; (2) the statements are otherwise consistent with the Code of Ethics and the Standards of Practice; and (3) the recipients of the information are not encouraged to infer that a professional counseling relationship has been established. (See C.6.b.)

e. Unjustified Gains.

Counselors do not use their professional positions to seek or receive unjustified personal gains, sexual favors, unfair advantage, or unearned goods or services. (See C.3.d.)

C.6. Responsibility to Other Professionals

a. Different Approaches.

Counselors are respectful of approaches to professional counseling that differ from their own. Counselors know and take into account the traditions and practices of other professional groups with which they work.

b. Personal Public Statements.

When making personal statements in a public context, counselors clarify that they are speaking from their personal perspectives and that they are not speaking on behalf of all counselors or the profession. (See C.5.d.)

c. Clients Served by Others.

When counselors learn that their clients are in a professional relationship with another mental health professional, they request release from clients to inform the other professionals and strive to establish positive and collaborative professional relationships. (See A.4.)

SECTION D: RELATIONSHIPS WITH OTHER PROFESSIONALS

D.1. Relationships With Employers and Employees

a. Role Definition.

Counselors define and describe for their employers and employees the parameters and levels of their professional roles.

b. Agreements.

Counselors establish working agreements with supervisors, colleagues, and subordinates regarding counseling or clinical relationships, confidentiality, adherence to professional standards, distinction between public and private material, maintenance and dissemination of recorded information, workload, and accountability. Working agreements in each instance are specified and made known to those concerned.

c. Negative Conditions.

Counselors alert their employers to conditions that may be potentially disruptive or damaging to the counselor's professional responsibilities or that may limit their effectiveness.

d. Evaluation.

Counselors submit regularly to professional review and evaluation by their supervisor or the appropriate representative of the employer.

e. In-Service.

Counselors are responsible for in-service development of self and staff.

f. Goals.

Counselors inform their staff of goals and programs.

g. Practices.

Counselors provide personnel and agency practices that respect and enhance the rights and welfare of each employee and recipient of agency services. Counselors strive to maintain the highest levels of professional services.

h. Personnel Selection and Assignment.

Counselors select competent staff and assign responsibilities compatible with their skills and experiences.

i. Discrimination.

Counselors, as either employers or employees, do not engage in or condone practices that are inhumane, illegal, or unjustifiable (such as considerations based on age, color, culture, disability, ethnic group, gender, race, religion, sexual orientation, or socioeconomic status) in hiring, promotion, or training. (See A.2.a. and C.5.b.)

j. Professional Conduct.

Counselors have a responsibility both to clients and to the agency or institution within which services are performed to maintain high standards of professional conduct.

k. Exploitive Relationships.

Counselors do not engage in exploitive relationships with individuals over whom they have supervisory, evaluative, or instructional control or authority.

l. Employer Policies.

The acceptance of employment in an agency or institution implies that counselors are in agreement with its general policies and principles. Counselors strive to reach agreement with employers as to acceptable standards of conduct that allow for changes in institutional policy conducive to the growth and development of clients.

D.2. Consultation (See B.6.)

a. Consultation as an Option.

Counselors may choose to consult with any other professionally competent persons about their clients. In choosing consultants, counselors avoid placing the consultant in a conflict of interest situation that would preclude the consultant being a proper party to the counselor's efforts to help the client. Should counselors be engaged in a work setting that compromises this consultation standard, they consult with other professionals whenever possible to consider justifiable alternatives.

b. Consultant Competency.

Counselors are reasonably certain that they have or the organization represented has the necessary competencies and resources for giving the kind of consulting services needed and that appropriate referral resources are available.

c. Understanding with Clients.

When providing consultation, counselors attempt to develop with their clients a clear understanding of problem definition, goals for change, and predicted consequences of interventions selected.

d. Consultant Goals.

The consulting relationship is one in which client adaptability and growth toward self-direction are consistently encouraged and cultivated. (See A.1.b.)

D.3. Fees for Referral

a. Accepting Fees from Agency Clients.

Counselors refuse a private fee or other remuneration for rendering services to persons who are entitled to such services through the counselor's employing agency or institution. The policies of a particular agency may make explicit provisions for agency clients to receive counseling services from members of its staff in private practice. In such instances, the clients must be informed of other options open to them should they seek private counseling services. (See A.10.a., A.11.b., and C.3.d.)

b. Referral Fees.

Counselors do not accept a referral fee from other professionals.

D.4. Subcontractor Arrangements

When counselors work as subcontractors for counseling services for a third party, they have a duty to inform clients of the limitations of confidentiality that the organization may place on counselors in providing counseling services to clients. The limits of such confidentiality ordinarily are discussed as part of the intake session. (See B.1.e. and B.1.f.)

SECTION E: EVALUATION, ASSESSMENT, AND INTERPRETATION

E.1. General

a. Appraisal Techniques.

The primary purpose of educational and psychological assessment is to provide measures that are objective and interpretable in either comparative or absolute terms. Counselors recognize the need to interpret the statements in this section as applying to the whole range of appraisal techniques, including test and non-test data.

b. Client Welfare.

Counselors promote the welfare and best interests of the client in the development, publication, and utilization of educational and psychological assessment techniques. They do not misuse assessment results and interpretations and take reasonable steps to prevent others from misusing the information these techniques provide. They respect the client's right to know the results, the interpretations made, and the bases for their conclusions and recommendations.

E.2. Competence to Use and Interpret Tests

a. Limits of Competence.

Counselors recognize the limits of their competence and perform only those testing and assessment services for which they have been trained. They are familiar with reliability, validity, related standardization, error of measurement, and proper application of any technique utilized. Counselors using computer-based test interpretations are trained in the construct being measured and the specific instrument being used prior to using this type of computer application. Counselors take reasonable measures to ensure the proper use of psychological assessment techniques by persons under their supervision.

b. Appropriate Use.

Counselors are responsible for the appropriate application, scoring, interpretation, and use of assessment instruments, whether they score and interpret such tests themselves or use computerized or other services.

c. Decisions Based on Results.

Counselors responsible for decisions involving individuals or policies that are based on assessment results have a thorough understanding of educational and psychological measurement, including validation criteria, test research, and guidelines for test development and use.

d. Accurate Information.

Counselors provide accurate information and avoid false claims or misconceptions when making statements about assessment instruments or techniques. Special efforts are made to avoid unwarranted connotations of such terms as IQ and grade equivalent scores. (See C.5.c.)

E.3. Informed Consent

a. Explanation to Clients.

Prior to assessment, counselors explain the nature and purposes of assessment and the specific use of results in language the client (or other legally authorized person on behalf of the client) can understand, unless an explicit exception to this right has been agreed upon in advance. Regardless of whether scoring and interpretation are completed by counselors, by assistants, or by computer or other outside services, counselors take reasonable steps to ensure that appropriate explanations are given to the client.

b. Recipients of Results.

The examinee's welfare, explicit understanding, and prior agreement determine the recipients of test results. Counselors include accurate and appropriate interpretations with any release of individual or group test results. (See B.1.a. and C.5.c.)

E.4. Release of Information to Competent Professionals

a. Misuse of Results.

Counselors do not misuse assessment results, including test results, and interpretations, and take reasonable steps to prevent the misuse of such by others. (See C.5.c.)

b. Release of Raw Data.

Counselors ordinarily release data (e.g. protocols, counseling or interview notes, or questionnaires) in which the client is identified only with the consent of the client or the client's legal representative. Such data are usually released only to persons recognized by counselors as competent to interpret the data. (See B.1.a.)

E.5. Proper Diagnosis of Mental Disorders

a. Proper Diagnosis.

Counselors take special care to provide proper diagnosis of mental disorders. Assessment techniques (including personal interview) used to determine client care (e.g., locus of treatment, type of treatment, or recommended follow-up) are carefully selected and appropriately used. (See A.3.a. and C.5.c.)

b. Cultural Sensitivity.

Counselors recognize that culture affects the manner in which clients' problems are defined. Clients' socioeconomic and cultural experience is considered when diagnosing mental disorders.

E.6. Test Selection

a. Appropriateness of Instruments.

Counselors carefully consider the validity, reliability, psychometric limitations, and appropriateness of instruments when selecting tests for use in a given situation or with a particular client.

b. Culturally Diverse Populations.

Counselors are cautious when selecting tests for culturally diverse populations to avoid inappropriateness of testing that may be outside of socialized behavioral or cognitive patterns.

E.7. Conditions of Test Administration

a. Administration Conditions.

Counselors administer tests under the same conditions that were established in their standardization. When tests are not administered under standard conditions or when unusual behavior or irregularities occur during the testing session, those conditions are noted in interpretation, and the results may be designated as invalid or of questionable validity.

b. Computer Administration.

Counselors are responsible for ensuring that administration programs function properly to provide clients with accurate results when a computer or other electronic methods are used for test administration. (See A.12.b.)

c. Unsupervised Test-Taking.

Counselors do not permit unsupervised or inadequately supervised use of tests or assessments unless the tests or assessments are designed, intended, and validated for self-administration and/or scoring.

d. Disclosure of Favorable Conditions.

Prior to test administration, conditions that produce most favorable test results are made known to the examinee.

E.8. Diversity in Testing

Counselors are cautious in using assessment techniques, making evaluations, and interpreting the performance of populations not represented in the norm group on which an instrument was standardized. They recognize the effects of age, color, culture, disability, ethnic group, gender, race, religion, sexual orientation, and socioeconomic status on test administration and interpretation and place test results in proper perspective with other relevant factors. (See A.2.a.)

E.9. Test Scoring and Interpretation

a. Reporting Reservations.

In reporting assessment results, counselors indicate any reservations that exist regarding validity or reliability because of the circumstances of the assessment or the inappropriateness of the norms for the person tested.

b. Research Instruments.

Counselors exercise caution when interpreting the results of research instruments possessing insufficient technical data to support respondent results. The specific purposes for the use of such instruments are stated explicitly to the examinee.

c. Testing Services.

Counselors who provide test scoring and test interpretation services to support the assessment process confirm the validity of such interpretations. They accurately describe the purpose, norms, validity, reliability, and applications of the procedures and any special qualifications applicable to their use. The public offering of an automated test interpretations services is considered a professional-to-professional consultation. The formal responsibility of the consultant is to the consultee, but the ultimate and overriding responsibility is to the client.

E.10. Test Security

Counselors maintain the integrity and security of tests and other assessment techniques consistent with legal and contractual obligations. Counselors do not appropriate, reproduce, or modify published tests or parts thereof without acknowledgment and permission from the publisher.

E.11. Obsolete Tests and Outdated Test Results

Counselors do not use data or test results that are obsolete or outdated for the current purpose. Counselors make every effort to prevent the misuse of obsolete measures and test data by others.

E.12. Test Construction

Counselors use established scientific procedures, relevant standards, and current professional knowledge for test design in the development, publication, and utilization of educational and psychological assessment techniques.

SECTION F: TEACHING, TRAINING, AND SUPERVISION

F.1. Counselor Educators and Trainers

a. Educators as Teachers and Practitioners.

Counselors who are responsible for developing, implementing, and supervising educational programs are skilled as teachers and practitioners. They are knowledgeable regarding the ethical, legal, and regulatory aspects of the profession, are skilled in applying that knowledge, and make students and supervisees aware of their responsibilities. Counselors conduct counselor education and training programs in an ethical manner and serve as role models for professional behavior. Counselor educators should make an effort to infuse material related to human diversity into all courses and/or workshops that are designed to promote the development of professional counselors.

b. Relationship Boundaries with Students and Supervisees.

Counselors clearly define and maintain ethical, professional, and social relationship boundaries with their students and supervisees. They are aware of the differential in power that exists and the student's or supervisee's possible incomprehension of that power differential. Counselors explain to students and supervisees the potential for the relationship to become exploitive.

c. Sexual Relationships.

Counselors do not engage in sexual relationships with students or supervisees and do not subject them to sexual harassment. (See A.6. and C.5.b.)

d. Contributions to Research.

Counselors give credit to students or supervisees for their contributions to research and scholarly projects. Credit is given through coauthorship, acknowledgment, footnote statement, or other appropriate means, in accordance with such contributions. (See G.4.b. and G.4.c.)

e. Close Relatives.

Counselors do not accept close relatives as students or supervisees.

f. Supervision Preparation.

Counselors who offer clinical supervision services are adequately prepared in supervision methods and techniques. Counselors who are doctoral students serving as practicum or internship supervisors to master's level students are adequately prepared and supervised by the training program.

g. Responsibility for Services to Clients.

Counselors who supervise the counseling services of others take reasonable measures to ensure that counseling services provided to clients are professional.

h. Endorsement.

Counselors do not endorse students or supervisees for certification, licensure, employment, or completion of an academic or training program if they believe students or supervisees are not qualified for the endorsement. Counselors take reasonable steps to assist students or supervisees who are not qualified for endorsement to become qualified.

F.2. Counselor Education and Training Programs

a. Orientation.

Prior to admission, counselors orient prospective students to the counselor education or training program's expectations, including but not limited to the following: (1) the type and level of skill acquisition required for successful completion of the training, (2) subject matter to be covered, (3) basis for evaluation, (4) training components that encourage self-growth or self-disclosure as part of the training process, (5) the type of supervision settings and requirements of the sites for required clinical field experiences, (6) student and supervisee evaluation and dismissal policies and procedures, and (7) up-to-date employment prospects for graduates.

b. Integration of Study and Practice.

Counselors establish counselor education and training programs that integrate academic study and supervised practice.

c. Evaluation.

Counselors clearly state to students and supervisees, in advance of training, the levels of competency expected, appraisal methods, and timing of evaluations for both didactic and experiential components. Counselors provide students and supervisees with periodic performance appraisal and evaluation feedback throughout the training program.

d. Teaching Ethics.

Counselors make students and supervisees aware of the ethical responsibilities and standards of the profession and the students' and supervisees' ethical responsibilities to the profession. (See C.1. and F.3.e.)

e. Peer Relationships.

When students or supervisees are assigned to lead counseling groups or provide clinical supervision for their peers, counselors take steps to ensure that students and supervisees placed in these roles do not have personal or adverse relationships with peers and that they understand they have the same ethical obligations as counselor educators, trainers, and supervisors. Counselors make every effort to ensure that the rights of peers are not compromised when students or supervisees are assigned to lead counseling groups or provide clinical supervision.

f. Varied Theoretical Positions.

Counselors present varied theoretical positions so that students and supervisees may make comparisons and have opportunities to develop their own positions. Counselors provide information concerning the scientific bases of professional practice. (See C.6.a.)

g. Field Placements.

Counselors develop clear policies within their training program regarding field placement and other clinical experiences. Counselors provide clearly stated roles and responsibilities for the student or supervisee, the site supervisor, and the program supervisor. They confirm that site supervisors are qualified to provide supervision and are informed of their professional and ethical responsibilities in this role.

h. Dual Relationships as Supervisors.

Counselors avoid dual relationships such as performing the role of site supervisor and training program supervisor in the student's or supervisee's training program. Counselors do not accept any form of professional services, fees, commissions, reimbursement, or remuneration from a site for student or supervisee placement.

i. Diversity in Programs.

Counselors are responsible to their institution's and program's recruitment and retention needs for training program administrators, faculty, and students with diverse backgrounds and special needs. (See A.2.a.)

F.3. Students and Supervisees

a. Limitations.

Counselors, through ongoing evaluation and appraisal, are aware of the academic and personal limitations of students and supervisees that might impede performance. Counselors assist students and supervisees in securing remedial assistance when needed, and dismiss from the training program supervisees who are unable to provide competent service due to academic or personal limitations. Counselors seek professional consultation and document their decision to dismiss or refer students or supervisees for assistance. Counselors assure that students and supervisees have recourse to address decisions made, to require them to seek assistance, or to dismiss them.

b. Self-Growth Experiences.

Counselors use professional judgment when designing training experiences conducted by the counselors themselves that require student and supervisee self-growth or self-disclosure. Safeguards are provided so that students and supervisees are aware of the ramifications their self-disclosure may have, on counselors whose primary role as teacher, trainer, or supervisor requires acting on ethical obligations to the profession. Evaluative components of experiential training experiences explicitly delineate predetermined academic standards that are separate and not dependent on the student's level of self-disclosure. (See A.6.)

c. Counseling for Students and Supervisees.

If students or supervisees request counseling, supervisors or counselor educators provide them with acceptable referrals. Supervisors or counselor educators do not serve as counselor to students or supervisees over whom they hold administrative, teaching, or evaluative roles unless this is a brief role associated with a training experience. (See A.6.b.)

d. Clients of Students and Supervisees.

Counselors make every effort to ensure that the clients at field placements are aware of the services rendered and the qualifications of the students and supervisees rendering those services. Clients receive professional disclosure information and are informed of the limits of confidentiality. Client permission is obtained in order for the students and supervisees to use any information concerning the counseling relationship in the training process. (See B.1.e.)

e. Standards for Students and Supervisees.

Students and supervisees preparing to become counselors adhere to the Code of Ethics and the Standards of Practice. Students and supervisees have the same obligations to clients as those required of counselors. (See H.1.)

SECTION G: RESEARCH AND PUBLICATION

G.1. Research Responsibilities

a. Use of Human Subjects.

Counselors plan, design, conduct, and report research in a manner consistent with pertinent ethical principles, federal and state laws, host institutional regulations, and scientific standards governing research with human subjects. Counselors design and conduct research that reflects cultural sensitivity appropriateness.

b. Deviation from Standard Practices.

Counselors seek consultation and observe stringent safeguards to protect the rights of research participants when a research problem suggests a deviation from standard acceptable practices. (See B.6.)

c. Precautions to Avoid Injury.

Counselors who conduct research with human subjects are responsible for the subjects' welfare throughout the experiment and take reasonable precautions to avoid causing injurious psychological, physical, or social effects to their subjects.

d. Principal Researcher Responsibility.

The ultimate responsibility for ethical research practice lies with the principal researcher. All others involved in the research activities share ethical obligations and full responsibility for their own actions.

e. Minimal Interference.

Counselors take reasonable precautions to avoid causing disruptions in subjects' lives due to participation in research.

f. Diversity.

Counselors are sensitive to diversity and research issues with special populations. They seek consultation when appropriate. (See A.2.a. and B.6.)

G.2. Informed Consent

a. Topics Disclosed.

In obtaining informed consent for research, counselors use language that is understandable to research participants and that: (1)

accurately explains the purpose and procedures to be followed; (2) identifies any procedures that are experimental or relatively untried; (3) describes the attendant discomforts and risks; (4) describes the benefits or changes in individuals or organizations that might be reasonably expected; (5) discloses appropriate alternative procedures that would be advantageous for subjects; (6) offers to answer any inquiries concerning the procedures; (7) describes any limitations on confidentiality; and (8) instructs that subjects are free to withdraw their consent and to discontinue participation in the project at any time. (See B.1.f.)

b. Deception.

Counselors do not conduct research involving deception unless alternative procedures are not feasible and the prospective value of the research justifies the deception. When the methodological requirements of a study necessitate concealment or deception, the investigator is required to explain clearly the reasons for this action as soon as possible.

c. Voluntary Participation.

Participation in research is typically voluntary and without any penalty for refusal to participate. Involuntary participation is appropriate only when it can be demonstrated that participation will have no harmful effects on subjects and is essential to the investigation.

d. Confidentiality of Information.

Information obtained about research participants during the course of an investigation is confidential. When the possibility exists that others may obtain access to such information, ethical research practice requires that the possibility, together with the plans for protecting confidentiality, be explained to participants as a part of the procedure for obtaining informed consent. (See B.1.e.)

e. Persons Incapable of Giving Informed Consent.

When a person is incapable of giving informed consent, counselors provide an appropriate explanation, obtain agreement for participation and obtain appropriate consent from a legally authorized person.

f. Commitments to Participants.

Counselors take reasonable measures to honor all commitments to research participants.

g. Explanations After Data Collection.

After data are collected, counselors provide participants with full clarification of the nature of the study to remove any misconceptions. Where scientific or human values justify delaying or withholding information, counselors take reasonable measures to avoid causing harm.

h. Agreements to Cooperate.

Counselors who agree to cooperate with another individual in research or publication incur an obligation to cooperate as promised in terms of punctuality of performance and with regard to the completeness and accuracy of the information required.

i. Informed Consent for Sponsors.

In the pursuit of research, counselors give sponsors, institutions, and publication channels the same respect and opportunity for giving informed consent that they accord to individual research participants. Counselors are aware of their obligation to future research workers and ensure that host institutions are given feedback information and proper acknowledgment.

G.3. Reporting Results

a. Information Affecting Outcome.

When reporting research results, counselors explicitly mention all variables and conditions known to the investigator that may have affected the outcome of a study or the interpretation of data.

b. Accurate Results.

Counselors plan, conduct, and report research accurately and in a manner that minimizes the possibility that results will be misleading. They provide thorough discussions of the limitations of their data and alternative hypotheses. Counselors do not engage in fraudulent research, distort data, misrepresent data, or deliberately bias their results.

c. Obligation to Report Unfavorable Results.

Counselors communicate other counselors the results of any research judged to be of professional value. Results that reflect unfavorably on institutions, programs, services, prevailing opinions, or vested interests are not withheld.

d. Identity of Subjects.

Counselors who supply data, aid in the research of another person, report research results, or make original data available take due care to disguise the identity of respective subjects in the absence of specific authorization from the subjects to do otherwise. (See B.1.g. and B.5.a.)

e. Replication Studies.

Counselors are obligated to make available sufficient original research data to qualified professionals who may wish to replicate the study.

G.4. Publication

a. Recognition of Others.

When conducting and reporting research, counselors are familiar with and give recognition to previous work on the topic, observe copyright laws, and give full credit to those to whom credit is due. (See F.1.d. and G.4.c.)

b. Contributors.

Counselors give credit through joint authorship, acknowledgment, footnote statements, or other appropriate means to those who have contributed significantly to research or concept development in accordance with such contributions. The principal contributor is listed first and minor technical or professional contributions are acknowledged in notes or introductory statements.

c. Student Research.

For an article that is substantially based on a student's dissertation or thesis, the student is listed as the principal author. (See F.1.d. and G.4.a.)

d. Duplicate Submission.

Counselors submit manuscripts for consideration to only one journal at a time. Manuscripts that are published in whole or in substantial part in another journal or published work are not submitted for publication without acknowledgment and permission from the previous publication.

e. Professional Review.

Counselors who review material submitted for publication, research, or other scholarly purposes respect the confidentiality and proprietary rights of those who submitted it.

SECTION H: RESOLVING ETHICAL ISSUES

H.1. Knowledge of Standards

Counselors are familiar with the Code of Ethics and the Standards of Practice and other applicable ethics codes from other professional organizations of which they are member, or from certification and licensure bodies. Lack of knowledge or misunderstanding of an ethical responsibility is not a defense against a charge of unethical conduct. (See F.3.e.)

H.2. Suspected Violations

a. Ethical Behavior Expected.

Counselors expect professional associates to adhere to Code of Ethics. When counselors possess reasonable cause that raises doubts as to whether a counselor is acting in an ethical manner, they take appropriate action. (See H.2.d. and H.2.e.)

b. Consultation.

When uncertain as to whether a particular situation or course of action may be in violation of Code of Ethics, counselors consult with other counselors who are knowledgeable about ethics, with colleagues, or with appropriate authorities.

c. Organization Conflicts.

If the demands of an organization with which counselors are affiliated pose a conflict with Code of Ethics, counselors specify the nature of such conflicts and express to their supervisors or other responsible officials their commitment to Code of Ethics. When possible, counselors work toward change within the organization to allow full adherence to Code of Ethics.

d. Informal Resolution.

When counselors have reasonable cause to believe that another counselor is violating an ethical standard, they attempt to first resolve the issue informally with the other counselor if feasible, providing that such action does not violate confidentiality rights that may be involved.

e. Reporting Suspected Violations.

When an informal resolution is not appropriate or feasible, counselors, upon reasonable cause, take action such as reporting the suspected ethical violation to state or national ethics committees, unless this action conflicts with confidentiality rights that cannot be resolved.

f. Unwarranted Complaints.

Counselors do not initiate, participate in, or encourage the filing of ethics complaints that are unwarranted or intend to harm a counselor rather than to protect clients or the public.

H.3. Cooperation With Ethics Committees

Counselors assist in the process of enforcing Code of Ethics. Counselors cooperate with investigations, proceedings, and requirements of the ACA Ethics Committee or ethics committees of other duly constituted associations or boards having jurisdiction over those charged with a violation. Counselors are familiar with the ACA Policies and Procedures and use it as a reference in assisting the enforcement of the Code of Ethics.

STANDARDS OF PRACTICE

All members of the American Counseling Association (ACA) are required to adhere to the Standards of Practice and the Code of Ethics. The Standards of Practice represent minimal behavioral statements of the Code of Ethics. Members should refer to the applicable section of the Code of Ethics for further interpretation and amplification of the applicable Standard of Practice.

Section A: The Counseling Relationship

Standard of Practice One (SP-1) Nondiscrimination

Counselors respect diversity and must not discriminate against clients because of age, color, culture, disability, ethnic group, gender, race, religion, sexual orientation, marital status, or socioeconomic status. (See A.2.a.)

Standard of Practice Two (SP-2) Disclosure to Clients

Counselors must adequately inform clients, preferably in writing, regarding the counseling process and counseling relationship at or before the time it begins and throughout the relationship. (See A.3.a.)

Standard of Practice Three (SP-3) Dual Relationships

Counselors must make every effort to avoid dual relationships with clients that could impair their professional judgment or increase the risk of harm to clients. When a dual relationship cannot be avoided, counselors must take appropriate steps to ensure that judgment is not impaired and that no exploitation occurs. (See A.6.a. and A.6.b.)

Standard of Practice Four (SP-4) Sexual Intimacies with Clients

Counselors must not engage in any type of sexual intimacies with current clients and must not engage in sexual intimacies with former clients within a minimum of two years after terminating the counseling relationship. Counselors who engage in such relationship after two years following termination have the responsibility to thoroughly examine and document that such relations did not have an exploitative nature.

Standard of Practice Five (SP-5) Protecting Clients During Group Work

Counselors must take steps to protect clients from physical or psychological trauma resulting from interactions during group work. (See A.9.b.)

Standard of Practice Six (SP-6) Advance Understanding of Fees

Counselors must explain to clients, prior to their entering the counseling relationship, financial arrangements related to professional services. (See A.10.a-d. and A.11.c.)

Standard of Practice Seven (SP-7) Termination

Counselors must assist in making appropriate arrangements for the continuation of treatment of clients, when necessary, following termination of counseling relationships. (See A.11.a.)

Standard of Practice Eight (SP-8) Inability to Assist Clients

Counselors must avoid entering or immediately terminate a counseling relationship if it is determined that they are unable to be of professional assistance to a client. The counselor may assist in making an appropriate referral for the client. (See A.11.b.)

Section B: Confidentiality

Standard of Practice Nine (SP-9) Confidentiality Requirement

Counselors must keep information related to counseling services confidential unless disclosure is in the best interest of clients, is required for the welfare of others, or is required by law. When disclosure is required, only information that is essential is revealed and the client is informed of such disclosure. (See B.1.a.-f.)

Standard of Practice Ten (SP-10) Confidentiality Requirements for Subordinates

Counselors must take measures to ensure that privacy and confidentiality of clients are maintained by subordinates. (See B.1.h.)

Standard of Practice Eleven (SP-11) Confidentiality in Group Work

Counselors must clearly communicate to group members that confidentiality cannot be guaranteed in group work. (See B.2.a.)

Standard of Practice Twelve (SP-12) Confidentiality in Family Counseling

Counselors must not disclose information about one family member in counseling to another family member without prior consent. (See B.2.b.)

Standard of Practice Thirteen (SP-13) Confidentiality of Records

Counselors must maintain appropriate confidentiality in creating, storing, accessing, transferring, and disposing of counseling records. (See B.4.b.)

Standard of Practice Fourteen (SP-14) Permission to Record or Observe

Counselors must obtain prior consent from clients in order to electronically record or observe sessions. (See B.4.c.)

Standard of Practice Fifteen (SP-15) Disclosure or Transfer of Records

Counselors must obtain client consent to disclose or transfer records to third parties, unless exceptions listed in SP-9 exist. (See B.4.e.)

Standard of Practice Sixteen (SP-16) Data Disguise Required

Counselors must disguise the identity of the client when using data for training, research, or publication. (See B.5.a.)

Section C: Professional Responsibility

Standard of Practice Seventeen (SP-17) Boundaries of Competence

Counselors must practice only within the boundaries of their competence. (See C.2.a.)

Standard of Practice Eighteen (SP-18) Continuing Education

Counselors must engage in continuing education to maintain their professional competence. (See C.2.f.)

Standard of Practice Nineteen (SP-19) Impairment of Professionals

Counselors must refrain from offering professional services when their personal problems or conflicts may cause harm to a client or others. (See C.2.g.)

Standard of Practice Twenty (SP-20) Accurate Advertising

Counselors must accurately represent their credentials and services when advertising. (See C.3.a.)

Standard of Practice Twenty-one (SP-21) Recruiting Through Employment

Counselors must not use their place of employment or institutional affiliation to recruit clients for their private practices. (See C.3.d.)

Standard of Practice Twenty-two (SP-22) Credentials Claimed

Counselors must claim or imply only professional credentials possessed and must correct any known misrepresentations of their credentials by others. (See C.4.a.)

Standard of Practice Twenty-three (SP-23) Sexual Harassment

Counselors must not engage in sexual harassment. (See C.5.b.)

Standard of Practice Twenty-four (SP-24) Unjustified Gains

Counselors must not use their professional positions to seek or receive unjustified personal gains, sexual favors, unfair advantage, or unearned goods or services. (See C.5.e.)

Standard of Practice Twenty-five (SP-25) Clients Served by Others

With the consent of the client, counselors must inform other mental health professionals serving the same client that a counseling relationship between the counselor and client exists. (See C.6.c.)

Standard of Practice Twenty-six (SP-26) Negative Employment Conditions

Counselors must alert their employers to institutional policy or conditions that may be potentially disruptive or damaging to the counselor's professional responsibilities, or that may limit their effectiveness or deny clients' rights. (See D.1.c.)

Standard of Practice Twenty-seven (SP-27) Personnel Selection and Assignment

Counselors must select competent staff and must assign responsibilities compatible with staff skills and experiences. (See D.1.h.)

Standard of Practice Twenty-eight (SP-28) Exploitive Relationships with Subordinates

Counselors must not engage in exploitive relationships with individuals over whom they have supervisory, evaluative, or instructional control or authority. (See D.1.k.)

Section D: Relationship With Other Professionals

Standard of Practice Twenty-nine (SP-29) Accepting Fees from Agency Clients

Counselors must not accept fees or other remuneration for consultation with persons entitled to such services through the counselor's employing agency or institution. (See D.3.a.)

Standard of Practice Thirty (SP-30) Referral Fees

Counselors must not accept referral fees. (See D.3.b.)

Section E: Evaluation, Assessment, and Interpretation

Standard of Practice Thirty-one (SP-31) Limits of Competence

Counselors must perform only testing and assessment services for which they are competent. Counselors must not allow the use of psychological assessment techniques by unqualified persons under their supervision. (See E.2.a.)

Standard of Practice Thirty-two (SP-32) Appropriate Use of Assessment Instruments

Counselors must use assessment instruments in the manner for which they were intended. (See E.2.b.)

Standard of Practice Thirty-three (SP-33) Assessment Explanations to Clients

Counselors must provide explanations to clients prior to assessment about the nature and purposes of assessment and the specific uses of results. (See E.3.a.)

Standard of Practice Thirty-four (SP-34) Recipients of Test Results

Counselors must ensure that accurate and appropriate interpretations accompany any release of testing and assessment information. (See E.3.b.)

Standard of Practice Thirty-five (SP-35) Obsolete Tests and Outdated Test Results

Counselors must not base their assessment or intervention decisions or recommendations on data or test results that are obsolete or outdated for the current purpose. (See E.11.)

Section F: Teacher, Training, and Supervision

Standard of Practice Thirty-six (SP-36) Sexual Relationships with Students or Supervisees

Counselors must not engage in sexual relationships with their students and supervisees. (See F.1.c.)

Standard of Practice Thirty-seven (SP-37) Credit for Contributions to Research

Counselors must give credit to students or supervisees for their contributions to research and scholarly projects. (See F.1.d.)

Standard of Practice Thirty-eight (SP-38) Supervision Preparation

Counselors who offer clinical supervision services must be trained and prepared in supervision methods and techniques. (See F.1.f.)

Standard of Practice Thirty-nine (SP-39) Evaluation Information

Counselors must clearly state to students and supervisees in advance of training, the levels of competency expected, appraisal methods, and timing of evaluations. Counselors must provide students and supervisees with periodic performance appraisal and evaluation feedback throughout the training program. (See F.2.c.)

Standard of Practice Forty (SP-40) Peer Relationships in Training

Counselors must make every effort to ensure that the rights of peers are not violated when students and supervisees are assigned to lead counseling groups or provide clinical supervision. (See F.2.e.)

Standard of Practice Forty-one (SP-41) Limitations of Students and Supervisees

Counselors must assist students and supervisees in securing remedial assistance, when needed, and must dismiss from the training program students and supervisees who are unable to provide competent service due to academic or personal limitations. (See F.3.a.)

Standard of Practice Forty-two (SP-42) Self-Growth Experiences

Counselors who conduct experiences for students or supervisees that include self-growth or self disclosure must inform participants of counselors' ethical obligations to the profession and must not grade participants based on their nonacademic performance. (See F.3.b.)

Standard of Practice Forty-Three (SP-43) Standards for Students and Supervisees

Students and supervisees preparing to become counselors must adhere to the Code of Ethics and the Standards of Practice of counselors. (See F.3.e.)

Sections G: Research and Publication

Standard of Practice Forty-four (SP-44) Precautions to Avoid Injury in Research

Counselors must avoid causing physical, social, or psychological harm or injury to subjects in research . (See G.1.c.)

Standard of Practice Forty-five (SP-45) Confidentiality of Research Information

Counselors must keep confidential information obtained about research participants. (See G.2.d.)

Standard of Practice Forty-six (SP-46) Information Affecting Research Outcome

Counselors must report all variables and conditions known to the investigator that may have affected research data or outcomes. (See G.3.a.)

Standard of Practice Forty-seven (SP-47) Accurate Research Results

Counselors must not distort or misrepresent research data, nor fabricate or intentionally bias research results. (See G.3.b.)

Standard of Practice Forty-eight (SP-48) Publication Contributors

Counselors must give appropriate credit to those who have contributed to research. (See G.4.a. and G.4.b.)

Section H: Resolving Ethical Issues

Standard of Practice Forty-nine (SP-49) Ethical Behavior Expected

Counselors must take appropriate action when they possess reasonable cause that raises doubts as to whether counselors or other mental health professionals are acting in an ethical manner. (See H.2.a)

Standard of Practice Fifty (SP-50) Unwarranted Complaints

Couselors must not initiate, participate in, or encourage the filing of ethics complaints that are unwarranted or intended to harm a mental health professional rather than to protect clients or the public. (See H.2.f.)

Standard of Practice Fifty-one (SP-51) Cooperation with Ethics Committees

Counselors must cooperate with investigations, proceedings, and requirements of the ACA Ethics Committee or ethics committees of other duly constituted associations or boards having jurisdiction over those charged with a violation. (See H.3.)

References

The following documents are available to counselors as resources to guide them in their practices. These resources are not a part of the Code of Ethics and the Standards of Practice.

American Association for Counseling and Development/Association for Measurement and Evaluation in Counseling and Development. (1989).

The responsibilities of users of standardized tests (revised). Washington, DC: Author.

American Counseling Association. (1988).

American Counseling Association Ethical Standards. Alexandria, VA: Author.

American Psychological Association. (1985).

Standards for educational and psychological testing (revised). Washington, DC: Author.

American Rehabilitation Counseling Association, Commission on Rehabilitation Counselor Certification, and National Rehabilitation Counseling Association. (1995).

Code of professional ethics for rehabilitation counselors. Chicago, IL: Author.

American School Counselor Association. (1992).

Ethical standards for school counselors. Alexandria, VA: Author.

Joint Committee on Testing Practices. (1988).

Code of fair testing practices in education. Washington, DC: Author.

National Board for the Certified Counselors. (1989).

National Board for Certified Counselors Code of Ethics. Alexandria, VA: Author.

Prediger, D.J. (Ed.). (1993, March).

Multicultural assessment standards. Alexandria, VA: Association for Assessment in Counseling.

POLICIES AND PROCEDURES FOR RESPONDING TO MEMBERS' REQUESTS FOR INTERPRETATIONS OF THE ETHICAL STANDARDS

Revised by Governing Council April 1994
Effective July 1, 1994

Section A:
Appropriate Requests

1. ACA members may request that the Committee issue formal interpretations of the ACA Code of Ethics for the purpose of guiding the member's own professional behavior.

2. Requests for interpretations will not be considered in the following situations:

    a. The individual requesting the interpretation is not an ACA member, or

    b. The request is intended to determine whether the behavior of another mental health professional is unethical. In the event an ACA member believes the behavior of another mental health professional is unethical, the ACA member should resolve the issue directly with the professional, if possible, and should file an ethical complaint if appropriate.

Section B:
Procedures

1. Members must send written requests for interpretations to the Committee at ACA Headquarters.

2. Questions should be submitted in the following format: "Does (counselor behavior) violate Sections _____ or any other sections of the ACA Ethical Standards?" Questions should avoid unique details, be general in nature to the extent possible, and be brief.

3. The Committee staff liaison will revise the question, if necessary, and submit it to the Committee Co-Chair for approval.

4. The question will be sent to Committee members who will be asked to respond individually.

5. The Committee Co-Chair will develop a consensus interpretation on behalf of the Committee.

6. The consensus interpretation will be sent to members of the Committee for final approval.

7. The formal interpretation will be sent to the member who submitted the inquiry.

8. The question and the formal interpretation will be published in the ACA newsletter, but the identity of the member requesting the interpretation will not be disclosed.

POLICIES AND PROCEDURES FOR PROCESSING COMPLAINTS OF ETHICAL VIOLATIONS

Section A: General

1. The American Counseling Association, hereafter referred to as the "Association" or "ACA," is dedicated to enhancing human development throughout the life span and promoting the counseling profession.

2. The Association, in furthering its objectives, administers the Code of Ethics that have been developed and approved by the ACA Governing Council.

3. The purpose of this document is to facilitate the work of the ACA Ethics Committee ("Committee") by specifying the procedures for processing cases of alleged violations of the ACA Code of Ethics, codifying options for sanctioning members, and stating appeals procedures. The intent of the Association is to monitor the professional conduct of its members to promote sound ethical practices, ACA does not, however, warrant the performance of any individual.

Section B: Ethics Committee Members

1. The Ethics Committee is a standing committee of the Association. The Committee consists of six (6) appointed members, including two (2) Co-Chairs whose terms overlap. Two members are appointed annually for three (3) year terms by the President-Elect; appointments are subject to confirmation by the ACA Governing Council. Any vacancy occurring on the Committee will be filled by the President in the same manner, and the person appointed shall serve the unexpired term of the member whose place he or she took. Committee members may be reappointed to not more than one (1) additional consecutive term.

2. One (1) of the Committee co-chairs is appointed annually by the President-Elect from among the Committee members who have two (2) years of service remaining and serves as co-chair for two (2) years, subject to confirmation by the ACA Governing Council.

Section C: Role and Function

1. The Ethics Committee is responsible for:

   a. Educating the membership as to the Association's Code of Ethics;

   b. Periodically reviewing and recommending changes in the Code of Ethics of the Association as well as the Policies and Procedures for Processing Complaints of Ethical Violations;

   c. Receiving and processing complaints of alleged violations of the Code of Ethics of the Association; and,

   d. Receiving and processing questions.

2. The Committee shall meet in person or by telephone conference a minimum of three (3) times per year for processing complaints.

3. In processing complaints about alleged ethical misconduct, the Committee will compile an objective, factual account of the dispute in question and make the best possible recommendation for the resolution of the case. The Committee, in taking any action, shall do so only for cause, shall only take the degree of disciplinary action that is reasonable, shall utilize these procedures with objectivity and fairness, and in general shall act only to further the interests and objectives of the Association and its membership.

4. Of the six (6) voting members of the Committee, a vote of four (4) is necessary to conduct business. In the event a Co-Chair or any other member of the Committee has a personal interest in the case, he or she shall withdraw from reviewing the case.

5. In the event Committee members recuse themselves from a complaint and insufficient voting members are available to conduct business, the President shall appoint former ACA Committee members to decide the complaint.

Section D: Responsibilities of the Committee

1. The Committee members have an obligation to act in an unbiased manner, to work expeditiously, to safeguard the confidentiality of the Committee's activities, and to follow procedures established to protect the rights of all individuals involved.

Section E: Responsibilities of the Co-Chairs Administering the Complaint

1. In the event that one of the Co-Chairs Administering the Complaint; conflict of interest in a particular case, the other Co-Chair shall administer the complaint. The Co-Chair administering the complaint shall not have a vote in the decision.

2. In addition to the above guidelines for members of the Committee, the Co-Chairs, in conjunction with the headquarters staff liaison, have the responsibilities of:

   a. Receiving, via ACA Headquarters, complaints that have been certified for membership status of the accused;

   b. Determining whether the alleged behavior(s), if true, would violate ACA's Code of Ethics and whether the Committee should review the complaint under these rules:

c. Notifying the complainant and the accused member of receipt of the case by certified mail return receipt requested;

d. Notifying the members of the Committee of the case;

e. Requesting additional information from complainants, accused members and others;

f. Presiding over the meetings of the Committee;

g. Preparing and sending, by certified mail, communications to the complainant and accused member on the recommendations and decisions of the Committee; and

h. Arranging for legal advice with assistance and financial approval of the ACA Executive Director.

Section F: Jurisdiction

1. The Committee will consider whether individuals have violated the ACA Code of Ethics if those individuals:

a. Are current members of the American Counseling Association; or

b. Were ACA members when the alleged violations occurred.

2. Ethics committees of divisions, branches, corporate affiliates, or other ACA entities must refer all ethical complaints involving ACA members to the Committee.

Section G: Eligibility to File Complaints

1. The Committee will receive complaints that ACA members have violated one or more sections of the ACA Code of Ethics from the following individuals:

a. Members of the general public who have reason to believe that ACA members have violated the ACA Code of Ethics.

b. ACA members, or members of other helping professions, who have reason to believe that other ACA members have violated the ACA Code of Ethics.

c. The Co-Chair of the Committee on behalf of the ACA membership when the Co-Chair has reason to believe through information received by the Committee that ACA members have violated the ACA Code of Ethics.

2. If possible, individuals should attempt to resolve complaints directly with accused members before filing ethical complaints.

Section H: Time Lines

1. The time lines set forth in these standards are guidelines only and have been established to provide a reasonable time framework for processing complaints.

2. Complainants or accused members may request extensions of deadlines when appropriate. Extensions of deadlines will be granted by the Committee only when justified by unusual circumstance.

Section I: Nature of Communication

1. Only written communications regarding ethical complaints against members will be acceptable. If telephone inquiries from individuals are received regarding the filing of complaints, responding to complaints, or providing information regarding complaints, the individuals calling will be informed of the written communication requirement and asked to comply.

2. All correspondence related to an ethical complaint must be addressed to the Ethics Committee, ACA Headquarters, 5999 Stevenson Avenue, Alexandria, VA 22304, and must be marked "confidential." This process is necessary to protect the confidentiality of the complainant and the accused member.

Section J: Filing Complaints

1. Only written complaints, signed by complainants, will be considered.

2. Individuals eligible to file complaints will send a letter outlining the nature of the complaint to the Committee at the ACA Headquarters.

3. The ACA staff liaison to the Committee will communicate in writing with complainants. Receipt of complaints and confirmation of membership status of accused members as defined in Section F.1, above, will be acknowledged to the complainant. Proposed formal complains will be sent to complainants after receipt of complaints have been acknowledged.

4. If the complaint does not involve a members as defined in Section F.1., above, the staff liaison shall inform the complainant.

5. The Committee Co-Chair administering a complaint will determine whether the complaint, if true, would violate one ore more sections of the ethical standards or if the complaint could be properly decided if accepted. If not, the complaint will not be accepted and the complainant shall be notified.

6. If the Committee Co-Chair administering the complaint determines that there is insufficient information to make a fair determination of whether the behavior alleged in the complaint would be cause for action by the Committee, the ACA staff liaison to the Committee may request further information from the complainant or others.

7. When complaints are accepted, complainants will be informed that copies of the formal complaints plus evidence and documents submitted in support of the complaint will be provided to the accused member and that the complainant must authorize release of such information to the accused member before the complaint process may proceed.

8. The ACA staff liaison, after receiving approval of the Committee Co-Chair administering a complaint, will formulate a formal complaint which will be presented to the complainants for their signature.

    a. The correspondence from complainants will be received and the staff liaison and Committee Co-Chair administering the complaint will identify all ACA Code of Ethics that might have been violated if the accusations are true.

    b. The formal complaint will be sent to complainants with a copy of these Policies and Procedures, a copy of the ACA Code of Ethics, a verification affidavit form and an authorization and release of information form. Complainants will be asked to sign and return the completed complaint, verification affidavit and authorizations and release of information forms. It will be explained to complainants that sections of the codes that might have been violated may be added or deleted by the complainant before signing the formal statement.

    c. If complainants elect to add or delete sections of the ethical standards in the formal complaint, the unsigned formal complaint shall be returned to ACA Headquarters with changes noted and a revised formal complaint will be sent to the complainants for their signature.

9. When the completed formal complaint, verification affidavit form and authorization and release of information form are presented to complainants for their signature, they will be asked to submit all evidence and documents they wish to be considered by the Committee in reviewing the complaint.

Section K: Notification of Accused Members

1. Once signed formal complaints have been received, accused members will be sent a copy of the formal complaint and copies of all evidence and documents submitted in support of the complaint.

2. Accused members will be asked to respond to the complaint against them. They will be asked to address each section of the ACA Code of Ethics they have been accused of having violated. They will be informed that if they wish to respond they must do so in writing within sixty (60) working days.

3. Accused members will be informed that they must submit all evidence and documents they wish to be considered by the Committee in reviewing the complaint within sixty (60) working days.

4. After accused members have received notification that a complaint has been brought against them, they will be given sixty (60) working days to notify the Committee Co-Chair (via ACA Headquarters) in writing, by certified mail, if they wish to request a formal face-to-face hearing before the Committee. Accused members may waive their right to a formal hearing before the Committee. (See Section P: Hearings).

5. If the Committee Co-Chair determines that there is insufficient information to make a fair determination of whether the behavior alleged in the complain would be cause for action by the Committee, the ACA staff liaison to the Committee may request further information from the accused member or others. The accused member shall be given thirty (30) working days from receipt of the request to respond.

6. All requests for additional information from others will be accompanied by a verification affidavit form which the information provider will be asked to complete and return.

7. The Committee may, in its discretion, delay or postpone its review of the case with good cause, including if the Committee wishes to obtain additional information. The accused member may request that the Committee delay or postpone its review of the case for good cause if done so in writing.

Section L: Disposition of Complaints

1. After Receiving the responses of accused members, Committee members will be provided copies of: (a) the complaint, (b) supporting evidence and documents sent to accused members, (c) the response, and (d) supporting evidence and documents provided by accused members and others.

2. Decisions will be rendered based on the evidence and documents provided by the complainant and accused member or others.

3. The Committee Co-Chair administering a complaint will not participate in deliberations or decisions regarding that particular complaint.

4. At the next meeting of the Committee held no sooner than fifteen (15) working days after members received copies of documents related to a complaint, the Committee will discuss the complaint, response, and supporting documentation, if any, and determine the outcome of the complaint.

5. The Committee will determine whether each Code of Ethics the member has been accused of having violated was violated based on the information provided.

6. After deliberations, the Committee may decide to dismiss the complaint or to dismiss charges within the complaint.

7. In the event it is determined that any of the ACA Code of Ethics have been violated, the Committee will impose for the entire complaint one or a combination of the possible sanctions allowed.

Section M: Withdrawal of Complaints

1. If the Complainant and accused member both agree to discontinue the complaint process, the Committee may, at its discretion, complete the adjudication process if available evidence indicates that this is warranted. The Co-Chair of the Committee, on behalf of the ACA membership, shall act as complainant.

Section N: Possible Sanctions

1. Reprinted Remedial requirements may be stipulated by the Committee.

2. Probation for a specified period of time subject to Committee review of compliance. Remedial requirements may be imposed to be completed within a specified period of time.

3. Suspension from ACA membership for a specified period of time subject to Committee review of compliance. Remedial requirements may be imposed to be completed within a specified period of time.

4. Permanent expulsion from ACA membership. This sanction requires a unanimous vote of those voting.

5. The penalty for failing to fulfill in a satisfactory manner a remedial requirement imposed by the Committee as a result of a probation sanction will be automatic suspension until the requirement is met, unless the Committee determines that the remedial requirement should be modified based on good cause shown prior to the end of the probationary period.

6. The penalty for failing to fulfill in a satisfactory manner a remedial requirement imposed by the Committee as a result of a suspension sanction will be automatic permanent expulsion unless the Committee determines that the remedial requirement should be modified based on good cause shown prior to the end of the suspension period.

7. Other corrective action.

Section O: Notification of Results

1. Accused members shall be notified of Committee decisions regarding complaints against them.

2. Complainants will be notified of Committee decisions after the deadline for accused members to file appeals or, in the event an appeal is filed, after a filed appeal decision has been rendered.

3. After complainants are notified of the results of their complaints as provided in Section O., Paragraph 2 above, if a violation has been found and accused members have been suspended or expelled, counselor licensure, certification, or registry boards, other mental health licensure, certification, or registry boards, voluntary national certification boards, and appropriate professional associations will also be notified of the results. In addition, ACA divisions, state branches, the ACA Insurance Trust, and other ACA-related entities will also be notified of the results.

4. After complainants have been notified of the results of their complaint as provided in Section O., Paragraph 2, above, if a violations has been found and accused members have been suspended or expelled, a notice of the Committee action that includes the sections of the ACA ethical standards that were found to have been violated and the sanctions imposed will be published in the ACA newsletter.

Section P: Hearings

1. At the discretion of the Committee, a hearing may be conducted when the results of the Committee's preliminary determination indicate that additional information is needed.

2. When accused members, within sixty (60) working days of notification of the complaint, request a formal face-to-face or telephone conference hearing before the Committee a hearing shall be conducted. (See Section K.6.)

3. The accused shall bear all their expenses associated with attendance at hearings requested by the accused.

4. The Committee Co-Chair shall schedule a formal hearing on the case at the next scheduled Committee meeting and notify both the complainant and the accused member of their right to attend the hearing in person or by telephone conference call.

5. The hearing will be held before a panel made up of the Committee and if the accused member chooses, a representative of the accused member's primary Division. This representative will be identified by the Division President and will have voting privileges.

Section Q: Hearing Procedures

1. Purpose.

   a. A hearing will be conducted to determine whether a breach of the ethical standards has occurred and, if so, to determine appropriate disciplinary action.

   b. The Committee will be guided in its deliberations by principles of basic fairness and professionalism, and will keep its deliberations as confidential as possible, except as provided herein.

2. Notice.

   a. The accused members shall be advised in writing by the Co-Chair administering the complaint of the time and place of the hearing and the charges involved at least forty-give (45) working days before the hearing. Notice shall include a formal statement of the complaints lodged against the accused member and supporting evidence.

   b. The accused member is under no duty to respond to the notice, but the Committee will not be obligated to delay or postpone its hearing unless the accused so requests in writing, with good cause reviewed at least fifteen (15) working days in advance. In the absence of such 15 day advance notice and postponement by the Committee, if the accused fails to appear at the hearing, the Committee shall decide the complaint on record. Failure of the accused member to appear at the hearing shall not be viewed by the Committee as sufficient grounds alone for taking disciplinary action.

3. Conduct of the Hearing.

   a. Accommodations. The location of the hearing shall be determined at the discretion of the Committee. The Committee shall provide a private room to conduct the hearing and no observers or recording devices other than a recording used by the Committee shall be permitted.

   b. Presiding Officer. The Co-Chair in charge of the case shall preside over the hearing and deliberations of the Committee. At the conclusion of the hearing and deliberations of the Committee, the Co-Chair shall promptly notify the accused member and complainant of the Committee's decision in writing as provided in Section O., Paragraphs 1 and 2, above.

   c. Record. A record of the hearing shall be made and preserved, together with any documents presented in evidence, at ACA Headquarters for a period of three (3) years. The record shall consist of a summary of testimony received or a verbatim transcript, at the discretion of the Committee.

   d. Right to Counsel. The accused member shall be entitled to have legal counsel present to advise and represent them throughout the hearing. Legal counsel for ACA shall also be present at the hearing to advise the Committee and shall have the privilege of the floor.

   e. Witnesses. Either party shall have the right to call witnesses to substantiate his or her version of the case.

   f. The Committee shall have the right to call witnesses it believes may provide further insight into the matter. ACA shall, in its sole discretion, determine the number and identity of witnesses to be heard.

   g. Witnesses shall not be present during the hearing except when they are called upon to testify and shall be excused upon completion of their testimony and any cross-examination.

   h. The Co-Chair administering the complaint shall allow questions to be asked of any witness by the opposition or members of the Committee if such questions and testimony are relevant to the issues in the case.

   i. The Co-Chair administering the complaint will determine what questions and testimony are relevant to the case. Should the hearing be disturbed by irrelevant testimony, the Co-Chair administering the complaint may call a brief recess until order can be restored.

   j. All expenses associated with counsel on behalf of the parties shall be borne by the respective parties. All expenses associated with witnesses on behalf of the accused shall be borne by the accused when the accused requests a hearing. If the Committee requests the hearing, all expenses associated with witnesses shall be borne by ACA.

4. Presentation of Evidence.

   a. The staff liaison, or the Co-Chair administering the complaint shall be called upon first to present the charge(s) made against the accused and to briefly describe the evidence supporting the charge. The person presenting the charges shall also be responsible for examining and cross-examining witnesses on behalf of the complainant and for otherwise presenting the matter during the hearing.

   b. The complainant or a member of the Committee shall then be called upon to present the case against the accused. Witnesses who can substantiate the case may be called upon to testify and answer questions of the accused and the Committee.

   c. If the accused has exercised the right to be present at the hearing, he or she shall be called upon last to present any evidence which refutes the charges against him or her. This includes witnesses as in Subsection (3) above.

   d. The accused will not be found guilty simply for refusing to testify. Once the accused member chooses to testify, however, he or she may be cross-examined by the complainant and members of the Committee.

   e. The Committee will endeavor to conclude the hearing within a period of approximately three (3) hours. The parties will be requested to be considerate of this time frame in planning their testimony.

   f. Testimony that is merely cumulative or repetitious may, at the discretion of the Co-Chair administering the complaint, be excluded.

5. Relevancy of Evidence.

   a. The Hearing Committee is not a court of law and is not required to observe formal rules of evidence. Evidence that would be inadmissible in a court of law may be admissible in the hearing before the Committee, if it is relevant to the case. That is, if the evidence offered tends to explain, clarify, or refute any of the important facts of the case, it should generally be considered.

   b. The Committee will not consider evidence or testimony for the purpose of supporting any charge that was not set forth in the notice of the hearing or that is not relevant to the issues of the case.

6. Burden of Proof.

   a. The burden of proving a violation of the ethical standards is on the complainant and/or the Committee. It is not up to the accused to prove his or her innocence of any wrong-doing.

   b. Although the charge(s) need not be proved "beyond a reasonable doubt," the Committee will not find the accused guilty in the absence of substantial, objective, and believable evidence to sustain the charge(s).

7. Deliberation of the Committee.

    a. After the hearing is completed, the Committee shall meet in a closed session to review the evidence presented and reach a conclusion. ACA legal counsel may attend the closed session to advise the Committee if the Committee so desires.

    b. The Committee shall be the sole trier of the facts and shall weigh the evidence presented and assess the credibility of the witnesses. The act of a majority of the members of the Committee present shall be the decision of the Committee. A unanimous vote of those voting is required for permanent expulsion from ACA membership.

    c. Only members of the Committee who were present throughout the entire hearing shall be eligible to vote.

8. Decision of the Committee

    a. The Committee will first resolve the issue of the guilt or innocence of the accused on each charge. Applying the burden of proof in subsection (5), above, the Committee will vote by secret ballot, unless the members of the Committee consent to an oral vote.

    b. In the event a majority of the members of the Committee do not find the accused guilty, the charges shall be dismissed. If the Committee finds the accused member has violated the Code of Ethics, it must then determine what sanctions, in accordance with Section N: Possible Sanctions, shall be imposed.

    c. As provided in Section O., above, the Co-Chair administering the complaint shall notify the accused member and complainant of the Committee's decision in writing.

Section R: Appeals

1. Decisions of the ACA Ethics Committee that members have violated the ACA Code of Ethics may be appealed by the member found to have been in violation based on one or both of the following grounds:

    a. The Committee violated its policies and procedures for processing complaints of ethical violations; and/or

    b. The decision of the Committee was arbitrary and capricious and was not supported by the materials provided by the complainant and accused member.

2. After members have received notification that they have been found in violation of one or more ACA Code of Ethics, they will be given thirty (30) working days to notify the Committee in writing by certified mail that they are appealing the decision.

3. An appeal may consist only of a letter stating one or both of the grounds of appeal listed in subsection 1 above and the reasons for the appeal.

4. Appealing members will be asked to identify the primary ACA division to which he or she belongs. The ACA President will appoint a three (3) person appeals panel consisting of two (2) former ACA Ethics Committee Chairs and the President of the identified division. The ACA attorney shall serve as legal advisor and have the privilege of the floor.

5. The three (3) member appeals panel will be given copies of the materials available to the Committee when it made its decision, a copy of the hearing transcript if a hearing was held, plus a copy of the letter filed by the appealing member.

6. The appeals panel generally will render its decision regarding an appeal which must receive a majority vote within sixty (60) working days of their receipt of the above materials.

7. The decision of the appeals panel may include one of the following:

    a. The decision of the Committee is upheld.

    b. The decision of the Committee is reversed and remanded with guidance to the Committee for a new decision. The reason for this decision will be given to the Committee in detail in writing.

8. When a Committee decision is reversed and remanded, the complainant and accused member will be informed in writing and additional information may be requested first from the complainant and then from the accused member. The Committee will then render another decision without a hearing.

9. Decisions of the appeals panel to uphold the Committee decision are final.

Section S: Substantial New Evidence

1. In the Event substantial new evidence is presented in a case in which an appeal was not filed, or in a case which a final decision has been rendered, the case may be reopened by the Committee.

2. The Committee will consider substantial new evidence and if it is found to be substantiated and capable of exonerating a member who was expelled, the Committee will reopen the case and go through the entire complaint process again.

Section T: Records

1. The records of the Committee regarding complaints are confidential except as provided herein.

2. Original copies of complaint records will be maintained in locked files at ACA Headquarters or at an off-site location chosen by ACA.

3. Members of the Committee will keep copies of complaint records confidential and will destroy copies of records after a case has been closed or when they are no longer a member of the Committee.

Section U: Legal Actions Related to Complaints

1. Complaints and accused members are required to notify the Committee if they learn of any type of legal action (civil or criminal) being filed related to the complaint.

2. In the event any type of legal action is filed regarding an accepted complaint, all actions related to the complaint will be stayed until the legal action has been concluded. The Committee will consult with legal counsel concerning whether the processing of the complaint will be stayed if the legal action does not involve the same complainant and the same facts complained of.

3. If actions on a complaint are stayed, the complainant and accused member will be notified.

4. When actions on a complaint are continued after a legal action has been concluded, the complainant and accused member will be notified.

For information on ordering the *ACA Code of Ethics and Standards of Practice* write to:

ACA Distribution Center
P.O. Box 531
Annapolis Junction, MD 20701-0531

or call 301-470-4ACA (301-470-4222) • toll free 1-800-422-2648 • fax (301) 604-0158

Appendix B

CONTACT INFORMATION

Counseling Professional Associations

American Counseling Association

5999 Stevenson Avenue
Alexandria, VA 22304-3300
800/442-2648
FAX 800/473-2329
membership@counseling.org (e-mail)
www.counseling.org (web page)

All divisions of the American Counseling Association may be contacted at this address.

National Certifying Boards for Counselors

National Board for Certified Counselors (NBCC)

3 Terrace Way, Suite D
Greensboro, NC 27403-3660
336/547-0607
FAX 336/547-0017
nbcc@nbcc.org (e-mail)
www.nbcc.org (web page)

NBCC offers the National Certified Counselor (NCC) credential.

Those who hold the NCC may also earn the following specialized credentials:

- Certified Clinical Mental Health Counselor (CCMHC)
- National Certified School Counselor (NCSC)
- Master Addictions Counselor (MAC)
- NBCC Approved Clinical Supervisor (ACS)

Commission on Rehabilitation Counselor Certification (CRCC)

1835 Rohlwing Road, Suite E
Rolling Meadows, IL 60008
847/394-2104
FAX 847/394-2108
www.crccertification.org (web page)

CRCC offers the Certified Rehabilitation Counselor (CRC) credential.

CRCC also offers the following specialized credentials:

- Master Addictions Counselor (MAC)
- Clinical Supervisor (CS)

Agencies that Accredit Counseling Facilities

Commission on Accreditation of Rehabilitation Facilities (CARF)

4891 E. Grant Road
Tucson, AZ 85712
520/325-1044
FAX 520/318-1129

International Association of Counseling Services (IACS)

101 S. Whiting Street, Suite 211
Alexandria, VA 22304
703/823-9840
FAX 703/823-9843

Joint Commission on Accreditation of Healthcare Organizations (JCAHO)

1 Renaissance Boulevard
Oakbrook Terrace, IL 60181
630/792-5000

Appendix C

EXAMPLES OF MANDATORY CHILD ABUSE REPORTING STATUTES

Louisiana

LSA-R.S. 14:403 (2000)

C. (1) Any person, including licensed physicians, interns or residents, nurses, hospital staff members, teachers, social workers, coroners, and others persons or agencies having responsibility for the care of children, having cause to believe that a child's physical or mental health or welfare has been or may be further adversely affected abuse or neglect or that abuse or neglect was contributing factor in a child's death shall report . . .

D. (1) Reports reflecting the reporter's belief that a child has been abused or neglect or that abuse or neglect was a contributing factor in a child's death shall be made to the parish child welfare unit or the parish agency responsible for the protection of juveniles and, if necessary, to a local or state law enforcement agency. These reports need not name the persons suspected of the alleged abuse or neglect . . .

(2) All reports shall contain the name and address of the child, the name and address of the person responsible for the care of the child, if available, and any other pertinent information.

(4) An oral report shall be made immediately upon learning of the abuse or neglect . . . and a written report shall follow within five days to the same agency or department.

Texas

V.T.C.A., Family Code § 261.101 (1999)

(a) A person having cause to believe that a child's physical or mental health or welfare has been adversely affected by abuse or neglect by any person shall immediately make a report . . .

(b) If a professional has cause to believe that a child has been abused or neglect or may be abused or neglected or that a child is a victim of an offense under Section 21.11, Penal Code the professional shall make a report not later than the 48th hour after the hour the professional first suspects that the child has been or may be abused or neglected or is a victim of an offense under Section 21.11, Penal Code. A professional may not delegate to or rely on another person to make the report . . .

(c) The requirement to report under this section applies without exception to an individual whose personal communications may otherwise be privileged, including an attorney, a member of the clergy, a medical practitioner, a social worker, a mental health professional, and an employee of a clinic or health care facility that provides reproductive services.

Wisconsin

W.S.A. 48.981 (1999)

(2) Persons required to report. A physician, coroner, medical examiner, nurse, dentist, chiropractor, optometrist, acupuncturist, other medical or mental health professional, social worker, marriage and family therapist, professional counselor, public assistance worker, . . . having reasonable cause to suspect that a child seen in the course of professional duties has been abused or neglected or having reason to believe that a child seen in the course of professional duties has been threatened with abuse or neglect and that abuse or neglect of the child will occur shall, . . . report as provided in sub. (3). Any other person, including an attorney, having reason to suspect that a child has been abused or neglected or reason to believe that a child has been threatened with abuse or neglect and that abuse or neglect of the child will occur may make such a report. Any person, including an attorney having reason to suspect that an unborn child has been abused or reason to believe that an unborn child is as substantial risk of abuse may report as provided in sub (3). No person making a report under this subsection may be discharged from employment for so doing.

(3) Reports; investigation. (a) Referral of report. A person required to report under sub. (2) shall immediately inform, by telephone or personally, the county department or, in a country having a population of 500,000 or more, the department or a licensed child welfare agency under contract with the department or the sheriff or city, village or town police department of the facts and circumstances contributing to a suspicion of child abuse, or neglect or of unborn child abuse or to a belief that abuse or neglect will occur . . .

Appendix D

CLIENT PERMISSION FORM
TO RECORD COUNSELING SESSION
FOR SUPERVISION PURPOSES

I, _____ [fill in name of client], hereby give my permission for my counselor, _____ [fill in your name] to audiotape/vidoetape [one or the other] our counseling session _____ [fill in date, or if over a period of time, fill in inclusive dates].

I understand that the purpose of this recording is for the clinical supervision of my counselor's work. I understand that only my client's clinical supervisor, _____ [fill in name of supervisor], will review the tape and that the tape will be erased after the supervisor has reviewed it.

_____ _____

Client's Signature   Date

Appendix E

Introduction[1]

The guidelines that follow are based on the General Guidelines, adopted by the American Psychological Association (APA) in July 1987 (*APA, 1987*). The guidelines receive their inspirational guidance from specific APA *Ethical Principles of Psychologists and Code of Conduct (APA, 1992)*.

These guidelines are inspirational and professional judgment must be used in specific applications. They are intended for use for providers of health care services.[2,3] The language of these guidelines must be interpreted in light of their aspirational intent, advancements in psychology and the technology of record keeping, and the professional judgment of the individual psychologist. It is important to highlight that professional judgment is not preempted by these guidelines; rather; the intent is to enhance it.

[1]In 1988 the Board of Professional Affairs (BPA) directed the Committee on Professional Practice and Standards (COPPS) to determine whether record keeping guidelines would be appropriate. COPPS was informed that these guidelines would supplement the provisions contained in the *General Guidelines for Providers of Psychological Services,* which had been amended two years earlier. The Council of Representatives approved the General Guidelines records provisions after extended debate on the minimum recordation concerning the nature and contents of psychological services. The General Guidelines reflect a compromise position that psychologists hold widely varying views on the wisdom of recording the content of the psychotherapeutic relationship. In light of the Council debate on the content of psychological records and the absence of an integrated document, BPA instructed COPPS to assess the need for such guidelines, and, if necessary, the likely content.

COPPS undertook a series of interviews with psychologists experienced in this area. The consensus of the respondents indicated that practicing psychologists could benefit from guidance in this area. In addition, an APA legal intern undertook a 50-state review of laws governing psychologists with respect to record keeping provisions. The survey demonstrated that while some states have relatively clear provisions governing certain types of records, many questions are often left unclear. In addition, there is a great deal of variability among the states, so that consistent treatment of records as people move from state to state, or as records are sought from other states, may not be easy to achieve.

Based on COPPS' survey and legal research, BPA in 1989 directed COPPS to prepare an initial set of record keeping guidelines. This document resulted.

[2] These guidelines apply to Industrial/Organizational psychologists providing health care services but generally not to those providing non-health care I/O services. For instance, in I/O psychology, written records may constitute the primary work product, such as a test instrument or a job analysis, while psychologist providing health care services may principally use records to document non-written services and to maintain continuity.

[3] Rather than keeping their own record system, psychologists practicing in institutional settings comply with the institution's policies on record keeping, so long as they are consistent with legal and ethical standards.

Underlying Principles and Purpose

Psychologists maintain records for a variety of reasons, the most important of which is the benefit of the client. Records allow a psychologist to document and review the delivery of psychological services. The nature and extent of the record will vary depending upon the type and purpose of psychological services. Records can provide a history and current status in the event that a user seeks psychological services from another psychologist or mental health professional.

Conscientious record keeping may also benefit psychologists themselves, by guiding them to plan and implement an appropriate course of psychological services, to review work as a whole, and to self-monitor more precisely.

Maintenance of appropriate records may also be relevant for a variety of other institutional, financial, and legal purposes. State and federal laws in many cases require maintenance of appropriate records of certain kinds of psychological services. Adequate records may be a requirement for receipt or third party payment for psychological services.

In addition, well documented records may help protect psychologists from professional liability, if they become the subject of legal or ethical proceedings. In these circumstances, the principal issue will be the professional action of the psychologist, as reflected in part by the records. At times, there may be conflicts between the federal, state or local laws governing record keeping, the requirements of institutional rules, and these guidelines. In these circumstances, psychologists bear in mind their obligations to conform to applicable law. When laws or institutional rules appear to conflict with the principles of these guidelines, psychologists use their education, skills and training to identify the relevant issues, and to attempt to resolve it in a way that, to the maximum extent feasible, conforms both to law and to professional practice, as required by ethical principles.

Psychologists are justifiably concerned that, at times, record keeping information will be required to be disclosed against the wishes of the psychologist or client, and may be released to persons unqualified to interpret such records. These guidelines assume that no record is free from disclosure all of the time, regardless of the wishes of the client or the psychologist.

1. Content of Records

Records include any information (including information stored in a computer) that may be used to document the nature, delivery, progress, or results of psychological services. Records can be reviewed and duplicated.

Records of psychological services minimally include (a) identifying data, (b) dates of services, (c) types of services, (d) fees, (e) any assessment, plan for intervention, consultation, summary reports, and/or testing reports and supporting data as may be appropriate, and (f) any release of information obtained.

As may be required by their jurisdiction and circumstances, psychologists maintain to a reasonable degree accurate, current, and pertinent records of psychological services. The detail is sufficient to permit planning for continuity in the event that another psychologist takes over delivery of services, including, in the event of death, disability, and retirement. In addition, psychologists maintain records in sufficient detail for regulatory and administrative review of psychological service delivery.

Records kept beyond the minimum requirements are a matter of professional judgment for the psychologist. The psychologist takes into account the nature of the psychological services, the source of the information recorded, the intended use of the records, and his or her professional obligation.

Psychologists make reasonable efforts to protect against the misuse of records. They take into account the anticipated use by the intended or anticipated recipients when preparing records. Psychologists adequately identify impressions and tentative conclusions as such.

2. Construction and Control of Records

Psychologists maintain a system that protects the confidentiality of records. They must take reasonable steps to establish and maintain the confidentiality of information arising from their own delivery of psychological services, or the services provided by others working under their supervision.

Psychologists have ultimate responsibility for the content of their records and the records of those under their supervision. Where appropriate, this requires that the psychologist oversee the design and implementation of record keeping procedures, and monitor their observance.

Psychologists maintain control over their clients' records, taking into account the policies of the institutions in which they practice. In situations where psychologists have control over their clients' records and where circumstances change such that it is no longer feasible to maintain control over such records, psychologists seek to make appropriate arrangements for transfer. Records are organized in a manner that facilitates their use by the psychologists and other authorized persons. Psychologists strive to assure that record entries are legible. Records are to be completed in a timely manner.

Records may be maintained in a variety of media, so long as their utility, confidentiality and durability are assured.

3. Retention of Records

Psychologists are aware of relevant federal, state and local laws and regulations governing records retention. Such laws and regulations supersede the requirements of these guidelines. In the absence of such laws and regulations, complete records are maintained for a minimum of 3 years after the last contact with the client. Records, or a summary, are then maintained for an additional 12 years before disposal.[4] If the client is a minor, the record period is extended until 3 years after the age of majority.

All records, active and inactive, are maintained safely, with properly limited access, and from which timely retrieval is possible.

4. Outdated Records

Psychologists are attentive to situations in which record information has become outdated, and may therefore be invalid, particularly in circumstances where disclosure might cause adverse effects. Psychologists ensure that when disclosing such information that its outdated nature and limited utility are noted using professional judgment and complying with applicable law.

---

[4]These time limits follow the APA's specialty guidelines. If the specialty guidelines should be revised, a simple 7 years requirement for the retention of the complete record is preferred, which would be a more stringent requirement than any existing state statute.

When records are to be disposed of, this is done in an appropriate manner that ensures nondisclosure (or preserves confidentiality). (See Section 3a.)

5. Disclosure of Record Keeping Procedures

When appropriate, psychologists may inform their clients of the nature and extent of their record keeping procedures. This information includes a statement on the limitations of the confidentiality of the records.

Psychologists may charge a reasonable fee for review and reproduction of records. Psychologists do not withhold records that are needed for valid healthcare purposes solely because the client has not paid for prior services.

References

American Psychological Association. (1987). *General guidelines for providers of psychological services.*

American Psychological Association. (1992). *Ethical principles of psychologists and code of conduct.*

Appendix F

CLIENT REQUEST FORM
TO TRANSFER RECORDS

I, _____ [fill in name of client], hereby request that copies of all of my counseling records [in the event only parts of records or limited information in records is to be copied and transferred, indicate that here, instead of "all"] in the possession of _____ [fill in name of agency] be transferred to _____ [fill in complete name and address of person to whom copies of records are to be sent]. I understand that personal and confidential information regarding my mental health treatment, including possible diagnoses of mental or emotional disorders and clinical impressions of my counselor could be included in these records.

I understand that this request authorizes a one time transfer of my records and that any further transfer of records requests must be authorized by a similar signed document.

_____   _____
Client's Signature   Date

NATIONAL BOARD FOR CERTIFIED COUNSELORS STANDARDS FOR THE ETHICAL PRACTICE OF WEBCOUNSELING

The relative newness of the use of the Internet for service and product delivery leaves authors of standards at a loss when beginning to create ethical practices on the Internet. This document, like all codes of conduct, will change as information and circumstances not yet foreseen evolve. However, each version of this code of ethics is the current best standard of conduct passed by the NBCC Board of Directors. As with any code, and especially with a code such as this, created for an evolving field of work, NBCC and CCE welcome comments and ideas for further discussion and inclusion. Further, the development of these WebCounseling standards has been guided by the following principles:

These standards are intended to address practices which are unique to WebCounseling and WebCounselors,

These standards are not to duplicate non-Internet-based standards adopted in other codes of ethics,

Recognizing that significant new technology emerges continuously, these standards should be reviewed frequently,

WebCounseling ethics cases should be reviewed in light of delivery systems existing at the moment rather than at the time the standards were adopted.

WebCounselors who are not National Certified Counselors may indicate at their Web-Site their adherence to these standards, but may not publish these standards in their entirety without written permission of the National Board for Certified Counselors.

The Practice of WebCounseling shall be defined as "the practice of professional counseling and information delivery that occurs when client(s) and counselor are in separate or remote locations and utilize electronic means to communicate over the Internet."

In addition to following the NBCC Code of Ethics pertaining to the practice of professional counseling, WebCounselors shall:

1. Review pertinent legal and ethical codes for possible violations emanating from the practice of WebCounseling and supervision.

Liability insurance policies should also be reviewed to determine if the practice of Web-Counseling is a covered activity. Local, state, provincial, and national statutes as well as the codes of professional membership organizations, professional certifying bodies and

Last modified: September 30, 1999.

state or provincial licensing boards need to be reviewed. Also, as no definitive answers are known to questions pertaining to whether WebCounseling takes place in the WebCounselor's location or the WebClient's location, WebCounselors should consider carefully local customs regarding age of consent and child abuse reporting.

2. Inform WebClients of encryption methods being used to help insure the security of client/counselor/supervisor communications.

Encryption methods should be used whenever possible. If encryption is not made available to clients, clients must be informed of the potential hazards of unsecured communication on the Internet. Hazards may include authorized or unauthorized monitoring of transmissions and/or records of WebCounseling sessions.

3. Inform clients if, how and how long session data are being preserved.

Session data may include WebCounselor/WebClient e-mail, test results, audio/video session recordings, session notes, and counselor/supervisor communications. The likelihood of electronic sessions being preserved is greater because of the ease and decreased costs involved in recording. Thus, its potential use in supervision, research and legal proceedings increases.

4. In situations where it is difficult to verify the identity of WebCounselor of WebClient, take steps to address impostor concerns, such as by using code words, numbers, or graphics.

5. When parent/guardian consent is required to provide WebCounseling to minors, verify the identity of the consenting person.

6. Follow appropriate procedures regarding the release of information for sharing WebClient information with other electronic sources.

Because of the relative ease with which e-mail messages can be forwarded to formal and casual referral sources, WebCounselors must work to insure the confidentiality of the WebCounseling relationship.

7. Carefully consider the extent of self disclosure presented to the WebClient and provide rationale for WebCounselor's level of disclosure.

WebCounselors may wish to ensure that, minimally, the WebClient has the same data available about his/her service provider as would be available if the counseling were to take place face to face (i.e., possibly ethnicity, gender, etc.). Compelling reasons for limiting disclosure should be presented.

WebCounselors will remember to protect themselves from unscrupulous users of the Internet by limiting potentially harmful disclosure about self and family.

8. Provide links to websites of all appropriate certification bodies and licensure boards to facilitate consumer protection.

9. Contact NBCC/CEE or the WebClient's state or provincial licensing board to obtain the name of at least one Counselor-On-Call within the WebClient's geographical region.

WebCounselors who have contacted an individual to determine his or her willingness to serve as a Counselor-On-Call (either in person, over the phone or via e-mail) should also ensure that the WebClient is provided with Local crisis intervention hotline numbers, 911 and similar numbers in the event that the Counselor-On-Call is unavailable.

10. Discuss with their WebClients procedures for contacting the WebCounselor-On-Call when he or she is off-line.

This means explaining exactly how often e-mail messages are to be checked by the WebCounselor.

11. Mention at their websites those presenting problems they believe to be inappropriate for WebCounseling.

While no conclusive research has been conducted to date, those topics might include: sexual abuse as a primary issue, violent relationships, eating disorders, and psychiatric disorders that involve distortions of reality.

12. Explain to clients the possibility of technology failure.

The WebCounselor

- gives instructions to WebClients about calling if problems arise,
- discusses the appropriateness of the client calling collect when the call might be originating from around the world,
- mentions differences in time zones,
- talks about dealing with response delays in sending and receiving e-mail messages

13. Explain to clients how to cope with potential misunderstandings arising from the lack of visual cues from WebCounselor or WebClient.

For example, suggesting the other person simply say, "Because I couldn't see your face or hear your tone of voice in your e-mail message, I'm not sure how to interpret that last message."

Appendix H

CLINICAL SUPERVISION MODEL AGREEMENT*

I, Theodore P. Remley, Jr., agree to provide supervision for you for the purposes of becoming a Licensed Professional Counselor in the state of Louisiana.

I am licensed by the state of Louisiana as a Professional Counselor. I am also licensed as a Professional Counselor in Virginia and Mississippi. I hold M.Ed., Ed.S., and Ph.D. degrees in counseling from the University of Florida. I am a National Certified Counselor (NCC). In the past, I have served as a high school counselor, community college counselor, university career counselor, counselor educator, community mental health center counselor, and counselor in private practice. My areas of counseling expertise include personal and social adjustment, relationship issues, career decision-making, work adjustment, divorce mediation, anger management, and serious mental illnesses.

It is your responsibility to obtain the degree necessary, meet the specific course content requirements, and complete the required practicum and internship necessary to register our supervision with the Louisiana Licensed Professional Counselors Board of Examiners (LPC Board) so that you may obtain the status of Intern. You must complete the LPC Board "Registration of Supervision" form and include all attachments. I will complete the section of the form for the supervisor, will provide you with a copy of my "Declaration of Practice and Procedures," and will sign where necessary. You must then submit the form to the LPC Board for approval.

The supervision I provide for you will be individual supervision. You will meet with me one hour each week during the time you are completing your required 3,000 hours of supervised experience as a counselor intern. The hourly fee for my services is $_____, which has been set according to a fee schedule based on the income of you and your spouse or partner. This fee schedule will be reviewed annually and adjusted as appropriate. Fees are payable by check before each supervision session begins. In the event you must reschedule a session for

---

*NOTE: This agreement was developed specifically to provide supervision to counselors preparing to be licensed as Professional Counselors in Louisiana. It should be modified to reflect the specific purpose and circumstances of supervision relationships.

some reason, you must notify me 24 hours in advance. If such notice is not received, you must pay the full fee for the missed session plus the fee for the current session prior to the next scheduled session. If you miss a session for circumstances beyond your control and were unable to contact me prior to missing the session, no fee will be charged.

Once our supervision relationship has been approved and you have been granted Intern status, our supervisory relationship will begin. Our professional relationship will be limited to the formal scheduled hours we have agreed to for your supervision. In the event situations occur in your role as counselor in which you need direction and advice, you should consult your immediate supervisor at the site where you are providing counseling services and follow his or her direction. My regular hourly fee for supervision must be paid by you for any telephone or face-to-face consultation requested by you outside our regularly scheduled supervision sessions.

My philosophy of supervision is that my role as your clinical supervisor is to assist you in practicing counseling in the most effective manner possible, given your choice of counseling theories, approaches, and interventions. I will review your work and give you my impressions of your strengths and weakness and will assist you in improving your skills as a counselor. In addition, I will evaluate your work on a continuing basis.

It is your responsibility to notify your administrative supervisor at the site or sites where you are collecting your hours of experience that you are receiving clinical supervision from me. You should explain the nature of our supervisory relationship. If your administrative supervisor wishes to consult with me regarding your work, ask him or her to contact me.

In order for me to supervise you, you must be able to audio-tape or video-tape one counseling session each week. You must follow any requirements your site or sites may impose regarding these tapes. At each meeting we have, you will provide me with a new tape. During the time the tape is in my possession, I shall ensure no one else has access to it. I will keep information revealed in the tape confidential. I will review the tape before our next meeting and will return the tape to you at that next meeting. It will then be your responsibility to erase or destroy the tape that has been reviewed.

During the time I am serving as your clinical supervisor, I will make every effort to review with you cases that you choose to bring to my attention for consultation. In addition, I will review the tapes you provide to me of counseling sessions. My duty to you is to provide you with professional clinical supervision. However, I will not be responsible for your day-to-day activities as a counseling intern. Your administrative supervisor or supervisors at your site or sites will be responsible for your on-going counseling activities.

Because I must evaluate your professional performance as a counselor intern, we will not have a personal friendship during the time I am serving as your supervisor. While we may have a congenial and collegial professional relationship and may attend social functions together, we should not include each other in social interactions one of us has initiated. Please do not offer me gifts or invite me to your home or nonprofessional social events you are hosting during the time I am serving as your clinical supervisor.

You must complete a total of 3,000 hours of supervised experience. When you have completed the first 1,000 hours, I will provide you with a written evaluation of your progress and performance, including my determination of whether you are progressing satisfactorily toward your goal of becoming a Licensed Professional Counselor. I will provide you with another written evaluation at the end of the second 1,000 hours. At the end of your total 3,000 hours of supervised experience, I will verify the supervision I have provided to you to the LPC Board and will either recommend or not recommend you for licensure as a Professional Counselor.

I agree to provide clinical supervision to you of your counseling responsibilities in a professional manner to the extent described within this agreement. Our relationship is limited to the terms and conditions set forth herein. Either of us, with a two-week written notice to the other, may cancel this agreement for any reason. In the event the agreement is canceled by either of us, you agree to notify the LPC Board immediately.

By signing below, I am agreeing to provide you with clinical supervision according to the terms of this agreement, and you are agreeing to pay my fee and comply with the terms of this agreement as well.

_____   _____   _____   _____
Theodore P. Remley, Jr.   Date   Supervisee's Signature   Date

REFERENCES

Abbott, A. (1988). *The system of professions: An essay on the division of expert labor.* Chicago: University of Chicago Press.

Abraham, S.C. (1978). *The public accounting profession: Problems and prospects.* Lexington, MA: Lexington Books.

Adarand Constructors, Inc. v. Pena, 515 U.S. 200, 115 S.Ct. 2097, 132 L.Ed.2d 158 (1995).

Age Discrimination in Employment Act of 1967, 29 U.S.C. §621 *et seq.* (1999)

Age Discrimination in Employment Act of 1975, 42 U.S.C. §§1601 *et seq.* (1999)

Ahia, C. E., & Martin, D. (1993). *The danger-to-self-or-others exception to confidentiality.* Alexandria, VA: American Counseling Association.

Akamatsu, T. J. (1988). Intimate relationships with former clients: National survey of attitudes and behavior among practitioners. *Professional Psychology: Research and Practice. 199,* 454–458.

Alberty, S. C. (1989). *Advising small business.* Deerfield, IL: Callaghan & Company.

Allison v. Patel, 211 Ga. App. 376, 438 S.E.2d 920 (1993).

Alton, W. G., Jr. (1977). *Malpractice: A trial lawyer's advice for physicians (how to avoid, how to win).* Boston: Little, Brown.

American Association for Marriage and Family Therapists, (1991). *Code of ethics.* Washington, DC: Author.

American Bar Association. (1999). Legal malpractice claims in the 1990s. [On-line] Available: *http://www.kvi-calbar.com/abaclaimdata.html.* Washington, DC: Author.

American Counseling Association. (1995). *Code of ethics and standards of practice.* Alexandria, VA: Author.

American Counseling Association. (1996). *Licensing requirements and scope of practice for counselors.* Alexandria, VA: Author.

American Counseling Association. (1997). *Licensing requirements* (2nd ed.). Alexandria, VA: Author.

American Educational Research Association. (1999). Standards for educational and psychological testing. Washington, DC: Author.

American Psychiatric Association. (1994). *Diagnostic and statistical manual of mental disorders* (4th ed.). Washington, DC: Author.

American Psychological Association. (1982). *Ethical principles in the conduct of research with human participants.* Washington, DC: Author.

American Psychological Association. (1992). *Ethical principles of psychologists and code of conduct.* Washington, DC: Author.

American Psychological Association. (1993). Record keeping guidelines. *American Psychologist, 48,* 984–986.

American Psychiatric Association. (1994) *Diagnostic and statistical manual of mental disorders* (4th ed.) Washington, DC: Author.

Anastasi, A. (1988). *Psychological testing* (6th ed.). New York: Macmillan.

Anderson, B. S. (1996). *The counselor and the law* (4th ed.). Alexandria, VA: American Counseling Association.

Anderson, D., & Swanson, C. D. (1994). *Legal issues in licensure.* Alexandria, VA: American Counseling Association.

Anderson, S. K., & Kitchener, K. S. (1996). Nonromantic, nonsexual post-therapy relationships between psychologists and former clients: An exploratory study of critical incidents. *Professional Psychology: Research and Practice, 27,* 59–66.

Appelbaum, P.S., Lidz, C. W., & Meisel, A. (1987). *Informed consent: Legal theory and clinical practice.* New York: Oxford University Press.

Applebaum, P. (1993). Legal liability and managed care. *American Psychologist, 48,* 251–257.

Application of Striegel, 92 Misc2d 113, 399 N.Y.S.2d 584 (1977).

Arthur, G. L., Jr., & Swanson, C. D. (1993). *Confidentiality and privileged communication.* Alexandria, VA: American Counseling Association.

Association for Counselor Education and Supervision. (1990). Standards for counseling supervisors. *Journal of Counseling and Development, 69,* 30–32.

Association for Counselor Education and Supervision. (1993, Summer). Ethical guidelines for counseling supervisors. *ACES Spectrum, 53*(4), 1–4.

Association for Specialists in Group Work. (1989). *Ethical guidelines for group counselors.* Alexandria, VA: Author.

Association for Specialists in Group Work. (1992). *Professional standards for the training of group workers.* Alexandria, VA: Author.

Association for Specialists in Group Work. (1998). ASGW best practice guidelines. *Journal for Specialists in Group Work, 23,* 237–244.

Atkinson, D. R., Molten, G., & Sue, D. W. (Eds.). (1993). *Counseling American minorities: A cross-cultural perspective* (4th ed.). Dubuque, IA: Brown and Benchmark.

Atkinson, D. R., Thompson, C. E., & Grant, S. K. (1993). A three-dimensional model for counseling racial/ethnic minorities. *The Counseling Psychologist, 21,* 257–277.

Austin, K. M., Moline, M. E., & Williams, G. T. (1990). *Confronting malpractice: Legal and ethical dilemmas in psychotherapy.* Newbury Park, CA: Sage Publications.

Axelson, J. A. (1993). *Counseling and development in a multicultural society* (2nd ed.). Pacific Grove, CA: Brooks/Cole.

Baird, K. A., & Rupert, P. A. (1987). Clinical management of confidentiality: A survey of psychologists in seven states. *Professional Psychology: Research and Practice, 18,* 347–352.

Bakke v. Regents of the University of California, 438 U.S. 265 (1978).

Bartell, P. A., & Rubin, L. J. (1990). Dangerous liaisons: Sexual intimacies in supervision. *Professional Psychology: Research and Practice, 21,* 442–450.

Beamish, P.M., Navin, S. L., & Davidson, P. (1994). Ethical dilemmas in marriage and family therapy: Implications for training. *Journal of Mental Health Counseling, 16,* 129–142.

Beauchamp, T.L., &: Childress, J.F. (1994). *Principles of biomedical ethics* (3rd ed.). New York: Oxford University Press.

Becker, R. F. (1997). *Scientific evidence and expert testimony handbook: A guide for lawyers, criminal iinvestigators and forensic specialists.* Springfield, Il: Charles C. Thomas.

Belli, Sr., M. M., & Carlova, J. (1986). *Belli for your malpractice defense.* Oradell, NJ: Medical Economics Books.

Belton, R., & Avery, D. (1999). *Employment discrimination law* (6th ed.). St. Paul, MN: West.

Beren, P., & Bunnin, B. (1983). *Author law and strategies.* Berkeley, CA: Nolo Press.

Bergan, J. R., & Kratochwill, T. R. (1990). *Behavioral consultation and therapy.* New York: Plenum.

Berge, Z. L. (1994). Electronic discussion groups. *Communication education, 43,* 102–111.

Berman, A. L., & Cohen-Sandler, R. (1982). Suicide and the standard of care: Optimal v. acceptable. *Suicide and Life-Threatening Behavior, 12,* 114–122.

Bernard, J. M., & Goodyear, R. K. (1992). *Fundamentals of clinical supervision.* Boston: Allyn and Bacon.

Berner, M. (1998). Informed consent. In L. E. Lifson, & R. I. Simon (Eds.), *The mental health practitioner and the law* (pp. 23–43). Cambridge, MA: Harvard University Press.

Bersoff, D.N. (1996). The virtue of principle ethics. *Counseling Psychologist, 24,* 86–91.

Biaggio, M., Paget, T. L., & Chenoweth, M. S. (1997). A model for ethical management of faculty-student dual relationships. *Professional Psychology: Research and Practice, 28,* 184–189.

Biele, N., & Barnhill, E. (1995). The art of advocacy. In J. C. Gonsiorek (Ed.), *Breach of trust: Sexual exploitation by health care professionals and clergy* (pp. 317–332). Thousand Oaks, CA: Sage.

Black, H. C. (1990). *Black's law dictionary* (6th ed.). St. Paul, MN: West Publishing.

Blackhall, L. J., Murphy, S. T., Frank, G., Michel, V., & Azen, S. (1995). Ethnicity and attitudes toward patient autonomy. *Journal of the American Medical Association, 274,* 820–825.

Blevins-Knabe, B. (1992). The ethics of dual relationships in higher education. *Ethics and Behavior, 2,* 151–163.

Blocher, D.H. (1987). *The professional counselor.* New York: Macmillan.

Bloom, B. L. (1977). *Community mental health: A general introduction* (2nd ed.). Monterey, CA: Brooks/Cole.

Bograd, M. (1993, January/February). The duel over dual relationships. *The California Therapist,* 7–16.

Bogust v. Iverson. 10 Wisc.2d 129, 102 N.W.2d 228 (1960).

Bok, S. (1983). *Secrets: On the ethics of concealment and revelation.* New York: Vintage Books.

Boling v. Superior Court. 105 Cal. App.3d 430, 164 Cal. Rptr. 432 (App. 1980).

Borders, L. D. (1991). A systematic approach to peer group supervision. *Journal of Counseling and Development, 69,* 248–252.

Borders, L. D., Cashwell, C. S., & Rotter, J. C. (1995). Supervision of counselor licensure applicants: A comparative study. *Counselor Education and Supervision, 35,* 54–69.

Borders, L. D., & Leddick, G. R. (1987). *Handbook of counseling supervision.* Alexandria, VA: Association for Counselor Education and Supervision.

Borow, H. (1964). Milestones: A chronology of notable events in the history of vocational guidance. In H. Borow (Ed.), *Man in a world at work* (pp. 45–64). Boston: Houghton Mifflin.

Borys, D.S. (1988). *Dual relationships between therapist and client: A national survey of clinicians' attitudes and practices.* Unpublished doctoral dissertation, University of California, Los Angeles.

Bouhoutsos, J., Holroyd, J., Lerman, H., Forer, B., & Greenberg, M. (1983). Sexual intimacy between psychologists and patients. *Professional Psychology, 14,* 185–196.

Bowman, V.E., Harley, L. D., & Bowman, R. L. (1995). Faculty-student relationships: The dual role controversy. *Counselor Education and Supervision, 34,* 232–242.

Braaten, E. E., Otto, S., & Handelsman, M. M. (1993). What do people want to know about psychotherapy.? *Psychotherapy, 30,* 565–570.

Bransford, S.D., & Stein, B.S. (1993). *The ideal problem solver* (2nd ed.). New York: Freeman.

Bray, J. H., Shepherd, J. N., & Hays, J. R. (1985). Legal and ethical issues in informed consent to psychotherapy. *American Journal of Family Therapy, 13,* 50–60.

Broverman, I. K., Broverman, D., Clarkson, F. E., Rosencrantz, P., & Vogel, S. (1970). Sex role stereotypes and clinical judgments of mental health. *Journal of Consulting and Clinical Psychology, 34,* 1–7.

Brown v. Board of Education, 347 U.S. 483 (1954).

Brown, D. (1993). Training consultants: A call to action. *Journal of Counseling and Development. 72,* 139–143.

Brown, D., & Srebalus, D. J. (1988). *An introduction to the counseling profession.* Upper Saddle River, NJ: Prentice Hall.

Bursztajn, H., Gutheil, T. G., Hamm, R. M., & Brodsky, A. (1983). Subjective data and suicide assessment in the light of recent legal developments. Part II: Clinical uses of legal standards in the interpretation of subjective data. *International Journal of Law and Psychiatry, 6,* 331–350.

Butler, S. F. (1998). *Assessment preparation and practices reported by mental health and related professionals.* Unpublished doctoral dissertation, University of New Orleans.

Caddy, R. G. (1981). The development and current status of professional psychology. *Professional Psychology, 12,* 377–384.

Calamari, J. D., Perillo, J. M., & Bender, H. H. (1989). *Cases and problems on contracts* (2nd ed.). St. Paul, MN: West.

Canterbury v. Spence, 464 F.2d 772 (D.C. Cir 1972).

Cantor, P. (1976). Personality characteristics found among youthful female suicide attempters. *Journal of Abnormal Psychology, 85,* 324–329.

Caplow, T. (1966). The sequence of professionalization. In H. M. Vollmer & D. L. Mills (Eds.), *Professionalization* (pp.19–21). Upper Saddle River, NJ: Prentice-Hall.

Capuzzi, D. (1994). *Suicide prevention in the schools: Guidelines for middle and high school settings.* Alexandria, VA: American Counseling Association.

Capuzzi, D., & Golden, L. (Eds.). (1988). *Preventing adolescent suicide.* Muncie, IN: Accelerated Development, Inc.

Carabillo, J. A. (1986). Liability for treatment decisions: How far does it extend? In C. M. Combe (Ed.), *Managed health care: Legal and operational issues facing providers, insurers, and employers* (pp. 341–407). New York: Practising Law Institute.

Carlson, J., Sperry, L., & Lewis, J. A. (1997). *Family therapy: Ensuring treatment efficacy.* Pacific Grove, CA: Brooks/Cole.

Carrese, J. A., & Rhodes, L. A. (1995). Western bioethics on the Navajo reservation. *Journal of the American Medical Association, 274,* 826–829.

Carroll, T. (1994). [On-line]. Available: http://www.usq.edu.au/faculty/arts/journ/copyus.htm

Cavanagh, M. E. (1982). *The counseling experience.* Monterey, CA: Brooks/Cole.

Chafee, Z. (1943). Privileged communications: Is justice served or obstructed by closing the doctor's mouth on the witness stand? *Yale Law Journal, 52,* 607–612.

Chamallas, M. (1988). Consent, equality and the legal control of sexual conduct. *Southern California Law Review, 61,* 777–862.

Chauvin, J. C., & Remley, T. P., Jr. (1996). Responding to allegations of unethical conduct. *Journal of Counseling and Development, 74,* 563–568.

Christie, G. C., Meeks, J. E., Pryor, E. S., & Sanders, J. (1997). *Cases and materials on the law of torts* (3rd ed.). St. Paul, MN: West.

Claim of Gerkin, 106 Misc.2d 643,434 N.Y.S.2d 607 (1980).

Clausen v. Clausen, 675 P.2d 562 (Utah, 1983).

Cleary. E. (Ed.). (1984). *McCormick's handbook on the law of evidence* (3rd ed.). St. Paul. MN: West.

Cohen, E. D. (1997). Ethical standards in counseling sexually active clients with HIV. *In Ethics in therapy* (pp. 211–233). New York: Hatherleigh.

Cohen, R. J. (1979). *Malpractice: A guide for mental health professionals.* New York: Free Press.

Cohen, R. J., & Mariano, W. E. (1982). *Legal guidebook in mental health.* New York: The Free Press.

Coleman, P., & Shellow, R. A. (1992). Suicide: Unpredictable and unavoidable–Proposed guidelines provide rational test for physician's liability. *Nebraska Law Review, 71,* 643–693.

Commonwealth ex rel. Platt v. Platt, 404 A.2d 410 (Pa. Super. 1979).

Connelly v. University of Vermont, 244 F.Supp. 156 (D.Vt. 1965).

Corcoran, M. E. (1989). Managing the risks in managed care. In M. E. Corcoran (Ed.), *Managed health care 1989* (pp. 7–70). New York: Practising Law Institute.

Corey, G. (2000). *Theory and practice of group counseling* (6th ed.). Pacific Grove, CA: Brooks/Cole.

Corey, G. (1991). *Theory and practice of counseling and psychotherapy* (4th ed.). Pacific Grove, CA: Brooks/Cole.

Corey, G., Corey, M., & Callanan, P. (1998). *Issues and ethics in the helping professions* (5th ed.). Pacific Grove, CA: Brooks/Cole.

Costa, L., & Altekruse, M. (1994). Duty-to-warn guidelines for mental health counselors. *Journal of Counseling and Development, 72,* 346–350.

Cottle, M. (1956). Witnesses—privilege-communications to psychotherapists. *University of Kansas Law Review, 4,* 597–599.

Cottone, R. R. (1985). The need for counselor licensure: A rehabilitation counseling perspective. *Journal of Counseling and Development, 63,* 625–629.

Cottone, R. R. (1992). *Theories and paradigms of counseling and psychotherapy.* Needham Heights, MA: Allyn & Bacon.

Cottone, R. R., & Tarvydas, V. M. (1998). *Ethical and professional issues in counseling.* Upper Saddle River, NJ: Merrill/Prentice Hall.

Council for Accreditation of Counseling and Related Educational Programs. (1994, January). *CACREP accreditation standards and procedures manual* (2nd ed.). Alexandria. VA: Author.

Council for Accreditation of Counseling and Related Educational Programs. (1998). *Directory of accredited programs.* Alexandria, VA: Author.

Cramton, R. C. (1981). Incompetence: The North American experience. In L. E. Trakman, & D. Watters (Eds.), *Professional competence and the law* (pp. 158–163). Halifax, Nova Scotia, Canada: Dalhousie University.

Crawford, R. L. (1994). *Avoiding counselor malpractice.* Alexandria, VA: American Counseling Association.

Curd, T. (1938). Privileged communications between the doctor and his patient—an anomaly of the law. *West Virginia Law Review, 44,* 165–174.

Curran, D. F. (1987). *Adolescent suicidal behavior.* Washington, DC: Hemisphere Publishing.

Custer, G. (1994, November). Can universities be liable for incompetent grads? *APA Monitor, 25*(11), 7.

Cynthia B. v. New Rochelle Hospital, 86 A.D.2d 256, 449 N.Y.S.2d 755 (App. Div. 1982).

Daniluk, J. C., & Haverkamp, B. E. (1993). Ethical issues in counseling adult survivors of incest. *Journal of Counseling & Development, 72,* 16–22.

Davidson, V. (1977) Psychiatry's problem with no name: Therapist-patient sex. *American Journal of Psychoanalysis, 37,* 43–50.

Davis, J. L., & Mickelson, D. J. (1994). School counselors: Are you aware of ethical and legal aspects of counseling? *The School Counselor, 42,* 5–13.

Davis, P. A. (1983). *Suicidal adolescents.* Springfield, IL: Charles C. Thomas.

Dawidoff, D. J. (1973). *The malpractice of psychiatrists: Malpractice in psychoanalysis, psychotherapy and psychiatry.* Springfield, IL: Charles C. Thomas.

Dean, L. A., & Meadows, M. E. (1995). College counseling: Union and intersection. *Journal of Counseling and Development, 74,* 139–142.

DeChiara, P. (1988). The need for universities to have rules on consensual sexual relationships between faculty members and students. *Columbia Journal of Law and Social Problems, 21,* 137–162.

Dedden, L., & James, S. (1998, Summer). A comprehensive guide to free career counseling resources on the Internet. *The ASCA Counselor,* pp. l7, 19.

DeFunis v. Odegaard, 507 P.2d 1169 (Wash. 1973), dismissed as moot, 416 U.S. 312 (1973), on remand, 529 P.2d 438 (Wash. 1974).

DeRonde v. Regents of the University of California, 625 P.2d 220 (Cal. 1981).

Deutsch, C. J. (1985). A survey of therapists' personal problems and treatment. *Professional Psychology: Research and Practice, 16,* 305–315.

Dinkmeyer, D., Jr., Carlson, J., & Dinkmeyer, D. (1994). *Consultation: School mental health professionals as consultants.* Muncie, IN: Accelerated Development.

Donigian, J. (1991). Dual relationships: An ethical issue. *Together, 19*(2), 6–7.

Dorken, H., & Webb, J. T. (1980). 1976 third-party reimbursement experience: An interstate comparison by insurance carrier. *American Psychologist, 35,* 355–363.

Dougherty, A. M. (1990). *Consultation: Practice and perspectives.* Pacific Grove, CA: Brooks/Cole.

Dougherty, A. M. (1995). *Consultation: Practice and perspectives in school and community settings* (2nd ed.). Pacific Grove, CA: Brooks/Cole.

Dougherty, A. M. (2000). *Psychological consultation and collaboration* (3rd ed.). Pacific Grove, CA: Brooks/Cole.

Driscoll, J. M. (1992). Keeping covenants and confidence sacred: One point of view. *Journal of Counseling and Development, 70,* 704–708.

Drukteinis, A. M. (1985). Psychiatric perspectives on civil liability for suicide. *Bulletin of American Academy of Psychiatry Law, 13,* 71–83.

Dugan, W. E. (1965). Preface. In J. W. Loughary, R. O. Stripling, & P. W. Fitzgerald (Eds.), *Counseling, a growing profession* (pp i–iii). Alexandria, VA: American Counseling Association.

Eisel v. Board of Education of Montgomery County, 597 A.2d 447 (Md. 1991).

Ellis v. Ellis, 472 S.W.2d 741 (Tenn. App. 1971).

Emener, W. G., & Cottone, R. R. (1989). Professionalization, deprofessionalization, and reprofessionalization of rehabilitation counseling according to criteria of professions. *Journal of Counseling and Development, 67,* 576–581.

Emerson, S., & Markos, P.A. (1996). Signs and symptoms of the impaired counselor. *Journal of Humanistic Education and Development, 34,* 108–117.

Engels, D. W., Minor, C. W., Sampson, J. P., Jr., & Splete, H. H. (1995). Career counseling specialty: History, development, and prospect. *Journal of Counseling and Development, 74,* 134–l38.

Enzer, N. B. (1985). Ethics in child psychiatry—An overview. In D. H. Schetky & E. P. Benedek (Eds.), *Emerging issues in child psychiatry and the law* (pp. 3–21) New York: Brunner/Mazel.

Epperson, D. L., & Lewis, K. N. (1987). Issues of informed entry into counseling: Perceptions and preferences resulting from different types and amounts of pretherapy information. *Journal of Counseling Psychology, 34,* 266–275.

Erickson, S. (1993). Ethics and confidentiality in AIDS counseling: A professional dilemma. *Journal of Mental Health Counseling, 15,* 118–131.

Etzioni, A. (1969). *The semi-professions and their organization.* New York: Free Press.

Ewalt, J. R. (1975). The birth of the community mental health movement. In W. E. Barton & C. J. Sanborn (Eds.), *An assessment of the community mental health movement* (pp. 13–20). Lexington, MA: D.C. Heath.

Family Educational Rights and Privacy Act of 1974, 20 U.S.C.A. §1232g (West, 1997).

Farber, B. A., & Heifetz, L. J. (1982). The process and dimensions of burnout in psychotherapists. *Professional Psychology, 13,* 293–301.

Fay v. South Colonie Cent. School Dist., C.A.2 (N.Y.) 1986, 802 F.2d 21.

Fazio, III, J. R. (1997). Wrongful termination law in Florida. [On-line] Available: *http://www.cafelaw.com/wrongfultermination.*

Finn, S. E., & Tonsager, M. E. (1992). Therapeutic effects of providing MMPI-2 test feedback to college students awaiting therapy. *Psychological Assessment, 4,* 278–287.

Fisher, R. M. (1964). The psychotherapeutic professions and the law of privileged communications. *Wayne Law Review, 10,* 609–654.

Ford, D. Y., Harris, J. J., & Schuerger, J. M. (1993). Racial identity development among gifted black students. *Journal of Counseling and Development, 71,* 409–417.

Forester-Miller, H. (1997). Dual relationships in training group workers. In B. Herlihy and G. Corey, *Boundary issues in counseling* (pp. 87–89). Alexandria, VA: American Counseling Association.

Forester-Miller, H., & Davis, T. E. (1995). *A practitioner's guide to ethical decision making.* Alexandria, VA: American Counseling Association.

Fox, R. E. (1994). Training professional psychologists for the twenty-first century. *American Psychologist, 49,* 200–206.

Friedman, J., & Boumil, M. M. (1995). *Betrayal of trust: Sex and power in professional relationships.* Westport, CT: Praeger.

Friedson, E. (1983). The theory of professions: State-of-the-art. In R. Dingwall & P. Lewis (Eds.), *The sociology of the professions.* New York: St. Martin's Press.

Gabbard, G. O. (1995, April). What are boundaries in psychotherapy? *The Menninger Letter, 3*(4), 1–2.

Garcia, J., Glosoff, H. L., & Smith, J. L. (1994). Report of the ACA ethics committee: 1993–1994. *Journal of Counseling and Development, 73,* 253–256.

Garcia, J., Salo, M., & Hamilton, W. M. (1995). Report of the ACA ethics committee: 1994–1995. *Journal of Counseling and Development, 72,* 221–224.

Gartrell, N., Herman, J., Olarte, S., Feldstein, M., & Localio, R. (1987). Reporting practices of psychologists who knew of sexual misconduct by colleagues. *American Journal of Orthopsychiatry, 57*(2), 287–295.

Gellhorn, W. (1976). The abuse of occupational licensing. *University of Chicago Law Review, 44,* 6–27.

Gelso, C. J., & Carter, J. A. (1985). The relationship in counseling and psychotherapy: Components, consequences, and theoretical antecedents. *The Counseling Psychologist, 13,* 155–243.

General Revision of the Copyright Law, 17 U.S.C. 101 *et seq.* (1999)

Gibson, R. L., & Mitchell, M. H. (1999). *Introduction to counseling and guidance* (5th ed.). Upper Saddle River, NJ: Merrill/Prentice Hall.

Gibson, W. T., & Pope, K. S. (1993). The ethics of counseling: A national survey of certified counselors. *Journal of Counseling and Development, 71,* 330–336.

Gilbert, L. A., & Rossman, K. M. (1992). Gender and the mentoring process for women: Implications for professional development. *Professional Psychology: Research and Practice, 23,* 233–238.

Gilbert, L. A., & Scher, M. (1987). The power of an unconscious belief: Male entitlement and sexual intimacy with clients. *Professional Practice of Psychology, 8,* 94–108.

Gilbert, S. P. (1992). Ethical issues in the treatment of severe psychopathology in university and college counseling centers. *Journal of Counseling & Development, 71,* 330–336.

Gladding, S. (1992). *Counseling as an art: The creative arts in counseling.* Alexandria, VA: American Counseling Association.

Gladding, S. T. (1995). *Group work: A counseling specialty* (3rd ed.). Upper Saddle River, NJ: Merrill/Prentice Hall.

Gladding, S. T. (1998). *Family therapy: History, theory, and practice.* (2nd ed.). Upper Saddle River, NJ: Merrill/Prentice Hall.

Gladding, S. T. (2000). *Counseling: A comprehensive profession* (4th ed.). Upper Saddle River, NJ: Merrill/Prentice Hall.

Glaser, R. D., & Thorpe, J. S. (1986). Unethical intimacy: A survey of sexual contact and advances between psychology educators and female graduate students. *American Psychologist, 41,* 43–51.

Glosoff, H. L. (1997). Multiple relationships in private practice. In B. Herlihy & G. Corey, *Boundary issues in counseling* (pp. 114–120). Alexandria, VA: American Counseling Association.

Glosoff, H. L. (1998). Managed care: A critical ethical issue for counselors. *Counseling and Human Development, 31*(2), 1–16.

Glosoff, H. L., Garcia, J., Herlihy, B., & Remley, T. P., Jr. (1999). Managed care: Ethical considerations for counselors. *Counseling and Values, 44,* 8–16.

Glosoff, H. L., & Herlihy, B. (1995, Winter). Teaching, training, and supervision standards in the 1995 ACA Code of Ethics: What's new, what's different? *ACES Spectrum,* 10–13.

Glosoff, H. L., Herlihy, S., Herlihy, B., & Spence, B. Privileged communication in the psychologist-client relationship. (1997) *Professional Psychology: Research and Practice, 28,* 573–581.

Glosoff, H. L. Herlihy, B., Spence, B. (In press.) Privileged communication in the counselor–client relationship. *Journal of Counseling and Development.*

Golden, L. (1990, March 1). In Schafer, C. Ethics: Dual relationships come under scrutiny. *Guidepost,* pp. 1, 3, 16.

Goldenberg, H., & Goldenberg, I. (1998). *Counseling today's families* (3rd ed.). Pacific Grove, CA: Brooks/Cole.

Goldenberg, I., & Goldenberg, H. (1996). *Family therapy: An Overview* (4th ed.). Pacific Grove, CA: Brooks/Cole.

Gostin, L. O. (1995). Informed consent, cultural sensitivity, and respect for persons [Editorial]. *Journal of the American Medical Association, 274,* 844–845.

Gould, D. (1998). Listen to your lawyer. In L. E. Lifson, & R. I. Simon (Eds.), *The mental health practitioner and the law* (pp. 344–356). Cambridge, MA: Harvard University Press.

Gould, J. W. (1998). *Conducting scientifically crafted child custody evaluations.* Thousand Oaks, CA: Sage.

Gray, L., & Harding, A. (1988). Confidentiality limits with clients who have the AIDS virus. *Journal of Counseling and Development, 65,* 219–226.

Greenburg, S. L., Lewis, G. J., & Johnson, J. (1985). Peer consultation groups for private practitioners. *Professional Psychology: Research and Practice, 16,* 437–447.

Grosch, W. N., & Olsen, D.C. (1994). *When helping starts to hurt.* New York: Norton.

Gumper, L. L. (1984). *Legal issues in the practice of ministry.* Minneapolis, MN: Ministers Life Resources.

Guterman, M. (1991). Working couples: Finding a balance between family and career. In J. M. Kummerow (Ed.), *New directions in career planning and the workplace* (pp. 167–193). Palo Alto, CA: Consulting Psychologists Press.

Gutheil, T. G. (1989). Borderline personality disorder, boundary violations, and patient-therapist sex: Medicolegal pitfalls. *American Journal of Psychiatry, 146,* 597–602.

Gutheil, T. G., & Gabbard, G. O. (1993). The concept of boundaries in clinical practice: Theoretical and risk-management dimensions. *American Journal of Psychiatry, 150,* 188–196.

Guttmacher, M., & Weihofen, H. (1952). Privileged communications between psychiatrist and patient, *Indiana Law Journal, 28,* 32–44.

Guy, J. D. (1987). *The personal life of the psychotherapist.* New York: Wiley.

Haas, L. J., & Alexander, J. R. (1981). *Ethical and legal issues in family therapy.* Paper presented at the meeting of the American Psychological Association, Los Angeles.

Haas, L. J., & Cummings, N. A. (1991). Managed outpatient mental health plans: Clinical, ethical, and practical guidelines for participation. *Professional Psychology: Research and Practice, 22,* 45–51.

Haas, L. J., & Malouf, J. L. (1995). *Keeping up the good work: A practitioner's guide to mental health ethics* (2nd ed.). Sarasota, FL: Professional Resource Exchange.

Hafen, B. Q., & Frandsen, K. J. (1986). *Youth suicide: Depression and loneliness.* Provo, UT: Behavioral Health Associates.

Hagan, M. A. (1997). *Whores of the court: The fraud of psychiatric testimony and the rape of American justice.* New York: Regan Books.

Haley, J. (1976). *Problem solving therapy.* San Francisco: Jossey Bass. Hare-Mustin, R. T. (1980). Family therapy may be dangerous to your health. *Professional Psychology: Research and Practice, 11,* 935–938.

Hamilton, R. W. (1990). *Cases and materials on corporations including partnerships and limited partnerships* (4th ed.). St. Paul, MN: West.

Handler, J. F. (1990). *Law and the search for community.* Philadelphia: University of Pennsylvania Press.

Hansen, J. C., Stevic, R. R., & Warner, R. W., Jr. (1986). *Counseling: Theory and process* (4th ed.). Boston: Allyn and Bacon.

Harding, A., Gray, L., & Neal, M. (1993). Confidentiality limits with clients who have HIV: A review of ethical and legal guidelines and professional policies. *Journal of Counseling and Development, 71,* 297–305.

Hare-Mustin, R.T. (1980). Family therapy may be dangerous to your health. *Professional Psychology, 11,* 935–938.

Haring-Hidore, M., & Paludi, M.A. (1989). Sexuality and sex in mentoring and tutoring: Implications for women's opportunities and achievement. *Peabody Journal of Education, 64,* 164–172.

Harrar, W. R., VandeCreek, L., & Knapp, S. (1990). Ethical and legal aspects of clinical supervision. *Professional Psychology: Research and Practice, 21,* 37–41.

Harris, A. D. (1997). *Licensing requirements* (2nd ed.). Alexandria, VA: American Counseling Association.

Hayman, P., & Covert, J. (1986). Ethical dilemmas in college counseling centers. *Journal of Counseling and Development, 64,* 315–317.

Haynsworth, H. J. (1986). *Organizing a small business entity.* Philadelphia: American Law Institute-American Bar Association Committee on Continuing Professional Education.

Hedges, L. E. (1993, July/August). In praise of dual relationships. Part II: Essential dual relatedness in developmental psychotherapy. *The California Therapist,* 42–46.

Hedlund v. Superior Court of Orange County, 34 Cal. 3d 695, 669 P.2d 41, 194 Cal. Rptr. 805 (1983).

La. Rev. Stat. Ann. § 37:1101–1115 (West, 1999).

Heller, M. S. (1957). Some comments to lawyers on the practice of psychiatry. *Temple Law Quarterly, 30,* 401–407.

Hendrick, S. S. (1988). Counselor self-disclosure. *Journal of Counseling and Development, 66,* 419–424.

Hendrix, D. H. (1991). Ethics and intrafamily confidentiality in counseling with children. *Journal of Mental Health Counseling, 13,* 323–333.

Henn, H. G. (1991). *Henn on copyright law: A practitioner's guide.* New York: Practising Law Institute.

Herlihy, B., & Corey, G. (1996). *ACA ethical standards casebook* (5th ed.). Alexandria. VA: American Counseling Association.

Herlihy, B., & Corey, G. (1997). Codes of ethics as catalysts for improving practice. In *Ethics in therapy* (pp. 37–56). New York: Hatherleigh.

Herlihy, B., & Remley, T. P. (1995). Unified ethical standards: A challenge for professionalism. *Journal of Counseling and Development, 74,* 130–133.

Herlihy, B., & Sheeley, V. L. (1988). Counselor liability and the duty to warn: Selected cases, statutory trends, and implications for practice. *Counselor Education and Supervision, 27,* 203–215.

Hermansson, G. L. (1997). Boundaries and boundary management in counselling: The never-ending story. *British Journal of Guidance and Counselling, 25*(2), 133–146.

Hershenson. D. B. (1993). Healthy development as the basis for mental health counseling theory. *Journal of Mental Health Counseling, 15,* 430–437.

Hershenson, D. B., Power, P. W., & Waldo, M. (1996). *Community counseling: Contemporary theory and practice.* Boston: Allyn and Bacon.

Hill, M., Glaser, K., & Harden, J. (1995). A feminist model for ethical decision making. In E. J. Rave & C. C. Larsen (Eds.), *Ethical decision making in therapy: Feminist perspectives* (pp. 18–37). New York: Guilford Press.

Hill, M. (1990). On creating a theory of feminist therapy. *Women and Therapy, 91,* 53–65.

Hilliard, J. (1998). Termination of treatment with troublesome patients. In L. E. Lifson, & R. I. Simon (Eds.), *The mental health practitioner and the law* (pp. 216–221). Cambridge, MA: Harvard University Press.

Hogan, D. B. (1979). *The regulation of psychotherapists.* Cambridge, MA: Ballinger Publishing.

Hollis, J. W. (1997). *Counselor preparation 1996–98: Programs, faculty, trends* (9th ed.). Muncie, IN: Accelerated Development.

Holroyd, J. C., & Brodsky, A. M. (1977). Psychologists' attitudes and practices regarding erotic and nonerotic physical contact with patients. *American Psychologist, 32,* 843–849.

Hopewell v. Adebimpe, 130 Pitt. L. J. 107 (1982).

Horowitz v. Board of Curators of the University of Missouri, 435 U.S. 78 (1978).

Houskamp, B. (1994). Assessing and treating battered women: A clinical review of issues and approaches. *New Directions for Mental Health Services, 64,* 79–89.

Howe, G. E. (1999, April 19). Safety net critical for health care of working poor. [On-line] Available: http://www.amcity.com/milwaukee/starts/1999/04/19/editoria14.html.

Howell, J. A. (1988). Civil liability for suicide: An analysis of the causation issue. *Arizona State Law Journal,* 573–615.

Hoyt, M. F. (1995). *Brief therapy and managed care: Readings for contemporary practice.*

Huber, C. H. (1994). *Ethical, legal, and professional issues in the practice of marriage and family therapy* (2nd ed.). Upper Saddle River, N J: Merrill/Prentice Hall.

Huber, C. H., & Baruth, L. G. (1987). *Ethical, legal and professional issues in the practice of marriage and family therapy.* Upper Saddle River, NJ: Merrill/Prentice Hall.

Huber, P. W. (1991) *Galileo's revenge: Junk science in the courtroom.* New York: Basic Books.

Huey, W. C. (1996). Counseling minor clients. In B. Herlihy & G. Corey, *ACA ethical standards casebook* (5th ed.) (pp. 241–245). Alexandria, VA: American Counseling Association.

Hughes, E. C. (1965). Professions. In K. S. Lynn (Ed.), *The professions in America* (pp. 1–14). Boston: Houghton Mifflin.

Hussain, S. A., & Vandiver, K. T. (1984). *Suicide in children and adolescents.* New York: SP Medical and Scientific Books.

Ideal Publishing Corp. v. Creative Features, 59 A.2d 862, 399 N.Y.S.2d 118 (1977).

In re marriage of Kovash, 858 P.2d 351 (Mont. 1993).

Jablonski v. United States, 712 F.2d 391 (9th Cir. 1983).

Jacobs, E. E., Harvill, R. L., & Masson, R. I. (1994). *Group counseling: Strategies and skills* (2nd ed.). Pacific Grove, CA: Brooks/Cole.

Jacobs, E. E., Masson, R. L., & Harvill, R. L. (1998). *Group counseling: Strategies and skills* (3rd ed.). Pacific Grove, CA: Brooks/Cole.

Jaffee v. Redmond et al., 1996 WL 314841 (U.S. June 13 1996).

Jagers, J. L. (1998). Record keeping. *The Examiner, 11*(2), 6–7.

Jago, J. D. (1984). To protect the public: Professionalism vs. competence in dentistry. *Social Science and Medicine. 19,* 117–122.

James, J. (1996, May 11). University to adopt rules that put limits on dating. *Register-Guard,* Eugene, OR, pp. 1, 6A.

John R. v. Oakland Unified School District, 48 Ca.3d 438, 256 Cal.Rptr. 766, 769 P.2d 948 (1989).

Johnson, S. W., & Maile, L. J. (1987). *Suicide and the schools: A handbook for prevention, intervention, and rehabilitation.* Springfield, IL: Charles C. Thomas.

Johnson, W. K., & Roark, D. B. (1996). *A copyright sampler.* Chicago: American Library Association.

Jones, P. A. (1996). Interstate testimony by child protective agency workers in the child custody context. *Vermont Law Review, 21,* 633–675.

Jordan, A. E., & Meara, N. M. (1990). Ethics and the professional practice of psychologists. *Professional Psychology: Research and Practice, 21,* 107–114.

Jorgenson, L. M. (1995). Sexual contact in fiduciary relationships. In J. C. Gonsiorek (Ed.). *Breach of trust: Sexual exploitation by health care professionals and clergy* (pp. 237–283). Thousand Oaks, CA: Sage.

Kain, C. (Ed.). (1989). *No longer immune: A counselor's guide to AIDS.* Alexandria, VA: American Counseling Association.

Kain, C. D. (1997). Coloring outside the lines: Multiple relationships in working with people living with HIV. In B. Herlihy & G. Corey, *Boundary issues in counseling* (pp. 131–134). Alexandria, VA: American Counseling Association.

Kane, A. W. (1995). The effects of criminalization of sexual misconduct by therapists. In J. C. Gonsiorek (Ed.), *Breach of trust: Sexual exploitation by health care professionals and clergy* (pp. 317–332). Thousand Oaks, CA: Sage.

Kaplin, W. A., & Lee, B. A. (1995). *The law of higher education* (3rd ed.). San Francisco: Jossey-Bass.

Katherine, A. (1991). *Boundaries: Where you end and I begin.* New York: Simon & Schuster.

Katz, J. (1977). Informed consent—A fairy tale? Law's vision. *University of Pittsburgh Law Review, 39,* 137–174.

Kearney, M. (1984). Confidentiality in group psychotherapy. *Psychotherapy in Private Practice, 2*(2), 19–20.

Keith-Spiegel, P. (1994). Teaching psychologists and the new APA ethics code: Do we fit in? *Professional Psychology: Research and Practice, 25,* 362–368.

Keith-Spiegel, P., & Koocher, G. P. (1985). *Ethics in psychology: Professional standards and cases.* New York: Random House.

Keller, E. (1988). Consensual amorous relationships between faculty and students: The Constitutional right to privacy. *Journal of College and University Law, 15,* 21–42.

Kemp, A. (1998). *Abuse in the family: An introduction.* Pacific Grove, CA: Brooks/Cole.

Kett, J. F. (1968). *The formation of the American medical profession: The role of institutions, 1780–1860.* New Haven, CT: Yale University Press.

Kitchener, K. S. (1984). Intuition, critical evaluation and ethical principles: The foundation for ethical decisions in counseling psychology. *Counseling Psychologist, 12,* 43–55.

Kitchener, K. S. (1988). Dual role relationships: What makes them so problematic? *Journal of Counseling and Development, 67,* 217–221.

Kitchener, K. S. (1992). Posttherapy relationships: Ever or never? In B. Herlihy & G. Corey, *Dual relationships in counseling* (pp. 145–148). Alexandria, VA: American Association for Counseling and Development.

Kitchener, K. S., & Harding, S. S. (1990). Dual role relationships. In B. Herlihy and L. Golden, *Ethical standards casebook* (4th ed.) (pp. 145–148). Alexandria, VA: American Association for Counseling and Development.

Knapp, S., & VandeCreek, L. (1987). *Privileged communications in the mental health professions.* New York: Van Nostrand Reinhold.

Knuth, M. O. (1979). Civil liability for causing or failing to prevent suicide. *Loyola of Los Angeles Law Review, 12,* 965–991.

Kottler, J. (1993). *On being a therapist.* San Francisco, CA: Jossey-Bass.

Kramer, D. T. (1994). *Legal rights of children* (2nd ed.). New York: McGraw-Hill.

Kurpius, D. J., & Fuqua, D. R. (1993). Introduction to the special issues. *Journal of Counseling and Development, 71,* 596–597.

Kutchins, H., & Kirk, S. (1987, May) DSM-IIIR and social work malpractice. *Social Work,* 205–211.

Ladany, N., & Friedlander, M. L. (1995). The relationship between the supervisory working alliance and trainees' experience of role conflict and role ambiguity. *Counselor Education and Supervision, 34,* 220–231.

Lakin, M. (1994). Morality in group and family therapies: Multiperson therapies and the 1992 ethics code. *Professional Psychology: Research and Practice, 25,* 344–348.

Lambert, M. J., & Cattani-Thompson, K. (1996). Current findings regarding the effectiveness of counseling: Implications for practice. *Journal of Counseling and Development, 74,* 601–608.

Langer, E. J., & Abelson, R. P. (1974). A patient by any other name. . . : Clinician group differences and labeling bias. *Journal of Consulting and Clinical Psychology, 42,* 4–9.

Leaffer, M. A. (1989). *Understanding copyright law.* New York: Matthew Bender.

Leahy, M. J., & Szymanski, E. M. (1995). Rehabilitation counseling: Evolution and current status. *Journal of Counseling and Development, 74,* 163–166.

Leatherman, C. (1993). In the debate over faculty-student dating, the talk turns to ethics, sex, even love. *Chronicle of Higher Education, 24*(37), A15–A17.

Lee, C. C., & Richardson, B. L. (Eds.) (1991). Multicultural issues in counseling: New approaches to diversity. Alexandria, VA: American Association for Counseling and Development.

Leong, F. T. L., & Wagner, N. S. (1994). Cross-cultural counseling supervision: What do we want to know? *Counselor Education and Supervision, 34,* 117–131.

Lerman, H., & Porter, N. (1990). The contribution of feminism to ethics in psychotherapy. In H. Lerman & N. Porter (Eds.), *Feminist ethics in psychotherapy* (pp. 5–13). New York: Springer.

Levy, C. S. (1972). The context of social work ethics. *Social Work, 17,* 95–101.

Lewis, J. (1993). Utilization review: Doctored decisions? *Trial, 29*(1), 83–87.

Lidz, C. W., Meisel, A., Zerubavel, M. C., Sestak, R. M., & Roth, L. H. (1984). *Informed consent: A study of decisionmaking in psychiatry.* New York: Guilford.

Lisa M. v. Henry Mayo Newhall Memorial Hosp., 12 Cal.4th 291, 48 Cal.Rptr.2d 510, 907 P.2d 358 (1995).

Litwack, T., Kirschner, S., & Wack, R. (1993). The assessment of dangerousness and prediction of violence: Recent research and future prospects. *Psychiatric Quarterly, 64,* 245–273.

Lloyd, A. P. (1992). Dual relationship problems in counselor education. In B. Herlihy and G. Corey, *Dual relationships in counseling* (pp. 59–64). Alexandria, VA: American Association for Counseling and Development.

Logan v. District of Columbia, D.C.D.C. 1978, 447 F.Supp. 1328.

Lonner, W. J., & Ibrahim, F. A. (1996). Appraisal and assessment in cross-cultural counseling. In P. B. Pedersen, J. G. Draguns, W. J. Lonner, & J. E. Trimble (Eds.), *Counseling across cultures* (4th ed.), (pp. 293–322). Thousand Oaks, CA: Sage.

Louisell, D. W., & Sinclair, K. Jr. (1971). The Supreme Court of California, 1969–70–Forward: Reflections on the law of privileged communications–The psychotherapist-patient privilege in perspective. *California Law Review, 59,* 30–55.

Louisiana Licensed Mental Health Counselor Act, La. Rev. Stat. Ann. §37. (West, 1999).

Ludes, F. J., & Gilbert, H. J. (1998). Fiduciary. *Corpus Juris Secundum, 36A,* 381–389.

Macbeth, J. E., Wheeler, A. M., Sither, J. W., & Onek, J. N. (1994). *Legal and risk management issues in the practice of psychiatry.* Washington, DC: Psychiatrists Purchasing Group.

MacNair, R. R. (1992). Ethical dilemmas of child abuse reporting: Implications for mental health counselors. *Journal of Mental Health Counseling, 14,* 127–136.

Madden, R. G. (1998). *Legal issues in social work, counseling, and mental health.* Thousand Oaks, CA: Sage.

Maloney, D. M. (1984). *Protection of human research subjects.* New York: Plenum.

Mannino, F. V., & Shore, M. F. (1986). Understanding consultation: Some orienting dimensions. *Counseling Psychologist, 13*(3), 363–367.

Manno v. McIntosh, 519 NW2d 815 (Iowa App. 1994).

Mappes, D. C., Robb, G. P., & Engels, D. W. (1985). Conflicts between ethics and law in counseling and psychotherapy. *Journal of Counseling and Development, 64,* 246–252.

Margolin, G. (1982). Ethical and legal considerations in marital and family therapy. *American Psychologist, 37,* 788–801.

Maslow, A. (1968). *Toward a psychology of being* (Rev. ed.). New York: Van Nostrand Reinhold.

Massachusetts Board of Retirement v. Murgia, 427 U.S. 307 (1976).

Matarazzo, J. D. (1986). Computerized clinical psychological test interpretations: Unvalidated plus all mean and no sigma. *American Psychologist, 41,* 14–24.

Mattie T. v. Johnson, D.C. Miss. 74 F.R.D. 498, (1976).

Mayfield, A. C. (1996). Receptivity of counselors to insurance fraud in mental health. Unpublished doctoral dissertation, University of New Orleans, Louisiana.

McCarthy, P., Sugden, S., Koker, M., Lamendola, F., Maurer, S., & Renninger, S. (1995). A practical guide to informed consent in clinical supervision. *Counselor Education and Supervision, 35,* 130–138.

McClarren, G. M. (1987). The psychiatric duty to warn: Walking a tightrope of uncertainty. *University of Cincinnati Law Review, 56,* (269–293).

McConnell, W. A., & Kerbs, J. J. (1993). Providing feedback in research with human subjects. *Professional Psychology: Research and Practice, 24,* 266–270.

McDonald v. Hogness, 598 P.2d 707 (Wash. 1979).

McGuire, J.M., Toal, P., & Blau, B. (1985). The adult client's conception of confidentiality in the therapeutic relationship. *Professional Psychology: Research and Practice, 16,* 375–384.

McKown, R. (1961). *Pioneers in mental health.* New York: Dodd, Mead.

McNeil, D., & Binder, R. (1991). Clinical assessment of risk of violence among psychiatric inpatients. *American Journal of Psychiatry, 148,* 1317–1321.

Meara, N. M., Schmidt, L. D., & Day, J. D. (1996). Principles and virtues: A foundation for ethical decisions, policies, and character. *Counseling Psychologist, 24,* 4–77.

Megargee, E. (1979). Methodological problems in the prediction of violence. In J.R. Hays, T. Roberts, & K. Solway (Eds.), *Violence and the violent individual* (pp. 179–191). New York: SP Medical and Scientific Books.

Meloy, J. (1987). The prediction of violence in outpatient psychotherapy. *The American Journal of Psychotherapy, 41,* 38–45.

Melton, G. B. (1991). Ethical judgments amid uncertainty: Dilemmas in the AIDS epidemic. *Counseling Psychology, 19,* 561–565.

Meneese, W. B., & Yutrzenka, B. A. (1990). Correlates of suicidal ideation among rural adolescents. *Suicide and Life-Threatening Behavior, 20,* 206–212.

Merluzzi, T.V., & Brischetto, C.S. (1983). Breach of confidentiality and perceived trustworthiness of counselors. *Journal of Counseling Psychology, 30,* 245–251.

Merta, R. J., Wolfgang, L., & McNeil, K. (1993). Five models for using the experiential group in the preparation of group counselors. *Journal for Specialists in Group Work, 18,* 143–150.

Mihaly, P. H. (1991). Health care utilization review: Potential exposures to negligence liability. *Ohio State Law Journal, 52*(4), 1289–1308.

Miller, I. J. (1996). Managed care is harmful to outpatient mental health services. A call for accountability. *Professional Psychology: Research and Practice, 22,* 349–363.

Miller, D. J., & Hersen, M. (1992). *Research fraud in the behavioral and biomedical sciences.* New York: Wiley.

Miller, D. J., & Thelan, M. H. (1986). Knowledge and beliefs about confidentiality in psychotherapy. *Professional Psychology: Research and Practice, 17,* 15–19.

Miller, G. M., & Larrabee, M. J. (1995). Sexual intimacy in counselor education and supervision: A national survey. *Counselor Education and Supervision, 34,* 332–343.

Miller, G. M., & Wooten, H. R., Jr. (1995). Sports counseling: A new counseling specialty area. *Journal of Counseling and Development, 74,* 172–173.

Mitchell, R. W. (1991). *Documentation of counseling records.* Alexandria, VA: American Counseling Association.

Mnookin, R. H., & Weisberg, D. K. (1995). *Child, family and state: Problems and materials on children and the law.* Boston: Little, Brown and Company.

Monahan, J. (1995). *The clinical prediction of violent behavior.* Northvale, NJ: Jason Aronson.

Moore, E. M. (1997). *The relationship between clinical graduate students' experiences with their educators and their views on therapist-client dual role relationships.* Unpublished dissertation, University of Windsor.

Morgan, E. (1943). Suggested remedy for obstructions to expert testimony by rules of evidence. *University of Chicago Law Review, 10,* 285–298.

Morris, W. O. (1984). *Revocation of professional licenses by governmental agencies.* Charlottesville, VA: Michie.

Muehleman, T., Pickens, B. K., & Robinson, F. (1985). Informing clients about the limits to confidentiality, risks, and their rights: Is self-disclosure inhibited? *Professional Psychology: Research and Practice, 16,* 385–397.

Mulvey, E., & Lidz, C. (1995). Conditional prediction: A model for research on dangerousness to others in a new era. *International Journal of Law and Psychiatry, 18,* 129–143.

Murphy, E. J., Speidel, R. E., & Ayres, I. (1997). *Contract law* (5th ed.). Westbury, NY: The Foundation Press.

Musto, D. (1975). The community mental health center movement in historical perspective. In W. E. Barton & C. J. Sanborn (Eds.), *An assessment of the community mental health movement* (pp. 1–11). Lexington, MA: D.C. Heath.

Myers, J. E. (1995a). From "forgotten and ignored" to standards and certification: Gerontological counseling comes of age. *Journal of Counseling and Development, 74,* 143–149.

Myers, J. E. (1995b). Specialties in counseling: Rich heritage or force for fragmentation? *Journal of Counseling and Development, 74,* 115–116.

Nagle v. Hooks, 295 Md. 133, 460 A.2d 49 (1983).

Napoli, D. S. (1981). *Architects of adjustment: The history of the psychological profession in the United States.* Port Washington, NY: Kennikat Press.

National Research Act of 1974, 42 U.S.C. 218 *et seq.* (Public Law 93-348).

National Research Act of 1974 Regulations, 45 Code of Federal Regulations 46.

Navin, S., Beamish, P., & Johanson, G. (1995). Ethical practices of field-based mental health counselor supervisors. *Journal of Mental Health Counseling, 17,* 243–253.

Neukrug, E. S., Healy, M., & Herlihy, B. (1992). Ethical practices of licensed professional counselors: An updated survey of state licensing boards. *Counselor Education and Supervision, 32,* 130–141.

Newman, J. L. (1993). Ethical issues in consultation. *Journal of Counseling and Development, 72,* 148–156.

Nixon, J. A. (1993). Gender considerations in the case of "The Jealous Husband:" Strategic therapy in review. *The Family Journal, 1,* 161–163.

Nugent, F. (1981). *Professional counseling: An overview.* Pacific Grove, CA: Brooks/Cole.

Orton, G. L. (1997). *Strategies for counseling with children and their parents.* Pacific Grove, CA: Brooks/Cole.

Page, R. C., & Bailey, J. B. (1995). Addictions counseling certification: An emerging counseling specialty. *Journal of Counseling and Development, 74,* 167–171.

Page v. Rotterdam-Mohanasen Central School Dist., 441 N.Y.S.2d 323, 109 Misc.2d 1049 (1981).

Paisley, P. O., & Borders, L. D. (1995). School counseling: An evolving specialty. *Journal of Counseling and Development, 74,* 150–153.

Pardeck, J. T. (1991). Using books in clinical practice. *Psychotherapy in Private Practice.* 9, 105–199.

Parham, T. A. (1997). An African-centered view of dual relationships. In B. Herlihy & G. Corey, *Boundary issues in counseling* (pp. 109–111). Alexandria, VA: American Counseling Association.

Patry, W. F. (1986). *Latman's the copyright law* (6th ed.). Washington, DC: The Bureau of National Affairs.

Pedersen, P. B. (1991). Multiculturalism as a generic approach to counseling. *Journal of Counseling and Development, 70,* 6–12.

Pedersen, P. B. (1994). *A handbook for developing multicultural awareness* (2nd ed.). Alexandria, VA: American Counseling Association.

People v. Cohen, 98 Misc.2d 874, 414 N.Y.S.2d 642 (1979).

People v. Lobaito, 133 Mich. App. 547, 351 N.W.2d 233 (App. 1984).

People v. Taylor, 618 P.2d 1127 (Colo. 1980).

Perr, I. N. (1985). Suicide litigation and risk management: A review of 32 cases. *The Bulletin of the American Academy of Psychiatry and the Law, 13,* 209–219.

Perritt, H. H., Jr. (1998). *Employee dismissal law and practice, Vol. 1* (4th ed.). New York: John Wiley & Sons.

Perry, S. (1989). Warning third parties at risk of AIDS: American Psychiatric Association's policy is a barrier to treatment. *Hospital and Community Psychiatry, 40*(2), 158–161.

Petersen v. State, 100 Wash. 2d 421, 671 P.2d 230 (1983) (en banc).

Peterson, C. (1996). Common problem areas and their causes resulting in disciplinary action. In L. J. Bass, S. T. DeMers, J. R. Ogloff, C. Peterson, J. L. Pettifor, R. P. Reaves, T. Retfalvi, N. Simon, C. Sinclair, & R. Tipton, *Professional conduct and discipline in psychology* (pp. 71–89). Washington, DC: American Psychological Association.

Petrashek v. Petrashek, 232 Neb. 212, 440 N.W.2d 220 (1989).

Phillips, B. N. (1982). Regulation and control in psychology. *American Psychologist, 37,* 919–926.

Piazza, N. J., & Baruth, N. E. (1990). Client record guidelines. *Journal of Counseling and Development, 68,* 313–316.

Pierce, K. A., & Baldwin, C. (1990). Participation versus privacy in the training of group counselors. *Journal for Specialists in Group Work, 15,* 149–158.

Pietrofesa, J. J., Hoffman, A., & Splete, H. H. (1984). *Counseling: An introduction.* Boston: Houghton Mifflin.

Pine, A. M., & Aronson, E. (1988). *Career burnout: Causes and cures.* New York: Free Press.

Pope, K. S. (1986). Research and laws regarding therapist-patient sexual involvement: Implications for therapists. *American Journal of Psychotherapy, 40,* 564–571.

Pope, K. S., Keith-Spiegel, P., & Tabachnick, B. G. (1986). Sexual attraction to clients: The human therapist and the (sometimes) inhuman training system. *American Psychologist, 41,* 147–158.

Pope, K. S. (1988). How clients are harmed by sexual contact with mental health professionals: The syndrome and its prevalence. *Journal of Counseling and Development, 67,* 222–226.

Pope, K. S. (1994). *Sexual involvement with therapists: Patient assessment, subsequent therapy, forensics.* Washington, DC: American Psychological Association.

Pope, K. S., & Bouhoutsos, J. C. (1986). *Sexual intimacy between therapists and patients.* New York: Praeger Press.

Pope, K. S., Butcher, J. N., & Sheelen, J. (1993). The MMPI, MMPI-2, and MMPI-A in court: A practical guide for expert witnesses and attorneys. Washington, DC: American Psychological Association.

Pope, K. S., Levinson, H., & Schover, L.R. (1979). Sexual intimacy in psychology training: Results and implications of a national survey. *American Psychologist, 34,* 682–689.

Pope, K. S., Sonne, J. L., & Holroyd, J. (1993). *Sexual feelings in psychotherapy: Explorations for therapists and therapists-in-training.* Washington, DC: American Psychological Association.

Pope, K. S., Tabachnick, B. G., & Keith-Spiegel, P. (1987a). Ethics of practice: The beliefs and behaviors of psychologists as therapists. *American Psychologist, 42,* 993–1006.

Pope, K. S., Tabachnick, B. G., & Keith-Spiegel, P. (1987b). Good and poor practices in psychotherapy: National survey of beliefs of psychologists. *Professional Psychology: Research and Practice, 19,* 547–552.

Pope, K. S., & Vasquez, M. J. T. (1991). *Ethics in psychotherapy and counseling: A practical guide for psychologists.* San Francisco: Jossey-Bass.

Pope, K. S., & Vetter, V. A. (1992). Ethical dilemmas encountered by members of the American Psychological Association: A national survey. *American Psychologist, 47,* 397–411.

Roeske, N.C.A. (1986). Risk factors: Predictable hazards of a health care career. In C. D. Scott & J. Hawk (Eds.), *Heal thyself: The health of health care professionals.* (pp. 56–70). New York: Brunner/Mazel.

Prochaska, J., & Norcross, J. (1983). Psychotherapists' perspectives on treating themselves and their clients for psychic distress. *Professional Psychology: Research and Practice, 14,* 642–655.

Prosser, W. (1971). *The law of torts,* St. Paul, MN: West.

Prosser, W. L., Wade, J. W., & Schwartz, V. E. (1988). *Cases and materials on torts* (8th ed.). Westbury, NY: The Foundation Press.

Purrington, W. (1906). An abused privilege. *Columbia Law Review, 6,* 388–422.

Randall, V. R. (1994a). Impact of managed care organizations on ethnic Americans and underserved populations. *Journal of Health Care for the Poor and Underserved, 5*(3), 224.

Randall, V. R. (1994b). Utilization review and financial risk-shifting: Compensating patients for cost containment injuries. *University of Puget Sound Law Review, 17*(1), 1–100.

Rave, E. J., & Larsen, C. C. (1995). *Ethical decision making in therapy: Feminist perspectives.* New York: Guilford.

Regents of the University of Michigan v. Ewing, 474 U.S. 214 (1985).

Remley, T. P., Jr. (1991). *Preparing for court appearances.* Alexandria. VA: American Counseling Association.

Remley, T. P., Jr. (1993). Consultation contracts. *Journal of Counseling and Development, 72,* 157–158.

Remley, T. P., Jr. (1995). A proposed alternative to the licensing of specialties in counseling. *Journal of Counseling and Development, 74,* 126–129.

Remley, T. P., Jr., Benshoff, J. M., & Mowbray, C. A. (1987). A proposed model for peer supervision. *Counselor Education and Supervision, 27,* 53–60.

Remley, T. P., Jr., & Fry, L. J. (1993). Reporting suspected child abuse: Conflicting roles for the counselor. *The School Counselor, 40,* 253–259.

Remley, T. P., Jr., Herlihy, B., & Herlihy, S. B. (1997). The U.S. Supreme Court decision in *Jaffee v. Redmond:* Implications for counselors. *Journal of Counseling and Development, 75,* 213–218.

Remley, T. P., Jr., Hulse-Killacky, D., Ashton, L., Keene, K., Kippers, S., Lazzari, S., Niemann, S., & Oprea, L. (1998, October). *Advanced students supervising other students.* Paper presented at Louisiana Counseling Association conference, Lafayette, LA, and Southern Association for Counselor Education and Supervision conference, Montgomery, AL.

Reppucci, N. D., Weithorn, L. A., Mulvey, E. P., & Monahan, J. (1984). *Children, mental health, and the law.* Beverly Hills, CA: Sage Publications.

Rice, P. R. (1993). *Attorney-client privilege in the United States.* Rochester, NY: Lawyers Cooperative Publishing.

Rios v. Read, D.C.N.Y. 73 F.R.D. 589 (1977).

Roberts v. Superior Court, 9 Cal.3d 330, 107 Cal. Rptr. 309, 508 P.2d 309 (1973).

Roberts-Henry, M. (1995). Criminalization of therapist sexual misconduct in Colorado In J. C. Gonsiorek (Ed.), *Breach of trust: Sexual exploitation by health care professionals and clergy,* (pp. 388–347). Thousand Oaks, CA: Sage.

Robertson, D. W., Powers, W., Jr., & Anderson, D. A. (1989). *Cases and materials on torts.* St. Paul, MN: West.

Rogers, C. R. (1961). *On becoming a person.* Boston: Houghton Mifflin.

Rosenbach, W. E. (1993). Mentoring: Empowering followers to become leaders. In W. E. Rosenbach & R. L. Taylor (Eds.), *Contemporary issues in leadership* (3rd ed.) (pp. 141–151). Boulder, CO: Wesview Press.

Rosenhan, D. L. (1973). On being sane in insane places. *Science, 179,* 250–258. Sleek, P. (1996, April). Ensuring accuracy in clinical decisions. *APA Monitor, 26,* 30.

Rosenstock v. Board of Governors of the University of North Carolina, 423 F.Supp. 1321, 1326–27 (M.D.N.C. 1976).

Rosenthal, R. (1994). Science and ethics in conducting, analyzing, and reporting psychological research. *Psychological Science, 5,* 127–133.

Rossi, R. L. (1995). *Attorneys' fees* (2nd ed.) (Vols. 1 & 2). Danvers, MA: Lawyers Cooperative Publishing.

Rottenberg, S. (Ed.). (1980). *Occupational licensure and regulation.* Washington, DC: American Enterprise Institute for Public Policy Research.

Salgo v. Leland Stanford Jr. Univ. Bd. of Trustees, 317 P.2d 170 (Cal. Ct. App. 1957).

Salisbury, W. A., & Kinnier, R. T. (1996). Posttermination friendship between counselors and clients. *Journal of Counseling and Development, 74,* 495–500.

Sampson, J. P., Jr. (1996). A computer-aided violation of confidentiality. In B. Herlihy & G. Corey, *ACA ethical standards casebook* (5th ed.) (pp. 213–215). Alexandria, VA: American Counseling Association.

Sampson, J. P., Jr., Kolodinski, R. W., & Greeno, B. P. (1997). Counseling on the information highway: Future possibilities and potential problems. *Journal of Counseling and Development, 75,* 203–212.

Schaffer, S. J. (1997). Don't be aloof about record-keeping; it may be your best liability coverage. *The National Psychologist, 6*(1), 21.

Schank, J. A., & Skovholt, T. M. (1997). Dual-relationship dilemmas of rural and small-community psychologists. *Professional Psychology: Research and Practice, 28,* 44–49.

Schmid, D., Applebaum, P., Roth, L. H., & Lidz, C. (1983). Confidentiality in psychiatry. A study of the patient's view. *Hospital and Community, Psychiatry, 34,* 353–356.

Schmidt, J. J., & Osborne, W. L. (1981). Counseling and consulting: Separate processes or the same? *Personnel and Guidance Journal, 59,* 168–171.

Schoener, G., & Gonsiorek, J. (1988). Assessment and development of rehabilitation plans for counselors who have sexually exploited their clients. *Journal of Counseling and Development, 67,* 227–232.

Schoener, G. R. (1989). Self-help and consumer groups. In G. R. Schoener, J. H. Milgrom, J. C. Gonsiorek, E. T. Luepker, & R. M. Conroe (Eds.). *Psychotherapists' sexual involvement with clients: Intervention and prevention* (pp. 375–399). Minneapolis, MN: Walk-In Counseling Center.

Schutz, B. M. (1990). *Legal liability in psychotherapy.* San Francisco: Jossey-Bass.

Schwab, R., & Neukrug, E. (1994). A survey of counselor educators' ethical concerns. *Counseling and Values, 39,* 42–45.

Scott, W. R. (1969). Professional employees in a bureaucratic structure: Social work. In A. Etzioni (Ed.), *The semi-professions and their organization* (pp. 102–156). New York: Free Press.

Section 504 of the Rehabilitation Act of 1973 (29 U.S.C. §794).

Sekaran, U. (1986). *Dual career families.* San Francisco: Jossey-Bass.

Seligman, L. (1986). *Diagnosis and treatment planning in counseling.* New York: Human Sciences Press.

Shuman, D. W., & Weiner, M. F. (1987). *The psychotherapist-patient privilege: A critical examination.* Springfield, IL: Charles C. Thomas.

Sieber, J. E. (1992). *Planning ethically responsible research—Methods series.* Newbury Park, CA: Sage.

Simon, R. I. (1987). *Clinical psychiatry and the law.* Washington, DC: American Psychiatric Press.

Simon, R. I. (1989). Sexual exploitation of patients: How it begins before it happens. *Psychiatric Annals, 19,* 104–112.

Simon, R. I. (1991). Psychological injury caused by boundary violations: Precursors to therapist-patient sex. *Psychiatry Annals, 19,* 104–112.

Simon, R. I. (1992). Treatment boundary violations: Clinical, ethical, and legal considerations. *Bulletin of the American Academy of Psychiatry and the Law, 20,* 269–288.

Simon, R. I. (1998). Boundary violations in psychotherapy. In L. E. Lifson & R. I. Simon (Eds.), *The mental health practitioner and the law* (pp. 195–215). Cambridge, MA: Harvard University Press.

Sims v. State, 251 Ga. 877, 311 S.E.2d 161 (1984).

Slater v. Baker & Stapleton, 95 Eng. Rep. 860 (K.B. 1767).

Slimp, P. A., & Burian, B. K. (1994). Multiple role relationships during internship: Consequences and recommendations. *Professional Psychology: Research and Practice, 25,* 39–45.

Sloan, I. J. (1992). *Professional malpractice.* Dobbs Ferry, NY: Oceana Publications.

Slovenko, R. (1960). Psychiatry and a second look at the medical privilege. *Wayne Law Review, 6,* 174–203.

Slovenko, R. (1966). *Psychotherapy, confidentiality, and privileged communication.* Springfield, IL: Charles C. Thomas.

Slovenko, R., & Usdin, G. (1961). The psychiatrist and privileged communication. *Archives of General Psychiatry, 4,* 431–444.

Slovic, P., & Monahan, J. (1995). Probability, danger, and coercion: A study of risk perception and decision making in mental health law. *Law and Human Behavior, 19,* 49–65.

Smith, D., & Fitzpatrick, M. (1995). Patient-therapist boundary issues: An integrative review of theory and research. *Professional Psychology: Research and Practice, 26,* 499–506..

Smith, H. B., & Robinson, G. P. (1995). Mental health counseling: Past, present, and future. *Journal of Counseling and Development, 75,* 158–162.

Smith, J. M., & Mallen, R. E. (1989). *Preventing legal malpractice.* St. Paul, MN: West.

Smith, R. L., Carlson, J., Stevens-Smith, P., & Dennison, M. (1995). Marriage and family counseling. *Journal of Counseling and Development, 74,* 154–157.

Snider, P. D. (1985). The duty to warn: A potential issue of litigation for the counseling supervisor. *Counselor Education and Supervision, 25,* 66–73.

Snider, P. D. (1987). Client records: Inexpensive liability protection for mental health counselors. *Journal of Mental Health Counseling, 9,* 134–141.

Sonne, J. L. (1994). Multiple relationships: Does the new ethics code answer the right questions? *Professional Psychology: Research and Practice, 25,* 336–443.

Squyres, E. (1986). An alternative view of the spouse of the therapist. *Journal of Contemporary Psychology, 16,* 97–106.

St. Germaine, J. (1993). Dual relationships: What's wrong with them? *American Counselor, 2,* 25–30.

Stadler, H. A. (1986). Making hard choices: Clarifying controversial ethical issues. *Counseling and Human Development, 19,* 1–10.

Stadler, H. A. (1990a). Confidentiality. In B. Herlihy & L. Golden, *Ethical standards casebook* (4th ed.) (pp. 102–110). Alexandria, VA: American Association for Counseling and Development.

Stadler, H. A. (1990b). Counselor impairment. In B. Herlihy & L. Golden, *Ethical standards casebook* (4th ed.) (pp. 177–187). Alexandria, VA: American Association for Counseling and Development.

Stadler, H., Willing, K., Eberhage, M., & Ward, W. (1988). Impairment: Implications for the counseling profession. *Journal of Counseling and Development, 66,* 258–260.

State of Louisiana through the Louisiana State Board of Examiners of Psychologists of the Department of Health and Human Services v. Atterberry. 664 So.2d 1216, La. App. 1 Cir., 1995.

State v. Andring, 342 N.W.2d 128 (Minn. 1984).

State v. Brown, 376 N.W.2d 451, review denied (Minn. App. 1985).

State v. Hungerford, 84 Wisc.2d 236, 267 N.W.2d 258 (1978).

State v. Kupchun, 117 N.H. 417, 373 A.2d 1325 (1977).

State v. Magnuson, 682 P.2d 1365, 210 Mont. 401 (Mont. 1984).

Stone, L. A. (1985). National Board for Certified Counselors: History, relationships, and projections. *Journal of Counseling and Development, 63,* 605–606.

Strasburger, L. H. (1998). Suggestions for expert witnesses. In L. E. Lifson & R. I. Simon (Eds.), *The mental health practitioner and the law* (pp. 281–298). Cambridge, MA: Harvard University Press.

Strickler, G. (1996). Psychotherapy in cyberspace. *Ethics and Behavior, 6*(2), 169, 175–177.

Stromberg, C. D. (1988). *The psychologist's legal handbook.* Washington, DC: Council for the National Register of Health Service Providers in Psychology.

Sudak, H., Ford, A., & Rushforth, N. (1984). Adolescent suicide: An overview. *American Journal of Psychotherapy, 38,* 350–369.

Sue, D. W. (1996). Ethical issues in multicultural counseling. In B. Herlihy & G. Corey, *ACA Ethical standards casebook* (5th ed.) (pp. 193–197). Alexandria, VA: American Counseling Association.

Sue, D. W. (1997). Multicultural perspectives on multiple relationships. In B. Herlihy & G. Corey, *Boundary issues in counseling* (pp. 106–109). Alexandria, VA: American Counseling Association.

Sue, D. W., & Zane, N. (1987). The role of culture and cultural techniques in psychotherapy: A critique and reformulation. *American Psychologist, 42,* 37–45.

Sullivan v. O'Connor, 363 Mass. 579 (1973).

Sumerel, M. B., & Borders, L. D. (1996). Addressing personal issues in supervision: Impact of counselors' experience level on various aspects of the supervisory relationship. *Counselor Education and Supervision, 35,* 268–285.

Suzuki, L. A., Meller, P. J., & Ponterotto, J. G. (1996). *Handbook of multicultural assessment.* San Francisco: Jossey-Bass.

Sweeney, T. (1995). Accreditation, credentialing, professionalization: The role of specialties. *Journal of Counseling and Development, 74,* 117–125.

Swenson, L. C. (1997). *Psychology and the law for the helping professions* (2nd ed.). Pacific Grove, CA: Brooks/Cole.

Tarasoff v. Regents of University of California, 529 P.2d 553, 118 Cal. Rptr. 129 (1974), *vacated,* 17 Cal. 3d 425, 551 P.2d 334, 131 Cal. Rptr. 14 (1976).

Tarka v. Franklin, C.A.5 (Tex.) 891 F.2d 102, certiori denied 110 S.Ct. 1809, 494 U.S. 1080, 108 (1989).

Taube, D. O., & Elwork, A. (1990). Researching the effects of confidentiality law on patients' self-disclosures. *Professional Psychology: Research and Practice, 21,* 72–75.

Taylor, K. (1995). *The ethics of caring.* Santa Cruz, CA: Hanford Mead.

Tayyari v. New Mexico State University, 495 F.Supp. 1365 (D.N.M. 1980).

Thoreson, R., Nathan, P., Skorina, J., & Kilberg, R. (1983). The alcoholic psychologist: Issues, problems, and implications for the profession. *Professional Psychology: Research and Practice, 14,* 670–684.

Thoreson, R. W., Morrow, K. A., Frazier, P. A., & Kerstner, P. L. (1990, March). *Needs and concerns of women in AACD: Preliminary results.* Paper presented at the annual convention of the American Association for Counseling and Development, Cincinnati, OH.

Thoreson, R. W., Shaughnessy, P., & Frazier, P. A. (1995). Sexual contact during and after professional relationships: Practices and attitudes of female counselors. *Journal of Counseling and Development, 74,* 84–88.

Thoreson, R. W., Shaughnessy, P., Heppner, P.P., & Cook, S. W. (1993). Sexual contact during and after the professional relationship: Attitudes and practices of male counselors. *Journal of Counseling and Development, 71,* 429–434.

Title I of the Americans with Disabilities Act of 1990, 42 U.S.C. §1211 *et seq.*

Title VI of the Civil Rights Act of 1964, 42 U.S.C. §2000e *et seq.*

Title VII of the Civil Rights Act of 1964, 42 U.S.C. §2000f *et seq.*

Title IX of the Education Amendments of 1972, 20 U.S.C. §12101 *et seq.*

Tomm, K. (1993, January/February). The ethics of dual relationships. *The California Therapist, 7–*19.

Toren, N. (1969). Semi-professionalism and social work: A theoretical perspective. In A. Etzioni, *The semi-professions and their organization,* pp. 12–63. New York: Free Press.

Truax v. Raich, 239 U.S. 33, 36 S.Ct. 7, 60 L.Ed. 131 (1915).

Truscott, D., Evens, J., & Mansell, S. (1995). Outpatient psychotherapy with dangerous clients: A model for clinical decision making. *Professional Psychology: Research and Practice, 26,* 484–490.

Tyler, J. M., & Tyler, C. (1994). Ethics in supervision: Managing supervisee rights and supervisor responsibilities. *Directions in Mental Health Counseling, 4*(11), 4–25.

Tylitzki v. Triple X Service, Inc., 126 Ill. App.2d 144, 261 N.E.2d 533 (1970).

U.S. CONST. amend. XIV.

Usher, C. H., & Borders, L. D. (1993). Practicing counselors' preferences for supervisory style and supervisory emphasis. *Counselor Education and Supervision, 33,* 66–79.

Van Hoose, W. H., & Kottler, J. (1985). *Ethical and legal issues in counseling and psychotherapy* (2nd ed.). San Francisco, CA: Jossey-Bass.

Van Hoose, W. H., & Paradise, L. V. (1979). *Ethics in counseling and psychotherapy: Perspectives in issues and decision-making.* Cranston, RI: Carroll.

Van Zandt. C. E. (1990). Professionalism: A matter of personal initiative. *Journal of Counseling and Development, 68,* 243–245.

VandeCreek, L., Miars, R. D., & Herzog, C. E. (1987). Client anticipations and preferences for confidentiality of records. *Journal of Counseling Psychology, 34,* 62–67.

Vasquez, M. J. T. (1988). Counselor-client sexual contact: Implications for ethics training. *Journal of Counseling and Development, 67,* 238–241.

Vasquez, M. J. T. (1991). Sexual intimacies with clients after termination: Should a prohibition be explicit? *Ethics and Behavior, 1,* 45–61.

Vidmar, N. (1995). *Medical malpractice and the American jury: Confronting the myths about jury incompetence, deep pockets, and outrageous damage awards.* Ann Arbor, MI: University of Michigan Press.

Virginia court ruling stirs concern about confidentiality protections in group therapy (1979). *Hospital and Community Psychiatry, 30,* 428.

Walden, S. L. (1997). Inclusion of the client perspective in ethical practice. In B. Herlihy & G. Corey, *Boundary issues in counseling* (pp. 40–47). Alexandria, VA: American Counseling Association.

Walsh, W. B., & Betz, N. E. (1995). *Tests and assessment* (3rd ed.). Upper Saddle River, NJ: Prentice Hall.

Walter, M. I., & Handelsman, M. M. (1996). Informed consent for mental health counseling: Effects of information specificity on clients' ratings of counselors. *Journal of Mental Health Counseling, 18,* 253–262.

Webb v. Quincy City Lines, Inc., 73 Ill. App.2d 405, 219 N.E.2d 165 (1966).

Wehrly, B. (1991). Preparing multicultural counselors. *Counseling and Human Development, 24*(3), 1–24.

Weil, R. I. (1983). Are professional corporations dead? *The North Carolina State Bar Quarterly, 30*(1), 8–9.

Weinapple, M., & Perr, I. (1979). The rights of minors to confidentiality: An aftermath of *Bartley v. Kremens. Bulletin of the American Academy of Psychiatry and the Law, 9,* 247–254.

Weinrach, S. G. (1989). Guidelines for clients of private practitioners: Committing the structure to print. *Journal of Counseling and Development, 67,* 299–300.

Weinrach, S. G., & Thomas, K. R. (1996). The counseling profession's commitment to diversity-sensitive counseling: A critical reassessment. *Journal of Counseling and Development, 74,* 472–477.

Welfel, E. R. (1998). *Ethics in counseling and psychotherapy.* Pacific Grove, CA: Brooks/Cole.

Wendorf, D. J., & Wendorf, R. J. (1992). A systemic view of family therapy ethics. In R. L. Smith & P. Stevens-Smith (Eds.), *Family counseling and therapy* (pp. 304–320). Ann Arbor, MI: ERIC/CAPS

West, J. J., & Idol, L. (1987). School consultation (Part 1): An interdisciplinary perspective on theory, models, and research. *Journal of Learning Disabilities, 20* (7), 388–408.

Wichansky v. Wichansky, 126 N.J. Super. 156, 313 A.2d 222 (1973).

Wickline v. California, 192 Cal.App.3d 1630 (1986); 239 Cal. Rptr. 810 (Ct. App. 1986).

Wigmore, J. H. (1961). *Evidence in trials at common law* (Vol. 8,)(McNaughton Rev.). Boston: Little, Brown.

Wilkinson, W. K., & McNeil, K. (1996). *Research for the helping professions.* Pacific Grove, CA: Brooks/Cole.

Williams, S., & Halgin, R. P. (1995). Issues in psychotherapy supervision between the white supervisor and the black supervisee. *The Clinical Supervisor, 13,* 39–61.

Wilson, F. R., Jencius, M., & Duncan, D. (1997). Introduction to the Internet: Opportunities and dilemmas. *Counseling and Human Development, 29*(6), 1–16.

Wilson v. Blue Cross, 271 Cal.Rptr. 876 (Ct. App. 1990).

Winston, M. E. (1991). AIDS, confidentiality, and the right to know. In T. A. Mappes & J. S. Zembaty (Eds.), *Biomedical ethics* (3rd ed.) (pp. 173–180). New York: McGraw-Hill.

Witmer, J. M., & Young, M. E. (1996). Preventing counselor impairment: A wellness approach. *Journal of Humanistic Education and Development, 34,* 141–155.

Woody, R. H. (1988a). *Fifty ways to avoid malpractice.* Sarasota, FL: Professional Resource Exchange.

Woody, R. H. (1988b). *Protecting your mental health practice: How to minimize legal and financial risk.* San Francisco: Jossey-Bass.

Wrenn, G. (1962). *The counselor in a changing world.* Washington, DC: American Personnel and Guidance Association.

Wylie, M. S. (1995, May/June). The power of DSM-IV: Diagnosing for dollars. *Networker,* 22–32.

Yalom, I. D. (1995). *The theory and practice of group psychotherapy* (4th ed.). New York: Basic Books.

Yaron v. Yaron, 83 Misc.2d 276, 372 N.Y.S.2d 518 (Sup. 1975).

Ziskin, J. (1995). *Coping with psychiatric and psychological testimony* (Vols. I, II, & III) (5th ed.). Los Angeles, CA: Law and Psychology Press.

Author Index

Subject Index